# INSIDERS' GUIDE® TO SANTA BARBARA

## Help Us Keep This Guide Up to Date

Every effort has been made by the author and editors to make this guide as accurate and useful as possible. However, many things can change after a guide is published—establishments close, phone numbers change, hiking trails are rerouted, facilities come under new management, etc.

We would love to hear from you concerning your experiences with this guide and how you feel it could be improved and be kept up to date. While we may not be able to respond to all comments and suggestions, we'll take them to heart and we'll also make certain to share them with the author. Please send your comments and suggestions to the following address:

The Globe Pequot Press
Reader Response/Editorial Department
P.O. Box 480
Guilford, CT 06437

Or you may e-mail us at:

editorial@globe-pequot.com

Thanks for your input, and happy travels!

INSIDERS' GUIDE® SERIES

# Insiders' Guide® to Santa Barbara

*Including Channel Islands National Park*

**SECOND EDITION**

By Karen Hastings

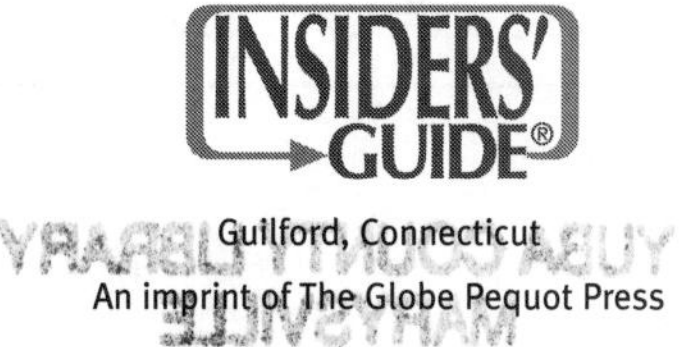


Guilford, Connecticut
An imprint of The Globe Pequot Press

The prices and rates in this guidebook were confirmed at press time. We recommend, however, that you call establishments before traveling to obtain current information.


A previous edition of this book was published by Falcon Publishing, Inc. in 1999.



Maps by Brandon Ray

ISBN: 0-7627-1023-3

Manufactured in the United States of America
Second Edition/First Printing

# Contents

## Directory of Maps

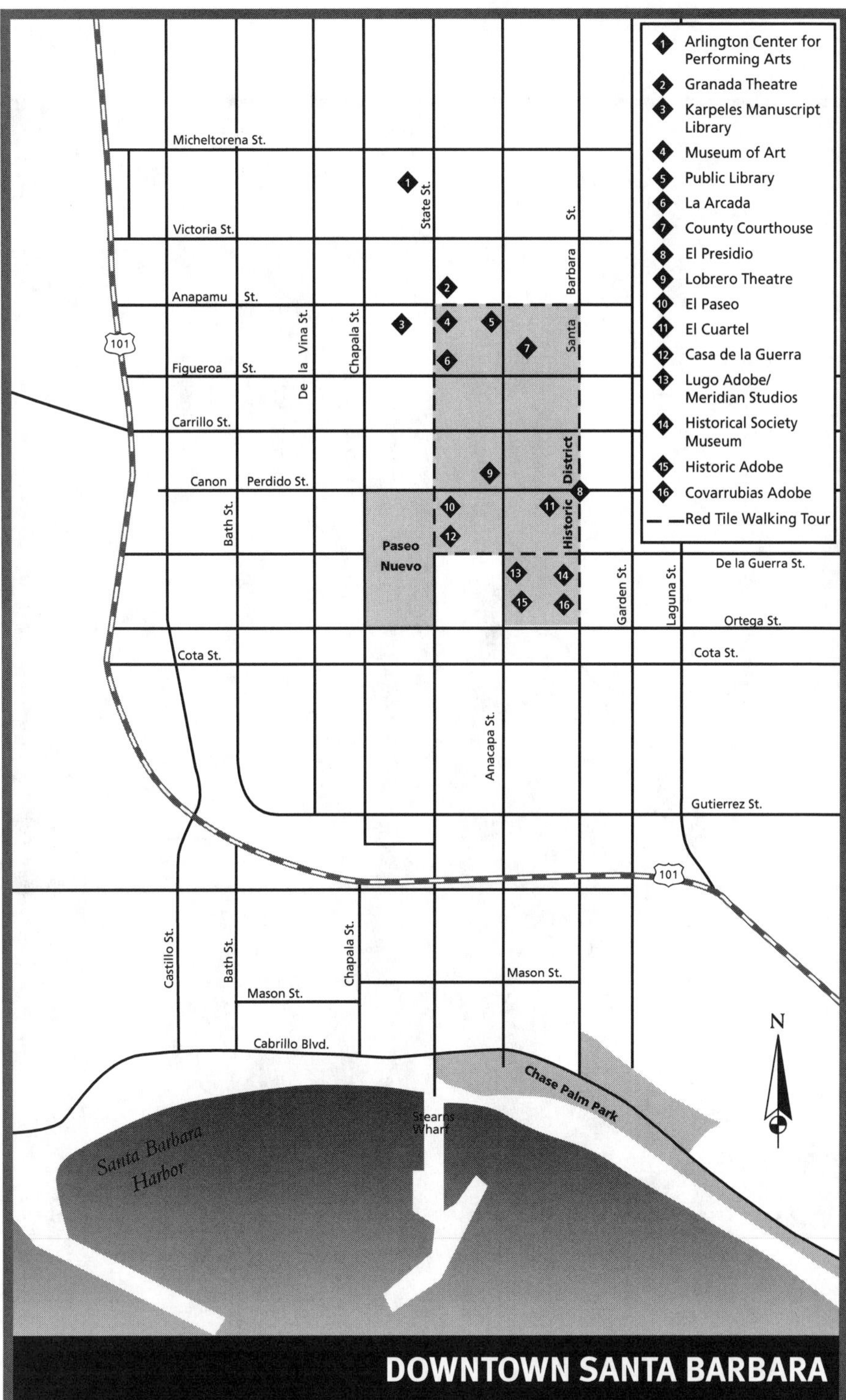
Arlington Center for Performing Arts
Granada Theatre
Karpeles Manuscript Library
Museum of Art
Public Library
La Arcada
County Courthouse
El Presidio
Lobrero Theatre
El Paseo
El Cuartel
Casa de la Guerra
Lugo Adobe/ Meridian Studios
Historical Society Museum
Historic Adobe
Covarrubias Adobe
Red Tile Walking Tour
Micheltorena St.
Victoria St.
Anapamu St.
Figueroa St.
Carrillo St.
Canon Perdido St.
De la Guerra St.
Ortega St.
Cota St.
Gutierrez St.
Mason St.
Cabrillo Blvd.
State St.
Santa Barbara St.
De la Vina St.
Chapala St.
Bath St.
Castillo St.
Anacapa St.
Garden St.
Laguna St.
Historic District
Paseo Nuevo
101
Chase Palm Park
Stearns Wharf
Santa Barbara Harbor
N
DOWNTOWN SANTA BARBARA

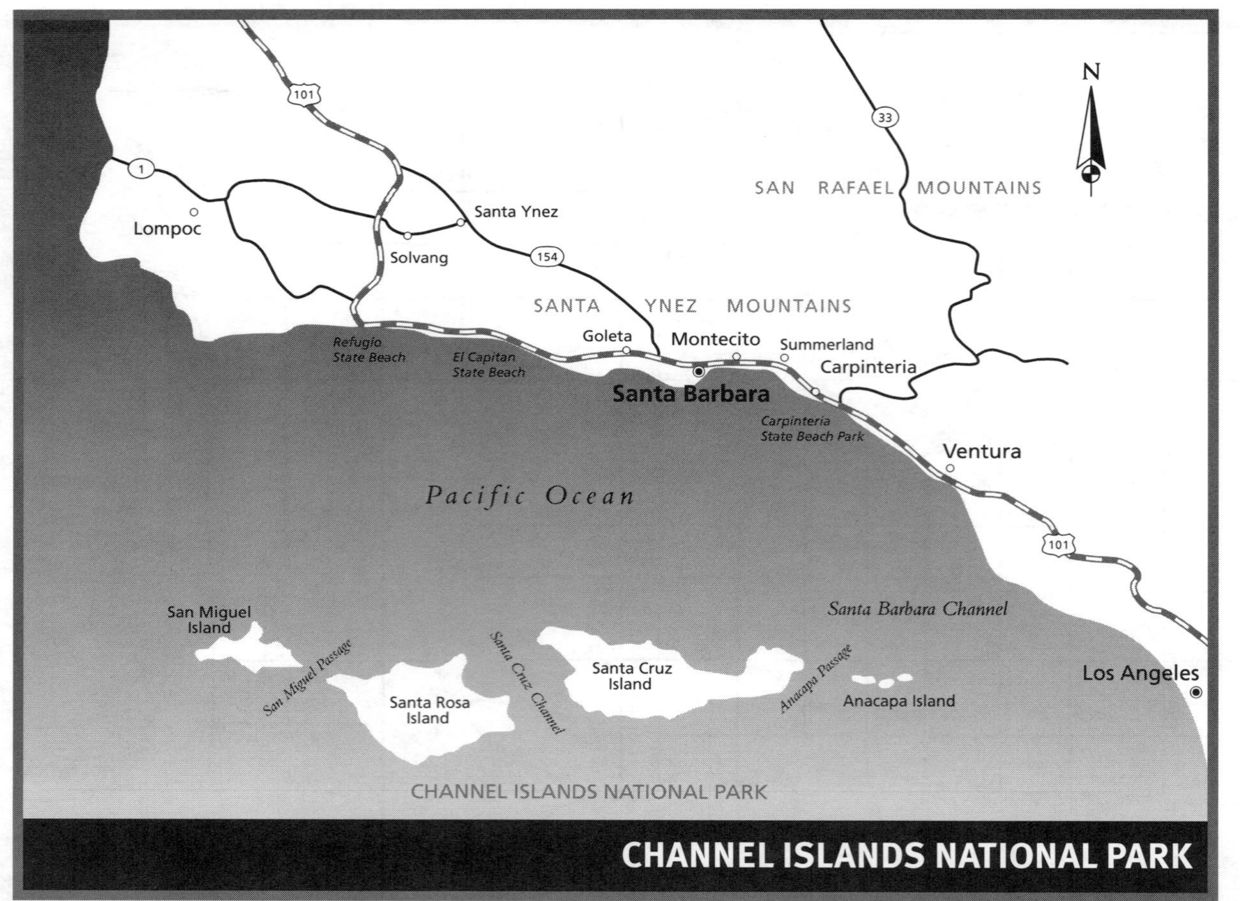
N
101
33
1
SAN RAFAEL MOUNTAINS
Santa Ynez
Lompoc
Solvang
154
SANTA YNEZ MOUNTAINS
Goleta
Montecito
Summerland
Carpinteria
Refugio State Beach
El Capitan State Beach
Santa Barbara
Carpinteria State Beach Park
Ventura
Pacific Ocean
101
Santa Barbara Channel
San Miguel Island
San Miguel Passage
Santa Rosa Island
Santa Cruz Channel
Santa Cruz Island
Anacapa Passage
Anacapa Island
Los Angeles
CHANNEL ISLANDS NATIONAL PARK
CHANNEL ISLANDS NATIONAL PARK

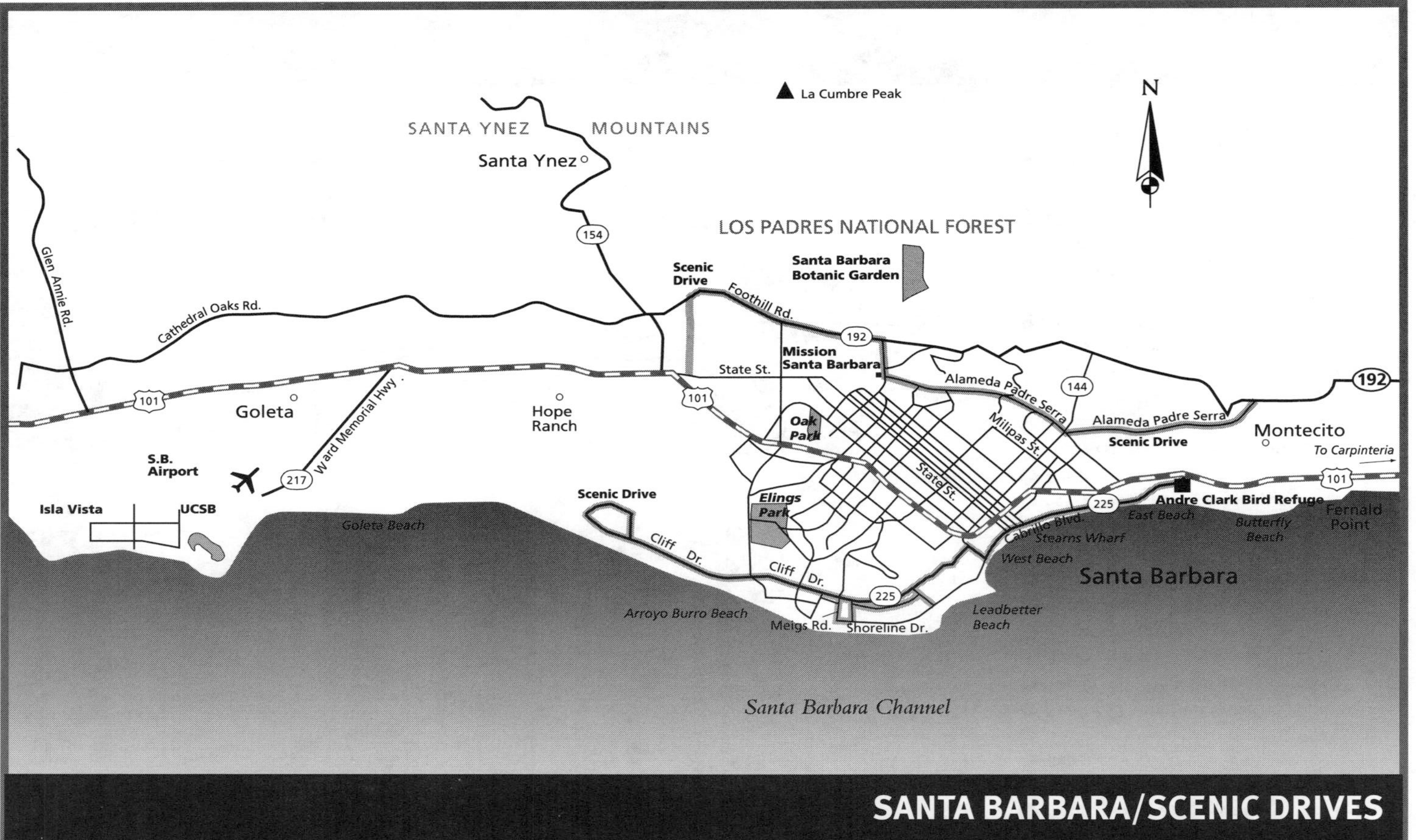
SANTA BARBARA/SCENIC DRIVES
N
La Cumbre Peak
SANTA YNEZ MOUNTAINS
Santa Ynez
LOS PADRES NATIONAL FOREST
Santa Barbara Botanic Garden
Glen Annie Rd.
Cathedral Oaks Rd.
154
Scenic Drive
Foothill Rd.
192
Mission Santa Barbara
State St.
Alameda Padre Serra
144
Alameda Padre Serra
Scenic Drive
Montecito
To Carpinteria
101
Goleta
Hope Ranch
Ward Memorial Hwy.
217
S.B. Airport
Isla Vista
UCSB
Goleta Beach
Scenic Drive
Oak Park
Milipas St.
State St.
Elings Park
Cliff Dr.
Cliff Dr.
225
Cabrillo Blvd.
Andre Clark Bird Refuge
East Beach
Butterfly Beach
Fernald Point
Stearns Wharf
West Beach
Santa Barbara
Arroyo Burro Beach
Meigs Rd.
Shoreline Dr.
Leadbetter Beach
Santa Barbara Channel

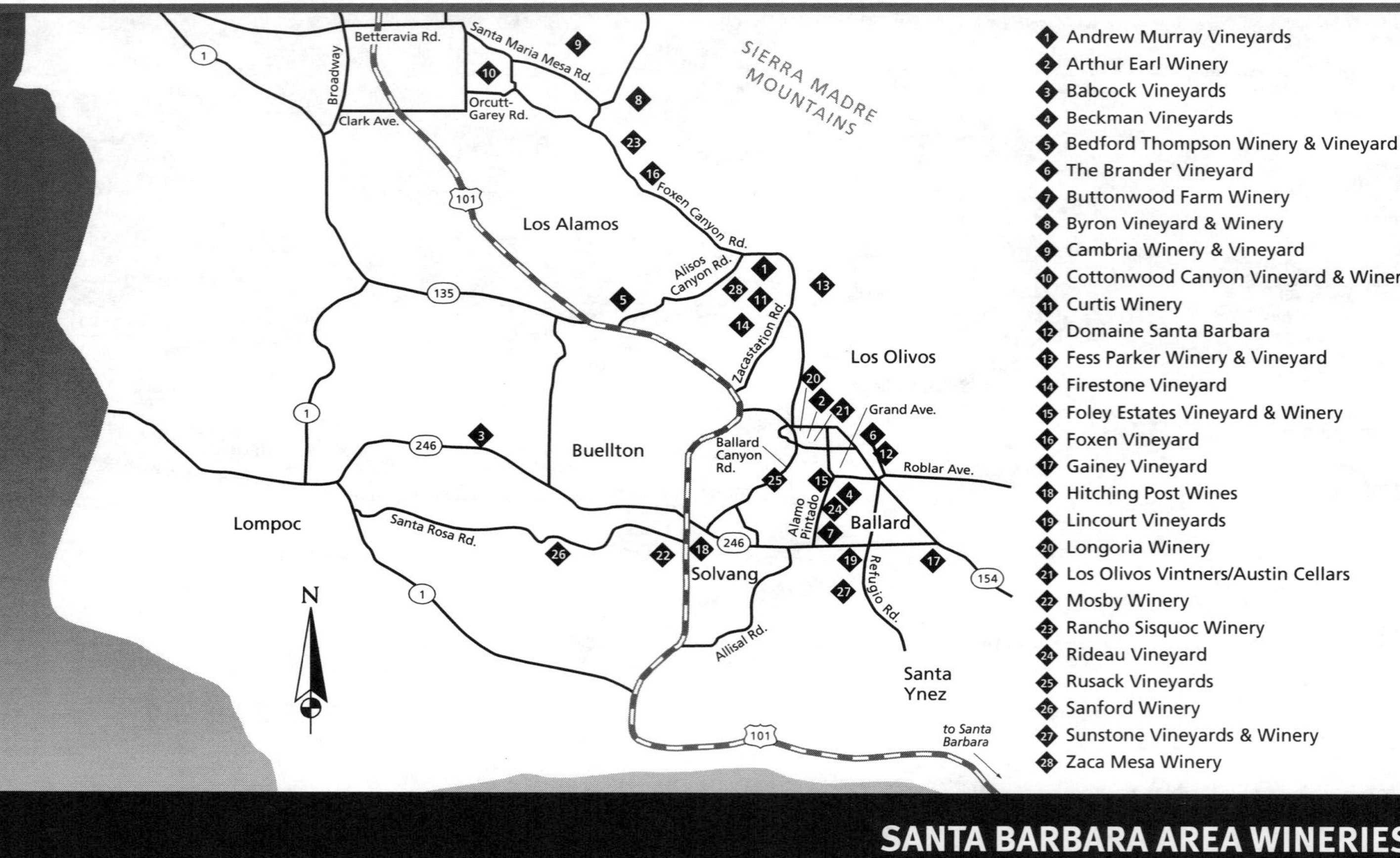
SANTA BARBARA AREA WINERIES
1 Andrew Murray Vineyards
2 Arthur Earl Winery
3 Babcock Vineyards
4 Beckman Vineyards
5 Bedford Thompson Winery & Vineyard
6 The Brander Vineyard
7 Buttonwood Farm Winery
8 Byron Vineyard & Winery
9 Cambria Winery & Vineyard
10 Cottonwood Canyon Vineyard & Winery
11 Curtis Winery
12 Domaine Santa Barbara
13 Fess Parker Winery & Vineyard
14 Firestone Vineyard
15 Foley Estates Vineyard & Winery
16 Foxen Vineyard
17 Gainey Vineyard
18 Hitching Post Wines
19 Lincourt Vineyards
20 Longoria Winery
21 Los Olivos Vintners/Austin Cellars
22 Mosby Winery
23 Rancho Sisquoc Winery
24 Rideau Vineyard
25 Rusack Vineyards
26 Sanford Winery
27 Sunstone Vineyards & Winery
28 Zaca Mesa Winery
Sierra Madre Mountains
Betteravia Rd.
Broadway
Clark Ave.
Santa Maria Mesa Rd.
Orcutt-Garey Rd.
Foxen Canyon Rd.
Alisos Canyon Rd.
Zacastation Rd.
Los Alamos
Los Olivos
Grand Ave.
Roblar Ave.
Ballard Canyon Rd.
Alamo Pintado
Ballard
Refugio Rd.
Buellton
Lompoc
Santa Rosa Rd.
Solvang
Allisal Rd.
Santa Ynez
to Santa Barbara
N
1
101
135
246
154

# Preface

Say "Santa Barbara" and what springs to mind? Is it beaches, blondes, and balmy weather? Or is it that infamous soap opera with the sultry vixens slinking across the set?

Visit Santa Barbara and no doubt you will see those idyllic palm-lined beaches where bronzed bodies spike volleyballs and jog along the shore without breaking a sweat. You'll see Spanish Revival architecture—bubbling fountains, cream stucco, and red-tiled roofs. You may even spot a celebrity or two. In fact, on the surface, Santa Barbara reminds us of one of the stars of its own soap opera—dazzlingly beautiful, seductive, and glamorous. But, read this book, get to know the town more intimately, and what you learn may surprise you.

Despite all the images of glittering materialism and the extremely high cost of living, Santa Barbara is actually quite conservative and unpretentious. Shunning the conspicuous consumption of big city life, the town prefers instead to bask in its wealth of natural beauty. And in this department, Santa Barbara is hard to beat.

Few spots on earth are blessed with such a fortuitous blend of attractive features—broad sunny beaches, rugged coastal peaks, picturesque valleys, giant kelp forests, and windswept islands. Cruise the sparkling waters and you might spot seals, dolphins, and migrating whales. Hike the canyons and you'll feel as though civilization is a million miles away.

Beneath this wildly beautiful visage Santa Barbara's culture and history run deep. It may have the soul of a small beach town but it exudes all the sophistication of a world-class city. Opera, theater, ballet, art galleries, museums, and top-notch restaurants are all within a short drive of residential areas, and Santa Barbara's excellent educational resources attract students from around the world. Look around and you will see the legacies of our colorful past—in the beautiful architecture, the food, the street names, and the people.

Today the town still celebrates its rich history and culture with a busy lineup of parades, street festivals, and events. Santa Barbara loves a party. No matter what time of year you visit, you're sure to find something fun to attend—whether it's the music and dance of the Chumash Indians, the "Old Spanish Days" celebration each August ("Fiesta" to the locals), the colorful floats of the Summer Solstice Parade, or the annual Santa Barbara Film Festival.

And then there's us—the people who live here. Many of us visited Santa Barbara long ago and fell in love. Others were lucky enough to be born here. We are artists and authors, students and professors, builders and gardeners, engineers and entrepreneurs. And yes, there are even a few celebrities and film folk among us. Though we come from diverse backgrounds, we all choose to live in Santa Barbara for the same reason—we simply cannot find the same quality of life anywhere else.

We especially love our Santa Barbara sunshine and spend our spare time lapping it up. In fact, as you explore our little piece of paradise, we'll be right beside you—hiking the wilderness trails, kayaking, cycling, surfing, fishing, and sailing. Rain is a welcome treat for us. Most of us don't even own an umbrella and we actually look forward to the few weeks of the year when we can bundle up in sweaters.

Thanks to all this sunny weather and crisp clean air we're a fairly relaxed and friendly bunch of people. So don't be surprised if we strike up a conversation or wave you ahead of us in traffic. We're proud of Santa Barbara and want you to enjoy it as much as we do.

So we invite you to get acquainted. If you're visiting, use this book to find the best of Santa Barbara. If you're moving here, thank your lucky stars. To ease your transition into Santa Barbara life, we've included detailed information on education and childcare, newspaper and television options, healthcare, and retirement opportunities. Don't let Santa Barbara's high cost of living scare you away. Bargains abound here, and we'll let you know where to find them.

Whether you're visiting or moving here, we hope this book serves as a trusty companion. Take it with you on all your adventures. As you flip the pages, you'll get to know the real Santa Barbara and the people who live here—our quirks and fancies, our pet peeves and our charms. You'll discover we're much more down-to-earth than you may have imagined. So relax, "kick back," and "Viva La Fiesta!"

# Acknowledgments

An old Chinese Proverb says, "A journey of a thousand miles begins with a single step." For me, updating this book was a journey that seemed far longer than a thousand miles at times. But from the beginning, there were two people in particular who stretched out their hands and helped me take the first step. They were the original authors—Cheryl Crabtree and Karen Bridgers.

Faced with the task of updating such a beautifully written book, I was scared to take that first step. But before I even began, Karen and Cheryl unselfishly pledged their support, a gesture that stayed with me throughout the entire journey. Chapter by chapter, my respect for their talent and hard work deepened. This book is their baby. I only hope I did it justice.

Many other people went out of their way to help, and I'd like to extend my deepest gratitude to them all. Special thanks to Timm Delaney from Coldwell Banker who shared his real estate expertise and supplied me with reams of current market information. Thanks to Captain Fred Benko from the *Condor* for his beautiful photographs and entertaining stories of the Santa Barbara Channel, to Alberta Brown who kindly reviewed copy on the Carpinteria seal sanctuary and provided expert feedback, and to the Santa Barbara Conference & Visitors Bureau.

Thanks also to my loyal friends and fellow scribes in the writers' group, who encouraged me to do this project in the first place—Nancy Shobe, Meg Miller, Sean Mason, Liz Podolinski, and Gina Rae Hendrickson. I appreciated all the tips and perceptive critiques.

I'd also like to thank my family in Santa Barbara and Australia for their love and support—especially my sister Cassie, whose brutal honesty I will always cherish. Finally, a big thanks to my husband, Brian. Armed with camera and tripod, he trekked across Santa Barbara snapping photos for this book. He also provided information for many of the chapters and critiqued page after page of text. But most importantly, he picked me up and carried me when the road got rocky. Brian, this book is for you and for all my family and friends.

# How to Use This Book

Whether you're lounging on the beach, hiking the mountains, cruising the ocean, or sightseeing in town, carry this book with you. It's meant to help you discover the best Santa Barbara has to offer, from entertainment and recreation to attractions, lodging, and more. We've arranged the book in straightforward, stand-alone chapters to give you quick and easy access to specific information. You can read the chapters in any order.

As you're planning your trip, you'll probably want to consult the Hotels and Motels, Bed and Breakfasts, and Vacation Rentals chapters. If you've just arrived and want to head straight for the sand, flip to the Beaches and Watersports chapter to decide which beach you'll visit first. When you're craving some mouth-watering Santa Barbara cuisine, turn to the Restaurants chapter for an overview of your options. If you're moving here, consider checking out the Neighborhoods and Real Estate chapter as soon as possible.

We've spiced up every chapter with handy Insiders' Tips and illuminating Close-ups on noteworthy people and places. We highly recommend that you read the Area Overview, Getting Here, Getting Around, and History chapters before embarking on your explorations.

The History chapter will shed light on Santa Barbara's unusual architecture and place names. The Area Overview chapter will help you understand who we are and what makes us tick (as well as what ticks us off). Armed with this information, you'll get a lot more out of what you see and do.

*Alice Keck Park Memorial Gardens is just one of Santa Barbara's many lovely outdoor spots.* PHOTO: BRIAN HASTINGS

The Getting Here, Getting Around chapter explains the layout of the city. Read this and you'll be less likely to get lost, which is easy to do when you're navigating our many one-way and dead-end streets for the first time. In our Attractions chapter, you'll find a list of our favorite things to see and do. We've also added some suggested itineraries at the end of the chapter to help you decide.

Worried about all those fires, earthquakes, and floods you've read about in the news? Our Living with Mother Nature chapter can ease your mind. We'll tell you how we locals live in tandem with nature's unusual gifts and whims, including El Niño patterns, Santa Ana winds, and earthquakes.

Traveling with your dog? To save you the hassle of calling around to find out whether Fido is welcome, we've noted pet-friendly places in our Hotels and Motels chapter.

The region covered in this book stretches along U.S. Highway 101 from Gaviota in the west to Carpinteria in the east. We've included a section on Channel Islands National

*Dusk falls on the Santa Barbara Harbor.* PHOTO: TOM TUTTLE, COURTESY OF THE SANTA BARBARA CONFERENCE & VISITORS BUREAU

Park and a chapter on the wineries in the North County, on the other side of the Santa Ynez Mountains. We also feature Cachuma Lake, a recreation area about 35 miles north of Santa Barbara.

Where appropriate, the chapters in this book are divided into geographic sections based on this west-east orientation. First, we cover Santa Barbara (the main city). Then we explore Goleta at the western end (including the beaches and rural areas between Gaviota and Goleta), followed by the towns east of Santa Barbara: Montecito, Summerland, and Carpinteria.

Most of the restaurants we've listed are located in the city of Santa Barbara, and because it takes no more than 15 or 20 minutes to drive from Santa Barbara to Goleta, Montecito, or Carpinteria, we've disregarded geographic orientation in the Restaurants chapter; instead, it's arranged by food type.

We've tried to make this guide so informative that you'll soon feel like an Insider, too. Stash it in your beach bag, your backpack, or your car. Mark it up, shake out the sand, and earmark the pages you turn to the most. Please write and tell us about your favorite discoveries or haunts, and be sure to let us know about any fantastic places we somehow overlooked. We also want to know when something doesn't match our description.

Write to us at: *Insiders' Guides*, The Globe Pequot Press, P.O. Box 480, Guilford, Connecticut 06437-0480. You can also contact us at the Insiders' Guide web site: www.insiders.com; go to the site's comments and suggestions page and send us your perspectives.

Welcome to Santa Barbara. Have a fantastic stay!

# Area Overview

**Nature Is Mostly Kind**
**Diversity Is Our Middle Name**
**Just a Few Caveats**

Santa Barbara has been called the American Riviera, the last unspoiled city in a Mediterranean climate, and even Paradise itself. Cruise our broad palm-studded drives and you will see no skyscrapers to mar the mountain views. Exotic trees and plants flourish, parklands pepper the city, and even downtown neighborhoods cascade with colorful blooms. Skim across the ocean to the wind-whipped Channel Islands and you will discover a whole other dimension of wilderness to explore. Secluded coves and sea caves lace the shores, and an amazing diversity of wildlife still thrives on these rocky isles and in the cool clear waters that splash their shores. Cradled between these rugged islands and towering coastal peaks, Santa Barbara is blessed with a gentle climate. For most of the year it is so bright and brilliant and sunny here that it's hard not to just stop and smile at the beauty of it all.

In addition to its natural riches, Santa Barbara shares its intriguing past with the world in ways that capture the heart and the imagination. The Spanish-Moorish architecture that is the city's hallmark is everywhere, from the facade of Mission Santa Barbara, known as the "queen" of the California missions for its exceptional beauty, to the Santa Barbara County courthouse, a breathtaking structure that lays claim to being one of the loveliest buildings in the country. Stroll the streets of Santa Barbara and you will discover that even modern buildings sport red-tile roofs, hand-painted tiles, open courtyards, and arched facades, a testament to a Spanish heritage that is widely celebrated today. Many streets bear the names of Chumash Indian chiefs, Spanish conquistadores, influential early residents, and even historical events, such as the "lost cannon" incident of 1848 that resulted in the naming of Canon Perdido Street. (See our Getting Here, Getting Around chapter for background information on many of Santa Barbara's unique street names.)

If Santa Barbara was for a time a well-kept secret, its days of anonymity are over. During the Reagan years, the president often visited his western retreat in the mountains above the city, and the press followed in droves. Hanging out in local hotels and restaurants (the Palace Grill was reportedly a White House press corps favorite) and reporting from scenic seaside overlooks, the media showcased the city incessantly. When the Queen of England visited the Reagan ranch in 1983, the international press moved in, and images of Santa Barbara were splashed across newspapers and television screens around the world. Adding to the mystique, the popular soap opera Santa Barbara was beamed to Europe and beyond, solidifying the city's image as a playground for the rich and famous and attracting hordes of foreign tourists to our sun-splashed shores.

Santa Barbarans are known to be exceptionally friendly and are practitioners of the laid-back California lifestyle. Beyond barring patrons without shirts or shoes, most shops and restaurants expect a casually dressed clientele, and shorts or blue jeans worn with sandals or athletic shoes are the norm. Even many conservatively dressed professionals look forward to "casual Friday," the one day a week when they can "dress down" in anticipation of the weekend. (Of course there are still a few stuffy offices in town, and several gala events require guests to dress to the nines, so it never hurts to ask before you show up in your baggy jeans and a sweatshirt.)

Grabbing a bagel and a cup of coffee (flavored, of course) and plopping down with a newspaper at an outdoor cafe is a popular local pastime, as are running, biking, and strolling along the waterfront. Extremely health-conscious as a whole, Santa Barbarans

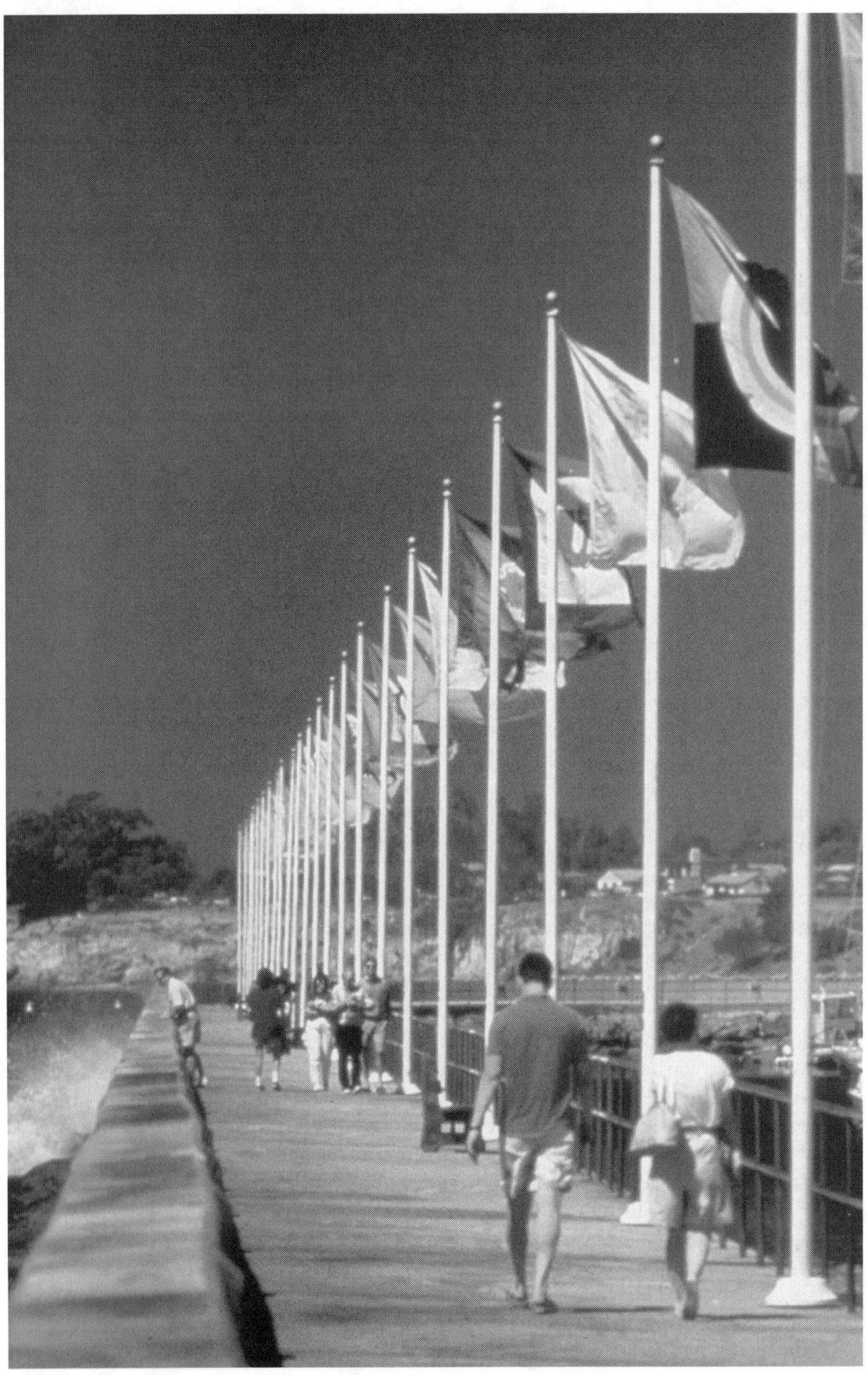

*Santa Barbara's beautiful flag-lined breakwater is a favorite spot for an afternoon stroll.* PHOTO: BILL DEWEY, COURTESY OF SANTA BARBARA CONFERENCE & VISITORS BUREAU

often pick up organic produce at one of several local farmers' markets, patronize the area's health food stores, or stop by for a fresh fruit "smoothie" (wheat grass, ginseng, and protein powder are some of the available add-ins) to drink on the way to the gym. By California law, smoking is not allowed in any public building, restaurant, or bar, an ordinance that suits most Santa Barbara residents fine. Santa Barbara is also big on culture. In addition to its excellent art museum, the city has dozens of local galleries that exhibit the work of local and nationally known artists. The city has its own symphony orchestra, ballet troupe, grand opera association, chamber orchestra, and several theater companies, all of which present a full lineup of excellent performances. In addition, the University of California at Santa Barbara Arts & Lectures program brings a world-class assortment of music, dance, theater, and lectures to local residents.

Fiercely protective of their beautiful home, Santa Barbarans work hard to preserve the qualities that make our region so special, and many issues are close to our hearts. Mention development, affordable housing, oil tankers, and power shortages and be prepared for a lively discussion. But you'll learn more about some of these issues as you flip through the pages of this book and chat with the locals when you visit.

## Nature Is Mostly Kind

Overall, Santa Barbara enjoys very pleasant weather: temperatures are generally balmy along the coast for most of the year, with monthly averages between 65 and 75 degrees. Inland, temperatures can be quite a bit higher during the day (especially in summer) and cooler at night. To cope with changing weather conditions, most Santa Barbarans have mastered the art of "layering" when dressing, a process that involves wearing a sweater or jacket over a long-sleeved shirt over a still lighter shirt in case the day warms up.

About 18 inches of rainfall is normal for the year, with most of it falling between December and March. Fog is often a factor in spring and early summer, when it can hang over the coastline until late morning or early afternoon. In some cases, it's a high fog that simply blocks out the sun, but the thick, drippy, wet, turn-on-your-windshield-wipers kind also occurs at various times of the year. On the other hand, in late summer and fall, mild and sunny conditions occasionally give way to temperatures in the 90s or 100s, especially if hot Santa Ana (or "sundowner") winds blow in from the north. (See our Living With Mother Nature chapter for more information on Santa Ana winds.) When temperatures rise, both literally and figuratively, overheated residents generally look to the sea and pray for the formerly unwelcome fog banks to return and deliver them out of their misery.

We tend to discount natural disasters, probably because they happen so seldom (or at least a lot less often than all the good stuff in Santa Barbara). Californians often joke about earthquakes and brush fires, referring to them as the "shake and bake" factor, but Insiders know that ignoring the potential for either is foolish. Find out all you can about being prepared for an emergency, then do something about it. Simply knowing what to do during an earthquake, having a map in case of an evacuation, or keeping shoes and flashlights next to your bed will help keep you safe if and when disaster strikes.

## Diversity Is Our Middle Name

The population of the city of Santa Barbara is about 92,000, roughly a quarter of the total population of greater Santa Barbara County. Several unincorporated areas lie outside the city boundaries, including parts of Goleta to the west; Montecito to the east, with about 10,000 residents; and Hope Ranch east of Goleta, a relatively small community nestled between the city of Santa Barbara and the sea.

With a population almost as large as

*Santa Barbara has the only south-facing coastline between Alaska and Cape Horn.* PHOTO: BRIAN HASTINGS

Santa Barbara's, Goleta has been debating for decades whether to become an incorporated city or be annexed to Santa Barbara. In November 2001, voters finally approved a proposal to incorporate parts of Goleta, creating the south county's second largest city (population 29,000) behind Santa Barbara (see our Neighborhoods and Real Estate Chapter for details). Montecito and Hope Ranch are the most expensive areas of Santa Barbara, with sprawling estates and ranch homes rimmed by gates and security fences, but you'll find few tourist attractions in either place. East of Montecito is the funky hillside community of Summerland (famous for its antique stores), and Carpinteria, a friendly, family-oriented community whose economy revolves largely around agriculture.

The large Latino population currently accounts for a sizeable 34 percent of Santa Barbara County. Some Latino families trace their roots to the city's original Spanish and Mexican occupants, and a strong sense of tradition permeates the city. Spanish dance studios are full of young women hoping to one day lead the Old Spanish Days parade as the "Spirit of Fiesta" in honor of their heritage. Because of this large Hispanic contingent, government and agency officials speak both English and Spanish. Human services, the retail trade, tourism, government, and agriculture employ the most workers locally. The heart of Santa Barbara's agricultural activity is the "North County," between 45 and 100 miles up the coast from the city of Santa Barbara. Broccoli, wine grapes, olives, lemons, flowers, strawberries, and avocados are all part of the local agricultural scene, and many of these crops are celebrated in annual festivals such as Lompoc's Flower Festival, Goleta's Lemon Festival, and the California Avocado Festival, held in the city of Carpinteria each fall. The University of California at Santa Barbara is a major local employer, as are several high-tech and software firms, government departments, school districts, and major healthcare facilities.

All things considered, Santa Barbara has a lot going for it, but the city has no plans to rest on its laurels. In 1997, a committee of 100 planners and civic leaders released a statement called "Downtown/Waterfront Santa Barbara: A Tradition in

Progress," which set forth its goal to "preserve and enhance the unique qualities" of Santa Barbara's downtown and waterfront areas while developing the city's reputation as a tourist mecca and a fine place to live. Six subcommittees continue to tackle issues ranging from traffic circulation to waterfront development, all in an effort to make the vision a reality. New, low-impact modes of transportation and expanded cultural facilities are all part of the plan. Preservation of the city's natural beauty tops the list of considerations as each project is proposed and carried out, and you can bet that Santa Barbarans are involved in and watching every move as they continue to fight for the environmental integrity of their beloved city.

## Just a Few Caveats

Santa Barbara would indeed seem to have it all: glorious weather, friendly people, beautiful ocean vistas, a healthy lifestyle, an impressive offering of cultural arts, and a collective consciousness dedicated to preserving it all for generations to come. Lest we besmirch our image as true Insiders, however, we feel obliged to let you know that the city probably falls a few notches short (but just a few, mind you) of being paradise. So, in the interest of full disclosure, here are a few things to watch out for. (Before you get discouraged, though, remember that most Santa Barbara residents had their eyes opened long ago, and they still wouldn't want to live anyplace else.)

In a time when travelers sometimes become victims, Santa Barbara is proud of its low crime rate. Violent crimes are rare, but common sense should be your guide. Despite the appeal of a late-night solitary stroll on the beach, unescorted women need to consider safety first. Also, local police recommend that cars be locked and valuables stowed out of sight or locked in the trunk.

It's easy to be seduced by our gorgeous beaches. Standing at the foot of Stearns Wharf and looking back at the mountains as the sun sets provides one of the most spectacular views in California. Residents and tourists alike look to the beaches for solace and beauty, and most times the beaches deliver. Recently, however, bacteria contamination, especially at Arroyo Burro Beach and Carpinteria, has become a concern. A chart of ocean testing results runs regularly in the *Santa Barbara News-Press*, and an Ocean Water Quality Hotline has been set up by Santa Barbara County Environmental Health Services, (805-681-4949). Although your day at the beach is not likely to be ruined by such pollution, it's wise to check the charts and watch for signs that indicate beach closure.

Tar is an all-too-familiar fact of life for Santa Barbara beachgoers. There is an ongoing disagreement about whether beach tar comes from natural seepage on the ocean floor or is somehow caused by oil drilling in the Santa Barbara Channel, but the reality is that it's everywhere, floating in the water, attaching itself to your swimsuit, and coating your feet. It's possible to avoid tar to some degree if you watch where you're stepping, but nearly every visit to the shoreline calls for tar removal. (We recommend wearing your crummiest shoes—or if you go barefoot, using baby oil to get the stuff off your skin.)

### Water, Water—Almost Everywhere

Santa Barbara doesn't really discuss its "water problem" these days because it seems as if it has been solved, and lately, the state's energy shortage has stolen the spotlight. The truth is, though, that rainfall varies from year to year, and long-term

**Insiders' Tip**

Santa Barbara averages 300 days of sunshine a year. No wonder we love it here!

**Insiders' Tip**

For a *Santa Barbara Visitor's Guide* with comprehensive information on accommodations, attractions, and events, call the Santa Barbara Conference & Visitors Bureau at (805) 966-9222 or (800) 676-1266, or visit www.santabarbaraCA.com and send an e-mail request.

droughts are often followed by exceptionally rainy seasons. After a series of drought years that left local reservoirs close to empty and required a ban on watering lawns and washing cars, citizens succumbed to the temptation of buying into California's state water system, a move that started costing local water districts $6.5 million per year beginning January 1, 1998. Of course, if California has another drought, there won't be enough water to satisfy the needs of all the new state water customers, but in the short run, developers are trying to cash in on the newfound availability of water to build, build, build. Problem is, available land in Santa Barbara is at an all-time low and the demand for real estate now far exceeds supply. That's where the laws of economics come in. . . .

## Unreal Estate

To put it succinctly, all real estate in Santa Barbara is expensive. A low-end price for a three-bedroom, 30-year-old tract home can run around $470,000, and you can easily pay $2,200 or more a month to rent a two-bedroom, two-bath unfurnished house, or $1,200 for a one-bedroom apartment. In 2000, the South Coast's median home price zoomed to $590,000, a 19-percent increase over the previous year. If that seems like small change, you're welcome to drop $5 or $6 million on a Montecito mansion, or $37 million on a Hope Ranch estate like one deep-pocketed buyer did in 2000. Sure it's expensive to live in Santa Barbara. But would so many people be looking for homes here if they were just putting out big bucks for wood and stucco? We doubt it. Insiders know that when you buy a house here, the price includes the beach, the sunsets, the art museum, the balmy weather, the palm trees, and many more delightful things you've yet to discover.

But there is a downside to this unquenchable demand. As property prices skyrocket, the lack of affordable housing has reached crisis proportions. According to a recent survey, only one in every 20 employees can afford to buy a home in Santa Barbara, and astronomical rents are forcing low-income workers out of the region. To solve the problem, the county is considering rent control and several high-density apartment projects are on the drawing board. But, while everyone agrees that something needs to be done, most residents don't want the increased development in their own backyard. Which brings us to the local political scene.

## To Grow or Not to Grow?

For years, "pro-growthers" and "no-growthers" have been at war in Santa Barbara, making every local election a down-and-dirty quest for power. Nearly every campaign addresses the issues of growth vs. quality of life, progress vs. stagnation, and developers' rights vs. preservation. Most of these political battles are the focus of races for mayoral or City Council seats in the City of Santa Barbara, and races for the Board of Supervisors, which administers the affairs of Santa Barbara County. When the balance of no-growthers and pro-growthers in a local governing body is at stake, you are guaranteed both a heated battle and a close election, and Insiders know that every vote counts when the future of the city or county is on the line.

And it isn't just growth issues that drive Santa Barbarans to the ballot box. To give you an idea of the kinds of issues that ignite Santa Barbarans, let's take a look back at the November 1997 city elections. The ballot issue of the day (besides the mayoral election and three City Council seats) was a proposal to ban gas-powered leaf blowers within the city limits. The "leaf blower war" began when a group known as BLAST (Ban Leaf blowers And Save our Town) went after the machines on the grounds that they stir up dust, release sickening fumes, and make too much noise. When the City Council refused to issue a full-scale ban, BLAST took its cause to the public, gathering 9,000 signatures to qualify the measure for the ballot. Howls of protest ensued from the opposition (known as Citizens Opposed to Radical Enactments, or CORE), which was largely made up of gardeners and landscape contractors. The ban bill passed with 54.5 percent of the vote, and BLAST has vowed to go after electric leaf blowers next, while CORE members, predicting that landscaping costs will rise 20 percent to 30 percent as a result of the ban, are still licking their wounds.

A tempest in a teapot? Not in Santa Barbara. With adamant advocates on both sides of almost any local issue, the political sparks are always flying. Often involved in the fray are the oil companies that continually fight for the right to drill and/or tanker in the oil-rich Santa Barbara Channel. Since 1969, when a Union Oil offshore platform blew out and sent waves of black crude onto Santa Barbara's beaches, watchdog groups such as G.O.O. (Get Oil Out) have fought to evict oil companies from the channel and spare Santa Barbara the risk of another devastating spill, something that oil executives continue to vow will never happen. Earth Day was born as a consequence of this and other catastrophes of the '60s, and a powerful force of environmentalism still pervades Santa Barbara today.

## Pushing the Comfort Zone

Santa Barbara is only 90 miles north of Los Angeles but often seems a world away in attitude. Life is slower here. Development is carefully controlled, and a laid-back approach is the order of the day. But locals are all very much aware that the Big City is knocking at our back door. For some residents, the ever-expanding megalopolis of L.A. is getting too close for comfort, but others enjoy the proximity for the cultural and recreational advantages. A trip to Disneyland or attending a big-league athletic event or museum opening is easily doable in a day, but after such an excursion, Santa Barbarans inevitably rush home and swear they wouldn't be caught dead suffering the indignities of L.A. gridlock on a daily basis. In addition, we're anxious to keep our own little piece of paradise to ourselves, refusing to budge on such highly charged issues as the proposed widening of U.S. Highway 101 at Milpas Street to accommodate heavier traffic. The expansion has still not been approved, and a vociferous group of Santa Barbarans are soundly against it. But people still flock to Santa Barbara, and you might find yourself sitting in bottlenecks during rush hours and on weekends. This

**Insiders' Tip**

In Spanish, Montecito means "little mountain." Goleta means "schooner" and Carpinteria was named after the Spanish word for "carpenter's shop," because the Chumash Indians used to build their canoes (*tomols*) there on the beach.

CLOSE-UP

## Santa Barbara Resources

**Santa Barbara Conference & Visitors Bureau and Film Commission**
**1601 Anacapa Street**
**Santa Barbara, CA 93101**
**(805) 966–9222, (800) 676–1266**
**www.santabarbaraCA.com**

**Santa Barbara Region Chamber of Commerce**
**12 East Carrillo Street**
**Santa Barbara, CA**
**(805) 965–3023**
**www.sbchamber.org**

worries many locals. The thought of Santa Barbara becoming "another L.A." is pretty unsettling, and residents cast anxious glances southward as a hazy cloud of smog continues its almost imperceptible crawl up the coast.

About 20 years ago, the economy was booming in Santa Barbara County. Large, defense-oriented companies were in their prime, and nearly everyone who worked for them was planning on staying 25 or 30 years and retiring with the traditional gold watch and some cushy lifetime benefits. Between 1991 and 1993, however, layoffs and cutbacks in the defense industry caused a downward spiral that naturally affected other areas of the local economy. For a time, homes stopped selling, families were squirreling away money against possible layoffs, no one was buying anything, and a sense of gloom and doom fell over Santa Barbara.

But wait! Just when it seemed that the economy couldn't sink any lower, things started to improve. Several high-tech computer firms moved to town, and the tourism and retail industries began to employ former defense workers and others who had lost their jobs. With the easing of water restrictions, construction picked up, and what was left of the defense industry began to diversify in order to snare profitable peacetime contracts. Santa Barbara enjoyed this economic prosperity into the early years of the 21st century. But it, like the rest of the country, faced economic uncertainty as 2001 drew to a close.

Santa Barbara is not perfect. What place is? But as long as the jobs, the power, and the water hold out, and Mother Nature behaves herself, we will continue to adore our beloved city and be forever grateful that we are perched (however precariously) on one of the most favored plots of land on the planet.

### Insiders' Tip

The shoreline juts sharply to the west just north of Ventura County, and all of southern Santa Barbara County's beaches are south-facing. Hence the name "South Coast," which is often used when referring to the South County.

# Getting Here, Getting Around



Before the 1870s, getting to and from Santa Barbara was pretty much limited to travel by stagecoach. The bulky vehicles lurched over San Marcos Pass or traveled south to Ventura, veering out onto the beach at low tide when they reached Rincon Point on their southward run. This was not the most comfortable way to travel, of course, nor the safest, as stages were held up on a regular basis, especially as they traversed bandit-ridden San Marcos Pass. After Stearns Wharf was completed in 1872, steamships had access to the city, and—with a little help from the adoring press—Santa Barbara started its transformation from a small town into a busy city with a lively tourist trade.

It was soon clear that a way was needed to accommodate all the visitors who were making their way from the wharf to the popular Arlington Hotel on State Street (see the introduction to our Hotels and Motels chapter for the history of the Arlington). So, in 1875, the Santa Barbara Street Railroad Company began operating mule-drawn railway cars that each held 12 passengers and followed a narrow gauge track that ran from the beach to the hotel. The completion of the Southern Pacific Railroad's link with Los Angeles in 1887 marked another transportation milestone for Santa Barbara. The resulting influx of visitors necessitated expansion of the street railway, which added two new lines and an additional 4 miles of track, including passing tracks that allowed more than one car to travel on State Street at once.

The street railway lasted in Santa Barbara until the 1890s, when a more modern mode of transportation, the electric trolley, began providing a convenient and inexpensive means of getting to and from just about anywhere in the city. The trolley era came to a close more than three decades later, when passenger automobiles became an attractive alternative form of transportation and began to compete for space on local streets. By 1929, it is estimated that 10,000 autos were buzzing around the city, and from then on, Santa Barbara was hooked on cars, an infatuation that continues in modern times. Not long after the automobile era got started, Santa Barbarans were able to take to the skies at the Santa Barbara Municipal Airport, which evolved from a small flight school near the corner of Hollister and Fairview Avenues in Goleta. The first commercial flight (via Pacific Seaboard Airlines), Los Angeles–bound, was made on August 1, 1931.

Today, of course, Santa Barbara has all the transportation options needed to get you here from almost anywhere (well, you may have to take a few detours, but you'll get here). Still, getting (and parking) around Santa Barbara proper is tricky for a number of reasons, so we've included everything you'll need to know to find your way around town as well as ideas on how to get in or out of town.

## Highways and Byways

U.S. Highway 101 is the West Coast's major north-south freeway and the "main drag" through Santa Barbara. You can take U.S. 101 south to the Mexican border or north to the Canadian border, and because it literally bisects Santa Barbara, it's within a few minutes' drive of anywhere in the city. If you're taking the freeway south, be aware that it narrows from six lanes to four in Montecito, which creates a huge backup on holidays and weekends. A proposal to widen the freeway to six lanes has been met with scorn by local residents, who don't want any more pieces of paradise bulldozed to accommodate what they perceive as a glut of weekending Los Angeles drivers. As of now, the issue is simmering on the back burner, but is far from dead.

Calif. Highway 154 (San Marcos Pass), which connects Santa Barbara's South County with Solvang, Cachuma Lake, the wine country, and the rest of the North County, is a mixed blessing. You can get to the same places by taking U.S. 101, but it takes longer than zipping over the pass. And, unfortunately, zipping is what people have a tendency to do on this winding narrow road, which has no center divider and no traffic lights. Combine a few impatient, speeding, or intoxicated drivers with darkness, high winds, fog, or other weather problems, and you have the potential for a serious accident.

This can be an extremely dangerous stretch of roadway, so if you take the pass, drive defensively, get over into one of the right lanes if traffic is stacking up behind you, and pass with extreme caution. In inclement weather, the pass is subject to rock or mudslides, which often close the road for hours or even days and add another element of danger.

In short, if you're going to drive the pass (and yes, Santa Barbarans do it all the time), be careful!

Calif. Highway 217 is a short stretch of highway that links northbound U.S. 101 with the University of California at Santa Barbara, the Santa Barbara Airport, and the rest of Goleta. The exit is just past the northbound Patterson Avenue off-ramp for U.S. 101, and from Calif. 217 you can reach the airport and Goleta Beach Park by taking the Sandspit Road exit. Downtown Goleta is off the Calif. 217 Hollister exit. The highway ends at the entrance to the UCSB campus.

### Insiders' Tip

Insiders know that gasoline is more expensive in Santa Barbara than just about anywhere else. So when traveling to Los Angeles, they leave Santa Barbara with half a tank, then fill 'er up in Los Angeles, returning with half a tank of bargain fuel.

## In Santa Barbara

"Blame It All On Captain Haley," wrote Barney Brantingham, a *Santa Barbara News-Press* columnist and local author, referring to Santa Barbara city streets. And, indeed, it seems that Capt. Haley has to shoulder most of the blame, even though he died decades ago and isn't around to hear the modern-day commentary on his 1851 survey. Salisbury Haley was a sea captain, after all, who just happened to be in port when the city was taking bids for the laying out of Santa Barbara's streets. Figuring he could make a quick $2,000 (which turned out to be the lowest bid), Haley became a landlubber just long enough to do the job, which looked good enough on paper to city planners. Problem was, Haley's survey chain had broken and been repaired with rawhide thongs that shrank and expanded depending on the weather. So by the time he was finished, everything was off by just a little—and sometimes by a lot. Later surveys showed that none of the city blocks Haley surveyed were the same size, with some being as much as 14 feet over the proposed size of 450 square feet. Haley, of course, had long since gone back out to sea.

Today, the streets are still crooked, city blocks are all different sizes, and there are enough one-way streets crisscrossing downtown to practically ensure that taking the most direct route to anywhere will still require going a block or two out of your way. Add the perennial road construction, potholes, cracks, torn-up streets, wooden barriers, and detours, and you have a typical day's drive in Santa Barbara.

It won't take you long to notice (whether you read the map or not) that Santa Barbara street names are both confusing and difficult to pronounce. Carrillo, Castillo, and Cabrillo are all U.S. 101 exits in close proximity to one another, and tongue-twisters such as Micheltorena and Salsipuedes are a mouthful. (See the Close-up in this chapter for an Insiders' look at the origins of the city's street names.) And then there is our unique geographical orientation. As one of the few stretches of Pacific coastline between Alaska and the South Pole that has mountains running east-west, Santa Barbara also has south-facing beaches. To everyone who knows that the Pacific Ocean is always to the west in California (and almost everyone does know that, don't they?), this state of affairs causes no end of confusion. Whether Salisbury Haley gave much thought to compass directions is debatable, but he chose to lay out the city's streets running diagonally from southeast to northwest and from southwest to northeast. In the middle is State Street, the main downtown business thoroughfare; once you've found your way there, you have a good point of reference for exploring the rest of the city.

Our best advice? Study your map before you go exploring, or—if all else fails—ask someone! We Santa Barbarans are unbelievably friendly and helpful.

An alternative for commuters is to contact Traffic Solutions (805-963-SAVE, www.sbcag.org/ts.htm), a division of the Santa Barbara County Association of Governments. The mission of Traffic Solutions is to help as many people as possible find an alternative to single-passenger car trips that clog the roads and pollute the air. Whether you're driving, walking, biking, or taking public transportation to work, Traffic Solutions wants to help you find the most efficient way to do it. The organization has a database of more than 1,100 commuters interested in carpooling, and you can be matched with someone going your way. It also dispenses information on bus routes and schedules, bicycle commuting, walking, and even telecommuting. More than 400 Santa Barbara and Goleta companies and 60 Carpinteria companies work with Traffic Solutions to provide transportation for their employees to and from work. The organization is a member of the Green Awards Consortium, which recognizes local companies for their voluntary efforts at saving energy and natural resources.

Santa Barbara Airbus recently acquired Traffic Solutions' Clean Air Express (805-964-7759 ext. 3), a fleet of nine 47-passenger buses that run clean on a mixture of compressed natural gas and diesel fuel. The fleet provides commuter bus service between Santa Barbara's North County south to Ventura. Cost for travel on any one of the nine routes is $100 a month, a wonderful savings when the price of gasoline soars.

## Parking

As much as we might want to, there's just no way to sugarcoat the daytime parking situation in downtown Santa Barbara. It's a nightmare. If you are going someplace with a private parking lot, count yourself blessed, because parking spaces are at a premium downtown, and public lots (there are 11 near State Street between

CLOSE-UP

## Car-free and Carefree

Sick of parking hassles and exorbitant gas prices? Below are a few local organizations that will help you explore Santa Barbara car-free.

- For an overview of alternative travel options, check out the "Take a Vacation From Your Car" project at www.santabarbaracarfree.org. Aimed at visitors, the project is a joint initiative between the Santa Barbara Air Pollution Control District and the American Lung Association.

- Traffic Solutions (805–963–SAVE or www.sbcag.org/ts.htm), a division of the Santa Barbara County Association of Governments, publishes commuter carpool match lists and lists of vanpool vacancies, and promotes the benefits of walking, cycling, and telecommuting.

- Santa Barbara Metropolitan Transit District (MTD, www.sbmtd.gov) operates local buses and electric shuttles. To plan your trip, use the online Trip Planner or call (805) 683–3702 and speak to a Transit Advisor. You can also purchase bus passes online.

- Santa Barbara Trolley Company (805–965–0353, www.sboldtowntrolley.com) operates narrated trolley tours of Santa Barbara attractions.

Victoria and Haley Streets, accessible from Chapala Street or Anacapa Street) are often filled to capacity. If you find a place in a public lot, the first 75 minutes of parking are free, with $1 charged for every hour or part of an hour thereafter, and a $10 maximum per day. Parking facilities are open 24 hours a day, seven days a week.

When public lots are full, you may be forced to find parking on a side street (no parking is permitted on State Street in the downtown district), which presents another challenge. Nearly all downtown streets have only 75- or 15-minute parking zones, and vigilant parking authorities regularly patrol the streets, giving tickets for infractions. As long as there's no solution on the horizon (the city has announced plans for a new downtown multilevel parking structure, but it is not expected to become a reality until the end of 2003), we suggest that you add an extra 15 minutes to your travel time to accommodate parking delays or the time it will take you to walk from your car to your downtown destination. But hey, you didn't expect everything to be perfect in paradise, did you?

## Take the Bus

If all this talk about traffic and parking woes has you feeling nervous about driving downtown, there are several other options to get you there and get you around. The Santa Barbara Metropolitan

Transit District provides bus service throughout the greater Santa Barbara area, from Carpinteria to Goleta. They also operate electric shuttles such as the Downtown-Waterfront Shuttle, the Seaside Shuttle in Carpinteria, and the seasonal Shopper Express and Field Trip shuttles (see below). The main transit center is at 1020 Chapala Street in Santa Barbara, and you can pick up a schedule there (or on an MTD bus), call (805) 683-3702 for help from a Transit Advisor to plan your route, or visit the MTD web site at www.sbmtd.gov and use the online trip planner. If you're already out and about, look for the bus stops with the yellow and black MTD signs every few blocks along the route. Exact change is required for all passengers. The standard one-way fare is $1; seniors 62 and older and disabled persons pay 50 cents, and the Downtown-Waterfront shuttle, which runs up and down State Street, costs just 25 cents. Blind passengers with an MTD ID card (ask your driver), UCSB and Santa Barbara City College students with a current ID card, and children 4 and younger accompanied by an adult ride free.

### Bike and Bus

If you'd like to take the bus and then bike your way around town, consider the Bike & Bus program, which allows you to stow your bike on a special rack on the bus, then disembark and ride away. Taking your bike incurs no extra charge, but Bike & Bus options are only available on certain lines. To find out which lines apply, call (805) 683-3702, visit MTD's web site, or pick up a *Routes & Schedules Guide* available at local businesses throughout the community.

### Downtown-Waterfront Shuttle

An extremely popular way to get around downtown and the waterfront is the Downtown-Waterfront Shuttle, also operated by the MTD. Making use of this service, you can shop State Street, tour the waterfront, then take the kids over to the zoo, all without the hassle of negotiating traffic jams or parking lots. The familiar little shuttles with the blue and black sailboat symbol are a familiar sight on State Street. Just hop aboard! The Downtown Shuttle runs from State Street at Sola Street to Stearns Wharf and back again, with service every 10 minutes between

*The Bike & Bus program makes it easier for cyclers to transport their wheels to some of Santa Barbara's scenic spots.* PHOTO: JOHN B. SNODGRASS

10:15 A.M. and 6:00 P.M. Fare is 25 cents one way (children 4 and younger ride free), and you can get on or off at any stop along the way (the shuttle stops on every block). Transfers to the Waterfront Shuttle are complimentary, but you need to ask your driver for a shuttle transfer when you board. The Waterfront Shuttle runs along Cabrillo Boulevard from the Santa Barbara Zoo to the harbor. Catch the shuttle at the zoo every 30 minutes between 10:00 A.M. and 5:30 P.M. daily, at the harbor every 30 minutes from 10:15 A.M. to 5:45 P.M. daily, or at any stop along the way. The fare is 25 cents for a one-way trip; children 4 and younger ride free. Note that during the busy summer months, the shuttle runs more frequently and the hours are extended.

### Seasonal Shuttles

#### *The Field Trip*

New to MTD in 2000, The Field Trip is a battery-electric shuttle that whisks travelers between downtown cultural attractions on weekends during the summer months. You can catch a ride to the Old Mission, the Santa Barbara Historical Museum, El Presidio, the Museum of Natural History, the County Courthouse, the Museum of Art, Alice Keck Memorial Park, and the Santa Barbara Botanic Garden. The shuttle runs between 10:00 A.M. and 5:00 P.M. weekends only from Memorial Day to Labor Day. One-way trips are $1, and you can purchase a day pass for $3. Call (805) 683-3702 for more information.

#### *Shopper Express*

Done the downtown shops and still haven't run out of steam? Conserve energy and catch a ride on MTD's Shopper Express. During the peak Christmas shopping season, this convenient electric shuttle provides nonstop service between the Paseo Nuevo Mall downtown and La Cumbre Plaza on Upper State Street (see our Shopping chapter). You can catch the shuttle at the bus stop adjacent to California Pizza Kitchen in Paseo Nuevo Shopping Center and at the Red Robin restaurant in La Cumbre Plaza. It usually runs every 30 minutes between 11:00 A.M. and 6:00 P.M. on weekends from the end of November until mid-December. After that, it runs every day until the end of December (excluding Christmas Day). Call (805) 683-3702 for exact schedules.

### In Carpinteria

Carpinteria Area Rapid Transit (CART), (805) 684-4554, has its own shuttle, which provides door-to-door service throughout the city. The fare is 75 cents; 30 cents for disabled passengers, seniors 65 and older, and children 17 and younger. The service runs from 8:30 A.M. to 5:00 P.M. Monday through Friday, and a reservation, which can be made up to two weeks in advance, is essential.

### Seaside Shuttle

Climb aboard the electric Seaside Shuttle and you can cruise in eco-friendly style between Carpinteria's downtown shopping district, residential areas, and the beach. The shuttle also connects with MTD's other lines for trips to downtown Santa Barbara, but make sure you ask your driver for a transfer when you pay. It's 25 cents for a one-way ride ($1 for a transfer), and the shuttle operates every 30 minutes Monday through Friday from 6:00 A.M. to 7:00 P.M. and Saturday and Sunday from 8:30 A.M. to 6:00 P.M., with more frequent service during peak commuter periods on weekdays. Call (805) 683-3702 for more information.

### For Disabled Passengers

Need a lift? Easy Lift Transportation (805-568-5114) provides curb-to-curb, wheelchair-accessible transportation for passengers with disabilities and covers the area between Summerland and west Goleta. Service is provided Monday through Friday from 6:00 A.M. to midnight, and on weekends and holidays from 6:00 A.M. to 9:00 P.M. The fare is $2 a ride. Reservations are essential and can be made up to two weeks in advance.

**Insiders' Tip**

While driving around town, if you see someone trying to pull out in heavy traffic, wave them ahead of you. Santa Barbara drivers are notoriously polite, and someone's bound to do the same for you.

## Taxis

Taxi fares, as is customary, are based on the distance you travel. The cost for a trip between the airport and downtown Santa Barbara will run you about $20. Call Orange Cab Company (805-964-2800), Rose Cab Company (805-564-2600), Santa Barbara City Cab Company (805-968-6868), or Yellow Cab Company (805-965-5111).

## Limousine Service

Since there are plenty of celebrities in Santa Barbara, there are more limo companies here than you might expect. Most provide everything from sedans to super-stretch limos, so if you have something special in mind, be sure to ask (being aware, of course, that the fancier you get, the more it will cost). In general, limo transportation from the airport to downtown runs between $75 and $90, plus tax and tip. Choose a company from the following list, and ride in style!

**Celebrity Transportation**
**(805) 683-1613, (800) 834-8911**

**Executive Limousine Service**
**(805) 969-5525**

**JLS Transportation**
**(805) 961-9111**
**www.jlslimo.com**

**Limousine Link & Sedan Services**
**(805) 898-9506**
**www.limolinksb.com**

**Lyons Limousine Service**
**(805) 683-3039**

**Mammoth Limousine Service**
**(805) 683-4807**

**Ocean Cities Limousine**
**(805) 564-2600, (800) 217-7364**

**Sammy's Express Limousine and Tours**
**(805) 962-0507, (800) 508-5466**
**www.sammyexpresslimo.com**

**Santa Barbara Limousine**
**(805) 964-5466, (877) 711-5466**
**www.sblimo.com**

**Spencer's Limousine**
**(805) 884-9700**
**www.spencerslimo.com**

**Sunset Limousine**
**(805) 963-0419**

**Walter's Limousine Service**
**(805) 964-7759**

## Rental Cars

You can find almost all the major rental car companies in the Santa Barbara area. Currently only Avis, Budget, Hertz, and National have counters at the airport, located in a building just south of the terminal. Not all companies provide pickup service, so you may have to hoof it a short distance to get to your car or take other airport transportation to the rental office if it's located downtown. Be sure to ask what the company policy is if you need pickup service either from the airport or from a downtown location.

CLOSE-UP

## Street Names

In addition to the tricky geographical orientation of Santa Barbara, visitors are often struck—and sometimes confused—by the interesting nature of the city's downtown street names. Spanish military men, Chumash Indian chiefs, and early settlers are all memorialized on city street signs, a fact that may leave you wondering whatever happened to Main Street, Maple Lane, and other classic American street names. (Well, we do have State Street.) Although we may not be able to walk you through all of the pronunciations (you can ask a local, but even they sometimes disagree), we can at least fill you in on the origins of the likes of Micheltorena, Salsipuedes, and Alameda Padre Serra. So read on for a crash course. (You can read more about many of these historical figures in our History chapter, or stop by the Santa Barbara Historical Society library, 136 E. De la Guerra Street, and do some research of your own.)

**Alameda Padre Serra**
Called simply APS by Insiders, this winding road just above Mission Santa Barbara leads to the city's Riviera. It was named in honor of Father Junipero Serra, the Franciscan friar who founded the mission.

**Anacapa Street**
Anacapa comes from the Chumash word meaning "ever-changing" or "mirage." The Indians noticed that, depending on the weather conditions, Anacapa Island, which is actually made up of three small islets, could also appear as one large mesa or, when the island was reflected in a mirage, a body of land much bigger than its actual size. Anacapa Street points in the direction of Anacapa Island.

**Anapamu Street**
Anapamu was a Chumash Indian chief.

**Arrellaga Street**
Joaquin Arrillega was one of California's Spanish governors, and this street was named for him, although the street name is actually spelled differently than the governor's name.

**Brinkerhoff Avenue**
This avenue is named for Samuel Bevier Brinkerhoff, the city's first medical doctor.

**Canon Perdido Street**
Literally "Lost Cannon Street," this downtown thoroughfare's name marks a famous local incident that happened in 1848. Four boys stole a cannon from the beach as a practical joke, but local military leaders were convinced that someone was trying to stockpile weapons for a rebellion against the American occupation forces. The military governor of California, Richard Mason, decided that if the cannon was not promptly returned, the people of Santa Barbara would have to pay a $500 fine (a pretty hefty fee in those days). Local residents were forced to cough up the money, and the cannon did not make another appearance until 1859, when it was found mired in Mission Creek.

**Cabrillo Boulevard**
Juan Rodriguez Cabrillo, the Portuguese explorer, sailed into the Santa Barbara Channel in 1542, becoming the first European to see the Santa Barbara coastline.

**Carrillo Street**
The name of this street reflects the role of the Carrillo family in Santa Barbara's history. Jose Raimundo Carrillo served as captain of the Presidio, and his son, Carlos Antonio de Jesus Carrillo, born at the Presidio, was appointed governor of California in 1837. The appointment was rescinded shortly thereafter, but he remained active in public life in Santa Barbara until his death in 1852.

**Castillo Street**
The name means "castle," and the street ends at a hill where a Spanish fortress once stood.

**De la Guerra Street**
The name literally means "of the war," but in this case it honors the family of Jose Antonio Julian de la Guerra y Noriega (better known simply as Jose de la Guerra), who became commandant of the Presidio in 1815, serving until 1842. His family's large adobe home was constructed facing what is now De la Guerra Plaza.

**Figueroa Street**
Jose Figueroa was a popular Mexican governor in early California.

**Gutierrez Street**
Benigno Gutierrez was a Chilean who came to California in 1849 to make his fortune in the gold fields. After amassing a substantial sum of money, he came to Santa Barbara in 1854 and became the city's first pharmacist.

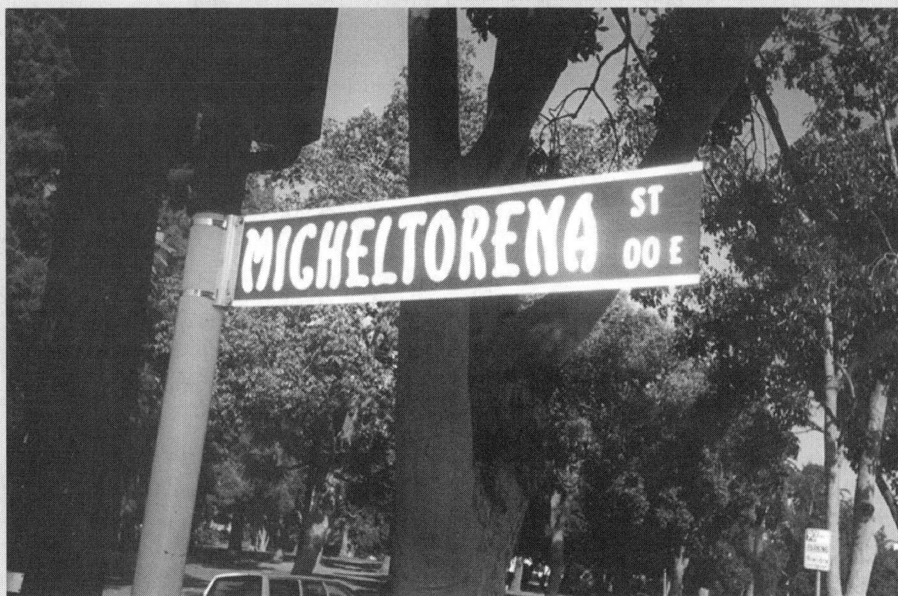


*Names and events in local history live on in Santa Barbara's street names.* PHOTO: KAREN BRIDGERS

**Haley Street**
This street is named for Salisbury Haley, a steamship captain who came to Santa Barbara as a surveyor in 1851 to lay out the city's streets.

**Indio Muerto Street**
The translation is literally "dead Indian"—Captain Haley found one here as he was doing his survey.

**Los Olivos Street**
"The Olives" Street once bisected the Mission's olive grove.

**Micheltorena Street**
Mexican governor Manuel Micheltorena took over as governor of California after Mexico overthrew the Spaniards in 1822.

**Milpas Street**
Milpas means "maize fields" or "sowing plot" in Spanish; the street is named for the farmland overseen by the Indians and padres from Mission Santa Barbara.

**Ortega Street**
Lieutenant Jose Francisco de Ortega was chosen in 1782 to be the builder and first commandant of the Presidio.

**Pedregosa Street**
The name is from the Spanish word meaning "stony"; this street was bisected by a stony creek.

**Salsipuedes Street**
In Spanish, *salsipuedes* literally means "leave if you can," a concept that residents continue to take literally when winter rains turn the area into a swamp.

**Sola Street**
Pablo de Sola was the last Spanish governor in California.

**Valerio Street**
Valerio was an infamous Indian robber who lived in a cave in the Santa Ynez Mountains and made forays into the city to steal from local residents.

**Yanonali Street**
This name is a variation on "Yanonalit," who was the Chumash chief when the Spanish arrived to establish the Presidio in 1769. After he was converted to Christianity, Pedro became his Christian name.

**Avis Rent-a-Car**
**(805) 965–1079, downtown Santa Barbara**
**(805) 964–4848, airport; (800) 331–1212**

**Budget Rent-a-Car**
**(805) 964–6791, airport; (800) 527–0700**

**Enterprise Rent-a-Car**
**(805) 966–3097, downtown Santa Barbara**
**(805) 683–0067, Goleta; (800) RENT–A–CAR**

**Hertz Rent-a-Car**
**(805) 967–0411, airport; (800) 654–3131**

**National Car Rental**
**(805) 967–1202, airport; (800) CAR–RENT**

**Thrifty Car Rental**
**(805) 681–1222, Goleta; (800) 367–2277**

**U-Save Auto Rental**
**(805) 963–3499, downtown Santa Barbara**

## The Santa Barbara Airport

"Quaint and charming" would be the words we'd use to describe the Spanish-style Santa Barbara Airport complex, which lies about 8 miles west of downtown. You, on the other hand, might think of something a bit more disparaging, especially if you're used to big-city technology and efficiency. But Santa Barbarans love their airport, and most visitors think its beautiful architecture and colorful Mission gardens are fitting for the gateway to a town so steeped in Spanish history. Big changes may be in store for the airport, however. A proposed expansion project, which will more than double the size of the terminal, is currently under environmental review. If approved, the first phase of the project should be completed by 2007 and will incorporate new FAA safety standards. In the meantime, we have a fancy new air-traffic control tower with state-of-the-art equipment, spanking-new restrooms, and a new aircraft rescue and fire-fighting station (not that you'd ever need it). The airport is often crowded, but in a friendly sort of way, and nearly everything is done the old-fashioned way, including the loading and unloading of baggage. There are no snug walkways out to your plane, so you have to cross the tarmac and go up the ramp. This means you'll need an umbrella if it's raining. Special assistance is available if you can't make the climb up the steps.

Departures and arrivals often happen in what seems like a simultaneous manner at adjacent gates, making the confining airport terminal a tight squeeze for everyone, but you're generally in and out so fast you hardly notice. Also keep in mind that air service is limited and generally requires a nonstop connecting flight to Los Angeles, San Francisco, San Jose, Denver, Salt Lake City, or Phoenix in order to board an international flight or even one that goes to the eastern half of the country. Unfortunately, connecting flights are often cancelled or delayed, causing no end of frustration for passengers who get hung up in L.A. or San Francisco. But if everything goes according to plan, you can enjoy a one-stop journey to one of 92 international destinations from our little airport.

Currently, the airport serves about 800,000 passengers per year with around 100 daily commercial flights. Major airlines servicing Santa Barbara include America West Express, American Eagle, Delta Airlines, and United Express, with air service provided by SkyWest Airlines and Air Wisconsin, but business in the commuter world is a bit volatile, so airline affiliations and service change from time to time. Santa Barbara's runways are relatively short, so air travel in or out of the city is always by turboprop or the smaller 737 jet. Most of the local airlines are linked to major airlines, so you can easily make connections, and you can even get a boarding pass and seating assignment for a longer trip as you board in Santa Barbara, saving time later.

Call these toll-free numbers for reservations: American Eagle/American Airlines, (800) 433-7300; United/United Express, (800) 241-6522; America West Express, (800) 235-9292. Information on

**Insiders' Tip**

The first road to be closed due to mudslides in a heavy rainstorm is almost always Calif. 154, so call for highway conditions, (800) 427-7623, before setting out.

airlines that serve the Santa Barbara area, the types of planes they fly, and their worldwide connections, as well as parking instructions and rates, are available from the Air Travel Hotline, (805) 683-4011. Better still, visit the Santa Barbara Airport web site at www.flysba.com.

## Airport Parking

The good thing about the short-term parking lot at the Santa Barbara Airport is that it's pretty much a hop, skip, and a jump from the terminal. You can whiz into the lot five minutes before Grandma's plane arrives and be at the gate in time to see her disembark. At peak travel seasons, however, part of the short-term lot (805-967-2745) may be used for long-term parking if the long-term lot, (805-967-4566) is full, which means you may drive around awhile before finding a spot. At such times (airport officials call it a "temporary overflow" situation), departing passengers are advised not to drive to the airport, but rather to take a taxi or shuttle or have someone drop them off to help alleviate the parking hassles.

This doesn't help you if you're picking up passengers, however, and you may find that your best bet is a quick stop in front of the terminal. If you do choose that option, be prepared to dodge a ton of traffic, don't leave your car unattended at the curb, and get in and out fast—it's a three-minute zone. (We find it's best to stay in the car, send the kids in to round up the arriving relatives, and just hope their plane is on time.) If you plan to park in the short-term parking lot, located to your left as you enter the airport, the first 15 minutes are free, you'll pay $1 for stays of 16 to 30 minutes, $2 if you park from 31 to 60 minutes, and $1 for each additional hour. Maximum charges are $10 per day in the daily section of the lot, and $15 in the hourly section. (If you eat at the Silver Wings Restaurant, on the second story of the terminal, you can get a validation for 90 minutes of free parking in the short-term lot—as long as you spend $6, excluding coffee and alcoholic beverages.)

The entrance to the long-term parking lot is farther east than the main airport entrance, which puts you farther away from the terminal, but it's still not much of a walk for the physically fit. Senior citizens, however, may find the trek a bit of a hardship, so you may want to drop them (and any heavy bags) off at the terminal before parking. As noted above, if the long-term lot is full, it may encroach on the short-term lot, and on the rare occasions that this occurs, a temporary parking lot is opened off Hollister Avenue adjacent to the Cinema Theater. A free airport shuttle will take you from there to the terminal, but you should arrive 90 minutes before your flight to allow enough time for parking and checking in. The overflow parking rate is $5 a day. Note that all the parking rates are raised periodically, and that all airport parking lots accept major credit cards.

## Leaving the Airport

To head to downtown Santa Barbara from the airport, turn right as you exit the parking lot and follow Sandspit Road past Goleta Beach Park, entering Calif. 217 where it merges with Sandspit Road. Stay in the left lanes, which merge with southbound U.S. 101 at Patterson Avenue. UCSB actually borders airport property on the west, so if you're going to the campus, turn right out of the airport parking lot, then take a quick left as the signs direct (if you go past Goleta Beach Park, you've gone too far). You will be linked with the last stretch of Calif. 217 and then find yourself at the entrance to the university. If you are staying in Goleta or want to go north, exit the airport to your left and follow Fairview Avenue to Hollister Avenue or Calle Real, major streets that should take you where you want to go. The northbound U.S. 101 on-ramp is on Fairview Avenue, on the north side of the overpass.

**Airport Shuttle Service**
**SuperRide Airport Shuttle**
**204 Moffett Place**
**Goleta, CA**
**(805) 683-9636, (800) 977-1123**

SuperRide provides on-demand, door-to-door shuttle service between the Santa Barbara Airport and the greater Santa Barbara area 24 hours a day. Reservations should be made 24 hours in advance, and the cost for one person varies from about $10 (Goleta) to more than $27 (Carpinteria), with fares based on the Zip code of origin or destination. Second passengers ride for $6.

**Shuttle Service to LAX**
**Santa Barbara Airbus**
**5755 Thornwood Drive**
**Goleta, CA**
**(805) 964-7759, (800) 423-1618**
**www.sbairbus.com**

Santa Barbara Airbus is a friendly local company that aims to save Santa Barbara travelers the hassles of driving to and departing from Los Angeles International Airport (LAX). It currently schedules seven daily round trips to LAX in comfortable buses originating at the company's Goleta office and stopping for pickups in Santa Barbara (at the Radisson Hotel) and Carpinteria (outside the International House of Pancakes on Casitas Pass Road). Long-term parking is available at the Goleta office by reservation only, but not at the Santa Barbara or Carpinteria stops. Trips to and from LAX generally take from two to two-and-a-half hours from Santa Barbara, depending on traffic. It seems that almost everyone in Santa Barbara has taken the Airbus at one time or another because the service is very reliable, it's generally cheaper than connecting with LAX via a commuter flight, and it's a pleasant drive. And what could be better than being dropped off in front of your LAX terminal? The fare to LAX for one person (if you make a reservation at least 24 hours ahead) is $34; it's $64 round-trip. You can show up without a reservation and hope there's room for you, but the fare goes up to $37 one-way and $69 round-trip. Discounts apply if two or more passengers travel together. Baggage is limited to two bags, plus a small carry-on, and an excess-baggage charge is levied if the limit is exceeded or if you transport unusual items such as bicycles, surfboards, or large boxes or trunks. Wheelchair-accessible vehicles require reservations 48 hours in advance, and charter services in 21-, 25-, and 47-passenger coaches are available.

The company also arranges Day Trip Adventures to Los Angeles destinations such as the Getty Museum, the Los Angeles Museum of Art, and Los Angeles basketball and baseball games. Call or visit its web site for further information.

> **Insiders' Tip**
>
> In accordance with California law, smoking is forbidden in any public building, which means you can't light up in the airport, bus station, or train station.

## Rail

**Amtrak**
**209 State Street**
**Santa Barbara, CA**
**(805) 963-1015, (800) USA-RAIL**
**www.amtrak.com**

Santa Barbara's lone Amtrak station, on lower State Street, flaunts an impressive face-lift, completed in Dec. 1999 at a cost of $8.4 million. Improvements included restoration of the historic old (1905) depot and upgrading of the Railway Express Agency, seismic upgrading, new platforms, landscaping, and the addition of taxi stands, bike racks, and 158 badly needed parking places. For the first time, long-term parking is now available at the

> **Insiders' Tip**
>
> Honking your horn while driving is just simply not done in Santa Barbara. According to state Motor Vehicle Code, it's illegal to blast your horn out of anger.

depot in a lot operated by the City of Santa Barbara. With all these improvements, traveling by train is an even more appealing alternative to sitting in traffic. Call the local number listed above for details on parking and other information, and for local schedules. Currently, the station is open from 5:45 A.M. to 9:00 P.M. daily and is fully staffed with ticketing, checked baggage, and package express service available. Separate, unstaffed, no-frills boarding platforms are in Carpinteria, at 475 Linden Avenue, and in Goleta, at the end of La Patera Lane between U.S. 101 and Hollister, but most passengers board at State Street.

Santa Barbara is served daily by Coast Starlight trains, which run between Seattle and Los Angeles, and the new Pacific Surfliner, which offers four round trips daily between here and San Diego, with one continuing to San Louis Obispo. The Pacific Surfliner trains are being upgraded, so you can ride in style with larger windows, laptop outlets, at-seat audio and video, reclining chairs with footrests, and complimentary wine and cheese. Other destination points along the routes are Oxnard, the San Fernando Valley, Los Angeles, and Orange County on southbound trains, and San Luis Obispo, San Jose, Oakland, Sacramento, and Portland on northbound trains. For a current schedule, pick up an Amtrak California Statewide Timetable (new ones are issued in May and October of each year), available at tourist stops around town or at the train station. Amtrak suggests that you call its toll-free number for fare information and be sure to ask about special packages. Generally, children ages 2 through 15 accompanied by an adult ride for half-price, and seniors 62 and older receive a 15-percent discount.

## Long-Distance Bus Service

**Greyhound Lines Inc.**
**Carrillo and Chapala Streets**
**Santa Barbara, CA**
**(805) 965-7551, tickets**
**(805) 962-2477, package express and baggage; (800) 231-2222**
**www.greyhound.com**

Greyhound has bus service that will eventually get you to almost anywhere in the United States. Direct service is offered to Los Angeles (up to 10 buses daily) and San Francisco (up to 6 buses daily). Information on all Greyhound routes and fares is available at the terminal or by calling the toll-free number shown above.

# History



Let's say you've just arrived in beautiful Santa Barbara for a week's vacation. You can't wait to get to the beach, you've been looking forward to sampling some local wines, and you plan to take in a concert or two. You couldn't care less about the history of Santa Barbara—you generally find history tedious and boring—and you'd just as soon skip the historical sights and get on with the good stuff.

Well, guess what? You don't have to go looking for history in Santa Barbara. It's right there every time you turn around.

Santa Barbara's roots are deep, and their evidence is everywhere: in the architecture, the street names, the celebrations, the shopping malls, the public parks and monuments, the food. Pretty soon you'll be so intrigued by everything around you that you'll be begging for a history lesson. Really.

## In the Beginning

Long before the celebrities and tourists hit the Santa Barbara beaches, the virgin stretches of sand and sea were home to the Chumash Indians, a gentle people who called their home "the land of the gods—the place where man was born."

Remains of Chumash villages have been found on both the mainland (the center of the Chumash capital city of Syukhtun was located on the present-day intersection of Cabrillo Boulevard and Chapala Street) and on the islands more than 20 miles offshore (now called San Miguel, Santa Rosa, Santa Cruz, Anacapa, and Santa Barbara or, collectively, the northern Channel Islands).

Ten thousand years ago, finely crafted 20-foot boats carried the Chumash back and forth across the Santa Barbara Channel as they brought their wares to market at Syukhtun or gathered to celebrate with dance, music, storytelling, and sacred ceremonies. The Chumash lived off the land and sea and developed a complex language, economy, and system of trade and taxation. When the Portuguese explorer Juan Rodriguez Cabrillo sailed to the Channel Islands in the fall of 1542, the Chumash paddled their massive canoes out to meet his two small ships, never realizing that this visit heralded changes that would eventually decimate their lives and culture.

## Santa Barbara, Protect Us!

Many seafaring explorers followed Cabrillo (who is reportedly buried somewhere on San Miguel Island), including Sir Francis Drake. On December 3, 1602, the eve of

**Insiders' Tip**

The Chumash population is estimated to have been about 22,000 before the arrival of the Spanish. Today, around 2,000 people in the area claim Chumash descent.

the feast day of Saint Barbara, patron saint of mariners, Sebastian Vizcaino's ship was in the channel when a violent storm erupted.

Fearing that he and his entire expedition were about to be swept to a watery grave, Vizcaino called upon the ship's friar to appeal to the saint, who was credited thereafter with sparing their lives.

In gratitude, the friar christened the channel Santa Barbara. None of the expedition disembarked, and it would be another 167 years before the land on either side of the channel was claimed for Spain.

## The Royal Presidio

On August 14, 1769, José Francisco de Ortega, a scout for the land expedition of Captain Gaspár de Portol, became the first non-Chumash of record to set foot in this area. The expedition, under the commission of King Carlos III of Spain, was sent with Father Junipero Serra to establish a series of both military and religious strongholds along the California coast in hopes of putting the entire region under the control of the Spanish crown.

Thirteen years later, Lieutenant Ortega brought a band of settlers and soldiers back with him and selected a spot for a fort approximately one mile inland from the south-facing shore. The last military outpost of the Spanish Empire in the New World thus originated on what is now the corner of Canon Perdido and Santa Barbara Streets. Father Serra celebrated a mass, and the fort was christened El Presidio Real de Santa Barbara (The Royal Fort of Saint Barbara).

## Mission Santa Barbara

By the late 1780s, several more structures had been added to the Presidio, including 12-foot-high walls with locked gates to surround it. Security had been one of the highest priorities of the Spanish, and with the settlement now enclosed and guarded, they were ready to turn their attention to building a mission for Father Serra. Unfortunately, the good father, knowing that construction of the mission would not begin until after the Presidio was completed, had already gone north to Monterey, where he died. His successor, Padre

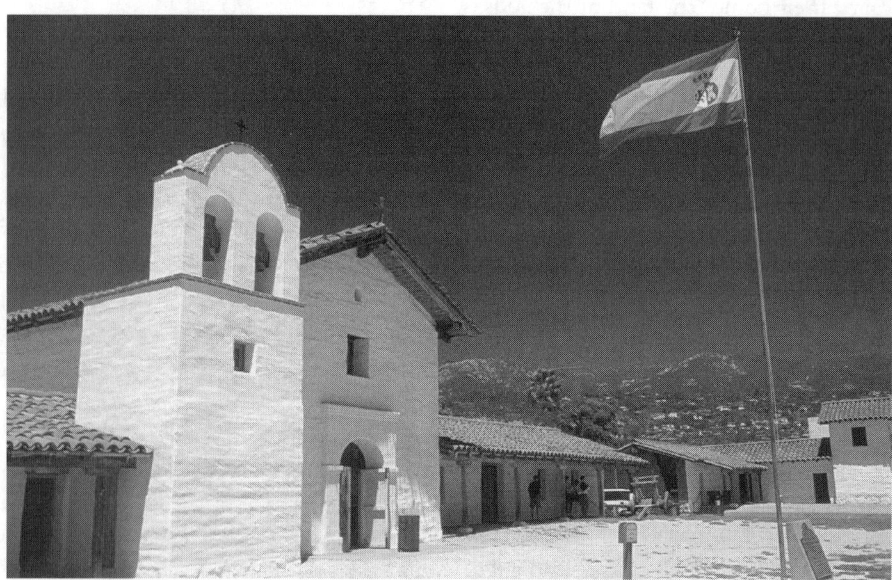

*The Spanish flag flies over El Presidio, the last military outpost of the Spanish Empire in the New World.*
PHOTO: BRIAN HASTINGS

**Insiders' Tip**

El Cuartel, built in 1782 and preserved in the El Presidio de Santa Barbara State Historic Park downtown, is the oldest residence in Santa Barbara and the second-oldest in California.

Fermín Francisco de Lasuen, raised and blessed the cross at Mission Santa Barbara on December 4, 1786. In addition to the dawning of organized religious life in Santa Barbara, the day's ceremonies marked the beginning of the end of the Chumash culture.

It was the Chumash Indians who had provided most of the labor for the building of the mission. The first structures were made of logs and mud, and the mission itself looked nothing like it does today. A small chapel, a kitchen, a granary, and separate quarters for the padres and the servants, arranged in a quadrangle, made up the early mission complex. Amid these humble surroundings, more than half of the Chumash population—including their chief, Yanonalit—eventually embraced Christianity, taking up residence nearby in a village that grew to include more than 250 adobe houses by the year 1800. Although the Chumash learned agriculture, animal husbandry, and other skills, the arrival of the Europeans took a terrible toll. Between 1787 and 1841, more than 4,000 Indians died, most from European diseases. By 1812, however, the faithful Indians had been instrumental in building two more churches on the mission site, including one adobe structure with six side chapels.

## Earthquake!

On December 12, 1812, a major earthquake wreaked havoc on the mission and surrounding areas. Following the initial shock, which caused most roofs to collapse, a series of tidal waves thundered as far inland as the Presidio, crushing and scattering what was left of the buildings. The Indians were terrified, and many fled the area, never to return.

In the ensuing weeks, aftershocks caused even more devastation, mud bubbled up from the ground, landslides buried many foothill canyons, and it seemed as though life would never be the same at Mission Santa Barbara. As the earth began to quiet, however, the rebuilding process began. In 1815, the remaining Indians, aided by soldiers and local artisans, started reconstructing the mission church using pink sandstone blocks and limestone mortar.

The new building, reportedly inspired by a drawing of a temple by Roman architect M. Vitruvius Polion from the first century B.C., had a single bell tower that was hung with six bells brought from Peru. On September 10, 1820, eight years after the disastrous quake, a formal dedication followed by a three-day fiesta celebrated its completion. A second tower was added just over 10 years later.

## The Rebellion

After the reconstruction of the mission, the Chumash Indians began to sorely resent their role as servants and builders. No longer free to roam the land they loved, they were sick, tired, and hungry, and they were often beaten for being lazy or disobedient.

The Mexicans, who took over the local government after the Mexican Revolution in 1822, were no kinder to the Indians than the Spanish had been, and in early

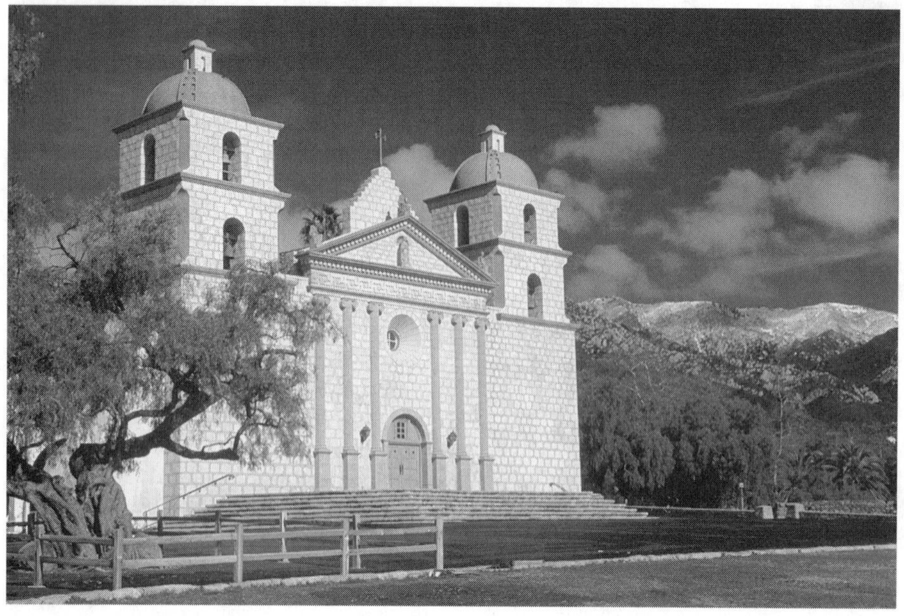

*Mission Santa Barbara is known as the "Queen of the Missions."* PHOTO: BRIAN HASTINGS

1824 the Santa Barbara Chumash joined forces with Chumash at the La Purísima, Ventura, and Santa Ines Missions to overthrow their oppressors.

After the severe beating of a young Chumash Indian in February, 1824, at Santa Ines, the Indians seized the mission and set fire to it. Demonstrations of support were staged at the three other missions, but the rebels were ultimately forced to flee when the military was called in to stop the revolt. After seeking refuge for a time with the Tulare tribe in the interior valley, the Chumash returned to Santa Barbara when the regional governor issued a guarantee of amnesty.

## The Mexican Period

Not long after Santa Barbara came under the political control of independent Mexico, foreign trade laws enforced under Spanish rule were abolished, and the city began to trade tallow and hides with the New England states, drawing Yankee traders such as William Goodwin Dana and his ship, *Waverly,* to the Santa Barbara area. (It was William Dana's cousin, Richard Henry Dana, who wrote *Two Years Before the Mast,* describing the latter's voyages to the area.)

The traders' visits were often filled with a whirlwind of social events arranged by hospitable Santa Barbara residents, including wealthy landowning Spanish dons and doñas whose families had stayed on after the Mexican Revolution.

On more than one occasion, dashing young sea captains fell in love with dark-eyed Santa Barbara señoritas and converted to the Catholic faith in order to marry them. William Dana himself fell for the charms of Josefa Carrillo, daughter of Carlos Antonio de Jesús Carrillo (better known as Don Carlos Carrillo), whose four sisters also married Americans.

Soon, it seemed everyone had heard of Santa Barbara, and its economic importance began to draw the attention of the U.S. government. During the Mexican War, in the late summer of 1846, a contingent of U.S. Marines led by Commodore Robert Field Stockton came ashore and raised the American flag over the Presidio. By Christmas Day, attempts by the Mexicans to regain control of the city had been put down by Captain John Fremont, and Santa Barbara belonged to the Americans.

The Californios (Hispanic residents who lived in Santa Barbara before it was captured by the United States) were furious about the takeover. As Americans continued to pour into Santa Barbara, Californios began to lose both their rights and their property; land was sold to the newcomers for 25 cents for an acre of farmland and $1 for a city lot.

Frustrated and angry, the Californios began to strike out at the Yankees by robbing and plundering them at every turn, but in the end their efforts were for naught. A drought in 1863–64 was the final economic blow to most of the remaining Californios, and many were forced to move to the poorer sections of town.

Soon after, displaced Chinese laborers from the California gold country moved into the city and often into the abandoned homes of the Californios. Shops, laundries, and gambling houses sprang up along Canon Perdido Street between State and Santa Barbara Streets. In response to some of the illegal activities of the Chinese, a law was eventually passed forbidding them to own land and thus forcing most of them to move to the outskirts of town. The social and economic future of Santa Barbara now rested squarely on the shoulders of the Americans, who by the late 1800s wielded most of the power and controlled nearly all of the land and the money.

**Insiders' Tip**

Santa Barbara's landmark Moreton Bay fig tree, planted at the junction of Highway 101 and Chapala Street in 1877, is the largest fig tree in the country. Stick the kids underneath, stand waaaaaay back, and you've got a great souvenir photo.

## The American Period

Full "Americanization," which included the adoption of English as the official language, slowly began to change Santa Barbara's character. By 1870 it was a growing American city with its own newspaper, boarding school, wharf, and expanding number of tourist attractions. Articles in major publications, including some New York City newspapers, praised the city's climate, hot springs, and other amenities, and before long tourists were coming in droves to stay at an increasing number of new hotels and boarding houses.

Stearns Wharf was completed in 1872 at a cost of $40,000, making Santa Barbara accessible by sea, and the Lobero Theatre, also completed in 1872, offered a new venue for the cultural arts. When the Southern Pacific Railroad connected Santa Barbara with Los Angeles in 1887 (the same year that State Street installed electric lights), the city became a full-blown tourist destination, hosting such luminaries as John D. Rockefeller, Sr., Andrew Carnegie, the Vanderbilts, and the DuPonts.

By the turn of the century, Santa Barbara was booming. In 1910, Santa Barbara became the "Film Capital of the World" when the American Film Company opened its Flying A Studio on the northwest corner of State and Mission Streets. The rugged backdrop of San Marcos Pass was often used for filming Westerns, and local beaches served as stand-ins for exotic island shores. Movie stars often sought respite in luxurious beachside hotels or relaxed in one of several local mineral springs.

With the continued Americanization of the city, Santa Barbara's Spanish

# Santa Barbara's Pearl

She was not a Santa Barbara native, never held a local office, and rarely dabbled in politics, but when it came to preserving, cleaning up, and beautifying Santa Barbara, Pearl Chase was a champion par excellence. She has been called tireless, persuasive, and selfless as well as bossy, arrogant, and curt, but no one disputes her lasting contribution to the city. At the time of her death in 1979 at the age of 90, Chase had received countless honorary degrees and national awards, was written up in a *Reader's Digest* article that dubbed her "Santa Barbara's Pearl," was voted the city's first Woman of the Year, and had done, according to one local writer, "more to beautify her adopted hometown of Santa Barbara than any other individual."

Born in Boston in 1888, Pearl Chase moved to Santa Barbara with her family when she was 12 years old. It wasn't until 1906, however, when she stepped off the train at Victoria Street Station with a degree from the University of California at Berkeley firmly in hand, that her commitment to civic activism was born. "I was," she said, "ashamed of the dirt and dust and ugly buildings and resolved then and there to devote my life to making Santa Barbara beautiful." And devote her life she did. Her resolve to dedicate herself to the public good got in the way of marriage and motherhood, but Chase had plenty to keep her busy during 70 years of public life. She had a magnificent vision of Santa Barbara's possibilities as a Mediterranean paradise or a "New Spain," and ferociously set about making her dream become a reality. She had little tolerance for laziness or excuses and handily took on anyone who got in her way.

Chase was instrumental in ridding the city of one of its worst eyesores, the local slaughterhouse, which she felt was both ugly and filthy. Then she started on the local dairies, which became veritable showplaces of sanitation and efficiency under her influence. She later took on the Southern Pacific Railroad, convincing corporate officials that the unsightly roundhouse on East Beach Boulevard should be rebuilt to resemble a Spanish bullring. It was done. She took up the cause of the poor, pushing for a new county hospital, collecting food and toys for underprivileged children at Christmas, and securing low-income housing in the city. Her dedication to the needs of Native Americans as vice president of the Santa Barbara Indian Defense Association for 14 years earned her the title of honorary Navajo Indian chief. In 1920 she helped form the Community Arts Association and placed herself on the Plans and Planting Committee, which heavily influenced almost all development within Santa Barbara at the time.

Despite her string of successes, however, that unpleasant hodgepodge of ugly commercial buildings downtown was a growing problem that even the formidable Pearl Chase seemed unable to remedy. Enter Mother Nature. On June 29, 1925, a magnitude 6.3 earthquake shook the Santa Barbara area, collapsing many of the downtown buildings that Chase and her committee found so objectionable. It was a golden opportunity. Almost immediately, the Plans and Planting Committee joined with the newly appointed Architectural Board of Review, and the "Santa Barbara look" was born. All reconstruction of buildings destroyed by the quake, as well as all new con-

*A plaque honoring Pearl Chase and her brother Harold sits prominently in Chase Palm Park.*
PHOTO: KAREN BRIDGERS

struction, was to conform to strict architectural standards. A Spanish-Mediterranean theme was to prevail, with red-tile roofs, arched facades, central courtyards, and muted plaster exteriors.

In 1927, Chase became chairwoman of the Plans and Planting Committee, a position she held until her retirement in the 1970s. She fervently pushed her agenda, advocating that no building in the city be taller than four stories and urging the banning of billboards along local highways. She convinced several major oil companies to construct their local gas stations in the Spanish style and took Standard Oil to task for plans to chop down a huge Moreton Bay fig tree at U.S. Highway 101 and Chapala Street, making the tree a public landmark in the process. In her spare time, Chase established the California Conservation Council, was a board member of the Save the Redwoods League, and continued to fight for the rights of the poor. In 1952, the *Los Angeles Times* named her its Woman of the Year, and in 1956, Santa Barbara bestowed the same honor. In 1963, Chase organized the influential Santa Barbara Trust for Historic Preservation, which remains dedicated to the preservation of historic buildings and sites in Santa Barbara County. Once a year in mid-November, a luncheon is held in Chase's honor, and the trust presents its annual Pearl Chase Award to a community activist who has dedicated his or her life to preserving and beautifying the city that Chase so loved.

The staggering impact that Pearl Chase had on the development of the city of Santa Barbara is in evidence everywhere today. Without any political authority whatsoever, Chase used pluck and determination (and her telephone) to fight for her causes. It is said that she knew just about everyone in town and prided herself on being a "burr under the saddle" of her opponents, many of whom gave in to her demands simply to end the tireless badgering. After her death, the hundreds of photographs and papers dealing with Chase's public life and service were donated to the

Special Collections Library at the University of California at Santa Barbara, which now bestows a scholarship in her name. Several plaques around town call grateful attention to her achievements, and Chase Palm Park, along the local waterfront, is named in her honor. Although many historians have paid her homage and young scholars continue to learn of her influence on the Santa Barbara of today, one question looms unanswered: Could Pearl Chase possibly have had anything to do with that fortuitous 1925 earthquake? Those who knew her don't doubt it for a second.

architecture began to be eclipsed by more "modern" buildings, resulting in a sort of hodgepodge look in the downtown area. Although many found this trend quite disturbing, no one was quite sure what to do about it. On June 19, 1925, a solution emerged in the form of a major earthquake that destroyed most of the downtown buildings, opening the way for reconstruction in what was to become the classic Santa Barbara style (see the Close-up in this chapter on Pearl Chase). During the 1930s, Santa Barbara's population continued to grow, and it remained a popular getaway for the rich and famous. Posh hotels such as Charlie Chaplin's Montecito Inn and Ronald Colman's San Ysidro Ranch catered to an upscale clientele.

Times were leaner during the Great Depression, and because the city was perched on the Pacific shoreline, there were many anxious moments during the war years that followed. In February 1942, a Japanese submarine fired on a beach approximately 10 miles west of the city, marking the first enemy shelling of the American mainland since 1812. Little damage was done, but tensions grew and coastal property values fell as a result of the incident. After World War II, Santa Barbara enjoyed the economic boom experienced by the rest of the country. The University of California at Santa Barbara campus accommodated young soldiers seeking an education on the GI Bill, and local government officials scrambled to secure enough water to meet the needs of the growing population. Bradbury Dam was completed in 1953, Cachuma Lake spilled over five years later, and the city's water problems seemed to be solved.

City boundaries expanded between 1960 and 1970, and Santa Barbara's population grew from 19,000 to more than 60,000. Research and development companies employed more than 160,000 workers by 1974, as families came to Santa Barbara from all over the country, drawn by the healthy economy and alluring lifestyle. The booming tourist economy was almost dealt a death blow in 1969 when a Union Oil platform five miles off the Santa Barbara coast blew out, sending thick waves of black crude oil onto local beaches. Tourism, as well as sea creatures and birds, took an extremely hard knock until the mess was cleaned up, and local environmentalists were livid, vowing to protect their beaches in the future. Since then, the activities of oil companies, who own drilling and tankering rights in the Santa Barbara Channel, have been under constant scrutiny.

Wildfires have also plagued Santa Barbara, the most recent being the 1990 fire that killed one person and destroyed hundreds of homes and several businesses. Started by an arsonist who was never caught, the blaze roared from the top of San Marcos Pass to the outskirts of Hope Ranch, driven by hot down-canyon winds. The threat of a brush fire is ever present in Santa Barbara, especially during drought years, when the canyons are overgrown with tinder-dry brush. (See our Living With Mother Nature chapter.) Fire was also a factor in November of 1998 when one of the city's most popular tourist attractions—Stearns Wharf—was hit by a $12-million blaze that destroyed 20 percent of the pier. Broadcast throughout the country, scenes of the spectacular blaze (as well as early reports that the wharf had been completely destroyed) led some to exclaim that Santa Barbara would never be the same. "Nonsense!" exclaimed city officials, who promptly plopped down a 70-foot Christmas tree on what was left of the rubble. With the burned-out section roped off, the pier reopened to public a few days after the fire, and repairs on the rest of the pier have now restored the landmark to its former glory.

Given that Santa Barbara's past is fraught with political skirmishes, water woes, environmental disasters, and economic downturns, the city has done well to maintain its reputation as a modern-day paradise. No matter how turbulent, every era of history has in some way left its mark, and Chumash Indians, Franciscan friars, Spanish dons, Mexican landowners, and irrepressible Yankee traders have all added something to the flavor of Santa Barbara. If you've any doubt, spend a few hours enjoying the festivities at the Old Spanish Days celebration, held each August (see our Annual Events chapter). On any given evening, you can watch Chumash dancers, see a living representation of Saint Barbara (a local woman is chosen to dress in costume and represent the saint), dance the fandango (complete with castanets), eat tacos washed down with tequila, and stop for a cappuccino on the way home. In no time at all, you'll be shouting "Viva la Fiesta!" right along with the natives.

**Insiders' Tip**

The last speaker of the Chumash language died in 1965.

# Hotels and Motels

**Santa Barbara**
**Goleta**
**Montecito**
**Carpinteria**

Santa Barbara has been known for its gracious hotels for more than 100 years. Many guests came to "take the cure" in the local mineral springs or benefit from the crisp ocean air. The first public lodging facility in the city, the Lincoln House, was built in 1871 and boasted 10 bedrooms, three bathrooms, and an adjacent stable for guests' horses and buggies. Today, that structure is part of The Upham Hotel, still one of the most charming lodging choices in Santa Barbara.

The most famous of Santa Barbara's grand hotels, the Arlington, was built four years later on State Street. A three-story structure with 90 luxurious rooms, the Arlington was known throughout the country as a retreat for discriminating guests and drew the rich and famous for more than 30 years until it burned to the ground in 1909.

In 1902, yet another grand hotel, the Potter, was constructed near the waterfront to attract wealthy winter visitors to what was quickly becoming one of California's most visited resort communities. The hotel was a five-story, 600-room respite for the rich and famous that charged $3 to $4 a night for a room and had its own vegetable garden and a country club with a racetrack, polo grounds, and a golf course. Unfortunately, the Potter also was destroyed by fire in 1921.

Despite these disasters, Santa Barbara has continued to build hotels and has big plans for the future. The most talked-about addition to the hotel scene is the 72-acre, $200-million Bacara Resort and Spa, in west Goleta. This glamorous Mediterranean-style resort opened its doors in September 2000 and has already lured a stream of celebrities and hosted high-profile weddings and conferences. You can read more about this in the listing below. Big changes are also brewing along the waterfront. In 2001, the owners of the Hotel Oceana in Santa Monica purchased four hotels opposite West Beach and transformed them into one sprawling beachfront resort that will go by the same name as its sibling. At press time, the hotel was still being revamped, but it looks set to make a huge splash on Santa Barbara's waterfront. In addition, the city recently approved a new hotel by Fess Parker (aka Davy Crockett) who already owns Fess Parker's DoubleTree Resort along this stretch. But construction of this hotel is not due to begin until summer 2002.

Even without these properties in the works, Santa Barbara has a lot to offer, and we've included some of the best and the brightest hotels and motels in our listings. Many of them have long and distinguished histories as well as fascinating guest lists, so we've tried to include the most interesting details and have even dropped a few names where appropriate.

Most of the older hotels are anxious to share their historic past with guests, and you can often find pamphlets or books in the lobby that will fill you in, so take the time to read them. (Who knows? Jacqueline Kennedy may have stayed in your very cottage!)

Even though you've probably read enough about Santa Barbara to entice you to come and visit, you may also be concerned about our city's high prices. Can you afford a vacation in paradise? Well, relax. Sure, we have a selection of exclusive resorts that are always written up in travel magazines and cost a small fortune, but there are plenty of moderately priced places too.

If you want a bare-bones kind of lodging option, you'll find an assortment of area Motel 6 accommodations: (805) 564-1392 or (805) 687-5400 in Santa Barbara; (805) 964-3596 in Goleta; (805) 684-6921 or (805) 684-8602 in Carpinteria; or call (800) 4-MOTEL-6 for toll-free reservations. There's also a Super 8 Motel in Goleta; call (805) 967-5591 or (800) 800-8000.

Also bear in mind that even the priciest accommodations can often be had for much less during the off-season (generally November through March, although many local hotels consider the Christmas holidays peak season), and several managers we talked to said they would often let rooms go for a song if they're available midweek at low season, so don't be afraid to haggle.

Before you pick up the phone, here are a few more facts that will help you make your decision. A 12-percent occupancy tax is added to all hotel room rates in the greater Santa Barbara area, so figure the extra into your total cost. Also, most hotels have a two-night minimum on weekends—especially during the high season. Unless we've indicated otherwise, the hotels and motels listed here offer discounts (AAA, corporate, AARP, etc.), cable television with at least one premium channel (HBO, Showtime, etc.), and smoking as well as nonsmoking rooms. They all accept major credit cards but only a few accept pets. We've noted the pet-friendly spots.

**Insiders' Tip**

Visiting Santa Barbara with Fido and want more information on pet-friendly spots? Go to www.allforanimals.com and click on the "Traveling to Santa Barbara with your pet" link. You'll find information on pet-friendly businesses in Santa Barbara, doggie daycare facilities, emergency hospitals, groomers, and specialty stores for pets.

Many hotels and motels offer a complimentary continental breakfast. Although the specifics may vary from place to place, this usually means pastries, muffins or bagels, fresh fruit, and coffee, tea, milk or juice. Generally this fare is available for a limited time each morning, so check the hours and realize that if you're a late sleeper, you may have to grab breakfast elsewhere.

All hotels are required by the Americans with Disabilities Act to provide fully accessible handicapped rooms (including bathrooms), so every lodging place we list has at least one. In addition, there may be several partially accessible rooms on lower floors, so if you are in need of any special facilities, make your needs known when you reserve your room.

Where we use the terms "full" or "fully stocked" kitchen, we mean a kitchen with everything you need to cook and serve a meal and clean up afterwards. A stove or stovetop, refrigerator, microwave, coffee maker, and pots, pans, dishes, and silverware will be on hand, and you'll have a sink to wash dishes in and towels to dry everything. If you have any question about kitchen facilities, ask.

One more thing: Many hotels offer privileges at local health clubs and golf courses. In some cases, this means you get to use the facilities for free or at a discounted price, but in others it means you get access but have to pay regular prices (this is especially true for privileges at private golf courses). Again, if you have any question about amenities, get a clear indication of what is complimentary and what you'll have to pay for. Finally, Santa Barbara has some of the highest hotel occupancy rates in Southern California, so if you're planning to visit at a busy time of year (long weekends, summer, and Christmas), try to book your hotel well in advance.

**Price-Code Key**

These prices are based on a one-night, double-occupancy stay in the high season and do not include taxes and fees for added services. Bear in mind that these are averages, so some rooms may be quite a bit more expensive. And, of course, fancy suites or cottages can run you into the several hundreds at the finest resorts.

| | |
|---|---|
| $ | $120 to $150 |
| $$ | $151 to $190 |
| $$$ | $191 to $250 |
| $$$$ | $251 and more |

# Santa Barbara

## By the Beach

**Cabrillo Inn at the Beach**
**931 E. Cabrillo Boulevard**
**Santa Barbara, CA**
**(805) 966–1641, (800) 648–6708**
**www.cabrillo-inn.com**
**$–$$**

This modest, family-run motel is not exactly deluxe, but it offers a clean, relaxed atmosphere and great oceanfront value. It's just a stone's throw from East Beach and the Cabrillo Bathhouse and about a mile from downtown. All but one of the 39 rooms have ocean and island views, and some have private balconies. Each has a king-size or two queen-size beds, an in-room refrigerator, and a phone (local and credit card calls are free).

You might find it hard to choose between the white sands across the street and the motel's two pools with two second-floor sundecks. Every morning you can head down to the ocean-view lounge for a complimentary continental breakfast and the morning paper.

Cabrillo Inn also has two Spanish-Mediterranean vacation cottages adjacent to the hotel. Each 1,600-square-foot unit has two bedrooms, two bathrooms, a large living room with a gas fireplace and sofa bed, a large, fully equipped kitchen with a dishwasher and microwave, direct-dial telephones with a private number and answering machine, laundry facilities, a VCR, and daily maid service.

Cottages rent weekly for between $1,575 to $2,675 depending on the season. Holiday rates are more. If you plan to stay awhile, ask about monthly rates. The cottages are nearly always booked, so make your reservations early. (Smoking is not allowed in the cottages.)

**Casa Del Mar**
**18 Bath Street**
**Santa Barbara, CA**
**(805) 963–4418, (800) 433–3097**
**www.casadelmar.com**
**$$**

If you walk just half a block from West Beach up Bath Street, you'll come to Casa Del Mar—a charming Mediterranean-style "house by the sea." It's a cross between a bed and breakfast inn and a small hotel, with very friendly service and helpful staff. Some of the 21 rooms and suites have full kitchens and 12 have mini-kitchens (a refrigerator and microwave), so this is a good spot for vacationing families, business travelers, and anyone who likes to prepare a few simple meals at "home." You can relax in the whirlpool spa or sit on the courtyard sundeck amid the flower gardens and winding pathways. All rooms have king- or queen-size beds and private baths, and some have a gas fireplace. Thoughtful touches include fresh flowers, hair dryers, coffee makers, and irons in every room.

There's a generous breakfast buffet every morning—rise and come down to the lounge and help yourself to homemade muffins, fresh croissants and cinnamon rolls, cereals, juices, and fruit. In the evening you can mix with other guests over wine and cheese. Business travelers appreciate the desk and telephone in every room and the fax service in the inn's office. All rooms at Casa Del Mar are non-smoking and golf and massage packages are available. Pets are welcome at an extra charge of $10 per night per pet, but they must never be left unattended.

**Country Inn by the Sea**
**128 Castillo Street**
**Santa Barbara, CA**
**(805) 963-4471, (800) 455-4647**
**www.countryinnbythesea.com**
**$$**

With its charming European country decor, the three-story Country Inn by the Sea provides a fresh bed-and-breakfast atmosphere a short walk from the beach. The inn is not in view of the ocean. It lies on a busy thoroughfare just a few blocks from West Beach, but car noise drops dramatically at night, when all the beachgoers are either out on the town or asleep.

When you're in your room you'll be in a reverie, anyway—you'll quickly float to dreamland under the cozy comforters in the canopy and four-poster beds. Four romantic spa rooms feature huge Jacuzzi tubs, and most rooms have air conditioning, refrigerators, balconies, and VCRs.

The remarkably friendly and hospitable staff is always happy to answer questions and direct you to the hotel's free video library, swimming pool, spa, redwood saunas, and sundeck. Every morning you can trot down to the sunny lounge for a tasty complimentary continental breakfast, and in the afternoons, the inn serves fresh-baked chocolate chip cookies with coffee and tea. The Country Inn by the Sea is completely smoke-free—no smoking is allowed anywhere on the premises.

**Eagle Inn**
**232 Natoma Avenue**
**Santa Barbara, CA**
**(805) 965-3586, (800) 767-0030**
**www.theeagleinn.com**
**$$$**

Set in a residential area a few blocks up Bath Street from the beach, this unique hotel features an exquisite exterior and a quiet, intimate atmosphere. It's considered a prime example of Spanish Colonial architectural style and has unusual Moorish-style doorways with pointed arches and cast-stone ornamentation, including a large eagle on the front wall (hence the name of the inn). The hotel has few recreational amenities, but it's a great base from which to explore the area. You can easily walk from here to restaurants, West Beach, the harbor, and Stearns Wharf.

Owners Alan and Janet Bullock once owned a hotel in England. They stopped in Santa Barbara while on vacation, fell in love with the area, and decided to move here (does this sound like a familiar story?). They purchased and converted a 1920s apartment building and transformed it into the Eagle Inn in 1981.

The inn's 30 light, spacious rooms feature fine period furnishings and details. About two-thirds have kitchens with dining areas (since it used to be an apartment complex), which makes the inn a good choice for long-term stays (weekly and long-term rates are available). All rooms are nonsmoking and have refrigerators, coffee makers, hair dryers, microwaves, ceiling fans, direct-dial phones with voice mail, and private baths. Rates include a complimentary continental breakfast. Thanks to a 2002 facelift, French windows and small balconies will add a touch of elegance to some of the front rooms. The lobby will be completely renovated to improve wheelchair accessibility, and many of the rooms will be enhanced with gas fireplaces.

**Fess Parker's DoubleTree Resort**
**633 E. Cabrillo Boulevard**
**Santa Barbara, CA**
**(805) 564-4333, (800) 879-2929 (outside 805 area code)**
**www.fpdtr.com**
**$$$$**

You won't find a swankier hotel on the main waterfront than the Doubletree. It's one of the city's largest and most eye-catching resorts, with 337 luxurious rooms and 23 deluxe suites, all set on 24 landscaped oceanfront acres about a half-mile east of Stearns Wharf. With its expansive meeting and banquet facilities, the resort draws large numbers of conferees, but it's also popular with tourists seeking plush waterfront digs. Even if you don't stay here, you can stroll, picnic, and people-watch in the grassy expanse that fronts the hotel (it's a city park, though you won't see too many signs announcing this fact).

"Extra oversize" is the best way to describe the guestrooms at the Doubletree—each averages 425 to 450 square feet and holds either a king-size or two queen-size beds with feather pillows. Dressed in ocean-inspired colors, each room has a patio or balcony, bathroom with a double vanity, mini-bar, sitting area, work desk, iron and ironing board, and coffee maker. Parking is complimentary if you park yourself; otherwise pay the valet service to do it for you.

In many ways, this resort resembles a health spa: you can play tennis on the lighted courts, swim some laps in the pool, hit a few balls on the putting green, work out in the fully equipped health center, or indulge in some relaxing treatments at Spa De Menicucci. Many guests rent bikes or in-line skates (for a fee) and cruise along the beachfront bike path across the street. You don't have to go far to replenish yourself after burning up all those calories. The two restaurants on the premises—Cafe Los Arcos and Rodney's Steakhouse (see the Restaurants chapter)—serve excellent food. If you're starving at 2:00 A.M., you can call upon the 24-hour room service to sate your hunger pangs. Believe it or not, pets are welcome on the first floor of this posh resort at no extra fee, so go ahead and bring Fifi and Fido along.

**Franciscan Inn**
**109 Bath Street**
**Santa Barbara, CA**
**(805) 963–8845**
**www.franciscaninn.com**
**$**

The Franciscan Inn is a charming and affordable Spanish-Mediterranean hideaway in a residential area just a few blocks from the beach. You can easily stroll to West Beach, the Santa Barbara Harbor, Stearns Wharf, State Street, and many shops and restaurants. The hotel's moderate size enables the owners to maintain a tranquil, private, family-style atmosphere and a high level of personalized service. Many guests return year after year, and a lot of them rave about the Franciscan's dedicated staff, many of whom have worked here for a decade or longer. Brightened with homey floral touches, the 53 rooms and suites were designed to meet a variety of budgets. Choices range from a cozy room with a single bed to spacious suites with a living room, wet bar, and fireplace. Many rooms feature comfortable sitting areas, and nearly all the suites provide fully stocked kitchenettes or full kitchens. All rooms and suites include direct-dial telephones with free local calls as well as TVs and VCRs with extended cable. Outdoors you can swim in the spacious pool or soak in the private spa tucked away in a secluded garden setting.

The Franciscan attracts many business travelers and extended-stay visitors. Many rooms feature dataports, computer hookups, and separate sitting areas. Weekly rates are available. Other extras at the Franciscan include complimentary continental breakfast, an afternoon tea-and-cookie hour, self-service laundry facilities, and valet service for dry cleaning.

**Harbor View Inn**
**28 W. Cabrillo Boulevard**
**Santa Barbara, CA**
**(805) 963–0780, (800) 755–0222**
**$$$$**

Luxurious yet casual, this Spanish-Mediterranean resort ranks among our favorite beachside hotels. It enjoys a prime waterfront location, overlooking Stearns Wharf and West Beach, just a half-block west of State Street (you can't get much closer to the tourist action than this). Originally built in 1985, it was renovated and expanded in the mid-1990s. In 2001, the east wing was expanded to include new luxury guest rooms and suites, most with ocean views. The owners also added a gift shop and business center.

The hotel now boasts 86 large, air-conditioned guest rooms and 10 suites, each decorated with specially designed fabrics, upholstery, tile, and artwork.

## Insiders' Tip

For quick reservations for Santa Barbara-area hotels, call Coastal Escapes Reservations Services at (800) 292-2222 or Santa Barbara Hot Spots at (800) 793-7666.

Many rooms feature oversize marble baths, sunken tubs, cathedral ceilings, wet bars, sliding louvered shutters, garden patios or balconies, and a choice of ocean or mountain views. Other touches include air conditioning, refrigerators, coffee makers, safes, robes, TVs, and an iron and ironing board in every room.

Outdoors, you can soak up the sun across the street at the beach or on the second-floor sundeck, then unwind in the large, glass-enclosed pool (young children can splash about in their own separate wading pool). Health buffs can work out in the fitness center and, at day's end, you can stroll in the gardens and stargaze while relaxing in the outdoor spa. Room service runs from 7:00 A.M. to 10:00 P.M. The lobby is always open and staffed by friendly professionals who really do go the extra mile to make your stay enjoyable.

**Hotel Oceana**
**202 W. Cabrillo Boulevard**
**Santa Barbara, CA**
**(805) 965–4577, (800) 965–9776**
**www.hoteloceana.com**
**$$$**

In 2001, a developer snapped up four established Spanish-Mediterranean–style hotels on Santa Barbara's waterfront (Beachcomber Inn, La Playa Motel, Ocean Palms Resort, and Sandy Beach Inn) and set about transforming them into one deluxe new 122-room hotel, Hotel Oceana. If its namesake sibling in Santa Monica is anything to go by, this new venture—completed at the end of 2001—will be a hit. It's in a prime location opposite West Beach, and with its low-rise red-tile roofs, palm-studded gardens, and pleasing swathes of green, it has plenty of potential. The rooms feature fully stocked mini-bars, hair dryers, irons and ironing boards, radios with CD players, and VCRs with DVD players. Amenities include two heated pools, a Jacuzzi, conference facilities, a breakfast cafe, and a fitness center.

**Inn by the Harbor**
**433 W. Montecito Street**
**Santa Barbara, CA**
**(805) 963–7851, (800) 626–1986**
**www.sbhotels.com**
**$**

Inn by the Harbor sits right next to the Tropicana Inn and Suites—they both belong to the same hotel family. However, the no-frills Inn by the Harbor is a little less expensive than its sister property. In 1999, the hotel was completely revamped. You enter the parking lot from a busy street, but most rooms are set back away from the street noise. From here you can walk three blocks to West Beach and the marina, then just a few more blocks to Stearns Wharf and State Street.

The inn offers 42 rooms, all nonsmoking and decorated in French country style, plus complimentary continental breakfast every morning. Room choices range from standard rooms with king- or queen-size beds to family suites with kitchens. One of the motel's nicest features is a peaceful, enclosed tropical courtyard pool area where you can sit and soak up some rays if you can't bring yourself to walk three blocks to the beach.

**Radisson Hotel Santa Barbara**
**1111 Cabrillo Boulevard**
**Santa Barbara, CA**
**(805) 963–0744, (800) 643–1994**
**www.radisson.com**
**$$$**

This sprawling Mediterranean-style oceanfront hotel is ideal for family vacations and relaxing getaways. East Beach, the Cabrillo

*Santa Barbara's waterfront hotels bask between mountains and sea.* PHOTO: BILL DEWEY, COURTESY OF THE SANTA BARBARA CONFERENCE & VISITORS BUREAU

Bathhouse, and a beachfront playground are just across the boulevard, and the zoo is a half-block walk away. To reach Stearns Wharf and State Street (about a mile down the road), hop on the electric shuttle that stops right in front of the hotel.

The hotel takes up an entire city block and the rooms are spread out in four buildings, so be sure to request accommodations close to the facilities if you have mobility problems. The Radisson offers 173 guest rooms, most with panoramic ocean or mountain views and either one king-size or two queen-size beds. Each room has a color TV with Nintendo games, a mini-bar, a telephone with voice mail and modem jack, climate control, a coffee maker, a hair dryer, robes, and an iron and ironing board. The ocean-view rooms were recently renovated. You and the kids can splash in the heated outdoor pool and gaze at the ocean at the same time. Or sink into the new Jacuzzi for a relaxing soak. When you feel like working out, just head for the hotel fitness center.

If you don't feel like venturing far away for meals, you can dine at the ocean-view Bistro Eleven Eleven, "where the food gets dressed up, but you don't have to." The restaurant serves breakfast, lunch, and dinner, and the lounge has live entertainment on weekends.

**Santa Barbara Inn**
**901 E. Cabrillo Boulevard**
**Santa Barbara, CA**
**(805) 966–2285, (800) 231–0431**
**www.santabarbarainn.com**
**$$$–$$$$**

Santa Barbara Inn is an elegant yet unpretentious upscale hotel that sits right across from East Beach and features some of the best unobstructed ocean views in the waterfront district. The hotel's biggest draw, apart from the view and the outstanding service, is Citronelle at the Beach, award-winning chef Michel Richard's renowned restaurant (see our Restaurants chapter).

Even if you don't stay at the inn, you should treat yourself to dinner or at least appetizers and drinks at Citronelle, which occupies a prime third-story corner of the hotel. You can savor the California French cuisine, acclaimed as some of finest in the nation, while taking in panoramic ocean views.

In 1998 the hotel was renovated inside and out. Each of the 71 deluxe rooms and suites features a large, private balcony, views of the ocean or mountains, and a refrigerator and coffee maker. The rooms are not air-conditioned, but they do have ceiling fans.

Suites have hair dryers and wet bars, and six rooms have fully equipped kitchens. The inn's other amenities include daily newspaper delivery, nightly turn-down service, a sundeck overlooking the ocean and lush gardens, and valet parking. Nonsmoking rooms are available. Should you decide to lounge close to home rather than across the street at the beach, you can relax in the heated pool and spa.

**Tropicana Inn and Suites**
**223 Castillo Street**
**Santa Barbara, CA**
**(805) 966–2219, (800) 468–1988**
**www.sbhotels.com**
**$–$$**

Done in cozy French country decor, The Tropicana offers an affordable yet comfortable alternative to the oceanfront Cabrillo Boulevard. Although Castillo Street handles a lot of beach traffic during the day, it quiets down at night, and most rooms are set back from the street. West Beach and the harbor are just two blocks away, and you can walk to restaurants and Stearns Wharf.

Your accommodation choices range from standard rooms with a king-size or two queen-size beds to family suites that can sleep up to eight persons and have full-size kitchens. Each room has a refrigerator; all are nonsmoking. Outdoors, you can dive into the heated pool, relax in the whirlpool, and lounge on the scenic sundecks. Start your day with a complimentary continental breakfast on the arbored patio and end it with milk and cookies or port wine and French brie. There's a coin-operated laundry on-site. Weekly and monthly rates are available.

**West Beach Inn at the Harbor**
**306 W. Cabrillo Boulevard**
**Santa Barbara, CA**
**(805) 963–4277, (800) 423–5991**
**www.westbeachinn.com**
**$$–$$$**

The three-story, Mediterranean-style West Beach Inn is fresh, cheery, and more affordable than most oceanfront accommodations. It's right across the street from the harbor and near West Beach. In 2000, management spruced up the guest rooms with new carpets and furnishings. Each has a refrigerator, coffee maker, hair dryer, iron and ironing board, bathrobes, and air conditioning. Many rooms also have views of the yachts bobbing in the harbor. Choose a one-bedroom suite if you'd like a kitchen. During the winter months, you might prefer a two-bedroom suite with a fireplace. The pool and spa overlook the ocean, so you can easily check out what's happening across the way. The inn serves a complimentary continental breakfast every morning and wine and cheese every afternoon.

## In Town

**Best Western Encina Lodge and Suites**
**2220 Bath Street**
**Santa Barbara, CA**
**(805) 682–7277, (800) 526–2282**
**www.sbhotels.com**
**$$**

We really like this well-managed hotel, which lies about two miles inland and one mile from downtown. It's cheerful, freshly painted, well kept, and very friendly (manager Carol Wolford is justifiably proud). Tucked into a residential neighborhood about a half-block from Santa Barbara Cottage Hospital and the renowned Sansum–Santa Barbara Medical Clinic (see our Healthcare and Wellness chapter), the property caters to older guests, many of whom are visiting local clinics or providing support to hospitalized friends or family.

The range of accommodations is exhaustive, with seven buildings housing

**Insiders' Tip**

The off-season in Santa Barbara is November through March, so you'll save money if you visit then.

regular guest rooms, apartments (some with two bedrooms and/or full-size kitchens), townhouses, pool suites, and efficiency units with kitchenettes. All rooms are decorated in a country style, and there are lots of nice decorative touches in every room.

Most of the units have a hair dryer, refrigerator, iron and ironing board, and coffee maker, and there is a wall safe in every room. The staff puts hard candy, apples, oranges, and packaged cookies in each room every day, which is another of those small touches that makes you feel at home.

A small pool, Jacuzzi, massage facility, and beauty shop are located on the grounds. Victoria's Cafe, across the parking lot from the office, serves breakfast, lunch, and dinner, and a flock of chattering finches fills the aviary outside.

In addition to the standard discounts, Encina Lodge offers discounts for anyone going to a Santa Barbara medical facility and will provide free transportation to doctor's appointments in the area as well as to the Santa Barbara Airport or the train station. Monthly rentals are available between October and mid-May.

**Best Western Pepper Tree Inn**
**3850 State Street**
**Santa Barbara, CA**
**(805) 687–5511, (800) 338–0030**
**www.sbhotels.com**
**$$**

Dotted with palms on Santa Barbara's busy main street, this well-maintained Spanish-Mediterranean mini-resort is similar in many ways to its sister, the Best Western Encina Lodge. With the friendly staff, comfortable rooms, central location, fountains, and reasonable rates, you can't go wrong by staying here. The inn is set on 5 landscaped acres in the heart of the Upper State Street shopping district, across the street from La Cumbre Plaza mall. Each of the 150 individually decorated guest rooms has a private patio or balcony overlooking garden courtyards with tiled pools and whirlpools. The rooms have air conditioning, coffee makers, and refrigerators, and fresh fruit and cookies are supplied. Extra amenities include two large tiled pools, an exercise room, a sauna, a massage room, hair salons, valet laundry service, and a gift shop.

K's Treehouse Restaurant and Lounge is right on the property. The restaurant serves breakfast, lunch, and dinner in a casual atmosphere and will also deliver to your room or poolside.

When you need a ride to or from the airport or train station, just make arrangements with the staff for complimentary transportation.

**El Encanto Hotel and Garden Villas**
**1900 Lasuen Road**
**Santa Barbara, CA**
**(805) 687–5000, (800) 346–7039**
**www.elencantohotel.com**
**$$$$**

Perched on Santa Barbara's Riviera, El Encanto (the name means "the enchanted" in Spanish) is a restored landmark complex that became a hotel in 1918. This venerable property was designated a charter member of Historic Hotels of America in 1990. The views of the city and ocean are stunning (even though you're several miles from the beach), and Mission Santa Barbara, the Botanic Garden, and the Santa Barbara Museum of Natural History are just down the road. Accommodations include 84 guest rooms, cottages, and villas in California Craftsman and Spanish Colonial Revival style, arranged among 7 acres of tropical gardens and quiet walkways. All are individually decorated, and several have fireplaces, porches, hardwood floors, and/or private balconies or patios. Most rooms only have one bed (king- or queen-size) so the hotel attracts many couples seeking a quiet respite.

The Presidential Villa, which has two bedrooms, two wood-burning fireplaces, and a spacious private patio with a fountain, was refurbished in 1996 and welcomed Prince Michael of Kent as its first guest (the going rate today is about $1,450 per night).

The hotel has several small meeting rooms, including the 660-square-foot Fireside Salon. Other amenities include a pool and tennis court, and guests are invited to an early evening Sunset Hour, which includes live entertainment, in the lounge Thursday through Saturday. The dining room (see our Restaurants chapter), which has some of the best views of any restaurant in the city, is open for breakfast, lunch, dinner, and Sunday brunch and boasts a wonderful outside terrace.

**El Prado Inn**
**1601 State Street**
**Santa Barbara, CA**
**(805) 966–0807, (800) 669–8979**
**www.elpradoinn.com**
**$**

Family-owned and -operated, El Prado is not one of those splashy Santa Barbara accommodations you read so much about, but rather a cozy and reasonably priced little motor inn on busy State Street offering value for your money and personalized service. All the rooms were recently revamped, with new furniture throughout, and a face-lift for the baths is underway. The lobby is homey and has its own resident cat, which welcomes new arrivals. Guests can also help themselves to coffee, tea, cocoa, apples, and cookies, which are available all day.

The inn has 62 well-kept rooms with queen- or king-size beds, and six suites with refrigerators, microwaves, sitting areas, and patios. Free continental breakfast is provided, and meeting space is available for 40. A heated pool and patio are about the only other amenities, but a coin-operated laundry and a market are right across the street, and you can reach nearly all of the area's attractions in just minutes.

Subject to availability, El Prado offers a variety of packages and discounts, including discounted rates for patients at Cottage and St. Francis Hospitals, so be sure to ask about specials when you reserve.

**Holiday Inn Express—Hotel Virginia**
**17 W. Haley Street**
**Santa Barbara, CA**
**(805) 963–9757, (800) 549–1700**
**www.hotelvirginia.com**
**$$$**

One of downtown Santa Barbara's newest boutique hotels is really one of its oldest—the 1926 Hotel Virginia, which is currently listed on the National Registry of Historic Places. It opened in January 1999 after undergoing a $5-million renovation and now combines the historic Spanish Colonial elements of the building with an Art Deco–style interior, including a mosaic fountain in the lobby and replicas of Malibu and Catalina tilework throughout. This is a great spot to stay if you're in town for

### Insiders' Tip

During Fiesta in early August, it's nearly impossible to find lodging in Santa Barbara. Make your reservations well ahead of time. For more affordable rates, try booking a room in Carpinteria or other areas outside the city.

business or want easy access to the shops, restaurants, and businesses downtown. You won't find a pool on-site, but the hotel is only four blocks from the beach. The 61 guestrooms feature 1920s Art Deco furnishings, advanced phone systems with dataports, hair dryers, ironing boards with irons, and air-conditioning. Guests also receive a complimentary continental breakfast of fresh pastries and can park their cars in a private lot for a fee—a big bonus in the downtown area. Call for information on discounts and special packages.

**Hotel Santa Barbara**
**533 State Street**
**Santa Barbara, CA**
**(805) 957–9300, (888) 259–7700**
**www.hotelsantabarbara.com**
**$$–$$$**

Before Hotel Santa Barbara opened in mid-1997 after a $4 million renovation to the 100-year-old building, there wasn't one hotel on lower State Street that we would have included on our "best and brightest" list.

This hotel has changed all that in a big way, providing well-appointed lodging in the heart of downtown's social scene. Walk into the elegant lobby with its tiled floor, large Grecian urns, and profusion of plants and flowers, and you'll get your first taste of how much work has gone into making this three-story property a showplace.

Seventy-five air-conditioned rooms and nine suites are appointed with queen- or king-size beds, with pullout sofas in the suites. All rooms are nonsmoking and have coffee makers and bottled water. Guests may request hair dryers, refrigerators, and ironing boards with irons. A complimentary continental breakfast is served to guests each morning, and coffee is available in the lobby throughout the day. Two conference rooms are also available. Although the hotel is on bustling State Street, the indoor corridors make it quiet and secluded. It's near downtown shops and restaurants and within five blocks of Stearns Wharf and the waterfront. If the view is important to you, ask for one of only four rooms that overlook State Street and the mountains. Guests who stay on a Saturday night don't have to check out until 6:00 P.M. Sunday upon request. When you call, be sure to ask about special packages that include discounts on local dining.

As we see it, the only drawback to Hotel Santa Barbara is its tricky parking situation. There is one pullout space in front of the hotel for loading or unloading, but the main parking lot is located behind the hotel with valet parking access in an extremely narrow driveway on Cota Street. If you opt to park your own car, turn into the small alley south of the valet parking driveway. Keep your eyes open or you'll miss it.

**Inn of the Spanish Garden**
**915 Garden Street**
**Santa Barbara, CA**
**(805) 564–4700, (866) 564–4700**
**www.SpanishGardenInn.com**
**$$$$**

Set deep in Santa Barbara's oldest neighborhood amid a mix of low-rise businesses and residences, this intimate Spanish-Mediterranean boutique hotel opened in 2001 just a few blocks from downtown. From here you can stroll to restaurants, businesses, shops, and theaters. It's a good choice for upscale leisure and business travelers seeking stylish accommodations close to downtown. The modern technology here is a nice counterpoint to the aura of Old World charm. All of the 23 spacious guest rooms and suites are air conditioned and come with king- or queen-size beds, DSL lines for high-speed Internet access, coffee makers, hair dryers, TVs and VCRs, and ceiling fans. The rooms also feature Spanish-style tiling, high ceilings, fireplaces, secluded garden patios or balconies, and private baths with deep tubs in most and deluxe toiletries. All are nonsmoking. In your free time, you can paddle in the lap pool, relax in the tropically landscaped courtyard, work out in the fitness room, or snuggle around the outdoor fire pit on cool nights. Continental breakfast and evening wine hour are included in the rates, the inn offers underground parking, and an intimate boardroom is available for business meetings.

**Lemon Tree Inn**
**2819 State Street**
**Santa Barbara, CA**
**(805) 687–6444, (800) LEM–ORNG**
**www.treeinns.com**
**$$–$$$**

Situated at the busy intersection of State Street and Alamar Avenue, the Lemon Tree (it actually has fruit-producing lemon trees growing across the front of the parking lot) offers a variety of fairly standard accommodations in 96 rooms and a deluxe wing (built in 1996) with a conference room and three suites. All of the rooms are nonsmoking and have king-, or two queen-size beds, air conditioning, and TV.

The poolside rooms have glass doors that open onto a patio facing the pool and are far more appealing than rooms that open onto the front of the building and face the parking lot. The pool area itself is delightful, with a tropical atmosphere, a Jacuzzi spa, and a giant chessboard.

You can visit the Crocodile Restaurant and Bar on the premises for breakfast, lunch, and dinner (see our restaurant chapter). The Crocodile serves drinks on the patio and offers live entertainment until 10:00 P.M. Wednesday through Saturday.

**Mountain View Inn**
**3055 De la Vina Street**
**Santa Barbara, CA**
**(805) 687–6636**
**www.mountainviewinnsb.com**
**$**

If you're on a budget and want to be in the center of town, this small no-frills motel will give you great value for the money. It's in the mid–State Street area right next to MacKenzie Park, close to Cottage Hospital, Sansum Medical Clinic, and Earl Warren Showgrounds, and within walking distance of a number of shops and restaurants.

The inn was completely renovated in 1997, and the 34 nonsmoking rooms are fresh, simple, and comfortable. Each room has a king-size, a queen-size, a queen-size and a double, or two double beds, air conditioning, a writing desk and chair, and direct-dial phones. When the weather's warm, cool off in the small outdoor pool. Complimentary continental breakfast is served daily.

**The Sandman Inn**
**3714 State Street**
**Santa Barbara, CA**
**(805) 687–2468, (800) 350–8174**
**www.thesandmaninn.com**
**$$**

The Sandman provides clean, comfortable accommodations in the Upper State Street area, close to La Cumbre Plaza mall and dozens of restaurants. All guests enjoy free access to the YMCA just a half-block away. Despite its busy location, the hotel has beautifully landscaped gardens and attractive recreational facilities. In your free time, you can splash about in the inn's two swimming pools or relax in the Jacuzzi. The inn has 112 air-conditioned rooms, including single and double rooms, suites, and family rooms with fully equipped kitchens. Each room has a hair dryer, a refrigerator, an iron and ironing board, cable TV, voice mail, and a coffee maker. A bar and grill on-site serves lunch and dinner, and room service is also available for those meals.

Business travelers appreciate the high-speed DSL Internet access in the lobby, and other amenities include a complimentary continental breakfast, ample free parking, and a laundry facility.

**The Upham Hotel**
**1404 De la Vina Street**
**Santa Barbara, CA**
**(805) 962–0058, (800) 727–0876**
**www.uphamhotel.com**
**$$$**

At the stately Upham Hotel, established in 1871, you can experience a bit of Santa Barbara history and enjoy easy access to

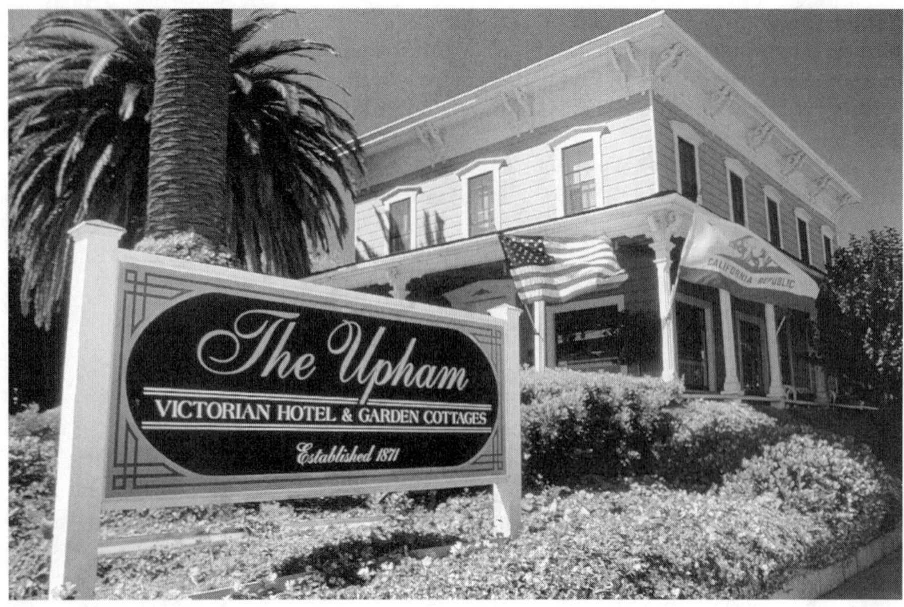


*Santa Barbara's accommodations range from affordable family lodgings and plush resorts to hotels steeped in history. An example of the latter is The Upham, circa 1871.* PHOTO: BRIAN HASTINGS

the arts and culture district. This elegant city landmark is the oldest continuously operating hostelry in Southern California. The Victorian hotel and garden cottages occupy a corner of De la Vina and Sola Streets, just two blocks from State Street and within walking distance of the Arlington Theatre, the Museum of Art, restaurants, and shops.

The Upham was built by Boston banker Amasa Lincoln (a distant cousin of Abraham Lincoln) in 1871. The Lincoln House (its original name) was an elegant, New England-style boarding house made of redwood timbers. Since it was built before mule-powered streetcars and the railroad came to town, the first guests arrived on foot or by horse or steamship. A subsequent owner, Cyrus Upham, changed the name to Hotel Upham in 1898.

Today the Upham tradition of hospitality is still going strong. The hotel was completely restored and refurbished in the 1980s and features a cozy lounge with a large fireplace, comfy sofas, and newspapers; tranquil gardens; and a resident cat, Henry, who will probably be the first staff member to greet you in the lobby. The atmosphere is very much bed and breakfast-style—in fact, the Upham Hotel frequently appears in bed and breakfast listings.

Fifty guestrooms and suites are contained in the original main building, three Garden Cottage buildings, the Lincoln Building, the Carriage House, and the Jacaranda and Hibiscus buildings. Each unit is individually decorated and filled with antiques and period furnishings. Fresh flowers and bedside mints add a homey touch.

All rooms have a private bath, direct-dial phone, and cozy comforters; VCRs and fax machines are available on request. Units in the Garden Cottages feature porches or secluded patios; several have gas fireplaces. For the ultimate splurge, book the luxurious Master Suite with a Jacuzzi tub, fireplace, wet bar, and private yard where you can nap peacefully in the hammock.

Rates include a sumptuous continental breakfast buffet (nutbreads and pastries, muffins, rolls, juices, cereals, fruits) and afternoon wine and cheese. Oreos await you in the lounge every evening, and coffee, tea, and fruit are always set out. Guest services include same-day valet laundry and dry cleaning services. The front office is staffed 24 hours a day. There is a two-night minimum stay for many weekends and holidays, and a one-night deposit is required. Louie's Restaurant—one of the best in town—adjoins the main lobby. Louie's offers innovative lunch and dinner menus featuring fresh seafood, pasta, and California cuisine. You can dine on the wide, wooden verandah year-round. (See our Restaurants chapter for details.)

## Goleta

**Bacara Resort & Spa**
**8301 Hollister Avenue**
**Goleta, CA**
**(805) 968–0100, (877) 422–4245**
**www.bacararesort.com**
**$$$$**

Set on 78 palm-studded beachfront acres, 13 miles north of Santa Barbara, the exclusive Spanish Colonial-style Bacara (that's "Ba-CAR-ah") Resort & Spa opened its doors in September 2000 after 18 years of red tape and revisions. Since its debut, the resort has shunned the riffraff, courting instead a star-spangled lineup of A-list celebs and corporate bigwigs who sometimes book the entire resort. (Be forewarned: If you're thinking of popping in for a few martinis, management suggests you make a reservation first.)

Bacara promises "The Good Life," and with its 311 luxury guest rooms, 49 suites, three gourmet restaurants, sprawling pools, impressive recreational facilities, grand ballroom, and multilevel spa, it certainly seems poised to deliver. This ambitious venture is the company's first foray into the hospitality business, and they've certainly spared no expense. Wander the light airy interior and you will see handwoven rugs imported from India, rich mahogany accents, and corridors full of commissioned art. Bacara's fine dining restaurant, Miró, uses fresh produce from the resort's 1,000-acre ranch (see our Restaurant chapter), and the Spa Café overlooking one of the pools serves up healthy fare. The landscaping is tropical meets the Mediterranean, with plenty of palms, bougainvillea, lush courtyards, and gushing fountains. In your spare time, you can pamper yourself in the opulent spa, relax on the beach, jog along the seaside running track, go horseback riding, play tennis on the har-tru courts, or hit a few rounds at the celebrated Sandpiper Golf Course next door. High-tech meeting facilities cater to everything from intimate cocktail soirees to large-scale conventions. The stylish guest rooms feature raised king-size or twin beds with Frette linens, warm-toned Spanish tiling, mahogany furnishings, video entertainment systems, high-speed Internet access, robes, Kiehl's toiletries, and fresh flowers. All have private balconies or patios with ocean, mountain, or garden views. Half are warmed by gas log fireplaces, and some of the suites boast romantic candle-lit Jacuzzi tubs. Bacara strives to evoke the beauty and glamour of a bygone era, but to stay here you'll have to pay a pretty price. Pooches are welcome, too (though the hotel doesn't advertise the fact); just be prepared to fork out an additional $125 per night.

**Best Western South Coast Inn**
**5620 Calle Real**
**Goleta, CA**
**(805) 967–3200, (800) 350–3614**
**www.bwsci.com**
**$**

This spiffy little inn lies only two miles from Santa Barbara airport and UCSB. It's a great choice if you're visiting the university or holding a small meeting or conference. In 2001, the entire hotel, including the pool and spa area, received a face-lift. Accommodations are now lighter and brighter, with fresh carpets and linens and a new decor. They include 121 guest rooms with queen- or king-size beds, and six two-room suites with microwaves and sitting areas. Each room is equipped with air conditioning, a refrigerator, a coffee maker, a hair dryer, and cable TV in a new armoire. Business travelers appreciate the voice mail and high-speed Internet access in each room, and complimentary continental breakfast is served in the lobby.

Pop into the lobby between 5:00 and 7:00 P.M. Monday through Thursday for beer, wine, and cheese, or help yourself to the coffee and tea anytime. For recreation you can splash about in the pool and spa, relax on lounge chairs around the sundeck, or play a few rounds of Ping Pong on the patio. Rose and topiary gardens and a bubbling fountain add a touch of elegance to the grounds. A great deal here is the free shuttle that whisks guests to the University of California at Santa Barbara campus and the airport. Guests also receive a complimentary pass to the Goleta Valley Athletic Club.

**Extended Stay America**
**4870 Calle Real**
**Santa Barbara, CA**
**(805) 692–1882, (800) EXTSTAY**
**www.extstay.com**
**$**

Extended Stay America is a relative newcomer to the local hotel scene, opening in early 1998 just off U.S. Highway 101 near the eastern edge of Goleta, about 10 minutes from downtown Santa Barbara. Geared to the business traveler who plans to stay for a week or more, the facility includes 104 rooms, most with queen-size beds, a kitchenette (with full-size refrigerator, electric stovetop, and dishes for two), desk, dataport phones, and voice mail. There are also three suites, each with a separate sitting area and king-size bed, but they're usually booked up. In fact, one has been occupied continuously by the same guest since the hotel opened.

There aren't a lot of frills here—no pool, Jacuzzi, or food service (but then, you'll be cooking in your room, remember?). The hotel doesn't honor room-rate discounts of any kind, but two people can stay for a week for less than $500, which is practically unheard of in Santa Barbara.

Everything's fresh and clean here. You have freeway access right out the front door, and there are enough restaurants and grocery stores nearby to meet your needs (a coin laundry is on the premises). We think this is a great bet for the business traveler or for anybody relocating to the area and needing transitional accommodations. Reservations are accepted no sooner than 90 days in advance.

**Insiders' Tip**

Hotels in Goleta are closer to the Santa Barbara Airport and the University of California at Santa Barbara than lodgings in the city of Santa Barbara.

**Holiday Inn**
**5650 Calle Real**
**Goleta, CA**
**(805) 964–6241, (800) HOLIDAY**
**www.holiday/inn.com**
**$$**

Completely renovated in 1996 and 1997, this property offers the standard Holiday Inn ambiance and amenities and represents a moderately priced lodging option in the Goleta Valley. In addition to 4,000 square feet of meeting space, there are 160 guest rooms, most with one king-size bed or two double beds. Four executive rooms have a king-size bed, pullout sofa, and wet bar. Some rooms have coffee makers and computer dataports, and refrigerators can be supplied on request for a small charge.

The grounds are nicely manicured and well kept, and you can loll around a large pool area, which has lots of lounge chairs for sunning. If you feel like a real workout, take advantage of a complimentary pass to the nearby Goleta Valley Athletic Club. If you're feeling hungry, you can enjoy breakfast and dinner at Remington's, the on-site restaurant. Or you can go across the street to Carrow's or visit one of several restaurants and fast-food establishments within walking distance on Calle Real. This hotel attracts corporate travelers as well as families looking for familiar Holiday Inn amenities.

**Pacifica Suites**
**5490 Hollister Avenue**
**Goleta, CA**
**(805) 683–6722, (800) 338–6722**
**www.pacificasuites.com**
**$$**

This unique property, with the restored 1880 Joseph Sexton House as its centerpiece, is absolutely charming and is currently the only all-suites property in the Santa Barbara area. Joseph Sexton was a successful Goleta Valley nurseryman. To design the home, he enlisted the services of Peter J. Barber, a local architect who also designed the first Arlington Hotel and the Upham Hotel.

After the Sextons died, the house had a number of owners but then fell into disrepair until the Invest West Financial Corporation acquired it in 1984. Before the complex was developed into a lodging property, the original home and grounds were completely restored, including the replacement of many of the large trees that had been lost over the years.

Today, the towering trees and expansive lawn create a parklike setting, and the old Sexton House is available for business or social functions. The plush sitting area just off the lobby has a fireplace and bar and is used for social functions or for guests to sit back and relax. The design of the rest of the complex echoes that of the Sexton House, with the same elegant architectural style and muted colors.

The hotel has 87 suites, each with a king-size bed or two double beds, a pull-out sofa, a refrigerator, a microwave, a coffee maker, a VCR, an AM/FM cassette player, and computer hookups. A full, cooked-to-order complimentary breakfast is served to guests in the breakfast room or on the outside terrace. Wine, beer, and soft drinks are available at the Manager's Mixers, which are held every day except Sunday from 5:00 to 7:00 P.M.

There is a pool and Jacuzzi, and guests also receive a half-off discount at Gold's Gym and the Goleta Valley Athletic Club. Golf packages for the new Glen Annie Golf Course, Sandpiper Golf Course, and Rancho San Marcos Golf Course are available in the off-season. The property is located adjacent to the Calif. 217 freeway, so there is some traffic noise, which is loudest on the west side of the complex. At press time, the hotel had plans to renovate the guest rooms making them predominantly nonsmoking.

**Ramada Limited**
**4770 Calle Real**
**Santa Barbara, CA**
**(805) 964–3511, (800) 2RAMADA**
**www.sbramada.com**
**$$**

Known locally as the Cathedral Oaks Lodge until it was acquired by Ramada, this 30-year-old motel has 126 rooms and three suites. Accommodations here are standard, but the courtyard in the middle of the complex features a lovely lagoon with waterfalls, a footbridge, water lilies, and a small population of resident ducks. Quiet walkways lead you through the surrounding gardens under swaying palms, a welcome respite for a hotel on a busy main street.

The rooms face indoor corridors and open onto patios or balconies that face either the courtyard or the parking lot (if you'd rather see the lagoon, you'll pay more for the privilege). All are air conditioned, and each comes with a coffee maker, iron and ironing board, desk, and two phones with voice mail. Upstairs rooms have higher ceilings, and there's a modest amount of meeting space on-site. A complimentary continental breakfast is served every morning, or if you feel more like pancakes, the International House of Pancakes is across the street. In your spare time, you can swim in the heated pool or relax in the hot tub.

The Ramada is near the eastern boundary of Goleta, about 10 miles from downtown Santa Barbara. You are not particularly close to any tourist attractions here, but the motel is moderately priced, and it's only a 10-minute drive to Santa Barbara's waterfront and other attractions.

## Montecito

**Coast Village Inn**
**1188 Coast Village Road**
**Montecito, CA**
**(805) 969–3266, (800) 257–5131**
**www.coastvillageinn.com**
**$$**

Modest by Montecito standards, this little motel is cheerful, well kept, and within walking distance of the exclusive boutiques and restaurants that line Coast Village Road (the local farmers' market is held right across the street on Fridays). The property was opened in the 1930s, but has been upgraded on a regular basis, and the guest rooms are constantly refreshed with new fabrics and linens. (You may want to avoid the back rooms, which open onto the parking lot.)

The 28 rooms and suites are decorated with country pine furniture and botanical prints. Typical features include ceiling fans, cable TVs, and phones with voice mail. The junior suite contains a queen-size bed and pullout sofa, and the deluxe suite has two bedrooms (one with a king bed and a second with two twins), a living room with a queen sofa bed, and a full kitchen. You won't find many amenities at this quiet little spot, but guests can enjoy the inn's heated pool, and the staff will gladly arrange in-room massages or facials. You can also take advantage of a 50-percent discount on a sightseeing tour on the Santa Barbara trolley. A complimentary continental breakfast is served daily at Peabody's, the on-site restaurant, which also serves lunch and dinner. The entire inn is nonsmoking and on-site parking is free.

**Four Seasons Biltmore**
**1260 Channel Drive**
**Montecito, CA**
**(805) 969–2261, (800) 332–3442**
**www.fourseasons.com**
**$$$$**

The Biltmore is the grande dame of Santa Barbara hotels, hands down. *Condé Nast Traveler* dubbed it a "sprawling pleasure palace on the edge of the Pacific," and an article in *Travel & Leisure* described it as "a 1920s fantasia of towers and arches and exotic gardens by the sea." It's actually a little more understated than these descriptions imply, but the bottom line is that this is a hotel that gets noticed, and it lives up to its reputation. Even with a train running through the back of the property, this is a place of elegance and romance, a place where the well-heeled love to stay.

Built in 1927, the Mediterranean-style complex has 217 guest accommodations that range from standard rooms to suites to private cottages. Each unit has a VCR, terry robes, a hair dryer, down pillows, a safe, two or more telephones, and a stocked bar and refrigerator.

The recreational opportunities are seemingly endless. In 2002, a brand new health club and spa will debut, along with a revamped pool area replete with lily ponds and lush landscaping. In the meantime, guests have free admission to the oceanfront Coral Casino Health Club across the street, which has an Olympic-size pool. Other amenities include tennis courts, a putting green, complimentary bicycles for touring, and watersports at the beach, which is directly across the street.

Preferred tee-time privileges are offered at some of the area's premier golf courses, and a full-service salon offers spa treatments and massage to help you relax after a day on the links.

Parents of young children will appreciate the babysitting services and children's activities, and pets are also welcome at the Biltmore at no extra charge. The services for business travelers are also generous. A 4,200-square-foot ballroom and 15,000 square feet of meeting space are available. Two fabulous restaurants—the Patio and La Marina—offer some of the best food in Santa Barbara (see our Restaurants chapter), making your holiday-by-the-sea complete.

**Montecito Inn**
**1295 Coast Village Road**
**Montecito, CA**
**(805) 969–7854, (800) 843–2017**
**www.montecitoinn.com**
**$$$**

The minute you drive up to the Montecito Inn, you know it's a different kind of small hotel. For one thing, you'll see Charlie Chaplin's face on the sign out front—a theme that is carried throughout, with statues of Chaplin in the lobby, his figure etched on the door of the meeting and banquet room, and original art posters hanging in the public areas.

Chaplin was one of the original investors in the hotel, which opened in 1928 and drew the rich and famous of the day, including Lon Chaney, Sr., Carole Lombard, Wallace Beery, and Norma Shearer, to name a few.

The hotel has undergone some changes over the years (a pool, spa, and enclosed parking garage were added, and the bathrooms and the lobby were refurbished) and now boasts 50 rooms and 10 elegant suites that were built in 1995. All the rooms are dressed in French Provincial style, most have a refrigerator and a hair dryer, and each is equipped with a VCR. The suites have a Jacuzzi, fireplace, separate sitting room with pullout sofa bed, refrigerator, two televisions, two VCRs, two-line phones, and Italian marble bathrooms.

There's a small pool, sauna, and Jacuzzi for guests, although their proximity to the freeway makes the area a bit noisy. There's also a complete library of Chaplin films if you feel like being nostalgic.

A complimentary continental breakfast is served each morning in the Montecito Café, just off the lobby (see our Restaurants chapter), or you can pay for a full cooked-to-order breakfast. Discount passes are given to guests for the local sightseeing trolley, or you can check out a bike if you want to explore on your own. Guests also enjoy golf privileges at the private Montecito Country Club, but there is no discount.

This charming little inn is truly unique for Santa Barbara, with a personalized, European feel. A two-night minimum stay is required on weekends, but come during the week and you can often get exceptionally good deals on rooms—just ask.

**San Ysidro Ranch**
**900 San Ysidro Lane**
**Montecito, CA**
**(805) 969–5046, (800) 368–6788 (from outside the 805 area code)**
**www.sanysidroranch.com**
**$$$$**

Set far from the touristy beachfront in the Montecito foothills, San Ysidro Ranch has been cloistering the rich and famous of the world for more than 100 years. The first cottages were built on the property in the 1890s, and guests began arriving in January 1893.

In the 1930s, actor Ronald Colman bought the property, and soon the likes of Gloria Swanson, Merle Oberon, David Niven, Fred Astaire, Groucho Marx, Lucille Ball, and other Hollywood luminaries were on the guest list. John Huston finished the script for *The African Queen* while ensconced in a ranch cottage, and Vivien Leigh and Lawrence Olivier were married in the Wedding Garden. Later, Jacqueline and John F. Kennedy honeymooned for a week in what is now the Kennedy Cottage.

Today, 21 cottages surrounded by gardens and mature trees hold 38 accommodations on the ranch property. There are several "standard" rooms (though nothing at the ranch can be considered standard in the traditional sense) as well as one- and two-bedroom suites and individual private cottages.

**Insiders' Tip**

Want to stay at the beach, but afraid you can't afford the prices? Even a block away from the ocean rooms are cheaper, so use your legs and save some cash.

All the cottages have fireplaces (wood is stacked by your door), king-size beds, luxurious bathrooms, and sunporches with ocean, mountain, or garden views. Thirteen cottages have private outdoor Jacuzzis, and two have marble floors and whirlpool baths. For the ultimate hideaway, the ocean-view Eucalyptus Cottage boasts its own swimming pool and Jacuzzi, a large living room, two bedrooms, three fireplaces, and a sprawling patio—all for the bargain price of $3,950 a night (ouch!).

If you want to do more than relax and soak up the ambiance (and many guests don't), take a dip in the pool, play a game of tennis, go horseback riding, or take advantage of golf privileges at the nearby Montecito Country Club. Can't leave home without your pooch? At San Ysidro Ranch, pets are welcome, so bring Fido along. The Stonehouse Restaurant on the property has received a plethora of culinary awards and is considered one of the finest restaurants in the state, if not the country (see our Restaurants chapter).

In short, if you're fleeing from the paparazzi, this is the spot to come.

Average price?—$695 a night.

## Carpinteria

**Best Western Carpinteria Inn**
**4558 Carpinteria Avenue**
**Carpinteria, CA**
**(805) 684–0473, (800) 528–1234**
**www.bestwestern.com/carpinteriainn**
**$**

Rimmed by colorful geraniums, this attractive Spanish-style hotel is a great choice for families, business travelers, and anyone who wants a comfortable yet affordable place to stay in the South County. It's just three blocks from downtown Carpinteria's main street, and you can walk to Carpinteria Beach. When you want to visit downtown Santa Barbara, just hop in your car and drive 9 miles up the freeway.

The 144 air-conditioned guest rooms and suites (90 percent are nonsmoking), are equipped with refrigerators, hair dryers, safes, irons and ironing boards, coffee makers, and cable TVs. Amid the red-tile roofs of the inn's main buildings you'll find a lovely courtyard with a swimming pool, Jacuzzi, fountains, and a koi pond. The hotel recently added a small workout room. When you're hungry, you can feast at the hotel's Sunset Grille Restaurant and quench your thirst at the full bar.

# Bed and Breakfast Inns

**Santa Barbara Beach Area**
**Santa Barbara**
**Summerland**
**Carpinteria**

Staying at an intimate bed and breakfast gives you an excellent opportunity to experience Santa Barbara's history and character. You can also mix with other guests and enjoy a more personalized level of service than most large hotels can offer. The area's first official bed and breakfast, The Old Yacht Club Inn, opened in 1980. A number of regional inns have since joined the ranks.

Each bed and breakfast listed here exudes its own unique personality and offers a range of services for visitors seeking a quiet respite from daily life. Most are splendidly restored, turn-of-the-century Victorian or California Craftsman homes filled with antiques, period pieces, and memorabilia.

The majority are located in historic residential areas close to mid-State Street, where you can escape from city noises but easily walk to restaurants, theaters, and shops. Several offer a peaceful refuge near the beach, while a few cater to those who prefer off-the-beaten-track hideaways.

Santa Barbara bed and breakfasts have much in common. You can expect gracious innkeepers to extend a warm welcome upon your arrival and provide excellent hospitality throughout your stay. Each inn serves either a full gourmet or a generous continental breakfast and has an afternoon or evening social hour, usually with wine and cheese and crackers or other appetizers. (If something more elaborate or unique is provided, we've noted it in the description.) Most also set out port or sherry, homemade cookies, or a snack in the evenings. Vegetarian or other special diets can usually be accommodated with advance notice.

Santa Barbara's high season typically starts in March and lasts through October. You should make your reservations as far in advance as possible, especially if you plan to visit on a weekend or holiday or in the summer months. Many of the inns are fully booked two or three months in advance. Also, the earlier you call, the better your chances of reserving the room of your choice.

When you call to make your reservation, be sure to inquire about the inn's minimum-stay and cancellation policies. Most require a two-night minimum stay on weekends and at least a week's advance notice if you cancel.

All inns listed here accept most major credit cards. Quoted rates usually are based on double occupancy. Additional guests pay anywhere from $15 to $40 per night. Although a few inns have daybeds or rollaways, most do not. If you have more than two people in your party, your best bet is to book a suite, if you can get one. Most establishments adhere to strict maximum capacity codes, so you should definitely inquire about these rules and other details before making your reservation. Children are welcome at all Santa Barbara bed and breakfast inns—it's the law. However, most innkeepers allow children only in certain rooms and discourage their presence at busy times when other guests may be honeymooning or escaping from their own kids. If you plan to bring the kids along, call ahead and discuss your options with the innkeeper.

Most bed and breakfast buildings were constructed many years ago, so they often have narrow stairs, walkways, and baths that may present problems for the physically

*Many Santa Barbara bed and breakfasts are beautifully restored Victorian homes.* PHOTO: BRIAN HASTINGS

challenged. If you have accessibility concerns, call ahead and discuss your particular needs and the building's layout with the innkeeper. Some buildings have one or two rooms that have worked out well for guests in wheelchairs or who have trouble negotiating flights of stairs.

Smoking is absolutely forbidden at all the bed and breakfasts listed here. If you're a smoker, you can usually light up outside in the garden or patio, but only if other nonsmoking guests aren't out there sharing your smoke. Some bed and breakfasts even enforce stiff fines on guests caught smoking in their rooms. So, however strong your urge to smoke, don't tempt fate by lighting up indoors.

Sorry pets—Santa Barbara's gracious bed-and-breakfast hospitality doesn't extend to you. None of the inns we've listed here allows animals of any kind. Try the establishments listed in our Hotels and Motels or Vacation Rentals chapters.

### Price-Code Key

Our pricing key indicates the average cost of double-occupancy accommodations on weekends during the high season (March through October) and does not include tax and fees for added services.

$ . . . . . . . . . . . . . . . . . . . . . . $135 to $170
$$ . . . . . . . . . . . . . . . . . . . . . $171 to $210
$$$ . . . . . . . . . . . . . . . . . . . . $211 to $260
$$$$ . . . . . . . . . . . . . . . . . . $261 and more

## Santa Barbara Beach Area

**The Old Yacht Club Inn**
**431 Corona del Mar Drive**
**Santa Barbara, CA**
**(805) 962–1277, (800) 549–1676 in California, (800) 676–1676 outside California**
**www.oldyachtclubinn.com**
**$–$$**

If you're longing for a convivial bed and breakfast experience, along with easy access to the beach, this friendly, turn-of-the-century inn will fulfill your wishes. Built as a private family home on East Beach in 1912, the Craftsman-style building served as the Santa Barbara Yacht Club's temporary headquarters for several years during the Roaring Twenties after the first clubhouse washed out to sea in a freak storm.

In 1928, the building was moved just a block inland to its current location tucked behind two olive trees on a peaceful residential street. In 1980, four schoolteachers purchased and meticulously restored the home, then opened it as Santa Barbara's first bed and breakfast inn. Two of the teachers, Nancy Donaldson and Sandy Hunt, remained as the innkeepers/owners for years before selling the inn to a local couple, Eilene Bruce and Vince Pettit, in 2000. The new owners and their manager, Astrid Ballard, intend to continue the inn's tradition of warm hospitality and fantastic food. Every morning you can indulge in a three-course gourmet breakfast that is guaranteed to please the palate. Banana pancakes and the scrumptious Santa Barbara omelet filled with two cheeses and topped with salsa are just two of the mouthwatering dishes on the breakfast menu. Special Saturday evening dinners, staged every few weeks, still feature former owner Nancy Donaldson's highly acclaimed recipes such as salmon with raspberry beurre blanc, and chocolate cheesecake.

The inn offers 12 rooms, including two suites, in the cozy main building and the adjacent Spanish-style Hitchcock House, built in 1926. All rooms have telephones and private baths, and the rooms in the Hitchcock House are equipped with cable TV. Both houses are filled with classic European and Early American antiques, Oriental rugs, historic photos, and memorabilia.

The inn's largest room is the spacious Santa Rosa Suite. It has a separate sitting room, a king-size bed, and a large bath with whirlpool tub. Other popular rooms include the Captain's Corner, which features a private "aft" deck, and the Castellamare Room, with a balcony and whirlpool tub. Fresh flowers and a decanter of sherry greet arriving guests in every room.

Since it takes only a minute to saunter over to East Beach, you should definitely take advantage of the inn's beach towels and chairs (available free of charge) and relax by the sea. You can also hop on one of the inn's bicycles and tool around the waterfront. A two-night minimum stay is required on weekends if a Saturday is included. Special business and midweek rates are available from October to May. This relaxed and unpretentious inn attracts a mixed bunch of couples, and it's a great choice for families seeking intimate accommodations a short stroll from the beach.

**Villa Rosa**
**15 Chapala Street**
**Santa Barbara, CA**
**(805) 966–0851**
**$$–$$$**

Although this cozy residence looks and feels like a small hotel, it has many characteristics of a typical bed and breakfast: a historic structure (built in 1932 in Spanish Revival style), personalized service, a satisfying continental breakfast, and the *Los Angeles Times* delivered to your door every morning. But the best thing about Villa Rosa is its location: it's also only 84 steps from West Beach and a hop, skip, and a jump from the marina and Stearns Wharf.

The building was remodeled in the early 1980s as a Santa Fe–style bed and breakfast. You can choose from 18 rooms in soft Southwestern color schemes with ocean, harbor, garden, or mountain views (but only two have glimpses of the sea). Several deluxe rooms feature fireplaces and/or private gardens, and the upstairs corner rooms are among the brightest units thanks to their extra windows and elevated views. Though the rooms lack televisions, all have tiny private baths, telephones, clock radios, bathrobes, hair dryers, and sitting areas.

When you're not exploring the town or sailing the sparkling harbor, you can relax

## Insiders' Tip

Celebrating a birthday or anniversary? With advance notice, most bed and breakfasts will provide fresh flowers, champagne, or a gift basket in your room. Ask when you book.

in the cozy lounge, take a dip in the small, heated pool and spa, or soak up some sun on the lovely outdoor garden patio. After a night on the town, you can look forward to sipping the complimentary port and sherry that are available in the lounge every evening. Nightly turndown is sweetened with Belgian chocolates. Children are welcome as long as they are at least 14 years old, due to the fact that the pool is unfenced. A conference room accommodates 15. The clientele is eclectic, but typically includes young couples and groups of friends looking for a more affordable option to the pricier beachside hotels in this area.

## Santa Barbara

**The Bayberry Inn**
**111 West Valerio Street**
**Santa Barbara, CA**
**(805) 569–3398**
**www.bayberryinnsantabarbara.com**
**$$**

If only the walls of this charming inn could talk. Built in 1894 in American Colonial Style, this grand old house was originally a residence for a prominent landowner, but it has since lived many colorful lives. In 1904 it became a private girls' boarding school. Then it was transformed into a school principal's residence, a sorority house, and finally, in 1980, a bed and breakfast. Today the building has been designated an historic "Structure of Merit," and if its walls could talk, they'd probably be thanking Kenneth and Jill Freeman. In 2000 this local couple snapped up the sunny house, freshened the decor, and are now lavishing their guests with warm hospitality and personalized service. Not only is this a labor of love for Jill and Kenneth, it's a family affair. Kenneth's mother-in-law fills the house with fresh flowers; Aunt Lillian works evenings and weekends; and Uncle Eddie whips up tasty treats in the kitchen. Not sure how to plan your day? Kenneth and Jill will gladly share their local knowledge and customize an itinerary for you.

Set on a quiet residential street across from Cheshire Cat Inn and Cottages and only a five-minute walk from downtown, The Bayberry houses eight beautifully decorated rooms. All are named after berries and feature motifs and Carlton Wagner color schemes in keeping with their namesake. Rich colors and thickly textured fabrics such as velvet and damask impart a formal feel to the rooms. All have queen-size canopy beds, private baths, TVs, and robes. Some of the rooms have decks and fireplaces, and two have baths across the hall. The upstairs Blueberry is one of the most popular rooms; it has a bright white-tiled bath, antique clawfoot tub, small balcony, and striking blue and white decor. Downstairs, Raspberry has a fireplace and private deck, and the newly decorated Teaberry, with its private entrance, skylight, and pretty pink color scheme, is also a popular pick.

Breakfast can be served in the privacy of your room, on the sunny outdoor deck, or under a crystal chandelier in the elegant dining room. Eddie uses fresh local produce to create such specialties as Bayberry Breakfast Bread Pudding, eggs Florentine, and vanilla almond french toast. When you return from a day of sightseeing or shopping, you can refuel with a home-baked dessert. Transfers between the airport and the downtown train station can be arranged between 9:00 A.M. and 5:00 P.M. with advance notice. Children under 10 stay free. Thanks to some nurturing by the Freeland family, this historic inn is now enjoying a new life as one of Santa Barbara's quintessential B&Bs.

**The Cheshire Cat Inn and Cottages**
**36 West Valerio Street**
**Santa Barbara, CA**
**(805) 569–1610**
**www.cheshirecat.com**
**$$–$$$**

An extremely popular destination for honeymoons and romantic getaways, Chesire Cat is set amid colorful English gardens in a quiet residential area just one block from State Street and a five-minute walk to restaurants, shops, and theaters. Owner Christine Dunstan, an experienced innkeeper from Cheshire, England, has done an incredible job of restoring and remodeling three neighboring Victorian homes (now more than 100 years old), a coachhouse, and three nearby cottages into a sophisticated, romantic retreat. She added modern conveniences and charming personal touches such as English antiques and Laura Ashley wallpaper and draperies. As a special bonus, the inn also now offers an enticing array of facials, massages, and spa treatments to soothe the mind and pamper the body. Treatments can be administered in your own room or in the new on-site spa rooms.

As you might guess, the inn's theme hails from the English classic *Alice's Adventures in Wonderland.* Most of the sparkling clean 21 rooms are named after characters in the book. For the ultimate romantic retreat, stay in Tweedledum, a luxurious two-room suite with a Jacuzzi, fireplace, sitting room with Oriental rugs, a king-size brass bed, and a wet bar/kitchen. If you don't need a kitchen, try the Queen of Hearts—an equally romantic but smaller room with a Jacuzzi.

Even if you don't have a Jacuzzi room, you can soak in the outdoor spa and enjoy the tranquil gardens. All rooms have private baths, robes, and direct-dial phones; some have TVs, VCRs, and beautiful potted orchids. A gourmet breakfast is served daily on Wedgwood china, either outside on the lovely brick patio or in the privacy of your room. Expect such mouthwatering treats as home-baked breads, freshly squeezed orange juice, artichoke frittata, and apples stuffed with cinnamon and raisins.

In 1997, the inn opened the Woodford, Prestbury, and Mobberly Cottages, named after three villages in Cheshire. Each has two bedrooms (one with a queen-size bed and one with a king-size), a private redwood deck, and a hot tub. Other features include a large living room with TV and VCR, a fireplace, a dining nook, a full bathroom, and a kitchen. The cottages may be rented by the day, week, or month. In the James House, dark wood, bay windows, and lovingly restored Victorian embellishments evoke the aura of days gone by. All the rooms here have a TV/VCR. The Unicorn has a balcony, White Queen and White King have Jacuzzi tubs for two, and an original wood-burning fireplace warms the Lion. Children are allowed only in the cottages; tots younger than 5 stay free. This meticulously maintained inn oozes personality and is a top choice for those who yearn for a historic bed and breakfast experience with a delightful English twist and a dash of whimsy.

**Glenborough Inn**
**1327 Bath Street**
**Santa Barbara, CA**
**(805) 966–0589, (888) 966–0589**
**www.glenboroughinn.com**
**$$–$$$**

One of the oldest bed and breakfasts in Santa Barbara, Glenborough Inn lies in a quiet residential area only a three-block walk from the heart of downtown. In 2000 the inn changed hands, and the new owners began freshening up the decor and adding down comforters and extra pillows to all the rooms. Privacy prevails here, and you could theoretically spend days in your room without having to leave. Your hot vegetarian breakfast comes directly to your door (you select the delivery time). Typical entrees include vegetable quiches, omelets, waffles, or croissants with scrambled eggs. Most

**Insiders' Tip**

If you want to avoid crowds, plan your trip to Santa Barbara during the winter months. The weather's still mild, fewer people are on the beach and the crisp winter skies make for fantastic views.

rooms have private entrances, fireplaces, in-room coffee service, and refrigerators; all rooms have direct-dial telephones and robes. Two boast private outdoor hot tubs, separate sitting areas, decks, gardens, and views. If you don't splurge on a room with a hot tub, you can reserve private time in the outdoor hot tub in the garden.

You can choose from 18 rooms and suites dispersed among five neighboring historic homes: The Craftsman Bungalow (c. 1906), The Victorian Cottage (c. 1885), The White Farm House (c. 1912), The Italianate (c. 1890), and La Casa Cottage (c. 1929). Each building has its own character, and the decor of the rooms varies widely too. One of the best picks is the Nouveau Luxury Suite—it has a private garden entry, brick patio with redwood hot tub, parlor sitting room with window seats, Franklin-stove fireplace, and a clawfoot tub and shower.

Do you shudder when you envision frilly lace canopy beds and floral wallpaper? Opt for the Captain's Quarters and you'll probably feel right at home. This room features a nautical theme, ship treasures and antiques, a private patio entry, a fireplace, a king-size bed, and a two-person Jacuzzi tub and shower.

Friday and Saturday evenings, wine and hors d'oeuvres are served between 5:00 and 6:00 P.M.

If you give the staff enough notice, you can arrange for flowers, champagne, massages, intimate dinners, and other special services. Children are welcome here at any time—the two-bedroom suites are ideal for families. Those seeking more solitude than the typical B&B experience allows can tuck themselves away here in comfort.

**The Parsonage**
**1600 Olive Street**
**Santa Barbara, CA**
**(805) 962–9336, (800) 775–0352**
**www.parsonage.com**
**\$–\$\$**

Originally built in 1892 for the parson of Trinity Episcopal Church, this restored Queen Anne Victorian conveys a sense of turn-of-the-19th-century Santa Barbara grandeur. The sunny hillside residence appeals to guests looking for a peaceful getaway spot close—but not too close—to downtown. Here you relax amid beautiful white fir floors and redwood moldings, period furnishings, and antique Oriental rugs while enjoying the serenity of the residential neighborhood.

The Parsonage is famous for its elaborate breakfasts and evening hors d'oeuvres. When it's sunny, breakfast is served on the outdoor patio overlooking the ocean and city. Expect such homemade delights as spinach and artichoke fritatta, sweet strata, waffles, and pancakes. Sleepyheads can breakfast anytime up until 10:00 A.M.

The Parsonage has six individually decorated rooms that are intentionally less frilly than some of the other Victorian-era B&Bs. Fresh flowers, king- or queen-size beds, private baths, robes, and telephones are in all. The pricier Honeymoon Suite offers fantastic ocean, island, and city views, as well as an elegant solarium, a spacious bath with a whirlpool tub, and breakfast delivered to your room. The suite's numerous windows attract the sun from morning to dusk. This is one of the loveliest bed and breakfast rooms we looked at for under \$300, and it's a relative bargain during the week at \$195 per night.

Next to the Honeymoon Suite is Majestic, which also boasts ocean views.

More affordable rooms include the Victorian, Alexandria, Lady Britni, and Versailles. The fact that the only TV on the premises is in the living room enhances the quiet atmosphere.

Children are welcome in certain rooms at certain times. Call ahead to discuss options for families. Casual elegance is the tone here. This is the kind of place where guests are treated like royalty but feel relaxed enough to dine in their robes if they wish.

**Secret Garden Inn and Cottages**
**1908 Bath Street**
**Santa Barbara, CA**
**(805) 687–2300**
**www.secretgarden.com**
**$**

The lush gardens of this secluded enclave aren't really secret, but they certainly enhance its peaceful, romantic atmosphere. In 1999, the inn was purchased by art-lover Dominique Hannaux, who is now adding a European flair to the inn with beautiful art and sleek decor inspired by her native France. Dominique also loves to cultivate local artistic talent. Works by local artists are displayed throughout the inn's common rooms, and every few months, Dominique hosts art openings, painting workshops, and performances by local musicians. Guests are invited to attend.

Set back off the street in a quiet residential area about six blocks from downtown, the Secret Garden includes 11 rooms and suites dispersed among a historic main house (c. 1905) and four charming cottages, all with private entrances. Five rooms feature private outdoor hot tubs. Many of the baths have antique clawfoot tubs. Other amenities in certain rooms include fireplaces, private decks, refrigerators, beautiful hardwood floors, Oriental rugs, and European art. Televisions can be added on request. A lovely choice is The Garden, with its striking French blue decor, honey-colored hardwood floors, skylit queen-size bed, and spacious bath done in white Italian tile. If you want to soak in your own private tub, Wood Thrush is a lovely option; it has a king-size bed and private walled deck with Jacuzzi.

Breakfast is a buffet of quiche, breads, scones, bagels, and croissants served in the kitchen. Those who prefer to dine in the privacy of their rooms can order room service in advance. Or, when the weather's nice, which is most of the time, you can savor your meal in the gardens, beneath the persimmon and avocado trees. Be prepared to commune with raccoons, possums, and birds.

The tranquility of this inn is hard to beat. None of the rooms have telephones, so you can easily escape the stress and strain of the workaday world. In the evening, you can help yourself to cookies, brownies, and hot cider. Children are welcome. Special midweek winter packages are available. This secluded inn appeals to couples, families, and artistic types who prefer chic European decor to fussy frills and ruffles.

**Simpson House Inn**
**121 East Arrellaga Street**
**Santa Barbara, CA**
**(805) 963–7067, (800) 676–1280**
**www.simpsonhouseinn.com**
**$$$$**

Just do it. You deserve it. Hang the cost and book a room today. This world-class inn is not just the empress of Santa Barbara bed and breakfasts, it's also one of the top bed and breakfast inns in North America according to industry peer rankings. When you stay here, you're guaranteed a fabulous, one-of-a-kind experience, well worth every dollar spent.

Scotsman Robert Simpson built this Eastlake Italianate Victorian with a wraparound porch in 1874. In the 1970s, the dilapidated but still beautiful estate fell into the hands of several development companies. It faced near-certain demolition until Glyn and Linda Davies purchased it as a family residence for themselves and their two children.

## Insiders' Tip

Many bed and breakfasts offer special packages as well as reduced rates on weekdays and/or in the low season (usually November through February). Be sure to inquire about possible deals when you make reservations.

Together, the family totally restored the home to its former elegance, scraping old paint, hunting down antique fixtures, and adding a foundation. The overgrown grounds were transformed into an acre of blissful, immaculate gardens, with historic trees and native California plants arranged in a formal English-style setting.

The Davies' painstaking restoration efforts resulted in the City of Santa Barbara declaring the Simpson House and its gardens a Historic Landmark in 1992. It is considered one of the most distinguished homes of its era in Southern California.

When the kids went off to college, the senior Davies decided to convert their historic home into a bed and breakfast inn. Located just a few blocks from State Street and the Arlington Center for the Performing Arts, Simpson House Inn's 14 rooms and suites are interspersed among several buildings. The original house contains six guest rooms, a formal dining room, and a living room with a fireplace.

The restored 1878 barn features four rooms, each with a king-size bed, sitting area, fireplace, TV and VCR, stereo, and wet bar. The three private garden cottages have Jacuzzis, fireplaces, and queen-size canopied feather beds. All rooms and suites have private baths and telephones. TVs and VCRs are in the rooms or available on request.

The sprawling gardens surround all the buildings. You can read, relax, and stroll among mature oaks, magnolias, exotic plants, and manicured lawns, serenaded by the soothing sound of flowing water from seven strategically placed fountains. Sandstone walls and tall hedges promote a sense of privacy and conceal the street from the oasis within.

The full gourmet breakfast at the Simpson House is a real treat, with organic California juices, fruits, and house specialties such as mushroom crepes and truffled eggs. You can choose to eat in your room or on the veranda or garden patios. Guests rarely notice that this is a vegetarian household, since all dishes are elegantly prepared and presented. In the afternoon, you can feast your eyes and palate at a lavish Mediterranean hors d'oeuvres buffet featuring local wines.

Why not go for the ultimate indulgences at this luxurious retreat? Pamper your body and settle your soul by arranging for the inn's European spa services in the privacy of your room. Choose from various types of massages and facials. You can also arrange for a guest pass to a nearby fitness facility.

Since the Simpson House is such a highly rated establishment, you might expect snootiness and snobbery to prevail among the staff and clientele. Not here—the casual atmosphere (jeans and shorts are just fine) and the super-friendly staff will make you feel at ease as soon as you arrive. Children are welcome in certain rooms. Call the inn to discuss your options if you plan to bring the young ones.

**Tiffany Country House**
**1323 De la Vina Street**
**Santa Barbara, CA**
**(805) 963–2283, (800) 999–5672**
**$$**

Honeymoon, wedding, getaway, business—whatever your reason for coming to Santa Barbara, you'll find an intimate getaway at Tiffany Country House. In late 1999, Vintage Hotels, owners of The Upham (see our Hotels and Motels chapter), purchased this grand century-old Victorian, stripped some of the frills and ruffles, and exposed more of the inn's dark woods, adding to its feel of formal elegance. Perhaps the best feature of this inn is its convenient location just three blocks from State Street and the heart of downtown, an easy walk to restaurants, shops, and museums.

The Tiffany's seven rooms all have telephones and private baths. The award for most spacious and comfortable quarters goes to the Penthouse Suite. It occupies the entire third floor and offers a sprawling bedroom with a fireplace, a private terrace and balcony, spectacular city, mountain and ocean views, a refrigerator, a TV and VCR, a double Jacuzzi tub, and a sitting area and writing nook.

Just got hitched or want to celebrate a special anniversary? Go for the romantic Honeymoon Suite, complete with a brass canopied bed, sunken double whirlpool tub, and fireplace. The staff delivers a full gourmet breakfast directly to both the Penthouse and Honeymoon suites every morning.

If you're staying in one of the less expensive rooms, you'll find your equally sumptuous breakfast of homemade granola, crepes, quiches, or waffles waiting in the dining room downstairs or out on the deck. Be sure to try some of the freshly baked cookies the cook sets out every evening and to stroll in the beautiful rose garden and patio, which are sometimes used for weddings. Children are welcome in the Penthouse Suite.

## Summerland

**Inn on Summer Hill**
**2520 Lillie Avenue**
**Summerland, CA**
**(805) 969–9998, (800) 845–5566**
**www.innonsummerhill.com**
**$$$**

Built in 1989 in California Craftsman style, the elegant Inn on Summer Hill rests on a hillside just off the freeway near the shores of Summerland. The out-of-town, seaview location makes it a great choice for a small-town romantic retreat. You can easily walk or bike the quarter mile to Summerland beach, while village shops, antique stores, and restaurants are a short stroll down the road. When you feel like exploring farther afield, hop in your car (the inn has plenty of on-site parking) and drive just 5 or 10 minutes to Montecito and downtown Santa Barbara.

What this inn lacks in history, it makes up for in creature comforts and delicious gourmet cuisine. The inn's skillfully decorated rooms evoke an English country feel with their king- or queen-size canopy beds, billowy down comforters, country pine antiques, and custom floral fabrics. Choose from upstairs balcony rooms with vaulted pine ceilings, or downstairs patio rooms. All have double-paned windows and double-insulated walls to block out noise from the outside world. The rooms are similar in layout and appointments, but each has a unique color scheme. All rooms include imported furniture, sitting areas, TV/VCRs, stereo cassette players, hair dryers, tea- and coffee-making facilities, mini-fridges, phones, fireplaces, and whirlpool tubs. Whichever room you choose, you can take in glorious sunset views across the ocean from your private balcony or patio.

If money's no object, you can't go wrong staying in The Suite, the inn's most spacious quarters. It features three ocean-view balconies, two fireplaces, a living room with hardwood floors and a wet bar, a bedroom with a king-size canopy bed, and his-and-her bathrooms with a whirlpool tub in between. Rates for other rooms vary according to location (patio or balcony) and bed size.

Wander out back and you'll find colorful gardens, English country benches, birdhouses, and a pergola with a spa—a great place to soak under the stars. Guests rave about the inn's gourmet food. The sumptuous breakfast, served in the downstairs dining room amid a collection of antique teapots, features such treats as Italian eggs Benedict with tomato cream sauce, black bean waffles, and shrimp and potato omelet in a lemon butter sauce. Feel like lounging around? For an additional fee, you can order breakfast in bed. In addition to the delicious breakfasts, you can feast on hors d'oeuvres throughout the day and end your evening with a complimentary dessert such as the Swiss apple tart or the Ticino chocolate torte.

The Inn on Summer Hill offers various special packages, some seasonal and a few throughout the year. Examples include golf, kayaking/cycling, horseback riding, honeymoon, and romantic getaway packages. Some are available Monday through Thursday, while others are for weekends. You can also order customized gift baskets and arrange for all sorts of special services through the concierge. Children are allowed only in certain downstairs rooms. This romantic inn appeals to anyone seeking the traditional flourishes of the bed and breakfast experience with a fresh country feel, outstanding cuisine, and sparkling sea views.

## Carpinteria

**Prufrock's Garden Inn**
**600 Linden Avenue**
**Carpinteria, CA**
**(805) 566–9696**
**www.prufrocks.com**
**$–$$**

Owners/innkeepers Jim and Judy Halvorsen converted a 1904 historic family home into this quaint inn, which provides a homey bed and breakfast experience in a small-town atmosphere. A glowing write-up in the *Los Angeles Times* helped the small, seven-room inn gain notoriety, so it's wise to make reservations well in advance. Prufrock's sits right on one of Carpinteria's main arteries from downtown to the beach, but it's in a quiet section. You can park your car at the side and walk nearly everywhere: to restaurants, a great playground, the "world's safest beach," and the Carpinteria pool. Or borrow the inn's "bicycle built for two" and explore the town. The Amtrak station is a few blocks away, and Santa Barbara proper lies just 12 miles north on the freeway.

The entire inn exudes an early California seaside ambiance, with hardwood floors, antiques, and soft color schemes. Feast on a full breakfast either in your room, in the lovely garden, or at the family-style dining table. Typical entrees include quiches, omelettes, or pancakes. Evenings, you can help yourself to the cookies, cake, fruit, crackers, cheese, iced tea, and lemonade that are left out for guests.

The cozy guest rooms are either in the house or in a jasmine-draped cottage out the back, renovated by the owners in 1998. They range dramatically in size and price so be sure to specify your needs when you book.

In the main house, the largest room, Garden Hideaway, has French doors that open to a private porch overlooking the colorful garden. Village Charm features a clawfoot tub and a private entry. Cottage Trellis offers a private view of the gardens. All three rooms have private baths, while the more affordable upstairs Ocean Breeze and Mountain View rooms share a full bath. The pricier cottage rooms are a little more secluded. They have private entrances, Jacuzzi tubs, and concrete patios with porch swings and fireplaces. The Afternoon Delight Suite here is perfect for families. Fling open the windows and the jasmine-scented breeze wafts through to cool the interior. You can also bask on your sunny patio with Tessie, the resident cat. It's fine to bring children to Prufrock's—three rooms have daybeds. Call to find out about special weekday rates and birthday and anniversary packages. This hospitable little inn is a home-away-from-home for all who stay here.

# Vacation Rentals



To find a vacation home for rent in Santa Barbara, you have to know who to ask, and you have to think ahead—and we mean way ahead. The high price of real estate discourages ownership of investment property, so the demand for seasonal rentals far outpaces supply in this fair city-by-the-beach. If you are planning a summer vacation, you need to start looking (and in some cases, making reservations) at least six months ahead. We've listed here some of the available options, which include rental units in complexes and on hotel grounds and, for those willing to forego staying in Santa Barbara proper, accommodations in seaside Carpinteria. Few local hotels offer "vacation rentals" as such, but they may offer weekly or monthly rates that represent a savings over the regular room rate, so ask when making reservations.

A few cautions: Always ask exactly what is included in the cost of your rental. Some places charge for the use of towels and other necessities, which will run your bill higher than just the cost of the lodging. Also ask what you are required to bring. When linens are not supplied (at a cost or otherwise), you may have to lug along towels, sheets, and other personal items. Find out what's in the kitchen, whether or not a VCR is included, and what the parking situation will be. Figure security deposits (usually refundable if you leave the rental in the same condition that you found it in) and occupancy taxes into your total cost. Be very sure to get an immediate confirmation of your reservation after you have made payment.

Finally, be aware that there are no truly "beachfront" homes in the city proper. Some may overlook a beach from a bluff or cliff, but you may have to drive 10 or 15 minutes to dig your toes in the sand.

A final thought: Yes, vacation rentals are expensive in Santa Barbara, but think of all that money you're going to save by not having to eat out all the time!

## Rental Agencies

In addition to the company listed below, which specializes in vacation rentals, several other real estate agencies in town handle vacation rentals as part of their services. Check our Real Estate chapter for a listing of local real estate firms and inquire about vacation rental opportunities.

**Coastal Getaways Realty, Inc.**
**1086 Coast Village Road**
**Montecito, CA**
**(805) 969–1258**
**768 Linden Avenue**
**Carpinteria, CA**
**(805) 684–8777**
**www.coastalrealty.com**

Coastal Getaways is the only vacation rental company in Santa Barbara that is a member of the National Vacation Rental Managers Association—and it's one of the only vacation rental companies in Santa Barbara, period. It handles upscale owner-occupied Santa Barbara properties that rent for between $2,000 and $7,500 a week while the owner is absent. Homes come with absolutely everything (including paid utilities), and if guests want something extra such as maid service or a chef, it can be arranged. The vast majority of the homes are nonsmoking, many do not allow pets, and all rentals require a cash payment 60 days in advance of occupancy (no credit cards are accepted except to hold a rental temporarily). Rental

*Many of the funky cottages fringing Miramar Beach make ideal vacation rentals in the summer.*
PHOTO: BRIAN HASTINGS

periods vary from a required three-day minimum (a week on beach properties) to leases of several years, and renters often love the area so much that they end up buying a home. Most of Coastal's summer rental properties are booked by December for the coming year. Winter rental of beach properties can cost as much as 33 percent less than summer rentals, but still require a reservation up to four months in advance.

## Rental Complexes

**Solimar Sands**
**4700 Sandyland Road**
**Carpinteria, CA**
**(805) 684–5613**
**www.solimarsands.com**

Located a half-block from the beach in Carpinteria, Solimar Sands includes 30 one- and two-bedroom, two-bath condos available for weekly (in summer) and monthly rental. One three-bedroom unit is also available. The condos include everything you need except sheets and towels, which you are expected to bring. There are no phones in the units, but pay phones are available on the grounds. The high season is July and August. High-season prices range from $900 weekly for a one-bedroom condo to $1,580 for a three-bedroom, two-bath unit; winter rates range from $1,150 to $1,950, respectively.

**Sunset Shores**
**4980 Sandyland Road**
**Carpinteria, CA**
**(805) 684–3682, (800) 343–1544**

Sunset Shores is an apartment complex across the street from the beach in Carpinteria. The 77 units include studios and one- and two-bedroom apartments that range in cost from $515 a week for a small studio in winter to $1,150 a week for a two-bedroom in summer. Furnishings and utilities are included, but you must bring your own towels and sheets. An up-front deposit of $700 is required for a monthly rental, $300 for a weekly.

**Villa Elegante**
**402 Orilla del Mar**
**Santa Barbara, CA**
**(805) 565–4459**
**www.villaelegante.com**

Just a block from East Beach in Santa Barbara, Villa Elegante comprises six newly built Mediterranean-style units with spacious two- and three-bedroom suites in duplexes. There's a minimum one-week stay, and prices range from $1,500 a week for a two-bedroom unit in winter to $2,700 a week for an ocean-view three-bedroom unit in summer. Everything is provided, including linens, and each suite has air conditioning, a gourmet kitchen, TV, VCR, stereo, washer and dryer, wood-burning fireplace, and individual parking garage. Upstairs units have balconies and ocean views. Book way ahead, as these might go fast once word gets around. A refundable $500 security deposit must be received within seven days of booking the reservation. Villa Elegante accepts pets in one of the units.

## Rentals at Hotels and Inns

A few hotels and bed and breakfast inns rent cottages or villas by the day, week, or month. All of the accommodations listed in this section are included in our Bed and Breakfasts or Hotels and Motels chapters, where you will find greater detail about the property and services of each.

**Cabrillo Inn at the Beach**
**931 E. Cabrillo Boulevard**
**Santa Barbara, CA**
**(805) 966–1641, (800) 648–6708**
**www.cabrillo-inn.com**

Behind the inn, which is across the street from the beach, a Spanish-style complex has two units available as vacation rentals. Each unit is a 1,600-square-foot, two-bedroom, two-bath apartment that will house up to five people. Gas fireplaces and built-in bookcases lend a homey feel, and the units have lots of French casement windows to let in the sunlight. Each unit has a private phone line with an answering machine, a TV/VCR, and daily maid service. They also feature a laundry plus full kitchen with a dishwasher and microwave, and you have access to the pool and other amenities available at the inn. The units are rented for Saturday arrivals and departures. Weekly rates range from $1,575 to $2,675 depending on the season. Holiday rates are more. Many families that stay here reserve for the next year, and the units are generally booked several months ahead. If you want to stay for longer than a few weeks, ask about the monthly rates.

### Insiders' Tip

A 12 percent tax on short-term accommodations is automatic everywhere in Santa Barbara County, so be sure to figure in the extra amount when assessing your rental costs.

**The Cheshire Cat Inn**
**36 W. Valerio Street**
**Santa Barbara, CA**
**(805) 569–1610**
**www.cheshirecat.com**

You'll vacation in style at this charming bed and breakfast inn, which has three cottages for rent by the week or month. Each two-bedroom cottage is individually furnished, and has a private front entrance, a large living room with a TV and VCR, gas fireplaces, a dining nook, and a kitchen stocked with everything you'll need. All have private decks with hot tubs. No more than four people can stay in any cottage at once, but children are welcome. Nightly low-season (October through May, Monday through Thursday) rates are $270 for a one-bedroom cottage to $300 for a two-bedroom. In high season,

## Insiders' Tip

Sometimes the *Santa Barbara News-Press* or *The Santa Barbara Independent* have vacation rental ads in their classified sections from local homeowners who are going on vacation and want to rent out their home while they're gone. Or, place your own "looking for . . ." ad. It's worth a try.

nightly rates are $325 for a one-bedroom to $375 for a two-bedroom. Call for weekly and monthly rates.

**Radisson Hotel Santa Barbara**
**1111 E. Cabrillo Boulevard**
**Santa Barbara, CA**
**(805) 963–0744, (800) 643–1994**
**www.radisson.com**

In addition to its regular guest rooms, the Radisson has five fully furnished apartments that can be rented for a minimum 30-day stay. Four of the units have one bedroom with a king-size bed in addition to a living area and kitchen. The fifth is a two-bedroom, 1,600-square-foot apartment on the third floor with ocean views and a deck. Maid service is provided twice a week, and all of the Radisson's amenities (including room service) are available to apartment guests. The apartments rent for between $2,225 and $3,500 a month, and reservations can be made no more than a year ahead. Sometimes units are available on the spur of the moment, but they are often booked far ahead for the summer months and Christmas holidays. Because of the 30-day minimum stay, the local 12 percent bed tax does not apply.

**San Ysidro Ranch**
**900 San Ysidro Lane**
**Montecito, CA**
**(805) 969–5046, (800) 368–6788 (from outside 805 area code only)**
**www.sanysidroranch.com**

One of the most exclusive resorts in the Santa Barbara area, San Ysidro Ranch offers seclusion for the well-heeled at several cottages located on the grounds. The largest cottage is the 2,200-square-foot Eucalyptus Cottage, a two-bedroom house with three wood-burning fireplaces, 2.5 bathrooms, and its own private heated swimming pool. Each cottage has a private patio, hot tub, and wet bar, but no kitchen. Actually, you might not care, because you can eat at the ranch's restaurant or order room service. And, just like the other guests, you can use the pool and tennis courts or arrange horseback riding. The price for living in such prestigious seclusion? A flat nightly rate runs from $695 to $3,750, depending on the cottage you choose.

# Restaurants

Cajun
California/American
Chinese
French
Health Food
Indian
Italian
Japanese
Mexican
Moroccan
South American
Thai

Few cities in the world can boast as many restaurants per capita as Santa Barbara. There are more than 400 in the greater Santa Barbara area, and during the busy summer months and holiday seasons, nearly all are filled to capacity with diners from around the world. Our restaurants represent all colors of the culinary spectrum. The mind-boggling array of international cuisine means you can always find the type of meal you're looking for, whether you're hankering for tacos or tournedos.

In recent years Santa Barbara has become a magnet for the haute gourmet, attracting some of the nation's best chefs as well as discerning diners looking for the types of meals they read about in *Bon Appetit* and *Gourmet* magazines.

Our burgeoning local wine industry has contributed to this restaurant renaissance, and many dining establishments offer pairings of acclaimed local wines with seasonal meals. (For more information on local wines, read our Santa Barbara Wine Country chapter.)

Don't worry if you're not an epicurean, though—you'll find plenty of restaurants to please your palate as well as your pocketbook. Wholesome fare reigns supreme in health-conscious Santa Barbara, and most menus include vegetarian and low-fat entrees. California cuisine—which features seafood, grilled meats, seasonal vegetables, and salads made with fresh, locally grown produce and herbs, arranged in a colorful, artistic presentation—dominates the current restaurant scene.

Here in Santa Barbara, chefs create their own versions of California cuisine, often adding local avocados, citrus fruits, and salsas to their concoctions.

Pacific Rim seafood, spices, and sauces are currently in vogue. Ahi tuna, for example, appears on hundreds of menus in about a million variations. You can order it as sashimi or a sushi roll, seared, pan-broiled, grilled, or coated with peppercorns. If your palate seeks adventure, you can take a culinary safari to our many international restaurants, from Mexican and Moroccan to South American and Thai. And restaurants serving traditional American fare—burgers, french fries, pizza, steak and potatoes and the like—will never go out of style here. Several local restaurants have been serving the same hearty American meals for more than 50 years.

According to our visiting friends and relatives, we locals are spoiled by all these choices, not to mention the convenience. It takes less than 15 minutes to drive to most restaurants—and the hard part is choosing one from among the many.

Sometimes we just park in a city lot and walk up and down State Street, Cabrillo Boulevard, or Coast Village Road in Montecito, savoring the aromas of steamed shellfish, grilled seafood, and bubbling stews. Then we let our appetites determine which restaurant we'll enter. So where will you dine this evening? To help you narrow down your choices, we've compiled an extensive list of our favorite restaurants, organized by the type of food they serve: Cajun, California/American, Chinese, French, health food, Indian, Italian, Japanese, Mexican, Moroccan, South American, and Thai.

In this chapter we focus on the dining experience. Several restaurants offer music, dancing, and/or other entertainment in addition to meals, and we've highlighted these in the Nightlife chapter. You can also find more information on hotel restaurants in the Hotels and Motels chapter. Nearly all the restaurants listed here accept reservations as well as credit cards. If not, we've noted it in the description. Speaking of reservations, we recommend that you always call ahead to reserve a table on weekends and holidays and at any time during the busy summer months. The most popular restaurants fill up quickly, and if you don't have a reservation, you might have to wait for an hour or two before you're seated.

Many restaurants have outdoor courtyards and patios, so you can dine alfresco, even in the evening and during the winter months. Which brings up two other important issues. The first is smoking. California law prohibits smoking in any restaurant or bar. If you want to light up, you will have to do so outdoors. Some restaurants have cigar terraces reserved for smokers. We've mentioned these in the individual write-ups.

The second issue is pets. When you strolled along State Street in the past, you would probably see more than a few happy pooches flopped by their owner's feet at the sidewalk cafes. Santa Barbarans love their pets and tend to bring them along everywhere they can—even to restaurants. But things are changing. Recently, Environmental Health Services cracked down on pets on restaurant patios. It's actually always been against the law to have animals in dining areas—inside or out—but many restaurant owners looked the other way as long as dogs were kept outdoors and under control. Now restaurateurs are being asked to comply with the state codes or face hefty fines. So be aware. If you take Fido out to lunch, you might have to settle for sitting at the edge of an outdoor patio and tying him to a nearby tree. To help you out, we've mentioned in the individual write-up if the restaurant offers an alfresco eating area. At least that way, you can sit where you can see your little buddy.

*Although dogs are welcome at some local beaches, no pets are allowed in Santa Barbara restaurants—not even outside on the patio.* PHOTO: BRIAN HASTINGS

Children's menus are available at many restaurants, and unless we've mentioned otherwise, the eateries listed here are wheelchair accessible. Casual dress is fine at most, and we know only a few that require a coat and tie. If you're going to an expensive restaurant for dinner, however, you probably want to change from your shorts, T-shirts, and flip-flops into somewhat dressier attire. So rev up the car and get started on your savory Santa Barbara safari. And be sure to let us know if you run into any fantastic restaurants we haven't mentioned. Bon appetit!

**Price-Code Key**

The price key symbol in each restaurant listing represents the average cost for a dinner for two, excluding appetizers, dessert, cocktails, beer or wine, tax, and tip. Keep in mind that many restaurants offer a range of entrees at varying prices. You could, for example, order a $10 pasta dish instead of the $25 lobster. These symbols provide only a general guide so you'll know whether a restaurant is basically inexpensive, upscale, or something in between.

$ ........................ Less than $20
$$ .......................... $20 to $40
$$$ ......................... $41 to $60
$$$$ .................... $61 and more

## Cajun

**Cajun Kitchen**
**901 Chapala Street**
**Santa Barbara, CA**
**(805) 965-1004**
**1924 De la Vina Street**
**Santa Barbara, CA**
**(805) 687-2062**
**420-E S. Fairview Avenue**
**Goleta, CA**
**(805) 683-8864**
**865 Linden Avenue**
**Carpinteria, CA**
**(805) 684-6010**
**$**

The casual, family-style Cajun Kitchen has long stood by its motto: "If you're in a hurry and can't wait for the best, try somewhere else and settle for less." It definitely lives up to its reputation for serving the best Cajun breakfasts and lunches in town, and all four locations are always crowded with locals and visitors. The extensive menu features Louisiana-style favorites: jambalaya and eggs, corn bread with apple butter, omelets, pancakes, Louisiana hot sausage, and blackened salmon Benedict with potatoes. Sleepyheads can order breakfast until closing time.

For lunch, you can spice up your day with blackened catfish or redfish, a po'boy sandwich, Bourbon Street chili, seafood gumbo, or shrimp Creole. We love the homemade corned-beef hash and eggs. The fantastic food and great service make the wait more than worthwhile.

All four Cajun Kitchens are open for breakfast and lunch daily. (Hint: go really early in the morning or after 1:00 P.M. and maybe you won't have to wait!)

**The Palace Grill**
**8 E. Cota Street**
**Santa Barbara, CA**
**(805) 963-5000**
**www.palacegrill.com**
**$$-$$$**

The good times roll in a big way every evening of the week at the Palace, which is consistently named one of the best Cajun restaurants in California. It's been written up in *Gourmet, Bon Appetit, Los Angeles Magazine,* and many other publications.

The colorful, lively Bourbon Street atmosphere provides a perfect complement to the spicy food. When Ronald Reagan was president and visited his nearby ranch, the secret service and press corps reportedly ate regularly at the Palace. We've also heard of people driving for five hours just to eat here. The Palace actually offers a mix of New Orleans, Creole, and pasta dishes plus steak, fish, and chicken dishes for those who prefer more subtle, less spicy seasonings. All meals are served by a waitstaff that works as a well-oiled team. Fresh seafood, typically redfish, crawfish, and prawns, is flown in direct from New Orleans.

The list of mouthwatering dishes is nearly endless: Cajun crawfish popcorn (one of our favorites), blackened redfish or ahi tuna, Louisiana prawns, gumbos, crawfish crab cakes, jambalaya, Caribbean coconut shrimp, and crawfish étouffée are just a few of the delicious options.

Quench your thirst with a Cajun martini or rum punch, or just head for the self-service wine bar. For dessert, save room for the sinful bread pudding soufflé (which you need to order before you order dinner because it takes a while to prepare) or the Key lime pie made with real Florida Key limes.

The Palace Grill is open for lunch and dinner seven days a week. Reservations are accepted for Sunday through Thursday, but on Friday and Saturday nights they're taken for the first seating only (5:30 P.M.)—after that, it's first come, first served. Without reservations, plan on a wait of an hour or longer during prime dinner hours. The time usually passes quickly, though, because it's lots of fun chatting with the interesting people in line, watching the magician who entertains on busy nights, and listening to the jazz musicians who often play here.

If you don't want to search for a parking place, take advantage of the Palace's valet parking. Just pull up to the front door (between State and Anacapa Streets) and ask for the service.

**Insiders' Tip**

Many Santa Barbara restaurants offer special, all-inclusive meals on holidays, often with live music and seasonal foods and wines. Why not treat yourself to epicurean delights on New Year's Eve, Valentine's Day, Easter, Oktoberfest and other special occasions?

## California/American

**Andria's Restaurant**
**214 State Street**
**Santa Barbara, CA**
**(805) 966–3000**
**$$**

Andria's has been a local favorite for more than a decade. In 2001 it moved from its harborside location, reappearing, under new ownership, in its original spot on State Street across from the train station. Despite the change in ownership, you'll still see the familiar faces of some of the old harborside crew, and probably the same loyal clientele. The specialty is still fresh fish, but Andria's also serves steak, baby back ribs, chicken, sandwiches, and salads. Some of the most popular dishes include the fresh fish entrees prepared with a pistachio-nut crust and lemon-herb beurre blanc, the New England sea scallops, the bacon-wrapped shrimp, and the New Zealand rack of lamb. You can also belly up to the oyster bar for a true taste of the sea. If you prefer to dine alfresco, choose a table on the enclosed patio fronting State Street. The restaurant also offers a club room out back seating 60 for banquets. The piano bar is definitely the place to be on weekends. Andria's serves 60 different types of beer on tap from its full bar and has an expansive wine list. It's open for lunch and dinner seven days a week.

**Arnoldi's Café**
**600 Olive Street**
**Santa Barbara, CA**
**(805) 962–5394**
**$$**

Master stonemason Joe Arnoldi and his wife, Ilda, opened this venerable Santa Barbara restaurant in a sandstone building at the corner of Olive and Cota Streets in 1940. For years, Joe and Ilda served pasta, red wine, and steaks to a steady stream of loyal locals. These days it's still a casual family restaurant, but it's owned and operated by longtime Arnoldi's bartender Jim Kershaw and his wife, Helen Daniels.

The couple renovated and updated the entire place and converted the former beer garden into a barbecue area with a bocce court. But they kept the checkered tablecloths, Italian-style booths, polished wood bar, deer and elk heads on the walls, and mural of Lake Como. The "new" Arnoldi's is quite the hip hangout for Santa Barbarans in their 30s or older. It's packed with locals nearly every weekend.

The menu has also been updated to include wild game, steaks, and seafood. Go wild and order the elk medallions or, if you're really hungry, the 22-ounce Angus beef porterhouse steak.

Arnoldi's creates fresh, handmade ravioli specials every day, for example, ravioli stuffed with butternut squash and goat cheese. A martini specialist is always on duty at the restaurant's popular bar. Arnoldi's is open for lunch Monday through Friday and for dinner every day.

**Arts & Letters Café**
**7 E. Anapamu Street**
**Santa Barbara, CA**
**(805) 730–1463**
**www.artsandletterscafe.com**
**$$**

At the romantic, intimate Arts & Letters Café, you can gaze at fine art, listen to live classical music, and feast on gourmet cuisine all at the same time. This small restaurant occupies a walled garden courtyard behind Sullivan Goss Books & Prints, Ltd. (see our Shopping chapter). Choose a table in the art gallery or in the courtyard by the bubbling fountain, order a glass of wine, and enjoy the casually elegant atmosphere.

The menu varies with the seasons and draws from fresh local bounty. Favorite lunch specialties include an array of salads: smoked duck, Mediterranean, diced chicken, and smoked turkey are a few examples. A typical dinner menu might include grilled salmon with a lime or dill sauce, roast chicken, herb-crusted tenderloin, or grilled swordfish with a tropical salsa.

The restaurant also offers special meals and events on holidays. Arts & Letters Café serves lunch daily, dinner Tuesday through Sunday, and breakfast on Sunday.

During the spring, summer, and fall, the Arts & Letters Troupe (a group of talented professional musicians from throughout Southern California) performs Tuesday through Thursday, presenting a different type of show each night of the week; classical guitar, contemporary music, and Opera Under the Stars are among the possibilities. Call for more information.

**Beachside Bar and Café**
**5905 Sandspit Road (in Goleta Beach Park)**
**Goleta, CA**
**(805) 964–7881**
**$$**

This is one of only a few area restaurants that is right on the beach. As you might expect, it draws a large crowd of locals and visitors looking for great seafood with a view. The Beachside boasts a fresh seafood bar with specialties such as bluepoint oysters, ceviche, and steamed mussels and clams. The seafood is wonderful, and you'll find a good selection of pastas and salads as well as chicken and beef dishes.

In the main dining room, large windows look out onto the beach (illuminated at night by floodlights), or you can opt for a table on the spacious patio, where you can smell the sea breeze and soak up the sun (there are umbrellas for shade, heaters for cold days, and a large fireplace that adds a cozy touch).

The restaurant has a lively bar scene (plus beer on tap and a good wine list), which means it can be pretty noisy inside, but everyone's having a good time and loving that food. Live jazz spices up the weekends. The Beachside is open daily for lunch and dinner. On weekends you might wait up to an hour for a table unless you have reservations.

**Be Bop Burgers**
**111 State Street**
**Santa Barbara, CA**
**(805) 966–1956**
**www.bebopburgers.com**
**$**

Pull into a parking space with a Hollywood star's name on it and get ready for some fun! At Be Bop Burgers, you're in a neon world of the '50s and '60s, with blaring vintage rock 'n' roll, old-fashioned photo booths, and a pristine classic car of the month on display.

This is the perfect place for families (see our Kidstuff chapter), with kid's food like chicken corn dogs and grilled cheese sandwiches, plus great fries and onion rings, milkshakes and malts; a piece of Bazooka bubble gum comes with each order. Parents will like the burgers (including the Beach Boys Veggie Burger, Be Bop Turkey Burger, and It's My Party Patty Melt), the salads (try Elvis' Breast of Chicken Salad), sandwiches (Buddy Holly's Tri-Tip BBQ Beef is a favorite), and small selection of beers and wines. The desserts are great, too, with appealing names like Mo Manna Banana Split and Slippin' 'n' Slidin' Sundae. Enjoy a retro reverie by browsing the rock 'n' roll memorabilia on the walls, then snuggle down in the nearest booth and chomp those fries.

Be Bop is open for breakfast, lunch, and dinner daily during the summer; breakfast is served on weekends only during the winter months.

**Blue Agave**
**20 E. Cota Street**
**Santa Barbara, CA**
**(805) 899–4694**
**$$**

This trendy, two-story restaurant and bar opened in 1995 and quickly became a popular hangout for young professionals, Hollywood celebrities, and chic singles and couples. Blue Agave's popularity has a lot to do with its winning combination of contemporary decor, romantic lighting, creative cuisine, a full bar stocked with dozens of different tequilas, and lively crowds.

The menu is eclectic, with a bit of everything: Pacific Rim, Mediterranean, Asian, Southwestern, and Mexican cuisine. Popular menu items include chicken mole, Chilean seabass, filet mignon, and anything with garlic mashed potatoes. Upstairs you can order a martini, lounge on couches around the fireplace, or head out to the cigar balcony overlooking Cota Street. For parties of four, we think the best dining nooks are the cozy and very private booths on this upper level. Blue Agave is open for dinner daily. Only parties of 6 or more can make reservations. If your party has fewer than 6 people, you'll be seated on a first come, first served basis. So it's best to show up before 8:00 P.M. if you don't want to wait for a table. Valet parking is available across the street.

**Bouchon**
**9 W. Victoria Street**
**Santa Barbara, CA**
**(805) 730–1160**
**www.bouchon.net**
**$$$**

If you can't make it to the wine country, come to Bouchon instead. The name is the French word for wine cork, and owner Mitchell Sjerven opened this very civilized eatery in the summer of 1998 with a desire to conjure a wine-country dining experience in the heart of downtown Santa Barbara. He must be doing something right. Since its launch, Bouchon has earned a place at the table with Santa Barbara's restaurant elite, receiving enthusiastic reviews from *Wine Spectator* and the local press. From his cozy exhibition kitchen, chef Charles Fredericks concocts an imaginative menu of regional wine-country cuisine using fresh local produce. Depending upon the season, you can feast on such specialties as lime seared sea scallops, roasted petit wild boar, and the popular bourbon and maple-glazed duck breast with fava bean, butternut squash, and applewood-smoked bacon succotash. And if that's not enough of a mouthful, Bouchon's wine list will dazzle your palate. Oenophiles can choose from an impressive lineup of more than 50 Central Coast wines by the glass as well as bottles from Northern California, the Pacific Northwest, the Central Coast, and France. You can sit in the bright and airy dining room or dine alfresco on the covered garden patio fronting Victoria Street. Plan-

*Many of Santa Barbara's dining spots have a nautical theme, like this building, which until recently housed Keeper's Lighthouse restaurant.* PHOTO: BRIAN HASTINGS

ning a special party? Reserve the private Cork Room and the chef will design a special menu just for you and your guests. Of course all this doesn't come cheap, but this is a special spot for special occasions. It's open for dinner seven nights a week.

**Brigitte's**
**1325 State Street**
**Santa Barbara, CA**
**(805) 966–9676**
**$$**

Brigitte's is one of our favorite places to eat in Santa Barbara (a local critic named Brigitte's the city's "Best American Bistro"). The reasonably priced gourmet cuisine is among the best in town, and it's served in a casual, unpretentious atmosphere. In August 2000 Richard Yates and Tina Takaya, the team from the popular Palace Grill, took over the helm, continuing Brigitte's tradition of warm conviviality and high-quality cuisine. If you like a truly eclectic menu with a wide selection of creative cuisine (and who doesn't?), you'll love it here. The menu shows a mix of Californian, Mediterranean, Italian, and Asian influences, and the daily specials add even more diversity. Brigitte's typically offers at least two meat and fresh fish specials as well as seasonal meals—hearty winter game dishes and lighter preparations in the summer. Favorite dishes are the chili-encrusted filet mignon cooked to order with a roasted garlic mushroom sauce, and the lemongrass-encrusted salmon with a Thai curry sauce. You can also order fresh homemade pastas risotto or gourmet pizzas cooked in a wood-burning oven. Be sure to leave room for one of Brigitte's incredible desserts. A popular pick is the Like Water for Chocolate Surprise, a decadent mix of white and milk chocolate mousse.

The wine list offers a good selection of international wines with a bent for bottles from California and France, plus you'll find a good variety of unusual beers and spirits. End your meal with a frothy cappuccino.

Brigitte's is open for lunch Monday through Saturday and for dinner nightly.

## Insiders' Tip

Santa Barbara's laid-back style means you can dress casually in almost every restaurant in town (but shirts and shoes are always minimum requirements).

**Brophy Bros.**
**On the breakwater at the harbor**
**Santa Barbara, CA**
**(805) 966–4418**
**$$**

So who wants to climb a flight of stairs, wedge into a tiny, crowded and noisy restaurant, and spend the next hour trying to hear yourself talk? Seafood lovers, that's who. Brophy Bros. has been around for a long time and is well-loved by locals for its salty, down-to-earth ambiance, fresh, simply served seafood, and spectacular harbor views. It also has the best clam chowder in town. Order up a shrimp cocktail and gaze out the open windows toward Stearns Wharf, or take in some of the local fishing and wharf memorabilia lining the walls.

You'll find a large selection of fresh seasonal fish on the menu, including mahimahi, salmon, and albacore. It's served with mountains of coleslaw and fries and your choice of salad or clam chowder. The clam bar is a favorite hangout, but you can also ask for a table on the small balcony, which is the perfect vantage point for watching the comings and goings in the harbor. If you can't climb the stairs to the main dining room, you can eat at the even smaller, downstairs version (same food).

Brophy Bros. is a natural magnet for tourists, so you may find it crowded on weekends and during the summer. If you don't want to wait too long for a table, we suggest you turn up early. The restaurant doesn't take reservations, but it will equip you with a pager so you can stroll around the harbor while you wait. It's open for lunch and dinner seven days a week.

**The Brown Pelican**
**2981½ Cliff Drive**
**Santa Barbara, CA**
**(805) 687–4550**
**$$**

Situated right on the sand, The Brown Pelican faces the surf on Arroyo Burro beach. The menu is as casual as the ambiance, with Mediterranean leanings and a choice of fresh seafood, free-range chicken, steak, pastas, salads, and sandwiches. Recently a new chef, who worked previously at Citronelle, has spiced up the menus. For lunch you can feast on a grilled fish ciabatta or tri-tip sandwich, and the new dinner favorites include the walnut-pecan salad, lobster linguine, and pistachio-crusted salmon. The clam chowder has been recognized by *Gourmet* magazine as some of the best on the West Coast, and kids will love the children's menu, which features all the old favorites, including a grilled cheese sandwich and fries.

The Brown Pelican also offers a full bar and a nice selection of local wines as well as espresso and cappuccino. It's a natural choice for beach lovers, who can sip a glass of wine on the patio and gaze out at the crashing waves. The Brown Pelican is open for breakfast, lunch, and dinner daily. It's especially crowded on weekends at breakfast and lunchtime. Reservations are recommended—especially Thursday through Saturday.

**Chad's**
**625 Chapala Street**
**Santa Barbara, CA**
**(805) 568–1876**
**www.chadsrestaurant.com**
**$$$**

If you're looking for a special-occasion meal in a festive (but not raucous) atmosphere, Chad's will more than fit the bill. When you enter the restaurant, you feel like you're entering someone's home. That's because it's in a renovated Victorian house built in 1876, with rambling porches, a living room with a full bar (that's packed for happy hour) and fireplace, and several dining rooms—some quieter and more romantic than others. Most people dress up a bit to come to Chad's, but the atmosphere is far from stuffy. In fact, owner Chad Stevens sometimes appears in a banana suit on weekend evenings and cajoles diners into joining him in a conga line that circles the restaurant.

Chad's menu features regional American dishes such as stuffed Montana pork chop, oysters Rockefeller, blackened or broiled seafood, chicken tchoupitoulas, filet mignon, braised lamb shanks, and pan-seared tri-tip. Accompanying most dishes are Chad's famous garlic mashed potatoes. Save room for the chocolate Jack Daniels soufflé. Chad's is open for dinner daily. If you're planning to eat at a traditional dinner hour on a weekend, you should make your reservations as early as possible. Chad's is sometimes fully booked several weeks in advance.

**Citronelle at the Beach**
**901 E. Cabrillo Boulevard, at Milpas Street**
**Santa Barbara, CA**
**(805) 963-0111**
**www.citronelle.com**
**$$$–$$$$**

Start with a fabulous location atop the Santa Barbara Inn, add an ocean view, throw in a nationally known chef, and you have the perfect dining experience. And "perfect" is a word often used in association with Citronelle, owned by chef Michel Richard, who won his fame at Hollywood's trendy Citrus.

Richard is not always on hand (he now has several other restaurants throughout the United States), but his fabulous French-California cuisine, in the hands of chef Felicien Cueff, has earned Citronelle the title of "Santa Barbara's Best Restaurant" according to more than one critic. In the past, readers of *Condé Nast Traveler* voted Citronelle one of six restaurants in the country with perfect food.

Start with a delectable appetizer like the avocado nest with fresh blue crab, the Santa Barbara black mussels, or the Camarillo mixed green salad, then begin the difficult process of choosing an entree from a fanciful menu of such delicacies as baked Norwegian salmon with a spinach crust and carrot curry sauce, braised lamb shank with a cabernet sauvignon sauce, or asparagus-crusted chicken. The restaurant has also added a new fixed price menu for lunch: appetizer, entree, and dessert for less than $20—not a bad deal. The desserts are always fabulous, as is the wine list. Groups can reserve one of four private areas, including the new upstairs space, the Penthouse at Citronelle, with panoramic views of the mountain and sea.

Citronelle is open for breakfast, lunch, and dinner daily, and for Sunday brunch. There's no dress code, but try to look as chic as you possibly can. And make a reservation—you'll probably need one! (Ask for a window table.)

**Comeback Café**
**324 State Street**
**Santa Barbara, CA**
**(805) 962-2889**
**$**

No, this isn't one of those tony Santa Barbara restaurants where you can discover a unique spin on California cuisine by some famous chef. The Comeback Café is just a good ol' down-home breakfast and lunch place where you can take the kids (there's a play area). Come on in after a walk on the beach, hang out on the patio, and eat fabulous food.

Try banana and wheat-germ pancakes, French toast drizzled with strawberry sauce or sprinkled with powdered sugar, or a delicious salad or sandwich. You won't find a bar here, but a small list of beer and wine is offered.

The Comeback Café is open for breakfast and lunch daily.

**Crocodile Restaurant & Bar**
**2819 State Street**
**Santa Barbara, CA**
**(805) 687–6444**
**www.treeinns.com**
**$$**

Upper State Street's Lemon Tree Inn has a great little bistro in the Crocodile Restaurant & Bar. The American fare ranges from club sandwiches to vegetarian dishes and pasta, but seafood and char-broiled steaks are the specialties. You'll also find sophisticated dishes such as rosemary chicken in a lemon cream sauce, and filet mignon with portabello mushroom wine sauce, as well as a special menu for the kids. All the breads, pastries, and desserts are baked fresh on the premises. Sit inside or opt for the tropical outdoor patio. The Crocodile is open for breakfast, lunch, and dinner daily. Pop in for the lively happy hour from 4:00 to 6:00 P.M. daily, with live entertainment Wednesday through Sunday.

**Downey's**
**1305 State Street**
**Santa Barbara, CA**
**(805) 966–5006**
**$$$**

Downey's is proof that good things come in small packages. Only 14 tables are tucked into this little dining room, but chef John Downey consistently serves up some of the finest cuisine in the city (just look at all the awards amassed on the wall).

The menu changes daily, incorporating the freshest local and seasonal ingredients. Such specialties as fresh swordfish with roasted red pepper sauce, Colorado lamb loin, and grilled duck with fresh mango chutney, wild rice, and ginger sauce have recently graced the menu, and once a month, a multicourse, prix-fixe chef's dinner draws a full house. For those trying to shy away from cholesterol-laden meals, a few heart-smart options are sprinkled throughout the menu.

In addition to the fabulous food (the *Zagat Restaurant Survey* once named it the "Best Restaurant in Santa Barbara"), Downey's offers a superb wine list and attentive service. Reserve ahead or you may be disappointed. Downey's serves dinner only, Tuesday through Sunday.

**Eladio's Restaurant & Bar**
**1 State Street,**
**Santa Barbara, CA**
**(805) 963–4466**
**$$$**

In a prime location directly across Cabrillo Boulevard from Stearns Wharf in the heart of the tourist district, Eladio's just emerged from a big bucks facelift. It's under the same ownership as the adjacent Harbor View Inn and draws many guests from that hotel and others nearby. Now exuding a more formal ambiance and wearing a bold new sea-themed decor with a dramatic frescoed ceiling, the restaurant serves up seasonal menus of high quality California cuisine prepared with fresh local produce. Sink into the well-cushioned banquettes and enjoy sweeping views of Stearns Wharf, the beachfront bike path, and the mountains while you dine. On warm days, you can also dine alfresco by a fountain in the courtyard. The lunch menu offers elaborate seafood, chicken, and beef dishes as well as gourmet salads and sandwiches. Scan the dinner menu and you'll find imaginative creations such as Lime Butter Basted Shrimp, Creamy Marscopone Risotto, and Pine Nut Crusted Aussie Rack of Lamb. The desserts sound just as delicious and the menu also offers a good selection of wines, ports, and single malt whiskeys. Eladio's has a full bar and is open for lunch and dinner daily.

**El Encanto**
**1900 Lasuen Road**
**Santa Barbara, CA**
**(805) 687–5000**
**www.elencantohotel.com**
**$$$**

The dining room at the El Encanto Hotel and Garden Villas boasts some of the best sunset views in town. Perched on the Riviera, El Encanto looks far out over the city and the Pacific Ocean beyond. On a balmy evening, sitting on the patio with a glass of wine, you'd be hard-pressed to find a more romantic spot in Santa Barbara. The restaurant and the hotel are scheduled for a face-lift, which will enhance the interior views as well.

Chef Mark Kropczynski delivers fine California cuisine with a Mediterranean influence. He is an avid fisherman who loves to catch and cook fresh fish, so you'll find lots of creative seafood options on the menu, all prepared with local seasonal fruit and vegetables. El Encanto's dining room has a full bar and a sterling wine list. It's open daily for breakfast, lunch, and dinner, and for Sunday brunch. Valet parking is available.

**The Endless Summer Bar and Café**
**113 Harbor Way**
**Santa Barbara, CA**
**(805) 564–4666**
**$$**

This surfing-inspired eatery is a bright new casual dining choice overlooking the Santa Barbara harbor. As with its downstairs fine-dining sibling, The Waterfront Grill, the emphasis here is on fresh-caught fish and seafood dishes, but you'll also find a great selection of juicy burgers, sandwiches, soups, and salads. Popular appetizers are the Channel Island mussels, popcorn shrimp, and the crispy calamari. The Hawaiian poke (marinated raw seafood) is also excellent. Slide into a banquette at a Hawaiian-print table, perch on stools at the full cocktail bar, or dine alfresco on the harbor-view terrace. The restaurant has an elevator for wheelchair access and is open for lunch and dinner daily.

**Enterprise Fish Company**
**225 State Street**
**Santa Barbara, CA**
**(805) 962–3313**
**www.enterprisefishco.com**
**$$**

Plop yourself down in a huge warehouse full of fishing memorabilia, laughter, and lively conversation and order up some really fresh seafood. One of Santa Barbara's old-time favorite seafood restaurants, Enterprise has some of the largest daily selections of fresh fish in town. Choose from the daily chalkboard specials (they change according to the season and which fish are available), which could feature Idaho catfish, Costa Rican mahimahi, Hawaiian ahi tuna, Chilean sea bass, or New Zealand orange roughy.

Everything is grilled over mesquite and served with your choice of potatoes Romano (a favorite), rice pilaf, fries, coleslaw, tossed green salad, or clam chowder. There's also an oyster and seafood bar and a sushi bar, plus a kids menu. Cocktails and a modest selection of wines and beers are also available. Enterprise Fish Company is open for lunch and dinner daily. Stop in for a bite, then head down to the wharf for an after-dinner stroll.

**Epiphany**
**21 West Victoria Street**
**Santa Barbara, CA**
**(805) 564–7100**
**$$$**

Tucked in a cozy 1800s cottage, this new fine-dining affair is the reincarnation of the former Blue Shark Bistro. New owners Alberto and Michelle Mastrangelo (with actor Kevin Costner as partner) revamped the interior, enlisted a top-rate chef and launched their sophisticated new eatery in the summer of 2001. So far it's a huge hit, drawing rave reviews for its creative California cuisine with a Mediterranean and Asian twist. Step inside and you'll feel like you've entered a cozy private home. The interior features an open-kitchen, a chic bar buzzing with handsome couples (wear something black), and multiple dining rooms with warm wooden floors and crisply-set tables well spaced for privacy. You can also sip cocktails or order from the bar menu by a bubbling fountain in the garden. The food is exquisite. Epiphany's chef, Michael Goodman, conjures up imaginative versions of Atlantic salmon, Alaskan halibut, chicken, rabbit, and wild boar among other things and you might even find sweetbreads (cow's thymus gland) on the menu. If you don't feel like a formal sit-down dinner, take a seat at the Raw Bar and savor Mediterranean sushi delights like Osetra caviar and a Belvedere vodka-cured salmon. Those with an adventurous palate will love it here. Epiphany is open for dinner seven nights a week.

**FisHouse**
**101 E. Cabrillo Boulevard**
**Santa Barbara, CA**
**(805) 966–2112**
**$$**

Thanks to its location on Cabrillo Boulevard, FisHouse (formerly the Charthouse) is another of those restaurants that's often filled with tourists. It's owned by Tom White of the popular Santa Barbara Shellfish Company on Stearn's Wharf, so it's no surprise that the focus here is on fresh local seafood. Wander into the light-filled, fish-themed dining room with its soaring ceilings, white-washed woods, and ocean views, and you'll feel like you're in Maui. The menu features such briny treats as fresh-shucked oysters (there's an oyster bar here), steamed mussels and clams, crab cakes, clam chowder, cioppino, and sometimes live local crab. When it's available, the lobster is a treat, and the calamari is also good. If you don't like seafood, you'll find plenty to please your palate including pasta, steak, and chicken. The front patio is a lovely spot to sit on warm summer evenings, and you can cozy up by the crackling fire here on cool nights. FisHouse is open daily for lunch and dinner.

**Frog Bar & Grill**
**405 Glen Annie Road (at the Glen Annie Golf Club)**
**Goleta, CA**
**(805) 968–0664**
**$$**

The Frog Bar & Grill is a relative newcomer to Goleta, tucked away on the grounds of the Glen Annie Golf Club. Since Goleta has few special-occasion restaurants, this one was a welcome addition.

The dining room is lovely and affords expansive views of the coastline. You can also pick a table on the spacious patio, which has a fireplace and heaters to ward off the chill if the day is cool. The food is upscale and well-prepared, with everything from sandwiches and salads to filet mignon, chicken fettucine alfredo, and New Zealand rack of lamb. The menu also offers a good selection of seafood such as the grilled salmon and shrimp scampi, and fresh fish specials are offered nightly. Order a cocktail at the full bar or choose a vintage from the wine list.

The Frog Bar & Grill is open for lunch daily and for dinner Monday through Saturday. The adjacent snack bar serves a full breakfast daily.

**The Harbor Restaurant**
**210 Stearns Wharf**
**Santa Barbara, CA**
**(805) 963–3311**
**$$$**

Halfway down Stearns Wharf, with ocean views to die for, The Harbor Restaurant can't help but be a touristy kind of place. It's always full of out-of-town visitors looking for fresh seafood and a seaside perch from which to enjoy the busy waterfront scene.

The restaurant's interior is upscale and nautical, but casual dress is perfectly acceptable, and The Harbor often draws diners from the busy Stearns Wharf foot traffic.

In addition to seafood, the menu offers steak, prime rib, and chicken, plus pastas, salads, and sandwiches. You'll also find a full bar here and a fair wine list. The Harbor is open for lunch and dinner daily, and breakfast on the weekends.

**Harry's Plaza Café**
**3318 State Street**
**Santa Barbara, CA**
**(805) 687–7910**
**$$**

Opened by Harry Davis in 1968, this lively, old-style restaurant has a 30-year tradition of serving down-home American food and very strong drinks. You can

*Perched on popular Stearns Wharf, The Harbor Restaurant offers priceless ocean views.* PHOTO: BRIAN HASTINGS

order steak, seafood, pastas, salads, sandwiches, and daily specials. The regulars at Harry's form an eclectic group that transcends all age groups: it's not unusual to see motorcycle riders, construction workers, and professionals in business suits seated side by side at the bar. A number of celebrities, including Wilt Chamberlain, Telly Savalas, and Bo Derek have popped into Harry's over the years. Harry's was recently sold to an experienced Santa Barbara restauranteur who plans to preserve the bar's unpretentious personalilty.

You'll find Harry's in Loreto Plaza at the corner of Las Positas Road and State Street. It's open daily for lunch and dinner.

**Intermezzo**
**813 Anacapa Street**
**Santa Barbara, CA**
**(805) 966–9463**
**www.winecask.com**
**$$**

A delightful little addition to the Wine Cask (see subsequent listing), Intermezzo offers light, bistro-style dining in a casual and intimate atmosphere. You can sip one of the cafe's interesting coffees or teas while relaxing on the patio, or cuddle on the couch inside near the fireplace and play chess while enjoying a glass of wine.

The menu is as casual as the surroundings, with an emphasis on salads, pastas, pizzas, and sandwiches—great for lunch or a late-night stop after the theater. Popular entrees include the homemade gnocchi with a porcini mushroom sauce and the veal ravioli with sage butter sauce. All of the desserts are homemade, and the wine list, drawn from the Wine Cask's selection, is one of the best in the city. Intermezzo also offers a martini menu and other mixed drinks from the bar and sells cigars, which can be smoked on the front patio.

Intermezzo is open for breakfast, lunch, and dinner Monday through Friday, and opens at 3:00 P.M. on weekends for dinner.

**Joe's Café**
**536 State Street**
**Santa Barbara, CA**
**(805) 966–4638**
**$$**

Joe's is one of the oldest and most famous

restaurants in all of Santa Barbara. Joe Ferrario opened the original restaurant at 512 State Street in 1928 during Prohibition, and according to local legend, Joe's was a popular speakeasy.

Joe's is still one of the area's most popular places to socialize, eat homestyle American/Italian food, and enjoy a drink from the famous bar (said to serve the stiffest, most generous drinks in town). In the 1980s, the restaurant moved just a few doors up from the original Joe's to larger quarters on the corner of Cota and State Streets.

The lively, informal atmosphere, excellent service, and hearty food will undoubtedly continue to attract steady crowds for decades to come. The menu still features many longtime favorites, including homestyle fried chicken, pot roast, Joe's spaghetti, calamari, prime rib, a great club sandwich, and charbroiled steaks. Joe's is open daily for lunch and dinner.

**La Marina**
**1260 Channel Drive**
**Montecito, CA**
**(805) 969–2261**
**www.fourseasons.com/santabarbara**
**$$$$**

La Marina is the formal dining room at the Four Seasons Biltmore. It's a kind of ultimate special-occasion place where you can spend a small fortune on food and wine, be treated like royalty, and go home feeling like you got your money's worth. The elegant ambiance, combined with the California cuisine of executive chef Martin Frost, is guaranteed to please.

Frost, a veteran of several Four Seasons properties, does many dishes well, but has a special flair for those with a British twist (he was born in London). You'll find everything from ahi tuna to roasted squab on the seasonal menu, with an extensive list of wines to pair with your food. A chef's four-course prix-fixe menu is also available each evening. It changes weekly and is also paired with wines.

La Marina is open for dinner only Tuesday through Saturday. Dress up for the occasion, and let the valet park your car. See also the Patio Restaurant, listed below, which is the Biltmore's less formal dining room.

**Left at Albuquerque**
**Paseo Nueveo Mall**
**803 State Street**
**Santa Barbara, CA**
**(805) 564–5040**
**$$**

Even before you start thinking about the Southwestern menu here, you can choose from more than 120 brands of tequila for a before-dinner drink (or try the housemade sangria). The restaurant will be bustling with fellow imbibers, many spilling out onto the patio, making it a friendly, noisy sort of place.

The food is a mix of Anglo, Mexican, and Native American cuisine with a bit of a trendy kick, as exhibited by dishes such as the crispy fried calamari with chipotle aioli. In addition to the tequilas, Left at Albuquerque has a full bar and microbrewed beers on tap. It's open for lunch and dinner daily.

**Louie's California Bistro**
**1404 De la Vina Street**
**Santa Barbara, CA**
**(805) 963–7003**
**www.uphamhotel.com**
**$$**

Pamper yourself at Louie's, a sophisticated California-style bistro in the historic Upham Hotel (see our Hotels and Motels chapter for a detailed description of Santa Barbara's oldest hostelry). The intimate, casually elegant atmosphere makes it a perfect place for a birthday lunch or dinner, business meeting, or romantic tête-á-tête.

Louie's is best known for gourmet cuisine at prices that won't make a huge dent in your budget. Signature dishes include Louie's famous Caesar salad, crab won tons, grilled ahi with tomatoes, potato-crusted sea bass, grilled pork chop with a sun-dried-cherry sauce, and spinach fettuccine with scallops. We know several Louie's regulars who always order the spinach-bacon quiche for lunch. Louie's serves beer and wine only. It's open for lunch Monday through Friday and for dinner seven days a week.

**Lucky's**
**1279 Coast Village Road**
**Montecito, CA**
**(805) 565–7540**
**$$$**

This sleek steakhouse in the old Coast Village Grill location is the hip new hangout in Montecito. Owner Gene Montesano (of Lucky jeans fame) and his partners have infused this place with some minimalistic glamour. From the old black-and-white photographs of celebrities adorning the walls to the smartly clad waiters, the valet parking, and the impressive list of champagnes, Lucky's exudes a kind of nouveau nostalgia. It's newly famous for its juicy steaks aged well and cooked to order—the filet porterhouse, an intriguing cut called a "flatiron," and the New York strip steak among them. Side selections include golden onion rings, home fries, and creamed spinach. You'll also find a few surprises on the menu, like the beef stroganoff, and a few enticing seafood options such as the steamed Maine lobster, jumbo shrimp cocktail, and swordfish brochette. If you're dining alone, you can perch at the bar and watch your favorite sports game or pick a people-watching spot on the street-side patio. The wine list is excellent and has a few big-ticket bottles that are a good indication of the clientele here. Lucky's is not for the miserly, but the beef is worth the bucks.

**Miró**
**Bacara Resort & Spa**
**8301 Hollister Avenue**
**Goleta, CA**
**(805) 968–0100**
**www.bacararesort.com**
**$$$$**

Perched on a bluff overlooking the Pacific at the ritzy new Bacara Resort & Spa, this sophisticated gourmet affair is a new high-point in Santa Barbara dining, with lofty prices to match. Since the resort's debut in 2000, many Hollywood celebrities have made the hike up here, including Pierce Brosnan, Jennifer Lopez, and Tom Hanks. Of the three restaurants at Bacara, Miró is the most formal. The restaurant is named for Joan Miró, the Spanish abstract expressionist, and the dining room displays some of the artist's original bronzes as well as reproductions of his whimsical paintings. Gazing at this evocative collection is a fitting prelude for the artistic California-French cuisine to follow. Distinguished French chef Remi Lauvand composes artful presentations that are almost as colorful as Miró's dramatic art. He uses organic vegetables grown at the Bacara ranch as well as fresh local seafood. A favorite here is the lobster with licorice. The sea scallops with a sauce of orange and black truffle also draw rave reviews, and the desserts, like the chocolate mousse layer cake, are divine. As soon as you slip into the red leather seats here, experienced staffers will cater seamlessly to your every whim. Obsessing over the wine selection? Enlist the services of the refreshingly unpretentious sommelier. She'll be happy to suggest the perfect pinot from the restaurant's 7,000-bottle cellar. You can also preface your meal with a creative cocktail from Miró's full bar. The restaurant is open for dinner Tuesday through Saturday and for brunch on Sundays. Private party areas are available and reservations are essential.

**Montecito Café**
**1295 Coast Village Road**
**Montecito, CA**
**(805) 969–3392**
**www.montecitoinn.com**
**$$**

There's a lot of history in the Montecito Inn (read more in our Hotels and Motels chapter), and some of it is preserved in the charming Montecito Café, just off the lobby. The beautiful wishing well, for example, is a replica of the one that once graced the inn's garden and was reportedly the inspiration for Richard Rodgers' 1936 love song, "There's a Small Hotel."

That sort of light, romantic atmosphere prevails in the cafe. The California cuisine is excellent, and the prices extremely reasonable for such high-quality fare. You'll find imaginative dishes such as grilled chicken breast with roasted Anaheim chilies, red onion, and tomato; grilled marinated flank steak with roast onion and peppercorn sauce; and black pepper fettuccine with grilled lamb sausage, red onions, sweet peppers, and cream—all under $15. An excellent list of wines and champagne provide the perfect accompaniment. The Montecito Café is open daily for lunch and dinner. The reservation policy is a bit unusual: no lunch reservations are taken, and only a third of the dining room can be reserved for dinner, while the other two-thirds are open for walk-in patrons. This can sometimes mean a wait, but it's worth it.

**The Nugget**
**2318 Lillie Avenue**
**Summerland, CA**
**(805) 969–6135**
**$$**

This saloon-style restaurant with an Old West theme is a casual place for lunch or dinner after a day at the beach. This is where Bill Clinton played the saxophone while on vacation just after the November 1992 presidential election.

The Nugget has a full bar and serves lots of traditional American food: chicken wings, curly french fries, steaks, burgers, seafood, and sandwiches. It's open for lunch and dinner daily.

**The Palms**
**701 Linden Avenue**
**Carpinteria, CA**
**(805) 684–3811**
**$**

This popular, informal Carpinteria hangout has been family-owned and -operated for some 40 years. Barbecue your own steak on the grill if you wish, or ask the chef to do it for you. You can also order fresh seafood and serve yourself from the salad bar. Park yourself by one of the two fireplaces, order a beer, and chat with the locals.

The Palms offers a full slate of traditional American food, including burgers, steaks, and fresh seafood. It's open for dinner seven evenings a week and has a cocktail lounge with live music Thursday through Saturday.

**Paradise Cafe**
**702 Anacapa Street**
**Santa Barbara, CA**
**(805) 962–4416**
**$$**

Many a local resident and visitor has wined and dined at this casual, quintessential Santa Barbara restaurant since 1983. It occupies a converted house on the corner of Anacapa and Ortega Streets, just a block from State Street.

The Paradise is best known for its tasty meats, burgers, and fresh local seafood grilled over a Santa Ynez oakwood fire. It's also noted for its extensive list of Santa Barbara County wines, including its own Paradise Chardonnay, made by Qupé winery. When the weather's warm, most people prefer to eat outside amid the tropical flowers. The separate bar area draws a hip singles crowd.

The Paradise Cafe is open for lunch and dinner daily and also for breakfast on Sunday.

**Patio Restaurant**
**1260 Channel Drive**
**Montecito, CA**
**(805) 969–2261**
**www.fourseasons.com/santabarbara**
**$$$**

One of two lovely dining rooms housed in the Four Seasons Biltmore, the Patio has all the ambiance of a seaside villa. Sun-splashed in the daytime, with tiled floors, tropical plants, and simply but elegantly set tables, the less formal of the hotel's restaurants is a wonderful spot for lunch.

Not surprisingly, the Patio has its own patio, which is directly across the street from the beach, and you can hear the crashing surf whether you are indoors or out. On Thursday through Sunday nights, a Flavors Around the World buffet is served, or you can order from the à la carte menu. Thursday is locals' night. So if you live in Santa Barbara, you'll score a discount on the Italian buffet. In addition to an excellent wine list, there is a full bar.

The Patio Restaurant is open for breakfast, lunch, and dinner daily and for a very popular Sunday brunch. Valet parking is available.

**Rocks**
**801 State Street**
**Santa Barbara, CA**
**(805) 884–1190**
**$$**

This contemporary, slightly upscale restaurant and bar is currently one of downtown's most popular nightspots. It's actually two bars—one upstairs and one downstairs—and you can dine on either level. We like to sit on the balcony overlooking State Street so we can people-watch—especially on a Saturday night.

The menu at Rocks features California cuisine with Pacific Rim accents and lots of fish in every way, shape, and form. The ahi tuna is excellent. You can also choose from a variety of pastas, salads, and meats. Order one of Rocks' famous martinis while you wait for your meal to arrive, then sit back and enjoy the scene. Rocks is open for lunch and dinner daily.

**Rodney's Steakhouse**
**Fess Parker's Doubletree Resort**
**633 E. Cabrillo Boulevard**
**Santa Barbara, CA**
**(805) 884–8581**
**www.rodneyssteakhouse.com**
**$$$**

Rodney's is one of Santa Barbara's first upscale steak houses, and many locals say it has the best beef in town. With its contemporary beach-inspired blue and gold decor, it's also a little more sophisticated than your average steak spot. Pining for a juicy porterhouse, grilled prime rib, or a thick slab of filet mignon? At Rodney's you order the cut. The USDA prime-grade beef is aged 21 to 28 days and presented before preparation. Then it returns to you cooked to order and smothered in the mouthwatering sauce of your choice—either bearnaise, green peppercorn, bordelaise, or maitre d' lemon-parsley butter. Not everyone's a meat lover. For those

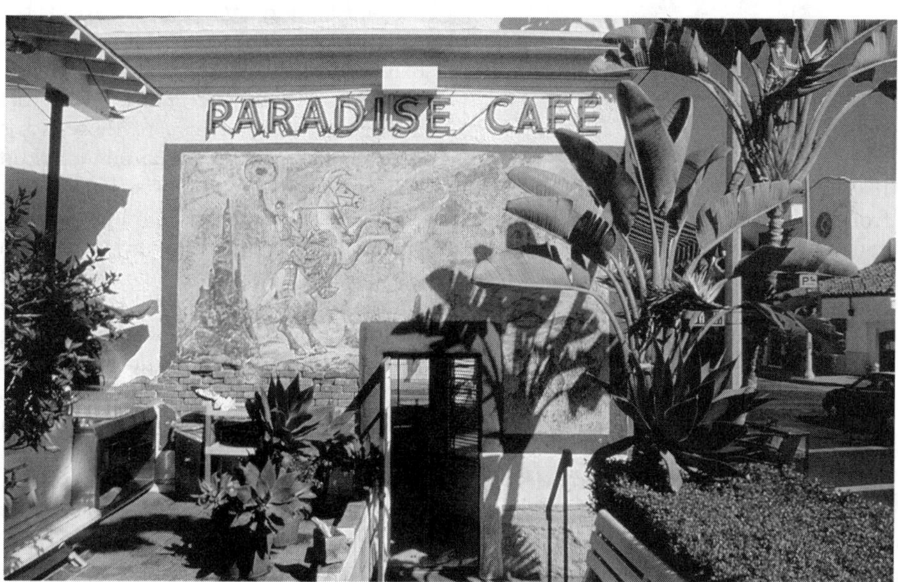


*A quintessential Santa Barbara restaurant, Paradise Cafe serves up some of the best burgers in town.*
PHOTO: BRIAN HASTINGS

**Insiders' Tip**

Don't forget to ask about daily specials, prix-fixe meals, and other discounts. Some restaurants, for example, offer early-bird dinners at a discount.

who prefer seafood, the menu offers some appealing alternatives such as the roasted halibut, cioppino, or baked Maine lobster plucked straight from the tank. Can't decide? Order the mixed grill platter with an eight-ounce filet, breaded garlic chicken, and spicy jumbo prawns. If you have any room left you can top off your evening with a vanilla bean soufflé, or some refreshing sorbet. The full-service cocktail bar specializes in martinis, and the wine list spotlights Californian and Santa Barbara County vintages (including some by Fess) as well as 15 wines by the glass. Rodney's serves dinner daily. Reservations are recommended.

**Roy**
**7 W. Carrillo Street**
**Santa Barbara, CA**
**(805) 966–5636**
**$$**

If you just walked by Roy, a little storefront hole-in-the-wall on Carrillo Street, you'd never get the idea that some of the best food in Santa Barbara is served within its funky and unpretentious interior. And we do mean unpretentious. The dining room is a sort of a retro 1950s affair, with mismatched vinyl booths, tables, and chairs, and an astounding chandelier that drops out of a black ceiling.

But then, your food starts arriving, and you'll think you've died and gone to heaven. Most of the entrees are a set price and come with warm homemade bread, soup, and a delightful salad of mixed greens topped with the house dressing. The menu changes every six weeks or so, and features such items as handmade cheese ravioli made with tomato pasta; vegetarian pasta with wild mushrooms, sun-dried tomatoes, artichoke hearts, and kalamata olives; and charbroiled king salmon with lemon hollandaise.

One item that's always on the menu is the bacon-wrapped filet mignon with portobello mushroom sauce. The desserts are wonderful, too. Add a great list of wines and ales, a full bar, and some lively entertainment, and you've got yourself a fabulous night out—at a bargain price! Roy is open until midnight for dinner seven nights a week.

**Sage and Onion**
**34 E. Ortega Street**
**Santa Barbara, CA**
**(805) 963–1012**
**www.sageandonion.com**
**$$$**

Voted "Best New Restaurant" in two local newspaper polls and the *Gault Millau* restaurant guide, this upscale fine dining establishment opened its doors in 1999 and has already garnered a string of rave reviews. If you want to splurge on some of the best food in Santa Barbara, this is the place to come. The man behind the magic here is British owner/chef Steven Giles. Trained in the classic French style, Chef Steven makes cooking an art. He describes the seasonal menu as European/American cuisine with an "English twist," a style best illustrated by the surprisingly light English stilton soufflé, which simply melted in our mouths. The dining room is cozy and contemporary—it feels like dining at a friend's house. You can also eat alfresco on the intimate street-side patio or, if you're dining alone, perch at the sleek wood bar. When you arrive, a single sage leaf on your fresh linen napkin sets the tone for an evening of simple elegance, crisp service, and exquisite cuisine. The menu changes with the seasons. The winter menu features such enticing creations as the succulent sage roasted chicken breast, hand-harvested scallops in a chardonnay sauce, and braised rabbit stew. The extensive wine list spotlights Californian wines, and the desserts like the molten lava chocolate cake and steamed maple sponge pudding are delicious—make sure you leave room. Sage and Onion serves beer and wine and is open for dinner daily. Walk-ins are welcome, but reservations are recommended.

**Santa Barbara Brewing Company**
**510 State Street**
**Santa Barbara, CA**
**(805) 730–1040**
**www.sbbrewco.com**
**$$**

Primarily known for its great selection of microbrewed beers (including Santa Barbara Blonde, Rincon Red, and Pacific Pale Ale), the Santa Barbara Brewing Company is a convivial place to hang out and enjoy some good food as well. Burgers, pizza, pasta, steak, and seafood are on the bill of fare, and there's a kids' menu with fish and chips, grilled cheese sandwiches, and other child-friendly foods. In addition to a wide choice of beers and ales, there's a full wine list. The Brewing Company is open for lunch and dinner daily and features a happy hour Monday through Friday from 3:00 to 6:00 P.M.

**Shoreline Beach Cafe**
**801 Shoreline Drive**
**Santa Barbara, CA**
**(805) 568–0064**
**$**

Since it's situated right on Leadbetter Beach, Shoreline Beach Cafe is a perfect place to grab a bite to eat before, during, or after a day in the sun and surf. You can come in your bathing suit or casual clothes and sit beneath colorful umbrellas on the deck, patio, or right on the beach. The kids can play in the sand while you eat.

Shoreline Beach Cafe is owned and operated by the same folks who run the popular Paradise Cafe downtown. Fill up on the famous half-pound Shoreline Burger, grilled shark burrito, tuna taco, or a bucket of steamed mussels and clams. You can also choose from various salads.

Shoreline Beach Cafe is open for breakfast, lunch, and dinner daily.

**Stella Mare's**
**50 Los Patos Way**
**Montecito, CA**
**(805) 969–6705**
**www.stellamares.com**
**$$–$$$**

Stella Mare's scores top points for its evocative French country ambiance and fresh seasonal wine country cuisine cooked on a wood-burning grill. This upscale bistro-style restaurant and bar in a historic (1872) Victorian house overlooks the tranquil Andree Clark Bird Refuge. With its intimate dining room, private party room, vine-draped patios, and solarium with a full bar, it's a popular venue for special events—many bridal showers and wedding receptions take place here.

It's one of our favorite spots to dine for a special family meal. People rave about the braised lamb shanks and seared pork tenderloin as well as the homemade pastas and desserts.

Stella Mare's offers live jazz on Wednesday nights. The restaurant is open for lunch and dinner Tuesday through Saturday and for brunch on Sundays.

**Stonehouse Restaurant**
**900 San Ysidro Lane**
**Montecito, CA**
**(805) 969–4100**
**www.sanysidroranch.com**
**$$$$**

The rustic look of the small stone house (formerly a fruit-packing house) nestled on the grounds of the San Ysidro Ranch (see our Hotels and Motels chapter) belies the elegance of its interior. The table settings are grand, as are the Persian rugs, copper doors, antiques, and the original art adorning the walls.

The food can be as wonderful as the surroundings. Chef Jamie West cooks up a variety of healthy but elegant dishes combining fresh ranch-grown herbs, fruit, and vegetables with flavorful seasonings, and adding influences from around the world. The seasonal menu might include coriander-crusted Muscovy duck breast, sea bass with roasted shallots and apple-smoked bacon, and truffled potato ravioli.

Desserts are as appealing as the entrees, and the wine list shines. The Stonehouse has received many culinary awards over the years, including a Wine Spectator Award of Excellence, the James Beard Foundation 10th Anniversary Award, and a Distinguished Restaurants of America Award. This is also one of the most expensive restaurants in Santa Barbara, so be prepared when the tab arrives!

The Stonehouse is open for breakfast, lunch, and dinner daily, and for Sunday brunch. This is one of the few places in town where you really ought to dress for dinner. More casual is the Plow and Angel Bistro downstairs.

**The Tee-off Restaurant and Lounge**
**3627 State Street**
**Santa Barbara, CA**
**(805) 687–1616**
**$$**

The Tee-off (a golf theme is carried throughout) has been at this upper State Street location for more than 40 years. It has a kind of old-fashioned steak house ambiance, with plush booths and red leather bar stools. The menu fits the theme, with steak, prime rib (a favorite), chops, chicken, and seafood topping the list. It's the perfect place to unwind after a game of golf, so order up a martini and a big juicy steak and enjoy! The Tee-off is open for dinner nightly.

**Waterfront Grill**
**113 Harbor Way**
**Santa Barbara, CA**
**(805) 564–1200**
**www.waterfrontgrill.net**
**$$$**

Craving some fresh-from-the-boat seafood and some dreamy harbor views? Come to the Waterfront Grill. Owned by experienced Santa Barbara restaurateurs Steve Hyslop and Larry and Nan Stone, this new fine dining seafood restaurant and its sibling Endless Summer Bar and Café upstairs (see previous entry) have a casual feel that suits their salt-tinged harbor setting. Lunch and dinner menus are the same at both, but the Waterfront Grill has a pricier dinner menu with more entree choices. You can relax on the raised outdoor terrace and gaze out at the boats bobbing on the harbor or dine inside and drink in the views. This is a popular spot with tourists, who pop in here for dinner after a stroll along the waterfront. The fish is so fresh it almost flops off your plate. Menu highlights are the fresh-shucked oysters, shrimp cocktail, tangy ceviche cocktail, and steamed Manila clams. We've also had some excellent halibut here—try the sesame-and-black-pepper-crusted halibut with lobster miso sauce. For those not in a seafood mood, the menu offers thick hand-cut steaks and hearty pasta dishes. Waterfront Grill has a full bar, so you can order up a fruity cocktail, sit back, and soak in the sunset while you wait for your meal. The restaurant serves up lunch and dinner daily and offers Sunset Dinner Specials from 5:00 P.M. to 6:30 P.M. Monday through Thursday. Valet parking is available in the lot out back.

**Wine Bistro**
**1280 Coast Village Road**
**Montecito, CA**
**(805) 969–3955**
**$$$**

The Wine Bistro combines a restaurant, wine shop, wine bar, and cigar shop in one location on Coast Village Road. The menu features fresh seafood dishes such as potato-crusted salmon and halibut with baby vegetables, Creole surprises like jamabalaya, and some classics such as beef stroganoff, filet mignon, and roasted rack of lamb. You also find a selection of gourmet salads. (Try the warm goat cheese salad.) The wine bar features more than 30 wines by the glass each day.

This is the perfect spot for a casual

lunch or dinner, with an outdoor patio on the Coast Village Road side. The Wine Bistro is open for lunch and dinner daily.

**Wine Cask**
**El Paseo**
**813 Anacapa Street**
**Santa Barbara, CA**
**(805) 966–9463**
**www.winecask.com**
**$$$**

If you're a wine connoisseur, you'll find nirvana at the Wine Cask, where more than 1,300 selections are available. Best of all, it's not just the wine list that merits an award; expect a warm and elegant European-style ambiance, a delightful stone patio, and fabulous food.

The menu changes seasonally and reflects the use of fresh local ingredients, including seafood. Recent menu selections included seared ahi tuna with ginger risotto (a favorite), grilled wild striped bass, and roasted Iowa pork chop. The five-course tasting menu, served on Sunday and Monday evenings, is extremely affordable and one of the best ways to taste the accomplished chef's cuisine paired with the best wines.

Be sure to stop at the next-door wine shop for a bottle to go. The inventory is amazing. The Wine Cask is open for lunch Monday through Friday and for dinner nightly.

**Woody's Bodacious Barbecue**
**5112 Hollister Avenue**
**Goleta, CA**
**(805) 967–3775**
**$**

The decor is strictly "old ranch house" at Woody's, consistently voted Santa Barbara's favorite barbecue restaurant by the locals. Get ready to have your senses assaulted the minute you walk in the door.

First, there are those tantalizing smells, as the kitchen whips up chicken, ribs, tri-tip, and burgers. Then there's the noise. You might be sitting next to an entire kids' soccer team, a clanging video game, or a blaring television.

Everything from a full slab of beef or pork ribs to a Caesar salad is available for the asking, and there's a kids' menu, too. Just step on up to the counter and order your food (which comes in a pie tin), and pick it up when your number is called. Then settle yourself down at a table and dive into a huge platter of smoked barbecue, which comes with a ton of fries or a baked potato plus your choice of BBQ beans, coleslaw, tossed salad, or pasta salad.

Woody's also offers microbrewed draft beers and free refills on soft drinks and coffee. If you don't feel like going out, Woody's will cater or deliver, or you can pick up a big ol' Jumbo Pak to go—made to order for 10 to 200 people!

Woody's is open for lunch and dinner daily.

## Chinese

**Empress Palace**
**2251 Las Positas Road**
**Santa Barbara, CA**
**(805) 898–2238**
**$$**

For flexibility and price, you can't beat the Empress Palace, Santa Barbara's only fine dining Chinese restaurant. Set aside some time for a meal here. It will take you a while just to read the menu. More than 200 items are featured including Cantonese and Szechwan dishes and classics like chow mein, imperial shrimp, and chop suey. For starters, the plump pan-fried pot stickers are a good choice, and the menu offers an expansive list of soups ranging from smooth green pea seafood soup to crab meat and corn. Expanding the options even further are barbecue dishes such as succulent roast duck and spare ribs. Lobster lovers can feast on a steamed whole specimen picked fresh from the tank and served with your choice of sauce such as black bean and chile, butter, or ginger and green onion. With its large tables, roomy banquettes, and affordable prices, this is a great spot to come with a group or family. You're sure to find something appealing from the mind-boggling menu, and you can also order special meal selections designed for three, four, or five diners so you can taste and share a variety of dishes. Empress Palace is open for lunch and dinner daily.

**Jimmy's Oriental Gardens**
**126 E. Canon Perdido Street**
**Santa Barbara, CA**
**(805) 962–7582**
**$$**

Jimmy Chung opened this restaurant in 1947 in a building that once was part of the city's old Chinatown. Now Jimmy's son Tommy Chung continues the 50-year family tradition of serving regional Chinese dishes (Mandarin, Szechwan, Cantonese) in a funky atmosphere. Diners enter into a dimly lit bar area decorated with Chinese lanterns, a pagoda, and booths covered in red vinyl. You can eat here or sit at a table in an adjacent dining room.

Jimmy's cooks up fantastic egg rolls, Mandarin orange chicken, and almond pressed duck. The chef uses cholesterol-free canola oil, and never adds MSG. Quench your thirst with Chinese beer or one of Jimmy's famous mai tais. Lunch is served Tuesday through Friday and dinner is available every evening except Monday.

**Mandarin Palace**
**3955 State Street**
**Santa Barbara, CA**
**(805) 683–2158**
**$$**

Sandwiched into the busy Five Points Shopping Center, the Mandarin Palace is always crowded with hungry shoppers as well as Chinese students from UCSB, a testament to the quality of its food. In recent years, the decor has gone upscale, but patrons dress in keeping with the restaurant's former, more casual style, and no one seems to object.

There's a great selection of Chinese specialties here—the sauces are delicious and the veggies are always done just right. The wine list includes about 10 wines, two Asian. Take-out is available and very popular. The restaurant is open for lunch and dinner daily, and the lunch special is always a good buy.

## French

**Mousse-Odile**
**18 E. Cota Street**
**Santa Barbara, CA**
**(805) 962–5393**
**$$**

Owner Yvonne Mathieu, who grew up in Alsace-Lorraine, used to run this charming downtown brasserie with her sister Odile, but now manages it on her own. Romantic in the evening, bright and airy during daylight hours, Mousse-Odile is a perfect place for casual dining in a classy atmosphere. It feels like a real French country home, with high ceilings, skylights, hardwood floors, and a charming patio out back.

Even the meals seem like those you might expect at home with friends in the French countryside: rustic fare with top-quality ingredients. For breakfast you can fill up on fresh fruits, a croissant with scrambled eggs, a waffle with crème anglaise, quiche, or an omelet—and, of course, cafe au lait. Lunch specialties include escargots, salad, soup, duck pâté, and ficelles (12-inch Parisian sandwiches). The dinner menu has remained relatively unchanged for nearly two decades, featuring escargots, veal, lamb, couscous, cassoulet, filet mignon, leg of lamb, Cornish game hen, duck, and fresh fish. The menu always has a vegetarian selection, too. You can even order a picnic basket to go: quiche, salad, lemon mousse with raspberry sauce, and a split bottle of white wine.

Mousse-Odile has a full bar and serves breakfast, lunch, and dinner Monday through Saturday.

**Restaurant Mimosa**
**2700 De la Vina Street**
**Santa Barbara, CA**
**(805) 682–2272**
**$$**

Mimosa is a charming little restaurant

with peach walls accented by hand-painted plates and crisp blue and white tablecloths. The food, which could be called French casual, is delicious. You can pick an entree from the very affordable bistro menu or choose from a variety of other entrees such as roasted venison, Camille's bouillabaisse (named for Mimosa's chef/owner Camille Schwartz), or sautéed beef medallions. Seafood options are also available.

Each main course comes with fresh vegetables and your choice of potatoes, risotto, or spaetzle, a wonderful German noodle. You'll start your meal with a basket of wonderful breads accompanied by little butterballs, and at meal's end, choose one of Camille's excellent desserts (we liked the crême brulée). There's a full bar and a satisfying wine list.

The place has a bit of a formal air, but stylish casual attire is fine. Parking is across Alamar Avenue in a small lot that is unfortunately very poorly lit at night. Restaurant Mimosa is open for lunch Monday through Friday and for dinner daily.

**Insiders' Tip**

For the latest buzz on the Santa Barbara restaurant scene, plus independent reviews, recipes, classifieds, and menus, see www.nippers.com. Can't choose a restaurant? Check out the Best Of section, which lists favorite eateries by cuisine and occasion—or play restaurant roulette. You can also chat with fellow food lovers on the Table Talk forum.

**William**
**230 E. Victoria Street**
**Santa Barbara, CA**
**(805) 966–7759**
**$$**

Wander into William (or "Will-yum" as some patrons like to call this place) and you'll feel as though you've arrived at a cozy bistro in a residential French neighborhood. Sultry jazz wafts over the speakers, and the staff greets you with a smile. The intimate ambiance and affordable classic French cuisine make this a perfect spot to bring a date. You can sit inside amid French art and photographs, or dine Parisian-style at one of the tiny linen-cloaked tables on the sidewalk. True to the French way, the menu has an emphasis on quality not quantity. Choose from French classics like hearty beef bourgignonne and a delightful version of grenouille (frogs legs), sautéed with asparagus, pistachios, and cream sauce, or savor some excellent seafood such as grilled ahi tuna, steamed mussels, or porcini-dusted halibut. Vegetarians will love the buckwheat crepes stuffed with asparagus, goat cheese, tomatoes, and walnuts. A list of delicious daily specials complements the regular menu, making your choice even harder. The lunch menu features a few smaller and more affordable variations of the dinner entrees as well as the kid-friendly croque monsieur, a grilled ham and cheese sandwich. Of course no French meal would be complete without a drop *du vin*, and luckily, William offers a discerning selection of both Californian and French wines. William is open for lunch Monday through Friday and for dinner Tuesday through Sunday.

## Health Food

**Good Earth**
**5955 Calle Real**
**Goleta, CA**
**(805) 683–6101**
**$$**

Good Earth is a great family restaurant with a relaxed, laid-back style and consistently good food. The emphasis is on healthy eating and high-quality ingredients, and you'll find a variety of delicious soups, salads, sandwiches, ethnic dishes, and fresh seafood. Breakfast is served all day, and the omelets are especially good. The breads and desserts are excellent, too (we love the lemon cake), and you can also buy them at the bakery case on your way out.

The dining room is spacious and airy, with an abundance of live plants and soothing New Age music wafting through the air. The outdoor patio is popular in nice weather. There's no bar, but the wine list is decent. Or try some Good Earth iced tea, which is a local favorite. Good Earth is open every day for breakfast, lunch, and dinner.

**The Main Squeeze**
**138 E. Canon Perdido Street**
**Santa Barbara, CA**
**(805) 966–5365**
**$**

The Main Squeeze is a popular cafe and juice bar just across the street from the Old Presidio. It's a great place for a quick, healthy meal or drink. Choose from a wide range of natural and nondairy foods, including chicken, pastas, and lots of vegetarian dishes made with local, seasonal organic produce. The wine list features award-winning local wines.

The Main Squeeze is open daily for lunch and dinner. Brunch is served on Saturday and Sunday. Reservations aren't necessary—waits are rarely long.

**The Natural Café**
**508 State Street**
**Santa Barbara, CA**
**(805) 962–9494**
**5892 Hollister Avenue**
**Goleta, CA**
**(805) 692–2363**
**$**

The Natural Café serves up great-tasting health food for vegetarians and health-conscious carnivores alike (you won't find red meat here, just turkey and chicken). In a recent local poll, the cafes scored awards for best sidewalk cafe, best veggie burger, and best health food. Pick a table, scan the extensive menu, and line up at the cash register to order your meal. When it's ready, one of the super-friendly, helpful staffers will deliver it to your table. There's something for everyone here: fish, chicken, pasta, vegetarian entrees, a kids' menu, a complete juice bar, beer, local wines, and desserts. Both locations of the Natural Café are open for lunch and dinner every day.

**Sojourner**
**134 E. Canon Perdido Street**
**Santa Barbara, CA**
**(805) 965–7922**
**$**

Voted "Best Spot to Dine Alone" in a recent local newspaper poll, Sojourner has served up natural food with flair since 1978. It's a stone's throw from the Old Presidio (across the street), just two blocks east of State Street. The menu includes mostly vegetarian dishes: soups, sandwiches, salads, pastas, polenta cakes, crispy tofu and onions, vegetarian stir fry, and lasagna.

For a protein pickup, try the Sojburger, a vegetarian protein patty with melted cheese, guacamole, sour cream, and sprouts. Beverages to complement your meal include juices, smoothies, chai, yogi tea, and vegan shakes. Sojourner also has an espresso bar, beer, local wines, and fantastic desserts. The "Soj" is open daily for lunch and dinner.

## Indian

**Flavor of India**
**3026 State Street**
**Santa Barbara, CA**
**(805) 682–6561**
**$$**

Santa Barbara has few Indian restaurants, so if you're craving some tandoori chicken, vegetable samosas, or a hearty lamb vindaloo, this is a great place to get

CLOSE-UP

## Best Breakfasts

Need some serious sustenance to kick-start your day? Below is a list of our six favorite breakfast nooks. Turn up in your shorts and flip-flops, refuel with some fresh-brewed java, and chow down on good old-fashioned breakfast grub.

**Esau's Coffee Shop,** 430 State Street, Santa Barbara (805) 965–4416. Slide into a vinyl banquette at this classic surfer joint and fill up on a pie-sized omelet. The French toast with crunchy cornflake batter will also do the trick. Park in the lot across the side street.

**Cajun Kitchen,** 1924 De La Vina Street, Santa Barbara (805) 687–2062; 901 Chapala Street, Santa Barbara (805) 965–1004; 865 Linden Avenue, Carpinteria (805) 684–6010; 420 S. Fairview Avenue, Goleta (805) 683–8864. Spice up your day with some Louisiana hot sausage, blackened catfish, and jambalaya. Cajun Kitchen serves breakfast all day.

**Comeback Café,** 324 State Street, Santa Barbara (805) 962–2889. Sweet-tooths can get their fix on sugar-dusted, strawberry-sprinkled French toast. Toddlers can tinker in the play area.

**East Beach Grill,** 1188 East Cabrillo Boulevard, Santa Barbara (805) 965–8805. Grab a table on the boardwalk, order the multigrain pancakes, and watch the bodies bronzing on the beach. Get there early though—tables fill up fast.

**Shoreline Beach Café,** 801 Shoreline Drive, Santa Barbara (805) 568–0064. Voted best spot to dine with your toes in the sand on the Nippers website, this casual spot owned by the folks at Paradise Cafe is true beachfront dining. Call first for hours.

**Summerland Beach Café,** 2294 Lillie Avenue, Summerland (805) 969–1019. Sleepyheads can score breakfast all day at this colorful old Victorian house. Pick a table on the sunny porch and feast on omelets, Belgian waffles, and huevos rancheros.

your fix. Tucked in an unassuming building on upper State, this casual eatery offers a wide selection of traditional Indian dishes at a pocketbook-pleasing price. Even on weeknights, Flavor of India draws a colorful and eclectic crowd of diners. You can sit on the raised patio facing State Street or pick a table inside. Never tried Indian cuisine before? Choose a combination dinner. These generous platters come with a variety of aromatic Indian specialties as well as salad or ratia, and naan bread so you can mop up all those delicious sauces. Every meal comes cooked to order–mild, medium, or spicy–and vegetarians will find a tempting lineup of meatless dishes. Looking for something different for lunch? The restaurant has an all-you-can-eat buffet lunch for $6.95, and you can wash it all down with some ice-cold Indian beer or a tangy mango lassi (yogurt drink). Flavor of India is open for lunch and dinner Monday through Saturday. It's closed Sunday.

## Italian

**Aldo's**
**1031 State Street**
**Santa Barbara, CA**
**(805) 963–6687**
**$$**

Aldo's is a quaint, Old World–style restaurant in a historic downtown adobe built in 1857. Here you can sit by the fountain in the stone courtyard and pretend you're in a trattoria in Florence, sipping chianti and watching the world go by. Or dine indoors by candlelight and tune out the world entirely. Wherever you choose to dine, you can order up first-rate traditional Italian seafood and meat dishes, pasta, salads, gourmet pizza, and local and Italian wines. Try Aldo's famous pork chops with various sauces, cioppino, or Venetian fish chowder, or one of the chef's daily specials. On weekends, guitar players and singers add to the Mediterranean ambiance.

Aldo's is open for lunch and dinner daily, as well as for brunch on Saturday and Sunday.

**Ca'Dario**
**37 E. Victoria Street**
**Santa Barbara, CA**
**(805) 884-9419**
**$$$**

Ca'Dario is a self-proclaimed "unpretentious Italian neighborhood restaurant filled with aroma, clever waiters, good friends, and rowdy conversation." In other words, you can expect a lively atmosphere and some really good Italian food.

Chef Dario Furlati offers such second courses as ossobucco con risotto (braised veal shank with saffron arborio rice), lombata al rosmarino (veal chop grilled with rosemary and olive oil), and sella d'agnello (grilled rack of lamb basted with garlic, olive oil, and fine herbs), to name a few. The daily special and the fresh fish of the day, available at market price, are other options. The wine list is excellent and heavy with Italian wines, and the service is attentive.

Whether you go for a meal, or just to sip wine or cappuccino at the bar, you'll be glad you discovered Ca'Dario. The restaurant is open for lunch Monday through Saturday and for dinner daily.

**Emilio's Ristorante and Bar**
**324 W. Cabrillo Boulevard**
**Santa Barbara, CA**
**(805) 966-4426**
**$$**

Cozy and convivial, Emilio's, located on Cabrillo Boulevard across from the beach, serves a seasonal menu of European country-style food using fresh organic vegetables and herbs. The appetizers and entrees are supplemented by both Italian and Santa Barbara County wines, and the bar serves everything from drink-of-the-moment martinis to grappas, vodkas, and scotches. Breads and pastas are made onsite, and paella is a specialty. Open for dinner nightly, Emilio's is usually crowded.

**Giovanni's**
**3020 State Street**
**Santa Barbara, CA**
**(805) 682-3621**
**1187 Coast Village Road**
**Montecito, CA**
**(805) 969-1277**
**5003 Carpinteria Avenue**
**Carpinteria, CA**
**(805) 684-8288**
**6583 Pardall Road**
**Isla Vista (Goleta), CA**
**(805) 968-2254**
**$**

Giovanni's bakes fantastic pizzas and sells them at great prices. Bring the family and watch the chefs twirl the dough and sprinkle the cheese with flair. You can also order salads, pasta, hot Italian sandwiches, cold sandwiches, beer, and wine. All Giovanni's locations are open for lunch and dinner daily.

**Olio e Limone Ristorante**
**17 West Victoria Street**
**Santa Barbara, CA**
**(805) 899-2699**
**$$$**

Owned and operated by chef Alberto Morello and his wife, Elaine, Olio e Limone serves up an imaginative menu of authentic Italian dishes—including a sprinkling of Sicilian specialties. Along with Bouchon (see above), this sophisticated little eatery is one of a few culinary gems to sprout up in this area of town, which seems to be the new hot spot for gastronomic ventures. The restaurant lies just around the corner from the Arlington Center for the Performing Arts and is often buzzing with the symphony crowd, which comes here to dine before performances. Tucked in a tiny space on Victoria Street, Olio e Limone feels like a cozy Florentine trattoria. Tables are set skirt by skirt, and passersby can peak in through the row of windows facing the street. The food is bright and fresh and bursting with flavor. Among the pasta dishes you'll find surprises like the ribbon pasta with morel mushrooms, asparagus, and cream, and the house-made duck ravioli. The swordfish is delicious, served lightly breaded with Sicilian ratatouille, and the filet of striped bass drizzled in lemon sauce and studded with capers is also superb. Olio e Limone serves only beer and wine. It's open for lunch and dinner daily.

**Palazzio**
**1151 Coast Village Road**
**Montecito, CA**
**(805) 969–8565**
**www.palazzio.com**
**$$**

Famous for its gargantuan portions, garlic rolls that emerge fresh from the oven every 10 minutes, lively atmosphere, and affordable prices, Palazzio is nearly always crowded with hip Montecito diners in their 20s, 30s, and 40s, and there's usually a long line of people waiting to get in on weekend evenings.

A few of the most popular entrees are spaghettini with meatballs; capellini with shrimp in a sauce of fresh artichoke hearts, sun-dried tomatoes, and garlic butter; and penne with smoked mozzarella, fresh tomato, sweet basil, and eggplant. Former president Ronald Reagan reportedly loved Palazzio's tiramisu, which has been named Presidential Tiramisu in his honor.

If you like Italian merlot or white wine, you can help yourself at the self-service wine bar (it operates on the honor system). The staff works as a team, so you can ask anyone who passes by to help you. The full orders of pasta are just right for sumo wrestlers, linebackers, and other hearty eaters. If these are too much for you, try the half-order dishes, which look more like normal-size portions.

Palazzio is open for dinner daily. One of the reasons the lines to get in are so long is that reservations are taken for the 5:30 seating only. After that, it's first come, first served. Plan to wait a little while unless you arrive early.

**Palazzio Downtown**
**1026 State Street**
**Santa Barbara, CA**
**(805) 564–1985**
**www.palazzio.com**
**$$**

This hip downtown restaurant, which opened in May 1998, is practically a carbon copy of its sister restaurant in Montecito (see above description), except it's slightly larger, has a full bar, and is open for lunch and dinner every day. As with the Montecito restaurant, you should count on waiting in line unless you arrive early.

**Pane e Vino**
**1482 E. Valley Road**
**Montecito, CA**
**(805) 969–9274**
**$$$**

We (along with practically everyone else in Santa Barbara) love the intimate atmosphere, charm, and high-quality meals at this small, authentic Italian trattoria. It's in the back of a shopping plaza parking lot in Montecito's Upper Village, near the intersection of San Ysidro and East Valley roads, not far from the post office.

You can choose a table in the softly lit interior or outside on the heated patio. Most of the waiters are Italian, and the Italian music that plays softly in the background adds an aura of romance. The menu features rustic, Northern Italian foods: pasta, seafood, veal chops, and meats (rabbits, duck) roasted on a spit.

Pane e Vino is open for lunch and dinner Monday through Saturday and for dinner only on Sunday.

## Insiders' Tip

Got the late-night munchies? Roy is consistently voted best spot for late-night dining in local newspaper polls. It's open until midnight daily. If you've had a big night bar-hopping and the clock's struck 12, head to Esau's for some serious grub (open 9:00 P.M. to 3:00 A.M. Friday and Saturday) or the downtown Carrows Restaurant at 210 W. Carrillo. It's open 24 hours.

**Pascucci**
**729 State Street**
**Santa Barbara, CA**
**(805) 963–8123**
**$**

The lively, contemporary atmosphere, good food at unbelievably affordable prices (at least for downtown Santa Barbara), and convenience of Pascucci make it one of the most popular eateries in the Paseo Nuevo area. It offers delicious pasta, soups, salads, sandwiches, appetizers, and pizzas—and many items are under $10. In fact, it recently scored awards in local newspaper polls for offering the "Best Meal Under $10." This is a great place to stop in for some sustenance after a busy day of shopping. You can dine in the cozy interior, perch at the bar, people-watch on the street-side patio, or order a glass of chianti, and relax on a comfortable sofa by the fireplace. Tip: the desserts here are among the best in town. Pascucci is open for lunch and dinner daily.

**Piatti**
**516 San Ysidro Road**
**Montecito, CA**
**(805) 969–7520**
**www.piatti.com**
**$$**

One of a chain of 15 restaurants throughout California and other western states, Piatti is an upscale Italian restaurant in a beautiful creekside setting. You'll find it near the Pierre Lafond & Co. store in Montecito's Upper Village, at the intersection of San Ysidro and East Valley Roads. Our favorite place to dine is outdoors by the creek (but bear in mind that the creek doesn't flow much during the dry summer months). You can also sit indoors by the fire, in the tastefully decorated dining area, or on the front patio. Wherever you sit, you'll be served an excellent Italian meal. Choose from fresh pasta, meat, and seafood dishes, risotto, and daily specials. Fine Italian and local wines are available, and there's also a full bar. If you're not too concerned about the cost (some work out to $5 or more per sip), try sampling the various types of grappa, a strong Italian brandy. Piatti is open for lunch and dinner daily, and for brunch on Sunday.

**Trattoria Mollie**
**1250 Coast Village Road**
**Montecito, CA**
**(805) 565–9381**
**$$$**

From simply delicious pizzas to delectable homemade breads and pastas to knockout gelatos, Mollie delivers fabulous Italian cuisine in her stylish Montecito trattoria. Mollie Ahlstrand is originally from Ethiopia, but she trained at Arturo's restaurant in Rome and has learned the fine art of creating splendid dishes from Padua, Umbria, Bologna, and Rome.

Pizzas and breads are baked in a wood-burning oven, meat dishes are tender and juicy, and the seafood is impeccable. If you really know Italian food, you'll love Mollie's perfectly executed renditions. Dress up a bit, and you'll fit right in with the upscale crowd.

Trattoria Mollie is open for lunch and dinner Tuesday through Sunday.

**Via Vai**
**1483 E. Valley Road, #20**
**Montecito, CA**
**(805) 565–9393**
**$$**

An offshoot of Pane e Vino, Via Vai in the Montecito Village shopping center offers a variety of authentic Northern Italian dishes, with an emphasis on pizza and pasta. Everything from pizze capricciosa to farfalle al salmone e piselli and salsiccia con polenta is on the menu. The grilled meats and seafood are every bit as good. You can dine in the bright cozy dining room or on the large heated patio. Via Vai is open daily for lunch and dinner.

## Japanese

**Arigato**
**1225 State Street**
**Santa Barbara, CA**
**(805) 965–6074**
**$$**

In a new location in the heart of downtown, opposite the Granada Theater, Arigato is still rolling out some of the freshest and best sushi in town. Voted the favorite Japanese sushi restaurant in a local poll, Arigato is best known for its wild combination rolls with equally wild names: California Sunset, Rock 'n' Roll, Swinging Roll, Wiki Wiki Roll, Wipeout Roll, and Sea Eel Goes Hollywood, to name a few. Can't choose? Get the "Whatever Roll" and your chef will prepare his favorite for the day. You can also get excellent soft-shell crab tempura and other traditional Japanese dishes. Popular choices include the succulent scallop in a black sesame sauce and spicy broiled mussels. The wait-staff are wonderful and very eager to please. If your fellow diners are not sushi fanatics, they can opt for the delicious crab cakes or the broiled chicken breast off the non-sushi menu. This is a great place to go before or after a movie or whenever you yearn for Japanese food. You can perch at the sushi bar, sit downstairs, or dine alfresco on the patio out front. The place is nearly always packed with young (20s and 30s) chic-looking diners. The beverage list offers more than 20 different types of hot or cold sake, imported Japanese beers, and some excellent wines—including the fruity plum wine. Arigato is open for dinner daily. Get there early if you can—the restaurant doesn't take reservations.

**Azuma**
**24 W. Figueroa Street**
**Santa Barbara, CA**
**(805) 966–2139**
**$$**

Famous for its sea urchin (uni), Azuma is a Japanese family-style restaurant serving up good sushi at a decent price. Slide into a wide booth or perch at the sushi bar. You can ask the master sushi chef to make just about any combination roll you like; he'll wrap it up in style in no time flat. In addition to sushi and sashimi, Azuma offers other traditional Japanese fare: noodles, tempura, seafood, beef and chicken dishes, and generous combination meals. Be sure to ask about the daily specials.

Azuma is open for lunch Monday through Friday and for dinner daily.

**Kyoto**
**3232 State Street**
**Santa Barbara, CA**
**(805) 687–1252**
**$$**

This serene Japanese restaurant on upper State Street between Alamar Avenue and Las Positas Road has been a popular neighborhood sushi spot for years. Kyoto's experienced chefs prepare generous proportions of high-quality traditional Japanese steak and seafood dishes, including sushi, sashimi, teriyaki, and tempura. A restaurant review web site has rated it the best local Japanese eatery for cooked cuisine. The private tatami rooms are great places to enjoy a romantic meal or a festive group celebration.

The parking lot is very small—be prepared to park on the street. Kyoto serves lunch Monday through Saturday and dinner daily.

**Morishima**
**1208 State Street**
**Santa Barbara, CA**
**(805) 568–1172**
**$$$**

At first glance, Morishima doesn't look at all like a fancy restaurant. The simple, unassuming atmosphere belies the delicious Japanese seafood that emerges from within. Owner Satoshi Morishima—a native of Okinawa who studied in Tokyo—used to work at a famous Japanese restaurant in Beverly Hills. Ever since he brought his culinary expertise to Santa Barbara, the community has raved about his delectable, new-style sashimi and specials. If you're daring, order the Omakase (Chef's Choice) for $40. The chef will prepare a truly amazing array of his best and most exotic dishes. You can also order sushi, sushi rolls, and tempura á la carte. Morishima is open for dinner Tuesday through Sunday and for lunch Tuesday through Saturday.

**Piranha**
**714 State Street**
**Santa Barbara, CA**
**(805) 965–2980**
**$$**

Dressed in sleek black and metallic accents, Piranha is a popular and trendy Japanese restaurant with a really long sushi bar and excellent food. If you don't sit at the bar for a close-up view of the master sushi chefs, you can sit tall on a barstool-height chair at one of the high tables lining the walls or at a lower table near the front windows. Piranha features numerous creative sushi combinations, plus a wide range of Japanese dishes. The soft shell crab is excellent. It's open for lunch Tuesday through Friday and for dinner Tuesday through Sunday (closed Monday).

## Mexican

**Acapulco Mexican Restaurant y Cantina**
**1114 State Street**
**Santa Barbara, CA**
**(805) 963–3469**
**$$**

Acapulco has good food and drinks and lots of lively Mexican music. It's a great place to hang out during Cinco de Mayo or Fiesta (see Annual Events chapter), when everyone is drinking margaritas and cracking confetti.

The menu is huge, with everything from traditional Mexican combination plates to soft tacos, sizzling fajitas, and shrimp enchiladas. Find a coveted spot near the fountain on the spacious outdoor patio, order a margarita from the long list of choices, and sit back and enjoy the evening.

If Mexican food is not your favorite fare, you can choose fresh fish entrees or salads, and there are several Heart Smart entrees for the health-conscious. Kids will be happy, too. The children's menu offers favorites like corn dogs, chicken tenders, and hamburgers. There's also a lively bar scene; margaritas are only $1.75 on Mondays, and happy hour runs 4:00 to 7:00 P.M. Monday through Friday.

Acapulco is open for lunch and dinner nightly.

**Café Del Sol**
**30 Los Patos Way**
**Santa Barbara, CA**
**(805) 969–3947**
**$$**

Café del Sol, in a pretty setting just across from the bird refuge, is an old Montecito favorite. Since 1965, this upscale Mexican eatery has attracted a loyal clientele of well-heeled locals who come here for the great food, earthy ambiance, and convivial bar. You can dine on the sunny wraparound patio, in the evocative split-level dining room, or join the crowd of cheery locals sipping cocktails at the bar. Order up a bowl of fresh guacamole. Then kick-start your meal with a Cadillac Margarita, an explosive blend of tequila, lime juice, and Grand Marnier. The menu offers a wide range of options, from traditional Mexican dishes such as snapper Veracruzano, chicken rellenos, fajitas, and enchiladas, to juicy steaks, pasta, chicken, and seafood dishes. You'll also find a few exotic twists like the sea scallops Manzanillo with white wine, cilantro, garlic, and fettuccine, and the Greek chicken with oregano and lemon. The food is reasonably priced and the restaurant is always humming with happy conversation. Café del Sol serves up lunch and dinner daily as well as Sunday brunch.

**Carlitos Café y Cantina**
**1324 State Street**
**Santa Barbara, CA**
**(805) 962–7117**
**$$**

The big brother of Carlitos Cava (listed next), Carlitos Café can be counted on to serve the same sort of upscale Mexican and Southwestern specialties as the Montecito restaurant. Fresh, homemade tortillas, meats cooked over an open-fire grill, and fresh chiles and spices combine to make all of Carlitos' dishes a sensation. Try the grilled chicken breast with mole poblano, tacos al carbón, or grilled carnitas, or select a traditional combination plate.

Carlitos has a full bar, including a large selection of Blue Agave tequilas and liqueurs and the requisite list of imaginative margaritas. Eat on the patio if it's a sunny day and enjoy the bubbling fountain. This is a fun place to bring a group. Kids can keep busy with crayons at the table, and live entertainment every evening from 7:00 to 10:00 P.M. enhances the festive ambiance.

Carlitos is open for lunch and dinner daily and for breakfast on Sunday.

**Carlitos Cava Restaurant and Bar**
**1212 Coast Village Road**
**Montecito, CA**
**(805) 969–8500**
**$$**

A relative newcomer to the Santa Barbara dining scene, Cava presents both traditional Mexican food and exotic dishes such as grilled chicken breast with Anaheim chiles, tomatoes, and onions with chipotle mashed potatoes. Choose a table on the small patio (there's a bit of traffic noise from Coast Village Road) or find a cozy spot inside, where a Santa Fe–style fireplace invites you to linger over cocktails. Your friendly waiter will bring a complimentary basket of chips and fabulous salsa (all salsas are made fresh every day) for dipping while you peruse the menu.

No matter what you choose, your food will be spicy and delicious. Entrees are served on huge plates with hot black beans and rice made with vegetable puree and chiles. For dessert, we loved the Posito de Cava, a chocolate torte with coffee, raspberry, and mango syrup, topped with whipped cream. The restaurant is quite kid-friendly, with brown paper and crayons on the tables to keep little hands busy. There is live entertainment every night, and Wednesday is Fiesta Paella night, when you can enjoy a three-course Spanish dinner featuring your choice of three paellas.

Cava is open for lunch and dinner daily and also serves breakfast on weekends. Complimentary valet parking is available.

**La Playa Azul Cafe**
**914 Santa Barbara Street**
**Santa Barbara, CA**
**(805) 966–2860**
**$$**

Family-owned and -operated La Playa Azul has offered first-rate Mexican cuisine since 1976. When renovation of the Old Presidio began a few years back, the restaurant building was torn down. Luckily for Santa Barbarans, La Playa Azul was able to move into another house on the same block. This one's larger and has a wonderful dining patio that's shaded by a colorful jacaranda tree.

La Playa Azul is best known for its fresh, high-quality ingredients, generous portions, and an intimate, slightly elegant

**CLOSE-UP**

## Tri-what?

If you're a newcomer to Santa Barbara, no matter how much experience you've had in the kitchen, you've probably never heard of tri-tip. But you soon will because everyone in Santa Barbara knows about tri-tip, has eaten it at family barbecues, school picnics, and political fund-raisers, and knows it's very likely to be on the menu at any sort of barbecue function involving from one to 5,000 people! (We're not kidding. Someone once cooked tri-tip for 5,000. Really.)

This unique cut of beef was born in Santa Barbara County, and as far as we know, no one else in any other part of the country has either heard of it or knows what to do with it. So if you're new to Santa Barbara, here's the scoop: A cow is a cow is a cow, of course, but tri-tip supposedly came to be in a now-defunct Safeway grocery store in Santa Maria way back in the '50s. (We can't be absolutely sure of its origins, of course. Santa Marians have been eating good barbecue for almost a century!)

Anyway, as the story goes, a butcher who was cutting beef loins into sections of top block sirloin and filet set aside the triangular shaped tip of the sirloin (as usual) to be cut into stew meat or ground up into hamburger. That fateful day, however, there was no need for more stew meat or hamburger, so the meat market manager, seeing that the triangular tip was going to be wasted, seasoned it with salt, pepper, and garlic salt and put it on the rotisserie. Much to the surprise of the butchers, after the meat had cooked for an hour or so, it came off the rotisserie succulent, tender, and delicious.

Of course stew meat is usually tough, but it seemed that the newly christened "tri-tip," when left in one piece and seasoned and cooked, was a different animal (so to speak). Tri-tip was born! Not that it caught on right away. People just couldn't figure out what in the heck it was, and they weren't all that comfortable with this new cut of meat that had suddenly materialized out of a cow when they thought they already knew everything about meat that comes out of a cow.

But, to its credit, tri-tip was a whole lot less expensive than those fancy cuts, a fact that was bound to pique some interest. It wasn't long before the Safeway meat manager opened his own meat market, and tri-tip became his baby. He let people sample it, promoted it, and even showed customers how to cook it, which was a major step forward.

Still, tri-tip wasn't available just anywhere, and even South County tri-tip aficionados would often get blank stares if they asked their Santa Barbara butcher for the cut. "Tri-what???" But then the word began to spread. Visitors and workers at Vandenberg Air Force Base began to tell other people about tri-tip, and soon, it was rumored, people from the San Joaquin Valley started coming over the hill to Santa Maria and buying tri-tip by the case, hauling it home for their own barbecues.

Once the secret was out, people started demanding tri-tip in grocery stores and meat markets all over the county. South County markets soon had tri-tip in their meat cases right along with those expensive cuts, sometimes pre-marinated and ready to put on the grill.

Soon caterers started serving tri-tip, and it was showing up at wedding receptions and church picnics. Certain groups—such as the Santa Maria Elks Club—developed reputations for being among the best tri-tip barbecuers in town and were in constant demand. They bought their own portable barbecue pits and charged to come out and put on a "Santa Maria–style Barbecue" for special events and get-togethers. (To this day, tri-tip barbecuing seems to be a sort of male bonding experience, although women can do it just as well.)

But you don't need a mess of men with barbecue forks to sample your own tri-tip barbecue. You can do it yourself. Here's how: First, buy enough tri-tip to feed your family. You can find it in most grocery stores and in local meat markets, and you can get pieces of it, or get the whole hunks. (Don't worry if you get too much—tri-tip sandwiches and tri-tip burritos are popular leftovers.)

*Santa Marians show off a perfectly done piece of tri-tip: brown on the outside, pink on the inside, and generously sliced.* PHOTO: COURTESY OF SANTA MARIA CHAMBER OF COMMERCE

If you don't buy the tri-tip already marinated, coat it with pepper and garlic salt. Leave the fat on, and put the meat on the grill fat side down to start with (old timers say red oak is the only fuel to use, but a lot of us cheat and use charcoal). Since the meat is so thick, it takes at least a couple of hours to cook a whole tri-tip, and you should flip it every half-hour or 45 minutes, but don't overcook it—a properly done tri-tip is rare in the middle.

Be sure to have some beans. The genuine Santa Maria–style barbecue requires little pink pinquito beans, which are grown only in Santa Barbara County, cooked fresh. (Again, some of us cheat and buy chili beans in cans, although it's not the "real thing.") Green salad and garlic bread round out the meal. Oh, and don't forget the fresh salsa, which most people use to douse their tri-tip. (Never—and we mean never—serve a tomato-based barbecue sauce with tri-tip. It would be sacrilege of the worst sort and old-time tri-tippers would laugh you to scorn.)

Add a bottle of Santa Barbara County wine, and you've got the tri-tip barbecue down pat! (Now don't go telling your East Coast relatives about tri-tip. All they're gonna do is look at you funny and say, "Tri-what???")

atmosphere. It's also famous for its excellent Jose Cuervo margaritas.

Specialties include scallops sauteed with onions, tomatoes, tomatillos, and pickled jalapeños; shrimp sauteed in tequila, garlic, cilantro butter, and fresh lime juice; veggie quesadillas; and halibut tacos. You might also try the crab and shrimp enchiladas or the great burritos. Nearly everything is served with fresh corn or flour tortillas.

La Playa Azul serves lunch and dinner every day.

**La Super-Rica Taqueria**
**622 N. Milpas Street**
**Santa Barbara, CA**
**(805) 963–4940**
**$, no credit cards**

This small, unassuming taco stand with a canopied patio serves up some of Santa Barbara's best and most authentic Mexican cuisine. After earning a master's degree in Spanish linguistics at UCSB in the late 1970s, owner Isidoro Gonzalez decided to abandon academia and venture into the restaurant business. First, though, he went to Mexico to collect regional recipes from relatives and other chefs—recipes that still form the basis of his 20-item chalkboard menu.

When you place your order, you have a full view of the tiny kitchen. It's a delight to watch the cooks roll out tortillas from fresh dough and toss sizzling steaks, chicken breasts, pork, and veggies onto the grill.

In addition to various tacos and quesadillas, Super-Rica offers many dishes rarely found in other Mexican restaurants, including roasted pasilla chile stuffed with cheese and served with pork (the Super-Rica Especial), melted cheese with bacon cooked in Mexicanware (the Tocino Especial), and cup-shaped corn tortillas filled with chicken, cheese, and avocado (Sopes de Pollo). Drinks include sodas, Mexican beer, and horchata, a popular Mexican rice beverage. Thanks to Julia Child's rave reviews and glowing write-ups in *Sunset,* the *Los Angeles Times,* and other publications, Super-Rica has achieved widespread notoriety. During prime dining hours, the line of people waiting to order nearly always stretches out the door and down the street.

The restaurant is open daily for lunch and dinner. Dine early or late if you want to avoid a 15-minute wait in the order line.

**Pollofino**
**6831 Hollister Avenue**
**Goleta, CA**
**(805) 685–1141**
**$**

We think Pollofino has the best charbroiled chicken in town. From a tiny storefront in the Kmart shopping center, it serves delectable chicken and beef cooked and seasoned to perfection.

With each order you get cooked pinto beans, warm tortillas, and fresh salsa. Or you can order a beef or chicken burrito (one is enough for a meal), tacos or quesadillas, or even ribs.

There are a few tables where you can eat on the spot, but lots of Pollofino's food gets taken home. The eatery is open daily for lunch and dinner.

**Rudy's**
**305 W. Montecito Street**
**Santa Barbara, CA**
**(805) 899–3152**
**Paseo Nuevo Mall**
**811 State Street**
**Santa Barbara, CA**
**(805) 564–8677**
**3613½ State Street**
**Santa Barbara, CA**
**(805) 563–2232**
**5680 Calle Real**
**Goleta, CA**
**(805) 681–0766**
**$**

Rudy's may look like a hole in the wall, but it cooks up some of the best Mexican food around. It's a great place to stop for a quick lunch or dinner before a movie, or just call up and order take-out. Rudy's is particularly famous for its great burritos, flautas, chimichangas, chile rellenos, and tamales. It also has great burgers. Rudy's is open for lunch and dinner daily.

## Moroccan

**Chef Karim's Moroccan Restaurant**
**1231 State Street**
**Santa Barbara, CA**
**(805) 899-4780**
**$$$**

Step into Chef Karim's dimly lit dining room and you step into another culture—a place filled with warm Moroccan hospitality, belly dancers, and belly laughs. It's a great choice if you're looking for an exotic culinary adventure and a fun night out with friends. As you sink into the comfy cushions amid jewel-toned tapestries and rugs, your Ceremonial Feast begins with the traditional orange-blossom hand-washing ceremony. It pays to partake because, as in Morocco, at Chef Karim's your fingers are your forks. Anchoring your multicourse Moroccan feast is your choice of 10 different entrees such as lemon chicken, beef or shrimp kebab, a vegetarian feast, succulent honey lamb, or the delicious white fish in red sauce. The meal begins with a hearty harira soup, Moroccan salads, and fresh baked bread. But the highlight is the scrumptious cinnamon and sugar-dusted b'stilla. This filo pastry pie filled with chicken, eggs, and almonds (or vegetables if you prefer) is a favorite with Chef Karim's guests. Then comes the entree, served up with a side dish of couscous and vegetables, followed by a dessert of honey-drizzled cookies, fruit, and nuts accompanied by Moroccan mint tea. You can also order imported Moroccan beer or wine and burn off the meal with some after-dinner belly dancing. Prices for the multicourse dinners range from $18.50 for the vegetarian feast to $30 for the meat-based spreads. Meals for children under 10 are half-price. If you're planning to bring a group, reserve the cozy private dining room in an arched alcove at the back—but you'll have to crane your neck a bit for the belly dancing (or join in!). Chef Karim's is open for dinner Wednesday through Sunday.

## South American

**Café Buenos Aires**
**1316 State Street**
**Santa Barbara, CA**
**(805) 963-0242**
**$$$**

For a taste of tango, romance, and South American flavor without having to fly to Argentina, head for Café Buenos Aires, right across from the Arlington Center for the Performing Arts. Owners Wally and Silvia Ronchietto, Argentine natives who have lived in Santa Barbara off and on for years, have managed not only to recreate the cuisine they grew up with, but also the casual, yet elegant Latin-European atmosphere of Buenos Aires.

Our favorite place to dine is in the spacious courtyard, which centers around a fountain and Old World street light. But we also love the beautiful interior, with hardwood floors that are perfect for tango dancing. The menu focuses on traditional Argentinian food plus popular dishes from Brazil and other South American nations. Definitely try the Argentine beef, which we think has more flavor than its typical American counterpart. Or fill up on calamari, fresh fish specials, Argentine barbecue meats, or hot and cold tapas (octopus, calamari, and traditional Argentine empanadas, among others).

The cafe offers a great selection of South American wines and exotic mixed drinks from the full bar (try the tangy lime caipirinha, Brazil's national drink). It also has live Latin music (diners are welcome to dance) several nights a week. Café Buenos Aires is open for lunch and dinner daily.

**Papagallo's**
**731 De la Guerra Plaza**
**Santa Barbara, CA**
**(805) 963-8374**
**$$**

Peru is known as the culinary capital of South America, and Papagallo's is the Peruvian culinary center of Santa Barbara. If you happen to be passing through De la Guerra Plaza (off De la Guerra Street between State and Anacapa Streets), the aroma of shellfish will surely lure you in.

Dishes include ceviche and clam chowder, paella, seafood pastas, skewered beef and chicken, and myriad variations of seafood. The fountain courtyard is a fantastic place to dine, especially on weekends, when you can listen to live South American music (there's a cover charge for the music). Papagallo's serves dinner Wednesday through Sunday.

## Thai

**Your Choice**
**3404 State Street**
**Santa Barbara, CA**
**(805) 569–3730**
**$**

Your Choice is our favorite uptown Thai restaurant. The spacious, contemporary dining room is always filled with the alluring aromas of coconut, lemongrass, and other savory Thai ingredients. The long menu features all sorts of appetizers, soups, salads, curries, seafood, beef, chicken, noodle, and rice dishes (the pad thai and the hot-and-sour soups are fantastic).

Your Choice serves lunch and dinner Tuesday through Sunday. (Closed Monday.)

**Your Place**
**22-A N. Milpas Street**
**Santa Barbara, CA**
**(805) 966–5151, (805) 965–9397**
**$**

Your Place is Santa Barbara's oldest Thai restaurant, and it's regularly voted the best Thai restaurant in town in local polls. The kitschy dining room is a treat in itself—you can gaze at the giant fish tank and the authentic Thai decorations while feasting on mouthwatering plates of exotic foods. Choose from more than 200 authentic Thai dishes, from satay and panang curry to coconut ice cream.

The restaurant sits right on Milpas Street, just a few blocks north of the freeway. It's open for lunch and dinner Tuesday through Sunday (closed Monday).

# Nightlife

**Bars/Lounges**
**Sports Bars and Brewpubs**
**Dance Clubs**
**Billiards**
**Coffeehouses/Bookstores**
**Country Music and Dance**
**Movie Theaters**
**Social Dancing**

When the sun goes down, Santa Barbara nightlife ignites. The afterglow from spending a day at the beach or on the water converts to social energy—and you'll find most of it centered between Stearns Wharf and the 1300 block of State Street. Even people who live in Goleta, Carpinteria, and Montecito head for downtown Santa Barbara just to be at the heart of the action.

Most dance clubs and bars that cater to the younger crowd (early 20s) are situated between the 300 and 600 blocks of State Street. As you walk north from there and approach the "arts and culture district" that extends to the 1300 block, you'll find dozens of restaurants, bars, theaters, bookstores, and coffeehouses along the way. Santa Barbara's cultural events calendar is busy every month of the year (see The Arts chapter for a broad overview of your many choices).

Many Santa Barbara nightspots appeal to a wide cross-section of people of all ages. We can, however, make a few generalizations: older people tend to go to the hotels; college students and people in their 20s tend to hang around the dance clubs on lower State Street.

At many places, the age group depends on the type of music played that evening. If a particular nightspot caters mostly to a single age group, we mention it in the listing. Otherwise, just pop your head in the door and find out whether the ambiance suits your style.

Many bars and restaurants host live music performances on Thursdays, Fridays, and Saturdays and sometimes other weekdays as well. Cover charges vary from $2 to $4 or sometimes more, depending on the band.

Something we've noticed in the last couple of years is that martinis have made a comeback here—in a big way. So have cigars, although the no-smoking law (see below) has put a damper on some of the wine and cigar bars that don't have outdoor patios. Most bars now advertise that their bartenders make the best martinis in town. Since so many of them present this claim to fame, we'll let you decide which will be your favorite.

In this chapter we've included some of the most popular nightspots in the area. We begin with our favorite bars, listed by geographic area. Then we list a few places according to their specialties: sports bars, comedy clubs, dance clubs, billiards, coffeehouses and bookstores, country music and dance, movie theaters, and social dancing (swing, ballroom, tango).

To find out what's happening on any given night, check the "Listings" section of *The Santa Barbara Independent* (a free weekly paper that comes out on Thursdays) or *Scene* magazine in the *Santa Barbara News-Press* (included in the Friday edition).

But before we send you on your nocturnal adventures, there are a few things you should know.

One of the most important is that California law forbids all smoking in bars and restaurants. Although many people applaud this restriction, others are mortally opposed. Some bar owners and smokers are still hotly contesting the no-smoking law, which went into effect in January 1998. Most bars are enforcing it, however, so expect to stand outdoors if you wish to light up.

Bars in the state of California are bound by law to stop serving alcohol by 2:00 A.M., so don't argue when the bartender shuts down. The minimum drinking age in California is 21. Be prepared to show legal identification (driver's license, passport) if you look younger than 30 years old.

Last, but certainly not least, know that any driver with a blood-alcohol level of .08 or higher is considered legally drunk. If you're caught driving drunk, you will be handcuffed, taken to jail, fingerprinted, and thrown into a detox cell for at least a few hours, usually overnight. You will also lose your license for a while—the length of time depends on how many times you've been previously arrested for drunk driving.

So now you're ready to walk, crawl, or dance your way through the Santa Barbara night hours. Have fun, and be sure to tell us about any places we might have missed.

## Bars/Lounges

### Downtown/ Beachside Santa Barbara

**Arnoldi's Café**
**600 Olive Street**
**Santa Barbara, CA**
**(805) 962–5394**
**www.arnoldiscafe.com**

Most locals have heard of Arnoldi's—it has served up homestyle Italian meals and steaks since 1940. But fewer people know that the historic restaurant in a quaint sandstone building was purchased several years ago by longtime Arnoldi's bartender Jim Kershaw and his wife, Helen Daniels.

The couple renovated and updated the entire place and converted the former beer garden into a barbecue area with a bocce court. The "new" Arnoldi's has become quite the hip hangout for Santa Barbarans in their 30s or older. It's packed with locals nearly every weekend. Arnoldi's always has a martini specialist on duty at the bar—in fact, it claims to serve the perfect martini.

**Arts & Letters Café**
**7 E. Anapamu Street**
**Santa Barbara, CA**
**(805) 730–1463**

Looking for culture? At the romantic, intimate Arts & Letters Café you can immerse yourself in a total artistic experience. The small restaurant/cafe occupies a courtyard behind Sullivan Goss Books & Prints, Ltd., which sells new, rare, and out-of-print art books and fine art.

In addition to serving intimate dinners, including pre-theater meals, six nights a week (closed Monday), the cafe organizes exhibitions in its gallery and offers a regular schedule of musical performances. It's a real treat to relax in the outdoor courtyard, sip fine wine, gaze at the art, and enjoy the music. A typical summer lineup would be "Contemporary Artists" on Tuesday, classical guitar on Wednesday, "Elegant Instrumentals" on Thursday, "The Best of Broadway" on Friday, "Opera Under the Stars" on Saturday, and piano music on Sunday. The entertainment schedule is typically shortened to two or three evenings a week during the winter months.

**Bar Los Arcos**
**633 E. Cabrillo Boulevard**
**Santa Barbara, CA**
**(805) 564–4333**

The Doubletree is one of Santa Barbara's high-end hotels, and its Bar Los Arcos matches the casual, yet sophisticated, character of the rest of the hotel. The bar offers a full range of drinks and light music, with live entertainment Tuesday through Saturday. During the week, pianists, guitarists, and trumpeters provide soft dance music, and live jazz spices up Friday and Saturday evenings.

**Bistro Eleven Eleven**
**1111 E. Cabrillo Boulevard**
**Santa Barbara, CA**
**(805) 730–1111**

Bistro Eleven Eleven is a casual-to-slightly-dressy restaurant and bar at the Radisson Hotel. On Friday and Saturday nights you can listen or dance to live music, which ranges from soft rock to jazz and rhythm and blues. The musical entertainment usually starts up around 9:30 P.M. Happy hour, with $2 margaritas, is from 4:00 to 7:00 P.M. seven days a week.

**Blue Agave**
**20 E. Cota Street**
**Santa Barbara, CA**
**(805) 899–4694**

We've noticed more than a few Hollywood celebrities popping into this small, two-story restaurant/bar with soft lights, contemporary decor, and a romantic ambiance. This is a great spot to take a first date. On weekends the place is packed with chic singles and couples in their late 20s, 30s, and 40s. You can choose from various types of margaritas (Blue Agave has an extensive tequila selection) as well as excellent martinis. Cigar smokers crowd the upstairs balcony. If you don't like standing, we suggest you go early for dinner. Valet parking is available across the street.

**Brophy Brothers**
**On the breakwater at the harbor**
**Santa Barbara, CA**
**(805) 966–4418**

Brophy's overlooks the yacht harbor and the mountains and is one of our favorite restaurants and watering holes. Many locals, especially those from the harbor community, quench their thirst and satisfy their hankering for seafood at the long cocktail and oyster bar. If you're lucky, you'll be seated at a table with fantastic views. Sometimes you'll be lucky to sit at all—the place is nearly always crowded. It's not a late-night spot, though, since everything closes around 10:00 P.M.

**Café Buenos Aires**
**1316 State Street**
**Santa Barbara, CA**
**(805) 963–0242**

Tango and romance are always in the air at Café Buenos Aires, a Latin restaurant and bar with a casually elegant atmosphere. Sit at a table in the spacious, open-air courtyard, sample exotic South American wine or mixed drinks, and let the live Latin music sweep you away to Argentina. Or choose an indoor table amid paned windows with mahogany frames and hardwood floors that are perfect for dancing the tango.

Wherever you're seated, you can dine on authentic regional cuisine from Argentina and South America or order fantastic tapas. Café Buenos Aires has somewhat flexible hours. It stays open as late as need demands—for example, after a symphony performance at the Arlington Center for the Performing Arts across the street. Happy hour is 2:30 to 5:30 P.M. Tuesday through Friday. The restaurant offers social tango dancing every Wednesday evening at 9:00 P.M. and hosts regular tango dancing events (see the Social Dancing section later in this chapter).

**Dargan's Irish Pub & Restaurant**
**18 E. Ortega**
**Santa Barbara, CA**
**(805) 568–0702**

This bright cheery, traditional Irish pub is one of our favorite pubs in Santa Barbara. You can wander in here any night of the week and usually find a lively crowd chatting over a few pints and shooting some pool. We've also noticed people pouring in here after special events. This is the kind of place where anyone can wander in and feel perfectly comfortable; where the classic, foot-tappin' tunes are loud enough to enliven the crowd but not so loud that they drown out conversation. You can come here and play a game of foosball with your buds, kick back with a Guinness stout by the fireplace, warm your belly with some hearty Irish stew, or listen to live folk music at least once a week. Dargan's has four pool tables in the spacious new section fronting Ortega Street and a great selection of draught beer and Irish whiskeys. Wednesday nights are trivia nights, and on Thursday evenings you can enjoy traditional Irish dancers and musicians and then try to steal the show at the "open mike" session. For easy access to Dargan's, park in Lot 10 on East Ortega.

**El Paseo Restaurant**
**10 El Paseo**
**Santa Barbara, CA**
**(805) 962–6050**

Many tourists and locals come to El Paseo to enjoy the historic Old Spanish/Mexican/Santa Barbara atmosphere. The courtyard has a retractable roof, so you can stare at the skies on balmy summer evenings. The bartenders make excellent margaritas, and the restaurant regularly books mariachi musicians to entertain the crowds. Settle down in a high-back chair, sip your margarita, and pretend you're reliving an 18th-century fiesta.

**Intermezzo**
**813 Anacapa Street**
**Santa Barbara, CA**
**(805) 966–9463**

The acclaimed Wine Cask Restaurant (which has a more upper-crust ambiance) opened this relaxed, next-door bistro in 1997. It caters to the late-night crowd and offers bistro-style dining, a full bar, and fine cigars, which you can smoke on the patio. This is the type of place you go to before or after a concert or theater performance. Relax and enjoy a martini by the fireplace.

**The James Joyce**
**513 State Street**
**Santa Barbara, CA**
**(805) 962–2688**

In this cozy bar you can order a pint of Guinness just as Joyce's Bloom would have done in 1904 Dublin. The James Joyce is a very popular, traditional Irish pub with a stone fireplace and a good selection of Irish whiskeys, single-malt scotches, cigars, and humidors. It serves up a heartwarming Irish coffee, too. Come here to shoot some pool, spark up the jukebox, play darts, or relax and chat with your buddies. On Sundays from 5:00 to 9:00 P.M. you can down your pint while enjoying live music.

**Jimmy's Oriental Gardens**
**126 E. Canon Perdido Street**
**Santa Barbara, CA**
**(805) 962–7582**

When the theaters close their curtains, the actors and stage hands (and all the locals who socialize with this crowd) head to Jimmy's, which is not only a great Chinese restaurant, but one of the town's best full bars (try the infamous mai tai). Jimmy's opened more than 50 years ago and the current owner, a son of the original Jimmy, is carrying on the tradition in his own style with great success.

**Joe's Café**
**536 State Street**
**Santa Barbara, CA**
**(805) 966–4638**

Joe's has been around forever (since 1928), and is said to be the longest-running restaurant and bar in Santa Barbara. As a restaurant, it delivers mom-and-pop-style steak, seafood, and Italian meals to your table. The bar, however, is another animal. The bartenders are known to pour the strongest cocktails in town, so the bar is nearly always packed. Joe's is also a popular meeting place for native Santa Barbarans who come here to catch up with old friends and prime themselves for a night on the town. While you're here, check out Shaq's huge shoe behind the bar.

**Mel's Cocktails**
**Paseo Nuevo**
**6 W. De la Guerra Street**
**Santa Barbara, CA**
**(805) 963–2211**

A colorful cross-section of locals and tourists (mostly in the 30-plus age group) have socialized at Mel's for 60 years. In a

*Both visitors and locals find plenty to do in Santa Barbara after the sun goes down.* PHOTO: TOM TUTTLE, COURTESY OF THE SANTA BARBARA CONFERENCE & VISITORS BUREAU

recent local newspaper poll it was voted best neighborhood bar. Mel's has two happy hours—7:00 to 10:00 A.M. (for the all-night worker) and 4:00 to 7:00 P.M. Monday through Friday. You'll also find a pool table, jukebox, and, some say, a very liberal attitude towards beefing up the booze content on the mixed drinks. The Bloody Marys are terrific. You'll find Mel's just a few doors down from State Street in one of the Paseo Nuevo courtyards.

**The Press Room**
**15 E. Ortega Street**
**Santa Barbara, CA**
**(805) 963–8121**

The Press Room, named for its location next to the *News Press* building, is where local bartenders head as soon as they're off work. This small cozy bar has a European feel and a great selection of beers. You'll find 12 brews on tap here, including Guinness, Tetley's, and Fullers. Best of all, The Press Room opens at all hours of the morning so that die-hard foreign sports fans can watch international football, rugby, and cricket matches on TV.

**Q's Sushi a Go Go**
**409 State Street**
**Santa Barbara, CA**
**(805) 966–9177**

Currently one of the hottest hangouts in the downtown area, Q's offers excellent sushi, pool, dancing, and drinks in an unusual turn-of-the-century, red-velvet atmosphere. The building dates back to 1899 and used to be a dinner theater, among other things. You can sit at tables on several levels surrounding a red-curtained stage, chow down on sushi, order any type of drink you like, challenge a friend to a game of pool at one of the nine tables on the third floor, and dance to live bands or recorded music played by a DJ. You can even watch major sports events on TV at the bars. Q's is open daily.

**Rocks Restaurant and Lounge**
**801 State Street**
**Santa Barbara, CA**
**(805) 884–1190**

When we polled friends about their current favorite nightspots, Rocks was consistently at the top of the list. This contemporary, slightly upscale restaurant and bar (actually two bars—one upstairs and one downstairs) serves excellent martinis. It's often packed with locals and tourists alike (mostly in their late 20s, 30s, and 40s) who come to socialize and be part of the "scene."

**Roy**
**7 W. Carrillo Street**
**Santa Barbara, CA**
**(805) 966-5636**

Roy is one of the few downtown restaurants that serves meals late in the evening (until midnight). It also offers late-night entertainment several nights a week featuring original compositions by folk, jazz, rock, and blues musicians. The food is delicious and inexpensive. Drinks are a bit less of a deal, but they're still affordable. Roy has a full bar, beer, wine, and gourmet coffee. Get here early if you plan to eat—or also plan to wait for a table.

**SOhO**
**1221 State Street**
**Santa Barbara, CA**
**(805) 962-7776**

If you enjoy music and want to get away from the hustle and bustle of lower State Street, chances are you'll love SOhO. It's a casual restaurant and bar up on the second floor of the Victoria Court shopping arcade. The site is ideal for all types of performances and dancing: high ceilings, lots of windows, red brick walls (sort of like those in a Soho loft), and an outdoor patio/deck.

Live music fills the restaurant nearly every night. The musical variety ranges from blues, jazz, folk, reggae, and rhythm and blues to rock and international. Many of the bands and entertainers are local talent.

The music usually starts at 7:30 or 8:00 P.M. during the week. On weekends you can dine with jazz tunes as a backdrop, then stay for the main billing, which begins at 9:00 or 9:30 P.M. If you want to make sure to get a good seat (or any seat at all when popular bands are playing) we suggest you eat dinner here first.

## Midtown/Upper State Street Area

**Harry's Plaza Café**
**3313B State Street**
**Santa Barbara, CA**
**(805) 687-7910**

Harry's is an uptown version of downtown Joe's—a traditional, family-style restaurant with big booths and long tables. Like Joe's, it's a Santa Barbara institution. It's always lively and packed with locals, mostly age 30 and older. Be forewarned: the bartenders serve very strong drinks that pack a mighty punch.

## Goleta

**Beachside Bar and Café**
**5905 Sandspit Road**
**Goleta, CA**
**(805) 964-7881**

At the Beachside, which sits right on Goleta Beach, you can take in fantastic ocean views while dining in the contemporary restaurant or relaxing in the lounge or at the oyster bar. An outdoor patio features glass walls, heaters, and a fireplace that keeps you warm when the ocean breezes pick up.

To get here, take U.S. Highway 101 to the UCSB off-ramp (Calif. Highway 217) and drive for about a mile to the Sandspit Road exit. Go left, then turn right into the Goleta Beach parking lot and bear left—you can't miss it.

**Elephant Bar**
**521 Firestone Road**
**Goleta, CA**
**(805) 964-0779**

This lively, safari-style restaurant just off Hollister Avenue near the airport is a local favorite. It serves a varied menu for lunch and dinner, but at night most people come here for the action-packed bar scene and the potent mixed drinks like Coco Locos.

> **Insiders' Tip**
>
> The parking lots between the 300 and 700 blocks of Lower State Street are often full on weekend nights. Try parking in one of the city lots just a few blocks farther north and walk back down along State Street.

## Montecito

**La Sala Lounge**
**1260 Channel Drive**
**Montecito, CA**
**(805) 969–2261**

The La Sala Lounge at the posh Four Seasons Biltmore hotel is the best "cheap date" in town. Order a drink, blend in with the crowd, and listen (or dance) to music every night, usually piano, swing bands, jazz or salsa, depending on the schedule. And there's never a cover charge.

**Lucky's**
**1269 Coast Village Road**
**Montecito, CA**
**(805) 565–7540**

Owned by the founder of Lucky Brand Dungarees, this swanky new cocktail bar and steak house opened in 2000 in the former Coast Village Grill location. Lucky's draws an upper-crust crowd of chic, well-groomed couples who come here to socialize or sit and sip while waiting for a table in the restaurant. (Meals can also be served in the bar.) Whilst quaffing your martini you can gaze at the old black-and-white photographs of movie stars on the walls, people-watch, or perch at the bar and view the big game on the flat-screen TV. Appropriately, valet parking is available in front.

## Carpinteria

**The Palms**
**701 Linden Avenue**
**Carpinteria, CA**
**(805) 684–3811**

The casual Palms restaurant has long held the title of Carpinteria's main local hangout. The cocktail lounge brings in live music Thursday through Saturday. Expect anything from rock 'n' roll and country music to covers of classic '60s and '70s tunes. Try the popular Tim's Titanic cocktail with Malibu rum and Midori and if you feel like dancing, just get up and boogie on the large dance floor.

## Up the Mountain

**Cold Spring Tavern**
**5955 Stagecoach Road**
**Santa Barbara, CA**
**(805) 967–0066**

For a real adventure, drive up Calif. Highway 154 about 20 minutes from Santa Barbara to Cold Spring Tavern. The rustic, 110-year-old cabin in the woods was once a stop on the main stagecoach route. Today it offers excellent food (fish, game, pastas, steaks) as well as a range of wines, beers, and mixed drinks.

The tavern has live music Wednesday, Friday, and Saturday nights. A tip: We usually designate a driver when we go here—Calif. 154 has only two lanes in most places and is very curvy.

# Sports Bars and Brewpubs

**O'Malley's**
**523 State Street**
**Santa Barbara, CA**
**(805) 564–8904**

When Michael Jordan popped into this wild sports bar several years ago, he created a huge ruckus. You can watch your favorite sports on the TVs, dance every night to a jukebox tune or music played by a DJ, or listen to some loud rock. If you want a

**Insiders' Tip**

Security is tight all along State Street, especially on weekends. The police patrol on foot and bicycle to ensure the safety of everyone visiting the downtown area. If you've overindulged, call Orange Cab (805-964-2800), Rose Cab (805-564-2600), Santa Barbara City Cab (805-968-6868), or Yellow Cab (805-965-5111).

more romantic spot to sit and chat, head upstairs to the cozy lounge. This is a rowdy bar that really gets going later in the evening. You'll see people spilling out onto the street-side patio after about 10:00 P.M.

**Santa Barbara Brewing Company and Restaurant**
**501 State Street**
**Santa Barbara, CA**
**(805) 730–1040**

This is the only combination microbrewery/restaurant in Santa Barbara County. It's a classy, American-style brewpub with eight large TVs broadcasting all major college and professional sporting events. You can wash down some hearty traditional American fare with a variety of homemade ales and lagers such as Santa Barbara Blonde and Rincon Red.

## Dance Clubs

**Calypso**
**514 State Street**
**Santa Barbara, CA**
**(805) 966–1388**

Calypso is a casual restaurant, bar, and dance spot with a tropical theme. It's famous for exotic drinks like the Calypso Cooler, a potent combination of three rums and three juices (pineapple, cranberry, and orange). You can sit indoors or on the lush outdoor patio and dance until you drop—or until Calypso closes. There are live reggae jams on Tuesday nights and other theme nights are staged throughout the week, including College Night, with half-price drinks from 10:00 P.M. to close, Ladies' Night, and '70s and '80s Dance Night. Take advantage of the two-for-one late-night happy hour from 10:00 to 11:00 P.M. every night.

**Club 634**
**634 State Street**
**Santa Barbara, CA**
**(805) 564–1069**

Dance devotees and live music lovers flock to Club 634 in the heart of the downtown bar district. You can usually feel the beat pulsing from within before you enter. This is one of those dimly lit, indestructible dance venues where hip 20-somethings come for College Night and Chemical Alternative Night, not soft music and quiet conversation. The club stages live music a couple of nights a week and the DJ spins the dance tunes on other evenings. Call for the weekly lineup or check the local newspaper, *The Independent*. Happy hour is 4:00 to 9:00 P.M. Wednesday through Friday.

**Zelo**
**630 State Street**
**Santa Barbara, CA**
**(805) 966–5792**
**www.zelo.com**

Zelo is nearly always voted best dance club in local polls. In the earlier evening hours it serves excellent food. After 10:00 P.M. a DJ spins dance tunes ranging from hits from the '70s, '80s, and '90s to hip-hop and reggae. Each day features a different music theme, and live bands perform on the palm-filled patio Saturdays after 10:00 P.M. Zelo becomes an 18-and-over dance club on certain nights of the week. Cover charges vary depending upon the evening, but you won't pay more than $10. Zelo is closed Mondays.

## Billiards

Many bars have pool tables. Here, though, are a few real live pool halls.

**Don Q Family Billiard Center**
**1128 Chapala Street**
**Santa Barbara, CA**
**(805) 966–0915**

Don Q is Santa Barbara's largest pool hall. It attracts billiards fans of all ages and serves beer to players 21 and older, as well as chips and sodas. Kids can play with video and pinball games if they don't want to play pool. Don Q has 11 excellent tables, including tournament and snooker tables. Rates range from $2.50 to $4.75 an hour per player depending on the time and day.

**Fig & Haley**
**14 W. Haley Street**
**Santa Barbara, CA**
**(805) 897–1840**

Fig & Haley is an upscale pool hall with eight championship tables. It's open only to persons 21 and older. The bar serves fine wines and beers. It will cost you $6 an hour to play before 7:00 P.M., $10 afterward. If you buy a pitcher of beer between 1:00 and 7:00 P.M. Tuesday through Friday or anytime on Sunday or Monday, you get a free hour of pool.

## Coffeehouses/Bookstores

Bookstores and coffeehouses serve as the main social hubs for many locals who seek alternatives to the bar scene. It's easy to find Starbucks, Peets, and other chain coffee shops: they're strategically located up and down all the popular shopping and restaurant streets. Here are a few of our favorite places in downtown Santa Barbara to browse shelves, listen to poetry, and meet with friends after dinner and the movies.

**Borders Books, Music & Cafe**
**900 State Street**
**Santa Barbara, CA**
**(805) 899–3668**
**7000 Marketplace Avenue**
**Goleta, CA**
**(805) 968–1370**
**www.borders.com**

Borders (a national chain of superstores) occupies a gigantic two-story former bank building on State Street and a new location in the Camino Real Marketplace in Goleta. The downtown location is the largest bookstore in town, with more than 200,000 book, music, and video titles and more than 2,000 periodicals in 10 different languages from 15 different countries. You're allowed to walk around with your coffee (as long as it has a lid on it) while browsing.

Borders arranges special events, including live music and readings, at both locations several evenings a week. Call to find out what's on the schedule.

**Hot Spots Espresso Company**
**36 State Street**
**Santa Barbara, CA**
**(805) 963–4233**

This coffee shop has lots of tourist information that you can peruse while sipping

### Insiders' Tip

When enjoying the nightlife on State Street, save your legs and hail a pedicab, Santa Barbara's version of a bicycle-driven rickshaw. It's a fast and fun way to cruise among the restaurants and bars.

your java. Plus, it's open 24 hours a day. You'll find it just a block up from Cabrillo Boulevard.

**Santa Barbara Roasting Company**
**321 Motor Way**
**Santa Barbara, CA**
**(805) 962–0320**

Insiders call this place "RoCo." It reminds us of the cozy coffeehouses where we used to meet friends and pretend to study when we were in college. RoCo is usually open until 11:00 P.M. daily. It's on the corner of State and Gutierrez Streets, set back from the city parking lot.

## Country Music and Dance

**The Galleon Room at Zodo's Bowling & Beyond**
**5925 Calle Real**
**Goleta, CA**
**(805) 967–0128**

This popular country-style lounge is in Zodo's Bowling & Beyond and offers live country music and dancing on Friday and Saturday nights at 9:30 P.M. The evening kicks off with a fun session of line dancing, then the music and dancing continue until well after midnight.

## Movie Theaters

Moviegoing is possibly Santa Barbara's favorite pastime. Every day of the week you can choose from a wide range of current films shown in the afternoons, evenings, and sometimes in the mornings as well. Metropolitan Theatres owns nearly all the theaters in the Santa Barbara area. You can call the Metropolitan Theatres Movie Hotline (805–963–9503) for locations and showtime information for all the following cinemas. If a theater also has a direct number, we've listed it.

### Santa Barbara

**Arlington Center for the Performing Arts**
**1317 State Street**
**Santa Barbara, CA**
**(805) 963–4408**

**Fiesta 5**
**916 State Street**
**Santa Barbara, CA**

**Metro 4**
**618 State Street**
**Santa Barbara, CA**

**Paseo Nuevo**
**8 W. De la Guerra Place (in the Paseo Nuevo Mall)**
**Santa Barbara, CA**

**Plaza de Oro**
**349 Hitchcock Way**
**Santa Barbara, CA**

**Riviera Theatre**
**2044 Alameda Padre Serra**
**Santa Barbara, CA**

### Goleta

**Camino Real Cinemas**
**Camino Real Marketplace**
**Goleta, CA**

**Cinema Twin**
**6050 Hollister Avenue**
**Goleta, CA**

**Fairview Twin**
**251 N. Fairview Avenue**
**Goleta, CA**

### Carpinteria

**Plaza Theatre**
**4916 Carpinteria Avenue**
**Carpinteria, CA**
**(805) 684–4014**

## Social Dancing

**Café Buenos Aires**
**1316 State Street**
**Santa Barbara, CA**
**(805) 963-0242**

You can tango under the stars in the courtyard or inside the beautiful restaurant at informal dances held at Café Buenos Aires every Wednesday at 9:00 P.M. throughout the year (dancing usually lasts about an hour to an hour and a half). An international dance teacher occasionally gives a seminar. Here's your chance to practice the Argentine tango, waltz, and Milonga! Call the restaurant for more information.

**Carrillo Recreation Center Ballroom**
**100 E. Carrillo Street**
**Santa Barbara, CA**
**(805) 897-2519**

The Carrillo Rec Center boasts one of the best dance floors anywhere—it's spring-loaded, which means you can dance for long periods of time without exhausting your leg muscles.

Practice your ballroom dancing to live orchestra music nearly every Saturday night from 8:00 to 11:00 P.M. Admission is $8 for members and $9 for non-members. Or you can turn up for the ballroom tea dance on the first Sunday of each month from 2:00 to 3:00 P.M.; dancers twirl to recorded Big Band music.

On the first and third Friday of every month, swing to live bands and DJs from 8:30 to midnight. Admission is $10. Free lessons are offered before the dance, from 7:00 to 8:00 P.M. For more swing dance information, call (805) 569-1952.

Contra dancing with live music and callers takes place every Sunday from 7:00 to 10:00 P.M. Admission is $7. Take advantage of the free lessons at 6:30 P.M. before each dance. Call the Santa Barbara Country Dance Society Hotline (805-969-1511) for information.

*Shops selling souvenirs, snacks, and sportswear line Stearns Wharf.* PHOTO: JOHN B. SNODGRASS

# Shopping



Shopping in Santa Barbara could conceivably qualify as an Olympic sport. We know many Insiders who spend hours happily dashing around hunting for exotic gifts, rare antiques, and the latest fashions. Strolling the outdoor paseos amid palm trees and fountains and stopping for an alfresco lunch or to sip a cappuccino in one of our streetside cafes are also part of the Santa Barbara experience—even if you don't buy anything. If you're on a mission, take this book with you to save time. Need help making a selection? Ask our friendly shopkeepers—most love to chat with customers and are happy to point out one-of-a-kind treasures for you to take home.

In addition to many nationally known retail stores, hundreds of specialty shops are sprinkled throughout the region. In this chapter, we first give you an overview of the region's main shopping areas. Then we take you on a brief tour of major shopping malls and arcades, followed by a list of homegrown stores that are unique to the area. Finally, we depart from our usual geographic listing format to point out a few of the most popular specialty stores by category—from antiques and bookstores to surfwear and women's clothing. All stores are open daily unless otherwise noted.

If you're planning a mall crawl during the busy Christmas season avoid parking hassles and catch the Shopper Express. This comfortable electric shuttle will whisk you between Santa Barbara's two major shopping malls—Paseo Nuevo and La Cumbre (see our Getting Here, Getting Around chapter for details on the shuttle). Happy shopping!

## Shopping Areas

### Santa Barbara

For the quintessential Santa Barbara shopping experience, head downtown to State Street. Many stores are concentrated on or near lower State Street, between the beginning of State Street at Stearns Wharf and the 1400 block. Paseo Nuevo Mall (the largest outdoor mall in this area) and the El Paseo shopping arcade are located around the 900 block. Victoria Court and La Arcada Court sit at the upper end of this district, between the 1100 and 1200 blocks. You can park in any of the city lots along Anacapa and Chapala Streets to access any part of this major shopping district. On upper State Street, which starts at about the 3000 block and continues through the 4000 blocks, you'll find a long stretch of shops, services, and businesses. La Cumbre Plaza mall is the main magnet in this area—it occupies the entire 3800 block of State Street.

Several strip malls are located here, as are a few shopping centers anchored by supermarkets: Five Points (across from La Cumbre Plaza on the 3900 block of State Street), Loreto Plaza (at the intersection of Las Positas Road and State Street), and

*Taking a break from shopping to chase bubbles on Stearns Wharf.* PHOTO: SALLY TURVEY

Ralph's (near the intersection of State Street and Alamar Avenue, between State and De la Vina streets).

## Goleta

Loads of stores, specialty shops, and services line both sides of Calle Real between Patterson and Fairview Avenues. The main strip mall in the area is the remodeled Calle Real Center, with nearly 50 merchants. These include Sonny's Fish Market (one of the best in all of Santa Barbara), Patty Montana (unique women's clothing), gift shops, the wholesaler chain store Trader Joe's, and restaurants such as Outback Steakhouse. Parking is plentiful along the strip that fronts the stores.

The Camino Real Marketplace—the largest shopping mall and discount center on the South Coast—opened in 1999 at the intersection of Hollister Avenue and Storke Road. (See the Shopping Malls and Arcades section of this chapter for a detailed description.)

## Montecito

Most Montecito residents head down the hill to Coast Village Road at some point every day to pick up their daily wares, gifts, clothes, coffee, ice cream, and pizza. This upscale shopping strip runs parallel to U.S. Highway 101, between Hot Springs and Olive Mill Roads. At the Hot Springs intersection you'll find a large shopping center with a Vons grocery store and drugstore, a French bakery, a health-food store, and other specialty shops.

As you drive along Coast Village Road toward Olive Mill Road, you encounter dozens of galleries, boutiques, specialty shops (tennis, stationery), restaurants, and services. You can park in the designated spaces in the parking lane right in front of the shops.

Montecito Village, at the intersection of San Ysidro and East Valley Roads, is a collection of exclusive boutiques, specialty shops, restaurants, a bookstore, a grocery store, and the post office. Insiders call this area the "Upper Village," the place where "real" Montecitans hang out and shop. Keep your eyes open if you're hoping to run into a film star or celebrity. Since many of them live nearby, this is where you're most likely to find one grabbing a cup of coffee, a newspaper, or a bite to eat.

## Carpinteria

Downtown Carpinteria is known for its small, quaint shops filled with antiques, collectibles, and gifts for home and garden. Many shoppers love the small-town atmosphere, the friendly shopkeepers, and the plentiful, easy-to-find parking. Most shops are located in the business district, which consists of several blocks radiating south, east, and west from the intersection of Linden and Carpinteria Avenues. You'll also find a couple of strip malls off Casitas Pass Road, between U.S. 101 and Carpinteria Avenue.

## Shopping Malls and Arcades

The historic **El Paseo** in the 800 block of State Street in Santa Barbara was reportedly California's first shopping center. It was built in the 1920s on the site of a historic residence that belonged to one of Santa Barbara's original Spanish families. Stroll through the cool courtyards with their fountains, tiles, and wrought-iron gates, and you'll feel as though you're in an old Spanish village. El Paseo's charming shops sell unusual items, from jewelry and lace to antiques and toys.

You'll know you're at the entrance to beautiful **La Arcada Court** when you see a giant clock on a pedestal in front of a broad, tiled walkway about a half-block down from the Museum of Art in the 1100 block of State Street. The Spanish-Mediterranean ambiance takes you back in time and makes you forget the hustle and bustle of adjacent State Street. Wander the cool paved corridors and you'll find art galleries, specialty shops, and cafe-style restaurants. Some consider the arcade a gallery in itself. Whimsical sculptures, fountains, and life-size bronzes provide fun photo opportunities, and the sounds of bubbling fountains fill the air. Sip a giant margarita at Acapulco Mexican Restaurant y cantina (see our Restaurants chapter), visit the old-fashioned barber shop, or browse the stores for quality men's and women's clothing, antiques, jewelry, gifts, and luggage.

**La Cumbre Plaza,** 121 S. Hope Avenue, is a convenient one-stop shopping venue. It's 3.5 miles north of downtown Santa Barbara, between U.S. 101 and State Street, bordered by Hope Avenue and La Cumbre Road. Completed in 1967, this complex was our only large-scale mall before Paseo Nuevo was built in 1990. Amble along the lovely outdoor walkway with its tiled fountains and colorful flowers, and you'll find shopping can be quite a relaxing experience—especially on warm summer evenings and at Christmastime when the carolers are singing. La Cumbre also attracts fewer tourists than State Street so it tends to be less crowded.

Robinson's-May and Sears department stores anchor the north and south sides of La Cumbre Plaza. In between stand many well-known chain stores such as Williams-Sonoma, Ann Taylor, The Disney Store, Kay Bee Toys, Brooks Shoes for Kids, The Limited, and a big new Pottery Barn. Parking is abundant except right before Christmas, when you could circle for quite a while before nabbing a prized spot.

**Paseo Nuevo Mall,** in the 700 and 800 blocks of State Street, was built in 1990 and is anchored by Nordstrom and Macy's. This spectacular Spanish-style mall is the most popular downtown shopping attraction. It covers two full city blocks in the heart of downtown, near many of the most popular restaurants, cafes, clubs, and bookstores.

The Paseo Nuevo complex includes more than 50 shops and restaurants plus a five-screen movie theater, the Contemporary Arts Forum gallery, and the Center

Stage Theater (see the Arts chapter for descriptions of the latter two). Palms and fountains grace the courtyards, which are typically filled with people dining alfresco and soaking up the sunshine. Jazz bands, singers, and other entertainers liven up the mall during the summer months and holiday seasons.

Paseo Nuevo merchants include well-known chains (Victoria's Secret, Gap, Banana Republic, and See's Candy) as well as a few that are unique to Santa Barbara and/or Southern California (for example, This Little Piggy Wears Cotton and Montana Mercantile). There's plenty of parking underneath and adjacent to the mall (enter on Chapala Street) as well as in the city lots on Anacapa and Chapala Streets.

Many Insiders like the small-scale, cozy ambiance of the two-story collection of shops and restaurants at **Victoria Court** in the 1200 block of State Street. The SOhO nightclub is upstairs, and Video Schmideo—with the best selection of foreign films and documentaries in town—is down below. Victoria Court is also home to *The Santa Barbara Independent*, the most popular weekly paper in the county (see our Media chapter). Pick up a croissant and a cappuccino, find a table in the peaceful courtyard, and relax and watch the world go by.

The biggest shopping attraction in Goleta is the **Camino Real Marketplace,** which opened in 1999. Located at the Hollister Avenue/Storke Road intersection, this sprawling "big box" mall introduced the first conglomeration of discount retail outlets to the region. With 83 acres and 3,000 parking spaces, it's also the largest shopping center on the South Coast. Though some residents wince at the increased traffic and loss of open space, most shoppers appreciate the discounted wares now available in our notoriously high-priced region. In addition to well-known stores such as Costco, Staples, Home Depot, Comp USA, Borders Books & Music, and Linens 'N Things, the mall includes restaurants such as Gina's Pizza and The New Baja Grill, a multiplex theater, and baseball fields.

*The Paseo Nuevo Mall offers more than 50 shops and restaurants and a five-screen movie theater.*
PHOTO: SANTA BARBARA CONFERENCE & VISITORS BUREAU

## Unique Santa Barbara Stores

These stores were all founded in Santa Barbara County and offer items you'll have a hard time finding anywhere else.

**As Seen on TV Store**
**1125 State Street**
**Santa Barbara, CA**
**(805) 564-4100**
**www.ontv2u.com**

You saw these items on TV, but until this infomercial store appeared, you couldn't check them out before ordering. The store opened in 1996 and is so popular the owners opened additional stores in Pismo Beach and Ventura. The store sells all the products you see on TV infomercials but at a lower price because it cuts out the shipping and handling fees—and you don't have to wait for delivery.

You can get all the current infomercial products here, plus the most popular and long-running items: unusual gadgets and doodads, kitchenware, hardware, health and beauty products, exercise equipment, audio and video products (including current CDs and videos), and automotive accessories. The store ships nationwide and credit card orders are now accepted over the phone, but it's much more fun to wander in and play with all the gadgets.

**Big Dog Sportswear Factory Outlet**
**6 E. Yanonali Street**
**Santa Barbara, CA**
**(805) 963-8728, (800) 642-DOGS**
**www.bigdogs.com**

As legend tells it, a group of friends conceived of the Big Dog idea in 1983 while on a river-rafting expedition. Everyone in the group received a pair of oversized shorts in vivid colors. Everyone loved the shorts, and one guy supposedly said "Man, these puppies are big!" That timely phrase launched Big Dog Sportswear, right here in Santa Barbara.

The Big Dog name and logo—a black-and-white Saint Bernard with a great big smile and bright red tongue—now appear on casual activewear and accessories for men, women, and children in the company's 140 stores across the United States and in England. Big Dog clothing is also sold through catalogs.

Big Dog's "casual activewear" is the type of clothing Santa Barbarans wear all the time: T-shirts, baggy shorts, and pants form the core of the wardrobe. At the outlet store, which sits on the corner of State and Yanonali Streets just a few blocks up from Cabrillo Boulevard, you can pick up Big Dog items at greatly reduced prices. Big dogs (and little dogs) are also welcome in the store.

**Crispin Leather**
**18 W. Anapamu Street**
**Santa Barbara, CA**
**(805) 966-2510**

For more than 30 years Crispin Leather has supplied Santa Barbarans and visitors from far and wide with top-quality leather goods. They specialize in "comfort footwear," carrying all major brands (e.g., Rockport, Birkenstock, Timberland) plus a few more. Locals shop here for snug sheepskin slippers and quality hiking boots, but Crispin also sells jackets, belts, hats, wallets, purses, keychains, and other items.

**Insiders' Tip**

Check out the latest sales, buy gift certificates, or print coupons at these great new local shopping web sites: www.shoppaseonuevo.com and www.shoplacumbre.com. Both sites are accessible via handheld cell phones and PDAs.

**Insiders' Tip**

For a gallery guide and map of Santa Barbara's antiques shops pick up a copy of *Tour* magazine. It's available at most local antiques stores, the visitor center, and many hotels and bed and breakfast inns.

**Jedlicka's**
**2605 De la Vina Street**
**Santa Barbara, CA**
**(805) 687–0747, (800) 681–0747**
**www.jedlickas.com**

Looking for real cowboy boots and hats? You won't find a better selection than at Jedlicka's. Started by George (Jed) Jedlicka in 1932, this nationally known Western store provides "everything for you and your horse." This is where real ranchers outfit themselves. You'll have a great time looking through the authentic Western clothes; belt buckles; Resistol, Stetson, and Akubra hats; custom-made saddles; and riding equipment for men, women, and children.

**Jordano's Marketplace**
**3025 De la Vina Street**
**Santa Barbara, CA**
**(805) 569–6262**
**1170 Coast Village Road**
**Montecito, CA**
**(805) 565–3001**
**www.jordanosmarketplace.com**

We love wandering through this popular store, wishing we could stock our entire kitchens with the gourmet cookware, appliances, home accessories, glassware, and crystal. In fact, Jordano's is so popular, in 1999 they opened another smaller store in Montecito. Items are pricey, but you can count on top quality and excellent customer service. Parking is plentiful—especially at the main store on De la Vina Street, which also has an espresso bar and a gourmet food section. Many Insiders buy gifts here for weddings, showers, and anniversaries, but bring extra money—you'll probably end up buying something for yourself.

**Magellan's**
**110 W. Sola Street**
**Santa Barbara, CA**
**(805) 568–5400**
**www.magellans.com**

America's leading mail-order source for travel products is headquartered right here in Santa Barbara. You can visit the showroom and view all the unique travel products featured in Magellan's catalogs, from alarm clocks and luggage to rain gear and water filters. Some items are discounted up to 50 percent. The store is closed Sunday.

**Santa Barbara Gift Baskets**
**Victoria Court**
**1221 State Street, #13**
**Santa Barbara, CA**
**(805) 965–1245**
**www.sbgiftbaskets.com**

Tucked in a corner across from the post office in Victoria Court, this small shop specializes in gift baskets featuring locally produced gourmet foods, wines, and gifts. Choose one of the pre-filled baskets such as the "Santa Barbara in a Basket," the "Pamper Me," or the "Gardener's Basket." Or you can custom-design a gift basket with your choice of local goods such as honey, chocolates, wines, olives, marmalades, salad dressings, marinades, notecards, and even shark jerky. Santa Barbara Gift Baskets also carries bath, wedding, and special-occasion gift items year-round, and you can have them delivered locally or shipped nationwide.

**The Territory Ahead**
**515 State Street**
**Santa Barbara, CA**
**(805) 962–5558 ext. 181**
**www.territoryahead.com**

Lots of people know about The Territory Ahead through their popular mail-order catalog. But here in Santa Barbara—the home of The Territory Ahead—you can see the clothes "up-close and personal" and try them on for yourself.

The shop specializes in casual yet classy men's and women's clothing and accessories in unique designs, made from high-quality natural-fiber fabrics and materials. These are the clothes you might wear for a special dinner while on safari or strolling the streets of Taipei. Park behind the store or in one of the city lots on Anacapa and Chapala Streets.

**This Little Piggy Wears Cotton**
**311 Paseo Nuevo**
**Santa Barbara, CA**
**(805) 899–2570**
**www.littlepiggy.com**

This is the type of store grandparents go wild in. The unique, top-of-the-line designer-style clothes for babies, boys, and girls are not inexpensive, but the quality and style are unsurpassed. The imported and domestic toys are also of the highest quality, and most are educational. Thanks to the store's success, the owners expanded and now have five "piggys" throughout California and Arizona plus a "Snoutlet" in Carpinteria (see our Outlets section towards the end of this chapter). This Little Piggy is a great place to shop for baby showers, birthdays, baptisms, and any occasion for which you can muster an excuse to lavish a child with "only the best."

**YES Store**
**Varying locations**
**Santa Barbara**

Can't figure out what to buy for someone who has everything or is hard to please? During the holiday season, Insiders flock to the YES Store. It's an excellent place to shop for unique, high-quality handcrafted items, all created by local artists and craftspeople. Handmade items include jewelry, textiles, pottery, glass, leather, basketry, toys, ornaments, clothing, photography, graphics, engraved rocks—you name it.

The YES Store began in December 1969, when 50 local artists and craftspeople banded together to sell their wares. Now the YES Store is a nonprofit cooperative group and a firmly entrenched Santa Barbara tradition. An elected screening committee holds a juried competition and selects approximately 80 artists to participate each season, which begins in mid-November and lasts through Christmas Eve.

The artisans stock, staff, and manage the store themselves. It's located in a different venue every year; a committee seeks out vacant downtown sites in which to set up displays. To find the current YES Store during the holiday season, check for ads in the *Santa Barbara News-Press* and *The Independent*.

## Antiques

**Antique Alley**
**706 State Street**
**Santa Barbara, CA**
**(805) 962–3944**

This antique collective is jam-packed with all kinds of collectibles and bric-a-brac. The aisles resemble a giant estate sale, with antique furniture, estate jewelry, china, glassware, pottery, fine art, paintings, prints, and vintage clothes.

**Antique Market Place**
**26 E. Ortega Street**
**Santa Barbara, CA**
**(805) 966–5655**

The Antique Market Place focuses on antiques rather than collectibles. You can buy (and sell) jewelry, porcelain, art objects, cut glass, silver, bronze figures, Oriental rugs, paintings, clocks, and dolls. We especially enjoy the ceramic beer steins with faces on them. The store is closed Sunday.

**Brinkerhoff Avenue (between State, W. Cota, W. Haley, and De la Vina Streets)**
**Santa Barbara, CA**

Stroll along this charming street and you can shop for antiques and admire the beautifully restored Victorian cottages at the same time. Brinkerhoff Avenue was named after Samuel Brinkerhoff, Santa Barbara's first physician. All the original Victorian houses still stand, and the city of Santa Barbara has designated Brinkerhoff Avenue as a special historic district. Some of the houses are now charming shops with antiques, wood carvings, collectibles, and/or specialty gifts. Recently, the district has experienced a renaissance as newcomers, like The Gentlemen Antiquarians below, open their doors here.

**The Gentlemen Antiquarians**
**502 Brinkerhoff Avenue**
**Santa Barbara, CA**
**(805) 965–9223**
**812 State Street**
**Santa Barbara, CA**
**(805) 965–5355**

In 2001, The Gentleman Antiquarians closed their Summerland location and opened a new store in an 1895 Victorian-style cottage on charming Brinkerhoff Avenue. Browse the front parlors of their shop/home and you will discover everything from grand pianos, vintage lighting, estate jewelry, and beautiful antique rugs. The store specializes in 18th- and 19th-century European furnishings but you will also find an eclectic mix of English, French, Oriental, and American antiques and accessories, Russian icons, and musical instruments. The State Street store features a sampling of the goods found at the main store. Both stores are open daily from 11 A.M. to 5 P.M.

**Heather House Antiques**
**2448 Lillie Avenue**
**Summerland, CA**
**(805) 565–1561**
**heatherhouse@home.com**

Set in a blue Victorian house with white trim, Heather House specializes in china and silver from Europe and America. It carries china sets, tea sets, silver dinnerware, teaspoons, and serving accessories as well as collections of Lalique and Royal Dalton figurines. Smaller pieces of furniture such as desks and end tables can also be found here. Open Friday through Monday or by appointment.

**State Street Antique Mall**
**1219 State Street**
**Santa Barbara, CA**
**(805) 965–2575**

With 65 dealers operating in the same 7,000-square-foot space, the State Street Antique Mall is one of Santa Barbara's largest antique collectives. It's a great place to find antiques and collectibles, furniture, decorator items, toys, lunchboxes, silver, linens, prints, paintings, jewelry, and vintage clothing. You can also purchase new items such as Crabtree & Evelyn soaps, women's casual clothes, and accessories like silk shawls and beaded bags.

**Summerland Antique Collective**
**2192 Ortega Hill Road**
**Summerland, CA**
**(805) 565–3189**

The 25 dealers who make up this well-organized collective have created a successful and very eclectic enterprise. The store looks as if someone rummaged through their grandmother's attic and put the entire contents up for sale. Among the hundreds of items found here are European and American antiques—especially furniture and accessories, decorative items, and jewelry.

**The Treasure House**
**1070 Fairway Road**
**Montecito, CA**
**(805) 969–1744**

Set on the Music Academy of the West campus, this high-end consignment shop sells "antiques and fabulous things" to benefit the Music Academy of the West. The Treasure House also gladly accepts donations. Open 1:00 to 4:00 P.M. Tuesday through Saturday.

## Bookstores

**Again-Books**
**16-A Helena Avenue**
**Santa Barbara, CA**
**(805) 966-9312**

For more than 20 years this small, general stock shop has sold used books and magazines on a wide range of subjects. It specializes in titles dealing with self-help, children, the Christian faith, and war. Again-Books is at the beach near the lighthouse, just three doors up from Cabrillo Boulevard between State and Anacapa Streets. Wander in and browse here any day of the week but note that the store usually opens after 3:00 P.M.

**Barnes & Noble Booksellers**
**829 State Street**
**Santa Barbara, CA**
**(805) 962-8509**
**www.barnesandnoble.com**

Whether you're looking for a bestseller, a classic, a magazine, or just about anything in print, you're likely to find it at Barnes & Noble, part of the well-known national chain. It's conveniently situated in a corner of Paseo Nuevo Mall, so you can easily pop in and browse the shelves between shopping and dining.

Barnes & Noble has an excellent children's section, an extensive selection of magazines, and a small cafe. The store hosts regular book signings, children's story hours, and special events. Call for information.

**Bennett's Educational Materials**
**Magnolia Shopping Center**
**5130 Hollister Avenue**
**Santa Barbara, CA**
**(805) 964-8998**

Parents, teachers, and anyone looking for quality books, toys, and school supplies will love this store, which has been in business in Santa Barbara since 1972. Bennett's sells a diverse range of children's books, workbooks, teaching resources, developmental toys, posters, and puzzles with an emphasis on educational items. The preschool section is particularly strong. Pop in and have a look. You're sure to find something fun and fascinating for your little ones.

**The Book Den**
**11 E. Anapamu Street**
**Santa Barbara, CA**
**(805) 962-3321**
**www.bookden.com**

The Book Den is Santa Barbara's oldest and best-stocked used bookstore, with 40,000 new, used, and out-of-print books (mostly used). Consistently voted "Best Used Bookstore" in a local poll, this popular store also provides online out-of-print search services. The titles encompass a wide range of subjects, including California history and architecture and books in foreign languages. You can browse the virtual shelves at their web site or wander in and look for yourself. To find the store, just walk across the street from the Museum of Art.

**Borders Books, Music & Cafe**
**900 State Street**
**Santa Barbara, CA**
**(805) 899-3668**
**7000 Marketplace Avenue**
**Goleta, CA**
**(805) 968-1370**
**www.borders.com**

When Bank of America moved across the street in 1996, Borders (of the national chain of superstores) took over the gigantic two-story former bank building. The store was so popular that in 2000, a new store with plenty of parking opened in the Camino Real Marketplace in Goleta. Both are favorite haunts of bibliophiles as well as weary shoppers who venture in to browse the shelves and relax with a coffee after a busy day at the mall.

The larger downtown store carries more than 200,000 book, music, and video titles and around 2,000 periodicals in 10 languages from 15 countries; the new store has a similar selection. Both stores offer a 30-percent discount on their current bestsellers.

## Insiders' Tip

Shopping downtown in Paseo Nuevo with a panting pooch? Stop in at Three Dog Bakery at 727 State Street (805-962-8220). They have a big dog's bowl full of clean cold water as well as lots of tasty fresh-baked treats for your furry friend.

It's sheer delight to wander through the seemingly endless aisles of books, CDs, and videos. Kids race to the well-designed children's sections, which have comfortable sitting areas with cushions and an extensive selection of children's videos as well as books. In the music sections you can listen to an assortment of CDs—from classical piano to the latest *Billboard* hits.

When you buy a cup of coffee in one of the cafes, you can sit down at a table to enjoy it or take it along with you while browsing. Borders also sponsors a busy schedule of children's story hours, book signings, seminars, lectures, and special events. Call for current program information.

**The Chandlery**
**132-B Harbor Way**
**Santa Barbara, CA**
**(805) 965–4538**
**www.chandlery.com**

If you're a sailor or a person looking for maritime books, this is the place to go. Established in 1946, The Chandlery offers an array of fiction and nonfiction books, charts, and maps, all related to boating, sailing, and nautical themes. Looking for a cookbook to take on a cruise or a book on sailing rules, repairing a boat, or tying knots? You'll find them all here, plus expert staff members who can point you to the exact books and charts you need.

The Chandlery overlooks the Santa Barbara Harbor, between the Yacht Club and Brophy Brothers restaurant.

**Chaucer's Books**
**Loreto Plaza**
**3321 State Street**
**Santa Barbara, CA**
**(805) 682–6785, (805) 682–4067**
**www.gtesupersite.com/chaucerbooks**

Insider bibliophiles rank Chaucer's as the best independent bookstore in town. It has a huge selection of titles—all stacked sky-high on shelves, floors, and any available space in the relatively small quarters. Chaucer's has extremely knowledgeable staff, an incredibly diverse selection of books, an outstanding children's section, and regular book signings by famous authors. The store is in Loreto Plaza, at the intersection of Las Positas Road and State Street.

**Front Page**
**5737 Calle Real**
**Goleta, CA**
**(805) 967–0733**

This small bookstore offers a great selection of magazines, newspapers, popular paperbacks, current bestsellers, maps, cards, and stationery. You'll also find postcards and a few children's titles.

**Isla Vista Bookstore**
**6553 Pardall Road**
**Santa Barbara, CA**
**(805) 968–3600**
**www.ivbooks.com**

Conveniently situated just down the road from UCSB, Isla Vista Bookstore is a complete off-campus college store. It primarily sells used textbooks and educational paperbacks, but also offers clothing and art and school supplies.

**Lost Horizon Bookstore**
**703 Anacapa Street**
**Santa Barbara, CA**
**(805) 962–4606**

Lost Horizon buys, sells, and appraises single copies and entire libraries of antiquarian books and maps. It has hundreds of books on the fine and decorative arts, monographs on artists, pencil-signed prints, paintings, and photographs. The store is particularly strong in California history and Western Americana.

**Metro Entertainment**
**6 W. Anapamu Street**
**Santa Barbara, CA**
**(805) 963–2168**

This shop seems to have every type of comic book published. It carries a full line of them, including Japanese animation, children's, and independents. It also has games, toys, and TV and movie merchandise and memorabilia.

**Pacific Travellers Supply**
**12 W. Anapamu Street**
**Santa Barbara, CA**
**(805) 963–4438, (888) PAC–TRAV**
**www.pactrav.com**

From books and maps to luggage and accessories, this store offers everything a traveler could want. Pacific Travellers Supply is best known for its excellent maps—its parent company is MAPLINK, the largest map wholesale distributor in the country. Whether you're going to Antarctica, the North Pole, or Mozambique, you can order a map of your destination through this store.

**Pacifica Graduate Institute Bookstore**
**249 Lambert Road**
**Carpinteria, CA**
**(805) 969–3626 ext. 121**
**www.pacifica.edu/bookstore**

Pacifica Graduate Institute offers advanced-degree programs in psychology and mythology (see our Education and Childcare chapter for more information on the school). Its bookstore carries more than 20,000 titles related to psychology, mythology, religion, and philosophy in ancient cultures and other cultural traditions. It also has tapes, cards, music, videos, drums, images, and jewelry.

The campus is between Summerland and Carpinteria; take the Padaro Lane exit, go south on Via Real, turn left on Lambert Road, and head toward the mountains.

**Paperback Alley Used Books**
**5840 Hollister Avenue**
**Goleta, CA**
**(805) 967–1051**

For more than 20 years, Paperback Alley has bought and sold thousands of fiction and nonfiction books, mostly paperbacks. The store carries more than 50,000 titles, so you're bound to find something you like at a very affordable price.

**Paradise Found**
**17 E. Anapamu Street**
**Santa Barbara, CA**
**(805) 564–3573**
**www.paradise-found.net**

If you're into metaphysics, you'll find paradise here in the form of metaphysical books, gifts, jewelry, incense, tapes, compact discs, and astrology charts. Listen to music, savor the incense, and watch the colored lights bounce through crystals. You'll soon be transported to a blissful spiritual realm.

**The Read 'N Post**
**1046-B Coast Village Road**
**Montecito, CA**
**(805) 969–1148**

An entire wall of The Read 'N Post is devoted to magazines of all types and sizes. The store also carries a wide selection of newspapers, maps, and paperbacks. Buy a magazine or paper, drop off your mail (there's a post office here), then head next door to Starbucks for a cup of coffee—that's what many Montecitans do every day.

**Sullivan Goss Books & Prints, Ltd.**
**7 E. Anapamu Street**
**Santa Barbara, CA**
**(805) 730–1460**
**www.sullivangoss.com**

Sullivan Goss boasts one of the largest selections of books on the fine and applied arts, architecture, and photography in the world. It buys and sells new, rare, and out-of-print books on architecture, art history, and photography as well as artists' biographies and catalogues raisonnés.

Artists, collectors, gallery owners, and art lovers all shop here regularly. The store also offers vintage and contemporary paintings, prints, and photographs by California artists.

The Arts and Letters Cafe, situated in a beautiful courtyard at the back of the store, provides excellent gourmet meals and classical music entertainment (see our Restaurants chapter for details).

**Tecolote Book Shop**
**1470 E. Valley Road**
**Montecito, CA**
**(805) 969–4977**

When it first opened for business in 1925, Tecolote was a carriage-trade bookstore—the staff would bring books to the carriage to show the customers. Today the small, intimate Tecolote remains a favorite bookstore among Insiders. Choose from a diverse selection of books, and pay extra attention to the many unusual art and coffee-table books, especially those on Montecito and Santa Barbara history.

Tecolote sits on the edge of a green lawn with a fountain in Montecito's Upper Village, an ideal spot to rest, read, and regroup.

**UCSB Bookstore**
**University Center**
**UCSB**
**Santa Barbara, CA**
**(805) 893–3271**
**www.bookstore.ucsb.edu**

Conveniently located on campus in the University Center, the UCSB Bookstore is a hot spot for students, teachers, and faculty members, and it's open to the public, too. The store specializes in academic support materials but you can also stock up on computer software, greeting cards, UCSB sweatshirts, gifts, and school and office supplies. To avoid a crowd, check out the scene at the shop by logging onto the web site, which has cameras that let you see the bookstore lines live. Closed Sunday.

**Valley Book & Bible**
**1200 State Street**
**Santa Barbara, CA**
**(805) 884–5166**
**www.vbb.com**

Part of a small, 40-year-old Southern California chain, Valley Book & Bible is a nondenominational Christian bookstore. It stocks books, bibles, magazines, software, T-shirts, videos, jewelry, gifts, and music for all Christian faiths. It's closed Sunday.

**Vedanta Book Shop (Sarada Convent Books)**
**925 Ladera Lane**
**Montecito, CA**
**(805) 969–5697**

Part of the Vedanta Temple, this religious bookstore offers an impressive variety of books covering all major religions, including Buddhism, Hinduism, Native American religions, Islam, and Sufism. It also has a huge selection of deity statues, for example Kuan Yen (a goddess of compassion), Buddha, and traditional Christian statues, santos, and angels.

## Farmers' Markets

**Santa Barbara Certified Farmers' Market Association**
**(805) 962–5354**

*Sunset Magazine* selected the Santa Barbara Farmers' Market as one of the "Top 10 Farmers' Markets in the West." It was started in 1973 by a handful of Santa Barbara growers who sold their produce at the Mission Rose Gardens. Now it's a nonprofit association with more than 200 growers.

The farmers' markets are great sources of fruits and vegetables (many are organic or not sprayed with pesticides), flowers, nuts, eggs, seafood, and plants. They're also fun places to browse and people-watch. Bring lots of change and small bills as well as sacks or baskets in which to haul your purchases.

The association currently sponsors the following local markets:

**Downtown Santa Barbara Market** (this is the largest and most popular one) is at the corner of Santa Barbara and Cota Streets and is open Saturday from 8:30 A.M. to 12:30 P.M.

**Old Town Santa Barbara Market,** in the 500 and 600 blocks of State Street, is open Tuesday from 3:00 to 6:30 P.M. (4:00 to 7:30 P.M. during the summer).

**Goleta Market,** in the 5700 block of Calle Real, is open Thursday from 3:00 to 6:30 P.M. (3:00 to 7:00 P.M. during the summer).

**Montecito Market** (Coast Village Market) is in the 200 block of Coast Village Road and is open Friday from 8:00 to 10:30 A.M.

**Carpinteria Market,** in the 800 block of Linden Avenue, is open Thursday from 3:00 to 6:30 P.M. (4:00 to 7:00 P.M. during the summer).

**Santa Barbara Fishermen's Market**
**Santa Barbara Harbor at the Breakwater**
**(805) 965–9564**

You can't get fish much fresher than this unless you catch it yourself. The market is usually held every Saturday from 7:30 to 11:30 A.M. at the harbor's main dock. You can only buy whole fish, so be prepared to feed a crowd or freeze what you don't eat. Take your fish to the adjacent Fish Market (run by the same association) at 117-F Harbor Way, and they'll filet your fish; fees are $1 for rockfish, $3 for halibut and $5 for tuna.

**Insiders' Tip**

The farmers' markets are the best places in Santa Barbara to buy fresh flowers.

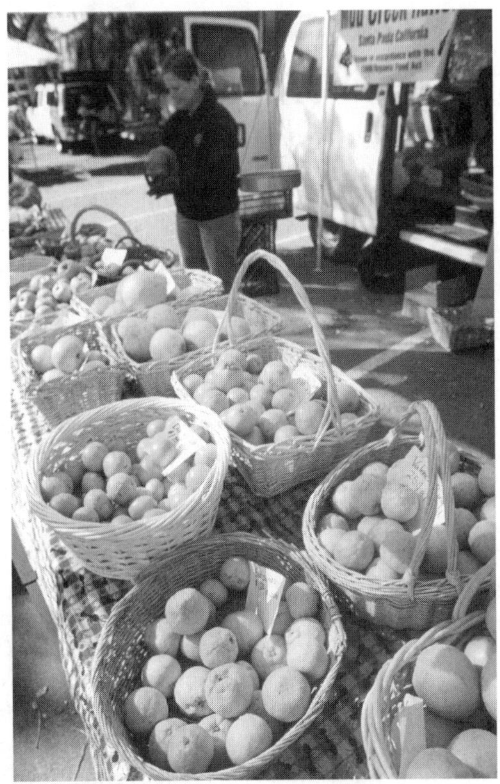

*A wide variety of fresh fruit tempts shoppers at the Old Town farmers' market.* PHOTO: BRIAN HASTINGS

If you're not an early bird or if it happens to be a day of the week other than Saturday, you can still purchase the association's fresh fish at the aforementioned Fish Market, which is open daily.

## Garden Delights

**Garden Market & Deli**
**3811 Santa Claus Lane**
**Carpinteria, CA**
**(805) 745–5505**

Zairean papaya, passionflower, and Persian mulberry are just some of the exotic plants you'll find at this charming new store. From the front it resembles a fruit market with its baskets of avocados, papayas, and mangoes, but wander in and you'll find a cute little cafe, gourmet gifts, and a courtyard nursery. Looking for a

CLOSE-UP

## A Garden of Eden for Organic Shopping

Organic foods, fiber, and other items are produced without chemical pesticides and fertilizers. They are also minimally processed without artificial ingredients, preservatives, or irradiation. Thirty years ago, the word "organic" was a term most people only heard in college chemistry classes. Many people considered the trend toward "natural" foods that started in the 1970s a fad, and an expensive one at that.

Today, however, statistics prove that the trend did not fade away along with bell bottoms and paisley shirts. Packaged Facts, a market research firm, estimates that organic food sales in the United States were $7.8 billion in 2000, a 20-percent increase over 1999 sales. It also reports that sales for organic products have grown steadily at a compound annual growth rate of 22 percent from 1996 through 2000. According to the industry publication *Organic and Natural News*, this trend is set to continue. Organic food sales could reach $20 billion by 2005. More people than ever are buying organic products because they are concerned about their own or their family's personal health, as well as the health of the Earth's ecosystems.

In health-conscious Santa Barbara, shopping for organic products is a firmly entrenched ritual for thousands of residents. Many people go out of their way to shop at supermarkets and produce stands stocked with natural and organic products. A few of the organic fruit and vegetable stands have been around for years. But the increasing interest in natural foods has spawned several new markets, as well as lower prices due to competition. This has all been great news for residents, who can now choose from many shops and stands rather than having to drive all over town just to find a head of organically grown lettuce.

Prices for organic foods are definitely dropping—one local market, for example, lowered its price for a half-gallon of organic milk by nearly a dollar after a supermarket chain began to offer the same brand of milk at a much lower price.

When shopping for organically grown produce in Santa Barbara (or anywhere in California for that matter), you should look at the labeling so you know what you're getting. Produce sold as organic in California must carry a label that states it was "grown in accordance with the California Organic Foods Act of 1990." The California Organic Foods Act defines what food can be legally marketed as organic in California. However, this label alone doesn't mean the food is "certified organic," which has stricter terms. If a label says "certified organic," it tells you that the product has been verified as organically grown by an independent third party.

If a grower is a member of the California Certified Organic Farmers (CCOF), that's a good sign. CCOF-certified produce meets standards beyond those set by California law. CCOF growers undergo annual farm inspections, must document all crop and soil additives and keep complete records. Watch for the CCOF label or ask the store or produce stand manager for documentation.

Also, be aware that some fruits and vegetable signs may say "no spray" or "pesticide free." This labeling means that the edible parts of the crop have not been sprayed with pesticides—but they could have been grown using synthetic fertilizers, insecticides, and fungicides.

*Organically grown produce is very popular with health-conscious Santa Barbarans.* PHOTO: KAREN BRIDGERS

If you're on the hunt for health foods, you'll be happy to know that Santa Barbara boasts an array of natural foods stores and fruit and vegetable stands. Here's a rundown of some of the best and brightest:

For convenient one-stop shopping, go to **Lazy Acres Market,** at 302 Meigs Road (near the intersection of Cliff Drive) in Santa Barbara (805–564–4410). Lazy Acres carries high-quality organic produce, grains, and dairy products, as well as all-natural (haven't been pumped with hormones or antibiotics) fish, poultry, and meats, a deli counter, a bakery, and all the usual things you would expect at a supermarket.

**Lassen's Health Foods,** at 5154 Hollister Avenue in Goleta's Magnolia Shopping Center (805–683–7696), and **Tri-County Produce Co,** at 335 South Milpas Street in Santa Barbara (805–965–4558) also offer a range of organic and natural products, but not fresh meats, fish, or poultry.

Our weekly farmers' markets are great places to find fresh organic produce (see the "Farmers' Market" section of this chapter). You can also stop in at the following stands—most are open daily: **Fairview Gardens Farms,** 598 North Fairview Avenue, Goleta (805–967–7369); **Lane Farms Green Stand,** 308 Walnut Lane, off Hollister Avenue, Goleta (805–964–3773); **Lane Farms-San Marcos Gardens,** 4950 Hollister Avenue, Goleta (805–964–0424); and **Mesa Produce,** 1905 Cliff Drive, Santa Barbara (805–962–1645).

## Insiders' Tip

If you're heading out to the farmers' market, take a big basket or bag. It's easier to carry all the fresh fruit and vegetables in one large carrier than to juggle a bunch of plastic bags.

gift for the gardener in your life? Take a peek in the gardening shed out back, where you'll find books, gloves, accessories, and gift baskets.

**Pan's Garden**
**2360 Lillie Avenue**
**Summerland, CA**
**(805) 969–6859**

Even if you're not a gardener, you'll love wandering through Santa Barbara's most unique nursery and garden and gift shop. It boasts an eclectic collection of plants, fountains, and garden ornaments and accessories, including hundreds of Tibetan statues, prayer flags, candles, and much more.

**Santa Barbara Botanic Garden**
**1212 Mission Canyon Road**
**Santa Barbara, CA**
**(805) 682–4726 ext. 127**
**www.sbbg.org**

The Garden Growers Nursery at the Botanic Garden is a great source for native California and Mediterranean plants. It's staffed by volunteers from 10:00 A.M. to 3:00 P.M. daily and is open on a self-serve basis during the garden hours (see Attractions). You can also shop for books, crafts, gift items, cards, and posters at the garden shop, which is open daily during Botanic Garden hours.

**Santa Barbara Orchid Estate**
**1250 Orchid Drive**
**Goleta, CA**
**(805) 967–1284**
**www.sborchid.com**

More than 100 varieties of orchids are in bloom at any given time at the 5-acre Orchid Estate, home of a vast selection of rare and exotic orchids from all around the world (including a large variety of cymbidiums). A stroll through the grounds will surprise and delight the senses. You can purchase orchid plants and bulbs as well as cut flowers, and all can be shipped anywhere in the U.S. The estate also hosts an Orchid Fair on the third weekend of July; more than 50 growers from around the world display their prized specimens.

## Outlet Stores

**Italian Pottery Outlet**
**19 Helena Street**
**Santa Barbara, CA**
**(805) 564–7655**
**www.italianpottery.com**

Less than a block up from the beach, between State and Anacapa Streets, is the largest selection of Italian ceramics in the western United States. You can buy all sorts of pottery firsts and seconds, from Sicilian folk art to classic designs, for up to 50 percent off retail prices. The store also carries other gift items from Italy, including Murano glass, jewelry, and garden accessories.

**Santa Barbara Ceramic Design**
**436 East Gutierrez Street**
**Santa Barbara, CA**
**(805) 966–3883**
**www.sbceramic.com**

Since 1976, this wholesale factory outlet has been dressing up homes and gardens nationwide with colorful ceramic art.

Bestsellers are the cheery address plaques and switch plates, but the store also sells other items such as clocks, doorbells, platters, plates, and coffee cups. This is a great place to shop for gifts. You can buy pieces decorated with in-house designs or with work by famous licensed artwork such as Disney's Classic Pooh and Beatrix Potter. Themed collections tailored to different areas of the country are also being developed, so you can pick up personalized gifts for faraway friends and relatives.

**Snoutlet**
**901 Linden Avenue**
**Carpinteria, CA**
**(805) 684–0462**

Love the designer children's wear sold at This Little Piggy Wears Cotton stores but wince at the price tags? Head to the "Snoutlet," where you'll find last season's stock at 50 to 90 percent off retail. See the This Little Piggy Wears Cotton entry in the "Unique to Santa Barbara" section earlier in this chapter. Note too that the toys here are sold at regular prices. Closed Monday.

**The Territory Ahead Outlet Store**
**419 State Street**
**Santa Barbara, CA**
**(805) 962–5558 ext. 185**

This outlet store carries discontinued and discounted clothing and accessories—the same stuff you see in Territory's regular store a block up State Street, only a few months later and a lot cheaper. Expect discounts of 30 to 80 percent. Some of their bestsellers are seconds sold at cost—especially leather goods such as shoes and jackets. See the store description in the "Unique to Santa Barbara" section earlier in this chapter.

## Skates and Skateboards

**Church of Skatan**
**336 Anacapa Street**
**Santa Barbara, CA**
**(805) 899–1586**

If you're obsessed with skateboarding or snowboarding, you'll be totally at home in this unusual shop. It provides top-quality equipment for hard-core skateboarders and snowboarders, including a large selection of shoes. There are no roller skates or in-line skates at this store (if you're looking for those items, see the following listing).

**A Skater's Paradise**
**537 State Street**
**Santa Barbara, CA**
**(805) 962–2526**

This mainstream, family-oriented store offers everything you need for skating. It sells roller and in-line skates, accessories, skateboards, clothing, backpacks, safety gear, and videos.

## Surf and Beachwear

If you want to look like a Santa Barbara Insider, you should wear the proper attire: shorts, T-shirts, sandals, bathing suits, hats, and sunglasses. Go to any of these shops and ask the staff for guidance—they'll be glad to deck you out in Santa Barbara style.

**A-Frame Surf**
**3785 Santa Claus Lane**
**Carpinteria, CA**
**(805) 684–8803**

Run by two local brothers, this new surf shop opened in 2000 on Santa Claus Lane. Heading for the waves and need some equipment? You can rent surfboards, body boards, wetsuits, fins, and skim boards here, and surfing lessons are available year-round. The store also sells short boards from local designers such as Progressive and Clyde Beatty as well as some hard-to-find smaller lines of surf and beachwear for men, women, and children. You'll also find Patagonia outdoor clothing and a great variety of women's sarongs.

**The Beach House**
**10 State Street**
**Santa Barbara, CA**
**(805) 963-1281**

Santa Barbara's quintessential beach store sells long and short surfboards, boogie boards, beachwear, and accessories. If you want to learn more about surfing, check out the books, videos, and the antique surfboards. The store also runs a great summer surf camp for kids. (See our Kidstuff chapter).

**The Bikini Factory**
**2275 B Ortega Hill Road**
**Summerland, CA**
**(805) 969-2887**
**www.bikinifactory.com**

The Bikini Factory is a funky little store just off the freeway exit in Summerland that has been saving women from the bathing suit blues for more than three decades. It has a fantastic selection of swimsuits and casual clothes for all ages and sizes. You can mix and match bikini tops and bottoms, and the store does alterations, so you'll find a suit that fits no matter what your dimensions. The Bikini Factory also manufactures its own line of Summerland Water Company swimwear, so you're sure to find something here that you won't see anywhere else.

**Channel Island Surfboards**
**29 State Street**
**Santa Barbara, CA**
**(805) 966-7213**
**www.cisurfboards.com**

Tourists and surf experts shop at Channel Islands Surfboards. The store specializes in high-performance short boards, but you can find a huge variety of surfboards here, all designed by Al Merrick, one of the best board designers and shapers in the surfing industry. You can also choose from a good selection of wetsuits, shirts, shorts, sundresses, and sandals.

**Surf Country**
**Calle Real Center**
**5668 Calle Real**
**Goleta, CA**
**(805) 683-4450**

Surf Country is a complete surf and beach shop, with a great selection of surfboards, wetsuits, skateboards, and beachwear for children and adults. You'll also find clothes, watches, sunglasses, hats, and accessories, and the staff is happy to dispense information about the best surf and beach spots. Surf Country rents soft and hard surfboards, snowboards, body boards, and wetsuits for $25 a day ($10 for each additional day). Surfing lessons are also available.

## Women's Clothing

**Angel**
**1221 Coast Village Road**
**Montecito, CA**
**(805) 565-1599**
**www.wendyfoster.com**

At Angel you'll find a hand-picked selection of hip clothes and accessories from small designer labels. Montecito darlings shop here for special events, but the store stocks everything from bikinis, jeans, and trendy sportswear to chic evening dresses and accessories.

**Montana Mercantile**
**Paseo Nuevo**
**811 State Street**
**Santa Barbara, CA**
**(805) 962-2494**

We know many husbands who shop here for anniversaries and birthdays because they're guaranteed to get something their wives will like. The casual, graceful, unstructured clothing looks great and feels comfortable. Montana Mercantile also sells home accessories, jewelry, and gifts.

**Patty Montana**
**5726 Calle Real**
**Goleta, CA**
**(805) 683-2733**

At Patty Montana you'll find a great selection of casual contemporary attire including dresses, separates, jackets, sweaters, and jewelry. The store offers a wide range of colors and styles and has now added lingerie to its collection.

**Pierre Lafond-Wendy Foster**
**833 State Street**
**Santa Barbara, CA**
**(805) 966-2276**
**516 San Ysidro Road**
**Santa Barbara, CA**
**(805) 565-1502**
**www.wendyfoster.com**

The clothes in this upscale boutique reflect Santa Barbara's casually elegant style. The store stocks sportswear as well as dressier outfits from small labels—stuff you can't usually find in other stores. It's very expensive, but the quality is high and the subdued colors and classic designs seem to stay in style. Guys, this is another great shop to buy gifts for the lady in your life. Or, if you can't decide, buy a gift certificate and give the gift of guilt-free shopping.

# Attractions



Santa Barbarans love showing visitors around their beautiful home. When you come here, you'll see why. For such a relatively small town, Santa Barbara offers an amazing diversity of things to see and do. Explore the region and you'll discover nationally acclaimed museums, rare wildlife sanctuaries, stunning gardens, fascinating historical sights, informative tours, and an exciting lineup of ocean adventures. Look around you. Chances are many of your fellow explorers are locals, who unabashedly proclaim that they'd rather spend their vacation discovering their own city than jet off to some exotic locale.

Of course the locals have "been there, done that," but they know that new exhibits, expansions, and upgrades make Santa Barbara attractions worth visiting again and again. The zoo, for example, has a long list of new exhibits, including the Channel Islands Fox exhibit, the Aquarium Complex, and Lorikeet Landing; two more projects—Cats of Africa and Wings of Asia—are in the works. The continual changing and upgrading of existing attractions, along with the addition of new ones (such as the multimillion dollar Maritime Museum), are why many Santa Barbarans are happy to spend their vacations at home.

If you're a history buff, you'll be pleased to know that most of the city's historical sights lie within a short stroll from each other in the downtown area. You can explore them in a couple of hours by taking the self-guided Red Tile Walking Tour (see entry in this chapter), which begins at the County Courthouse, one of Santa Barbara's most famous landmarks.

If you're more interested in some seaside fun, head for Stearns Wharf and the Santa Barbara Harbor, where you can go for a stroll in the crisp sea air, grab some fresh seafood, and browse the specialty shops.

Tired of trying to see it all on your own? Let someone else show you around on a special tour by trolley, limousine, private car, or van. (We have listed a few of the best-known sightseeing tour companies towards the end of this chapter.) Most will customize itineraries to suit your particular interests.

Finally, to save you time, we've crafted a few itineraries featuring "must-do" Santa Barbara attractions. Flip to the end of this chapter and you'll find suggestions for one-, three-, and five-day stays. Use them as a guide. If you have a particular passion not covered in these suggestions, you can supplement or substitute them with other activities covered elsewhere in this book.

Attractions outside the greater Santa Barbara area are discussed in our Daytrips chapter, which covers destinations both north and south of the city. But we think you'll find enough right here to keep you happily occupied for quite a long time. Enjoy!

## Cultural Attractions

**Arlington Center for the Performing Arts**
**1317 State Street**
**Santa Barbara, CA**
**(805) 963-4408**

The Arlington Center is one of Santa Barbara's most beloved performance venues, and both its name and its location speak volumes about Santa Barbara history. In 1875 the tony Arlington Hotel occupied the current site of the Arlington Center. The hotel was a magnet for the rich and famous of the day, including several presidents, movie stars, military heroes, and foreign guests.

*The Arlington Center for the Performing Arts is set in an elaborate, Moorish-style, 1930s movie palace.* PHOTO: ROY NORTHCUTT—DEE WELSCH—TERRELL FOSS

In 1909 a fire of undetermined origin burned the hotel to the ground. A "new" Arlington was built on the site, but it never quite lived up to the original and was razed in 1925. In 1931, an impressive Moorish-style building was erected on the site by Fox West Coast Theatres as a movie palace. That historic structure is now occupied by the Arlington Center for the Performing Arts.

The seats on the main floor of the elaborate theater provide the illusion of being under an open sky in the central courtyard of a Spanish village. Slanted tile roofs, arched doorways, and balconies surround the perimeter, and above the rooftops are mountain vistas and twinkling stars arranged as they might appear in the night sky. So realistic is this scene that Santa Barbarans have often been able to convince a newcomer that this is indeed an outdoor theater-under-the-stars.

These days, in addition to featuring first-run films, the Arlington is home to the Santa Barbara Symphony and hosts a plethora of other special events, many under the auspices of the Community Arts Music Association. No formal tours are offered, and the theater is open regularly to the public only during the screening of movies or other public events. Plan to go early so you can explore a bit before the lights go down.

**Karpeles Manuscript Library Museum**
**21 W. Anapamu Street**
**Santa Barbara, CA**
**(805) 962-5322**
**www.rain.org/~karpeles/sbfrm**

A small museum dedicated to historical documents, the Karpeles has a significant collection of rare manuscripts from such authors as H. G. Wells, Mark Twain, Sir Arthur Conan Doyle, and John Steinbeck. In addition, the Karpeles has historical documents from the fields of history, music, science, and art, including works by Einstein, Darwin, and Newton. Since the Karpeles family's acquisitions are rather staggering, exhibits change periodically, so you may see new documents each time you visit. Occasionally, the museum hosts special events such as a past exhibition on Anne Frank and the rise of Hitler. The museum is open daily from 10:00 A.M. to 4:00 P.M. Admission is free.

**Santa Barbara Museum of Art**
**1130 State Street**
**Santa Barbara, CA**
**(805) 963-4364**
**www.sbmuseart.org**

One of the top 10 regional museums in the country, the Santa Barbara Museum of Art has permanent collections of Asian, American, and European art, including works by such well-known artists as Eakins, Monet, Chagall, Picasso, and O'Keefe. It opened a stunning new wing in 1998. See our chapter on The Arts for more details.

## Historic Places and Historical Museums

**El Paseo**
**15 E. De la Guerra Street**
**Santa Barbara, CA**
**(805) 965-0093**
**www.sbthp.org**

Spanish Colonial Revival-style architecture is shown off beautifully in El Paseo, a small shopping complex (reportedly California's first "shopping center") built in the 1920s around the historic De la Guerra adobe. The adobe was built between 1819 and 1826 by Jose de la Guerra y Noriega, who was, at the time, commander of El Presidio de Santa Barbara. De la Guerra and his wife, Doña Maria Antonia, raised 12 children here, and the house was the social center of Santa Barbara for years.

The wedding reception of De la Guerra's daughter, Anita, took place at Casa De la Guerra in 1836 and was described in Richard Henry Dana's book, *Two Years Before the Mast.* The adobe house was restored by the Santa Barbara Trust for Historic Preservation and opened as a museum in March 1998. The museum is open noon to 4:00 P.M. Thursday through Sunday. Admission is free, but donations are appreciated. The recently restored casa contains furniture and artifacts of the era.

The rest of the El Paseo complex includes shops, galleries, and restaurants. The charming Old World courtyard is a fabulous spot for lunch. Browsing is free anytime at El Paseo, but most shops and galleries don't open until 10:00 A.M. The main entrance is on the 800 block of State Street, but it's also accessible from De la Guerra and Anacapa Streets.

**El Presidio de Santa Barbara State Historic Park**
**123 E. Canon Perdido Street**
**Santa Barbara, CA**
**(805) 966-9719**
**www.sbthp.org**

Sitting incongruously in the middle of bustling downtown Santa Barbara is a nearly block-long complex of stark adobe buildings that represent the city's beginnings. Founded in 1782 by Lieutenant Jose Francisco de Ortega, the Royal Presidio was the last military outpost of the Spanish Empire in the New World.

An ongoing restoration process by the Santa Barbara Trust for Historic Preservation has preserved the spirit of the place. The bell tower that was destroyed by an earthquake in the 19th century was recently replaced, along with two huge bells, one of which is believed to be the original Presidio Bell rung by Father Junipero Serra at the first mass said here in 1782. (See our History chapter for more information.) The careful restoration makes it easy to imagine the Spanish padres sitting in their sparsely furnished quarters or Santa Barbarans of 200 years ago worshipping in the Presidio Chapel, reconstructed on its original foundations.

Also of note here is El Cuartel, the guard's house. It is the oldest building in Santa Barbara and the second oldest in the state of California.

Visits to the site are self-guided, although groups may call to arrange a

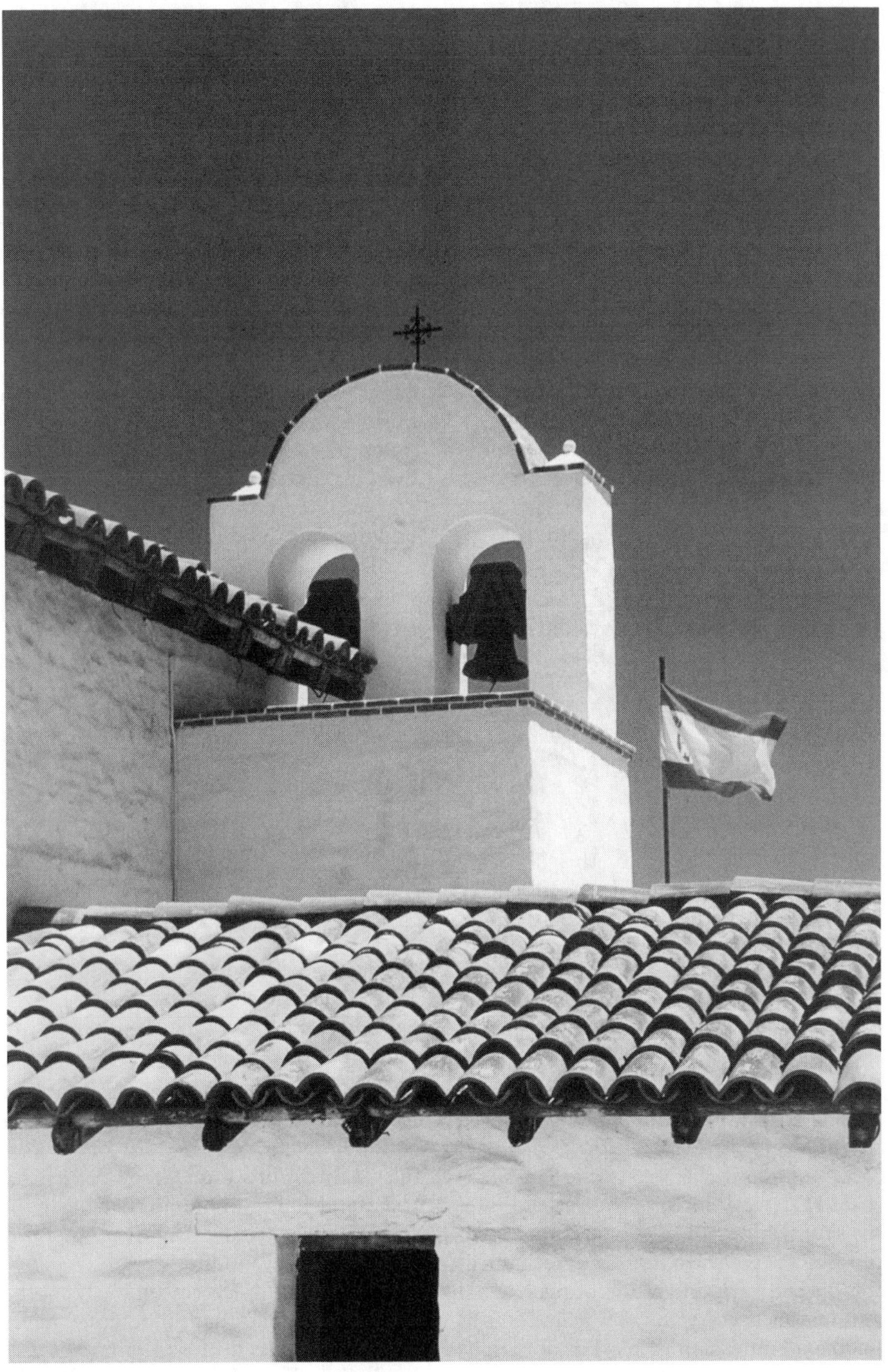

*El Presidio's newly restored bell tower is graced by what is thought to be one of the original bells rung during the first mass here in 1782.* PHOTO: BRIAN HASTINGS

### Insiders' Tip

The restored chapel bells at El Presidio de Santa Barbara State Historic Park, the birthplace of Santa Barbara, chime every day at noon. If you want the honor of ringing them, call (805) 965-0093. Everyone is welcome.

docent-led tour. A 15-minute slide show is well worth seeing, and a scale model of the Presidio offers a detailed look at life in Spanish California. The Presidio is open every day from 10:30 A.M. to 4:30 P.M. Admission is free.

**Fernald Mansion**
**414 W. Montecito Street**
**Santa Barbara, CA**
**(805) 966-1601**

Situated next door to the Trussell-Winchester Adobe (see subsequent entry), the 14-room Fernald Mansion is one of just a few Victorian homes preserved in Santa Barbara. An example of the traditional "gingerbread" Victorian, the gabled mansion was built in 1826 by local lawman Charles Fernald for his wife, Hannah.

The mansion was originally located on lower Santa Barbara Street but was moved to the Montecito Street address, where it is now a museum operated by the Santa Barbara Historical Society. The Fernald family's furnishings and personal effects are of interest, as are the hand-carved ornamentation, staircase, and wainscoting.

It's open every Sunday from 2:00 to 4:00 P.M. Admission is free, but donations to the Santa Barbara Historical Society are appreciated.

**Lobero Theatre**
**33 E. Canon Perdido Street**
**Santa Barbara, CA**
**(805) 963-0761**
**www.lobero.com**

When Jose Lobero set out to build his dream opera house in Santa Barbara, he had the financial backing and the necessary artistic flair, but he made a mistake when he chose the neighborhood.

When the opera house opened on February 22, 1873 (with the premiere performance of an opera written by Lobero), Santa Barbarans came in droves. But soon business fell off due to the venue's proximity to Chinatown's opium dens and brothels. Eventually, Lobero lost the theater and committed suicide, and the building was razed in 1923.

The elaborate Spanish-style theater that occupies the site today was built in 1924 and named in Lobero's honor. It currently serves as home to the Santa Barbara Chamber Orchestra and the Santa Barbara Grand Opera, and as the venue for countless other community events and performances. The neighborhood's just fine these days, so buy yourself a ticket and be there when the doors open to give yourself some time to get a sense of the place. Tours are available by appointment only.

**Mission Santa Barbara**
**2201 Laguna Street**
**Santa Barbara, CA**
**(805) 682-4713**

Known as the "Queen of the Missions" for its beauty and hilltop setting, Mission Santa Barbara was the 10th of California's 21 missions founded by Franciscan friars and is the only one that has been continuously occupied by the Franciscan order since its founding.

Dedicated on December 16, 1786, the mission complex has undergone many changes since its humble beginnings as a small chapel and living quarters for missionaries and Chumash Indians. In December 1812, a major earthquake nearly leveled the chapel and surrounding

> **Insiders' Tip**
>
> To see some authentic relics from Santa Barbara's Spanish period, wander across the road from the Mission Church. Starting on the corner of Alameda Padre Serra and Mission Canyon Road, and continuing up Mountain Drive, you'll find ruins of the old waterworks and adjacent structures built by the Chumash Indians in the early 1800s.

buildings. The present pink sandstone church—with one bell tower—was constructed around the old chapel and dedicated in 1820. The second bell tower was added more than a decade later.

In 1925, the mission suffered the shock of another major earthquake, and the towers and living quarters had to be repaired and reinforced. The building remained intact until the years following World War II, when deterioration called for complete reconstruction of the mission facade, which was done in the early 1950s.

Reportedly inspired by a drawing of a church designed by the Roman architect M. Vitruvius Polion in the first century B.C., Mission Santa Barbara, with its thick adobe walls, tiled roof and floors, and open courtyards, has strongly influenced the architectural style of the city. Inside, rooms are preserved in the style of the 1700s, with artifacts and displays relating to early mission life.

The self-guided tour includes eight rooms, the cloister gardens, the chapel, the cemetery, and the beautiful Moorish fountain and courtyard. A gift shop near the entrance sells religious items and educational materials on Santa Barbara and the California missions. For a moment of quiet reflection after your tour, wander down to the beautiful Mission rose gardens. You can also explore the ruins of the old Mission aqueduct built by the Chumash Indians in 1806—just wander across the street from the church. Mission Santa Barbara is open seven days a week from 9:00 A.M. to 5:00 P.M. Admission is $4 for adults, free for children 12 and younger.

**Old Spanish Days Carriage Museum**
**129 Castillo Street**
**Santa Barbara, CA**
**(805) 962–2353**

When Santa Barbara's historic carriages and stagecoaches are not making their annual appearance in the Old Spanish Days parade (see our Annual Events chapter), they're housed at this museum, which contains one of the most extensive collections of antique carriages in the country.

You'll see a variety of horse-drawn carriages (sans the horses, of course), many owned by early Santa Barbara families and restored by the museum. The museum also houses an impressive collection of saddles, a horse-drawn fire truck, an antique hearse, and an old wine cask cart.

The Carriage Museum is open Monday through Friday from 8:00 A.M. to 3:00 P.M. and Sunday from 1:00 to 4:00 P.M. There is no admission fee, but a donation to the nonprofit museum is appreciated.

**Painted Cave**
**Off Calif. Highway 154 on Painted Cave Road**
**Santa Barbara, CA**

A remnant of the culture of the Chumash Indians, Santa Barbara's first residents, has been preserved in this ancient 22-foot-deep cave, which contains brightly colored pictographs from pre-Columbian times. Unfortunately, the other Stone Age artifacts found in the cave—including arrowheads, axes, and baskets—were removed by unscrupulous marauders in the 1870s. The rock paintings remain intact, now protected by a locked metal screen.

The cave is on the edge of the road, but you have to look carefully or you'll drive right by. Watch for the sign on Painted Cave Road off E. Camino Cielo Road.

**Red Tile Walking Tour**
**Downtown Santa Barbara**
**(805) 965–3021**

Called the "Red Tile Tour" because of the red-tiled roofs you will see on Santa Barbara's oldest buildings, this 12-block, self-guided excursion provides a great opportunity to brush up on local history. Turn to the Downtown Santa Barbara map at the beginning of this book, then start your tour at the Santa Barbara County Courthouse.

Along the way, you'll see some of the oldest adobes in Santa Barbara in addition to the Historical Museum, El Presidio de Santa Barbara State Historic Park, and the architecturally interesting Public Library, Main Post Office, Museum of Art, and Lobero Theatre. The walk concludes back at the courthouse, and if you time it just right, you can take in a guided courthouse tour as well.

You can embark on the free walking tour anytime, but check the hours of the historic parks and museums to make sure they'll be open when you come by, and be aware that some of them charge for admission.

**Santa Barbara County Courthouse**
**1100 Anacapa Street, at Anapamu Street**
**Santa Barbara, CA**
**(805) 962–6464**

Hundreds of historic courthouses grace this fair country, but it would be difficult to find another as stunning—both inside and out—as the Santa Barbara County Courthouse, a magnificent Spanish-Moorish structure that is one of the most photographed landmarks in the city.

Completed in 1929 (fortuitously just before the stock market crash), the ornate structure features handpainted ceilings, a spiral staircase, wrought-iron chandeliers, imported tiles, carved doors, and beautiful historical murals.

Outside, spacious lawns and swaying palm trees surround the building, set off by a unique sunken garden. In the words of Charles H. Cheney, who in 1929 wrote the preface to *Californian Architecture in Santa Barbara,* "romance ran riot" in the courthouse, an assessment that was not altogether a compliment, as Cheney deemed it too large and overdone to "belong" to what he viewed as the low-key, intimate style of the city.

Still, Cheney acknowledged the "extraordinary number of intriguing bits of design" found both inside and outside the structure, and it is these unique features that continue to draw visitors more than 70 years after the building was completed.

Free hour-long guided tours are offered Monday through Saturday at 2:00 P.M., with an additional 10:30 A.M. tour on Monday, Tuesday, and Friday, or you can wander around on your own. Be sure to go to the top of the 80-foot clock tower, which affords a panoramic view of the city. The courthouse is open weekdays 8:00 A.M. to 5:00 P.M. and weekends 10:00 A.M. to 5:00 P.M., but the doors close to new visitors at 4:45 P.M. Admission is free.

**Santa Barbara Historical Museum**
**136 E. De la Guerra Street**
**Santa Barbara, CA**
**(805) 966–1601**

Art, textiles, furniture, clothing, and other artifacts from Santa Barbara's rich, multicultural past have been preserved in this complex of adobe structures under the auspices of the Santa Barbara Historical Society. Step back in time as you view the collected remnants of the area's Spanish, Mexican, and American periods, or stroll the inner courtyard, which seems far removed from the busy streets that surround the museum and adjacent historical adobes (including Casa Covarrubias, constructed in 1817). You can browse on your own (all exhibits are carefully labeled) or take a guided tour, offered Wednesday and Saturday at 11:30 A.M. and Sunday at 1:30 P.M.

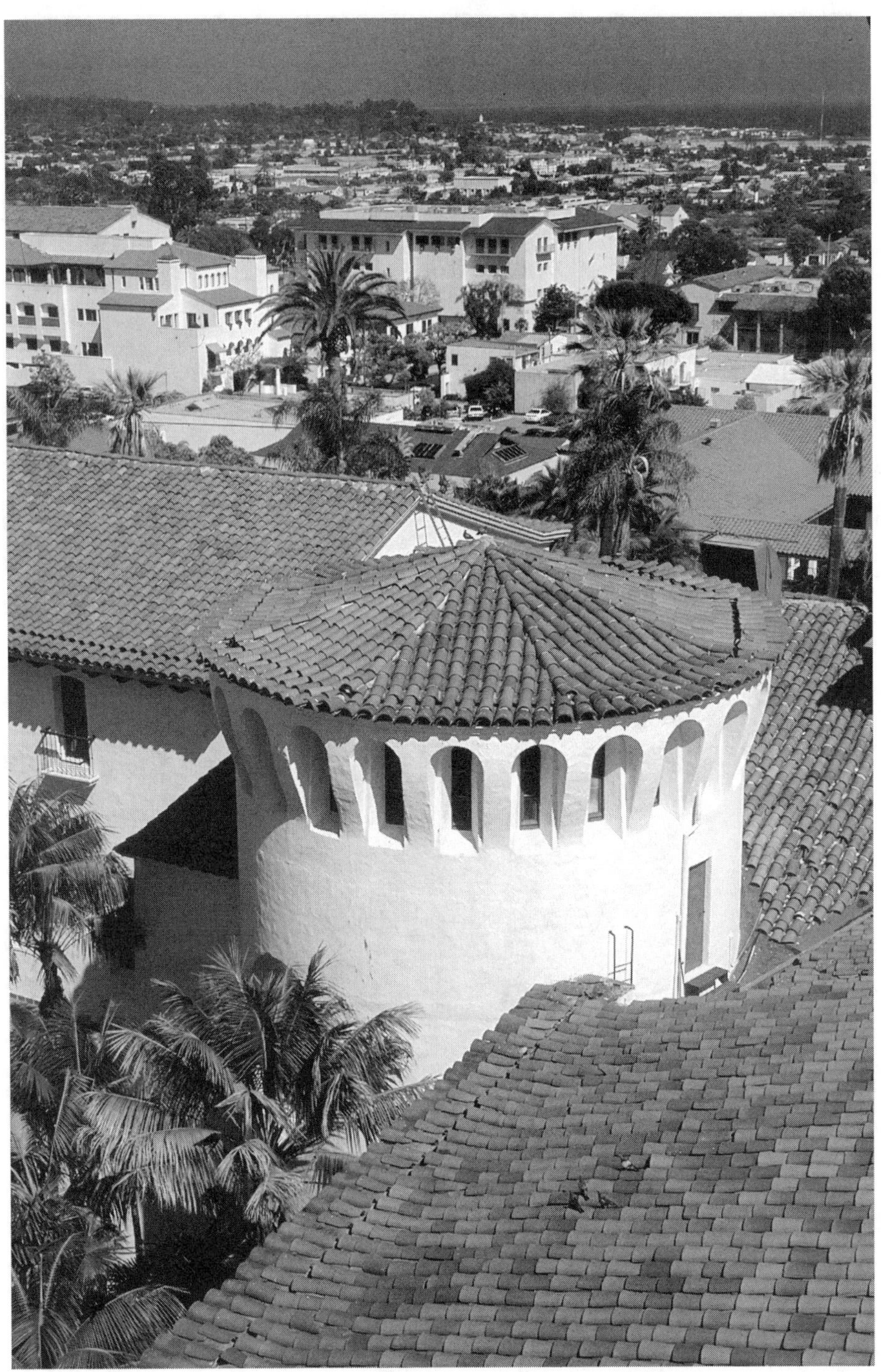

*The Red Tile Walking Tour takes its name from the roofs of some of Santa Barbara's oldest buildings.*
PHOTO: BRIAN HASTINGS

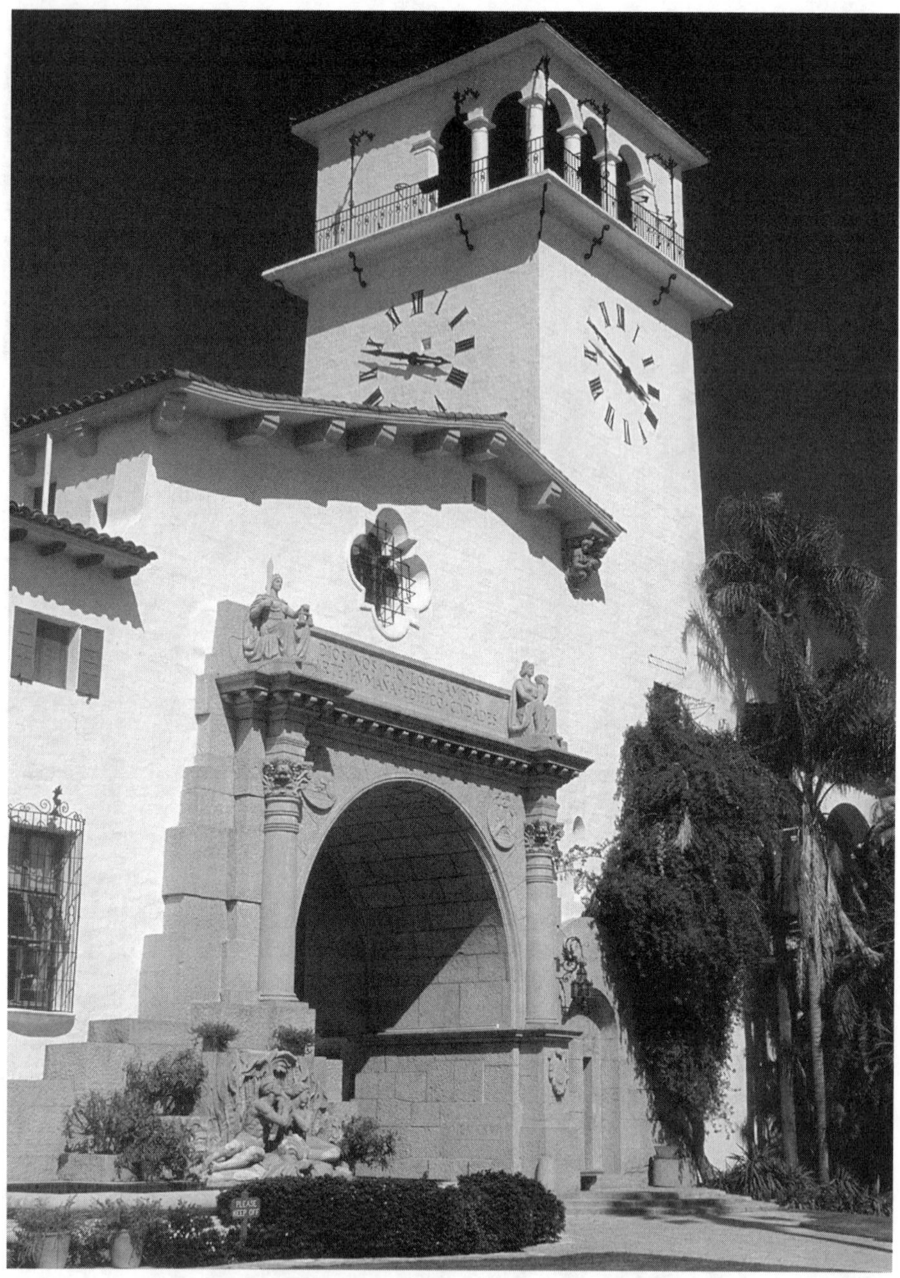


*Opened in 1929, the Spanish-Moorish Santa Barbara County Courthouse is considered one of the greatest public buildings in America.* PHOTO: BRIAN HASTINGS

The Gledhill Library, on the museum grounds, houses an impressive collection of books, maps, and photographs chronicling Santa Barbara's history. It's open to the public 10:00 A.M. to 4:00 P.M. Tuesday through Friday and 10:00 A.M. to 1:00 P.M. the first Saturday of the month. (An hourly library research fee is charged for persons who are not members of the Historical Society.)

The museum is open Tuesday through Saturday from 10:00 A.M. to 5:00 P.M. and Sunday from noon to 5:00 P.M. Admission is free, but a donation is appreciated. If you can't find a parking space on the adjacent street, watch for the small driveway next to the museum on De La Guerra Street; there are parking spaces in back.

**Trussell-Winchester Adobe**
**412 W. Montecito Street**
**Santa Barbara, CA**
**(805) 966–1601**

In 1853, the sidewheel steamer *Winfield Scott* sank off Anacapa Island. The ship's captain, Horatio Trussell, salvaged a ridge pole from its mast as well as other useful timber and brass and used the objects along with adobe bricks in the construction of this home, built in 1854. Later the home was occupied by Dr. Robert F. Winchester, a local physician, until his death in 1932.

Now under the auspices of the Santa Barbara Historical Society, the home is a small museum that includes period furnishings and other items used by the Trussell and Winchester families. The museum welcomes visitors every Sunday between 2:00 and 4:00 P.M. If you would like to arrange a group tour at another time, call the Historical Society at the listed number to make a reservation. Admission is free, but donations are appreciated.

## Local Landmarks and Outdoor Attractions

**Moreton Bay Fig Tree**
**Chapala Street at U.S. Highway 101**
**Santa Barbara, CA**

The Moreton Bay Fig Tree (and yes, everyone in Santa Barbara knows exactly which tree you are talking about when you say "the" Moreton Bay Fig Tree) was planted on July 4, 1876, by a young girl who had been given the seedling by a sailor fresh off the boat from Australia. A year later, when the girl moved away, she gave the little tree to a friend, who transplanted it to its current location. The rest, as they say, is history.

The tree is now huge (some say it is the largest specimen of Ficus macrophylla in the country), and it has had quite a life here in the fertile soil of Santa Barbara. In the 1930s, the tree was nearly cut down to make way for a gas station until Pearl Chase (read all about her in the Close-up in our History chapter) put a stop to that nonsense.

In 1961, the Parks Department measured the tree and announced that more than 16,000 people could stand in the shade beneath the 21,000 square feet covered by its outstretched branches. In the 1970s it was a home of sorts to the city's homeless people, who camped on the lawn until they were finally evicted. In 1982, it was declared a city landmark.

In recent years, the venerable tree underwent some special treatment to ensure that it continues to flourish. Both the Santa Barbara Parks Department and the Historic Landmark Commission approved the installation of a chain barrier to keep people at a distance (branches have been broken by climbing children, and people have carved their initials in the trunk). Interpretive signs tell you about the tree and politely ask that you admire it from afar.

The Moreton Bay Fig Tree is always open, and there is no admission fee. Bring your camera.

**Santa Barbara Harbor and Breakwater**
**Entrance at Harbor Way, off Cabrillo Boulevard west of Castillo Street**
**Santa Barbara, CA**

You'll find everything from rowboats to expensive yachts tied up at the harbor, which is nestled inside a protective breakwater. Watch the boats come in, observe sailboarders offshore, browse the shops, or visit one of the harbor's restaurants. The breakwater, constructed in 1924, is paved and wide enough to accommodate you, your friends, and a baby stroller, so go for a walk!

**Insiders' Tip**

A walk along the flag-lined breakwater at the Santa Barbara Harbor is a welcome diversion for Santa Barbara residents and visitors alike. Be careful, however, when the surf is high. More than one unsuspecting person has been doused when waves crashed over the wall. (It's not dangerous—just wet and cold.)

Wednesday through Sunday, weather permitting, colorful flags line the breakwater until sunset, with each flag representing one of Santa Barbara's service organizations.

At the east end of the harbor is SEA Landing, where the seagoing *Condor* departs for whale-watching excursions and Truth Aquatics' three boats anchor (see our Beaches and Watersports chapter). The harbor is open every day, and there is no admission price for exploring.

**Stearns Wharf**
**State Street and Cabrillo Boulevard**
**Santa Barbara, CA**

When Santa Barbara lumberman John Stearns completed his namesake pier in 1872, he could hardly have imagined that more than 100 years later it would be the most visited landmark in town. For decades after its completion (it was then the longest deep-water pier between Los Angeles and San Francisco), the wharf was used for loading and unloading freight and passengers, but in 1941 The Harbor Restaurant was built, marking the beginning of the wharf's transition into a tourist attraction. Today its seaside location, restaurants, shops, and festive atmosphere draw visitors by the thousands. Limited parking (including valet parking) is available on the wharf itself, or you can park in the nearby public lots on Cabrillo Boulevard and walk the half-mile to the end of the pier.

As you enter, stop for a look at the Dolphin Fountain, formally known as the Santa Barbara Bicentennial Friendship Fountain, which was created by local artist Bud Bottoms in 1982 under the sponsorship of the Santa Barbara/Puerto Vallarta Sister City Committee. A replica of the fountain has been installed in all of Santa Barbara's sister cities, including Puerto Vallarta, Mexico; Toba, Japan; and Yalta.

Continuing on, you'll find several excellent restaurants (this is the place to get really great seafood), and shops selling confections, souvenirs, and sportswear. The Sea Center is on the pier, as is the embarking point for harbor cruises and parasailing. You can even do a little wine tasting here! Stearns Wharf is always open, and there is no admission fee.

## Natural Attractions and Science Museums

**Santa Barbara Botanic Garden**
**1212 Mission Canyon Road**
**Santa Barbara, CA**
**(805) 682–4726**
**www.sbbg.org**

In 1926, rather than see a pristine Santa Barbara canyon turned into a housing development, Anna Blaksley Bliss snapped up the land and declared it a botanical preserve in memory of her father, Henry Blaksley.

Today the 65 acres that make up the Santa Barbara Botanic Garden provide a superb setting for the study of native California flora. More than 5 miles of trails meander along the banks of upper Mission Creek and through the garden's meadows and canyons, which are planted with wildflowers, cacti, oak, sycamore trees, and more than 1,000 species of rare and indigenous plants. There's an entire section devoted to flora found on the

*The Santa Barbara Bicentennial Friendship Fountain (a.k.a. the Dolphin Fountain) stands at the entrance to Stearns Wharf.* PHOTO: BRIAN HASTINGS

Santa Barbara Channel Islands as well as a forest of redwood trees and display areas on the California desert and mountains.

"The garden" is best dressed in spring, when the wildflowers are in bloom, but it's the perfect spot for a peaceful stroll (or an invigorating hike) at any time of year. Although most plants are labeled, you may find it helpful to take a one-hour, docent-led tour, offered daily at 2:00 P.M. and also at 10:30 A.M. on Thursday, Saturday, and Sunday.

Of special interest to history buffs is the sandstone dam that spans Mission Creek near the redwood grove. Built in 1806 by Chumash Indians to harness irrigation water for nearby grain fields, the structure remains intact. The gift shop has a particularly good collection of botanical books and offers handcrafted items for sale. The Home Demonstration Garden is dedicated to teaching groups and individuals about using and caring for California native plants in Southern California gardens. One of the garden's biggest events is its fall plant sale held each October (see our Annual Events chapter).

The Botanic Garden is open 9:00 A.M. to 4:00 P.M. weekdays and 9:00 A.M. to 5:00 P.M. weekends. From March though October, hours are extended to 5:00 P.M. weekdays and 6:00 P.M. weekends. Admission is $5 for adults; $3 for seniors 60 and older, teens 13 through 17, and students with current ID; and $1 for children ages 5 through 12. Children younger than 5 are admitted free. Dogs on leashes are welcome.

**Santa Barbara Maritime Museum**
**Harbor Way**
**Santa Barbara Harbor**
**Santa Barbara, CA**
**(805) 965–8864**
**www.sbmm.org**

Opened in the summer of 2000, this impressive multimillion dollar tribute to the sea is a treat for the whole family. The museum displays fascinating military history exhibits, model ships, fishing and diving equipment, antique instruments,

CLOSE-UP

# Suggested Itineraries

Can't choose from all the attractions in this chapter? To save you time, we've listed our recommendations for one-, three-, and five-day stays. If you're visiting, use these itineraries as a guide—you can tweak them to suit your interests and time limits. If you live here, they might come in handy when friends and family visit.

Need transportation? See our Getting Here, Getting Around chapter. You can also read the individual listings in this chapter for more details on each attraction. So pack your sunglasses and camera, slather on the sunscreen, and enjoy!

## Snapshot

Only have one day in paradise? The following itinerary will give you a taste of Santa Barbara's history, shopping, architecture, and waterfront.

- Visit the beautiful Mission Santa Barbara, "Queen of the Missions." Take the self-guided tour through the museum, cloister gardens, cemetery, and chapel. If you have time, stop to admire the roses in the beautiful Mission rose garden.
- Bike, bus, or drive downtown to State Street. Stroll amid the fountains and flowers of Paseo Nuevo Shopping Mall. Then wander four blocks up State Street, browsing the specialty shops and quaint Spanish-style paseos along the way (see our Shopping chapter).
- Enjoy an alfresco lunch in a street-side cafe. Continue up State Street (about three blocks) to Anapamu Street. Turn right, walk one block to Anacapa Street, and you'll see the magnificent Santa Barbara County Courthouse on the right-hand corner. Take a self-guided or docent-led tour (see the listing in this chapter) then climb up the clock tower and enjoy the panoramic views.
- Bike, bus, or drive to Stearns Wharf. Browse the gift shops and Sea Center or sample some wines in the ocean-view tasting room. Bike or stroll a quarter of a mile west along the beachfront bike path to the Santa Barbara Harbor. (If you have time, visit the Maritime Museum.) Sip a cocktail at a waterfront restaurant (see our Restaurants chapter) and/or enjoy a fresh seafood dinner while you gaze out at the sunset and the silhouetted yachts.

## Short and Sweet

A three-day stay captures the contrast between Santa Barbara's coastal attractions and the quiet countryside of the Santa Ynez Valley. You can mix and match these activities and swap the days depending on the weather. Remember, if it's foggy on the coast, it's usually warm and sunny in the wine country.

### Day One

See the Snapshot itinerary above.

### Day Two

Consider renting a limousine so you can sip your way through the Santa Ynez wine country in style (and safety). If you're driving, take San Marco Pass over the mountains and into the valley. Linger for lunch in small-town Los Olivos or the quaint Danish village of Solvang. Then follow the Foxen Canyon Wine Trail through the oak-studded countryside, stopping to sample some wines along the way. (See our Santa Barbara Wine Country chapter.)

### Day Three

Weather permitting, board a whale-watching cruise. In the winter, you can see migrating gray whales; in the summer, blue whales, humpbacks, and minkes. (See our Beaches and Watersports chapter.)

*And/or*

Follow the self-guided Red Tile Walking Tour (see the individual listing in this chapter and the map at the front of this book). If you did the *Snapshot* tour you can skip the Courthouse but be sure to stop at the Santa Barbara Historical Museum, El Presidio de Santa Barbara State Historic Park, El Paseo, and the Art Museum.

## Stay a While

Ocean, islands, history, shopping, architecture, and the arts are all covered in our five-day stay.

### Days One to Three

Follow the *Short and Sweet* itinerary.

### Day Four

Explore the Santa Barbara Zoo, Museum of Natural History, and/or the Santa Barbara Botanic Gardens.

### Day Five

Take the scenic drive (see the map at the front of this book) and explore the affluent neighborhoods of Montecito and Hope Ranch.

*or*

Sail a yacht or charter a plane to the rugged Channel Islands. Spend the day hiking the Nature Conservancy Trails, diving the kelp forests, or kayaking around the sea caves and rocky coves. (See our Channel Islands chapter.)

*In summer Stearns Wharf draws thousands of visitors.* PHOTO: JOHN B. SNODGRASS

rare artifacts, and historical photos. After reading about life on the sea, visitors can experience it through a host of fun interactive exhibits. Spy through a real submarine periscope and see a 360-degree view of the harbor, learn to sail a yacht, experience a simulated dive, take a virtual submarine ride under the channel, and then "catch the big one" at the sport-fishing exhibit. Shaped like a ship's hull, the 86-seat Munger Theater presents documentaries on nautical topics such as the America's Cup, El Niño, and deep-sea archeological expeditions and adventures. After your visit, browse the gift shop for maps, nautical books, clothing, toys, and gifts. The museum is open Wednesday through Sunday from 11:00 A.M. to 5:00 P.M. Admission is $5 for adults; $3 for seniors, students, and kids ages 6 to 17; and $1 for children ages 1 to 5. Families of five or more pay only $15. There's no charge for children under 1 and members. For membership information, contact the museum.

**Santa Barbara Museum of Natural History**
**2559 Puesta del Sol Road**
**Santa Barbara, CA**
**(805) 682–4711**

Tucked inconspicuously among the oaks in Mission Canyon, the Santa Barbara Museum of Natural History is thought by many to be one of the most beautiful small museums in the country. Founded in 1916 on the banks of Mission Creek, the low-roofed, Spanish-style structure includes several exhibit halls dedicated to the study of California and Santa Barbara County natural history.

Your adventure begins outside the entrance, where the magnificent 72-foot skeleton of a blue whale provides a perfect photo op. Pass through the entrance into a quaint courtyard, then follow the signs to the areas that interest you most.

The museum is a treasure trove of Chumash Indian artifacts (don't miss the baskets and the full-scale model of a Chumash canoe) and features small but impressive exhibits on mammals, birds, insects, reptiles (stop by the Lizard Lounge to visit live critters), gems and minerals, plants, and marine life. Kids love pushing a button to make a coiled rattlesnake's tail "rattle," and creating waves with the hands-on wave machine is a favorite diversion in the marine life exhibit hall.

In addition to its many permanent attractions, the museum offers a dynamic schedule of special exhibits and events for the whole family (see our Kidstuff chapter for details on activities of interest to children).

Gladwin Planetarium, on the grounds, features a changing lineup of programs reflecting the seasonal skies or other astronomical happenings and invites you to bring the whole family to survey the night sky through its high-powered telescope (dress warmly!). The museum gift shop sells books, jewelry, and lots of cool stuff for kids.

The museum is open 9:00 A.M. to 5:00 P.M. Monday through Saturday and 10:00 A.M. to 5:00 P.M. Sunday and holidays. Admission is $7 for adults; $6 for teens 13 through 17 and seniors 65 and older; and $4 for children ages 2 through 12. Admission is free to all on the last Sunday of each month. There's a nominal charge in addition to the museum admission fee for planetarium shows: $2 for adults and $1 for seniors 65 and older and children 12 and younger.

**Santa Barbara Zoological Gardens**
**500 Niños Drive**
**Santa Barbara, CA**
**(805) 926–5339, (805) 962-6310, recorded information**

Zoos and kids seem made for each other (and indeed, this one is amply discussed in our Kidstuff chapter), but the Santa Barbara Zoo is such a charming place that we think it's worth a visit whether you have the kids in tow or not. To begin with, there's a fabulous ocean view from its grassy hilltop, which is believed to have once been the site of a Chumash Indian camp.

Long after the Chumash were gone, a grand mansion was built on the hill and was the centerpiece of a 16-acre estate. The original home was built by John Beale in 1896, but after his death in 1914, his widow, Lillian, married John Child, and the property became known as the Child Estate. After Mr. Child's death, the land was presented to the Santa Barbara Foundation, which in turn transferred management to the Child Estate Foundation.

In 1962, the land was cleared, making way for the very humble Child Estate Zoo, which opened in August 1963. A llama, two sheep, a goat, a turkey, and a pair of spider monkeys were the only inhabitants of the new zoo, but the community had a vision of what the zoo could become and set about making it a reality. In 1972, the zoo joined the American Zoo and Aquarium Association and has continued its development in keeping with the AZA's goals and objectives. In 1981, the zoo was accredited by the AZA—a status it currently maintains.

Over the years, Santa Barbara's zoo has added an impressive number of new animals and exhibits, and it continues to be dedicated to preserving a high-quality environment for both visitors and the zoo's permanent residents. More than 700 animals currently reside at the zoo, which attracts more than a half-million visitors every year, many of them longtime Santa Barbarans who go back often to see what's new.

Some of the most recent additions include the Channel Island Fox exhibit; the Aquarium Complex, home to freshwater stingrays, a Malayan water monitor, and small sharks; and Lorikeet Landing, where you can buy a cup of nectar and hand-feed these brilliantly colored parrots. New additions in the works include the Cats of Africa and Wings of Asia exhibits. One of the most popular exhibits is the Karisoke Research Outpost, a replica of Dian Fossey's gorilla research station in Rwanda, which overlooks the zoo's gorilla compound. Inside, you'll find information on gorilla conservation efforts and habitat preservation.

**Insiders' Tip**

Don't walk too far on Stearns Wharf without stopping to turn around. The view toward the mountains is breathtaking and quintessentially Santa Barbara. Add a sunset and you have the perfect setting for a romantic stroll.

You can easily "do the zoo" in a few hours, but if you have kids you may want to make a day of it. Don't miss Max, the male silverback gorilla, the giraffe with the kinky neck (no, it doesn't hurt), the elephants, and the monkey island. And a stop at the gift shop is a must. The zoo is open every day (except Thanksgiving and Christmas) from 10:00 A.M. to 5:00 P.M., with ticket sales ending at 4:00 P.M.

Admission is $8 for adults, and $6 for children ages 2 through 12 and seniors 60 and older; tiny tots are admitted free of charge. A year's family membership is $60; it entitles you to a quarterly newsletter, discounts on education programs and at the Gift Shop, and free admission to dozens of other zoos across the country (including the Los Angeles Zoo). Parking is $2 per vehicle and free for members.

**Sea Center**
**211 Stearns Wharf**
**Santa Barbara, CA**
**(805) 962–0885**

Operated by the Santa Barbara Museum of Natural History, the Sea Center is the city's "window on the Santa Barbara Channel." Unfortunately, it closed at the end of 2001 for an 18-month renovation. But the good news is that the new and improved Sea Center, slated to reopen in summer 2003, will be more than double its former size with a fascinating collection of hands-on exhibits. Call for more information.

**Whale-Watching**

Whale watching in the Santa Barbara Channel is one of the most popular family recreational activities in town. Several local companies offer trips from December through April, when California gray whales migrate along the coast, and from June through September, when blue and humpback whales come to feed in the channel. For details, see our Beaches and Watersports chapter.

## Goleta

**South Coast Railroad Museum and Goleta Depot**
**300 N. Los Carneros Road**
**Goleta, CA**
**(805) 964–3540**
**www.goletadepot.org**

The Goleta Depot, built in 1901, has been restored on this site, adjacent to the Stow House (below). The museum is very small, but includes railroad memorabilia, photos, and a 300-foot model railroad. Movies are screened in the theater room. You can send a telegraph or climb aboard the real caboose displayed on tracks outside.

A big draw is the miniature train that circles the grounds and offers rides Wednesday and Friday between 2:00 and 3:45 P.M. and Saturday and Sunday between 1:00 and 3:45 P.M. (see the Kidstuff chapter for details on train rides and birthday parties at the museum). A small museum shop sells gifts and educational materials with a railroad theme. The museum is open 1:00 to 4:00 P.M. Wednesday through Sunday. Admission is by donation.

**Stow House**
**304 N. Los Carneros Road**
**Goleta, CA**
**(805) 964–4407**

The Stow House, a restored Victorian home built in the 1870s, is the oldest frame home in Goleta and is filled with furniture, clothing, kitchenware, and other items from the period. Its interior is especially charming when adorned for Christmas. A blacksmith's shop and other small outbuildings have also been preserved.

The grounds are lovely, with various exotic plantings (many labeled) and a wide expanse of shaded lawn that is often used for special events such as weddings, an annual Fourth of July celebration, and other community events. Lake Los Carneros, a small artificial lake located east of the house, is a popular site for walking or birding.

The Stow House is open for 30-minute guided tours 2:00 to 4:00 P.M. Saturday and Sunday; it's closed in January. A $2 donation is requested.

## Montecito

**Lotusland**
**695 Ashley Road**
**Montecito, CA**
**(805) 969–9990**
**www.lotusland.org**

Lotusland is one of Santa Barbara's rarest and most unique gems. You have to do some planning in order see it, but you will never forget your visit. Overseen by the Ganna Walska Lotusland Foundation, the 37-acre estate is named for the sacred Indian lotus, which was planted there in the early 1890s by nurseryman R. Kinton Stevens.

In 1941, the estate was purchased by well-known Polish opera singer Mme. Ganna Walska, who shaped Lotusland into what it is today: a series of breathtaking theme gardens filled with rare botanical specimens that delight the eye and renew the spirit.

Your two-hour guided tour will take you through an imaginative Theatre Garden displaying 16th-century German and Viennese sculptures of dwarves and hunchbacks; the delightful Blue Garden, planted with blue fescue, blue Atlas cedars, and blue Mexican fan palms; a breathtaking Aloe Garden, with its centerpiece Shell Pond lined with abalone and South Sea Island giant clam shells; a forest of dragon trees from the Canary Islands; a serene Japanese Garden; and the second-finest collection of rare cycads in the world, including 11 of the 12 genres.

Other highlights include a working horticultural clock, a 12th-century baptismal font, and topiary, fern, palm, and succulent gardens. This is far more than an interesting tour for garden buffs; it is an invitation to the fascinating world of Mme. Walska and her botanical wonders. Don't miss it. Tours are conducted Wednesday through Saturday at 10:00 A.M. and 1:30 P.M. from mid-February to mid-November.

Reservations can be made up to a year in advance; call between 9:00 A.M. and noon Monday through Friday to book. The reservation office is open year-round.

The cost is $15, and visitors must be 10 or older. Becoming a member of Lotusland ($50 a year) entitles you to some flexibility in reserving a tour time and includes two free admission passes. Call (805) 969–3767 for information on membership.

## Carpinteria

**Carpinteria Harbor Seal Colony**
**Below Carpinteria Bluffs**

Carpinteria is home to one of only two publicly accessible harbor seal colonies in Southern California. To see these fascinating creatures, hike a half-mile down the spectacular bluff-top trail at the southern end of Bailard Avenue. You'll see the viewing area perched on a bluff just before the Venoco pier. For more information, see the Close-up in the Parks chapter.

**Carpinteria Valley Museum of History**
**956 Maple Avenue**
**Carpinteria, CA**
**(805) 684–3112**

Although it may not have the glamour of Santa Barbara, Carpinteria is a delightful little city with deep historical roots. Its small museum depicts the lives of Carpinteria's earliest residents, with exhibits on the Chumash Indians, the city's pioneer families, and its agricultural history.

Furniture, clothing, farm tools, and other historical artifacts are on display, along with exhibits on oil production, a turn-of-the-century schoolhouse, and a quilt depicting local historical events.

The museum is open 1:00 to 4:00 P.M. Tuesday through Saturday. Admission is by donation.

**Insiders' Tip**

Adobe is the Spanish word for a sun-dried brick and for the clay soil used to make such a brick. Santa Barbara's best-known historical adobe dwelling is Casa de la Guerra in El Paseo.

## Sightseeing Tours

**Blue Sky Tours**
**204 Moffett Place**
**Goleta, CA**
**(805) 564–1811, (800) 977–1123**

See the city aboard a limousine, minibus, or town car. Blue Sky offers a wide range of tours, including a two-hour Santa Barbara Magic tour; the Montecito Medley, which takes you past the elegant homes of local celebrities and other landmarks; the Sunset Extravaganza; and the Santa Barbara County Wine Tour. Prices vary according to the type of vehicle and size of the party. A variety of other specialty tours are also available, so call for complete details and prices.

**Personal Tours, Ltd.**
**(805) 685–0552**

You get just what you'd expect from this well-established Santa Barbara company, which offers affordable in-depth private tours with a personal touch. Choose one of the prepackaged tours or custom design a tour to suit your own special interests, be they estates and gardens, natural history, fine arts, real estate, photography, or shopping. Local specialty tours include a wine-tasting tour to the Santa Ynez Valley, and a three-hour Santa Barbara Tour that explores the history, architecture, and horticulture of the region. Looking for a whole day adventure? Take the six-hour package that includes walking tours of the County Courthouse and the Old Mission plus lunch. Tours are priced according to the duration of the trip and the vehicle used but range from $95 for a basic tour in your own car to $350 for a basic coach tour. You can also choose from sedans, convertibles, custom vans, and minibuses. Charter tours to out-of-town attractions such as Hearst Castle, Big Sur, and Los Angeles events are also available, and international language tours can be arranged with advance notice. If you don't find your dream tour on the list, call Personal Tours, Ltd., and they'll assist you in designing an itinerary. Vehicles are equipped for the physically challenged and all tours require reservations in advance.

**Santa Barbara Old Town Trolley**
**120 State Street**
**Santa Barbara, CA**
**(805) 965–0353**
**www.sboldtowntrolley.com**

Hop aboard the 30-passenger Santa Barbara Trolley for a 90-minute narrated tour of the city, including drive-bys of major tourist attractions.

Montecito, the Moreton Bay Fig Tree, downtown Santa Barbara, and the County Courthouse are included in the tour, and there's a 15-minute stop at Mission Santa Barbara so you can stretch your legs and get a closer look.

This is the only scheduled stop, but there are five tours daily, and you can get off and explore on your own anytime you want, then get back aboard when another trolley comes by. Even if you opt to stay on for the full 90 minutes, you'll have all the information you need to strike out on your own after the ride.

The trolley operates seven days a week, with tours departing from Stearns Wharf at 10:00 and 11:30 A.M. and 1:00, 2:30, and 4:00 P.M. Admission is $12 for adults and teens and $7 for children 12 and younger.

**Spitfire Aviation**
**204 Moffett Place, Suite P**
**Santa Barbara, CA**
**(805) 967–4373**
**www.flyspitfire.com**

Unique to Santa Barbara, this touring company lets you see the city and environs from the sky. Board a four-seat Cessna at the Santa Barbara Airport for your tour and you're up, up, and away! Lasting just over an hour, the excursion includes an aerial view of Santa Barbara, the coastline, the Santa Ynez Valley, and the mountains. Cost is $99 for adults and teens, $89 for seniors 55 and over, and $49 for children 12 and under. A 45-minute Express Tour, which includes Santa Barbara and the coastline, is available for $79 for adults and teens, $69 for seniors, and $39 for children.

# Kidstuff



## Voyage to Planet Santa Barbara

Hey, kids! Welcome to Mission Control, where we'll prepare you for a trip to a really cool place: Planet Santa Barbara. Your assignment: to find out as much as you can about the planet and its people. This will involve lots of hands-on exploration, like going to the younger natives' favorite beaches, playgrounds, and camps. It also means having lots of fun along the way.

Are you up for this action-packed adventure? Then let's get started! Don't forget to bring your parents along. They might come in handy when you're renting equipment and buying admission tickets.

## How to Avoid Looking Like an Alien

First, we need to help you look and act like a Santa Barbara kid so you'll fit right in. Most local kids (both boys and girls) wear T-shirts, shorts, and sandals nearly every day. When it's too cold for shorts, they wear sweatshirts and jeans or cotton pants.

If you really want to look like a Santa Barbara kid, wear surfer-style flip-flops. (Tell your parents to check out the "Surf and Beachwear" section in our Shopping chapter to find shops that sell the proper attire.) A Santa Barbara kid wouldn't be caught dead with a bright-red sunburn, so make sure you slather on that sunscreen! Baseball caps and shades are always "in."

When it comes to language, Santa Barbara kids mostly speak just like everyone else in Southern California. Throw in the word "like" between lots of words (". . . and she's like swimming down at the . . . and then he's like mad . . . ") and you'll sound just like a young Insider.

## What's Happening on Planet Santa Barbara

Several publications have listings of the many daily, weekly, ongoing, and special events for kids in the Santa Barbara area. In the *Santa Barbara News-Press,* look for the "Public Square" section of the daily paper. On Sundays, look for the "What's Doing on the South Coast" section, which lists "For the Kids" happenings for the week.

The *Santa Barbara Independent,* a free weekly paper available at newsstands all over the county, also lists events for kids. Read the day-by-day listings for the week; each day's listings has a kids' section. Also check out the listings for ongoing community events.

*Santa Barbara with Kids!* by Susan Applewood Cam is a locally produced and published book with comprehensive information about places to go and things to do with youngsters. It's available at most bookstores in the area as well as at many museums and attractions. A free monthly magazine, *Santa Barbara Family Life*, includes lots of feature articles, parenting tips, book and software reviews, a calendar of events, and a section just for kids. You can find it at grocery stores, bookstores, the library, toy shops, and many other places frequented by families.

After you've done your prep work, you're ready to embark on your mission. Take this manual along—it has lots of tips about where to go and what to do. Grab your gear, strap yourself in, and get ready for a voyage you won't forget. Ten, nine, eight, seven, six, five, four, three, two, one... we're off!

## The Mission Begins!

Now that you've landed, it's time to explore. In this chapter you'll find information about Santa Barbara kids' favorite haunts and activities. Many of these also appear in more complete detail in other chapters, for example, Beaches and Watersports, Recreation, and Attractions. In these cases, we provide a brief description tailored for kids in this chapter and refer you to the appropriate chapter for other details.

Good luck and have fun. Don't forget to report back to us about what you see and do!

## Getting Wet and Wild

When the weather's warm (which is often), Santa Barbara kids like to cool down by the ocean or in one of our many community pools.

### Favorite Beaches

Most young Insiders hang out at the beach a lot. You'll always find a pack of them boogie-boarding and surfing at most beaches every day during the summer and on warm-weather weekends the rest of the year. The following are their favorite beach haunts (see our Beaches and Watersports chapter for detailed descriptions). Lifeguards are generally on duty at these beaches daily from early or mid-June until Labor Day.

#### Santa Barbara

**Arroyo Burro Beach**
**2981 Cliff Drive**
**Santa Barbara, CA**
**(805) 687–3714**
**www.sbparks.org**

This is the place to find Insider kids, who call it "Henry's" (spelled Hendry's) beach. Even when the surf's not up, dozens of children float around in wetsuits, hoping for a swell. Parents like to hang out at the Brown Pelican restaurant at the beach entrance, while kids line up at the snack bar. It's also a great beach for tidepooling when the tide is low, and you can reserve a group area here for birthday parties.

**East Beach/Cabrillo Pavilion Bathhouse**
**E. Cabrillo Boulevard near Niños Drive**
**Santa Barbara, CA**
**(805) 897–2680**
**www.sbparksandrecreation.com**

Although East Beach isn't the best beach for surfing and boogie-boarding, you can't beat the services and activities. There's a playground, snack shop/restaurant, bathrooms, showers, and volleyball courts. You can rent boogie boards, beach chairs, volleyballs, and more at the bathhouse.

**Insiders' Tip**

Before you take the kids to a park or beach, check out www.sbparks.org for information on facilities and printable maps.

*For Santa Barbara kids, a sunny Christmas morning can be the perfect time to make sand angels on the beach.* PHOTO: BRIAN HASTINGS

**Leadbetter Beach**
**Shoreline and Loma Alta Drives**
**Santa Barbara, CA**
**(805) 897-2680**
**www.sbparksandrecreation.com**

"Leds" is a broad stretch of sandy beach between the yacht harbor and Shoreline Park. Since it's a favorite local sailboarding spot, you can watch the sailboards and catamarans ply the waves while you're digging for crabs and building sand castles.

If you don't want to picnic, you can order great food at the Shoreline Beach Café, with tables either right in the sand or just above on the patio. The waves near the point are often ideal for pint-size surfers: not too big, but big enough for fun boogie-board and surf rides. Picnic and barbecue areas, restrooms, and outdoor showers are also available here.

### Goleta

**Goleta Beach Park**
**5986 Sandspit Road**
**Goleta, CA**
**(805) 967-1300**
**www.sbparks.org**

This 29-acre county park is very popular with local families. It lies right near the entrance to UCSB and offers boating, fishing, restrooms, a playground, and picnic and barbecue areas on a grassy expanse under a stretch of palm trees. You can fish off the Goleta Pier and munch on snacks from the snack bar.

The popular Beachside Bar and Café, located on the beach inside the park, provides excellent food and views in a casual atmosphere.

### Summerland

**Lookout Park/Summerland Beach**
**2297 Finney Road**
**Summerland, CA**
**(805) 568-2460**
**www.sbparks.org**

You'll find this park and beach between U.S. Highway 101 and the ocean, near the Summerland exit. Romp in the large playground and picnic on the bluffs above the beach. When you're ready for a swim or a beach walk, just head down the path to the beach. The park has barbecue facilities, restrooms, and on-site parking.

### Carpinteria

**Carpinteria City Beach**
**End of Linden Avenue**
**Carpinteria, CA**
**(805) 684-5405**

This is billed as the "world's safest beach." That's because the natural reef breakwater along the shore tames large waves and eliminates rip tides. The gently sloping shore and mild waves make it a great beach for safe swimming, surfing, and boogie-boarding. You can rent bikes, kayaks, and other equipment, buy snacks and lunch at the snack bar, and play volleyball on one of the beach courts.

**Carpinteria State Beach Park**
**Entrance at Linden Avenue near Sixth Street**
**Carpinteria, CA**
**(805) 684-2811**
**www.parks.ca.gov**

Carpinteria's 48-acre state park is right next to the City Beach. It has day-use and camping facilities, and a visitor center with natural history exhibits and nature programs. It's a fantastic place to explore tidepools, watch birds, swim, fish, hike, picnic, and splash around. There's an excellent swimming beach and a fairly good area for surfing.

Day-use hours are 7:00 A.M. to 7:00 P.M. during the winter and 7:00 A.M. to 9:00 P.M. during the summer. For camping information, read the Camping section in our Recreation chapter.

## Surf and Boogie-Board Lessons

If you want to learn to surf or boogie-board or just to improve your skills, we recommend you take lessons from the experts. They'll teach you about safety, surf etiquette, and a whole lot more. See our Beaches and Watersports chapter for information on renting or buying boards, wetsuits, and other equipment.

### Santa Barbara

**Davey Smith's Surf Academy**
**222 Meigs Road #20**
**Santa Barbara, CA**
**(805) 965-7341, (877) 543-2839**
**www.surfinstruction.com**

Davey offers a hugely popular surf camp during the summer (see the Summer Camp section later in this chapter). During the fall, winter, and spring months, however, he gives private lessons ($50 for an hour and a half) to kids of all ages. The fee includes equipment—a wetsuit and board.

### Goleta

**Surf Country**
**5668 Calle Real**
**Goleta, CA**
**(805) 683-4450**

Sign up for Surf Country's lessons and learn to paddle a board, maneuver it quickly, gain balance, read a wave, and surf as safely as possible. A 90-minute lesson costs $45 for an individual and $75 for two people. The shop supplies the surfboard, wax, leash, and wetsuit. Surf Country offers lessons by appointment for all levels, from beginner to advanced.

## Swimming Pools

When warm weather makes you want to dive, splash, and cavort, you can head to one of Santa Barbara's clean, safe community pools. Lifeguards are always on duty. These are all outdoor pools; we don't have any public indoor pools. However several private organizations offer swim instruction for infants and children in warm, private indoor pools year-round. Call the Anacapa Dive Center (805-963-8917), Santa Barbara Aquatics (805-964-0180), or Wendy Fereday Swim School (805-964-7818).

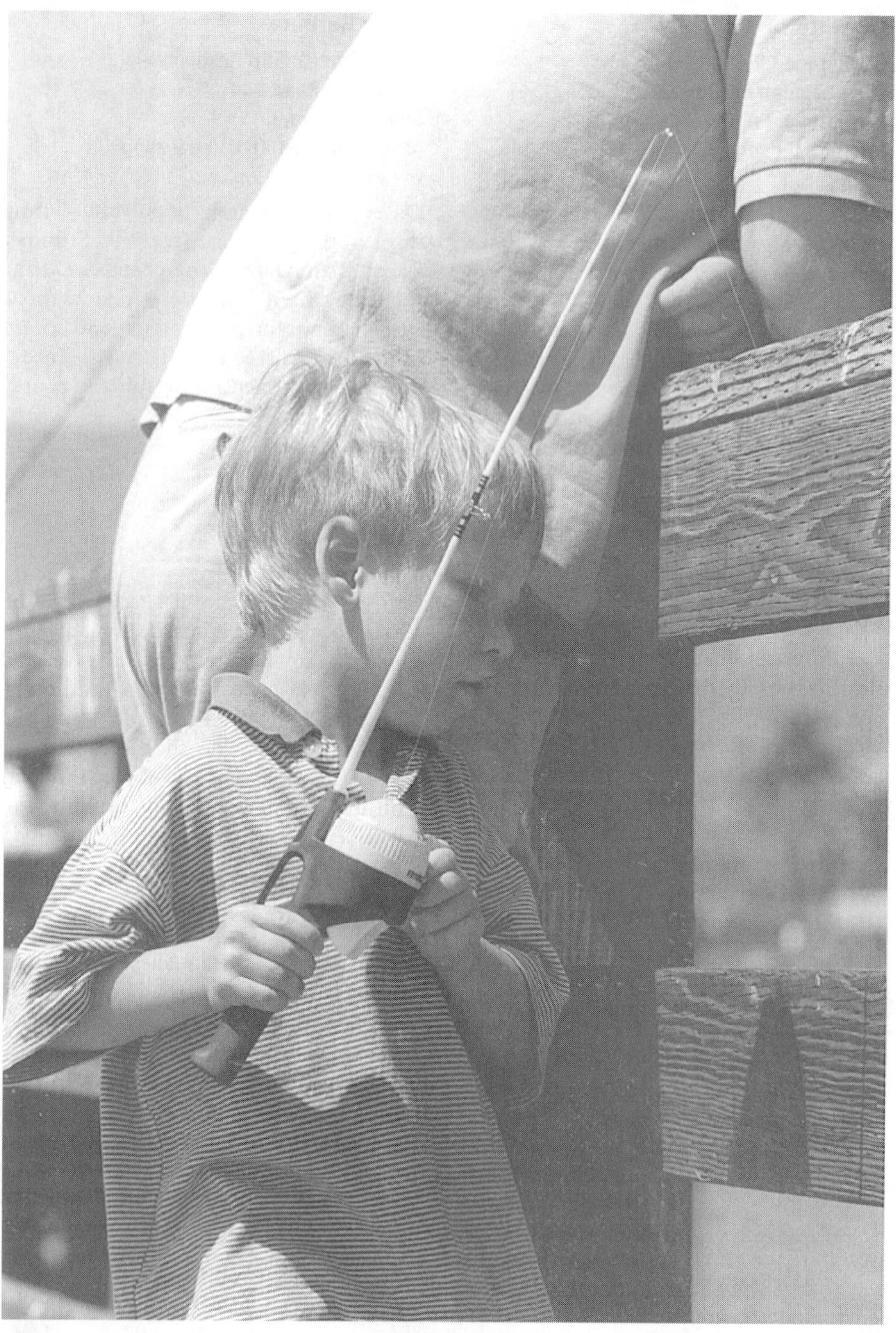

*Fisherkids can cast a line at the Santa Barbara breakwater and at the Goleta and Gaviota Beach piers.*
PHOTO: SALLY TURVEY

### Santa Barbara

**Los Baños del Mar Pool**
**401 Shoreline Drive**
**Santa Barbara, CA**
**(805) 966–6110**

Built in 1914, this historic 50-meter pool underwent a total renovation in 1997. The pool, deck, and mechanical systems were completely redone, and the facility now boasts updated showers, lockers, benches, plumbing, fixtures, and more.

Los Baños is located next to West Beach at the harbor (where Castillo Street ends). From mid-June to Labor Day weekend, the pool is open for recreational swimming weekends from 1:15 to 5:00 P.M. and weekdays from 1:45 to 3:45 P.M. Fees are $2.50 for adults and teens, $1 for children 13 and younger. Parking is available in the harbor lot and on the street. (See our Recreation chapter for information on other Los Baños programs.)

**Oak Park Wading Pool**
**Oak Park, Alamar and Junipero Avenues**
**Santa Barbara, CA**
**(805) 966–6110**

A fountain sits in the middle of this large, sparkling pool. You can splash and float here if you're younger than 7. The pool is open 11:00 A.M. to 5:00 P.M. daily from the second week of June through Labor Day; in May to mid-June and from Labor Day to the end of September it's open 2:00 to 5:00 P.M. on weekdays and 11:00 A.M. to 5:00 P.M. on weekends. Bathing suits are required. Admission is free.

**West Beach Wading Pool**
**401 Shoreline Drive**
**Santa Barbara, CA**
**(805) 966–6110**

This spacious 18-inch-deep pool sits right next to the "big" pool complex, Los Baños del Mar. It's open to kids 7 and younger daily from the second week of June through Labor Day weekend from 11:00 A.M. to 5:00 P.M. Bathing suits are required. Park in the harbor lot or on the street. Admission is free.

### Goleta

**UCSB Campus**
**Goleta, CA**
**(805) 893–7619**

UCSB opens its gorgeous outdoor pool complex to the public every afternoon during the summer months and on weekends during the school year. It includes a 50-meter pool, a diving pool, plus an additional lap pool with a shallow area for kids. The fee is $5 for adults and teens, $3 for kids younger than 18. Call for specific hours.

### Carpinteria

**Carpinteria Valley Community Swimming Pool**
**5305 Carpinteria Avenue**
**Carpinteria, CA**
**(805) 566–2417**

For just $1.50, kids younger than 12 can splash and play in Carpinteria's large outdoor pool every afternoon and evening during the summer and every afternoon the rest of the year. Adults pay $3. See our Recreation chapter for specific hours.

## Life on the Planet's Wild Side

Planet Santa Barbara isn't just inhabited by people—lots of exotic animals, plants, and other natural wonders live here too! Following are some of the best places to see, touch, feel and experience all these things for yourself.

### Santa Barbara

**Santa Barbara Botanic Garden**
**1212 Mission Canyon Road**
**Santa Barbara, CA**
**(805) 682–4726**
**www.sbbg.com**

The Botanic Garden is much more than a collection of plants and flowers—it's a great place to dive headlong into the world of nature. Walk (or run) along the 5.5 miles of trails, and you'll discover a

**Insiders' Tip**

Shoreline Park, just above Leadbetter Beach, is one of the best places to fly a kite when the breeze picks up.

redwood grove, meadows, canyons, a historic dam, and a bubbling creek.

There's a picnic area near the entrance and a gift shop filled with books, games, and interesting items for kids as well as adults.

The Botanic Garden also sponsors workshops and special events for children throughout the year. Call and ask for the Education Department for details. (Also see our Attractions chapter for additional details and hours and admission fees.)

**Santa Barbara Museum of Natural History**
**2559 Puesta del Sol Road**
**Santa Barbara, CA**
**(805) 682–4711**

Listen to insects talk, walk beneath a giant blue whale skeleton, and learn all about the Chumash Indians, the Native Americans who lived in the Santa Barbara region for thousands of years. This museum has lots of exhibits on birds, marine life, mammals (including grizzly bears, coyote, and deer), shells, and lizards. Many of the exhibit halls feature interactive computers or displays.

You can explore the wonders of the universe in the museum's Gladwin Planetarium, which has regular shows throughout the year. Call (805) 682-3224 for showtimes. Star parties are held the second Saturday of every month from 8:30 to 10:00 P.M.

At the planetarium you can also check out an observatory and the E. L. Weigand SpaceLab, a fun, interactive space exploration center. Get inside a telescope, find out how much you would weigh on another planet, and hear about the latest news from space!

Be sure to stroll over to the creek and the picnic areas in the museum's backyard. It's a great place to hang out and watch squirrels, birds, and lizards in action. And before you leave, make sure you and your parents take a spin through the museum gift shop, which has books, puzzles, crafts, and lots of interesting items related to the world of nature.

The museum sponsors after-school and weekend workshops for kids and adults throughout the year. Call (805) 682-4711, extension 308, for information. See our Attractions chapter for a full museum description, including hours and admission prices.

**Santa Barbara Zoological Gardens**
**500 Niños Drive**
**Santa Barbara, CA**
**(805) 962–5339**
**(805) 926–6310 recorded information**

Get up-close and personal with lions, gorillas, elephants, leopards, and other animals! Considered the finest small zoo in California, the Santa Barbara Zoological Gardens is as wild as Santa Barbara gets. It's also one of the best places for kids to spend free time on fair-weather days. Lots of Insider kids go there at least once a week year-round and attend at least a week or two of Zoo Camp in the summer (see the "Summer Camps" section later in this chapter).

Once part of a grand estate, the beautifully landscaped grounds include palm gardens, exotic plants, and an expansive hilltop knoll overlooking the ocean. More than 700 animals live amid the lush botanical gardens—river otters, lions, leopards, giraffes, sea lions, and llamas to name just a few. Most exhibits have low enclosures and windows or open space, so shorter visitors (even toddlers and babies in strollers) can easily see and interact with the animals. Don't miss the new lorikeet interactive exhibit, where you can buy cups of nectar and hand-feed the brilliantly colored parrots.

*Animal-loving kids might see elephant seals at the Channel Islands.* PHOTO: CONDOR PHOTOS

As part of the international Species Survival Plan, the zoo received three lowland gorillas in 1996: Max, Goma, and Kivu. At the gorilla habitat you can tour the Karisoke Research Outpost, a replica of the station established by Dian Fossey to research the highly endangered mountain gorillas.

Here you can read field reports from the real Karisoke Research Station in Africa and peer over the gorilla's "backyard" before heading for the main viewing windows. Max, a silverback male, tends to hover in a cave, but Kivu and Goma regularly play near the viewing window and often interact with visitors, especially children.

You can see nearly all the animals in an hour or two, but you'll probably want to spend at least a half-day just enjoying the grounds. Take a spin on the handmade Dentzel miniature carousel—you can ride on a sea serpent, unicorn, horse, pig, frog, rabbit, or a fish. It's for kids only (sorry mom and pop!) and costs only $1. The carousel is open 11:00 A.M. to 4:30 P.M. daily in the summer and 11:00 A.M. to 4:00 P.M. on weekends the rest of the year.

You can also hop aboard one of the miniature C. P. Huntington trains that circle the zoo every half-hour. Train tickets for kids ages 2 through 12 cost 50 cents; adults and teens pay $1 a ride. From the train you can see toucans, giraffes, gibbons, behind-the-scenes areas, and the adjacent Andree Clark Bird Refuge.

If you're bursting with energy, head up to the zoo playground. During certain hours of the day you can feed the llamas and sheep. When your own tummy growls, spread out a picnic lunch on the grassy knoll. Or you can buy salads, sandwiches, burgers, corn dogs, zoo fries, and other fare at a restaurant at the zoo entrance, or hot dogs and snacks at a stand near the elephants.

Don't leave without browsing the gift shop, which has everything from African artifacts, puzzles, books, and games to jewelry, clothing, and exotic stuffed animals.

During the school year, the zoo offers fun workshops for kids, adults, and families. Some of the more popular kids' workshops include the Zoo Snooze, an overnight adventure where you learn all about animal nightlife; Night Prowl (same as the Snooze but without the overnight); Junior Zookeeper, a chance to tour behind the scenes; and So You Want to Be a Vet?—a chance to find out what it's like to be a zoo veterinarian. Families are welcome on the zoo's annual Whale Watch every March.

Preschoolers (ages 3 through 5) with a parent in tow are invited to join Kinderfari, a behind-the-scenes journey through the world of zoo animals. Toddlers (18 months to 3 years) accompanied by a parent can sign up for Baby and You at the Zoo, which features close encounters with zoo animals and activities. And hey, Mom and Dad—here's something just for you! Rounds with the Vet offers grown-ups a fantastic opportunity to go on morning rounds with the staff veterinarian.

For information on workshops, call (805) 962-5339 and ask for the Education Office. See our Attractions chapter for zoo hours and admission prices.

**Sea Center**
**211 Stearns Wharf**
**Santa Barbara, CA**
**(805) 962-0885**

"What's under all that water anyway?" The Sea Center on Stearns Wharf is a fantastic place for kids to actually see for themselves. Unfortunately though, the center closed at the end of 2001 for an 18-month renovation. It will reopen in summer 2003 with even better interactive exhibits that will keep little hands busy and little brains buzzing.

## Goleta

**Ellwood Grove Monarch Butterfly Roosting Site**
**End of Coronado Street**
**Goleta, CA**

This dense eucalyptus grove is one of several places along the California coast that attracts wintering monarch butterflies. The black-and-orange butterflies usually start to arrive in October and can be seen hanging from the trees and fluttering about. Peak butterfly-watching season is mid-winter.

The grove is in the Santa Barbara Shores neighborhood near the Winchester Canyon exit of U.S. 101. To find it, drive along Coronado Street from Hollister Avenue toward the ocean. This will dead-end at the eucalyptus grove. Park on the street and follow the trail to the right about 100 yards. Look up in the trees—you can't miss them!

## Carpinteria

**Carpinteria Harbor Seal Colony**
**Carpinteria Bluffs**
**End of Bailard Avenue**
**Carpinteria, CA**

Hey kids! Want to see a real wild seal colony? Well you're in luck, because Carpinteria is home to one of only two publicly accessible harbor seal rookeries in California. Best of all, the rookery is tucked in a cove below the beautiful Carpinteria bluffs—a fantastic place to hike and look for other wildlife, too. The best time to visit is from December 1 to May 31 when the seals haul out on land to rest, give birth, and nurse their pups. From January to May, volunteers are there to answer your questions. Visit from late February to April and you might even be lucky enough to see a chubby little seal pup coming into the world!

To find the rookery, tell mom and dad to take the Bailard Freeway exit in Carpinteria, turn right, and park in the lot at the end of the street near the hot dog stand. Follow the path to the right along the ocean and you'll see breathtaking views of Rincon point to the east and the Channel Islands to the south. Watch for red-tailed hawks. They hover here looking for ground squirrels and gophers. But don't get too close to the edge. It's very steep!

About half a mile down the track you'll see the viewing area just before the pier. Dogs scare the seals, so if you happen to be walking one, tie it up before you enter the area. Shhh! Be very quiet. Creep up to the railing slowly and you should be able to spot the seals way down on the beach below. Look for some in the water and on the rock. See how well their big blubbery bodies blend with their natural surroundings? To find out more about the harbor seals—including what they eat and what eats them—see our Close-up in the Attractions chapter.

### North of Santa Barbara

**Cachuma Lake**
**Ca. Highway 154, 20 miles northwest of Santa Barbara**
**(805) 568–2460**
**www.sbparks.org**

Take a cruise on Cachuma Lake and spot bald eagles, deer, and other animals. Park naturalists lead two-hour guided Eagle Cruise tours from November through February. When the eagles leave, you can still take the cruise to spot other wildlife. See our Parks and Recreation chapters for a detailed description of the lake.

## Wiggle Mode

You've got the wiggles and you just can't sit still any longer. What's a kid to do? Luckily, there are many places on Planet Santa Barbara where kids can run around and expend excess energy. Here are a few safe, fun ways to shake your sillies out and develop your motor skills.

## Bowling

**Zodo's Bowling & Beyond**
**5925 Calle Real**
**Goleta, CA**
**(805) 967–0128**

Open 24 hours a day, the smoke-free Zodo's Bowling & Beyond offers daily bumper bowling. It's a great place to let off steam, especially when it's cold, rainy, or foggy outside. It costs $2.75 a game for each child, or bowl as many games in an hour as you like for $15. Juniors (teens and under) are $15 an hour anytime. Call for special themed bowling sessions such as Rock and Bowl, Galactic Bowl, and Glow Bowling with disco strobes and luminous bowling balls. The bowl provides 6- and 8-pound balls for kids. Weekends can be crowded, so you may have to wait a bit for a lane. The cafe is open 6:00 A.M. to 9:00 P.M. Monday through Friday and 6:00 A.M. to 2:00 P.M. on weekends.

*Kids can spot harbor seals from the beautiful Carpinteria bluffs.* PHOTO: KAREN HASTINGS

**Insiders' Tip**

Hop on the open-air, electric Downtown/Waterfront shuttle for a fun cruise along Cabrillo Boulevard or State Street. It costs just a quarter and stops every block or two.

## Indoor Play

**Gymboree Play & Music**
**5148 Hollister Avenue**
**Goleta, CA**
**(805) 683–7780**
**www.sbgymbo.com**

Santa Barbara's only Gymboree program is in the Magnolia Shopping Center between Turnpike and Patterson. Gymboree offers classes, music programs, and open-play opportunities using specialized equipment for newborns, infants, and children 4 years and under. Classes cost $143 for a 13-week session and $256 for a 26-week session. Music classes for children from 16 months through 4 years feature singing, finger play, creative movement, and instrument play with styles of music from around the world.

Children enrolled in a current 13-week session may attend a free open gym session once a week; unlimited free gym sessions are allowed for those enrolled in the 26-week session. Non-enrolled children pay $11 per session. Call or check the web site for the current schedule.

**Kindermusik**
**1213 State Street, Suite 1**
**Santa Barbara, CA**
**(805) 884–4009**

Bring out the song in your child at Kindermusik, which offers music-appreciation classes for children from 3 months to 7 years. Depending on the age group, the sessions typically involve creative movement, instrument exploration, singing, dancing, and storytelling through music. Classes range from about $135 to $210, plus materials fees. Kindermusik is tucked back behind MacDonald's near Victoria Court.

**2000 Degrees**
**1206 State Street**
**Santa Barbara, CA**
**(805) 882–1817**
**www.2000degrees.com**

2000 Degrees is a fantastic rainy day hangout for budding little artists. At this ceramics workshop, you purchase greenware (unfinished ceramics such as cups, plates, and bowls), paint it with your own creative designs, and select a special glaze. Prices range from $2 for a tile to $60 for a platter. Not the artistic type? Don't worry. Experienced staffers are on hand to help you out. Included in the $7 workshop fee is the use of brushes, paints, stencils, and other materials. 2000 Degrees will do all the glazing and firing. They'll even ship the piece to you if you leave town before it's ready. This is a great place to make personalized gifts for friends and family.

## Playgrounds

Our Parks chapter provides complete details on the area's best parks. Here, though, we'd like to point out a few of the local kids' favorite playgrounds. They're all in Santa Barbara and they all have safe, modern play structures plus unique atmospheres that spark your imagination. Romp on!

**Chase Palm Park Shipwreck Playground**
**Cabrillo Boulevard, between Santa Barbara Street and Calle Cesar Chavez**
**Santa Barbara, CA**
**(805) 564–5418**

Designed for toddlers through 12-year-olds, this amazing playground opened in May 1998, replete with spouting whales, a shipwreck village, talking tubes, and bridges. As a whole, the 15,000-square-foot playground represents Santa Barbara, from the Santa Ynez Mountains (represented by a tall back wall) all the way to the Channel Islands.

Beneath the mountains stretches a cityscape—a series of facades adorned with Spanish/Mexican tile artwork. From the spongy "shore," a pier juts out in the sandy "ocean." A ramp leads to one of the coolest play structures around—a ship that appears to have crashed on rubber-coated rock.

Cross another couple of bridges and you come to an island—a mounded grass area with a deck and pole like Robinson Crusoe's. In the sand area you can ride statues of whales, dolphins, and other sea creatures as well as a spring-mounted raft and buoy.

Toddlers can make sand castles and dig around in a contained area shaped like breaking waves. Water mists sprinkle the sand (and any kids sitting nearby) every few minutes, timed by embedded computer chips. The playground also has picnic areas and restrooms.

**Kids' World**
**Alameda Park, corner of Micheltorena and Garden Streets**
**Santa Barbara, CA**
**(805) 564–5418**
**www.sbparksandrecreation.com**

Sit on a shark, ride a whale, hide in the turrets of a magic castle, and race across suspension bridges! This one-of-a-kind playground is 8,000 square feet of pure fun. It was designed by Santa Barbara children and constructed by community volunteers in 1993.

Very small children can scramble around in the toddler area, which has pint-size swings, slides, and climbing equipment. Older, more agile kids can tear through tunnels, slip through slides, swing on ropes, and generally have the time of their lives. (Be sure to wear brightly colored clothes so Mom and Dad can spot you between the wooden castle slats.)

Just across the street, at Alice Keck Park Memorial Garden, you can watch the goldfish circle the pond and turtles bask in the sun.

**Oak Park Playground**
**300 W. Alamar Avenue at Junipero Street**
**Santa Barbara, CA**
**(805) 564–5418**

"Take me to the oak tree park!" Our own children made this request many a time. It has two great playgrounds—one perfect for toddlers and small children and another for the agile and daring. During the summer months, kids 7 and younger can cool off in the wading pool (see the Swimming Pools section earlier in this chapter). It has restrooms, shady picnic sites, and convenient parking in the lot or on the street.

**Shoreline Park Playground**
**Shoreline Drive and San Rafael Avenue**
**Santa Barbara, CA**
**(805) 564–5418**

This small playground, near the parking lot and restrooms at the west end of Shoreline Park, is ideal for younger children. It's where Insiders take their little ones to practice riding trikes and two-wheelers. From here you can take in fantastic views of the ocean and the Channel Islands. At certain times of year you can spot whales, and throughout the year you can often watch the schools of dolphins that regularly play nearby.

**Stevens Park**
**258 Canon Drive**
**Santa Barbara, CA**
**(805) 564–5418**

Twenty-five-acre Stevens Park lies at the entrance to the foothills near the intersection of San Roque and Foothill Roads. Here you can picnic, go on short nature walks, and hike along creekside and canyon trails. It has swings and two play structures (one for toddlers and one for older kids), restrooms, barbecue and picnic areas, and on-site parking.

**Tar Pits Park**
**East end of Carpinteria State Beach**

The Chumash Indians built their canoes and boats here and caulked the planks with natural asphalt. You can see gooey black stuff oozing down the cliffs, plus

**Insiders' Tip**

Sign up for summer camp sessions as early as possible. The most popular camps fill up early, sometimes by May.

lots of sea creatures on the reef. To get here, take Concha Loma to Calle Ocho. Park and walk over the railroad tracks to the lookout point. Walk down the steps to reach the beach. Make sure you wear old shoes and swimsuits—the natural asphalt can really stick to them.

## Roller Skating/ Skateboarding

The best places to in-line skate or skateboard are along the Cabrillo Bike Path or the new Skater's Point Skate Park (see our listing below). You can rent equipment at a number of beachside locations—see our Recreation chapter for details. No one's allowed to skate or skateboard on any public street or on many city sidewalks or public ways in the downtown and beach area. When you see signs with pictures of skates and skateboards with a big line painted through them, you'll know you're in a restricted area. It's okay to skate on sidewalks elsewhere. When you rent or buy equipment, ask for information on prohibited areas.

**Skate Depot**
**Linden Avenue at Fifth Street**
**Carpinteria, CA**
**(805) 684–5405**

Skate Depot, which operates much like any other city park, opened in December 1998, much to the delight of skateboarders in the eastern reaches of the county. It includes ramps, a half-tube, a pyramid, and other obstacles. Skateboarders are required to file a liability waiver with the city and adhere to all posted rules. Call the above city hall number for information. Helmets and knee and elbow pads are also required. Although the facility is unsupervised, officials often drop in to make sure skateboarders have the appropriate sticker on their helmets—evidence of the filed waiver. If you don't have one (or if you don't have the proper safety attire), you'll be fined. Skate Depot is located at the west end of the Amtrak station parking lot in downtown Carpinteria and is open from 8:00 A.M. to sunset.

**Skater's Point Skate Park**
**Chase Palm Park**
**236 East Cabrillo Boulevard (near Stearns Wharf)**
**Santa Barbara, CA**
**(805) 897–2650**

Completed in 2000, this brand new skate park by the beach is a popular hub for Santa Barbara's skating community. You can't beat the location. It's right on the beachfront. Head toward Stearns Wharf and you'll see it on the east side. Kids of all ages flock here to ride the 12,000 square feet of ramps, bowls, and rails. While they're waiting, they can practice on Cabrillo Bike Path or watch all the action from the observation decks. Helmets and knee and elbow pads are required, and admittance is free.

## Youth Sports

Santa Barbara offers countless opportunities for kids to participate in individual and team sports. The city's Parks and Recreation Department sponsors dozens of youth sports programs for boys and girls, both classes and teams; among them are aquatics, baseball, flag football, golf, softball, T-ball, tennis, track and field, and volleyball. Call (805) 564–5495 or (805) 564–5418 for information.

The Santa Barbara Family YMCA (805–687–7727, www.ciymca.org) and the Montecito Family YMCA (805–969–3288, www.ymca.net) also offer a range of youth sports programs. If you're interested in joining a sports league or would like private instruction, we recommend you call the Page Youth Center at (805) 967–8778. You can also look through the Yellow Pages and call for information. Popular youth sports include Little League, BMX Motor Cross, football, roller hockey, soccer, swimming, diving, and water polo. A number of private organizations offer training and specialized instruction in gymnastics, martial arts, horseback riding, and tennis.

One club worth special mention is the Santa Barbara Sea Shell Association (www.sbssa.org), Santa Barbara's oldest youth sports club. It promotes the sport of sailing by teaching its members racing skills, seamanship, and the art of being a good sport. You have to celebrate your eighth birthday by Labor Day to participate the following season (April through October). Sea Shell skippers learn to race Sea Shells and Sabots, smaller boats just under 8 feet in length. Registration fees are approximately $100 a year.

## Thinking Mode

### Libraries

Nearly all branches of the Santa Barbara Public Library offer a weekly Preschool Story Time. They also sponsor many special events for children, for example puppet and magic shows, films, and drumming workshops. You can pick up a monthly calendar of events at any branch. You can also check out videos and connect to the Internet at any branch.

**Insiders' Tip**

Taking the gang to the zoo? Rent a wagon for $6, pop the kids and your bags inside, and you can whiz around the exhibits with ease.

If you have any questions or need help finding something, the experienced children's librarians are more than happy to help out. Hours vary by branch; call for information or visit the library web site at www.ci.santa-barbara.ca.us/library//. If the branch locations aren't convenient, you can always visit the Bookmobile, a huge traveling library that goes all over the city: to schools, shopping centers, retirement centers, and other locations throughout the community. Call the Goleta branch for schedules.

**Preschool Story Times**
**Santa Barbara Central Library**
**40 E. Anapamu Street**
**Santa Barbara, CA**
**(805) 962–7653**
**10:30 A.M. Tuesday and Thursday**

**Santa Barbara Eastside Branch**
**1102 E. Montecito Street**
**Santa Barbara, CA**
**(805) 963–3727**
**10:30 A.M. Wednesday, 11:00 A.M. Saturday; bilingual story times 10:00 and 10:30 A.M. Thursday and 11:30 A.M. Saturday**

**Goleta Branch**
**500 N. Fairview Avenue**
**Santa Barbara, CA**
**(805) 964–7878**
**10:30 A.M. Tuesday and Wednesday**

**Montecito Branch**
**1469 E. Valley Road**
**Santa Barbara, CA**
**(805) 969–5063**
**10:30 A.M. Thursday**

**Carpinteria Branch**
**5141 Carpinteria Avenue**
**Santa Barbara, CA**
**(805) 684–4314**
**10:30 A.M. Thursday**

### Bookstores

Many area bookstores offer children's story hours at least once a week—and they're free! Check the newspapers and magazines listed at the beginning of this chapter for information, or pick up a calendar of events at the store. The following Santa Barbara bookstores have the best children's book sections. For hours and additional information about these bookstores, see our Shopping chapter.

**Borders Books, Music & Cafe**
**900 State Street**
**Santa Barbara, CA**
**(805) 899–3668**
**7000 Marketplace Avenue**
**Goleta, CA**
**(805) 968–1370**
**www.borders.com**

Borders arranges children's story hours several times a week in the morning, afternoon, and evening. They also have an excellent selection of children's books as well as music and videos for the younger set. The children's sections feature a comfortable sitting areas where you can curl up on a pillow and read as long as you like.

**Chaucer's Books**
**Loreto Plaza**
**3321 State Street**
**Santa Barbara, CA**
**(805) 682–6787, (805) 682–4067**
**www.gtesupersite.com/chaucerbooks**

Chaucer's has an outstanding children's section. The knowledgeable staff can tell you all about the best books for kids. Though there isn't an area for sitting and reading, you'll have fun just browsing the well-stocked shelves. Chaucer's is in Loreto Plaza at the intersection of State Street and Las Positas Road.

## Just Plain Fun

### Goleta

**South Coast Railroad Museum and Goleta Depot**
**300 N. Los Carneros Road**
**Goleta, CA**
**(805) 964–3540**
**www.goletadepot.org**

Hop aboard a miniature train, clamber through a real caboose, and check out cool train artifacts from long ago. Built in 1901, the Victorian Goleta Depot is a historical landmark as well as a fun place to picnic and hang out. It's located at Lake Los Carneros County Park, right next to the historic Stow House (see our Attractions chapter). The museum is dedicated to the history and adventure of railroading, emphasizing American rural railroad stations.

The miniature train ride is by far the most popular attraction for children at the museum. It operates year-round on Wednesday and Friday through Sunday. The rides are usually offered from 2:00 to 3:45 P.M. during the week and from 1:00 to 3:45 P.M. on weekends.

It costs $1 for a single ride. Ticket prices are usually higher during special events at Easter, Christmas, and other holiday times. Infants aren't allowed on the train; you have to be able to get on and off by yourself and be at least 34 inches tall. Parents may ride with their children.

Other popular attractions include a 300-square-foot HO-scale model railroad exhibit, working railroad communications and signaling equipment, a small theater that shows films and documentaries, a bay-window caboose, a station yard track, and a gift shop with train history–related gifts for all ages. On the third Saturday of every month, you can ride a handcar around the grounds.

The museum is open Wednesday through Sunday 1:00 to 4:00 P.M. Admission is free, but donations are requested.

## Hunger Mode

Since Santa Barbara is such a laid-back place, many restaurants have children's menus, crayons, and comfortable seating for wiggly bodies. We want to tell you about a couple of our favorites—places where the food is good, kids won't get bored, and parents can relax, too.

*The South Coast Railroad Museum at the old Goleta Depot is a fun stop for young Thomas the Tank Engine fans.* PHOTO: JOHN B. SNODGRASS

**Be Bop Burgers**
**111 State Street**
**Santa Barbara, CA**
**(805) 966–1956**
**www.bebopburgers.com**
**$**

Blast to the past—the '50s and '60s, to be specific—at this fun family diner. It's regularly voted one of the "Best Restaurants to Take Kids," "Best Kid's Dinner," and "Best Burger" in local Santa Barbara newspaper polls. Kids like to come here to play in the coin-operated Fun Zone with games, rides, and pinball machines. Mom and Dad like to look at the memorabilia and listen to the vintage rock 'n' roll jukebox tunes.

On display are a "Classic Car of the Month," movie stars' pictures and autographs, old posters and news clippings, and vintage rock guitars. You can have your picture taken at the Fun Fifties photo booth and the Surfin' USA Photo Area. At certain times, a DJ is available to play requests.

Besides the great atmosphere and activities, Be Bop offers good food—and it's inexpensive too. The classic Be Bop Burger is the most popular item on the menu. There are also turkey, veggie, and chili burgers, various sandwiches, and fantastic onion rings.

Healthier fare includes a variety of salads, for example Caesar, chicken Caesar, and Oriental, and a soup of the day. Quench your thirst with shakes, floats, and sodas (Mom and Dad can indulge in beer or wine if they want).

Kids' meals cost around $2 to $3, and you can choose a Wee Bop Burger, turkey hot dog, chicken corn dog, grilled cheese sandwich, fish and chips, or chicken bits. Be Bop is open for lunch and dinner. It also serves an all-American breakfast daily (weekends only during the winter months).

**Comeback Café**
**324 State Street**
**Santa Barbara, CA**
**(805) 962–2889**
**$**

Looking for some serious sustenance and a place the kids will love? This low-key cafe serves up wicked portions of homestyle cooking such as French toast drizzled with strawberry sauce, and banana and wheat germ pancakes. It's right on lower State Street, so you can pop in for a quick bite after a morning at the beach. The kids' menu includes fun treats like Mickey Mouse pancakes, peanut butter and jelly sandwiches, and quesadillas. Toddlers can tinker in the play area and moms and dads can send postcards to faraway friends and family. Comeback Café is open for breakfast and lunch daily.

**Woody's Bodacious Barbecue**
**5112 Hollister Avenue**
**Goleta, CA**
**(805) 967–3775**
**$**

Voted "Best Barbecue Restaurant" in a local poll for 15 years in a row, Woody's is a fun place to take the kids. The rugged Wild West decor (you wash your hands in a bathtub in the center of the room) and great kid's menu of dino ribs, chicken strips, hamburgers, and hot dogs, are sure to be a hit with the young ones. Moms and dads will love the prices and the portions. The huge servings of succulent barbecue chicken, baby back ribs, and oak-smoked prime rib and duckling will satisfy even the hungriest of bellies. Vegetarians can graze at the salad bar. Woody's is open for lunch and dinner daily.

## Summer Camps

The hardest task facing Santa Barbara kids every summer is deciding which camps to attend. Santa Barbara has dozens of day camps and a few overnight camps in the area. Some are general summer camps that typically offer arts and crafts, sports, and activities. Others focus on a particular theme or sport, for example music, arts, sailing, basketball, or aquatic activities.

Your best bet for choosing a camp is to pick up a regional camp guide. Both *The Santa Barbara Independent* and the *Santa Barbara News-Press* publish a summer camp/youth activity guide every spring. The *News-Press Youth Activity Guide* is also published online at www.newspress.com. Another excellent resource is the City of Santa Barbara's *Parks & Recreation Guide* (spring/summer issue). You can pick up the latest issue at any library or call (805) 564–5418. The following camps are the most popular among Insider kids. Happy camping!

### Santa Barbara

**Davey Smith's Surf Academy**
**222 Meigs Road #20**
**Santa Barbara, CA**
**(805) 965–7341, (877) 543–2839**
**www.surfinstruction.com**

Hundreds of youths ages 8 through 14 have honed their surf skills at Davey Smith's summer surf camp. The one-week sessions (Monday through Friday 8:30 A.M. to 5:00 P.M.) teach safety, etiquette on the water (for example, when to take a wave if others are waiting), style, and technique.

Davey usually offers about 12 sessions from mid-June to September. He sends out information at the beginning of March, and the sessions fill up fast. The sooner you can reserve a spot, the better. This is a mobile camp; the group meets at a designated location and heads for a beach that's conducive to the day's weather and swell. The academy provides wetsuits and boards. The cost is $350 a session.

**Santa Barbara Family YMCA**
**36 Hitchcock Way**
**Santa Barbara, CA**
**(805) 687–7727**

The Santa Barbara YMCA has offered an affordable day camp for years. Activities typically include field trips, games, swimming, arts and crafts, drama, music, and sports. It's open to children in kindergarten through sixth grade, and campers are grouped by grade. Fees range from $115 to $125 a week for members and $125 to $135 a week for nonmembers.

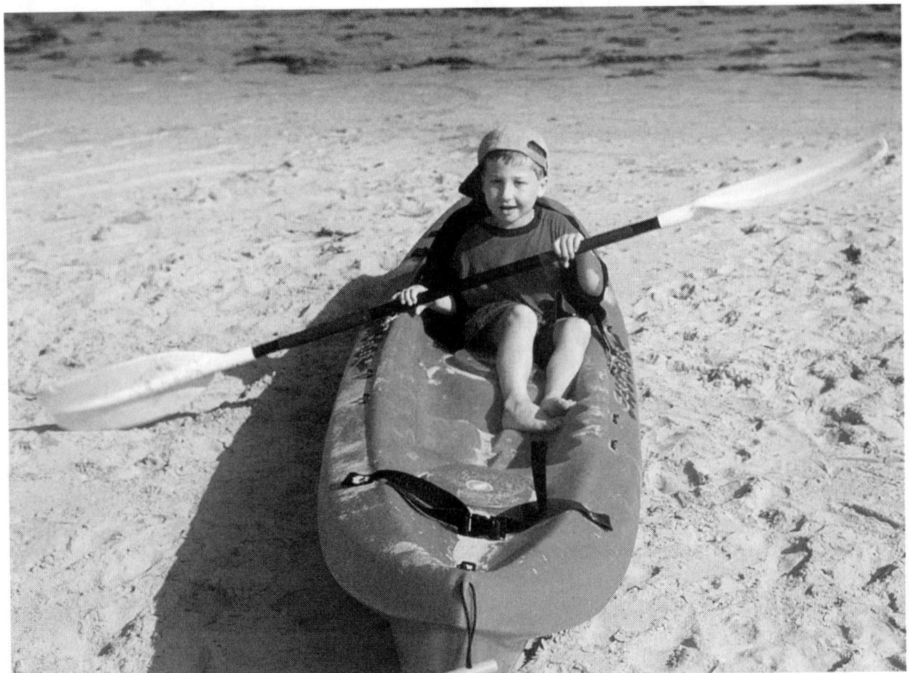

*Summer camp can include kayaking classes in Santa Barbara.* PHOTO: BRIAN HASTINGS

**Youth Sailing/Kayaking Camp**
**Santa Barbara Harbor**
**(805) 962–2826**
**www.sbsail.com**

The Santa Barbara Sailing Center has offered this popular camp since 1985. Both sailing and kayak camp programs are for kids ages 8 through 16. The week-long sessions (Monday through Friday) include 20 hours of hands-on instruction and are offered from mid-June to the end of August. Kayaking sessions are held from 8:30 A.M. to 12:30 P.M. Sailing sessions meet in the afternoons from 1:00 to 5:00 P.M. Sessions cost $140.

**ShowStoppers**
**(805) 682–6043**

ShowStoppers offers summer performance workshops for kids ages 6 through 15. It usually has two three-week sessions, in the morning and/or afternoon. Participants acquire musical-theater skills through practical workshops where they learn to perform in a musical production. Call for more information. See our The Arts chapter for information on ShowStoppers' year-round programs.

**Santa Barbara Surf Adventures**
**10 State Street**
**Santa Barbara, CA**
**(805) 963–1281**

Run out of the Beach House in Santa Barbara, this popular one-week summer surf camp is geared to first-time and beginner surfers who want to brush up on their surfing skills. Classes, taught by professional lifeguards and experienced long-time Santa Barbara surfers, also cover beach safety, first aid, and marine biology. One-week Leadbetter Beach camps start at about $220 and include a soft surfboard, wetsuit, and camp T-shirt. One-week travel camps cost about $250. Participants meet at Leadbetter Beach and venture to the day's surfing destination depending on swell and weather conditions.

**Zoo Camp**
**Santa Barbara Zoological Gardens**
**500 Niños Drive**
**Santa Barbara, CA**
**(805) 962–5339**
**www.santabarbarazoo.org**

Zoo Camp is regularly voted the "Best Kids' Camp in Santa Barbara" in local newspaper polls. It's open to all kids from age 3 to 12. Campers are grouped by age; group size ranges from 10 to 15 kids, with one counselor and two to four counselors-in-training per group.

Each week-long session (Monday through Friday, 9:00 A.M. to 2:00 P.M.) focuses on a particular theme, for example Habitats, Diversity, and Conservation. Themes are repeated every three weeks. You can sign up for as many sessions as you like or register for one or more individual days (excluding Friday).

Each week's activities revolve around the theme-of-the-week and include animal encounters, group play, behind-the-scenes visits, games, stories, educational activities, and art projects. Special activities such as conservation fairs and beach excursions are held every Friday. Zoo Camp costs $110 a week ($100 for zoo members). An extended day (8:00 A.M. to 5:00 P.M.) is now available at $155 a week ($145 for members). Cost includes a T-shirt, which campers must wear daily (so it's easy to spot them amid all the visitors).

### Insiders' Tip

During Old Spanish Days in August you can watch—or join—the Children's Fiesta Parade. Hundreds of kids dress up in traditional costumes and jaunt down State Street. (See our Annual Events chapter for more information.)

### Goleta

**University of California at Santa Barbara Summer Camps**
**UCSB Campus**
**Goleta, CA**
**(805) 893–3913**

Since 1981, UCSB has provided excellent summer programs for local and visiting youth. The UCSB Day Camp is open to kids ages 5 through 14; it's led by UCSB coaches, local teachers, and students earning teaching credentials. The one-week sessions introduce kids to various sports, games, and activities appropriate for the specific age group and skill level.

Typical activities include arts and crafts, gymnastics, swimming, field trips, beach days, archery, and sports. Groups are sorted into four divisions: Freshman Camp (ages 5 through 6), Sophomore Camp (ages 7 through 9), Junior Camp (ages 10 through 12), and Senior Camp (ages 12 through 14). UCSB Day Camp costs between $100 and $120 a week.

UCSB coaches also run specialized volleyball and basketball camps for girls and boys (day and overnight). There are also UCSB tennis, golf, soccer, water polo, baseball, drama, and swing dance camps. UCSB Ocean Camps offer one-week surf and kayak sessions for boys and girls ages 9 through 17. Fees are $85 a session (Monday through Friday, half-day). There's also a seven-week Junior Lifeguard camp for $300. Call for information.

### Montecito

**Montecito Family YMCA**
**591 Santa Rosa Lane**
**Montecito, CA**
**(805) 969–3288**
**www.ymca.net**

This camp is smaller than the one at the main YMCA—approximately 100 kids attend the camp at a time. It's also open to middle school-age campers. The Y offers special activities such as off-site camping and horseback riding. Each session has a theme and lasts two weeks. Typical activities include arts and crafts, swimming, barbecues, and field trips to local parks and beaches. Fees start at $250.

**Westmont College Sports Camp**
**Westmont College**
**955 La Paz Road**
**Montecito, CA**
**(805) 565–6010**
**www.westmont.edu**

Kids from ages 5 through 12 can sign up for half-day programs in basketball, soccer, volleyball, tennis, track and field, archery, and general sports skills. Kids ages 7 through 14 can enroll in a full-day sports camp for basketball, soccer, or baseball. Age groups vary depending on the sport. Half-day sessions cost $125; full-day sessions, $175. Sessions last one week.

## Best Places for a Birthday Party

When the big day comes along, you can choose from dozens of places to celebrate with friends and family. During fair-weather months, parties take place at just about every park in the county (see our Parks chapter to review your options). Here are a few other Insider kids' favorite party locations.

### Santa Barbara

**Gymboree Play & Music**
**5148 Hollister Avenue**
**Goleta, CA**
**(805) 683–7780**
**www.sbgymbo.com**

At a Gymboree party, kids 4 and younger can spend two hours romping on the play equipment and joining in music, movement and games. Gymboree supplies invitations, party bags, an air jumper, a zipline, and staffers to lead the songs and activities.

**Kindermusik**
**1213 State Street, Suite 1**
**Santa Barbara, CA**
**(805) 884–4009**

Kids love music, and good tunes are sure to set the tone for a successful birthday party. Kindermusik will create a theme and design musical activities and creative games for your child's party. You can stage the event in their studio or they'll come to you.

**Santa Barbara Zoological Gardens**
**500 Niños Drive**
**Santa Barbara, CA**
**(805) 962–5339 ext. 27, Birthday Party Hotline**
**(805) 962–5339 ext. 54 (recorded message)**
**www.santabarbarazoo.org**

You can reserve one of six picnic areas at the zoo for your private use for the entire day. The Ridley-Tree House Restaurant can cater the party with special kids meals such as pizza and sandwiches, and the gift shop can provide gift bags for guests. You can even purchase a special party bag complete with animal print invitations, plates, cups, napkins, a tablecloth, and decorative banners. For a minimal extra charge, you can also arrange for a zoo docent to bring an animal to the party. This is a favorite spot for kids' parties, so you need to book at least two weeks in advance.

### Goleta

**Zodo's Bowling & Beyond**
**5925 Calle Real**
**Goleta, CA**
**(805) 967–0128**

You can bumper bowl the day away at Zodo's Bowling & Beyond. Choose from three children's birthday packages. The first is $8.95 per child for an hour of bowling, the second includes lunch for $12.95 per child, and if you throw in a birthday cake and party bags it's $15.95 per child. This is a popular place so you'll need to book lanes a week or two in advance.

**South Coast Railroad Museum and Old Goleta Depot**
**300 N. Los Carneros Road**
**Goleta, CA**
**(805) 964–3540**
**www.goletadepot.org**

Hop aboard the party train! The South Coast Railroad Museum offers a Party Pack, which lets you buy tickets for miniature train rides in advance and reserve picnic tables. You also receive a coupon that's good for a 10-percent discount on any purchase at the museum's Trackside Shop.

## Especially for Teens

**Teen Programs**
**100 E. Carrillo Street**
**Santa Barbara, CA**
**(805) 897-2650**
**www.sbparksandrecreation.com**

The Santa Barbara City Parks and Recreation Department sponsors a Teen Programs club for local youth from ages 13 through 19. Activities are planned by teens themselves and include sports tournaments, drug-free and tobacco-free dances with DJs and live bands, special classes, field trips, teen-produced TV shows, murals, and conferences. The fee for each activity varies from $5 to $25.

During the summer months, Teen Programs organizes a Summer Late Nights Program. Various sites throughout the city (for example public swimming pools, Boys and Girls Clubs, and the YMCA) stay open for late-night activities exclusively for teens on Friday, Saturday, and Sunday nights between 8:00 P.M. and midnight. Just hop aboard a free shuttle bus to any of the designated sites and join in the fun.

# Living with Mother Nature

Rockin' and Rollin'
Devil Winds
Fire!
And—Would you Believe—Floods!

With all of Santa Barbara's wonderful qualities, you wouldn't think there would be anything to worry about besides high prices and an occasional foggy morning. But local residents know that Mother Nature occasionally imparts a cruel blow, and rather than burying our heads in the proverbial sand, we try to learn as much as we can about every possibility. Knowledge is power, as they say, and being prepared could literally save your life.

Visitors to California are probably more afraid of earthquakes than anything else. No matter how sophisticated the science of earthquake prediction has become, the fact is that no one knows exactly when a quake will hit—or how earthshaking it will be. Although you just never know when the ground underneath you will start heaving and jolting, we hope that reading this chapter will allow you to rest a little easier. In addition to earthquakes, the chapter deals with several other unsettling natural phenomena, including Santa Ana winds, brushfires, and El Niño, a warm ocean current that causes a huge increase in seasonal rainfall followed by inevitable floods, mudslides, and one great big mess. Before you decide to move to or spend your vacation on the East Coast, however, remember that most of us have lived for decades in Santa Barbara without being directly affected by any of these natural disasters. And we've all survived an earthquake or two with nothing more than a few broken knickknacks and frayed nerves. So relax! We still think you'd be hard-pressed to find a nicer place to vacation—or live in—at any time of year.

## Rockin' and Rollin'

Santa Barbara has had its share of earthquakes, and we mean big earthquakes (as well as lots of little shakers). This is mostly due to the fact that California's main earthquake fault, the San Andreas, sits right under the Santa Ynez Mountains, which border Santa Barbara to the north. It is along the San Andreas that seismologists have predicted the proverbial "Big One" : that massive earthquake that is supposed to suddenly let loose after years of pressure buildup along the fault line. Of course, no one knows when this will happen, and predictions run the gamut, from "imminent" to "within the next 100 years," and, lately, some scientists have said that perhaps they were all wrong about the San Andreas after all. Even if a large quake does happen, the fault stretches from Southern California clear up to the San Francisco Bay Area, so the hardest-hit areas could be anywhere along the fault line. While we're realistic about earthquakes, we like to think the Big One will leave Santa Barbara relatively unscathed.

The above philosophy might be wishful thinking, however, because Santa Barbara has been hit by large quakes before, both along the San Andreas Fault and on smaller faults in the area. Of course, back in the old days, structures were built of adobe bricks and fell down in a heartbeat. On the morning of December 12, 1812, for example, a major quake destroyed Mission Santa Barbara and the Presidio, and frightened local residents half to death. It was more than a century before the next major quake struck, on June 29, 1925,

*A storm approaches Santa Barbara Harbor.* PHOTO: BRIAN HASTINGS

destroying most of downtown Santa Barbara's buildings, cracking Sheffield Reservoir, and killing several people. The largest temblor in recent times happened in 1978 when a fault under the Santa Barbara Channel gave way, rupturing to the northwest. Goleta sustained the most damage in the quake, which hurled one-third of the books in the UCSB library onto the floor, shattered windows, dislodged dozens of mobile homes from their supports and derailed a freight train. The most famous of California's earthquakes in recent years is probably the Northridge quake of 1994, which killed 55 people and caused more than $9 billion in property damage in the San Fernando Valley. Who can forget those news shots of a three-story apartment building that collapsed down to one story, killing 16 people who were asleep in their beds? Could the same thing be in store for Santa Barbara?

California is earthquake country! But before you panic, remember that the Hollywood film depictions of people being swallowed up by huge cracks in the ground during earthquakes take it to the extreme. Unless something falls on you or you go running around with no shoes through a room littered with broken glass, you'll probably be able to ride the thing out with no problem. Seismic retrofitting (which is essentially strengthening buildings to withstand major quakes) is a continuous process in the city and the state, and most of our public buildings, highway bridges, and schools would be able to stand some pretty heavy shaking without falling down.

Around the house, we suggest protecting your family heirloom china by storing it carefully wrapped in a low cupboard or in a box on the garage floor, out of the way of other objects that might fall on it. Bolt or strap heavy bookcases or cabinets to the wall so they don't fall on you, and do the same to your water heater, which will be one of the first things to topple over in a major quake. Some people go so far as to put latches on kitchen cabinets to keep dishes and food from spilling out onto the floor during a quake. Household chemicals should be sealed tightly and stored so they won't tip over, and flammable liquids should be stored well away from your water heater if it has a pilot light.

For more tips on earthquake safety, see the Survival Guide in the Pacific Bell Smart Yellow Pages or contact the local office of the American Red Cross at (805) 687-1331. When you feel an earthquake happening (and yes, you'll know when it happens), here are a few basic survival tips: First, stay calm! (Okay, okay, we know this is pretty unrealistic.) If you are inside, stand under a doorway or take shelter under a sturdy desk or table away from windows or falling heavy objects or appliances. If you are outside, stand as far away as possible from buildings (which usually fall outward if they are going to fall), trees, and telephone or electrical lines. If you are on the road, get away from overpasses, bridges, and tunnels and stop in a safe area, then stay in your car until the shaking stops and it is safe to proceed. If Santa Barbara is hit with a major earthquake, fire, or flood, possibilities include loss of electrical power and/or telephone service, evacuation, contaminated drinking water, and lack of access to retail stores. To prepare for such a state of affairs, you should have a basic emergency kit for your family. Suggested items include a portable radio with extra batteries; a flashlight for each member of the family plus extra batteries; a first aid kit, including a book with instructions for dealing with injuries; enough bottled water to sustain your family for several days; and canned and dried foods to sustain your family for a week (rotate these, making sure that shelf life is not exceeded), and a manual can opener. You can add other items you feel are appropriate for your family.

**Insiders' Tip**

Until 1934, Santa Barbara had a record high temperature on the U.S. Weather Bureau's books. It occurred on June 17, 1859, when a simoom (scorching wind) swept down from the northwest and the mercury soared to 133 degrees Fahrenheit. Cattle dropped dead and birds fell from the sky. The record was topped when the mercury hit 134 in Death Valley in 1934.

## Devil Winds

Nearly every year, in late fall and early winter, the wind pattern shifts ominously along the Southern California coast. Ocean breezes that keep us cool and gently sway the trees give way to hot, dry, and powerful Santa Ana winds out of the northeast. The change doesn't happen in an instant, and forecasters are usually able to see the winds coming, but they are stifling and unsettling at best, and the threat of wind-driven brushfires lingers oppressively on everyone's mind until the winds abate. Reportedly named for Santa Ana Canyon near Los Angeles, where they blow particularly strong, Santa Ana winds are created when high pressure develops over the Great Basin, forcing air downslope from the high plateau to the coast. The air warms as it rushes through the canyons of Southern California, and it also picks up speed. Temperatures may rise into the 90s or 100s, and winds typically gust between 15 and 40 miles per hour, with isolated gusts reaching hurricane force. The winds tend to blow hardest at night and in the early morning, rattling nerves as they play havoc while you're trying to sleep.

It is during the ferocious Santa Ana wind storms that the California fire season roars into everyone's consciousness. Chaparral-covered hillsides that have dried out through the summer are tinder-dry in fall, and all it takes is a careless moment to ignite a wind-driven fire that can be virtually unstoppable. See the next section for suggestions on what to do to

CLOSE-UP

# Birding in Santa Barbara

If all you've been doing since you got to town is sunning yourself, going for strolls on the beach, and browsing museums, you've missed one of the activities for which Santa Barbara is renowned. We're talking about birding. More than 450 species of birds have been recorded in Santa Barbara County, making it one of the premier birding spots in the country. Santa Barbara's combination of ocean, coastal wetlands, freshwater marshes, coastal sage scrub, native grasslands, riparian woodland, oak woodland, chaparral, and pine forest make it a magnet for birds. Due to its location along the Pacific Flyway, the area also sees large numbers of migrating birds in spring and fall, which is when you are most likely to see local birders out in force.

While most tourist publications tout the city's fabulous restaurants, shops, and cultural offerings, birders often eschew all that for a day in the field. Even if you're not a field birder, you can join the hundreds of local backyard birders who religiously stock feeders for their feathered friends. In short, birding is big in Santa Barbara.

## Getting Started

If you're just getting started in birding, we recommend taking one of the Adult Education birding classes offered by Santa Barbara City College's Continuing Education Division (805–687–0812). Both beginning and intermediate classes on birds of the Santa Barbara region are offered two or three times a year for a small fee. Classes, usually held on weekday mornings, span six weeks and are led by experienced birders. You'll learn to recognize local birds and take several field trips to various habitats, including beaches, sloughs, and creeks. All you need is a little free time and a pair of binoculars.

The Santa Barbara Museum of Natural History (805–682–4711) schedules birding classes and sponsors field trips. We also recommend joining the Santa Barbara Audubon Society (805–964–1468), which offers free field trips at least once a month and puts on monthly programs that cover all aspects of birding and nature in general. Introductory membership is $20 and includes a subscription to *El Tecolote,* the monthly newsletter that lists all field trips and programs. If you are a member of the National Audubon Society, membership in the local chapter is free. Finally, every beginning birder needs a field guide. Two excellent choices if you're just starting out are Herbert Clarke's *An Introduction to Southern California Birds* and Roger Tory Peterson's *A Field Guide to Western Birds.*

Once you've mastered all the local species (give yourself a couple of years for this), you'll be ready to graduate to the National Geographic Society's more comprehensive *Field Guide to the Birds of North America.* Commonly referred to as the "Geo guide," this is the favorite of most birders and includes birds from all regions of the country. (Believe it or not, most of the eastern birds—especially the warblers—have made their way to Santa Barbara County at one time or another, causing no end of excitement for local listers.)

## Best Birding Spots

While you may not have to go looking for birds in Santa Barbara (there are usually plenty in your yard, especially if you have a feeder), there are a few local hot spots that are frequented by both local and out-of-town birders. Here are a few of our South County favorites:

### Rocky Nook Park

With mature oaks and sycamores as well as the riparian woodland bordering Mission Creek, Rocky Nook Park, located just above Mission Santa Barbara in Mission County, is a great birding spot during every season. It's especially good in early spring, when warblers tend to gather before migration. Yellow-rumped, Townsend's, and black-throated gray warblers are usually singing by April, and warbling vireos, western tanagers, Bullock's, and hooded orioles, Pacific-slope flycatchers, black-headed grosbeaks, and western kingbirds are always present in the spring. Oak titmice, wrentits, and several varieties of woodpeckers are just some of the species that inhabit the park year-round, and an occasional rarity such as a black-and-white warbler may lurk in the oaks.

### Andree Clark Bird Refuge

Situated at the east end of Cabrillo Boulevard, the refuge offers a close-up look at waterfowl as well as land birds that frequent the introduced trees and plants north of the refuge. This is one of the few places in the county where you can sometimes find great-tailed grackles and wood ducks, and you'll occasionally see eastern kingbirds on the islands during migration. Observation platforms along the north side of the refuge allow for clear viewing of the water, and a trail runs from the Los Patos Way parking lot west.

### Garden Street Outfall

Where Garden Street (formerly known as Santa Barbara Street) meets Cabrillo Boulevard, the beachfront is especially good for spotting shorebirds, gulls, and terns. This is the favorite resting spot of black skimmers in the winter, and Santa Barbara's only recorded black-headed gull showed up at the outfall for several winters beginning in 1992.

### Atascadero Creek

Atascadero Creek is accessible at the south end of Turnpike Road, Walnut Drive, Patterson Avenue, and Ward Memorial Drive. It is especially good in fall for migrating warblers and sparrows. Blue grosbeaks and lazuli and indigo buntings are often found in the weedy grasses here in fall, and occasionally a rarity such as painted bunting, bobolink, or dickcissel turns up. It's an easy walk along the hard-packed dirt of the edge of the creek, and an adjacent bike trail runs the entire distance.

## San Jose Creek

San Jose has been a favorite birding creek for years. Right on the border between Santa Barbara and Goleta, it offers the best birding between Cathedral Oaks Road and north Patterson Avenue and above and below the Berkeley Road bike bridge. During migration, it's especially good for warblers, tanagers, orioles, and humming birds, which frequent the bottlebrush trees along Merida Drive.

## Stow House and Lake, Los Carneros

Located off Los Carneros Road between Calle Real and Cathedral Oaks Road, this county park features exotic plantings, an artificial lake, and plenty of open space. One of the best places in the South County to see all the California specialties (wrentit, California towhee, California thrasher, and often California quail), it is frequented by Adult Ed birding classes and area birders. In the garden of Stow House, look for an abundance of orioles (both hooded and Bullock's) in the spring as well as hummingbirds, vireos, and warblers. Sparrows, including white-crowned, Lincoln's and golden-crowned, are plentiful in winter, and berry-eaters such as cedar waxwings, American robins, and western tanagers feed in pyracantha and toyon. The lake affords views of a variety of wintering ducks and herons, egrets, and bitterns. You can hike around the lake and garden in about an hour, or stop on the footbridge at the north end of the lake and watch the reeds below for soras, Virginia rails, and least bitterns. In spring and fall, Lake Los Carneros is a perfect spot for observing seasonal comings and goings.

## Central Coast Birding Trail

Recently, the National Audubon Society of California and the Santa Barbara and La Purisima local chapters became partners in forming the Santa Barbara County section of the Central Coast Birding Trail, which in its entirety runs from the northern edge of Ventura County up the coast to Monterey. A brochure outlining Santa Barbara County's best birding spots along the trail is available from the Santa Barbara Audubon Society. Some of the places we've mentioned previously are included, along with several North County sites.

# Christmas Count

Every year, the National Audubon Society sponsors a Christmas Bird Count. The CBC happens during a designated two-week period from mid-December to early January, and each local Audubon Society chapter picks one day during the count period to stage its count. On that day, birders fan out over the designated count circle (each count must be conducted within the perimeter of a predetermined circle with a 15-mile diameter), recording every species and individual bird they see. Although it is impossible to be exact, data from counts held all over North America are used to determine the relative stability of certain species and the expansion or shrinking of their ranges. All of this sci-

*Local birders focus on local birds during a Santa Barbara Audubon Society outing to Lake Los Carneros in Goleta.* PHOTO: KAREN BRIDGERS

entific stuff aside, over the years the CBC has evolved into a kind of Super Bowl of birding during which different count circles vie for the honor of recording the most species of birds. Santa Barbara inevitably does itself proud in this winter census, virtually always finding enough species to rate a place in the top five counts in the country. In 1981, 1983, and 1988, Santa Barbara recorded more species of birds than any other count, further bolstering its reputation as a North American birding hot spot. Only experienced birders generally participate in the count, but feeder watchers can also contribute. Look for details in *El Tecolote,* the Santa Barbara Audubon Society's newsletter.

## Listing

Listing is big with birders. As the name implies, listing is simply keeping a list of all of the species of birds you have seen in a particular context. Most local birders keep a life list (a list of every species they have ever seen), a North America list, a California list, and a Santa Barbara County list as well as a yard list (a list of every species they've seen in or from their yard). Listing is made easier by the availability of checklists, which you will find in most field guides or can pick up from the local Audubon Society chapter. The checklist to the birds of Santa Barbara County, for example, has 445 species on it, with places where you can check off those you have seen. It is available for a small fee from the Santa Barbara Audubon Society.

**Insiders' Tip**

The *Santa Barbara News-Press* publishes a column called Bird Watch in the Thursday "Life" section that focuses on local bird species and news of interest to local birders. On the prowl for species rare in these parts? Call the Santa Barbara Audubon Society's Rare Bird Alert hotline at (805) 964-8240.

protect yourself and your property from fire damage. Thus prepared, the next time those devil winds come thundering down the canyons, perhaps you can sit on your deck with a tall glass of iced tea and not worry your little head about it.

## Fire!

Santa Barbara is no stranger to fires. Many neighborhoods in the city have either been destroyed or threatened, with homes in the brushy canyons being especially vulnerable. One of the most devastating fires in Santa Barbara's history happened in June 1990, when an arsonist hurled an incendiary device into the dry brush above Painted Cave Road. Driven by gusting Santa Ana winds, the blaze swept down the canyon and threatened to burn its way to the sea. Exclusive homes burned to the ground as residents barely escaped with their lives, and horses and other animals wandered the streets, dazed and confused. When the winds finally died down and the fire was put out, more than 450 homes had been destroyed and nearly 5,000 acres consumed, leaving a black scar on the hills above Santa Barbara for years. If you are lodging along the coast or live in the midst of a well-populated area free of brush and chaparral, brushfires are not much of a threat. But if you live in the foothills or canyons above the city, you need to do all you can to protect yourself against fires. There is much you can do to prepare for a brushfire or possible evacuation.

First, remove all hazardous brush to within 100 feet of your house and any outbuildings. If you have a wooden shake roof (which is a veritable fire trap), replace it with fire-resistant roofing material. Ask your contractor or a building supply store for options. If you have a swimming pool, get a pump for it that will divert water into a hose for firefighting. Since people tend to panic in emergencies, make a prioritized list now of what you want or need to take with you if you have to evacuate suddenly. Post it in a convenient place (like on the inside of a cupboard door), and make sure the items listed are easily accessible. During periods of high fire danger, keep your car's gas tank at least half full so you don't have to stop and get gas in order to get out of the area. Also, have at least two sets of keys for each vehicle, and leave one set at home and easily accessible so parked cars can be moved out of harm's way. Finally, be careful out there! Do not discard lighted cigarettes carelessly, never set off personal fireworks, and be extremely careful when using outdoor machinery that could send sparks flying into dry brush. The neighborhood you save may be your own.

## And—Would You Believe—Floods!

If you've never lived in California, you might not have heard of Santa Ana winds, but we'd bet our bottom dollar you've heard of El Niño. This benignly named weather phenomenon has wreaked havoc on the world a couple of times in the last several years and has been blamed for floods, droughts, fires, and just about

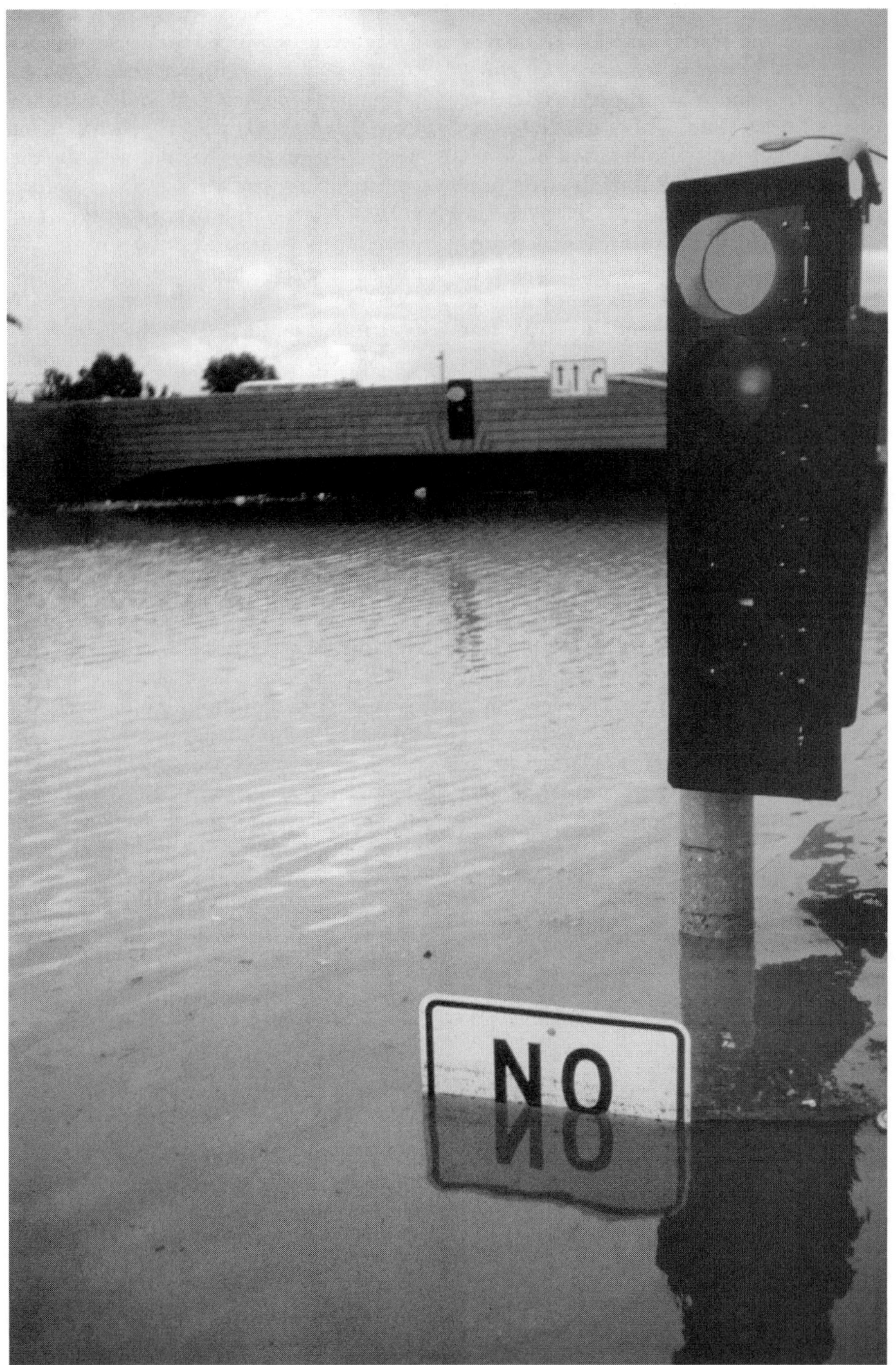


*Freak heavy rains flood the Garden Street underpass.* PHOTO: BRIAN HASTINGS

every other natural disaster, including the plunge of the stock market (well, maybe that's a slight exaggeration). El Niño, which is a Spanish name used in reference to the Christ child, was originally recognized by fishermen off the coast of South America. Since it tended to show up near the Christmas holiday, it was given the name of the baby whose birth is celebrated at that season. Over the years, however, El Niño has lost whatever innocent connotation it once had and tends to strike fear into the hearts of just about everyone who has something to lose from its effects.

El Niño is quite a complex phenomenon, but basically it has to do with the interaction between the atmosphere in the tropical Pacific and the surface layers of the ocean. That somehow results in warmer temperatures at the surface of the ocean off Southern California, which causes storms to be warmer, resulting in a lot more rain than normal. Also, it causes big waves that tend to take out piers and crash through the windows of beachfront homes. While it's interesting to read about the causes of El Nino, people are more concerned about the impact it will have in their own backyard. In fall 1997, scientists started warning Californians that the winter of 1997–98 was going to be a big El Niño season. Everyone got all worked up and creeks were cleared, the harbor was dredged, sandbags were amassed, roofs were replaced, emergency agencies planned their strategies, and then. . . nothing. Halloween and Thanksgiving came and went and hardly a drop fell from the sky. And then, just when everyone was on the verge of gleefully declaring that the scientists were wrong, Santa Barbara got slammed with a major storm in early December. "Not an El Niño storm," said meteorologists. "Just wait." The rest of December and nearly all of January were practically bone dry.

We were almost out of the woods. Then, in February, El Niño hit with a vengeance. High waves ripped 150 deck planks off Stearns Wharf and loosened 50 foundation pilings, requiring a half-million dollars in repairs. Then the rains pounded Santa Barbara, sometimes dropping 4 or 5 inches per storm. Near the end of the rainy season, Santa Barbara had already received nearly 47 inches, beating the former record of 45.2 inches in the 1940–44 season. As a result, the hotel occupancy rate dropped, rain-soaked hillsides slid onto roads and houses, and many areas of the city and county were flooded at various times. Everything was, in short, a great big mess. Luckily, El Niño only comes around every three to seven years, so it may not hit again for a while. So pack your lucky rabbit's foot along with your sunscreen and come on over!

# Santa Barbara Wine Country



Are you a wine lover in search of a Santa Barbara excursion? Just hop in your car and drive north, and within 45 minutes of leaving downtown Santa Barbara you'll land smack dab in the heart of one of California's premier wine regions.

The North County (which is how most Santa Barbarans refer to the region on the north side of the Santa Ynez Mountain range) is a tranquil and beautiful area, with scenic roads that wind through rolling, oak-studded hills, valleys, and mountains. It's home to ranchers, farmers and, in recent years, more than a few celebrities escaping the glare of Hollywood—including Michael Jackson and Bo Derek.

Agriculture dominates the North County scene, and much of Santa Barbara County's produce originates here. Recently, broccoli nudged strawberries out of the top spot for the annual revenue totals of county crops.

The second most valuable crop is wine grapes, whose market value exceeded $90 million in 2000, making the wine industry one of the largest agricultural businesses in Santa Barbara County. In less than 30 years, this scenic region has evolved into a world-class hot spot for premium wine production. In 1970 fewer than 200 acres in the area were planted with grapevines. Today more than 20,000 acres are planted with nearly all types of wine-producing grapes. Wineries large and small are scouting for new vineyard locations, buying land, digging in, and planting those vines. It's almost like a Grape Rush—everyone wants a piece of the gold-nugget action.

Santa Barbara County's wine-making and grape-growing history spans more than 200 years. It started in 1782 when Father Junipero Serra carried grapevines from Mexico all the way to Santa Barbara. Mission Santa Barbara maintained several vineyards, and there was even a winery on Santa Cruz Island. Justinian Caire planted 150 acres with imported French grape slips and shipped his wines up the coast to San Francisco for bottling.

By the 1920s there were about 250 acres of land planted with wine grapes. Prohibition effectively shut down all winery operations in the area, and it would be more than 30 years before the local wine industry would reestablish itself. But then it did so with a vengeance.

In the early 1960s, researchers at the University of California at Davis discovered that the unusual geography, topography, and climate of the Santa Barbara County region held great promise for growing wine grapes. This substantiated the suspicions of several winemaking pioneers, who were already scoping out the region for places to plunk their vines.

So now for a geography, topography, and climate lesson. (Don't yawn—it's important!) By now, you're probably used to hearing about the unusual east-west orientation of the Santa Barbara coastline. Well, the Santa Ynez and the San Rafael mountain ranges also run east-west. No other coastal mountain ranges on the West Coast of North America, except for some in parts of Alaska, run in this direction—they all run pretty much north-south.

The valleys between these east-west-running mountains run perpendicular to the coastline—also an unusual phenomenon. The cool ocean breezes and fog flow steadily through the valleys in the late afternoon or evening, then retreat about mid-morning. The result: hot sunny days and cool nights, perfect for growing wine grapes.

The region is basically a grower's paradise: All the classic grape varieties thrive here, thanks to the numerous microclimates and the long, cool growing season. The region is far enough south to avoid the early winter storms that sometimes threaten late harvests up north. And since the winters are usually temperate, bud break on the vines occurs much earlier than up north. The grapes here hang on the vines longer, which allows them to develop rich, intense, concentrated flavors.

In 1962 Pierre Lafond established Santa Barbara Winery, the first commercial winery in Santa Barbara County since Prohibition. Stearns Wharf Vintners followed suit in 1965. The 1970s gave birth to several more fledgling wineries, including Firestone Vineyard, Rancho Sisquoc Winery, Zaca Mesa Winery, and the Brander Vineyard.

By the 1980s the word about the great wine potential of Santa Barbara County was starting to spread, and the wine industry's roots were firmly entrenched in local soil. Today there are more than 60 wineries in Santa Barbara County and more than 20,000 acres of vineyards. Most are small operations, run by families or individuals rather than large corporations.

Until just a few years ago, the majority of grapes grown here were shipped to wineries outside the county. That trend is now reversed—the grapes are mostly being used by wineries within Santa Barbara County or by wineries outside the county that own vineyards here, such as Kendall-Jackson and Robert Mondavi in Northern California.

Nearly everyone here grows and produces Chardonnay—it's the area's signature wine. But Santa Barbara County has also been singled out for producing world-class Pinot Noir—a fragile, delicate varietal that requires not only ideal growing conditions, but also careful management. Other popular Santa Barbara County wines include Riesling, Sauvignon Blanc, Syrah, Merlot, Cabernet Sauvignon, and Gewürztraminer.

While great grapes form the basis of great wines, they wouldn't amount to much without the expertise of an experienced wine-maker. The winemakers of Santa Barbara County have earned a reputation in the wine world not only as wizards in the technical sense, but also as creative innovators who aren't afraid to experiment with new methods and varietals. Here, you'll notice some unique and intriguing blends that you won't find anywhere else.

Santa Barbara County wines have earned great respect in the wine world and have won numerous awards in regional, national, and international competitions. Once you taste them, you'll be raving, too.

To learn more about the region's phenomenal growth and leap to stardom in the world of wine, get a copy of *Aged in Oak: The Story of the Santa Barbara County Wine Industry*. It covers the entire 200-year history of the Santa Barbara County wine industry, focusing on the grape-growers and wine-makers whose pioneering efforts set the stage for today's vibrant industry. The text was researched and written by faculty and students at UCSB, and the nonprofit Santa Barbara County Vintners' Association contributed to the winery profiles, sidebars, and maps. The book also features fantastic photos by Kirk Irwin, a renowned Santa Barbara photographer. You can purchase the book at local bookstores, at many wineries, and through the Santa Barbara County Vintners' Association (805-688-0881, 800-218-0881).

## Wine Country Information

**Santa Barbara County Vintners' Association (805) 688–0881, (800) 218–0881**

The Santa Barbara County Vintners' Association is a nonprofit organization founded in 1983. It supports and promotes Santa Barbara County as a premium wine-producing and wine grape-growing region. It also strives to enhance the position of Santa Barbara County wines in the world marketplace. Current members include 56 wineries, 29 independent vineyards, and 5 vineyard consultant/management companies.

The Vintners' Association sponsors festivals, seminars, and tastings and provides information to the media and consumers. Call for specific information about wineries and events and to request a current Santa Barbara County wine country map.

### Insiders' Tip

In the summer, when it's foggy and cool on the coast, it's usually hot and sunny in the wine country. So if you're heading to the valley for a day of wine tasting on a foggy summer day, dress in cool, light clothing.

## Touring and Tasting through Wine Country

Santa Barbara wine country is not Napa or Sonoma, but we think that's a blessing. It's not nearly as touristy, crowded, and built-up, and we think the wines rank up there with the best.

When you go touring here, you can relax and enjoy gorgeous scenery and outstanding wines without the crowds and the hype. Many wineries welcome visitors year-round, most on a daily basis and others at least on weekends.

Tasting rooms range from tiny spaces in historic farmhouses and rustic cabins to spacious, contemporary buildings with various amenities. You can sample the wines and buy a few bottles (or cases) to bring home; at some places you can sample and purchase gourmet foods such as pasta sauces, salsas, grapeseed oils, and other winery products.

Several wineries offer tours of the winemaking facilities and/or caves, and one or two will take you through the vineyards at certain times of year. Reservations for tasting and tours are usually required for groups of 10 or more—you will need to call ahead and make an appointment.

Most Santa Barbara County wineries are part of one of two outstanding wine trails, the Santa Ynez Valley Wine Trail and the Foxen Canyon Wine Trail (see the "Wineries" section of this chapter). You can also visit a few wineries that lie west of U.S. Highway 101, and several tasting rooms right in downtown Santa Barbara by the beach.

In this chapter we give you an overview of most of the area's main tasting rooms. We also let you know about a few of our favorite hotels, inns, and restaurants in Santa Barbara wine country. And if you'd like someone to guide you through the wine country—and do all the driving—we recommend a few tour companies.

If you'd like more information on what to see and do while on a daytrip to Solvang and other parts of the North County, be sure to read our Daytrips chapter. Have a wonderful time tasting your way through the bounty of Santa Barbara County!

## How to Get There

Before heading out on your wine-tasting adventure, be sure to get an up-to-date wine touring map featuring all Vintners' Association member wineries, restaurants,

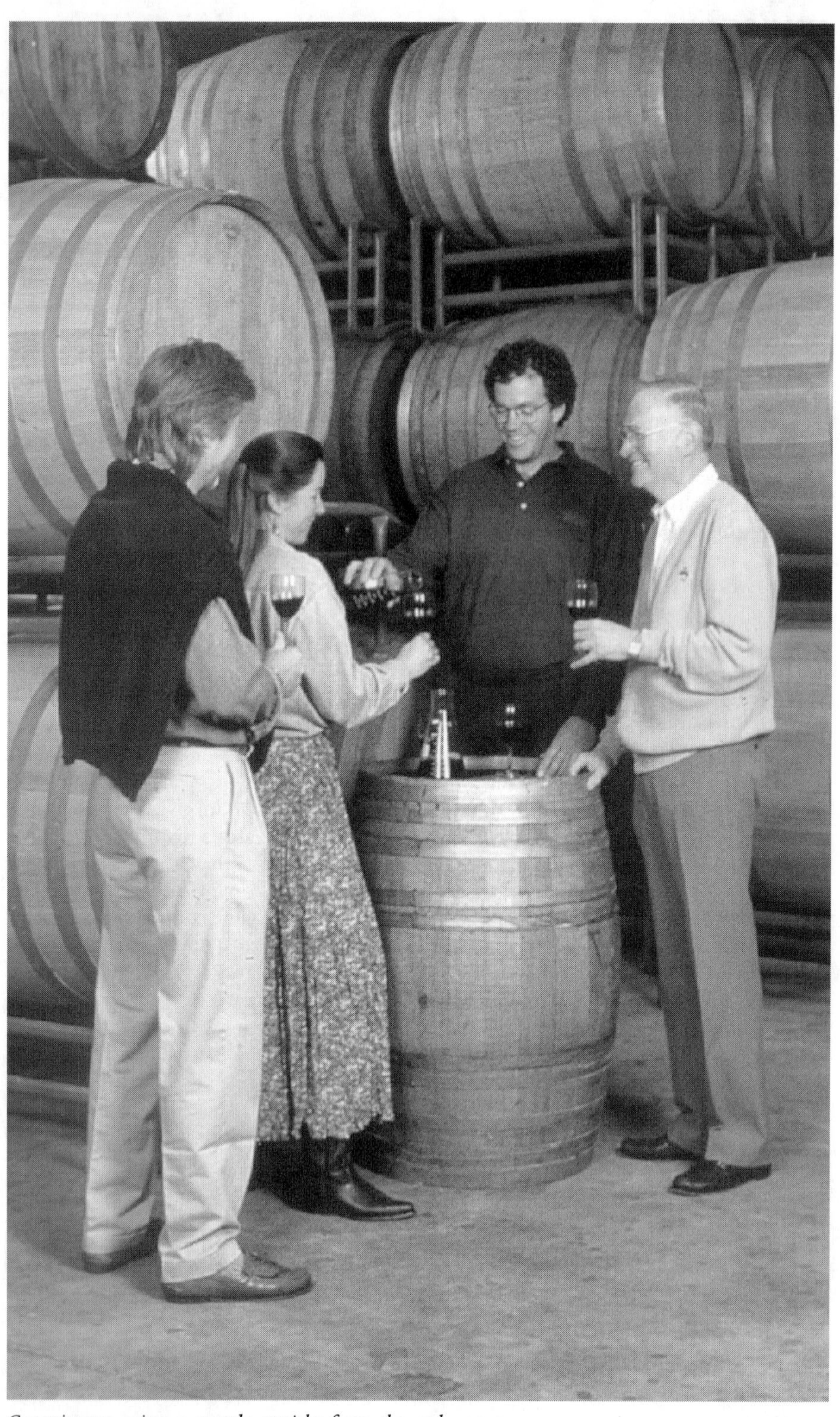

*Connoisseurs enjoy a sample straight from the cask.* PHOTO: KIRK IRWIN, COURTESY OF THE SANTA BARBARA VINTNERS' ASSOCIATION

lodgings, wine shops, and touring services. The association is adding members all the time, and they produce a new map at least once a year, sometimes more often. You can pick up the map at winery tasting rooms, visitor centers, restaurants, and hotels throughout Santa Barbara County and by calling the Vintners' Association at (805) 688-0881 or (800) 218-0881.

From Santa Barbara you have two travel options. The first is to drive north along U.S. 101 about 45 miles to Calif. Highway 246 in Buellton, then turn east. We suggest you begin by stopping in the historic town of Santa Ynez, about 10 miles east of U.S. 101. From there it's just a short drive to many of the wineries on the Santa Ynez Valley Wine Trail.

If you're planning to go on the Foxen Canyon Wine Trail, you should continue driving north on U.S. 101 past Buellton, up to the Calif. Highway 154 turnoff. Turn right and head east a few miles to Foxen Canyon Road. Actually, we suggest that you first drive just a few miles farther on Calif. 154 to historic Los Olivos, where you can visit a few tasting rooms and stock up on picnic items and gas before you head out on the 20-mile wine trail.

Alternatively, you can drive along the "scenic" route to wine country—Calif. 154, which cuts over the mountains and drops into the west side of the Santa Ynez Valley. From downtown Santa Barbara, take U.S. 101 to the State Street/Calif. 154 exit and take Calif. 154 up the mountain. As you descend, you'll be treated to a fantastic overview of the Santa Ynez Mountains, the Los Padres National Forest, and Cachuma Lake.

About 40 minutes after leaving Santa Barbara, you'll arrive at the point where Calif. 154 intersects with Calif. 246. Turn left to go to Santa Ynez and begin the Santa Ynez Valley Wine Trail or continue on about 5 miles to Los Olivos to explore the town before starting your journey along either the Santa Ynez Valley or the Foxen Canyon Wine Trail.

## Tours and Transportation Services

Taking an escorted tour is a great way to cruise through wine country. Just sit back, relax, and sample wine to your heart's content.

**Blue Sky Tours**
**204 Moffett Place**
**Goleta, CA**
**(805) 564-1811, (800) 977-1123**

Blue Sky Tours will customize guided wine country tours to suit your preferences. Vehicles range from town cars and plush limousines to minivans and 47-passenger buses. Tours operate seven days a week and the prices vary depending on the number of passengers. Call for more information.

**Breakaway Tours and Event Planning**
**(805) 783-2929, (800) 799-7657**
**www.breakaway-tours.com**

If you want to come away from a wine country tour feeling like you've learned something about the region, Breakaway Tours is a good choice. This company is a corporate and group tour specialist, but they also customize fun educational tours for individuals. You set the pace—you can learn as little or as much as you please. Vehicles range from 14-passenger vans to 47-passenger motor coaches, and there's door-to-door service. Fees depend on the tour, number of passengers, and whether you want meals and other extras included. The company also organizes winery dinners and other group functions. Call for more information.

**Personal Tours**
**(805) 685-0552**

This excellent local company will customize a wine country tour to suit your needs. All tours are narrated so you'll learn some interesting tidbits about the vineyards, celebrity ranch estates, and other attractions in the area. Vehicles range from sedans, convertibles, and custom vans to minibuses and motor coaches with restrooms. The company also provides step-on guide service (aboard your own vehicle). Call for prices.

**Spencer's Limousine & Tours**
**(805) 884–9700**
**www.spencerslimo.com**

Spencer's offers tours in the luxury of a limousine, minibus, or van. It can customize tours to suit your needs. Each tour is tailored to your tastes, both in wines and places of interest. A four-hour tour might cost $50 per person (four-person minimum); the price would increase if you wanted a longer tour and extra amenities. Spencer himself is an avid historian, so you can expect excellent narration along the way.

**Wine Tours of Santa Barbara**
**(805) 965–0353**
**www.sboldtowntrolley.com**

Santa Barbara Old Town Trolley Co. started running these affordable wine tours in 2000 and business is already booming. Hop aboard the operation's comfortable 27-passenger air-conditioned mini-coach for your narrated tour of the wine country. Along the way, you'll visit Bridlewood, Foley, Gainey, and Rideau vineyards. Tours range from $59 to $69 per person and include lunch and wine-tasting fees. Champagne and hors d'oeuvres are also provided on the bus so you can relax, sip some bubbly, and learn a bit about the region's winemaking history without having to worry about driving. Tours depart daily from Stearns Wharf at 9:40 A.M. and pick up passengers at major hotels before heading into the valley. Customized tours are also available. Call for more information.

**Winetours 101**
**2890 Tepusquet Canyon Road**
**Santa Maria, CA**
**(805) 937–3290**
**www.Winetours101.com**

Pamper yourself for a day and let Jill be your designated driver. She'll pick you up at your North County doorstep and take you on an action-packed, full-day trip to the wineries. Pick-ups in Santa Barbara are available for an extra fee. The tour includes visits to several wineries and other local attractions, refreshments, a delicious lunch, a personal local guide, and unique souvenirs.

Tours are limited to your personal group of two to six persons. The all-inclusive fee for two is $300. Additional guests are $100 each. Discounts for multiple days are available.

## Tasting in Los Olivos

Los Olivos is a small, historic town at the north end of the Santa Ynez Valley Wine Trail and near the beginning of the Foxen Canyon Wine Trail. It's a great place to stop for a snack or a meal or to shop for high-quality art at its famous galleries.

The downtown area covers just a few square blocks, so you can park your car and walk wherever you need to go. You can taste an array of local premium wines right in town at tasting rooms on Grand Avenue, the main street in Los Olivos. Some of the rooms feature wines made by wineries without visitor facilities, and several are part of the Santa Ynez Valley Wine Trail.

Here are two independent tasting rooms that give you the chance to sample various local wines.

**Los Olivos Tasting Room and Wine Shop**
**2905 Grand Avenue**
**Los Olivos, CA**
**(805) 688–7406**
**www.losolivoswines.com**

Here you can sample various wines from wineries that either don't have their own tasting rooms or have limited quantities of wine or limited tasting room hours—including Au Bon Climat, Lane Tanner, Qupé, Foxen, and many others. Ten different wines are always uncorked and ready for tasting. The tasting room is open from 11:00 A.M. to 6:00 P.M. daily (last tasting at 5:30 P.M.).

*Old Western-style facades still line the streets of Los Olivos, a charming small town in the heart of the wine country.* PHOTO: BRIAN HASTINGS

**Los Olivos Wine and Spirits Emporium**
**2531 Grand Avenue**
**Los Olivos, CA**
**(805) 688–4409, (888) SB–WINES**
**www.sbwines.com**

The Los Olivos Wine and Spirits Emporium represents many of the area's smaller premium wineries that produce wine in limited amounts. Most of these wineries do not have their own tasting rooms. You can taste the quality wines of Whitcraft, Qupé, Lane Tanner, Jaffurs, Fiddlehead Cellars, and many others.

You can also purchase wines as well as brandies, distilled agave, small-batch bourbons, and other spirits. The emporium is open daily from 11:00 A.M. to 6:00 P.M. You'll find it in the middle of a field just a half-mile south of the town of Los Olivos (look for the windmill).

## The Wineries

Now that you're a bit familiar with the area, you're ready to start your wine-tasting tour. What follows are brief descriptions of the main wine trails and the wineries along them, including tasting room hours. Some tasting rooms offer 5 to 10 free samples of wines. Most wineries charge a nominal tasting fee (usually $3.50), which typically includes a wine glass. Some also offer you the chance to taste special reserve wines for a fee.

It's best to devote at least a day to each trail so you can take your time tasting, relaxing, and taking in the views. Veteran wine tasters recommend focusing on just one or two varietals at each winery rather than trying every single type. Also, you should eat a bit before each session and remember to drink lots of water—wine can dehydrate you quickly, especially in warm weather.

### Foxen Canyon Wine Trail

The Foxen Canyon Wine Trail connects two wine-growing regions: the Santa Ynez Valley and the Santa Maria Valley. The trail begins on Foxen Canyon Road, just

## Insiders' Tip

Don't start on the Foxen Canyon Wine Trail with an empty gas tank—there aren't any services along the way. It can take up to an hour just to drive the length of Foxen Canyon Road, so make sure you leave enough time to get to the final winery on your list before the bottles are corked up.

north of Los Olivos. From there, the road twists and turns through 20 miles of gently rolling hills and vineyards until it ultimately reaches the end station in Santa Maria, the northernmost area of the county. (We personally think that Foxen Canyon Road is one of the most scenic country roads in the state.)

As you drive along the country roads, you can stop at trail wineries along the way. This is a fantastic tour if you want to feel as if you've stepped back in time and left the workaday world far behind.

**Andrew Murray Vineyards**
**Tasting Room at 2901 Grand Avenue**
**Los Olivos, CA**
**(805) 693-9644**

Andrew Murray Vineyards is Santa Barbara County's only exclusively Rhone estate. It grows grapes on 25 separate hillside blocks on Foxen Canyon Road, each with a distinct microclimate. Individual blocks are handpicked, vinified, and aged separately. The vineyards consistently produce wines of uncommon character, richness, and longevity. The tasting room is in downtown Los Olivos and is open from 11:00 A.M. to 6:00 P.M. Wednesday through Monday (closed Tuesday).

**Bedford Thompson Winery & Vineyard**
**9303 Alisos Canyon Road**
**Los Alamos, CA**
**(805) 344-2107**
**www.bedfordthompsonwinery.com**

Bedford Thompson's tasting room in a rustic old farmhouse is off Alisos Canyon Road between U.S. 101 and Foxen Canyon Road. This small winery, established in 1994, produces just 4,300 cases a year of Chardonnay, Pinot Gris, Syrah, Grenache, Mourvedre, and Cabernet Franc. The Bedford Thompson tasting room is open 10:00 A.M. to 5:00 P.M. daily. You can also enjoy lunch in the small picnic area.

**Byron Vineyard & Winery**
**5230 Tepusquet Road**
**Santa Maria, CA**
**(805) 937-7288, (888) 303-7288**
**www.byronwines.com**

Founded in 1984 by winemaker Byron "Ken" Brown, this highly respected winery is now owned by Robert Mondavi. Ken, however, is still the wine-maker in charge. Byron Winery focuses on Chardonnay and Pinot Noir produced in traditional Burgundian style. It also produces small amounts of Pinot Blanc and Pinot Gris. The estate includes Santa Barbara County's oldest commercial vineyard, and you can picnic in a lovely spot overlooking Tepusquet Canyon. The tasting room is open daily from 10:00 A.M. to 5:00 P.M. from April through October, and from 10:00 A.M. to 4:00 P.M. from November through March. Sometimes the road leading to the winery closes in the winter and spring due to flooding—during those months, you should call ahead to see whether you'll have to take a detour.

**Cambria Winery and Vineyard**
**5475 Chardonnay Lane**
**Santa Maria, CA**
**(888) 339-9463**
**www.cambriawines.com**

From its name, many people assume this winery is located in the coastal town of Cambria (see our Daytrips chapter if you're interested in visiting the town, not the winery). Actually, Cambria Winery is located about 12 miles east of downtown Santa Maria, at the base of Tepusquet Canyon, a former Chumash Indian encampment.

This was the original vineyard in the area, and as Tepusquet Vineyard it produced top-quality wine grapes from the early 1970s to the mid-1980s. Current owner Jess Jackson purchased the property in 1987 and established Cambria Vineyards. The winery is best known for its distinct and intense Chardonnay, Pinot Noir, and Syrah. It also produces Viognier, Barbera, Pinot Blanc, Sangiovese, and a sparkling wine.

The winery tasting room is open 10:00 A.M. to 5:00 P.M. Saturday and Sunday and weekdays by appointment.

**Cottonwood Canyon Vineyard**
**3940 Dominion Road**
**Santa Maria, CA**
**(805) 937–9063**
**www.cottonwoodcanyon.com**

This is the end of the line—or the beginning, depending on which end of the Foxen Canyon Wine Trail you start at. Cottonwood Canyon is a small ultra-premium winery specializing in Estate Chardonnay and Pinot Noir. It was founded in 1988 by the Beko family, and you can sample their wines here in the vineyard tasting room.

The winery sits on a hilltop overlooking the valley, and the picnic area boasts fantastic views of the northern end of the Foxen Canyon Wine Trail. Tours of the wine caves, which are dug into the hillside, are offered on Saturdays. The tasting room is open from 10:30 A.M. to 5:30 P.M. daily.

**Curtis Winery**
**5249 Foxen Canyon Road**
**Los Olivos, CA**
**(805) 686–8999**
**www.curtiswinery.com**

Curtis Winery opened in April 1998 right next door to Firestone (see subsequent listing). In fact, Curtis is owned by Firestone and specializes in handmade boutique wines. Winemaker Chuck Carlson selects handpicked grapes purchased from various Santa Barbara County vintners with a focus on the Rhone Varietals.

The tasting room usually sets out at least one Viognier, a Viognier blend, a Heritage rose, a Syrah, and a Syrah blend. Curtis is also producing small lots of wine in a new gravity-flow facility. The winery is open for tours, tasting, and sales from 10:00 A.M. to 5:00 P.M. daily. If you have a picnic lunch, you can spread it out in the picnic area.

**Fess Parker Winery & Vineyard**
**6200 Foxen Canyon Road**
**Los Olivos, CA**
**(805) 688–1545**
**www.fessparker.com**

Fess Parker (a.k.a. Davy Crockett) and his family own this large, contemporary winery. Fess, the founding visionary, recently turned the reins over to his son and daughter. In fact his son, Eli Parker, is the wine-maker. The vast tasting room is set amid 700 acres of vineyards, lawns, manicured rose gardens, and winery facilities. Step inside and you can browse the antiques and Hollywood memorabilia or relax by the massive stone fireplace.

If you're sampling wines, try the Syrah, Viognier, Pinot Noir, Chardonnay, and White Riesling. The gift shop offers gourmet items, signature winery merchandise, picnic snacks, and Davy Crockett and Daniel Boone items, including Fess's trademark coonskin caps and coonskin bottle toppers.

Winery tours begin at 11:00 A.M. and 1:00 and 3:00 P.M. daily. Tastings and sales are available from 10:00 A.M. to 5:00 P.M. daily.

**Firestone Vineyard**
**5000 Zaca Station Road**
**Los Olivos, CA**
**(805) 688–3940**
**www.firestonewine.com**

Founded in 1972, Firestone is the oldest winery and vineyard in the county. It sits atop a secluded mesa overlooking the valley and vineyards and is best known for its excellent Chardonnay. It also makes high-quality Cabernet Sauvignon and Merlot.

You can picnic in a secluded courtyard or in a picnic area on the hillside overlooking the scenic valley below. Firestone is open for tours, tasting, and sales from 10:00 A.M. to 5:00 P.M. daily. Tours begin every hour at 15 minutes past the hour (last tour at 3:15 P.M.). Don't miss the vineyard tours during harvest time.

**Foxen Vineyard**
**7200 Foxen Canyon Road**
**Santa Maria, CA**
**(805) 937–4251**

Foxen Vineyard's small, rustic winery and tasting room are in a 100-year-old converted barn and other historic buildings right off the side of the road. Foxen makes small amounts of handcrafted Chenin Blanc, Chardonnay, Pinot Noir, Cabernet Sauvignon, Cabernet Franc, Merlot, Syrah, Viognier, and Sangiovese using traditional French methods. It's open for tasting and sales noon to 4:00 P.M. Friday, Saturday, Sunday, and Monday. Note: We arrived after the 4:00 P.M. closing time one Saturday and couldn't find the winery—that's because they bring in the Foxen sign from the side of the road at the end of the day and then the buildings look like someone's private property. (Make sure you plan to arrive well before they shut the doors!)

**Rancho Sisquoc Winery**
**6600 Foxen Canyon Road**
**Santa Maria, CA**
**(805) 934–4332**
**www.RanchoSisquoc.com**

This rustic winery on a 37, 000-acre cattle ranch uses only the finest grapes from its 308-acre estate vineyard—one of the oldest in the county. When you arrive at Rancho Sisquoc, you really feel like you're out on a homestead in the Old West—there's nothing around for miles except pastures, vineyards, and a few ranches and farms here and there. The picnic tables on a grassy area are a great spot to relax and eat.

In the rustic tasting room you can sample various Rancho Sisquoc wines, for example Sauvignon Blanc, Chardonnay, Sylvaner, Riesling, Merlot, Cabernet Sauvignon, and a Meritage blend. The Rancho Sisquoc tasting room is open from 10:00 A.M. to 4:00 P.M. daily.

**Zaca Mesa Winery**
**6905 Foxen Canyon Road**
**Santa Maria, CA**
**(805) 688–9339, (800) 350–7972**
**www.zacamesa.com**

Spanish settlers called this area *la zaca mesa* (the restful place), and the name truly fits the bill. This is one of our favorite wineries, not just for its fantastic wines, but also for the gorgeous natural setting—an unobtrusive, environmentally correct building that blends in perfectly with the surroundings.

The 750-acre property includes 246 acres of mesa vineyards, tranquil dirt roads, nature trails, herb gardens, and native landscaping. You can picnic at tables in the grassy courtyard picnic area or up on the nature trails.

Established in 1973, Zaca Mesa produces about 45,000 cases of wine a year, including Chardonnay, Viognier, and Syrah. The winery is known as a trendsetter because of its unique blends of Rhone varietals, for example the Z Cuvée, a blend of Grenache, Mourvedre, Syrah, Cinsant, and Counoise.

But Zaca Mesa is best known for its famous Syrah. In 1995, *Wine Spectator* said that Zaca Mesa's 1993 Syrah was the sixth best in the world. Zaca Mesa is open for tasting from 10:00 A.M. to 4:00 P.M. daily.

## Santa Ynez Valley Wine Trail

The Santa Ynez Valley Wine Trail winds through the southern end of Santa Barbara wine country, where most of the population lives. You'll see horse farms and orchards, historic towns and quaint villages.

The trail is a loop that takes you to all the major wineries in the Santa Ynez Valley. You can start in Buellton, then head over to Santa Ynez, go up to Los Olivos, and wind back through historic Ballard to Solvang. Or follow the route in reverse.

Either direction you take, you can spend a day (or longer) stopping at the premium wineries along the trail. Pick up a flier at any of the wineries—if you have the bottom of it stamped at six of the wineries, you qualify for a monthly drawing for a free case of wine.

**Insiders' Tip**

Many wineries have wine clubs, and membership often gives you access to limited-release premium wines that never get as far as the stores or restaurants.

**Arthur Earl Winery**
**2921 Grand Avenue**
**Los Olivos, CA**
**(805) 693–1771**

This small winery opened in 1996 and produces about 2,500 to 3,000 cases a year of Italian and Rhone varietals. The winery purchases all its grapes from Santa Barbara County growers, usually in small lots. Many of these lots are bottled separately and are labeled with the source vineyard's name. Other Arthur Earl wines are blends of wine grapes from different vineyards.

You can taste Arthur Earl's current selection of wines inside a charming little tasting room in Los Olivos. It's open for tasting and sales daily from 11:00 A.M. to 6:00 P.M.

**Beckmen Vineyards**
**2670 Ontiveros Road**
**Los Olivos, CA**
**(805) 688–8664**
**www.beckmenvineyards.com**

Beckmen Vineyards is a small, friendly family-owned and -operated winery. Owner Thomas Beckmen and wine-maker Steve Beckmen currently focus on Rhone varietals, producing about 20,000 cases a year. The winery is probably best known for its excellent Syrah. To boost production of its estate wines, Beckmen recently purchased a new vineyard, Purisima Mountain, in Ballard Canyon. Beckmen Vineyards has a beautiful picnic area overlooking a duck pond; the picnic tables are tucked in their own private arbor enclosures. The Beckmen tasting room is open 11:00 A.M. to 5:00 P.M. daily from June 15 to September 15, and from 11:00 A.M. to 5:00 P.M. Friday through Sunday the rest of the year.

**The Brander Vineyard**
**2401 Refugio Road**
**Los Olivos, CA**
**(805) 688–2455**
**www.brander.com**

The Brander Vineyard was established in 1975 and has always been acclaimed as a top producer of premium Sauvignon Blanc. Today the winery produces about 10,000 cases of estate wine each year with grapes from its 40-acre vineyard. Along with the Sauvignon Blanc, Brander makes a Bouchet (a blend of red Bordeaux varietals), Merlot, and Cabernet Sauvignon. Its sister winery, Domaine Santa Barbara, produces Chardonnay, Pinot Gris, and Pinot Noir. The Brander Vineyard is open for tasting and sales daily from 10:00 A.M. to 5:00 P.M. during the summer and 11:00 A.M. to 4:00 P.M. the rest of the year.

**Buttonwood Farm Winery**
**1500 Alamo Pintado Road**
**Solvang, CA**
**(805) 688–3032**
**www.buttonwoodwinery.com**

Established in 1989, Buttonwood Farm Winery produces about 8,000 cases a year of first-rate Sauvignon Blanc, Merlot, Cabernet Sauvignon, Cabernet Franc, Syrah, Marsanne, and red and white blends. You can sample Buttonwood

CLOSE-UP

## What's in a Name?

Ever looked at bottles of wine from Santa Barbara County and wondered about the different regions on the labels? These appellations, also known as American Viticultural Areas (AVAs), can divulge much about the character of the wine you are about to drink. If a label says "Santa Ynez Valley," this means at least 85 percent of the grapes were grown in that federally recognized region. It's a guarantee of geographic origin. Once you know a bit about the growing conditions in these areas, you'll have a richer appreciation for the differences in climate and soils that create the flavor of the wine. California has 69 appellations, three of which belong to Santa Barbara County. We've described these three AVAs briefly below so you can impress your friends next time you buy a bottle.

**Santa Rita Hills**—In 2001 the Bureau of Alcohol, Tobacco and Firearms approved this AVA to differentiate wines made from grapes grown in the cooler western edge of the Santa Ynez Valley. Conditions here mirror those found in Reims in Champagne, France. Morning fog is frequent, winds are strong, and soils typically contain less clay and more calcium than those in the eastern Santa Ynez Valley. World-class Pinot Noir and Chardonnay are produced in this region, which encompasses most of the vineyards lying west of U.S. Highway 101.

**Santa Ynez Valley**—Lying predominantly east of Highway 101, this region is generally warmer than the Santa Rita Hills area with well-drained soils ranging from sandy loams and clay loams to shaly and silty clay loams. The area primarily produces high quality Cabernet Sauvignon, Cabernet Franc, Merlot, Syrah, Grenache, and Sauvignon Blanc.

**Santa Maria Valley**—This funnel-shaped region in the northern part of Santa Barbara County has a cool climate thanks to its prevailing ocean winds. The area's well-drained soils range from sandy loam to clay loam and its cool temperatures make it one of California's best AVAs for Pinot Noir and Chardonnay. Rhone varietals also thrive here, showing great clarity and depth of fruit.

Farm wines every day from 11:00 A.M. to 5:00 P.M. and picnic in the pretty gardens surrounding the tasting room.

**Foley Estates Vineyard & Winery**
**1711 Alamo Pintado Road**
**Solvang, CA**
**(805) 688–8554**

Originally called J. Carey Cellars, Foley Estates has produced limited amounts of handcrafted premium wines for more than 20 years. Nestled under a graceful pepper tree, the tasting room is in a lovely old yellow farmhouse. Within its cozy interior, you can sample and purchase some excellent wines including Pinot Noir, Chardonnay, Cabernet Sauvignon, Merlot, Sauvignon Blanc, and Rosé. You can also relax outdoors on the covered deck or at the picnic tables on the lawn. Take your glass over to LinCourt Vineyards (see subsequent listing) and you'll receive a complimentary tasting. (The two vineyards are owned by the same family.)

Foley Estates is open 10:00 A.M. to 5:00 P.M. daily. Tours are by appointment.

**The Gainey Vineyard**
**3950 E. Calif. Highway 246**
**Santa Ynez, CA**
**(805) 688–0558**
**www.gaineyvineyard.com**

The *Los Angeles Times* has written that "Gainey Vineyard is one of the most beautiful wineries in the world." It's part of the 1,800-acre Gainey Ranch in the Santa Ynez Valley, and the location has been used for a number of Hollywood films and TV shows.

A father-son team of Daniel J. and Daniel H. Gainey runs the winery. It's one of the only wineries in Santa Barbara County to own vineyards in both warm and cool microclimates: one for top-quality Bordeaux varietals and the other for Burgundian varietals. It produces about 18,000 cases annually. Varietals include Sauvignon Blanc, Chardonnay, Riesling, Merlot, Pinot Noir, Cabernet Sauvignon, and Cabernet Franc.

Rising at the end of a long drive lined with pepper trees, the beautiful Spanish-style tasting facility was built in 1984. Within its cool tiled interior, you can taste and purchase the wines and buy delicious tapenades, pasta, gourmet vinegars, and bread-dippers. Be sure to pick up some of the complimentary gourmet recipe sheets near the counter. If you're looking for a place to eat lunch, you can relax and dine at picnic tables overlooking the vineyards. Each year the winery hosts an extensive program of events, including cooking classes, outdoor concerts, winemaker's dinners, and an annual harvest "crush party." The tasting room is open 10:00 A.M. to 5:00 P.M. daily (last tasting at 4:45). Free tours begin at 11:00 A.M. and 1:00, 2:00, and 3:00 P.M.

**LinCourt Vineyards**
**343 N. Refugio Road**
**Santa Ynez, CA**
**(805) 688–8381**

William P. Foley II, owner of Foley Estates Vineyard & Winery, purchased the Santa Ynez Winery in 1996 and renamed it Lin-Court Vineyards after his two daughters, Lindsay and Courtney. The winery produces about 15,000 cases of wine a year and is best known for its Chardonnay and Pinot Noir. Once you pay for a tasting here, you can take your glass over to Foley Estates Vineyard for a complimentary tasting (and vice versa).

The picnic tables on a velvety patch of grass offer fantastic views of the Santa Ynez River Valley. The tasting room is open 10:00 A.M. to 5:00 P.M. daily in the summer and Friday through Monday the rest of the year.

**Longoria Winery**
**2935 Grand Avenue**
**Los Olivos, CA**
**(805) 688–0305**
**www.longoriawine.com**

Few local winemakers know more about local grapes than Rick Longoria. He's been involved in the local wine industry since 1976.

Rick and Diana Longoria's own wine business was a part-time endeavor for 15 years, but now they are fully devoted to their growing winery, which produces about 4,000 cases of handcrafted wines a year. Rick concentrates on Chardonnay, Pinot Noir, Merlot, and Cabernet Franc and has recently added Syrah and Pinot Grigio to the list.

In spring 1998 the Longorias opened a tasting room in a turn-of-the-century building in the center of the quaint village of Los Olivos. It's open for tasting and sales Monday, Wednesday, and Thursday from noon to 4:30 P.M., and Friday through Sunday from 11:00 A.M. to 4:30 P.M. (closed Tuesday).

**Los Olivos Vintners/Austin Cellars**
**2923 Grand Avenue**
**Los Olivos, CA**
**(805) 688–9665, (800) 824–8584**

Austin Cellars was established in 1981. New owners acquired the winery in 1992, and while they continued to produce wines under the Austin Cellars label, they

*Wine country visitors sip wines in the scenic courtyard at Sunstone Vineyards and Winery.*
PHOTO: BRIAN HASTINGS

began using Los Olivos Vintners as their business name and the brand name for their reserve wines. The winery produces about 2,500 cases of wine a year and is best known for its Pinot Noir, dessert wine, Chardonnay, and Cabernet. The tasting room is in downtown Los Olivos and is open from 11:00 A.M. to 6:00 P.M. daily.

**Rusack Vineyards**
**1819 Ballard Canyon Road**
**Solvang, CA**
**(805) 688–1278**
**www.rusackvineyards.com**

Geoff and Alison Rusack's winery is the closest one to downtown Solvang and produces about 5,500 cases of handcrafted premium wines a year. If you're curious about the wine-making process, you might be interested to know that this is a gravity-flow winery, so the wine is treated as gently as possible throughout all stages of production. Rusack Vineyards is perhaps best known for its Cabernet Sauvignon and Chardonnay, but it also produces Pinot Noir, Riesling, Syrah, Merlot, Bordeaux varietals, Cabernet Franc, and a dessert wine made from Riesling and Muscat grapes frozen after harvest. The setting is beautiful. You can relax and sip your wine on a redwood deck overlooking the vineyards and oak-studded hills. Tastings are offered Friday through Sunday from 11:00 A.M. to 5:00 P.M. or by appointment.

**Sunstone Vineyards and Winery**
**125 Refugio Road**
**Santa Ynez, CA**
**(805) 688–WINE, (800) 313–WINE**
**www.sunstonewinery.com**

Sunstone's name comes from its sun-colored stone embankment overlooking the Santa Ynez River Valley, and it's one of the most gorgeous wineries and tasting rooms in the area. Completed in 1993, the spacious, Provençal-style facility offers an elegant tasting bar, stone floors, an arbored porch, beautiful landscaping with French lavender and rosemary, a courtyard with umbrella tables, and a unique 120-foot stone cave dug into the hillside and packed with French oak barrels filled with aging wines. You can also purchase gourmet pasta sauces, vinegars, and grilling oils from the display in the rustic tasting room.

The winery was established in 1989 and produces about 15,000 cases of wine a year using only organically grown grapes. Its signature wine is Merlot, but it also makes excellent Cabernet Sauvignon, Syrah, Viognier, Sauvignon Blanc, Chardonnay, and Muscat Canelli. The tasting room is open 10:00 A.M. to 4:00 P.M. every day.

## West of U.S. Highway 101

**Babcock Vineyards**
**5175 E. Calif. Highway 246**
**Lompoc, CA**
**(805) 736–1455**
**www.babcockwinery.com**

Dentist Walt Babcock and wife, Mona, established this winery in 1984, and son Bryan has been making highly lauded premium, handcrafted wines ever since. He creates around 20,000 cases a year of Chardonnay, Pinot Noir, Cabernet Franc, Syrah, Gewürztraminer, Pinot Gris, and two varieties under the Eleven Oaks label, Sauvignon Blanc and Sangiovese. During the summer, special wine discovery tours, including barrel tastings and lunch, are arranged by appointment for the experienced wine taster. The Babcock tasting room is open Friday through Sunday from 10:30 A.M. to 4:00 P.M. and other days by appointment.

**Mosby Winery**
**9496 Santa Rosa Road**
**Buellton, CA**
**(805) 688–2415, (800) 70–MOSBY**
**www.mosbywines.com**

This 206-acre vineyard and winery was once part of the old Rancho de la Vega land grant and has been owned and operated by Bill and Jeri Mosby since 1975. The rustic, restored 1860s carriage house now serves as the tasting room. No other Santa Barbara County winery produces as many Italian varietals or brandies as Mosby (about 10,000 cases total).

It's mainly known for its Pinot Grigio, Sangiovese, and brandies, which include Grappa di Traminer (from estate-grown Traminer), Distillato di Prugne Selvaggie (made from wild Pacific plums), and Acqua di Lampone (made from Oregon raspberries). It's also one of the few wineries in the country to produce Teroldego and Cortese. The tasting room is open Monday through Friday 10:00 A.M. to 4:00 P.M. and Saturday through Sunday 10:00 A.M. to 5:00 P.M.

**Sanford Winery**
**7250 Santa Rosa Road**
**Buellton, CA**
**(805) 688–3300, (800) 426–9463**
**(toll-free in California only)**

Sanford is one of our favorite wineries. It's a little further out than some of the others, but we think it's worth the drive for the breathtaking scenery, rich historic ambiance, and fantastic wines. Best of all, the tasting is free. You'll find Sanford Winery just outside of Buellton, 5 miles west of U.S. 101 on Santa Rosa Road.

The winery site, part of the original Santa Rosa land grant, is a 738-acre property known as Rancho El Jabali. Look carefully for the small sign near a cactus garden lined with California poppies then follow the drive a half-mile, over a tiny stream, to the tasting room.

Established in 1981 by Richard and Thekla Sanford, the winery was the first in Santa Barbara County to have its estate vineyards certified as organic. It currently produces about 41,000 cases a year of Chardonnay, Sauvignon Blanc, Pinot Noir, and Vin Gris. Surrounded by golden meadows and geranium gardens, the tasting room is in a rustic but beautiful building that was artfully converted from an old milking shed in 1983. You might also meet Luna, the winery's well-fed Labrador. She'll also happily escort you to the picnic area, a pretty spot to relax and eat lunch. The tasting room and adjoining picnic facilities are open daily from 11:00 A.M. to 4:00 P.M.

## Santa Barbara

If you can't make it over the mountains to the North County, just go down to the beach area and sample wine at two of the oldest wineries in the county.

**Santa Barbara Winery**
**202 Anacapa Street**
**Santa Barbara, CA**
**(805) 963–3646, (800) 225–3633**
**www.sbwinery.com**

Established in 1962, Santa Barbara Winery is the oldest winery in the county. It produces about 30,000 cases a year of Chardonnay, Pinot Noir, Sauvignon Blanc, Syrah, Zinfandel, and Cabernet Sauvignon wines. The vineyard is up in Santa Ynez, but the winery is down by the beach, on the corner of Yanonali and Anacapa Streets, just two blocks north of Cabrillo Boulevard and one block east of State Street.

You can taste wine while viewing the wine-making activity in the barrel room.

The winery is open for tasting from 10:00 A.M. to 5:00 P.M. daily. Tours are at 11:30 A.M. and 3:30 P.M.

**Stearns Wharf Vintners**
**217G Stearns Wharf**
**Santa Barbara, CA**
**(805) 966–6624**
**www.stearnswharfvintners.com**

The Stearns Wharf Vintners tasting room on Stearns Wharf opened in 1981. Here you can sample Stearns Wharf Vintners wines (including Chardonnay, Pinot Noir, Muscat Canelli, and Merlot) and other wines while taking in wonderful views of Santa Barbara, the ocean, and the islands. The room is open for tasting from 9:00 A.M. to 9:00 P.M. daily (9:00 A.M. to 6:00 P.M. in the winter).

## Restaurants

Very few wineries provide food of any type, and few of the country roads in the more remote areas of wine country offer any services. If you plan to picnic along the way, you should definitely make a point of stopping for provisions before you set out. Touring through wine country truly works up an appetite, and besides, it's much better to sample wine with food in your stomach.

### Price-Code Key

For your convenience, we've included typical pricing for a dinner for two, excluding such extras as appetizers and dessert, tax, and tip. These codes are general guidelines only.

| | |
|---|---|
| $ | Less than $20 |
| $$ | $20 to $40 |
| $$$ | $41 to $60 |
| $$$$ | $61 and more |

You'll find a number of great restaurants and food stores in all North County towns, including Solvang, Buellton, Santa Ynez, Los Olivos, Los Alamos, and Santa Maria. Following are descriptions of a few favorite watering holes. You can also ask North County Insiders—they'll be happy to point you toward the closest and best cafes, restaurants, and shops.

**The Ballard Store Restaurant and Bar**
**2449 Baseline Avenue**
**Ballard, CA**
**(805) 688–5319**
**$$$**

Now under new ownership the classy, yet cozy, Ballard Store lies on a quiet country street opposite the Ballard Inn. A local purchased the restaurant in May 2000, freshened up the interior decor, and revamped the menu. It's now eclectic, with an emphasis on California cuisine. Popular dishes include bouillabaisse and the lobster filet with blue cheese sherry sauce, but you can also order pasta, New Zealand lamb, macadamia-nut-crusted halibut, steaks, salmon, and more. The chef bakes his own bread and pastries, and the restaurant boasts a discerningly stocked wine cellar and a full bar. You can also have martinis made to order at your table (just beckon the traveling cart). If you're wine touring or attending a concert, you can call ahead and order a box lunch. The Ballard Store Restaurant is open for dinner Tuesday through Sunday and for Sunday brunch.

**Cafe Chardonnay**
**2436 Baseline Avenue**
**Ballard, CA**
**(805) 688–7770**
**$$**

This elegant but unpretentious country restaurant at the Ballard Inn prepares some of the best gourmet meals in the area. It offers an outstanding selection of Santa Barbara County wines to complement its creative wine country cuisine featuring seafood, pasta, grilled meats, and fresh local produce. Expect such mouthwatering dishes as New Zealand lamb loin marinated and grilled with roasted garlic and Cabernet sauce, filet mignon, blackened ahi tuna, and linguini scampi with fresh artichokes and garlic butter sauce. Make sure you leave room for dessert. Chef Humberto's Chocolate Mousse "Martini" is sure to seduce the sweet-toothed. Cafe Chardonnay serves dinner Tuesday through Sunday only. Reservations are highly recommended—the restaurant fills up fast.

**Cold Spring Tavern**
**5995 Stagecoach Road**
**Santa Barbara, CA**
**(805) 967–0066**
**$$**

More than a century ago, when stagecoaches pulled up to the Cold Spring relay station at the top of San Marcos Pass, travelers could always count on a delicious Old West meal at the tavern. It's still a great place to stop on the way to or from the wine country. You can dine by romantic lamplight in the rustic cabin and order some unusual fare.

The hearty lunch choices include buffalo burgers, venison sausage burgers, and venison steak sandwiches. For dinner, you can stick with traditional favorites like rack of lamb, fresh fish, roast chicken, steaks, and pasta. Or, if you're daring, go for the wild game: medallions of rabbit, stuffed pheasant breast, roast black bear, or wild boar tenderloin. Wind up the meal with Jack Daniel's pecan pie or apple cobbler just like Mom used to make.

Cold Spring Tavern is open for lunch and dinner daily and for country breakfast on Saturday and Sunday. To get there, take U.S. 101 to Calif. 154 and head up the mountain (it's about 7 miles to the top). Once you start downhill on the valley side, continue about a mile and turn left onto Stagecoach Road. Take a direct right and go down the canyon about 1.5 miles to the tavern. If you're coming from the opposite direction, turn right on Stagecoach Road, then take another immediate right and follow the road about a quarter-mile.

**The Hitching Post**
**406 E. Highway 246**
**Buellton, CA**
**(805) 688–0676**
**www.hitchingpost2.com**
**$$$**

Where do local and visiting vintners head when they want a great Santa Maria–style steak, great company, and great wines all in one place? The Hitching Post, a casual, cowboy-style steakhouse and bar, is at the top of the list. It's been written up in *Gourmet,* the *Los Angeles Times,* and other publications, and restaurateurs and vintners from around the world rave about the quality of the meat, cooking, and service.

Choose the cut and size of steak you'd like (all are from Midwestern corn-fed beef and nearly all are certified Angus), and the cook will grill it to perfection over oak. Reviewers also rave about the wine list, which features Santa Barbara County wines, of course, including those made by the owner and main chef, Frank Ostini.

Complete steak dinners include a fresh vegetable tray, choice of soup or bay shrimp cocktail, organic mixed green salad, choice of rice pilaf, baked potato, or french fries, salsa, and homemade bread. Prices vary by the steak's size and type. You can also order combination meals of steak with quail, shrimp, or duck.

Don't worry if you're not a beef eater—the menu also features pork ribs and chops, seafood, quail, turkey, ostrich, and various other entrees. You can also order a children's meal of steak or chicken for $8.

The Hitching Post is conveniently situated right off Calif. 246, just a mile or so east of U.S. 101. You can't miss it: look for the sign that says "World's Best BBQ Steaks."

**Los Olivos Café**
**2879 Grand Avenue**
**Los Olivos, CA**
**(805) 688–7265**
**www.losolivoscafe.com**
**$$**

On the main street in the heart of Los Olivos, this cute Mediterranean-style cafe is a popular spot with the locals. The menu is seasonal but typically includes pasta dishes such as pesto ravioli, grilled fish and meats, and salads like the delicious raspberry pecan salad. The cafe also offers an impressive selection of local and international

**Insiders' Tip**

When wine tasting, experts recommend focusing on a particular varietal so as not to confuse the palate. Also try to taste earlier in the day. Your palate is at its freshest around midday.

wines by the glass. Wander in and dine in the cozy Tuscan interior or people-watch on the picket-fence-lined patio out the front. If you're planning a picnic lunch, you can order food to go. Los Olivos Café is open for lunch and dinner daily.

**Massimi's Ristorante**
**2375 Alamo Pintado Avenue**
**Los Olivos, CA**
**(805) 693–1941**
**$$**

This upscale Italian eatery opened in May 1999 at the site of the old Side Street Café. It serves a range of delicious antipasto dishes such as carpaccio, calamari, and polenta, as well as gourmet sandwiches, classic pasta dishes, and meat, chicken, and fish entrees smothered in mouthwatering Italian-style sauces. Popular choices include osso bucco, lobster salad, and seafood ravioli. You can dine in the air-conditioned interior or relax out back on the shady garden patio amid the palms, grape vines, and honeysuckle. Massimi's is open for lunch and dinner Tuesday through Saturday and for dinner on Sunday.

**Mattei's Tavern**
**2350 Railway Avenue**
**Los Olivos, CA**
**(805) 688–4820**
**$$**

When the stagecoach pulled out from Cold Spring Station, it rolled down the hill, forded the Santa Ynez River, and eventually arrived in Los Olivos, home of Mattei's Tavern. After the restaurant opened more than a century ago, four generations of Mattei's presided over the business. Then in 1971, the Firestone family purchased the property, and it's remained in their hands ever since.

Today you can travel back in time at Mattei's, dining on American-style cuisine in an Old West atmosphere. The menu includes steaks, prime rib, seafood, and many other entrees; the restaurant also offers a salad bar and a children's menu. Don't miss the mud pie, with a chocolate graham cracker crust, mocha ice cream, fudge, whipped cream, and nuts. You can dine inside by the native-rock fireplace or relax at an outdoor table.

Even when they're not interested in a complete meal, lots of locals and visitors stop at Mattei's lounge for a cool drink at the full Western-style bar. Mattei's is open for dinner Wednesday through Sunday. Dress is casual.

To get to Mattei's, take Calif. 154 and turn west onto Grand Avenue in Los Olivos. Take an immediate right on Railway Avenue and just head north a few blocks.

**Panino**
**2900 Grand Avenue**
**Los Olivos, CA**
**(805) 688–9304**
**$**

This laidback little corner cafe sells an excellent selection of hot and cold gourmet sandwiches with fresh-baked bread as well as salads featuring locally grown produce. Try the smoked turkey with sliced brie; the tuna, artichoke, and black olive pesto; or pick one of the many vegetarian selections. If you're looking for a lighter meal, the goat cheese and roasted pepper salad or the Insalada Caprese are good choices. Dine inside or at one of the tables that spill onto the sidewalk. If you're in a hurry, you can order food to go. Panino is open for lunch daily.

**The Vintage Room**
**2860 Grand Avenue**
**Los Olivos, CA**
**(805) 688–7788**
**$$$**

Awarded the "Wine Spectator Award of Excellence" in 2000 for its outstanding wine list, the Vintage Room is an elegant restaurant in the Fess Parker Wine Country Inn and Spa. Guests come here to feast on gourmet California cuisine made with fresh local produce. The lunch menu offers salads, pastas, sandwiches, fresh fish, gourmet appetizers, and grilled meats. For dinner, some of the chef's appetizer and entree specialties include oak-smoked tomato bisque, coriander-crusted salmon filet, and grilled prime filet with portabello mushroom butter. The Vintage Room is open for breakfast, lunch, and dinner daily as well as for brunch on Sunday.

**Zaca Creek Restaurant & Saloon**
**1297 U.S. Highway 101 Frontage Road, one mile north of Buellton**
**(805) 688–2412**
**$$**

This popular local restaurant serves hearty steaks and ribs cooked over an oak barbecue, prime rib, and a wide selection of fresh fish. It offers a children's menu as well as an early-bird menu (5:00 to 6:00 P.M.). On Saturday nights, the bar usually hosts live country music. Zaca Creek is open for dinner seven nights a week.

## Accommodations

After a day in the North County, you can easily drive back to Santa Barbara—it's just an hour or less down U.S. 101. But if you'd like to spend more than a day or two exploring wine country, we recommend staying overnight at a hotel or bed and breakfast inn. (After a day of sampling wine in the sun, most people just want to take a nap rather than a long car ride.)

If you stay, you can choose from a number of fine lodging places. Unless otherwise noted, the accommodations below provide at least one specially equipped room for the physically challenged. A few allow small dogs in certain rooms.

To make quick arrangements, call a free reservation service: Santa Barbara Hotspots (805-564-1637 or 800-793-7666) or Coastal Escapes (805-684-7679 or 800-292-2222). They'll be happy to provide information on availability and rates and make your reservations. You can also call the Solvang Conference and Visitors Bureau at (805) 688-6144 or (800) 468-6765.

### Price-Code Key

Prices for these accommodations are based on a one-night, double-occupancy stay in the high season and do not include taxes and fees for added services. Remember that these are just averages—some rooms may be more expensive (especially suites), while others may cost less.

$ . . . . . . . . . . . . . . . . . . . . . . . $100 to $120
$$ . . . . . . . . . . . . . . . . . . . . . . $121 to $170
$$$ . . . . . . . . . . . . . . . . . . . . . $171 to $225
$$$$ . . . . . . . . . . . . . . . . . . . $226 and more

Our Daytrips chapter also offers suggestions on places to stay and dine in Solvang and other nearby towns. Here, we'll tell you about a few of our favorite wine country inns and resorts. Some are a bit pricey, but well worth the money spent.

**The Alisal Guest Ranch and Resort**
**1054 Alisal Road**
**Solvang, CA**
**(805) 688–6411, (800) 4–ALISAL (from outside the 805 area code)**
**www.alisal.com**
**$$$$**

This exclusive, 10,000-acre resort and working cattle ranch has 73 comfortable California ranch-style cottages, studios, and suites, each with a wood-burning fireplace. Voted one of the "50 Best Dude Ranches in the West" by *Sunset Magazine,* this popular resort has been pampering guests—many of them loyal returnees—since 1946. The resort has played host to

**Insiders' Tip**

Heading out for a day of wine tasting? Appoint a designated driver before you begin the tour and take a bottle of water. Sipping wines in the sun all day can leave you feeling dehydrated.

an impressive list of celebrities ever since Clark Gable and Lady Ashley exchanged vows here back in 1949 in the original library. Today, it is a favorite hideaway for active couples and families who enjoy all the cozy comforts of home but want to remain incommunicado for a while—all the rooms are telephone- and television-free. The room rate is $385 to $475 a night and includes breakfast and dinner. The resort offers an incredible array of recreational facilities, including seven tennis courts; two 18-hole golf courses; a private 100 -acre spring-fed lake for boating, sailboarding, and fishing; guided horseback rides; and miles of spectacular nature trails. At certain times of the year, the resort offers a special package that includes unlimited horseback riding, golf, tennis, and fishing.

Dining in the Ranch Room is reserved for guests, but the Alisal's River Grill is open to the public for dinner Monday through Saturday.

**The Ballard Inn**
**2436 Baseline Avenue**
**Ballard, CA**
**(805) 688–7770, (800) 638–2466**
**www.ballardinn.com**
**$$$–$$$$**

Fronted by picket fences and fragrant rose gardens, this charming inn on a quiet street in the tiny town of Ballard is a popular getaway for couples seeking a romantic weekend retreat. The inn enjoys an excellent reputation for down-to-earth hospitality and personalized service. All of the 15 comfy guest rooms are uniquely decorated with themes reflecting the region's colorful history. Davy Brown's Room feels like a cozy wood cabin with its stone fireplace and wood-paneled walls, the Western Room has a cowboy theme, and the larger-but-pricier Mountain Room boasts a small balcony overlooking the street. Typical appointments include antique furnishings, king-size beds, and hand-pieced quilts or down comforters. Phones and televisions are available upon request, but most guests here don't want them. All rooms have full private baths and seven rooms have wood-burning fireplaces.

Rates include a full cooked-to-order breakfast and afternoon wine and hors d'oeuvres. The inn's Cafe Chardonnay, which serves dinner Wednesday through Saturday, is considered one of the finest restaurants in the entire region (see "Restaurants" section of this chapter). Although The Ballard is a nonsmoking inn, smoking is permitted on the verandah.

**Fess Parker Wine Country Inn & Spa**
**2860 Grand Avenue**
**Los Olivos, CA**
**(805) 688–7788**
**www.fessparker.com**
**$$$$**

Tucked behind olive trees on the main street in Los Olivos, this posh bed and breakfast-style hotel has 21 beautifully appointed rooms, a pool, a spa, and a fleet of bicycles for your use. Fess Parker (a.k.a. Davy Crockett) purchased the hotel in summer 1998 and remodeled it to reflect a wine country theme. You might even bump into him during your stay, as he regularly pops in to shake hands with the guests. Fess's wife, Marcella, infused a personal touch by decorating each room differently. Some are bright and airy, with potted palms and light color schemes, others are warm and cozy. All the rooms have antique furnishings, gas fireplaces, down comforters, TVs in armoires, wet

*The Fess Parker Wine Country Inn & Spa pampers its guests with plush accommodations and rejuvenating spa treatments.* PHOTO: KIRK IRWIN, COURTESY OF FESS PARKER WINE COUNTRY INN & SPA

bars, hair dryers, and plush robes. Four rooms in the complex across the street are equipped with Jacuzzi tubs. A new annex with 25 additional rooms is slated for completion in 2002. If you really want to pamper yourself, stroll down the street to Spa Vigne for all sorts of rejuvenating facial, body, and massage therapies. The resort also offers meeting space with audiovisual equipment. Downstairs are the bar, Le Saloon, and The Vintage Room restaurant. (See the "Restaurants" section in this chapter.) Room rates start at $400 per night, with a two- and sometimes three-night minimum on weekends and certain holidays. Breakfast is included in these rates Sunday through Thursday.

**Rancho Santa Barbara Marriott**
**555 McMurray Road**
**Buellton, CA**
**(805) 688–1000, (800) 638–8882**
**www.santaynezhotels.com**
**$$–$$$**

This midsize Marriott offers good-value accommodations in a convenient location, just north of the U.S. 101/Calif. 246 intersection. It's right next to the freeway, but you really don't hear much of the traffic when you're indoors. There are 149 deluxe guest rooms (including 27 two-room executive suites), a swimming pool, and tennis, racquetball, and squash courts, as well as several restaurants. Room rates range from $99 to $220 per night, depending upon the time of your visit.

**Santa Ynez Inn**
**3627 Sagunto Street**
**Santa Ynez, CA**
**(805) 688–5588, (800) 643–5774**
**www.santaynezinn.com**
**$$$–$$$$**

Opened in the fall of 2001, this $2-million Victorian-style boutique hotel in the Old West town of Santa Ynez is a fresh choice for visitors seeking luxury accommodation in the wine country. The elegant two-story inn offers 14 plush guest rooms and suites, a fitness facility with sauna, an outdoor heated whirlpool and sun deck, meeting rooms, catering facilities, and extensive gardens. Each room is uniquely decorated. Expect antique furnishings, queen- or king-size beds, TVs with DVD/CD entertainment systems, coffee makers, hair dryers, robes, and thoughtful touches such as fresh cut flowers. Some rooms also come

*Fine wines and great food make the annual Santa Barbara County Vintners' Festival a popular event.*
PHOTO: COURTESY OF THE SANTA BARBARA VINTNERS' ASSOCIATION

with gas fireplaces, balconies or patios, double steam showers, and whirlpool tubs. Rates are from $195 to $395 per night and include a full gourmet breakfast, afternoon tea, and evening wine and hors d'oeuvres.

## Festivals

Santa Barbara wine country takes advantage of every opportunity to host a celebration. (Wouldn't you if you had such great wine and food to serve?) Dinners, concerts, open houses, harvest parties, and other special events take place at various wineries practically every month of the year.

For a current schedule of events, contact the Santa Barbara County Vintners' Association at (805) 688–0881 or (800) 218–0881. Also watch for announcements in *The Santa Barbara Independent* or the *Santa Barbara News-Press.* The following are brief descriptions of two major events that almost always sell out beforehand. Get your tickets early! Call (800) 218–0881 for information; also see our Annual Events chapter.

### Santa Barbara County Vintners' Festival

This epicurean extravaganza is one of the most popular annual events in the valley. Member wineries dispense their wines, and local restaurants and caterers set out fantastic food for a week of special tastings, outings, and dinners. The main event is held the third weekend in April in a beautiful outdoor setting such as Firestone Meadow.

Visitors spend the afternoon sampling fine wines and dishes prepared by top restaurant chefs, watching demonstrations (for example, wine barrel building), and listening to live music. The festival usually takes place from 1:00 to 4:00 P.M. on a Saturday and Sunday. The $60 admission fee covers all tasting and sampling.

### A Celebration of Harvest

This colorful outdoor festival is held the second Saturday in October and showcases the foods and wines grown and produced in Santa Barbara County. Join the wineries as they celebrate the grape harvest, taste fine wines, and fill up on gourmet dishes emphasizing locally grown ingredients prepared by area chefs. The celebration also features music, demonstrations, and exhibits. Tickets are $60 and must be purchased in advance from the Vintners' Association.

# Daytrips

Heading North
Heading South

With all the people coming to Santa Barbara to escape the rigors of big-city life, you wouldn't think Santa Barbarans would be looking for a getaway of their own. The fact is, even we enjoy a change of scenery every now and then.

There are basically two choices for a daytrip or getaway out of Santa Barbara: drive north or drive south.

If you head north on U.S. Highway 101 (which will eventually take you to San Francisco), you're basically eschewing the big city and looking for some peace and quiet in northern Santa Barbara County or in the little beach towns that dot the coast between here and Monterey. This drive is far less hectic than the southbound route and avoids most of the L.A. traffic that tends to rattle the nerves of Santa Barbarans. We'll give you a peek at the charming Danish town of Solvang in the Santa Ynez Valley plus some information on the Morro Bay area and one of the Central Coast's most popular attractions, Hearst Castle.

Traveling south on U.S. 101 will take you to Los Angeles, where you'll find all the sights and entertainment you've come to expect from a large cosmopolitan city. We've included information on some of the most-visited attractions in L.A. as well as a look at the artsy town of Ojai, an off-the-beaten-path destination south of Santa Barbara with a Bohemian feel.

No matter which way you decide to go, there are plenty of options within a few hours' drive of Santa Barbara's borders that can pleasantly fill a day or a weekend.

## Heading North

### Velkommen til Solvang!

Solvang, one of the most popular daytrip destinations with Santa Barbarans, is just a 45-minute drive up the coast. From either U.S. 101 or Calif. Highway 154, take Calif. Highway 246 into the heart of this self-proclaimed "Danish Capital of America."

Here you can get a good look at Danish-style architecture (including windmills), check out the **Hans Christian Andersen Museum** at 1680 Mission Drive (805–688–2052) and the **Elverhoj Danish Heritage and Fine Arts Museum** at 1624 Elverhoj Way (805–686–1211), ride the **Copenhagen street car** powered by two large Belgian draft horses, or allow yourself to be seduced by the smells emanating from one of the Danish bakeries.

The specialty and gift shops are fabulous, and the art galleries and antique stores make browsing irresistible. All of these attractions draw hordes of tourists, so plan to wade through the crowds at this Disneyesque Danish town, especially on weekends and during the summer. If you really want to get a taste of Denmark, visit during the Danish Days celebration in September (see our Annual Events chapter).

Solvang is particularly charming when decorated for Christmas (see the Winterfest listing in our Annual Events chapter), which is a great time to shop and pick up some incredible Danish pastries to tempt Santa. (First you have to get them home without devouring them—quite a challenge for most of us.) Summertime brings the **Pacific Conservatory of the**

*Oak-studded hills and fields of wildflowers lie just beyond Santa Barbara's coastal mountains.*
PHOTO: KIRK IRWIN, COURTESY OF THE SANTA BARBARA CONFERENCE & VISITORS BUREAU.

**Performing Arts Theaterfest** (800-549-PCPA, www.pcpa.org) to Solvang, and several productions are staged in the city's outdoor **Festival Theatre** each season from June through October. This is not small-town entertainment by any means. Well-known professional actors are often in the cast, and productions are always first-rate. Santa Barbarans frequently make a round-trip excursion to Solvang on a summer evening to eat dinner and catch a show.

Golfers will love the beautiful **River Course at the Alisal** (805-688-6042, www.rivercourse.com), a public 18-hole championship course on the banks of the Santa Ynez River near the exclusive 10,000-acre Alisal Guest Ranch and Resort, at 1054 Alisal Road (805-688-6411, 800-4-ALISAL from outside the 805 area code, www.alisal.com; see our Santa Barbara Wine Country chapter).

You'll also find many lodging options within the city of Solvang. Most have Danish architecture and charming names such as the Chimney Sweep Inn, the Storybook Inn Bed and Breakfast, and the Danish Country Inn. Contact the Solvang Conference and Visitors Bureau, at the corner of Mission Drive and Calif. 246 (805-688-6144,

800-468-6765, www.solvangusa.com) for information.

Also in Solvang is **Mission Santa Inés,** on Mission Drive just east of Alisal Road (805-688-4815, www.missionsantaines.org). The 19th of California's missions, founded in 1804, it's worth a look (if you can tear yourself away from the sights and smells of downtown Solvang).

Or you can explore the nearby wine country (see our Santa Barbara Wine Country chapter).

**Insiders' Tip**

If you snag a seat to one of Solvang's PCPA Theaterfest outdoor performances, dress warmly and take a heavy coat and blanket. Yes, we know it was 90 degrees in Solvang this afternoon, but it's going to get cold tonight!

## More of the North County

Just a hop, skip, and a jump from Solvang (3 miles to the east on Calif. 246 to be exact), is the **Chumash Indian Casino** (800-728-9997), operated by the local Chumash tribe. Touted as "the best place to play from L.A. to the Bay," the casino has become a gambling and entertainment hot spot, offering a large range of gaming options and big-name entertainment.

Five miles northwest of Solvang is **Lompoc** (correctly pronounced LOM-poke), where flower seeds are big business. More than 15 miles of private flower fields bloom in the summer, including wide expanses of sweet peas, lavender, marigolds, calendula, and larkspur. You can get a map of the flower fields from the Lompoc Chamber of Commerce at 111 S. I Street (805-736-4567). Also in Lompoc, along Calif. 246, is **La Purisima Mission State Historic Park** (805-733-3713). La Purisima is the most fully restored of all California's missions, and all of the main buildings are filled with furniture and other artifacts. Living-history tours and craft demonstrations are just some of the activities here.

In downtown Lompoc, it's hard to miss the dozens of murals depicting the city's culture and history. You can drive by and admire them, or call the Chamber of Commerce for information on walking tours.

Also here is **Vandenberg Air Force Base,** where missile launches often light up the sky. In the past, bus tours, which included a stop at the base's Space and Missile Museum, were given at 10:00 A.M. on Wednesdays only by appointment. The tours were dicontinued after September 11, 2001. For up-to-date information, call (805) 606-3595. The base's main gate is at the end of Calif. Highway 1.

Approximately 80 miles north of Santa Barbara on U.S. 101 is **Santa Maria,** home of the Santa Maria-style barbecue known as tri-tip (see a brief discussion of this delicacy in our Restaurants chapter), and the Santa Barbara County Fair (see our Annual Events chapter).

## The Central Coast

Just north of Santa Maria, you'll cross the line into San Luis Obispo County, which marks the halfway point between Los Angeles and San Francisco. As you meander along U.S. 101, you'll come to the small beach towns of **Grover Beach, Pismo Beach, Shell Beach,** and **Avila Beach** just before the freeway makes a wide curve inland.

Any of the beach cities are good places to stop for a bite to eat or a seaside stroll. **F. McLintocks Saloon and Dining House** (805-773-1892, www.mclintocks.com) just off U.S. 101 on Mattie Road in Shell Beach, is a popular stopping-off point for steaks and seafood, and there's a great kids' menu too.

*La Purisima is the most completely restored of California's missions.* PHOTO: SALLY TURVEY

Pismo has a great family beach and some good seafood restaurants with excellent clam chowder and fish and chips. Just south of Pismo Beach is the **Pismo Dunes State Vehicular Recreation Area,** where motor vehicles are permitted to drive on the beach and off-road vehicles have access to the expansive sand dunes.

Stay on U.S. 101 and you'll come to the city of San Luis Obispo. Just outside the city limits, you'll pass the famous **Madonna Inn** (805-543-3000, 800-543-9666, www.madonnainn.com), a fantasy lodging built in 1959. Every room is uniquely decorated at this hotel—and we don't mean with a different color of chintz. The list of imaginative theme rooms includes the Cave Man Room, which is literally carved out of stone.

San Luis Obispo is home to the **Central Coast campus of California Polytechnic State University,** at the north end of Grand Avenue, and is a pleasant mix of college town and historic California. You can take a campus walking tour (805-756-5734), visit the city's historical sights, including **Mission San Luis Obispo de Tolosa** at 751 Palm Street (805-543-6850), or pick up some of the local bounty at the Thursday night farmers' market, held downtown. Stop by the Chamber of Commerce Visitor Center at 1039 Chorro Street (805-781-2777, www.visitslo.com) for maps and complete information on local sights and celebrations.

Take Los Osos Valley Road west through Los Osos and you'll come to the beautiful 8,000-acre **Montaña de Oro State Park** (805-528-0513), with its rugged coastal beaches, large eucalyptus groves, and miles of hiking, biking, and horseback-riding trails. Check in at the park headquarters in the old Spooner Ranch House just above Spooner's Cove for information about camping, nature walks, and other park activities.

## Insiders' Tip

For a real National Geographic experience, stop by the Piedras Blancas elephant seal rookery along scenic Calif. 1, the Pacific Coast Highway. About 8,000 seals come here to mate, molt, and give birth on the beach 4.4 miles north of Hearst Castle and 11.7 miles north of Cambria. For more information and maps, visit www.elephantseal.org or call (805) 924-1628.

## Morro Bay

If you take scenic Calif. 1 out of San Luis Obispo, you'll soon find yourself in Morro Bay, a beautiful little town by the sea. The waters of Estero Bay lap at the shore, providing more than 2,000 acres of mudflats, eelgrass beds, tidal wetlands, and open water. As you might imagine, the birding is excellent here, and there are plenty of opportunities for kayaking, fishing, surfing, and boating.

**Morro Rock,** a volcanic remnant that towers more than 575 feet above the bay, looms over the harbor and is itself a wildlife preserve and home to nesting peregrine falcons. If you watch the waters at the base of the rock, you may get your first glimpse of some delightful Central Coast characters, the California sea otters—so bring your binoculars and camera.

On Main Street on the south side of the city is **Morro Bay State Park** (805-772-2694), which includes a great blue heron rookery, a museum of natural history, and plenty of opportunities for birding (pick up a birding guide at the museum), hiking, and camping.

If roughing it isn't your idea of a good time, consider a stay at **The Inn at**

## Insiders' Tip

Dreaming of a romantic and affordable midweek escape? Insiders pop up to the Cambria Pines Lodge, 2905 Burton Drive, Cambria (800-445-6868, www.cambriapineslodge.com) for their fantastic weekday special (Sunday through Thursday). The Escape Plan includes a spacious suite with a fireplace (subject to availability), dinner for two, a bottle of house wine, and a buffet breakfast all for $119 to $149 a night (depending on the season). Book early!

**Morro Bay** (805-772-5651, 800-321-9566, www.innatmorrobay.com), a Cape Cod-style inn overlooking the bay at the park's entrance (and right across the street from a golf course).

Even if you're not into birding, you'll find plenty to do in Morro Bay, from watching the fishing boats come in to browsing the unique shops on the Embarcadero to lingering over some delicious seafood at one of the local restaurants. In October, the Harbor Festival is a great excuse for a weekend getaway.

Contact the Morro Bay Chamber of Commerce, 880 Main Street (805-772-4467, 800-231-0592, www.morrobay.org) for complete information on things to do, local festivals, and lodging and dining options.

## Cambria

Once you've had your fill of Morro Bay, continue up Calif. 1 to the little village of **Cambria,** voted the No. 1 getaway spot for Santa Barbarans (it's a little more than two hours from home) and beginning to catch on with L.A. residents as well.

This is too bad in a way, for sleepy little Cambria used to be a true respite from the world; now it's crowded on weekends, and you can scarcely get a room reservation unless you call weeks ahead. This situation does little to deter Cambria-lovers, however, so plan ahead if you want to spend the weekend.

Lodging choices on Moonstone Beach Drive will put you across the street from the beach and just a few steps from a romantic evening stroll at sunset, but you'll pay less for a room in town. Also, although fog may blanket the coast in winter and early spring, you'll save money by visiting in the off-season. Besides its appealing shops and art galleries, Cambria has some excellent restaurants, including the eclectic **Robin's,** 4095 Burton Drive (805-927-5007, www.robinsrestaurant.com), with a wonderful international menu; **Ian's,** 2150 Center Street (805-927-8649), which has a California gourmet menu and serves wonderful lamb; **The Brambles Dinner House,** 4005 Burton Drive (805-927-4716, www.bramblesdinnerhouse.com), offering steak, seafood, and prime rib; and **The Sow's Ear Café,** 2248 Main Street (805-927-4865, www.thesowsear.com), touting a menu that includes everything from "contemporary American to Southwestern Tropical" cuisine.

One of our favorite dinner spots is the **Sea Chest Oyster Bar and Restaurant** (805-927-4514), housed in a no-frills sea shack on Moonstone Beach Drive. You'll get some of the best seafood imaginable here, including fabulous fresh oysters, clams, mussels, lobster, and fish from waters around the world. The restaurant opens every night at 5:30 P.M. (except from mid-September to May 1, when it's closed Tuesdays), and there's always a line of people waiting to enter.

All Cambria restaurants have excellent wine lists, most with a good variety of local wines.

Just a few miles up the coast from Cambria is **San Simeon,** home of William Randolph Hearst's lavish castle on the hill. Now one of the most popular tourist attractions in California, **Hearst Castle** (its official name is La Cuesta Encantada, "The Enchanted Hill") is now a State Historical Monument overseen by the California State Parks system. The hilltop estate was voted the top U.S. monument in a 2000 *Condé Nast Traveler* survey.

It took almost 28 years to build Hearst's magnificent estate, which has 165 rooms and 127 acres of gardens, terraces, pools, and walkways. Spanish and Italian antiques fill the rooms, and the pure opulence of the place is staggering.

Except for marveling at the sheer size of the thing as you gaze up from Calif. 1, you can't get near the castle without a ticket for one of the tours. Four daytime tours are offered daily beginning at 8:20 A.M., with the last tour scheduled for about 3:20 P.M. Each tour focuses on different areas of the castle, but first-time visitors usually choose The Experience Tour, which includes the main house and gardens, the Assembly Room, the Refectory, the Morning Room, the Billiard Room, and the Theater as well as a 40-minute National Geographic IMAX film.

Tours last just over two hours, and each requires a half-mile walk and climbing 150 to 400 stairs, depending on the tour you choose. In spring and fall, an evening tour is added on Friday and Saturday. Reservations are strongly recommended and can be made by calling (800) 444-4445 (major credit cards are accepted). You can also buy tickets at the Hearst Castle ticket office when you arrive, but you'll be lucky to find a vacancy. Some of the tours sell out months in advance.

Prices for any of the four tours are $14 for adults and $8 for children 6 through 12. Children 5 and younger are admitted free as long as they don't occupy a seat on the bus to the castle. Evening tours are $20 and $10, respectively. Wheelchair-accessible and foreign-language tours may be arranged by calling (805) 927-2020. For more information on Hearst Castle as well as directions and a map see www.hearstcastle.org.

## Heading South

### Ojai

Ever heard of the 1930s film **Lost Horizon?** Well, if you have, you can be in Shangri-la within 45 minutes of leaving downtown Santa Barbara. The famous movie was filmed in Ojai (pronounced OH-hi), a lush valley surrounded by vast groves of orange trees, the majestic Topa Topa Mountains, and millions of acres of Los Padres National Forest lands. It's one of the most scenic spots in all of California (besides Santa Barbara, of course) and an ideal destination for a daytrip.

Ojai resembles Palm Springs in some ways: It's a resort town (population 7,600) where you can golf on championship courses, pamper yourself with all variations of spa services, and shop for quality artwork and antiques. But it's also a Shangri-la for artists and for outdoor-recreation and nature lovers. You can hike along hundreds of miles of trails and go mountain biking, horseback riding, boating, fishing, and camping. Ojai is also home to a number of unique centers of philosophy and spirituality—in fact, it's a New Age capital of sorts.

To get to Ojai, just drive south from Santa Barbara about 12 miles to Carpinteria. Right at the Ventura/Santa Barbara County line, you'll see an exit for Calif. Highway 150. If the road is open (mudslides sometimes close this scenic country road during the winter months), you can take it all the way to Ojai, about 20 miles to the southeast (just follow the signs).

Call the Ventura CalTrans office at (805) 389-1565 before setting out to find out whether the road is open. If it's not, you need to drive another 20 or so miles to Ventura, then take the Calif. Highway 33 exit and head up to the mountains for 11

**Insiders' Tip**

The Santa Barbara Airbus arranges a regular schedule of daytrips to popular L.A.-area destinations, for instance the Getty Center, Dodger games, and the Los Angeles County Museum of Art. Call (805) 964-7759 or (800) 423-1618 for fares and schedules.

miles. Along the way you pass through a few small towns: Casitas Springs, Oak View, and Mira Monte. The road forks just a mile or two before downtown Ojai. Just keep heading east. The road will become a combination of Calif. 33 and Calif. 150 for a while.

Just before you reach downtown Ojai, you'll come to another major intersection: the "Y." This is where Calif. 33 turns to continue its trek over the mountains to the northwest. To reach downtown, though, you should veer right and stay on Calif. 150 heading east. The first thing you should do is stop in at the **Visitor Center** of the **Ojai Valley Chamber of Commerce,** at 150 W. Ojai Avenue (805-646-8126, www.the-ojai.org). It has maps and tons of information on accommodations, restaurants, special events, things to see and do, shopping, art galleries, and lots of other useful stuff.

It's fun to walk around the small, quaint town of Ojai. Many people drive hundreds of miles just to poke around the galleries and antique shops, which are said to be among the best in Southern California. Be sure to browse at **Bart's Books,** which sets out more than 100,000 used books on tree-shaded patios. You'll find it one block north of Ojai Avenue on the corner of Cañada and Matilija Streets (805-646-3755). Bart's is closed Monday.

The **Ojai Valley Museum,** 130 W. Ojai Avenue (805-640-1390), is a fun place to explore if you're interested in finding out about the colorful local history. Admission is $3. Call for opening times, as they vary.

It's easy to get around Ojai—just hop aboard the air-conditioned, wheelchair-accessible **Ojai Trolley Service,** which traverses the valley's main strip Monday through Friday from 7:15 A.M. to 5:40 P.M., and Saturday and Sunday from 9:00 A.M. to 5:00 P.M. The one-hour town ride costs only 25 cents, and if you're 65 or older or younger than 2, you ride free. The trolley stops near most of the hotels, motels, restaurants, and shops.

Ojai offers a year-round calendar of events, and many visitors arrange their visits to coincide with them. A few major events include the **Ojai Music Festival,** a renowned series of classical music concerts that usually takes place over three days at the end of May; the **Ojai Wine Festival,** an afternoon in early June that you can spend tasting the favorite wines of 40 wineries, sampling cuisine from Ojai Valley restaurants, and browsing through displays of works by local and regional artists and artisans; and the **Ojai Shakespeare Festival,** which takes place in August.

Fifteen-acre **Libbey Park,** in the center of town, is the site of many special events. The park includes the Libbey Bowl (where most performances take place), picnic areas, tennis courts, and a playground.

If you've come to Ojai to enjoy the great outdoors, you have many options. The scenic, 9-mile **Ojai Valley Trail** has wide pathways for horseback riding, biking, walking, and jogging. It links Ventura's Foster Park (7 miles north of Ventura near Casitas Springs) to Ojai's Soule Park, at the eastern edge of town, so you can park your car at Foster Park and ride your bike to Ojai, if you wish. Ask for a trail map at the Chamber of Commerce. You can rent bikes at Bicycles of Ojai, 108 Cañada Street (805-646-7736).

Hiking in the mountains near Ojai can be sheer bliss—the vistas from the peaks over the valley, ocean, and islands below are spectacular. At the **Ojai Ranger Station,** 1190 E. Ojai Avenue (805-646-4348), you can pick up free maps of dozens of backcountry hiking and mountain-bike trails in the Los Padres National Forest. You should also contact the ranger station if you'd like a campground listing or to make camping reservations; call (800) 280-CAMP. You can also make reservations online at www.reserveusa.com.

Adventure Passes are required if you want to park in the Los Padres National Forest. You can purchase them at the ranger station. A day pass costs $5; an annual pass is $30.

Horses and equestrian trails abound in Ojai. **Western Trail Riding** (805-640-8635) offers guided trail rides for one or two people (maximum) and riding lessons, and **Ojai Valley Inn's Ranch and Stables** offers guided trail rides, lessons, and a children's petting farm—call (805) 646-5511, extension 51, for information.

Hoping for a few hours trolling for trout in a beautiful lake? Head for the **Lake Casitas Recreation Area,** 11311 Santa Ana Road, just 5 miles southwest of Ojai. In 1984, the Olympic rowing and canoeing events were held here. You can rent boats (805-649-2233) and fish for bass, catfish, trout, and crappie from sunrise to sunset.

If golf is your game, you can tee off at the legendary par-70 PGA course at the **Ojai Valley Inn & Spa,** 905 Country Club Road (805-646-2420, www.golfojai.com), or the **Soule Park Golf Course,** an 18-hole, par-72 public course at 1033 E. Ojai Avenue (805-646-5633).

Ojai is where Insiders go for an ultimate pampering experience—for a birthday, wedding, or anniversary treat, or just for a massive dose of R&R. The most exclusive, luxurious spa is the new **Spa Ojai,** a 31,000-square-foot spa village at the Ojai Valley Inn & Spa, 905 Country Club Road (805-640-2000, 800-422-6524, www.spaojai.com).

Spa Ojai offers innovative treatments and programs for creativity, self-discovery, and fitness. It has 28 treatment areas (some with fireplaces), a cardiovascular fitness center, a weight room, a pool, an art studio, and a hair and nail salon. Take your pick of massages, body treatments, facials, programs, and classes in an elegant setting.

Another famous spot is **The Oaks at Ojai,** a residential health spa where you can check in to lose pounds and inches and indulge in facials, body scrubs, and paraffin treatments. It's at 122 E. Ojai Avenue (805-646-5573, 800-753-6257, www.oaksspa.com).

Anyone interested in philosophy and spiritual traditions may want to check out a couple of renowned centers located here. **The Krishnamurti Library,** at 1070 McAndrew Road (805-646-4948, www.kfa.org), has a comprehensive collection of the writings and tapes of philosopher J. Krishnamurti—call if you're interested in arranging a visit or check out their Web site for opening hours and directions.

The **Krotona Institute of Theosophy,** at 2 Krotona Hill (Calif. 33 at Hermosa Road, 805-646-2653), includes a library, bookstore, and school of theosophy. The public is invited to check out the institute's beautiful grounds—a 115-acre wooded estate with Spanish-style buildings, lily ponds, and magnificent views. The Krotona Institute is open daily; call for hours.

Other popular visitor sites include the **Old Creek Ranch Winery,** 10024 Old Creek Road in Oak View (805-649-4132), which offers wine-tasting Friday, Saturday, and Sunday from 11:00 A.M. to 5:00 P.M., and **The International Center for Earth Concerns,** 2162 Baldwin Road (805-649-3535). The center is a nonprofit organization that works to enhance people's appreciation of nature, understand the Earth and its systems, and promote effective environmental programs. It offers regular guided tours and bird walks in its gorgeous botanical gardens with South African, Australian and native Californian plants and oak groves. Call for dates, times, fees, and reservations.

## Daytrip Resources

For more information on any of the destinations in this chapter, contact the organizations below.

**Solvang Conference & Visitors Bureau**
**www.solvangusa.com**
**(805) 688–6144, (800) 468–6765**

**San Luis Obispo Chamber of Commerce**
**www.visitslo.com**
**(805) 781–2777**

**Lompoc Valley Chamber of Commerce and Visitor's Bureau**
**www.lompoc.com**
**(805) 736–4567**

**Santa Maria Valley Chamber of Commerce and Visitor & Convention Bureau**
**www.santamaria.com**
**(805) 925–2403**

**Morro Bay Visitor's Center & Chamber of Commerce**
**www.morrobay.org**
**(805) 772–4467, (800) 231–0592**

**Cambria Chamber of Commerce**
**www.cambriachamber.org**
**(805) 927–3624**

**Ojai Valley Chamber of Commerce**
**www.the-ojai.org**
**(805) 646–8126**

**Los Angeles Convention and Visitors Bureau**
**www.lacvb.com**
**(213) 624–7300, (800) 228–2452**

### Where to Eat in Ojai

If all the scenery and fresh air trigger your appetite, Ojai has a good selection of restaurants that range from the ultimate gourmet experience to excellent taco stands and pizza parlors. You can pick up a detailed restaurant list from the Chamber of Commerce.

The area's most famous restaurant is **The Ranch House,** on S. Lomita Street (805-646-2360, www.theranchhouse.com), which offers gourmet dining in a gorgeous garden setting with meandering streams. It's open for dinner Wednesday through Sunday and for brunch on Sunday (closed Monday and Tuesday).

Another famous gourmet spot is **Suzanne's Cuisine,** at 502 W. Ojai Avenue (805-640-1961, www.suzannes cuisine.com). Suzanne's is open for lunch and dinner every day except Tuesday.

### Where to Stay in Ojai

While you can easily return to Santa Barbara (it's just 45 minutes away), you might be tempted to overnight in Shangri-la. For accommodation arrangements, contact the Ojai Valley Chamber of Commerce, (805) 646-8126, for an Ojai Valley area accommodations guide.

If you're looking for a luxurious resort, you can't go wrong by choosing Ojai's most famous hotel: the **Ojai Valley Inn & Spa,** 905 Country Club Road (805-646-5511, 800-422-6524, www.ojairesort.com). It's a full-service, 220-acre luxury resort with spectacular views, 208 deluxe guest rooms and suites, an 18-hole championship golf course (site of many Senior PGA events), and three heated swimming pools, including a 60-foot lap pool.

The inn offers tons of activities—horseback riding, tennis, swimming, hiking, biking, and jeep tours—along with a children's program, a golf academy, and a fitness center. The new Spa Ojai (see spa description above) has a huge range of services. Room rates start at $275 a night and climb to $330 to $ 2,500 for suites and cottages.

Slightly more affordable is **The Oaks at Ojai,** 122 E. Ojai Avenue (805-646-5573, 800-753-6257, www.oaksspa.com), a resident fitness spa. It has 46 rooms, including cottages and a main lodge plus a pool. The American Plan includes gourmet, low-calorie meals (1,000 calories a day), snacks, and 16 fitness classes daily. It also offers massages, facials, and a hair and nail salon. Room rates range from $150 to $240, including meals and optional fitness classes.

For a bed and breakfast experience, try the **Theodore Woolsey House,** 1484 E. Ojai Avenue (805-646-9779, www.theodorewoolseyhouse.com), a historic bed and breakfast inn on a 7-acre estate in a peaceful, secluded setting. Room rates start at $70 and go up to $175 per night.

**The Blue Iguana Inn** is an affordable, artsy place to hang your hat and explore. This Southwestern-style villa is right on Calif. 33 at 11794 N. Ventura Avenue (805-646-5277, www.blueiguanainn.com), 2 miles west of downtown Ojai. It has 11 individually decorated guest rooms, fully equipped kitchen suites, a pool, and a spa. Room rates start at $95 and go up to $179.

## Los Angeles

We Santa Barbarans hate to admit it, but Los Angeles does have some attractions well worth getting in the car and driving two hours for. Where else in Southern California can you find such a great concentration of world-class museums, concerts, and performances? The greater Los Angeles region—a huge metropolitan area with nearly 5 million people—is just 90 miles south of Santa Barbara on U.S. 101. There's so much to see and do there, we can't possibly tell you about everything. But we will point out some sources of general information and highlight our favorite places to visit. We'll also give you pointers about when and how to travel to L.A.—the freeways can be confusing, not to mention super-crowded.

If you want to find out what's happening in the Los Angeles area, be sure to pick

**Insiders' Tip**

Avoid the freeways Friday afternoons and any afternoon preceding a major holiday. Also, U.S. 101 is nearly always packed with visitors leaving Santa Barbara to go home to L.A. on Sunday from 4:00 P.M. on, so try to avoid that time as well.

up a copy of the Sunday *Los Angeles Times,* available at newsstands and supermarkets around Santa Barbara County. The weekly "Calendar" section gives detailed information on current performance and exhibition schedules for art, music, theater, dance, theme parks, and much more. Listings include information on where and how to purchase tickets.

For general tourist information on the greater Los Angeles region, contact the Los Angeles Convention and Visitors Bureau, 633 W. 5th Street, Suite 6000, (213) 624-7300 or (800) 228-2452, www.lacvb.com. You'll get an information packet with suggestions for entertainment, lodging, dining, special events, and more. If you're already in L.A., stop by the visitor information centers in downtown Los Angeles, 685 S. Figueroa Street, (213) 689-8822, or in Hollywood, 6541 Hollywood Boulevard, (213) 689-8822.

### Getting There

To get to Los Angeles from Santa Barbara, just drive south on U.S. 101, which becomes the Ventura Freeway as soon as you cross the southern Santa Barbara County line. Drive for 90 miles, and you will be at the edge of the city of Los Angeles. From there, you have a mind-boggling array of freeway choices, depending on where you're going. We suggest you purchase a good map of the Los Angeles-area freeway system before heading south—they're available at most gas stations and convenience stores.

If you're going to the Westwood-Beverly Hills-Los Angeles Airport region, take Interstate 405 south. If you're heading for downtown Los Angeles or Hollywood, just continue on U.S. 101 until you see signs for the Hollywood Freeway, then go south (it will still be U.S. 101).

If you have time and would like to follow a less stressful, scenic route to the city, you can take Calif. 1, the Pacific Coast Highway, which follows the coastline through Malibu. Watch for the Calif. 1 signs as you enter Oxnard, about 40 miles south of Santa Barbara. The highway winds through the city of Oxnard until it reaches the coast. Follow the road all the way to Santa Monica, where you will take U.S. Highway 10 east to reach I-405, Beverly Hills, and downtown Los Angeles.

We Insiders carefully plan our departures to and from Los Angeles. Most of us hate having to sit in bumper-to-bumper traffic and heavy congestion, which is pretty much a given during rush hours and a possibility at any time of day or evening because of freeway construction, accidents, and other factors.

On weekdays, it's best to leave Santa Barbara either very early in the morning (5:00 A.M.) or wait until about 8:30 A.M. When returning to Santa Barbara, it's best to get back on the freeway before 3:00 P.M. or to have dinner and wait until 7:00 or 8:00 P.M. Otherwise, you're risking a severe bout of frustration while stuck in gridlock and traffic that moves at a snail's pace. Another alternative is to make it to Calif. 1 on the coast before 5:00 P.M., then head back north. Weekend traffic is generally lighter, but you never know when or if you'll run into traffic, so always leave plenty of time to arrive at your destination.

Unfortunately, Los Angeles is a car-oriented city, and public transportation pales in comparison with systems in other cities its size. But from Santa Barbara you can take an Amtrak train to sparkling, newly renovated Union Station in downtown Los Angeles (800-872-7245)—there are four or five trains every day.

Once you arrive, you can walk around or hop on the Metro Red Line, which runs 4.5 miles and makes five stops on its way through downtown to MacArthur Park. The Metro Blue and Red Lines will take you to Long Beach and to Redondo Beach and eastern suburbs, respectively. But they don't really stop close to many major tourist attractions.

## Things to See and Do

Among all the things to see and do in Los Angeles, here's a rundown of our favorite museums and attractions.

Los Angeles boasts excellent museums, and many are situated on Museum Row on Wilshire Boulevard, between I-405 and downtown Los Angeles. Museum admission fees range from $2 to $9.

The **Los Angeles County Museum of Art,** 5905 Wilshire Boulevard (323-857-6000, www.lacma.org), has more than 150,000 works of art and is one of the largest art museums in the country. It features impressive permanent collections, special exhibitions, lectures, films, and concerts. The museum is closed Wednesday.

The **Natural History Museum of Los Angeles County,** 900 Exposition Boulevard (213-763-3466, www.nhm.org), is a great place to see dinosaurs, fossils, gems, minerals, animal exhibits, and pre-Columbian artifacts.

Another fascinating museum focusing on natural history is the **George C. Page Museum of La Brea Discoveries,** on Museum Row at 5801 Wilshire Boulevard (323-934-7243, www.tarpits.org). This museum houses prehistoric fossils recovered from the La Brea Tar Pits, the world's richest source of Ice Age mammal and bird fossils. You can view some of the pits up-close and personal (from behind a fence, of course).

We think that if everyone visited the **Museum of Tolerance,** war would disappear from the planet. Conveniently situated at 9786 W. Pico Boulevard, on the corner of Pico and Roxbury Drives, just south of Beverly Hills, this high-tech, hands-on experiential museum focuses on two themes through interactive exhibits: the dynamics of racism and prejudice in America and the history of the Holocaust.

In the Tolerancenter you learn all about stereotypes and prejudice through hands-on exhibits and the displays offering a historical perspective on pursuit of tolerance (for example, Reverend Martin Luther King, Jr., and the struggle for civil rights in America) and intolerance (e.g., genocides in the 20th century).

In the Holocaust section, you go back in time to witness the events before and during World War II. Every visitor receives a different passport photo with the story of a child whose life was changed by the events of the Holocaust. The passport is updated throughout the tour, and at the end you find out the ultimate fate of that child.

Although the themes of this museum may sound depressing, parts of it are actually very uplifting, as they focus on courageous acts of people fighting against intolerance. It's an eye-opening experience for anyone 8 and older. (Younger children are welcome, but they probably won't absorb the full impact of the exhibits.)

The museum is closed Saturday and on major Jewish holidays. Call (310) 553-8403 for information or visit www.weisenthal.com. Advanced reservations are recommended.

The fabulous new **Getty Center** sits on a hill overlooking Brentwood, Beverly Hills, and the sprawling city of Los Angeles. It includes the J. Paul Getty Museum plus a host of organizations funded by the J. Paul Getty Trust. Take a tram ride to the summit, then visit the museum, which consists of five two-story pavilions that house the permanent collection.

The museum's masterpieces include Mantegna's *Adoration of the Magi,* four paintings and the best group of drawings by Rembrandt in the United States, Vincent van Gogh's *Irises,* and paintings by Monet, Renoir, and Cézanne. It also boasts one of the finest collections of

## Insiders' Tip

Scurrying around the Magic Kingdom? Save time by using Disney's new FASTPASS system. This free guest service saves your place in line at the most popular rides so you can explore more of the park's attractions or grab a bite to eat. Look for the FASTPASS machines near select rides.

photographs in existence, with works from 1839 to the present.

The Getty Center opened in early 1998 and has been absolutely packed with people ever since. To get there, take U.S. 101 to I-405, then head south just a few miles and exit at Getty Center Drive. The museum is closed Monday and major holidays.

Admission is free, but you do have to make a reservation for parking and pay a $5 parking fee. If you arrive by taxi, bus, motorcycle, or bicycle, you don't need a reservation, but you may not be admitted due to site capacity restrictions. Parking on surrounding streets is restricted—residents of this posh neighborhood do not enjoy having the public hanging about near their properties. To make a parking reservation or for more information, call (310) 440-7300, or (310) 440-7305 for the deaf or hearing-impaired.

Museums appeal to our intellectual sides. Now we'll tell you about the Los Angeles attractions that provide high-charged entertainment for visitors of all ages who just want to have some fun.

We start off with what is probably the main attraction in all of Southern California—**Disneyland.** If you have children and they discover Santa Barbara is just two-and-a half hours from the Magic Kingdom in Anaheim, they will probably never forgive you if you don't make the effort to take them there—especially now that Disneyland's new neighbor, **California Adventure,** has opened its doors. Launched in February of 2001, this new Disney venture boasts a bevy of adrenaline -pumping attractions like Soarin' Over California, which gives riders the sensation of hang-gliding over forests, mountains, and oceans, and the California Screamin', a knuckle-clenching roller-coaster ordeal. You'll also find plenty of opportunities to experience the glamorous world of the silver screen.

Both Disneyland, and California Adventure are open daily. Admission for a day at one of these parks (which includes all the rides) is $43 for adults, and $33 for children ages 3 through 11. Children younger than 3 get in free. If you want to visit both parks, you have to buy a Multi-Day Park Hopper Ticket, which will set you back $111 for adults and $87 for children ages 3 through 11. Call (714) 781-4565 or visit www.disneyland.com for hours and all other information.

To get to Disneyland, take U.S. 101 south to Interstate 5 and continue south. Exit at Harbor Boulevard and go southwest (just follow the signs to the park).

Although you could conceivably drive to Disneyland, spend the day, then head back to Santa Barbara, it would be an exhausting enterprise. Also, the best way to avoid crowds is to stay at the **Disneyland Hotel** or **Disney Pacific Hotel,** right next to Disneyland. That's because on many days you can enter the park 90 minutes before the public is allowed in. Only certain rides are open during those pre-opening hours, but they're usually the ones with the longest lines (e.g., Indiana Jones Adventure, and Pirates of the Caribbean). If you have small children, you can do all of Fantasyland during early admission hours without having to wait in line at all, which is a real plus. (An hour-long line in the summer heat would try any kid's patience.) The hotel rates are not cheap, but you can't beat the convenience. Check out online reservations at www.disneyland.com for package prices. Drive from Santa Barbara the night before, check into the hotel, get up early, ride the monorail to the park and do Disneyland with as little stress as possible.

For more theme-park fun, head to **Six Flags Magic Mountain.** It's an amusement park with 100 acres of rides, shows, and entertainment, including lots of roller coasters. You'll find it at 26101 Magic Mountain Parkway, off I-5 near Valencia. Admission is $42.99 for adults and $21.50 for children 4 feet tall and shorter. Children 2 and younger are free. Call (661) 255-4100 or visit www.sixflags.com/magicmountain for hours.

Next door to Magic Mountain is **Six Flags Hurricane Harbor Water Park.** It's a pirate's dream come true: lagoons, ruins, and more than 20 water slides, open selected days in May and September then daily through June, July, and August. Younger children will like Castaway Cove, which has waterfalls and slides perfectly sized for little ones. Admission is $21.99 for adults and $14.99 for children 4 feet tall and shorter. Children 2 and younger are free. Call (661) 255-0208 or visit www.sixflags.com/hurricaneharborla for hours and information.

At **Universal Studios Hollywood** you can take a thrilling tour through the 420-acre Universal Studios complex—the largest TV and film studio in the world. The tour lasts five to seven hours, so plan on a full day. Go behind famous movie scenes, ride through Jurassic Park, meet King Kong, and watch a Flintstones show. Admission is $43 for adults, $37 for seniors 60 and older, and $33 for children ages 3 through 11. Children younger than 3 get in free. Call (818) 508-9600 or visit www.universalstudios.com for more information. Universal Studios is located just off U.S. 101; either the Universal Center Drive exit or the Lankershim Boulevard exit.

# Annual Events

Santa Barbara is event-happy. Really. No matter what month of the year, you'll find enough galas, fund-raisers, benefits, ethnic festivals, and celebrations to keep you busy every weekend. Luckily, the local press does a great job of publishing everything, so you can look ahead and pick and choose events that appeal to you.

As you glance through our list, you will notice that many events are related to the local agricultural bounty. For example, there's the International Orchid Show (March), the Lompoc Flower Festival (July), the Goleta Lemon Festival (October), the California Avocado Festival (also in October), and a host of festivals and parties that celebrate the local wine-making industry.

A colorful line-up of ethnic festivals also graces the list. Many of these have become Santa Barbara favorites over the years, mostly because they are fun, free, offer fabulous food, and have a delightful international flavor. Many of the fund-raisers involving wine and wine tasting are expensive. Although you might think $45 is a bit steep for a few hours of sipping wine and eating hors d'oeuvres, these events are extremely popular with Santa Barbarans, and nobody minds the cost because the money goes to various good causes (besides, you can fill up on excellent wine and hors d'oeuvres). If you can't afford fancy wine dinners, you'll find plenty of events to attend that are inexpensive and even free. In addition to the ethnic and agricultural festivals noted above, many family-oriented events offer free admission.

Maybe tickets to a reception or a symposium at the Santa Barbara International Film Festival are out of your price range, but you can probably afford a film screening for $7.50, which puts you right in the middle of the action. If even that's too much, stand outside the ropes with other fans and watch the celebrities arrive. Hey, it's Hollywood!

In general, nobody dresses up for anything in Santa Barbara, so casual dress is acceptable everywhere unless you're attending a fancy "gala" of some sort. If you have any questions about what to wear or are concerned about any aspect of the event, by all means call and ask. We can guarantee that you'll receive friendly advice. We Insiders have dialed every number on the list, and we found a lot of gracious and helpful folks on the other end of the line. (Well, actually we sometimes found recorded events lines, but even they always gave us the option of talking to a real person.)

The following listings are in alphabetical order under each month. Unless indicated otherwise, admission to all events is free (although you'll probably have to pay for food and maybe some activities). Prices listed are correct as we go to press, but they have a tendency to creep up from year to year. But the events that cost are always worth the money. Enjoy!

## January

**New Year's Day Hang Gliding and Paragliding Festival**
**South side of Elings Park**
**Cliff Drive**
**Santa Barbara, CA**
**(805) 965–3733**
**www.flyaboveall.com/newyear1.htm**

If you're not into football, spend a pleasant New Year's Day afternoon observing experienced hang glider and paraglider pilots maneuver their crafts down one of the oldest training hills in the country. This is a grassroots, low-key, no-frills festival organized by pilots who return to the place where they first learned to glide and celebrate the new year with a day of flying.

Instructors are on hand to explain the sport or to arrange lessons, but the day is for experienced pilots only and no "rides" are given to the uninitiated. For the best viewing, enter the park on the unmarked dirt Cliff Drive entrance road located on the north side of Cliff Drive, 300 yards east of Las Positas. Bad weather cancels the festival, but if the weather holds, most gliders are launched between 11:00 A.M. and 3:00 P.M.

Organizers encourage a donation to the nonprofit Elings Park Foundation.

## February

**Fantasy Wedding Faire**
**Earl Warren Showgrounds**
**U.S. Highway 101 and Las Positas**
**Santa Barbara, CA**
**(805) 963–8862**
**www.earlwarren.com**

Everything you need to plan the perfect wedding is offered at this Sunday extravaganza, a benefit for the Santa Barbara Division of the American Heart Association.

Fashion shows offer the latest in wedding attire, catering firms and bakeries tempt you with luscious samples, and vendors representing photographers, florists, jewelers, video production companies, wedding and reception venues, furniture stores, limousine services, and nearly everything else you can think of vie for your business with demonstrations and free giveaways. This is a must for brides-to-be and a heck of a lot of fun for everyone else. Admission is $8.

## March

**International Orchid Show**
**Earl Warren Showgrounds, U.S. Highway 101 and Las Positas**
**Santa Barbara, CA**
**(805) 967–6331**
**www.sborchidshow.com**

Santa Barbara produces more orchids than any other region of the country, and local growers introduce their finest blooms at this three-day event, which is the longest-running orchid show in the state. Upwards of 5,000 spectators attend the show, which features a stunning array of orchids brought in by more than 75 exhibitors from around the world. Booths are designed around each year's theme, and both commercial and private growers compete for the top awards.

A selection of blooming plants, corsages, supplies, commemorative pins, and limited-edition posters are on sale. In conjunction with the show, many local growers host open houses and greenhouse tours. Admission is $8 for adults; $6 for seniors 65 and older and students with ID; children 12 and under are admitted free. Buying tickets in advance saves you a few dollars.

**Kite Festival**
**Shoreline Park, Shoreline Drive**
**Santa Barbara, CA**
**(805) 963–2964**

The kite festival has been a March tradition in Santa Barbara for more than 15 years. It's always held the third Sunday in March. Contests include stunt flying and highest-flying, and there are awards for the most beautiful and largest kite. Kids can participate in a tail-chasing event, in which a kite is flown close to the ground

**Insiders' Tip**

For a list of upcoming festivals and events, visit the Santa Barbara Conference & Visitor's Bureau at www.santabarbaraCA.com and click on the link to the Calendar of Events.

and they try to catch the tail. Food is available at booths.

**Santa Barbara International Film Festival**
**Various locations**
**Santa Barbara, CA**
**(805) 963–0023**
**www.sbfilmfestival.org**

Okay, so it's not Cannes—yet—but over the past several years, this local film festival has received worldwide recognition for its diverse programming and screenings of more than 100 films from around the world. It has a strong local following, and enthusiastic fans, industry professionals, and celebrity guests take part in an exciting 10 days of screenings and other special events held all over town.

Independent films made in the United States and abroad are screened at local theaters, and workshops and symposiums focusing on films and filmmaking are held at various venues in the city.

A well-known actor or actress is honored each year (Rob Reiner was feted in 2001), and many celebrities come to town to join in the festivities, which include a star-studded opening night. Even if you don't get in to see a film, you can ogle the celebs from the sidelines. You'll find schedules for all festival events on the website and at local hotels; you can also check listings in the local newspapers or call to get on the mailing list.

Passes for festival events range from $750 for a platinum all-inclusive transferable pass to $400 for a gold nontransferable pass and $225 for a film pass. You can also buy a ticket for any six films for $48 or for a single film for $8. Tickets for symposiums are $35 each.

Get tickets early for the special events, as they often sell out ahead of time. You can reserve tickets for these as early as January by calling the above number. Tickets to individual films are sold on a first come, first served basis.

**Whale Festival**
**Stearns Wharf (at the south end of State Street), and Santa Barbara Museum of Natural History**
**2559 Puesta del Sol**
**Santa Barbara, CA**
**(805) 897–3187**
**www.sbwhalefestival.com**

Benefiting the Santa Barbara Marine Mammal Center and the Channel Islands National Marine Sanctuary, this two-day street fair draws throngs of locals and visitors. Talks by naturalists from the Sea Center and educational materials from the museum and marine sanctuary are available. Food booths, a crafts sale, a beer garden, and live music add to the festivities.

## April

**Earth Day Festival**
**(805) 963–0583**
**www.communityenvironmentalcouncil.org**

In 1969, an oil rig ruptured off the coast of Santa Barbara spewing 200,000 gallons of crude oil into the sea. The spill devastated marine habitats and fueled an environmental movement that culminated in the designation of Earth Day in 1970. Today half a billion people around the globe commemorate the occasion. It's officially observed on April 22, but the festivities in Santa Barbara usually take place on the closest Sunday (and sometimes Saturday). Thousands turn up for the free day of live music on a solar-powered stage (Jackson Brown, Kenny Loggins, and Jeff Bridges performed in past celebrations), and more than 100 nonprofit environmental organizations dispense information on earth-friendly practices and "green" technology. You can feast at the food booths, and the kids will have a ball at the special children's activities. The venue for Earth Day 2002 is the beautiful sunken gardens at the Santa Barbara County Courthouse, an appropriately evocative venue for such a poignant event.

**Garden Egg Hunt and Children's Festival**
**Santa Barbara Botanic Garden**
**1212 Mission Canyon Road**
**Santa Barbara, CA**
**(805) 682–4726 ext. 102**
**www.santabarbarabotanicgarden.org**

It's an eggstravaganza! Garden staff dye eggs donated by local markets and tuck them into nooks and crannies throughout the expansive grounds. Kids are taken on a nature walk, then turned loose for the egg hunt, which is followed by refreshments and craft activities. Proceeds go towards the garden's children's programs.

The egg hunt takes place from 10:00 to 11:30 A.M. on the Saturday before Easter, or sometime in April if Easter falls in March. The cost is $12 per child for members of the Botanic Garden and $15 for nonmembers. Egg hunters should bring their own baskets.

**Jewish Festival**
**Oak Park**
**300 West Alamar Avenue**
**Santa Barbara, CA**
**(805) 957–1115**
**www.sbjf.org**

Sponsored by the local Jewish Federation, the Jewish Festival features a Klezmer band playing the traditional music of Eastern Europe, recitations in Yiddish, wine tasting, dancing, and booths with Jewish food and crafts. Admission is free.

**Presidio Days**
**El Presidio de Santa Barbara**
**123 East Canon Perdido Street**
**Santa Barbara, CA**
**(805) 965–0092**
**www.sbthp.org**

The place where Santa Barbara began celebrates the city's birthday with a reenactment of the founding of the Presidio,

*Presidio Days, Santa Barbara's birthday celebration, takes place in April at the city's birthplace, El Presidio.* PHOTO: DEANNE MUSOFF CROUCH

historical tours, and a big birthday cake. Usually Presidio and Chumash descendents ring the bells in the newly restored bell towers, and multicultural dance and music performances brighten the festivities.

**Santa Barbara County Vintners' Festival**
**Various locations**
**Santa Ynez Valley**
**(805) 688–0881, (800) 218–0881**
**www.sbcountywines.com**

Wine connoisseurs will think they've died and gone to heaven at this extremely popular celebration of local food and wine. More than 50 wineries in Santa Barbara County offer samples of their vintages and local restaurants cook up luscious fare.

A ticket entitles you to a signature wine glass and a buffet plate; all you have to do is sip and sample your way through four hours of tasting in an idyllic setting in the Santa Ynez Valley while live music wafts through the air. We can't imagine a better way to spend a springtime afternoon. Wine and gift baskets can be bid on at a silent auction, or you can take home a souvenir T-shirt or poster.

Tickets for the festival are $60 and must be bought in advance directly from the Santa Barbara County Vintners' Association, which suggests you purchase them in January, before the event sells out, which it does every year. Choose either Saturday or Sunday; tasting is from 1:00 to 4:00 P.M., rain or shine. (Wine-maker dinners and open houses are also held in conjunction with the festival, but individual wineries handle the arrangements, so call them directly for ticket information.) The festival is held the third weekend of April.

**Santa Barbara Fair & Expo**
**Earl Warren Showgrounds**
**U.S. Highway 101 and Las Positas**
**Santa Barbara, CA**
**(805) 687–0766**
**www.earlwarren.com**

Held in late April, the city's annual Fair & Expo is five days (usually Wednesday through Sunday) of fun with an old-fashioned county-fair ambiance. Exhibits, crafts, art, games, live animals, and carnival rides, along with live entertainment and food booths, are the hallmarks of this event.

A special area is dedicated to the younger set, offering puppet shows, jugglers, a petting zoo, and pony rides. Teenagers will enjoy the thrill rides, while smaller kids can find tamer fare at the Kiddie Carnival. A Junior Livestock Auction happens on Saturday afternoon, and there are special exhibits aimed at young adults. Tickets are $5 for adults, $4 for seniors 55 and older, and $3 for kids 6 through 12. Children 5 and under are admitted free.

**Spring Plant Sale**
**Santa Barbara Botanic Garden**
**1212 Mission Canyon Road**
**Santa Barbara, CA**
**(805) 682–4726**
**www.santabarbarabotanicgarden.org**

The garden's biggest plant sale happens in the fall (see October), but you can pick up some native California plants for your spring garden at this downscaled version. Attendance at the sale is free with admission to the Botanic Garden ($5 for adults; $3 for seniors 60 and older, teens, and students with current IDs; $1 for children 5 through 12).

## May

**Children's Festival**
**Alameda Park West**
**Micheltorena and Anacapa Streets**
**Santa Barbara, CA**
**(805) 965–1001**
**www.fsacares.org/spotlight.htm**

You'll find free entertainment as well as a ton of fun stuff to do all day long at the Children's Festival. The most popular activity is the pony ride, which usually has a long line of would-be cowboys and cowgals waiting for their turn. There's also face painting, kids' crafts, carnival games, magicians, clowns, and Sportsworld, with games to test athletic skills in kids ages 6 and up. Food booths tempt you to splurge on a variety of treats. The festival is always held the Saturday after Mother's Day, with proceeds benefiting the Family Service Agency of Santa Barbara.

**Cinco de Mayo**
**Various locations**
**Santa Barbara**
**(805) 965-8581**

Several local venues have Cinco de Mayo celebrations to mark the anniversary of the Mexican defeat of the French at the city of Puebla. La Casa de la Raza, at 601 E. Montecito Street (phone number above), has a spirited multicultural festival with poetry readings, dance, theater, and music that ranges from reggae to pop.

Food booths and entertainment are offered at De la Guerra Plaza (on De la Guerra between State and Anacapa Streets), and various cultural and educational events take place at Santa Barbara City College, 721 Cliff Drive (805-965-0581 ext. 2292), and the University of California at Santa Barbara—call the Office of Student Life at (805) 893-4569 for information.

Some activities are held on the day of Cinco de Mayo (May 5), while others are scheduled on the closest weekend. It's best to call each number listed above for the specifics, as they change from year to year.

**I Madonnari**
**Mission Santa Barbara**
**2201 Laguna Street**
**Santa Barbara, CA**
**(805) 569-3873**
**www.rain.org/~imadonna/festival.htm**

Held annually on Memorial Day weekend, I Madonnari is a charming Italian street-painting festival held in the Mission courtyard. More than 200 artists get down on their hands and knees to create colorful chalk masterpieces on the asphalt and cement, and although some are rather amateurish, there are always several that are truly stunning.

Spectators stroll the courtyard at their leisure, then walk down to the lawn where an "Italian marketplace" features food booths and entertainment. After the festival is over, the street paintings remain, so you can browse later if you don't want to brave the crowds on the weekend (parking is a pain). If there's rain in the forecast, of course, the paintings are in danger of becoming chalk puddles, so don't wait too long.

## June

**Big Dog Parade & Canine Festival**
**State Street and Chase Palm Park**
**Santa Barbara, CA**
**(805) 963-8727**
**www.bigdogs.com**

Ever had a secret urge to dress up your pooch in a ridiculous outfit? This is your chance. Enter Fido in the annual Big Dog Parade and Canine Festival, make him look really silly, and you might even win a prize. Over 2,000 participants (people and pooches) strut down State Street in this popular event, and prizes are awarded for the Best in Parade, Best Costume, and Most Humorous. After the procession, you can take your pooch to meet the "Paw Reader," test his agility in the Canine Challenge Course, and enjoy live music and great food. It costs about $10 to $15 to enter the parade. All participants receive a bag of Big Dog goodies, and proceeds go to the Big Dogs Foundation to help children, dogs, and dogs helping people. If you just want to turn up and have a giggle on the sidelines, it's free.

**Jose Cuervo Volleyball Tournament**
**East Beach**
**Santa Barbara, CA**
**(805) 564-5555**

Beach volleyball is big in Santa Barbara, and a beach chair and some sunblock are the only requirements for watching this competition. There are men's, women's, and co-ed divisions, and if you get tired of

## Insiders' Tip

The Summer Solstice Parade is only half the fun. After the parade, head to Alameda Park for the wild free party with food, drink, and dance.

watching the game, there are always lots of beautiful people around to hang out with.

**Lompoc Flower Festival**
**Various locations**
**Lompoc, CA**
**(805) 735–8511**
**www.flowerfestival.org**

The Lompoc Valley, known for its thriving flower seed industry, turns into splashes of vibrant color during June, July, and August. This self-proclaimed "greatest little free festival in the West" celebrates the valley's blooming harvest with a weekend's worth of arts and crafts, flower field tours, and—what festival would be without it?—lots of delicious food.

A parade features floats decorated with local flowers, a carnival offers rides and attractions for the whole family, and you'll find free entertainment at several local venues.

The festival's highlight is the flower show, which has been judged one of the highest-ranking shows in the state and is held at the Veterans Memorial Building. More than 200 amateur flower arrangements and 500 specimens are on display, and there are arrangements by commercial growers and a children's section. (Needless to say, it all smells heavenly!)

Visit the tea room for a taste of homemade baked goods and tea or punch, or watch one of several demonstrations going on in the hall. Admission to the show is $2.50 in advance or $3 at the door; children 11 and younger are admitted free.

Other events held in conjunction with the festival include guided bus tours departing from Ryon Park and rolling past 1,000 acres of local flower fields (a nominal fee is charged), and an arts and crafts show displaying the works of more than 100 artists and artisans in oil paints, watercolors, stained glass, wood, jewelry, leatherwork, and ceramics.

There's food aplenty at the 35 booths, all operated by nonprofit organizations, selling ethnic specialties, full dinners, and treats galore.

**Santa Barbara Writers Conference**
**Westmont College**
**955 La Paz Road**
**Montecito, CA**
**(805) 684–2250**
**www.sbwc-online.com**

Sit at the feet of successful authors during this week of writing workshops, lectures, and other special events designed to sharpen your writing skills. After almost three decades at the beachfront Miramar Hotel, the conference moved to Montecito's oak-studded Westmont College campus in 2001.

This is a nationally known and well-respected conference and seminar that is open to the public and includes workshops on biography, humor, nonfiction, fiction, screenwriting, poetry, science fiction, mysteries, children's books, and many more subjects of interest to writers. Such literary luminaries as Alex Haley, William Styron, and Ray Bradbury have been guest speakers in the past.

The cost for all events (including the opening and closing banquets) and lodging at Westmont is $1,245 for a single room or $945 per person for a double. You can also pay a fee of $400 for the entire week as a day participant.

**Summer Solstice Celebration**
**State Street and Alameda Park**
**Santa Barbara, CA**
**(805) 965–3396**
**www.solsticeparade.com**

If you're looking for Spanish dancers and historical parades here, you can forget it.

*Summer Solstice dancers celebrate South Pacific style.* PHOTO: BRIAN HASTINGS

Summer Solstice, held at high noon on the Saturday nearest June 21, is when the city throws its distinguished past out the window and goes completely wacko. A whimsical theme is chosen for the parade each year, and participants walk, cycle, in-line skate, or use some other creative form of transportation (no motorized vehicles or live animals are allowed) up State Street dressed in imaginative and colorful costumes that relate to the theme. (Well, actually, some people ignore the theme, using the occasion to parade around half-dressed and body-painted, or just half-dressed, period.) After the parade, the whole party moves up the block to Alameda Park for a free celebration with food, drink, and dance that continues for the rest of the afternoon. You can also attend the free Saturday night music and dance event at the Santa Barbara County Courthouse sunken gardens from 7:00 to 10:00 P.M.

This is Santa Barbara's largest single-day arts event and it's about as wild and unpretentious a parade as you can get. Its popularity was reflected in the 2000 *Santa Barbara News-Press* Reader's Choice Awards, wherein the Summer Solstice Parade got more votes than Fiesta (see Old Spanish Days, below) as the "Best Summer Event." Everyone has fun at Summer Solstice, and parade-watchers are often as wild and crazy as the participants. If you don't have a thing to wear or want to design your own float, sign up for the public workshop held in the weeks prior to the parade and make your own ensemble with the help of artists-in-residence. The workshop is $25 for adults, $10 for kids 4 through 12.

## July

**California Outrigger Championships**
**Off Leadbetter Beach**
**Santa Barbara, CA**
**(805) 964–6890**

You'll think you're in Hawaii when you see the big outrigger canoes compete in one-mile sprints just offshore. More than 20 California teams join the race for the championship, which takes place from 8:00 A.M. to 4:00 P.M., and the competition is fascinating to watch. More than 1,000 spectators are usually on hand, and live entertainment and food vendors add to the festive atmosphere. Bring your binoculars.

**French Festival**
**Oak Park**
**300 West Alamar Avenue**
**Santa Barbara, CA**
**(805) 564–5418**
**www.frenchfestival.com**

Held to coincide with Bastille Day weekend, the French Festival is the largest French celebration in the western United States. It features everything from a French poodle parade to a miniature Eiffel Tower. Entertainment includes can-can dancers and live music, and the food is wonderful. French pastries, fresh croissants, savory hunks of French bread, and

*Wacky costumes are the norm at the Summer Solstice Celebration.* PHOTO: BRIAN HASTINGS

**Insiders' Tip**

To avoid the horrendous gridlock that accompanies the Fourth of July festivities on the waterfront, park at a city parking lot on middle State Street, then pay 25 cents for a shuttle ride to the beach.

a variety of French wines are on the menu, and all can be enjoyed at a European-style outdoor cafe. With the puppet shows, storytellers, and wading pool, there's plenty to keep the kids entertained too. Admission is free.

**Greek Festival**
**Oak Park**
**300 West Alamar Avenue**
**Santa Barbara, CA**
**(805) 683–4492**
**www.saintbarbara.net/GreekFestival.htm**

Always held the week before Fiesta (which can land it in late July or early August), the Greek Festival is far and away the favorite ethnic festival of Santa Barbarans. Who can resist the moussaka, shish kebob and baklava, not to mention that infectious music? You'll be dancing like Zorba by the time you leave. It's great fun and always crowded. Admission is free.

**Independence Day Celebration**
**Various locations**
**(805) 884–8200**
**www.sparklesb.org**

"The Fourth" is always celebrated in a grand way in Santa Barbara, thanks mostly to S.P.A.R.K.L.E. (Santa Barbara Patriotic Association for the Return of Kabooms to Light the sky for Everyone). This grassroots organization has made the Fourth of July a celebration truly "by the people and for the people" (to borrow an appropriately patriotic phrase).

There's partying on the waterfront all day long, and fireworks are launched from the end of the breakwater at 9:00 P.M., accompanied by music blaring from beachside loudspeakers. What a show! This is the largest fireworks display between Los Angeles and San Francisco. Many events are free. (Note: All personal fireworks are illegal everywhere in Santa Barbara.)

**Santa Barbara County Fair**
**County Fairgrounds**
**937 S. Thornburg Street**
**Santa Maria, CA**
**(805) 925–8824**
**www.sbcofair.com**

A local tradition for more than 100 years, the Santa Barbara County Fair is an old-fashioned kind of celebration. You'll find kids auctioning off stock, displays of local agricultural bounty, exhibits galore, top-flight entertainment, and a popular carnival midway in addition to a plethora of food. Lots of fun is in store for the whole family. Admission is $6 for adults, $3 for seniors 62 and older and children 6 through 11.

**Santa Barbara National Horse and Flower Show**
**Earl Warren Showgrounds**
**U.S. Highway 101 and Las Positas**
**Santa Barbara, CA**
**(805) 687–0766**
**www.earlwarren.com**

The year 2001, saw a return to the Santa Barbara tradition of combining the Flower Show with the Horse Show. After more than 80 consecutive years in Santa Barbara, the National Horse Show has a long and distinguished tradition. It draws horses from eight western states and riders from around the world, making it one of the top multibreed shows in the nation and the only one in the West to appear on the American Horse Shows Association's short list of "Major National and International Equestrian Competitions."

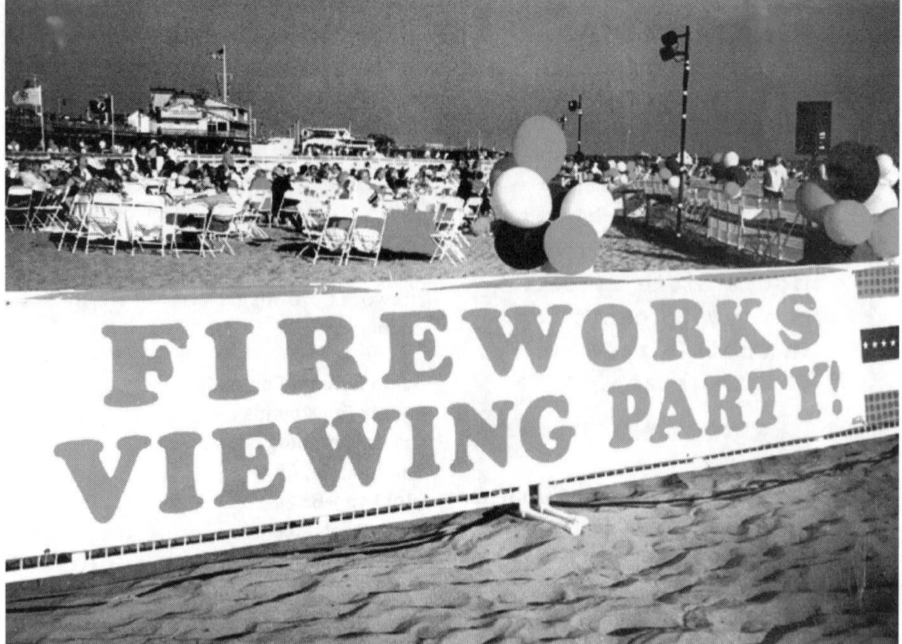


*Festooned with balloons and banners, the S.P.A.R.K.L.E. Beach Party provides a ringside seat for the July 4th fireworks show on West Beach.* PHOTO: KAREN BRIDGERS

The two-week-long show features American Saddlebred, Morgan, Hackney, Roadster, and Plantation Walking Horses the first week and jumpers and hunters the second. Ages of the participants vary from 5 to 85, making this a decidedly family event. Even if you don't understand a thing about horse shows, the arena performances at this one are both entertaining and enjoyable. For garden-lovers, the Flower Show captures all the beauty Santa Barbara has to offer in one building, with lush gardens, creative landscapes, colorful cut-flower arrangements, and homegrown vegetables. Tickets are $3 for adults, $1 for children 6 through 12; children under 5 are admitted free.

**Santa Barbara Wine Auction Weekend**
**Various locations**
**Santa Barbara, CA**
**(805) 969–WINE**
**www.musicacademy.org**

One of the more distinguished events held in Santa Barbara, the annual Wine Auction Weekend benefits the Music Academy of the West and is a must for wine connoisseurs. It's held in mid-August each year. The weekend encompasses three days of events including a gourmet dinner and concert on the grounds of the Music Academy, Masterpiece Dinners in estate homes throughout Santa Barbara, and the wine auction itself, preceded by special food and wine tastings. Tickets for each event range from $150 to $250.

**Semana Nautica**
**Various locations**
**Santa Barbara, Goleta, and Carpinteria**
**(805) 897–2680**
**www.semananautica.com**

A 10-day summer sports festival that spans both sides of the July 4 holiday, Semana Nautica offers for your participation or observation just about every sport you can imagine, from beach volleyball to cardboard kayak races to sandcastle building (okay, so some of them aren't exactly sports). More than 40 events are scheduled at venues throughout the South County, including swimming, yachting, softball, cycling, and running. Get off that couch and start training! Schedules are available starting June 1. There is a small fee for participation in each event, but the spectating is free.

## August

**Festa Italiana**
**Oak Park**
**300 West Alamar Avenue**
**Santa Barbara, CA**
**(805) 565-2968**
**www.festaitaliana.org**

A Santa Barbara tradition for more than 20 years, Festa Italiana is one of the most beloved of local ethnic festivals. You'll find everything Italian here, from cappuccino and espresso to pasta, pizza, and homemade pastries. Italian chefs demonstrate the art of cooking Italian, and accordions play classic Italian songs. There's even a bit of opera for you Puccini fans.

*A furry friend leads the way at El Desfile de los Niños, the Children's Parade of Old Spanish Days.*
PHOTO: MICHAEL D. ROBERTSON, COURTESY OF OLD SPANISH DAYS

**Old Spanish Days**
**Various locations**
**Santa Barbara, CA**
**(805) 962-8101**
**www.oldspanishdays-fiesta.org**

Old Spanish Days (the locals call it "Fiesta") is quintessentially Santa Barbara. A distinguished annual tradition that began in 1924, the five-day event is a colorful feast for the eyes, ears, and palate as residents and thousands of tourists celebrate the city's Spanish roots.

So many things happen around town in conjunction with Fiesta that you need a program to keep track of them all. Luckily, schedules of events are widely available (50,000 copies of the free official brochure are put out all over town). The *Santa Barbara News-Press* and the *Santa Barbara Independent* both publish annual Old Spanish Days special editions that list virtually everything, allowing you to pick and choose.

Some of the most popular events are the two parades, El Desfile Historico (The Historical Parade) and El Desfile de los Niños (The Children's Parade); Noches de Ronda, a free program of dance and music held every evening in the sunken gardens of the Santa Barbara County Courthouse; the two Mercados (marketplaces), one in De la Guerra Plaza downtown and one at MacKenzie Park on upper State Street, where vendors sell everything from Mexican food to T-shirts; and the Competicion de Vaqueros, a stock horse show and rodeo held at Earl Warren Showgrounds.

Some locals steer clear of downtown during Fiesta, especially during the parades, because of the traffic snarls, parking problems, and crowds. But most look forward to it. Wander down to the Mercado at lunch and you'll see locals in business suits snacking side-by-side with the tourists. You haven't really done Santa Barbara until you've done Fiesta, so pour

CLOSE-UP

## Spirit of Fiesta

Every year, on a warm summer night, thousands gather beneath the steps of Mission Santa Barbara. Then, as the moon rises from the lavender peaks, and the crowd falls silent, a proud senorita lights up the stage. She stands tall. Her gaze fixed, her chin up, she stretches her slender arms to the sky. Guitars strum a crisp glissando. Then with a swirl of her skirt and a staccato of clicks from her castanets, flamenco fills the air. This is Fiesta-Pequena, "Little Fiesta," prelude to the annual five-day Old Spanish Days celebration ("Fiesta" to the locals), and this beautiful senorita dances for all Santa Barbara. Tomorrow she will lead the parade, smiling and waving in her white satin dress. But tonight, as her mother watches with her heart in her throat, she dances in the footsteps of three generations. She is an ambassador picked for her passion and poise. She is the Spirit of Fiesta.

For many Santa Barbarans, Fiesta means a four-day margarita-fest. It means fat burritos in El Mercado, long bar lines, late nights, and cracking cascarones (confetti-filled eggs) on the heads of unsuspecting friends. Some think it's too commercialized. Many envision traffic snarls and sweaty crowds and vow to steer clear of all the commotion. But to most Santa Barbarans, Fiesta is a proud tradition. It's one of the few times of the year when the community comes together to celebrate its diverse heritage regardless of social status, religion, or race. But for all the thousands of locals and visitors from around the world who take part in the festivities each year, few know much about the true spirit of the past that inspired the celebration and the history of how it all came to be.

Like the celebration today, the first Fiesta was spawned from a mix of history, art, and commerce. The descendents of the families who first settled in Santa Barbara wanted a way to preserve the gracious Old Spanish Days culture of the past. Old Spanish Days refers to the Rancho Period of the early 19th century, when Santa Barbara was an isolated patchwork of pueblos and ranches under both Mexican and American rule. By all accounts, the residents of Santa Barbara during this time lived in harmony, and the spirit of charity and hospitality was strong. Rancheros (ranchers) welcomed visitors into their homes and shared their food and their friendship—"mi casa es su casa" (my home is your home) was the popular sentiment of the time. It was a life less hurried, when the arrival of visitors or the return of old friends and family prompted huge celebrations. It was a life of simplicity, generosity, and warmth. This romantic notion of the past hung heavy in the minds of the descendents of these Californianos, as they were called. So they organized special festivals such as La Primavera (the spring party) with colorful costumes, music, and dance to keep the spirit of the Old Spanish Days alive.

Against this background of nostalgia came the imminent opening of the new Lobero Theater. It was 1924. The theater had just been restored and civic leaders wanted to celebrate its debut with a gala event, something the whole community could enjoy. With this in mind, the Community Arts Association conceived an idea. Why not organize a festival to mark the occasion? Representatives from Community Arts shared the idea with the merchants' association and received an enthusiastic response. For years, the business folk in town had dreamed of staging an annual summer festival to entertain and attract tourists in the relatively quiet warmer months. Celebrating the opening of the Lobero was the perfect occasion.

As a result of these mixed motivations, representatives from three diverse groups—art lovers, business people, and descendents of early Spanish settlers—all came together and formed a committee to plan the celebration. Working side by side with a budget of only $5,000, they came up with many ideas of their own and decided to incorporate many elements of La Primavera as well. They wanted the five-day celebration to include food stalls, a Western rodeo, activities for children, an arts and crafts fair, and free nightly performances of music, song, and dance. The committee also envisioned a large parade as a critical component of the celebration and enlisted Dwight Murphy, a noted horseman of Santa Barbara, to organize the event.

*The beautiful senorita who is named the "Spirit of Fiesta" will lead the Old Spanish Days Fiesta Parade.* PHOTO: MICHAEL D. ROBERTSON, COURTESY OF OLD SPANISH DAYS

Endowed with a modest $200 budget, Dwight met with other members of the community and came up with the idea of having a historical theme for the parade. To learn more about the old way of life, they met with descendents of the Spanish settlers, the De le Guerra and Ortega families, who shared their history, culture, and traditions with the men. Dwight then appointed committees to arrange floats, carriages, horsemen, and costumes. Back in the Old Spanish Days, the rancheros held their horses in high regard. Travel was by horseback and children learned to ride at a very early age. Dwight shared this love of horses. In particular, he had a passion for palominos and possessed some of the finest specimens of the breed. So it was fitting that his beautiful palominos should feature prominently in the parade.

That first Fiesta Parade was a walking history book, albeit a romanticized version. Chumash Indians, Spanish explorers, and soldiers marched down State Street re-enacting important events from Santa Barbara's past. The arrival of the Spanish pioneers, the founding of the Presidio and the Mission, the raising of the Mexican flag, and the Gold Rush, among other events, were all represented in the parade. Golden palominos, saddled in silver, pulled the beautifully decorated floats. Spectators dressed in the colorful costumes of Old Spanish Days, and a spirit of unity prevailed. The festival was a huge success.

Today, the Historical Parade (El Desfiles Historico) is the biggest equestrian parade in the United States and most of the elements of that original festival still survive. Visit Santa Barbara in the first week of August (when Fiesta traditionally takes place) and you can still enjoy the free nightly entertainment with costumes, song, and dance (known today as Las Noches de Ronda), a children's parade (El Desfile de los Ninos), open-air marketplaces filled with the aromas of authentic Old Spanish Days cuisine (El

Mercado), an arts and crafts show, and a Western rodeo (Competicion de Vaqueros), the same events that brought thousands of locals and visitors together more than three-quarters of a century ago.

Over the years, Old Spanish Days/Fiesta has evolved and expanded. Two years after the first Fiesta celebration, Dwight Murphy was elected as the first "El Presidente" of the Old Spanish Days festival. In this role, he presided over its organization and acted as spokesperson for all the events. This custom continues today. Each year, the volunteer board of directors selects a respected member of the community to act as El Presidente or La Presidente. He or she is honored at many of the Old Spanish Days events and acts as an ambassador to visitors and residents.

Fiesta Pequena also originated two years after the original festival. In 1925, a massive earthquake rocked Mission Santa Barbara, but it was restored by the following year. So on a warm summer's night in 1926, on the eve of Old Spanish Days Fiesta, the people of Santa Barbara gathered beneath the steps of the Mission to celebrate its restoration. Today this event, known as "Little Fiesta," is the official opening of the five-day celebration. It is a night of blessings, dance, music, and song. For the next five days the community will come together to celebrate and recapture the rich traditions and culture of the past.

So as you sit sipping your margarita, watching the beautiful senorita twirl across a moonlit stage, think of the true spirit of Fiesta. It's not just the costumes, the crowds, and confetti. It's a ritual that reflects the friendliness of the people of Santa Barbara. It's a time to share our love of music, art, and dance. But most importantly, it's the gracious spirit of old Santa Barbara passed from generation to generation, a spirit of tolerance, hospitality, and warmth. Viva La Fiesta!

yourself a margarita, grab your castanets, and party! Oh, and watch out for those cascarones, decorated eggs filled with confetti that are sold on the street. You haven't been initiated into Fiesta until someone has cracked one over your head, spilling all those teeny tiny bits of paper right into your hair and down your back, and into your clothes, your car, your house, and . . . well, you get the picture. Admission to most of the public events is free. (Also see the Close-up on Fiesta in this chapter.)

## September

**Danish Days**
**Various locations**
**Solvang, CA**
**(805) 688–6144, (800) 468–6765**
**www.solvangcc.com**

It's almost as good as being in Denmark when you visit the annual Danish Days festival held in mid-September in Solvang. Folk dancing, music, parades, storytelling, demonstrations of Old World Danish crafts, and plenty of good food (we recommend the deliciously delectable aebleskivers smothered in jam and powdered sugar) contribute to the charm of this weekend festival. Everyone dresses up in native costumes, and a roving beer wagon adds to the ambiance.

If you're interested in seeing the real thing, enter the raffle for a round-trip ticket for two to Denmark. Even if you find ethnic festivals ho-hum, the aebleskivers alone make this one worth going to.

**Santa Barbara International Jazz Festival**
**Various Locations**
**(805) 969–5038, (800) 480–FEST**
**www.sbjazz.com**

Starting in 2001, the Jazz Festival will become a biennial, rather than an annual, event. But it is still a popular one. The

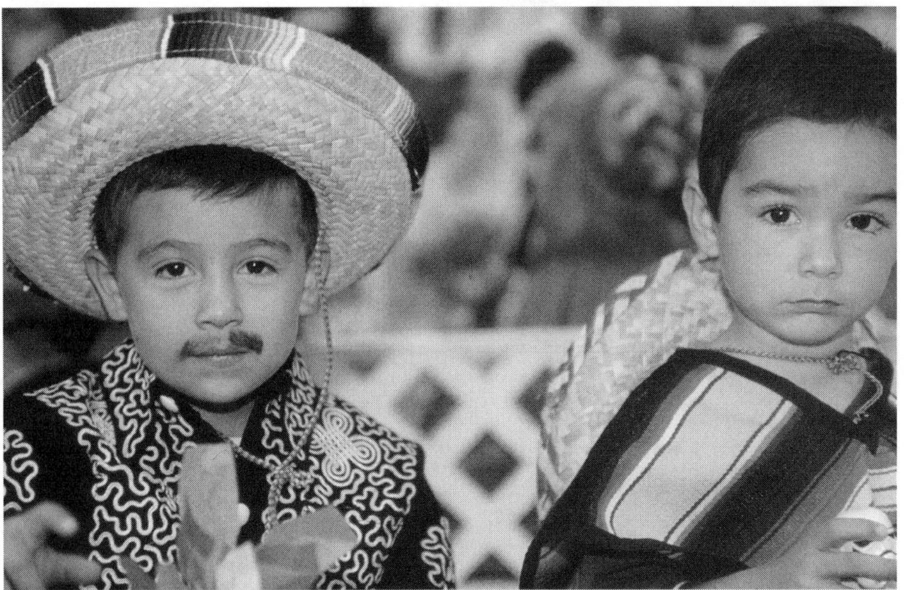

*During Old Spanish Days, little hombres can join in the fun at the Children's Parade.*
PHOTO: MICHAEL D. ROBERTSON, COURTESY OF OLD SPANISH DAYS

organizers bring some of the world's top jazz performers into town for a weekend of band jazz, Dixieland, Latin jazz, blues, and a plethora of other delights. Locations tend to change from year to year so call the numbers above or check the website before heading out.

**Zoo-B-Que**
**Santa Barbara Zoological Gardens**
**500 Niños Drive**
**Santa Barbara, CA**
**(805) 962-5339**
**www.santabarbarazoo.org**

If you're looking for something that's fun for the whole family, you won't do much better than the annual Zoo-B-Que, a benefit held at the zoo in late September. Kids of all ages will enjoy camel rides, crafts, magicians, puppet shows, and—of course—all of the zoo animals and attractions. In addition, there's a delicious tri-tip barbecue and a raffle with prizes that range from a small stuffed toy to dinner at local restaurants and hotel getaway weekends. Admission is $15 for adults and $10 for children 2 to 12.

## October

**Artwalk**
**Santa Barbara Museum of Natural History**
**2559 Puesta del Sol**
**Santa Barbara, CA**
**(805) 682-4711**
**www.sbnature.org**

A major fund-raiser for the museum, Artwalk opens with a Friday-night reception and then proceeds with two days of art exhibitions and a juried fine arts show and sale. Paintings, jewelry, glass, photographs, and ceramics by more than 100 artists from California and the West are displayed on the museum grounds along scenic Mission Creek, and visitors browse at their leisure. A celebrity artist is featured each year in a special indoor show. Proceeds from the sale inject new life into museum programs. Admission to Artwalk is $6.

## Insiders' Tip

Best warm summer night hangout during Fiesta: the Santa Barbara County Courthouse. Bring a blanket, a picnic dinner, and binoculars for a close-up view, and enjoy a (free!) evening of Spanish, Mexican, and Indian dance, music, and song.

**California Avocado Festival**
**Linden Avenue**
**Carpinteria, CA**
**(805) 684-0038**
**www.avofest.com**

"The best time you'll ever have with an avocado" is the theme and pledge to festival-goers at this weekend affair. The world's largest bowl of guacamole (200 gallons requiring more than 2,000 avocados, 700 cloves of garlic, the juice of 80 lemons, and 40 pounds of grated cheese) lures celebrants to this annual tribute to the "love fruit."

In addition to the guacamole, you'll be able to sample a wide variety of dishes you never thought you'd see an avocado in, including avocado ice cream. Sit in the papier-mâché avocado "love pit," browse the selection of hand-carved avocado pits, and see the pear-shaped fruits dressed up for judging. Other highlights are fabulous food and good music dubbed—what else?—"guac 'n' roll."

**Celebration of Harvest**
**Various locations**
**Santa Ynez Valley**
**(805) 688-0881, (800) 218-0881**
**www.sbcountywines.com/festivals.htm**

Local vintners celebrate the grape harvest at this fall festival held on the second Saturday of October from 1:00 to 4:00 P.M. Similar to the Santa Barbara County Vintners' Festival held in April, the Celebration of Harvest features local wines and food from area restaurants. Tickets, which go on sale at the end of July, are usually around $60 and must be purchased in advance from the Santa Barbara County Vintners' Association.

**Fall Plant Sale**
**Santa Barbara Botanic Garden**
**1212 Mission Canyon Road**
**Santa Barbara, CA**
**(805) 682-4726**
**www.santabarbarabotanicgarden.org**

Insiders know there's no better place to find native plants than at the Fall Plant Sale at the Botanic Garden. On Saturday and Sunday, regular admission to the Botanic Garden ($5 for adults; $3 for seniors 60 and over, teens, and students with current IDs; $1 for children 5 through 12) gets you into the plant sale, where you'll find everything from tiny seedlings to trees, most grown at the garden's own nursery and some that you can't find anywhere else in town.

Experts are on hand to answer questions, but all plants are varieties that grow well in the Santa Barbara area, so how can you miss? This is a must for gardeners.

**Goleta Lemon Festival**
**Stow House**
**304 N. Los Carneros Road**
**Goleta, CA**
**(805) 967-4618, (800) 646-5382**
**www.goletavalley.com/lemonfestival**

Lemonade, lemon cake, lemon bars, lemon soft tacos, and some delectable lemon meringue pies are just some of the lip-smacking choices at the Goleta Lemon Festival, a tribute to the citrus crop that has been a staple of Goleta's economy for years. In addition to sampling the food, you can browse through a variety of arts and crafts and enjoy entertainment that varies from Elvis impersonators to magic shows to clowns and jugglers. Kids will enjoy a ride on the historic fire engine or a turn at the petting zoo.

*The Old Spanish Days parade moves down palm-studded Cabrillo Boulevard.* PHOTO: MATT STRAKA, COURTESY OF OLD SPANISH DAYS

If you think you have the best lemon pie recipe on the planet, enter it in the lemon pie baking contest. If you're clueless in the kitchen, pick up a copy of *If You Love Lemon,* the festival's official cookbook. All booths are run by local community organizations, so when you buy that yellow cotton candy, your money goes to a good cause.

**Old-Time Fiddlers' Convention**
**Stow House**
**304 N. Los Carneros Road**
**Goleta, CA**
**(805) 966–1191, (805) 682–1593**
**www.sbsunriserotary.f2s.com/fiddler**

Held on a Sunday afternoon in mid-October, the fiddlers' convention is a celebration of old-time music. No piece of music less than 50 years old is allowed. The contestants, playing fiddles, banjos, and other instruments, compete in 15 categories, which also include singing and group performance. It's a foot-stompin', hand-clappin' good time for everyone, with more than 100 musical artists and the requisite good food. Tickets are $9 for adults, $6 for seniors, and $3 for children 12 and older.

**Santa Barbara Air Fair**
**Santa Barbara Municipal Airport**
**Santa Barbara, CA**
**(805) 967–7111**

Vintage war birds, aerial acrobatics, demonstrations, and hands-on exhibits are all part of the fun at the airshow, held every other year on a Saturday in early October. The next one is scheduled for 2003. Sponsored by several local organizations as a benefit for the Santa Barbara Children's Aviation Scholarship Fund, this is great family fun, especially for budding pilots and daredevils. When you get tired of looking at airplanes, grab a bite at a food concession and chow down.

## November

**Santa Barbara National Amateur Horse Show and Holiday Fair**
**Earl Warren Showgrounds**
**U.S. Highway 101 at Las Positas**
**Santa Barbara, CA**
**(805) 687–0766**
**www.earlwarren.com**

Always held around Thanksgiving, this major event is an important training show for future Olympian equestrians. Junior and amateur riders compete in English and Western divisions. Starting in 2001, a Holiday Fair was added to the event. Now you can watch the horses then stroll around a magical old-fashioned Christmas village with carolers and Yuletide entertainment. Food booths will tempt you with roasted chestnuts, turkey, and other Christmas treats. You can also see a live Nativity scene and visit Santa with your wish list.

***Santa Barbara News-Press* Half-Marathon, and Cally's 5K Fun Run & Walk**
**Leadbetter Beach, Santa Barbara**
**(805) 892–2250 ext. 5050, (805) 964–2591**
**www.newpress.com/halfmarathon**

A benefit for the United Boys & Girls Clubs of Santa Barbara and the Santa Barbara County Athletic Association, this popular event is for the whole family, with awards given in more than 60 categories. The half-marathon begins at 8:00 A.M., and the course winds its way through some of Santa Barbara's most beautiful scenery.

The Half-Marathon wheelchair division starts at 8:10 A.M. and the 5K Fun Run & Walk begins at 8:12 A.M. After the races, a buffet breakfast is served, and massage therapists stand by to work out the kinks in those sore muscles. The awards ceremony follows at 10:30 A.M. The fee to participate in the half-marathon is $25 (includes T-shirt); the 5K Fun Run & Walk fee is $20 (includes T-shirt).

## December

**Celebrity Waiters Luncheon**
**Fess Parker's Doubletree Resort**
**633 E. Cabrillo Boulevard**
**Santa Barbara, CA**
**(805) 963–1426**
**www.californialung.org**

For more than 15 years, the Celebrity Waiters Luncheon has raised money for the American Lung Association of Santa Barbara County. In addition to the money raised through ticket sales, big bucks are generated by local celebs acting as waiters; they'll literally stand on their heads if need be in an effort to influence diners to leave huge tips, which are also donated to the charity (the highest tip on record is $3,000).

The waitstaff usually includes some pretty impressive help, including stars such as Santa Barbara's own Kenny Loggins and local political leaders. It's a great cause and a lot of fun. Tickets are $35 for the luncheon—and plan to reach deep into your pockets for a big tip.

**Downtown Holiday Parade**
**State Street**
**Santa Barbara, CA**
**(805) 962–2098 ext. 22**
**www.santabarbaradowntown.com**

This is a traditional holiday parade in which many local kids strut their stuff, with bands playing Christmas songs and a few floats, one of which carries a smiling Santa Claus. Real snow is usually trucked to a nearby spot so that the kids can make snowmen and throw snowballs after the parade.

It's no coincidence that this parade winds its way down State Street, where most of Santa Barbara's retail stores are located, so after the parade, browse the shops and spend some money. Christmas is coming, after all! The parade usually starts at 6:30 P.M. For more information, visit the web site and click on "What's Happening?"

**Insiders' Tip**

What are the best seasonal events in Santa Barbara? According to a local poll, Summer Solstice and Fiesta take the top honors for summer, while the Parade of Lights and the Christmas Parade are the winter favorites.

**Folk and Tribal Arts Marketplace**
**Santa Barbara Museum of Natural History**
**2559 Puesta del Sol**
**Santa Barbara, CA**
**(805) 682–4711**
**www.sbnature.org**

You can shop the world in a weekend at this three-day arts and crafts marketplace, which is usually held the first weekend in December in the museum's auditorium. It's the perfect place to find an unusual gift for the holidays, with booths featuring jewelry, baskets, clothing, art, and other objects from around the world. Highlights include textiles from Guatemala, carvings from Africa and Asia, and jewelry from India. Prices for the art and crafts range from as low as 50 cents up to $500 for more elaborate pieces. Admission is free.

**The Nutcracker**
**Arlington Theatre**
**1317 State Street**
**Santa Barbara, CA**
**(805) 963–4408**

A Santa Barbara tradition for more than 20 years, the enchanting *Nutcracker* ballet is presented each December by the Santa Barbara Festival Ballet and the Santa Barbara Ballet Center, with celebrated guest artists and imaginative sets and costumes. Take your budding little ballerina and watch her eyes shine.

Performances are on a Saturday and Sunday, with matinees both days and an evening performance on Saturday. Ticket prices range from about $8 to $32.

**Parade of Lights**
**The waterfront off Stearns Wharf**
**Santa Barbara, CA**
**(805) 969–5217**

This Yuletide parade features dozens of boats adorned with holiday lights and other festive decorations cruising around Stearns Wharf and the local waterfront. There's a theme chosen for the parade each year, and entries range from the whimsical to the elaborate.

If the weather is bad or the swells are high, the parade is canceled and boats will stay securely in their slips, but they'll still be decked out, so walk around the harbor and breakwater for a look.

**Winterfest (Solvang)**
**Various locations**
**Solvang, CA**
**(805) 688–6144, (800) 468–6765**

The Danish town of Solvang is appealing at any time of year, but it's especially delightful when dressed up for Christmas. The Winterfest celebration is marked by millions of lights adorning the downtown area, live entertainment, and special events.

A tree-lighting ceremony kicks off the weekend, followed by a Christmas Tree Walk led by Santa and Mrs. Claus. A parade follows on Saturday, and a Christmas pageant rounds out the Winterfest offerings. Now that you're in the Christmas spirit, stop in at the city's many unique shops in search of that special Christmas gift—and don't forget to sample the fabulous Danish pastries and cookies. Your nose will lead the way.

# The Arts



The Santa Barbara arts scene has been hopping since the 1870s. Spurred by reports of the glorious climate and gorgeous scenery, wealthy families from the East, South, and Midwest began moving here in droves in the late 1800s and the first half of the 20th century. Rather than do without the established opera houses, museums, theaters, and orchestras to which they were accustomed, they decided to bring world-class culture right here.

Numerous patrons poured large amounts of money into local community groups. (The Fleischmanns, Peabodys, McCormicks, and Ridley-Trees, as well as Lotte Lehmann and Michael Douglas are just a few of the many generous financial supporters of Santa Barbara arts over the years.)

These groups in turn developed arts schools, theater and dance companies, orchestras, and other performing arts groups. They also invited the world's best performers, teachers, musicians, and writers to Santa Barbara.

This tremendous local support continues to this day and is largely responsible for the big-city variety and quality of arts and culture in our relatively small community. We have our own symphony, two chamber orchestras, choral groups, a professional ballet company, and several theater companies that present everything from Shakespeare and Broadway-style musicals to contemporary dramas and comedies.

We have several major art museums, a natural history museum, and a number of historical museums.

The area's institutions of higher education also contribute to the rich variety of community arts. The dance, music, theater, and art departments at the University of California at Santa Barbara, Westmont College and Santa Barbara City College present regular concerts, exhibits, and events that showcase student talent. Aspiring professional photographers from the Brooks Institute of Photography exhibit their thought-provoking pieces at various locations on the institute's two campuses and around town.

For more than 50 years the Music Academy of the West has brought together master musicians and talented music students for a summer of intensive study—and a popular eight-week festival that wows the public year after year.

A great thing about Santa Barbara is that you don't have to travel far to enjoy performances by world-class artists. The world comes here instead—and it doesn't seem to take much to convince it to come. Santa Barbara is a perfect stopover on a trip to Los Angeles or San Francisco. And who wouldn't want to hang out on the beach or wander the streets of a beautiful town between performances?

More than 90 organizations are currently bringing the arts to the region. Santa Barbara has hosted all sorts of traveling stars, from Mae West and the Marx Brothers to the Vienna Philharmonic and Sting.

The area's stimulating intellectual environment has attracted both emerging artists and those whose names are already internationally renowned. Just sit for a while in a downtown cafe and look around. You're bound to see budding photographers, screenplay writers, artists, and musicians. You might also run into one of our many resident celebrities, including film stars, directors, producers, and novelists.

To be honest, however, it's tough to be an artist just starting out here. There are few garrets to rent, and the cost of living isn't exactly cheap. Also, the Santa Barbara audience as a whole is highly educated and culturally diverse, i.e., it can be very critical and demanding of artistic quality.

Still, many young people manage to eke out a living in our fair city and establish a foundation for a future career in their chosen artistic field. In fact, Santa Barbara currently enjoys an international reputation as a destination point for vanguard art.

Our thriving rock 'n' roll scene serves as a case in point. Agents come regularly to Santa Barbara to check out new Santa Barbara bands, which have established a national reputation for creating cutting-edge music. Many local bands have signed contracts with major agencies in recent years, including Toad the Wet Sprocket (now disbanded), Nerfherder, and Summer Camp.

While we couldn't possibly include everything related to the arts in this chapter, we've tried to give you a good idea of the depth and breadth of our cultural offerings. The chapter isn't arranged geographically because nearly all the groups and venues are in Santa Barbara.

To find out what's happening in Santa Barbara while you're here, we recommend that you pick up any of the following publications. The *Santa Barbara Independent* is a free weekly newspaper that comes out every Thursday and includes a detailed events calendar for the entire week. It also has a popular arts section with reviews, information, and gallery listings. The *Santa Barbara News-Press* features a daily listings calendar. The Friday issue includes a special *Scene* magazine with a day-by-day events listing for the week as well as reviews and other arts information. The *Santa Barbara Performing Arts Guide* is a quarterly pamphlet that includes complete local theater, event, and gallery listings. You can find it as a pullout inside *Santa Barbara Magazine,* or at hotels, the Visitor Information Center on Cabrillo Boulevard, or through the Conference & Visitors Bureau.

## One-Stop Cultural Shopping

Santa Barbara has a number of arts organizations and centers that sponsor a wide range of exhibits, events, programs, and activities throughout the year.

**Cabrillo Pavilion Arts Center**
**1118 E. Cabrillo Boulevard**
**Santa Barbara, CA**
**(805) 897–1982**
**www.sbparksandrecreation.com**

Located on East Beach overlooking the sand and sea, the Cabrillo Arts Center presents a range of art exhibits at the pavilion and organizes a variety of fun classes and events at other sites around town. All are sponsored by City Parks and Recreation. Visit the gallery at the Art Center itself and you'll see a new exhibit each month by a local group or organization, such as the Santa Barbara Art Association and the Los Padres Watercolor Society. The center also presents special art exhibits coinciding with ethnic and cultural celebrations like African American, Hispanic, and Native American Heritage Months. The Arts Center gallery is open Monday through Friday 9:00 A.M. to 5:00 P.M. Admission is free.

Classes arranged by the center at other locations around town include children's creative dance and ceramics, yoga, and instruction in a variety of dance styles including swing, folk, tap, Argentinian tango, ballroom, and belly dancing. Locals love the events. In July and August, you can attend free concerts in Alameda Park on Sunday afternoons and music concerts at Chase Palm Park on Thursday evenings.

You can also book the Cabrillo Pavilion Arts center for private special events.

**Santa Barbara Arts and Crafts Show**
**Chase Palm Park, along Cabrillo Boulevard east from State Street**
**Santa Barbara, CA**
**(805) 897–1982**
**www.sbparksandrecreation.com**

You can shop for culture here—literally. Established in 1965 by local artists, the Santa Barbara Arts and Crafts Show is called the "Art Center of the West." Sponsored by City Parks and Recreation since 1966, the show is now the only continuous, nonjuried arts festival of original drawings, paintings, sculpture, crafts, and photography in the world. Approximately 300 Santa Barbara County resident artists display their own works in an informal atmosphere under the palms of Chase Palm Park. All items are original art, created by the artists you meet. The show is held on all fair-weather Sundays and holidays from 10:00 A.M. until dusk.

**Santa Barbara Contemporary Arts Forum**
**653 Paseo Nuevo, 2nd floor**
**Santa Barbara, CA**
**(805) 966–5373**
**www.sbcaf.org**

Founded in 1976, CAF presents provocative, innovative contemporary art that explores aesthetic and social issues of our time. It has earned an international reputation as a leading alternative art space and is the primary contemporary arts center on California's Central Coast.

CAF presents the work of local, regional, national, and international artists in 15 to 20 exhibitions annually as well as a broad variety of performance and media art. In addition, it operates extensive education and outreach programs, including classes in contemporary art, lectures, poetry readings, panel discussions, workshops, catalogs, video programs, artists' gallery talks, and mentorship programs.

The CAF gallery is actually three galleries in one: the main Klausner Gallery, the Norton Gallery (reserved for area artists), and the Partridge Gallery (reserved

*Held on Sundays and holidays along the palm-lined waterfront, the Santa Barbara Arts and Crafts Show is a great place to buy original art and imaginative gifts.* PHOTO: SANTA BARBARA CONFERENCE & VISITORS BUREAU

for art by community residents, e.g., children's groups, elderly artists). The gallery is located in a striking second-story space in the Paseo Nuevo Mall and is open to the public Tuesday through Saturday from 11:00 A.M. to 5:00 P.M. and Sunday noon to 5:00 P.M. Admission is free.

**University of California at Santa Barbara Arts & Lectures**
**UCSB Campus**
**Goleta, CA**
**(805) 893–3535**
**www.artsandlectures.ucsb.edu**

For more than 40 years the UCSB Arts & Lectures program has brought a unique and lively array of performing arts, films, lectures, and writers' readings to the university campus—and to the entire Santa Barbara community.

Performances feature world-class touring artists: dance companies, chamber musicians, theater companies, and traditional musicians from all over the world. Examples of the diverse range of invitees include the Parsons Dance Company, the Tokyo String Quartet, Spalding Gray, the National Theatre of the Deaf, and the Whirling Dervishes.

Arts & Lectures also presents international cinema, rarely seen documentaries, independent films, and top Hollywood movies. Lectures and readings bring distinguished people from every area of public life to the stage, for example veteran civil rights activist Julian Bond, dancer Suzanne Farrell, and the Dalai Lama of Tibet, as well as acclaimed writers, including poet laureate Robert Pinsky and novelist Toni Morrison.

Most events are presented in the 860-seat Campbell Hall on the UCSB campus, although recently productions and programs have been making more frequent appearances in downtown venues such as the Lobero Theatre and Arlington Center (see the "Venerable Venues" section later in this chapter).

## Bells on Their Toes

Dance in all its forms is a favorite local activity. Although many talented local dancers have found it difficult to earn paychecks for their expertise, they have found numerous ways to practice dance and create high-caliber performance groups. The Santa Barbara Dance Alliance arranges for the country's best choreographers to visit the city and promotes local choreographers and dancers.

A number of local amateur dance companies—the Santa Barbara Festival Ballet, West Coast Ballet, and the Santa Barbara Chamber Ballet, among others—also give seasonal performances. These companies often invite professional guest artists to perform along with locals.

**State Street Ballet**
**322 State Street**
**Santa Barbara, CA**
**(805) 965–6066**
**www.statestreetballet.com**

Currently, State Street Ballet is the only fully professional ballet company in the Santa Barbara area. This small ensemble made its debut in 1994 and has already succeeded in its goal to bring the Santa Barbara community "high-quality ballet with a flair." About 20 dancers make up the company during its six-week spring

*The State Street Ballet performs both contemporary and classical ballets.*
PHOTO: DAVID BAZEMORE

*Some 300 Santa Barbara County artists exhibit their work at the weekly Santa Barbara Arts and Crafts Show.* PHOTO: JOHN B. SNODGRASS

and fall seasons—a potpourri of nationalities, sizes, and backgrounds. The company strives to present energetic contemporary ballets mixed with the classics, showcasing professional work by professionals. It tours nationally, but is in residence at the Lobero Theatre and also performs at the Granada Theatre, at 1216 State Street (805-966-2324, 800-366-6064).

State Street Ballet manages to attract top-notch dancers thanks to the extensive dance-world contacts of its founder, Rodney Gustafson. Gustafson is a former American Ballet Theatre dancer who first came to Santa Barbara while on tour with the ABT in the 1970s. He noticed Santa Barbara was rich in all the arts except professional ballet. The beauty and potential of the area drew him back here in 1993 to start a professional company and affiliate school with his partner and wife, Allison Gustafson, also a professional dancer. The Gustafsons maintain warm relations with the ABT, the Joffrey Ballet, and other internationally known troupes—hence the depth and quality of State Street's members and guest artists.

The company maintains an active repertory of contemporary ballets (Balanchine's *Who Cares?,* Gustafson's *Bolero*) and the classics (*Giselle, Paquita Variations, La Vivandiere*). In the 2001–2002 season, State Street Ballet performances included *Alice in Wonderland, Ballroom,* and Gustafson's version of *The Nutcracker.*

**Insiders' Tip**

For a current schedule of art, music, and theater events go to www.newspress.com and click on "Arts and Entertainment." You can search by date, name, or category.

## The Camera's Rolling All Over Town

Since it's only 90 miles from Hollywood, Santa Barbara attracts not only celebrity residents from the motion picture industry but also visiting film crews. It's not unusual to run across a group filming a scene at the beach, the zoo, on the courthouse lawn, or on State Street.

At one time, Santa Barbara was the film capital of the world. In 1912, the Flying A Studio built the best-equipped and most innovative motion picture studio in the nation on the corner of Mission and State Streets. Flying A produced hundreds of films—from Westerns to dramas set on tropical islands and the Arabian desert.

Hollywood eventually succeeded in drawing the motion picture industry farther south, and grand-scale film production in Santa Barbara ceased by 1921. Today you can satisfy your appetite for great film at a number of Santa Barbara movie theaters, film festivals, and other venues.

## Movie Theaters

Metropolitan Theatres has a monopoly on just about all the movie theaters in this town. All theaters show the usual Hollywood releases as well as a few major foreign films. The Riviera Theatre tends to present popular artsy foreign films. The less popular or more offbeat films are often sent to Plaza de Oro.

Call the Metropolitan Theatres Movie Hotline, (805) 963-9503, for locations and showtime information for all the following cinemas except the Riviera and the Arlington, which have their own box office numbers: Santa Barbara Fiesta 5, 916 State Street; Metro 4, 618 State Street; Paseo Nuevo, 8 W. De la Guerra Place (in the Paseo Nuevo Mall); Riviera Theatre, 2044 Alameda Padre Serra (805-965-3886); Arlington Center for the Performing Arts, 1317 State Street

(805-963-4408); Plaza de Oro, 349 Hitchcock Way; and in Goleta, Goleta Cinema Twin, 6050 Hollister Avenue; Camino Real Cinemas, Camino Real Marketplace, and Fairview Twin, 251 N. Fairview.

## Film Festivals and Other Movie Venues

**Santa Barbara International Film Festival**
**1216 State Street, Suite 710**
**Santa Barbara, CA**
**(805) 963-0023**
**www.sbfilmfestival.org**

Every March Santa Barbara turns into a mini Cannes, with film professionals, celebrities, press, and thousands of fans dashing from screen to screen for 11 straight days. Best known for its discovery of independent films, documentaries, shorts, and videos, the Santa Barbara Film Festival continues a tradition of diverse programming, showcasing independent films from around the world. More than 125 films from 20-plus countries are presented.

The festival's cornerstone series are World Cinema, Documentaries, and U.S. Independents. It also features seminars with respected industry professionals and a screenplay competition sponsored by producer Ray Stark.

You can purchase festival film tickets individually or by the series. For more information on the festival, call the above number, visit the web site, or turn to the listing in our Annual Events chapter.

**University of California at Santa Barbara Arts & Lectures**
**UCSB**
**Goleta, CA**
**(805) 893-3535**
**www.artsandlectures.ucsb.edu**

The UCSB Arts & Lectures program sponsors a series of excellent films from around the world—internationals, documentaries, and independents—as well as top Hollywood movies. Films are shown weekly (except during school breaks).

### Insiders' Tip

Did you know that Oscar—the most famous statuette in history—has ties to Santa Barbara? Oscar's designer, Greg Stanley, studied at the nationally known Santa Barbara School of the Arts in the early 1920s.

## Gallery Gazing

**Arlington Gallery**
**(805) 898-2005**

The Arlington Gallery has attracted discriminating collectors since 1977, specializing in works by famous Western painter Edward Borein and other American paintings of the 19th and 20th century. The gallery no longer operates in a public space; call the above number if you'd like to arrange a viewing.

**Brooks Institute of Photography Galleries**
**Jefferson Campus (main gallery)**
**1321 Alameda Padre Serra**
**Santa Barbara, CA**
**(805) 966-3888**
**Montecito Campus**
**Graholm Estate**
**801 Alston Road**
**Montecito, CA**
**(805) 966-3888**
**www.brooks.edu**

Brooks Institute of Photography is an internationally renowned school for professional photographic education (see our Education and Child Care chapter for details on the school and its programs). Brooks hosts numerous cultural events for the Santa Barbara community, including exhibits by world-renowned photographers, international multimedia slide shows, student film festivals, undersea slide shows, and educational lectures. On most Fridays throughout the year the public is invited to attend the institute's All-Campus Tours and International Slide Shows at the Montecito campus. These award-winning multimedia shows are produced by student participants in the school's international photodocumentary project. They take two-month photo expeditions to exotic locales, for example, China, India, and West Africa. Call or visit the institute's web site for details. The public is invited to tour the campuses and view the numerous photographic images produced by students, faculty, and alumni. Brooks' two photographic galleries are open Monday through Friday 8:00 A.M. to 5:00 P.M., and admission is free.

**Delphine Gallery**
**1324 State Street, Suite F**
**Santa Barbara, CA**
**(805) 962–6625**
**www.delphinegallery.com**

You'll find Delphine Gallery in Arlington Plaza, across the street from the Arlington Center for the Performing Arts. The gallery showcases the work of California artists (most of them modern) and is open Monday through Friday from 10:00 A.M. to 5:00 P.M. and Saturday from 10:00 A.M. to 3:00 P.M.

**The Easton Gallery**
**557 Hot Springs Road**
**Montecito, CA**
**(805) 969–5781**
**www.eastongallery.com**

Ellen Easton's gallery focuses on contemporary landscapes by local artists. Easton represents about half the artists involved in The Oak Group (see the Close-up in this chapter). The gallery is open weekends from 1:00 to 5:00 P.M. and by appointment weekdays.

**Faulkner Gallery**
**Santa Barbara Public Library**
**40 E. Anapamu Street**
**Santa Barbara, CA**
**(805) 564–5608**

Any art group can book this gallery for month-long shows. The Santa Barbara Art Association sponsors eight or nine shows a year at the Faulkner. All types of art are shown here, including weaving, sculpture, and ceramics. The gallery is open Monday through Thursday 10:00 A.M. to 9:00 P.M., Friday and Saturday 10:00 A.M. to 5:30 P.M., and Sunday 1:00 to 5:00 P.M.

**The Frameworks and Caruso/Woods Fine Art**
**131 E. De la Guerra Street**
**Santa Barbara, CA**
**(805) 965–1812**

This small, intimate gallery has been around since the early 1980s (previously under the name De la Guerra Gallery) and offers thought-provoking, eclectic exhibits. It presents a new show approximately every eight weeks. The museum-quality framing and design business at the same location helps support the gallery space. The gallery is open Tuesday through Friday 10:00 A.M. to 5:00 P.M. and Saturday 11:00 A.M. to 3:00 P.M.

**Gallery 113**
**1114 State Street (La Arcada Court)**
**Santa Barbara, CA**
**(805) 965–6611**
**www.gallery113.com**

The Santa Barbara Art Association runs this cooperative enterprise, which is billed as Santa Barbara's oldest fine art gallery. Founded in 1973, the gallery presents a new show every month featuring a local artist. Shows represent a variety of art forms, including sculpture, painting, jewelry, and ceramics. It's open Monday through Saturday 10:00 A.M. to 5:00 P.M., Sunday 1:00 to 4:00 P.M.

CLOSE-UP

## The Oak Group: Artists Making a Difference

Santa Barbara's natural beauty has long enticed plein air artists, who strive to record their connection with nature through landscape paintings. The same beauty has also attracted scores of housing-tract developers, oil companies, and others who lust after prime open land and resources for a less altruistic reason: easy money.

In the opinion of most Santa Barbara residents, far too many scenic landscapes disappeared forever in the 1900s. Rows of luxury homes, hotels, and golf courses have replaced the meadows and groves where people once roamed freely.

This constantly encroaching development has always been a subject of much local debate, especially since the major oil spill off the coast in 1969. Some residents sit back and watch as environmentalists, developers, and oil companies wage battle after battle. Others take their written and vocal views to hearings, courtrooms, and the media. But one of the area's most powerful environmental allies is not a group of attorneys or politicians, but a collection of 23 local landscape artists: The Oak Group.

Since 1986, The Oak Group has effectively used the power of visual art to protect and preserve the county's few remaining areas of wilderness and open space. Through their art, members have made thousands of people aware of the endangered natural landscapes that surround them. This awareness, in turn, has generated much public support for conservation.

The Oak Group has also raised much-needed funds for environmental protection. All members have pledged to donate 50 percent of their profits from benefit shows to environmental organizations, thus raising nearly $400,000 for environmental purposes in the last 12 years.

The group played a pivotal role in the "rescue" of the Douglas Family Preserve, an open-space area on the bluffs overlooking Arroyo Burro Beach, as well as the preservation of the Sedgwick Ranch in the North County. An article in *The Santa Barbara Independent* once called The Oak Group "the community's most visible environmental force."

So who are these valiant heroes, armed with paint and brushes?

The Oak Group was spawned by conversations between two well-known local artists: Ray Strong and Arturo Tello. Strong, now in his 90s, still paints with the vigor and passion that has long distinguished his work. Educated at Stanford University and the Art Student's League in New York, he formerly shared a gallery with Ansel Adams.

Since moving to Santa Barbara in 1960, Strong has established himself as a leader and mentor in the plein air painting scene.

*"Garden Path" by Glenna Hartmann, a member of The Oak Group.*

*"Fall Reflections" by Oak Group artist Richard Schloss. Group members support environmental causes.*

You can see his works all around Santa Barbara: the dioramas in the Bird Habitat Hall at the Museum of Natural History as well as paintings on permanent display at the Museum of Art and other locations.

While working together on some frames, Strong and Tello (born in 1954) chatted about a book they both were reading about the artist Pisarro's life. The book described the way Pisarro, Gauguin, and Cézanne painted together in the countryside, sharing artistic experiences and helping each other find ways to further develop their art.

Tello and Strong thought it would be a great idea to start such a group of their own. They began with a small contingent of seven artists who called themselves the "Open Airing Klub," or OAK Group. The group first met in early 1986 and has been meeting for painting outings, group shows, lectures, and other functions ever since.

From the beginning, the artists' mission has been to capture the beauty of the landscape on canvas. Their efforts to preserve the landscape are a natural outgrowth of the act of painting. They don't just glance at a landscape, splash some color, and move on. They observe, feel, hear, and immerse themselves in the scenes before them. To these artists, whose lives are so intimately and emotionally entwined with nature, it seems a moral obligation to fight to protect the land they love to paint from development and destruction.

The Oak Group's initial exhibitions focused on endangered lands, then expanded to include places that have been successfully protected, at least for the time being. Their impressive works continue to celebrate the "wild" areas of Santa Barbara, the Channel Islands, and elsewhere—raising our awareness of the beauty we often take for granted and spurring efforts to protect it.

Current members of The Oak Group include Meredith Abbott, Whitney Abbott, Donald Archer, Joseph Areno, Marcia Burtt, Chris Chapman, Patricia Chidlaw, Michael Drury, Erika Edwards, Karen Foster, Karen Gruszka, Glenna Hartmann, John Iwerks,

Larry Iwerks, Manny Lopez, Eric Parfit, Hank Pitcher, Richard Schloss, Skip Smith, Thomas Van Stein, Ray Strong, Arturo Tello, and Sarah Vedder.

For more information on The Oak Group, contact Ellen Easton at the Easton Gallery at 557 Hot Springs Road, Montecito (805–969–5781), or Oak Group member Glenna Hartmann (805–965–5526). Easton represents about half of the members of The Oak Group and has published a commemorative book titled *The Oak Group: The First Ten Years 1986–1996.* You can also visit the group's web site at www.theoak group.org.

**Reynolds Gallery**
**Westmont College**
**955 La Paz Road**
**Montecito, CA**
**(805) 565–6162**
**www.westmont.edu**

Reynolds showcases all types of art by local and national artists. It offers a number of shows throughout the year, including an invitational theme show, a faculty show, a local artists' show, and an end-of-year senior exhibit. It also has an annual show with judging, in which the entire community is invited to exhibit. Reynolds is open Monday through Friday 8:30 A.M. to 4:30 P.M. and Saturday 11:00 A.M. to 2:00 P.M. year-round except the month of August, when it often closes for summer break.

**Sullivan Goss Books & Prints Ltd./Arts & Letters Café**
**7 E. Anapamu Street**
**Santa Barbara, CA**
**(805) 730–1460**
**www.sullivangoss.com**

A combination bookstore/cafe/gallery, this establishment opened in 1995 and offers a small print gallery featuring Old Masters, American printmakers, original prints, antique maps, photographs, and natural history prints. It also organizes revolving exhibitions on various subjects, for example, photographs of Tibetan exiles in India. You'll find one of the largest art-book collections in the world here (see our Shopping chapter for details). Stay to enjoy live music—Broadway songs, classical guitar, opera, classical piano—offered many evenings in the cafe.

## A Wordsmith's Wonderland

Writers abound in Santa Barbara. The literary community bursts with the extraordinary talents of novelists, poets, and screenwriters, including T. C. Boyle, Fannie Flagg, Thomas McGuane, Sue Grafton, Gerald Brown, and Dennis and Gayle Lynds. Famous authors of children's books who live in the area include Audrey and Don Wood and Lee Wardlaw. Santa Barbara also has more small publishers than any other U.S. region of its size.

Nearly every day brings a reading, lecture, or book signing at bookstores, cafes, colleges, and libraries. The *Santa Barbara News-Press* devotes a full page to books in the "Life" section of the Sunday paper and publishes a a detailed schedule of local literary events. The *Santa Barbara Independent* also includes book signings and other literary happenings in the weekly events listings.

For a fascinating look at Santa Barbara history through the voices of its literati, pick up a copy of *Literary Santa Barbara: Between Great Mountains and a Great Sea,* by Stephen Gilbar and Dean Stewart. It includes a wide spectrum of voices, from Chumash storytellers to famous writers who took up residence here, and it's filled with nuggets of trivia (e.g., did you know W. B. Yeats was here?).

The book is available at local booksellers. If you're moving here and want to get involved in a writer's group, we suggest you attend a reading at one of the locales listed below and speak with other writers. They can point you in the right direction.

You can also meet other budding scribes through Santa Barbara City College adult education classes. Each year, the continuing education division offers excellent writing courses in a number of different genres. After attending these courses, many students get together and form their own writers' groups. (See our Education Chapter for more information on this program or visit www.sbcc.net/ce).

Here are a few highlights of our literary scene.

**Santa Barbara Writer's Conference**
**(805) 684–2250**
**www.sbwc-online.com**

After almost three decades at the beachfront Miramar Hotel, this nationally renowned conference moved to Montecito's oak-studded Westmont College campus in 2001 while the Miramar gets a face-lift. The conference aims to sharpen the skills of aspiring writers and launch them along the path to publication. About 350 people attend this June week of writing workshops and evening lectures by literary celebrities. In the past, guest speakers have included such esteemed literati as Ray Bradbury, Charles Schultz, Amy Tan, Sue Grafton, Lisa See, and Aimee Liu. You can register as a day student or for a package including full board, but either way, apply early. Registration is limited to the first 350 who apply. (See our Annual Events chapter for more details.)

**Small Publishers, Artists & Writers Network (SPAWN)**
**(805) 643–2403**
**www.spawn.org**

SPAWN is a nonprofit organization providing education, information, resources, and a supportive networking environment for artists, writers, and other creative people interested in the publishing process. The organization participates in book festivals, arranges occasional seminars held at the Karpeles Manuscript Library Museum, and holds field trips to areas of literary interest such as book manufacturing facilities. SPAWN membership dues are $45 per year and include a regular newsletter, printed member directory, a personal web page, and steep discounts at several literary organizations as well as seminars and workshops. Nonmember subscriptions to the newsletter are $15 per year. The newsletter is the best source of information but you can also access schedules for upcoming events at the organization's web site. Tax-deductible donations are appreciated.

**Speaking of Stories**
**Lobero Theatre**
**33 E. Canon Perdido Street**
**Santa Barbara, CA**
**(805) 966–3875, (805) 963–0761**
**www.speakingofstories.org**

Pages come alive on stage during these magical evening performances, when professional actors read classics and short stories to an attentive audience. In winter/spring 2001, director Karin de la Peña and producer Steven Gilbar presented four performances, which featured stories by such distinguished authors as Jack London, Somerset Maugham, Alice Walker, Anton Chekhov, and William Faulkner. In the past, performers have included celebrities such as John Cleese, Jane Seymour, Jeff Bridges, and other talented local actors.

Readings focus on world literature and take place on Monday evenings about once a month from February through May at the Lobero Theatre (805–963–0761). You can also attend special presentations at other times of the year. The Christmas presentation of *Holiday Chestnuts & Some Surprises* is always popular. Tickets range from $13 to $25 and are available an hour before each performance. Season subscriptions are also available.

## Treasures From Art and Nature

Art in a variety of guises can be found in several Santa Barbara museums.

**Insiders' Tip**

To purchase tickets in advance for many events, call TicketMaster at (805) 583-8700 or visit the website at www.ticketmaster.com.

**Karpeles Manuscript Library Museum**
**21 W. Anapamu Street**
**Santa Barbara, CA**
**(805) 962–5322**
**www.rain.org/~karpeles/sbfrm**

The Karpeles Manuscript Library is the world's largest private holding of important original documents and manuscripts. David and Marsha Karpeles established the museum because they wanted American children to gain a sense of destiny and hope for the future. They believe this can be accomplished by helping people look closely at important accomplishments in various disciplines—particularly history, literature, science, government, art, and music. They opened the original Manuscript Library in Montecito in 1983 but now operate out of the above location.

In addition to the Santa Barbara location, the library now operates museums in Tacoma, Washington; Jacksonville, Florida; Duluth, Minnesota; Charleston, South Carolina; and Newburgh and Buffalo, New York.

The library features rotating exhibits that focus on about 25 documents at a time. Topics are drawn from fields of history, music, science, literature, and art. Highlights of the museum's permanent collection include the original draft proposal for the U.S. Bill of Rights and documents penned by such stellar scientists as Einstein, Galileo, Darwin, and Newton.

Exhibits in recent years include: "Anne Frank in the World 1929–1945," "Space," and "Women's Rights and Women in Literature." Every three months the museum features different painting and photography exhibits showcasing the works of the community. The museum is open daily 10:00 A.M. to 4:00 P.M., and admission is free.

**Santa Barbara Historical Museum**
**136 E. De la Guerra Street**
**Santa Barbara, CA**
**(805) 966–1601**

To gain a sense of what it was like to live in the Santa Barbara of yesteryear, come here. The Santa Barbara Historical Society constructed this museum, and for over three decades it has celebrated Santa Barbara's artistic and cultural heritage through displays of unique artifacts, photographs, furnishings, and textiles dating as far back as the 15th century.

Artifacts from the Chumash, Spanish, Mexican, American, and Chinese cultures attest to Santa Barbara's multicultural heritage. The museum library holds rare literary and visual documents, including 30,000 historic photographs. Adjacent to the museum are two early 19th-century buildings, the 1817 Casa Covarrubias and the 1836 Historic Adobe.

Museum hours are Tuesday through Saturday 10:00 A.M. to 5:00 P.M., Sunday noon to 5:00 P.M. The museum is closed Monday. Admission is free, but donations are appreciated. (See the listing in the Attractions Chapter for more information).

**Santa Barbara Museum of Art**
**1130 State Street**
**Santa Barbara**
**(805) 963–4364**
**www.sbmuseart.org**

Santa Barbara's recently expanded Museum of Art ranks among the top 10 regional museums in the country. Its permanent collection includes Asian, American, and European treasures spanning more than 4,000 years, from ancient bronzes to vanguard contemporary art.

American art ranges from early portraits through 19th- and 20th-century landscapes, still life, and portraiture to Modernist painting and sculpture. The Asian collection encompasses the art of China, Japan, India, Tibet, and Southeast Asia.

While roaming the halls, you can view works by numerous well-known artists such as Eakins, Monet, Chagall, Picasso, and O'Keeffe. The museum also brings touring exhibits to the community several times a year. The museum opened its stunning Peck Wing in February 1998 and now features three spacious galleries, a gift shop, a cafe, and a children's gallery. The Constance and George Fearing Library stocks a wide range of reference books, art periodicals, and art exhibition and auction catalogs. Library hours vary, so call before you visit.

Museum hours are Tuesday through Saturday 11:00 A.M. to 5:00 P.M. (Friday until 9:00 P.M.) and Sunday noon to 5:00 P.M. Admission is $6 for adults, $4 for seniors 65 and older, and $3 for students and children ages 6 through 17. Children younger than 6 are admitted free. Admission is free on Thursday and on the first Sunday of each month.

**University Art Museum**
**UCSB**
**Goleta, CA**
**(805) 893–2951**
**www.uam.ucsb.edu**

Established in 1959, the University Art Museum is known for its creative programs focusing on vanguard contemporary art. In 2000, the museum completed an extensive renovation and expansion project and now has six new galleries, three of which are dedicated to showing the museum's permanent collections. The museum's 7000-object fine art collection ranges from antiquity to the present. Of special note is the Sedgwick Collection of Old Master Paintings and the Morgenroth Collection of Renaissance Medals and Plaquettes. Modern holdings include sculpture by Henry Moore, Sam Francis, and George Rickey; paintings by Joan Mitchell and Robert Therrien; and works by Georgia O'Keeffe and Jean Tinguely.

One of the museum's particular strengths is works on paper, with drawings by Jonathan Borofsky and prints by Jean Arp, Richard Diebenkorn, and 1930s WPA artists. You will find more than 300 paintings and drawings by early 20th-century Santa Barbara artist Fernand Lungren and a substantial group of 19th- and 20th-century photographs here.

Among the museum's past exhibitions are: "Japanese Fishermen's Coats from Awaji Island," "Just Another Poster? Chicano Graphic Arts in California," and "Survival System Train and Other Sculpture by Kenji Yanobe."

The museum's architecture and design collection, which focuses on the work of Southern California–based architects and designers, is considered one of the most comprehensive of its type in the country. It includes more than 500,000 historic drawings and related documents such as correspondence and writings, photographs, models, casts, and furniture.

A diverse educational outreach program of lectures, tours, films, performances, and symposia is scheduled throughout the year, and special educational programs are offered for school children. In addition, the Museum Store offers an array of unique art, design, and fashion items that reflect the museum's changing exhibitions. For information about current exhibitions and programs, call the numbers above or visit the museum's web site. The museum's hours are noon to 8:00 P.M. Tuesday, and noon to 5:00 P.M. Wednesday through Sunday. The museum is closed Monday. Admission is free.

## The Scintillating Sounds of Music

**Camerata Pacifica Santa Barbara**
**(805) 961–0570 for information**
**(805) 961–0571 or (800) 557–BACH for tickets**
**www.cameratapacifica.org**

A sonorous little Santa Barbara gem, Camerata Pacifica is a chamber music ensemble with a refreshingly relaxed approach and a sharp sense of humor. The ensemble's eight-program concert series is often spiced with witty banter between the group's founder, Adrian Spence, and the other musicians. Performances range from The Coffeehouse Series of casual performances to more formal special events. They are staged in four different venues including the Music Academy of the West's Abravanel Hall and Santa Barbara City College's Fé Bland Forum. The group's diverse repertoire includes the classics as well as more obscure musical treats and contemporary pieces. Known for its educational emphasis, the organization also presents an entertaining lecture series, "The Hitchhiker's Guide to Classical Music . . . or When to Clap and Other Mysteries Revealed" as well as outreach programs to retirement communities and schools. For program information visit their web site or call the number above.

**Community Arts Music Association**
**111 East Yanonali Street**
**Santa Barbara, CA**
**(805) 966–4324; tickets for individual performances through the Arlington Box Office, (805) 963–4408**
**www.camasb.org**

Founded in 1919, CAMA is the grande dame of Santa Barbara arts groups. It is devoted to bringing the world's greatest symphony orchestras, maestros, and soloists to Santa Barbara's balmy shores.

The roster of artists and orchestras presented by CAMA over the past 80 years represents a Who's Who of music in this century: Horowitz, Rachmaninoff, Segovia, Mehta, the New York and Berlin Philharmonics, and the Concertgebouw Orchestra, to name just a few. The Los Angeles Philharmonic has performed in Santa Barbara every decade since 1920. A recent season featured performances by the English Chamber Orchestra, the Kirov Orchestra, the Los Angeles Philharmonic Orchestra, and pianist André Watts.

CAMA's season runs October through May, and concerts tend to sell out quickly; in fact, it's sometimes hard to get tickets to certain performances at all unless you're a season subscriber. Call right away if you have any interest in attending a performance. All concerts are held at the Arlington Center for the Performing Arts, at 1317 State Street.

**Music Academy of the West**
**1070 Fairway Road**
**Montecito, CA**
**(805) 969–4726, (805) 969–8787 box office**
**www.musicacademy.org**

The Music Academy of the West is internationally renowned and widely considered one of the finest summer music festivals and schools in the country. Every summer it offers eight weeks of richly varied music performed by exceptional musicians—much to the delight and benefit of Santa Barbara residents and visitors.

The academy was established in 1947 by a group of dedicated arts patrons and celebrated musicians, including legendary German opera singer Lotte Lehmann and Dr. Otto Klemperer, music director of the Los Angeles Philharmonic from 1933 to 1939. The group wanted to create a summer music academy on a par with such East Coast institutions as Juilliard and Tanglewood.

The academy has provided gifted young musicians with the opportunity for advanced study and performance under the guidance of internationally known faculty artists (including Metropolitan Opera star Marilyn Horne, director of the Music Academy's voice program, and piano pedagogue Jerome Lowenthal).

In 1951, the academy took up permanent residence at Miraflores, an elegant,

*Set on a gorgeous bluff-top estate, the Music Academy of the West attracts some of the country's finest musicians.* PHOTO: BRIAN HASTINGS

Mediterranean-style estate on a bluff overlooking the Pacific Ocean. Today the campus occupies 9 acres of wooded, beautifully landscaped grounds and gardens.

More than 175 events are open to the public during the academy's Summer Festival, which starts in mid-June and ends in mid-August. Highlights include weekend Festival Orchestra concerts led by distinguished guest conductors, the Tuesdays at Eight chamber music series, a fully staged opera, and Concerto Night, during which the winners of the academy's concerto competition perform with the Festival Orchestra. Call (805) 897-0300 for daily concert updates.

Picnic Concerts at the Miraflores campus are popular events. Concertgoers enjoy a picnic supper in the gardens followed by a concert showcasing brilliant young musicians in Abravanel Hall.

Master classes—the academy's signature program, in which faculty artists give feedback to students after they perform—are held in piano, strings, brass, winds, percussion, and voice and are open to the public. Call or visit the above web site for more information. Also, free community-outreach concerts are presented at various locations around town, including the Santa Barbara Mission, the Botanic Garden, and the Santa Barbara Museum of Art. Some of the Summer Music Festival events are free of charge. For those that aren't, subscriptions are available or you can purchase single tickets from the Music Academy Box Office (805-969-8787) or the Lobero Box Office (805-963-0761). You can also order tickets online at www.lobero.com.

**Music Theatre of Santa Barbara**
**Granada Theatre**
**1216 State Street**
**Santa Barbara, CA**
**(805) 966-2324, box office; (800) 366-6064**
**www.mtsb.org**

In 2001, Santa Barbara Civic Light Opera reinvented itself. Flying under a new banner as the Music Theatre of Santa Barbara, the organization now imports touring shows under the title "Broadway By the Sea" instead of producing them locally. Some local actors are a bit peeved

**Insiders' Tip**

If you like the blues, visit www.sbblues.org and sign up for the free Blues Lovers e-mail updates. You'll receive all the latest information on blues events in Santa Barbara.

by the change, but many theatergoers are pleased to see nationally acclaimed shows right here in our own backyard. The 2001–2002 MTSB season offered such diverse performances as the Peking Acrobats, *Chicago—The Musical, Tap, The Rat Pack, Knight Life,* and the circus extravaganza *Apogee.* Season subscriptions are available. Some shows may have to be relocated while the Grandada Theatre is renovated; call the box office numbers above for more information.

**Opera Santa Barbara**
**123 W. Padre Street, Suite A**
**Santa Barbara, CA**
**(805) 898–3890, (800) 563–7181**
**www.operasb.com**

Formerly the Santa Barbara Grand Opera Association, Opera Santa Barbara has changed its name but not the high quality of its stunning productions. When this nonprofit organization opened its first official season in 1996, it was the first opera company in the region in nearly 35 years. It is now an acclaimed, established presence in the community.

Opera Santa Barbara is the dream child of opera singers Marilyn Gilbert, a lawyer by profession, and her husband, Nathan Rundlett, a retired teacher. They wanted to bring opera on a grand scale back to town and started making the dream a reality in 1993. They staged five full operas and countless operatic excerpts at many locations to build an audience. A following emerged and the company opened its first official season in fall 1996.

Opera Santa Barbara attracts first-rate singers, technical staff, conductors, and stage directors. Many of the stars sing with major opera companies, for example, the Metropolitan, San Francisco, and Munich operas. The orchestra is composed of professional players from Santa Barbara and Los Angeles led by concertmaster Gilles Apap, an internationally known violinist.

Productions are fully staged, thanks to set designers from California and New York, choreographers, award-winning costume designers, and a large chorus. Musical direction is currently under the leadership of the company's principal conductor, Valéry Ryvkin, who was an assistant conductor at the Metropolitan Opera in New York. The season runs from August through March. For tickets, call the Lobero Theatre Box Office (805) 963–0761 or visit the opera company's web site at www.lobero.com.

**Santa Barbara Blues Society**
**(805) 897–0060**
**www.sbblues.org**

Founded in 1977, Santa Barbara Blues Society is the oldest society of its kind in the United States. This nonprofit organization sponsors and produces regular performances of well-known blues musicians—such as Alvin Youngblood Hart, harmonica player Charlie Musselwhite, and guitarist/singer Woody Mann—at various locales around town.

**Santa Barbara Chamber Orchestra**
**(805) 687–7820**
**www.sbco.org**

Directed by renowned violist Heiichiro Ohyama, this acclaimed orchestra consistently presents classical chamber music of the highest standards and spotlights world-renowned guest soloists. A recent season featured six chamber orchestra concerts at the Lobero Theatre, including performances by guest pianist David Golub. A second concert series called the

Chamber Players Series featured the Music Director Ohyama as violist.

The orchestra's season runs fall through spring, with concerts taking place on Tuesday evenings. Seats are almost always sold out through season subscriptions, but when they are available, individual tickets can be ordered through the Lobero Theatre Box Office (805-963-0761). To order subscriptions, call the Santa Barbara Chamber Orchestra at the number above.

**Santa Barbara Choral Society**
**(805) 965-6577**
**www.sbchoral.org**

The Santa Barbara Choral Society, founded in 1948, is the oldest performance organization in Santa Barbara. It's renowned for the high quality and discipline of its singers and its challenging, innovative repertoire. Composed of about 120 members, the society aims to open up avenues for study and performance to all qualified singers and to encourage public interest in choral music. The society has presented several world premieres and devotes a significant number of its programs to 20th-century music by American composers.

The Choral Society has performed a range of great works, from Orff's *Carmina Burana* to Mozart's *Grand Mass in C minor.* Often it collaborates with other musical groups, including the Santa Barbara Symphony, Santa Barbara Chamber Orchestra, and Music Academy of the West. Performances take place fall through spring.

**Santa Barbara Master Chorale**
**(805) 967-8287**
**www.sbmasterchorale.org**

The Santa Barbara Master Chorale was created in 1984 and performs major choral works in the oratorio tradition. The professional orchestra and soloists, conducted by Phillip McLendon, present concerts three or four times a year. Performances have included Bach's *Magnificat in D,* Schubert's *Mass in E flat,* Stravinsky's *Symphony of Psalms,* Mozart's *Requiem,* and a summer Pops Concert.

**Santa Barbara Symphony**
**1900 State Street, Suite G**
**Santa Barbara, CA**
**(805) 898-9626, season tickets;**
**(805) 963-4408, Arlington Center box office**
**www.thesymphony.org**

The Santa Barbara Symphony performs traditional symphonic, choral, and popular music. Varujan Kojian, director of the symphony during the 1980s, played a major role in developing the orchestra into a professional ensemble that rivals those of major metropolitan areas. Following Kojian's sudden death in 1993, Gisèle Ben-Dor was chosen to continue Kojian's efforts to provide world-class performances to community audiences.

An annual seven-concert subscription series forms the core of the symphony's offerings. Internationally recognized musicians and conductors often participate in the series as guest artists. Most performances take place at the Arlington Center for the Performing Arts. Recently the symphony added two new series: the Pop Series and the Family Series. The Pop series includes a New Year's Eve concert and party and other performances by pop artists. The Family Series includes three performances throughout the year aimed at introducing children and their families to the symphony. Free outdoor concerts are held on special occasions, and the organization offers a range of valuable educational programs such as the Santa Barbara Youth Symphony and Concerts for Young People. For more information, call the number above or visit the symphony's web site. You can also order both season tickets and single concert tickets online.

**Sings Like Hell**
**Lobero Theatre**
**33 E. Canon Perdido Street**
**Santa Barbara, CA**
**(805) 963-0761**
**www.singslikehell.com**

The promoters call this year-round series of monthly performances "very hot music in a really cool place." Top singers/

songwriters come to the Lobero Theatre to play a range of music, from folk rock, jazz, reggae, and pop to hip-hop and country. The targeted audience is people who want to listen to live contemporary music concerts in a comfortable theater setting rather than a bar. Typically, hip 30- to 50-year-olds attend.

Performers in this radical series are chosen for their talent, regardless of fame or fortune. In the past they have included Peter Case, Tom Russell, The Persuasions, David Crosby, Tracy Chapman, Charlie Musselwhite, Greg Brown, Laura Love, and Shawn Colvin. Season ticket holders receive a backstage pass for a meet-the-artist reception after each show. Tickets are available at the Lobero Theatre Box Office (see above) or online at www.lobero.com.

## Curtain Call

It's not New York, but Santa Barbara comes pretty darn close to offering a similarly wide range of high-quality dramas, musicals, contemporary plays, and offbeat comedies.

**Circle Bar B Dinner Theatre**
**Circle Bar B Guest Ranch**
**1800 Refugio Road**
**Goleta, CA**
**(805) 965–9652**
**www.circlebarb.com/dinnertheater**

The Circle Bar B Guest Ranch in the mountains northwest of Santa Barbara hosts a lively dinner theater every Friday and Saturday evening and Sunday afternoon from April through November. Tickets cost $32 for general admission, $28 for seniors, and $11 for guests of the ranch and include the show plus a tri-tip barbecue dinner served family-style (Friday and Saturday evenings) or a Cornish game hen brunch (before the Sunday matinee). Vegetarian meals are also available with advance notice.

The theater usually offers four shows every season, typically comedies, farces, and musical comedies. It doesn't have a liquor license, but guests are welcome to bring along a bottle of wine if they wish.

**Ensemble Theatre Company of Santa Barbara**
**(805) 962–8606, box office**
**www.ensembletheatre.com**

Founded in 1979, the award-winning Ensemble Theatre Company is Santa Barbara's oldest professional theater group. Directed by Robert Grande-Weiss since 1985, ETC has built an excellent reputation for producing a range of classic and modern comedies, dramas, and premieres. It produces five fully staged productions each season from October through May. The 2000–2001 lineup included *Art* by Yasmine Reza, *The Aspern Papers* by Michael Redgrave from the story by Henry James, *A Doll's House* by Henrik Ibsen, *Collected Stories* by Donald Margulies, and *The Weir* by Conor McPherson. ETC's professional company members have performed on Broadway and appear regularly in film and television. Guest directors come from major regional theaters. Set designers work in regional theater, film, and television.

Outside the mainstage season, ETC presents annual short-run experimental productions by local and emerging playwrights. It also offers a Storybook Theatre, which stages two original musical plays for children every year. The Saturday public performances, where children can enjoy box lunches with the Storybook actors, are a big hit with family members of all ages. The company resides at the intimate 140-seat Alhecama Theatre in the Presidio State Park. Call the number above for tickets.

**Pacific Conservatory of the Performing Arts Theaterfest**
**(805) 922–8313, box office; (805) 686–1789; (800) 549–PCPA**
**www.pcpa.org**

This unique regional theater group is not technically within the geographic region we're focusing on in this book. However, lots of Santa Barbarans head up to Solvang and Santa Maria in the North County for the excellent performances of comedies, dramas, and musicals.

PCPA is based at Allan Hancock College in Santa Maria and appears at three different North County facilities, the closest being the 700-seat Solvang Festival Theatre, an outdoor amphitheater. PCPA is the only training program of its kind in the country offered by a community college. It supports a unique, fully accredited vocational training program for aspiring actors and theater technicians.

PCPA Theaterfest is home to a core company of resident and visiting professionals. During a recent summer, the company presented such classics as *42nd Street, The Tempest, My Fair Lady, Rope,* and *On Golden Pond.* You can order season subscriptions or tickets to individual performances from the PCPA web site or by calling the box office number above. Note that arrangements for patrons with special needs are subject to availability and must be made in advance.

## Venerable Venues

A number of area arts centers, auditoriums, theaters, and halls host a wide range of performances by local and traveling companies and troupes.

**Alhecama Theatre**
**914 Santa Barbara Street**
**Santa Barbara, CA**
**(805) 962–8606**

The Alhecama, a cozy 140-seat theater next to the Old Presidio, was originally the centerpiece of the Santa Barbara School of the Arts. The school, which was a branch of the Community Arts Association, boasted a powerhouse teaching staff of nationally known artists, including Buckminster Fuller, Carl Oscar Borg, Ed Borein, and Colin Campbell Cooper. The school closed when its director died in 1932, and the association handed over the property to a bank during the Depression to pay off creditors.

Philanthropist and civic leader Alice Schott saved the arts complex from becoming a parking lot when she bought the property in 1939. She renamed the property and the theater Alhecama—a word coined from the first two letters of her four daughters' names: Alice, Helen, Catherine, and Mary Lou. Later she deeded the property to what's now called the Adult Education Program, which held well-attended classes there from 1945 to 1981.

The California Department of Parks and Recreation purchased the property in 1981, handing management over to the Santa Barbara Trust for Historic Preservation. Today the theater is home to the Ensemble Theatre Company. The facilities feature a climate-control system and free parking next to the theater.

**Arlington Center for the Performing Arts**
**1317 State Street**
**Santa Barbara, CA**
**(805) 963–4408**

This exquisite city landmark is probably the most unusual theater you'll ever visit. It's also Santa Barbara's main performing arts venue, and it has held that title for more than 50 years. It's built on the site of the grand Arlington Hotel, which opened in 1875. Arlington was the name of the Virginia mansion owned by Robert E. Lee and later used by General Ulysses S. Grant, and the posh hotel was so named to appeal to post–Civil War sympathizers of both the North and the South.

The hotel burned to the ground in 1909, and a new Arlington rose from the ashes in 1911. Bad luck befell that building too, as it was heavily damaged in the 1925 earthquake and subsequently demolished.

The site lay as a patch of weeds until Fox West Coast Theatres erected the third and present structure as a showcase movie house in 1930–31. The stunning tile-roofed building was designed to resemble the Moorish kings' Alcazar in Seville. The unique architectural style is actually a combination of numerous styles from Spanish architecture. The Andalusian exterior features a tall spire and an arched courtyard with fountains.

The interior is adorned with sweeping staircases of glazed Tunisian tiles, antique chandeliers, and iron lanterns that are copies of Catalonian street lamps from the 14th through the 16th centuries. The walls depict authentic Spanish villages, each building completely detailed with roof, chimney, lighted windows, balconies, stairways, and ironwork. The ceiling boasts a moonlit sky and twinkling stars.

Metropolitan Theatres Corporation restored the Arlington as a center for the performing arts in the mid-1970s, increasing the seating capacity in the process to attract top artists. It opened in 1976 with Benny Goodman and the Santa Barbara Symphony Orchestra as featured performers. Many famous artists and groups have performed here since, including the Vienna Choir Boys, The National Theatre of the Deaf, Mummenschanz, Maya Angelou, and Fiona Apple.

**Campbell Hall**
**UCSB**
**Goleta, CA**
**(805) 893–3535**

Opposite the University's Cheadle Hall administration building, Campbell Hall is the main venue for Arts & Lectures performances by comedians, musicians, dance troupes, and all types of touring artists. This 860-seat facility on the UCSB campus was originally designed as a recital hall, and the acoustics and sight lines are excellent.

**Center Stage Theater**
**751 Paseo Nuevo**
**Santa Barbara, CA**
**(805) 963–0408**
**www.centerstagetheater.org**

When negotiating permission from the city to build the Paseo Nuevo Mall, mall developers agreed to provide space for the visual and performing arts. The intimate Center Stage Theater now occupies some of this space on the top level of the mall. The theater is a great little black box venue. Because of its diminutive size (it seats a maximum of only about 150 people), you're always close to the action on stage. At intermission, you can sip drinks in the Spanish-style courtyard out front overlooking the palms and fountains of the mall below. It's a lovely spot to gather on warm summer evenings. Center Stage Theater is run by Santa Barbarans for Santa Barbarans. The main mission is to provide an accessible venue for performances, 90 percent of which are local theater, dance, and music groups that rent the space. Top professionals appear at Center Stage only about 12 weeks a year. Tickets are usually very reasonable.

**Granada Theatre**
**1216 State Street**
**Santa Barbara, CA**
**(805) 966–2324**

Built in the 1920s, the Granada is housed in the only commercial building that exceeds six stories in Santa Barbara. In recent years, the structure has been looking a bit faded but a much-needed facelift might be just around the corner. In 2001, the nonprofit Santa Barbara Center for the Performing Arts offered to buy the theater and embark upon a vigorous fund-raising effort to return the venue to its former glory. Plans for this $14- to $16-million revamp include restoring the balconies (which are now walled in and serve as cinemas), expanding the lobby, improving the acoustics, and adding seats. Capacity would swell from 950 seats to 1,500. The Music Theater of Santa Barbara calls the Granada home, but it would move to new digs while the renovations take place, a project that could take 24 to 30 months. Call for current information. If all goes well this grand old theater may gleam again one day as a jewel in Santa Barbara's crown of evocative arts venues.

**Lobero Theatre**
**33 E. Canon Perdido Street**
**Santa Barbara, CA**
**(805) 963–0761**
**www.lobero.com**

In the 1870s there were no opera houses in California south of San Francisco. A Santa

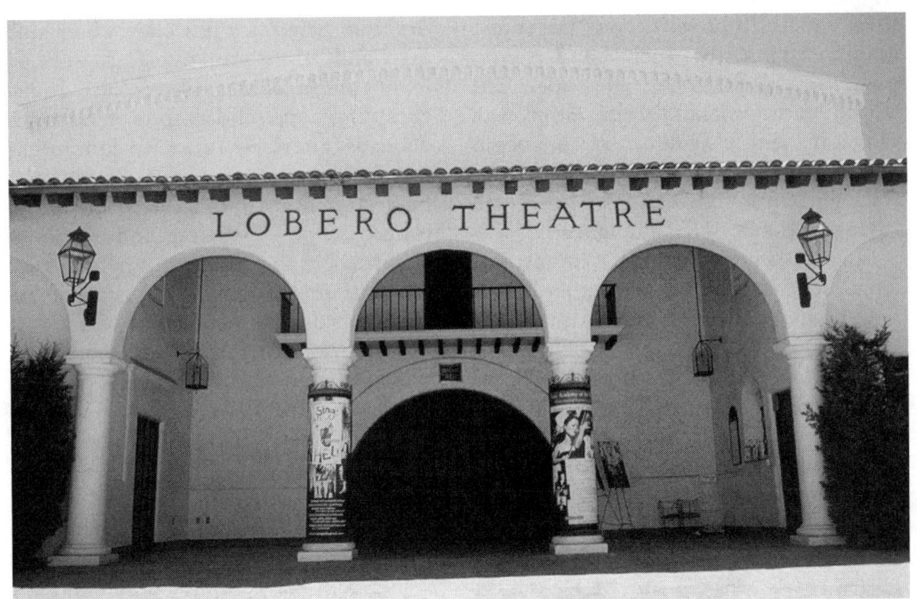


*Santa Barbara's Lobero Theatre is California's oldest continuously operating theater.* PHOTO: BRIAN HASTINGS

Barbara opera aficionado named José Lobero changed all that by establishing the first opera house in Southern California. He raised money and built the original theater—supposedly the largest adobe structure in existence at the time—in 1873. It soon became a major cultural center, attracting traveling shows, vaudeville, and performances by community groups.

Unfortunately, Lobero eventually went bankrupt and, unwilling to live without money and in poor health, committed suicide. The building fell into disrepair and was condemned in 1922. The Community Arts Association purchased the structure and tore it down. The group then contracted famous local architects George Washington Smith and Lutah Maria Riggs to design the "new" Lobero, a stately Spanish Revival structure with soaring columns, graceful arches, and a red tile roof. The new theater opened in August 1924.

Today the Lobero Theatre is not only a major performing arts center for the community, but a city and state historic landmark that enjoys the title of California's oldest continuously operating theater. The nonprofit Lobero Theatre Foundation has operated the 680-seat theater since 1938. It provides an intimate setting for many types of performances and events, from chamber music, ballet, and opera to lectures, contemporary music, and children's theater. The theater recently completed a four-year renovation project and further renovations are planned for the future.

Regular performers include the Santa Barbara Chamber Orchestra, the Contemporary Music Theater, Opera Santa Barbara, and the Santa Barbara Festival Ballet. Many other artists have appeared on the Lobero stage, including Bonnie Raitt, Lynn Redgrave, The Flying Karamazov Brothers, The Chieftains, and Queen Ida.

**Santa Barbara Bowl**
**1122 N. Milpas Street**
**Santa Barbara, CA**
**(805) 962–7411**
**www.sbbowl.com**

Music lovers of all types flock to the Bowl for excellent concerts from April through October. Built in 1936 of local stone, the 4,400-seat outdoor amphitheater in the

Riviera foothills provides an outrageously scenic setting for rock bands, symphonies, and singers of all stripes. The sloped seating makes for fantastic views. On clear evenings, you can see the ocean shimmering in the distance, and with the stars glittering above and on stage, you can't beat the bowl for ambiance.

Itzhak Perlman, Joan Baez, Jimmy Buffet, Bruce Springsteen, and James Taylor have performed here. In recent years, the Bowl has hosted a long list of popular stars, including Sting, Sheryl Crow, Alanis Morisette, Bob Dylan, the B-52s, the Gypsy Kings, Tom Petty and the Heartbreakers, and Toad the Wet Sprocket (our most famous local band, which has since disbanded).

## Art for Kids (and Grownups, Too)

**2000 Degrees**
**1206 State Street**
**Santa Barbara, CA**
**(805) 882–1817**
**www.2000degrees.com**

At this ceramics workshop you can choose from more than 200 pieces of bisqueware, then paint it, bake it, and take it home. Prices for the pieces (cups, plates, platters, and more) range from $2 to $60. Your purchase allows you to select up to four colors for each piece from a palette of 60 hues ($1 per additional color).

For $4, kids age 9 and younger can paint as long as they like. Adults pay a workshop fee of $7. When you're done, the staff coats the piece with a high-gloss finishing glaze and fires it in the kiln. Pieces are ready for pickup in one to four days; you can have them shipped if you won't be in town when they're done.

**Art from Scrap**
**302 E. Cota Street**
**Santa Barbara, CA**
**(805) 884–0459**
**www.communityenvironmentalcouncil.org/afs**

Art from Scrap is a fun place where children and adults can transform springs, foam rubber, plastic neon-colored squigglies, yarn, paper, and all sorts of industrial doodads into works of art. An educational program of the nonprofit Community Environmental Council, Art from Scrap promotes conservation and reuse of discarded materials through hands-on exploration. Regional businesses and manufacturers donate materials.

Art from Scrap Fun Workshops have varying themes and are offered every Saturday from 10:30 A.M. to noon for ages 6 years and older. The cost is $5 per person. Art from Scrap's office and retail store are open Tuesday, Wednesday, and Friday from 10:00 A.M. to 2:00 P.M., Thursday 10:00 A.M. to 6:00 P.M., and Saturday 10:00 A.M. to 3:00 P.M. (Children 5 and younger must be accompanied by a parent.)

**Lobero Theatre Foundation Family Series**
**33 E. Canon Perdido Street**
**Santa Barbara, CA**
**(805) 963–0761**
**www.lobero.com**

The Lobero Theatre Foundation sponsors a popular Family Series of shows for children and teenagers. It's billed as "great entertainment for the entire family." In 2001, the series presented *It's Magic!, Santa Barbara Dance Theater,* and *Actors from the London Stage.* If your child is interested in performing, check out the Lobero's summer circus camp. Call (805) 966–4946 for information.

**Ridley-Tree Education Center**
**1600 Santa Barbara Street**
**Santa Barbara, CA**
**(805) 962–1661**
**www.sbmuseart.org**

Ridley-Tree is the Santa Barbara Museum of Art's education center. Primarily involved with studio art, it sponsors many art classes and events for children, as well as exhibitions of children's artwork including sculpture, painting, ceramics, and drawings. The center also offers adult and family workshops and children's art adventure camps. Fall, winter, spring, and summer classes and events are held. Call or visit the museum's Web site for details.

**ShowStoppers**
**(805) 682–6043**

Since 1993 this private organization has been filling a void left by disappearing drama programs at public schools. It is Santa Barbara's only year-round theater experience for students, and it's a great way to build confidence and help kids grow up without stage fright. ShowStoppers presents six shows a year. Participants range in age from 6 to 15, and they learn the art, craft, and ethics of musical theater production, including singing, acting, stage direction, and choreography. Every child gets a chance to shine to the best of his or her ability. Recently, Showstoppers added a youth program in which students perform in a real Broadway show—in 2001 it presented *Big River.*

ShowStoppers operates out of La Colina Junior High, but it also takes shows on the road to places all over town: auditoriums, the Botanic Garden, day camps, and libraries. Every spring it presents a Gilbert and Sullivan show at La Colina (not bad for such a young troupe).

# Parks

Santa Barbara
Goleta
Montecito
Summerland
Carpinteria
West of Goleta
Santa Ynez Valley

It's true that Santa Barbarans love their beaches, but eventually we all get a hankering for a change of scenery, a wide expanse of green grass, and a shady grove for picnicking. Luckily, maintaining a thriving system of parks has always been a high priority in Santa Barbara, and whether you're looking for a tranquil garden or a rugged spot to hike, you'll find enough wide-open spaces to fit your every mood (not to mention plenty of room for the kids to run around).

In this chapter, we show you the best of our beautiful parks, covering Santa Barbara first, and then heading west to east from Goleta to Carpinteria. Next we'll go inland for a look at Cachuma Lake Recreation Area, one of the county's most popular parks. City, county, and state parks are listed according to the geographical area in which they are found, along with their major features and other useful information.

For information about parks within the city of Santa Barbara, contact Santa Barbara Parks and Recreation (805–564–5418), which administers the daily workings and programs at more than 57 parks citywide (a total of 1,764 acres). The Adaptive Programs Office (805–564–5421) can answer questions about wheelchair accessibility to the parks; call between 8:00 A.M. and 5:00 P.M. weekdays.

All city parks are open from 6:00 A.M. until a half-hour after sunset, except where posted otherwise. During summer daylight saving time, many parks remain open until 10:00 P.M., but be sure to check the posted hours when you arrive. All city park restrooms are closed at dark, and no overnight camping is allowed.

Reservations for city park facilities such as ballfields or group picnic areas with barbecue pits are taken on a first come, first served basis and can be made up to 30 days before an event by calling Parks and Recreation at (805) 564–5418. Fees vary according to the facility you wish to rent, with charges for staff services, group-picnic-site maintenance, and recreational facilities. If you want to take your chances and not make a reservation, the area is yours if you show up first and no one else has reserved, but popular areas are often reserved ahead, so don't count on one being available.

If you're planning a big party, be aware that consumption of alcoholic beverages in city parks is prohibited at all posted sites, and you should apply in advance for a special permit if you're planning to haul along a cooler full of beer. Call for information on the city ordinance that may cut into the fun unless you know how to get around it (legally, of course).

Nearly 20 county parks fall under the auspices of the Santa Barbara County Park Department (805–568–2460), headquartered at Rocky Nook Park in Mission Canyon. You can make reservations for facilities at any county park by calling (805) 568–2465. You can also read about park facilities or download printable maps at the department's excellent web site at www.sbparks.org. Park hours are from 8:00 A.M. to sunset year round.

Southern Santa Barbara County has four California state parks and all are on the beach. We include a short write-up on each in this chapter, but refer to our Beaches and Watersports and Recreation chapters for complete information on facilities and camping. A parking fee of $5 or less a day is charged for day-use of all state parks; it's payable at the entrance kiosk. (If you pay an entrance fee to one state park, you can use the permit to enter another park the same day.)

Annual passes ($35 a year) are also available and entitle you to unlimited passenger-vehicle or motorcycle entry and parking at any state park for a 12-month period. Discount passes are available for the disabled and for seniors 62 and older. For complete information on all California state park passes, call (916) 653-4000, visit www.parks.ca.gov or write to P.O. Box 942896, Sacramento, CA 94296-0001. The Channel Islands National Park and Marine Sanctuary are so spectacular, they get their own separate chapter in this book—don't miss it!

If Fido is part of the family outing, you'll want to make a note of these rules. Dogs must be on a leash at all times in county parks, and there are only two leash-free parks in the city of Santa Barbara: the Douglas Family Preserve and a posted off-leash area of Elings Park. Even then, the dog's human companion must be at least 18 years of age, be able to leash the dog immediately if there are any signs of trouble, and keep the dog out of picnic sites, sports fields, and playgrounds. Any damage done to a park by an unleashed dog is the owner's responsibility, and doggie messes must be cleaned up immediately using "poop station" supplies, which are found in most city and county parks.

You can bring your dog with you to a California state park, but you must be able to show the dog's rabies vaccination certificate or license. During the day, dogs must be on a leash no more than 6 feet long, and dogs are not allowed on trails or in buildings unless they are seeing-eye dogs.

## Santa Barbara

**Alameda Park**
**1400 Santa Barbara Street**
**Santa Barbara, CA**
**(805) 564–5418**
**www.sbparksandrecreation.com**

One of the city's oldest parks, Alameda is best known today as the site of Kids' World (see the "Playgrounds" section in our Kidstuff chapter), a very cool 8,000-square-foot fun zone for—who else?—kids. But while the kids are playing, mom and dad will appreciate the park's unique collection of more than 70 species of trees, the bandstand, and the acres of shady lawn. Since this park is close to downtown, it provides a good respite from the hustle and bustle, even though the street-only parking can sometimes present a problem. Many downtown workers grab a sack lunch, hoof it over from their offices, and relax in the shade.

**Alice Keck Park Memorial Gardens**
**1500 Santa Barbara Street**
**Santa Barbara, CA**
**(805) 564–5418**
**www.sbparksandrecreation.com**

A relative newcomer on the city parks scene, Alice Keck Park Memorial Gardens is a gorgeous 4.6-acre sanctuary right in downtown Santa Barbara. With the focus on an impressive botanical collection complemented by a koi-filled lily pond

*The koi pond in lovely Alice Keck Park Memorial Gardens is a tranquil spot to sketch.*

PHOTO: BRIAN HASTINGS

and small streams, the park has an especially tranquil feel. It's the perfect spot to contemplate the meaning of life. A Sensory Garden for the visually impaired opened recently in the park, one of few such areas on the Central Coast. Within the garden, visitors can touch trees and bubbling water as well as smell the flowers and enjoy other nonvisual experiences. Alice Keck also boasts a low-water demonstration garden. Pick up a pamphlet here and you'll find lists of all the plant species used in its creation. The only parking is on the street.

**Andree Clark Bird Refuge**
**1400 E. Cabrillo Boulevard**
**Santa Barbara, CA**
**(805) 564–5418**
**www.sbparksandrecreation.com**

Once a tidal marsh known as the Salt Pond, the bird refuge was donated to the city in 1909. Mary Clark, a local philanthropist, had the pond drained and converted to a freshwater lake, then named it after her deceased daughter, Andree. You can ride your bike to the refuge, which sits at the east end of Cabrillo Boulevard. Be sure to pack your binoculars. This is one of the best spots in town for observing waterfowl, migrating songbirds, and resident species that thrive in the water and surrounding foliage. Stroll around the pond and you'll find interpretive signs and observation platforms. It's an easy walk.

Although the city has done its best to remove domesticated fowl from the refuge, there are always a few hanging around, and you should be aware that feeding the birds here is against the law (not to mention unhealthy for the birds). If you choose not to walk or bike, you can park your car in the small lot on Los Patos Way.

**Arroyo Burro Beach Park**
**2981 Cliff Drive**
**Santa Barbara, CA**
**(805) 687–3714**
**www.sbparks.org**

Better known as Hendry's Beach, Arroyo Burro is one of the most popular county parks in Santa Barbara. It was part of the original lands that the King of Spain granted to Santa Barbara in 1782. For more information on recreational facilities, see our Beaches and Watersports chapter.

**Chase Palm Park**
**E. Cabrillo Boulevard**
**Santa Barbara, CA**
**(805) 564–5418**
**www.sbparksandrecreation.com**

Named in honor of the venerable Pearl Chase (see the Close-up on Miss Chase in our History chapter), Chase Palm Park stretches along the beachfront from Stearns Wharf to East Beach. The 35 acres include a bike path and walkway, large stretches of lawn, a soccer field, and restrooms. Ultimate Frisbee is often played here on weekends.

Once consisting mainly of just palm trees and grass, the park seems to be ever evolving. The Chase Palm Park Expansion, completed in early 1998, includes a fascinating children's playground with a nautical theme (read more about it in the "Playgrounds" section of our Kidstuff chapter), a carousel, and a public pavilion. Arts and crafts booths line the park each Sunday and holiday, and the rest of the time you'll see people of all ages enjoying the lovely seaside setting.

The only problem is—you guessed it—parking. Street parking is almost impossible to find on weekends and holidays.

**Douglas Family Preserve**
**End of Linda Road on the Mesa**
**Santa Barbara, CA**
**(805) 564–5418**
**www.sbparksandrecreation.com**

The Douglas Family Preserve is one of the last undeveloped pieces of oceanfront property in Santa Barbara. At one point developers wanted to change that, but in late 1996 the citizens of Santa Barbara had a chance to save the property from development when the owners, tired of trying to get financing, offered to sell it for $3.5 million.

*Serenity reigns at Andree Clark Bird Refuge, home to both native and migrating species.*

PHOTO: BILL DEWEY, COURTESY OF SANTA BARBARA CONFERENCE AND VISITORS BUREAU

**Insiders' Tip**

Some of Santa Barbara's parks are favorite weddings spots. Among the most popular are the ocean-view bluffs of Shoreline Park, the Rose Garden near the Mission, Alice Keck Memorial Garden with its koi-filled lily pond, Manning Park, and the panoramic hilltop at Elings Park.

The fate of what was formerly known as the Wilcox Property (it was once owned by nurseryman Roy Wilcox) had been a subject of public debate for years, and preservation-minded Santa Barbarans were not about to let this chance go by. So they started sending in money. Cash, checks, and even pennies from children's piggy banks flooded in from all parts of the city and county.

When the total didn't quite add up to enough, actor and local resident Michael Douglas chipped in $600,000 to put the fund-raising campaign over the top. On March 1, 1997, the 70-acre Douglas Family Preserve, named by the largest contributor in honor of his father, Kirk, became the property of the City of Santa Barbara.

Truly a "people's park," it's basically undeveloped, but it's a good place for a solitary stroll on bluffs overlooking the ocean, and it's one of only two parks in the city where dogs can run free. Park on the 300 block of Linda Road and enter through the metal gate. There are no restrooms or recreational facilities.

**Elings Park**
**1298 Las Positas Road**
**Santa Barbara, CA**
**(805) 569–5611**
**www.elingspark.org**

Run by the Elings Park Foundation, which has donated untold amounts of money and time to make it one of the city's most beloved recreational areas, beautiful Elings Park comprises 230 acres. Of these, 135 remain undeveloped. Facilities include three lighted fields, jogging and hiking trails, picnic and barbecue facilities, a playground, and restrooms. Stand on the hilltops here and you can breathe in panoramic views of the city and ocean.

The undeveloped south part of the park boasts the area's best hang-gliding and paragliding training hill and is the site of the annual New Year's Day Hang Gliding and Paragliding Festival (see our Annual Events chapter). Soaring gliders are a common sight in this area of the park, and you are welcome to watch.

If you're planning a get-together, you can reserve one of three picturesque special event areas. Godric Grove boasts a 300-seat amphitheater, a sprawling lawn, and a deck area shaded by oak trees. Singleton Pavilion has a lovely gazebo in the middle of a meadow as well as picnic tables tucked in a grove of liquid amber. The Canopy at the softball field is a great place for children's birthday parties due to its shaded picnic area and large playground. These areas are often booked on weekends, so be sure to make a reservation well in advance (up to a year ahead if you want a group area on a weekend during the months of June, July, August, and September). Parking is usually ample, but when several events are going on at once, cars can spill out onto the adjoining streets.

The park is one of only two in Santa Barbara that allow off-leash dogs in certain areas. But you'll need to pay for a permit and tags. The yearly fee is $52. For information, contact the Elings Park Dog Owners Group (EPDOG) at P.O. Box 3971, Santa Barbara, CA 93130 or e-mail epdogsb@yahoo.com.

Park hours are 8:00 A.M. to sunset. Once you've enjoyed this wonderful place, you might be moved to make a donation to the Elings Park Foundation, which will gladly accept your contribution. Just walk into the office and write a check, or send your donation to the foundation at P.O. Box 30818, Santa Barbara, CA 93130-0818.

**Franceschi Park**
**1510 Mission Ridge Road**
**Santa Barbara, CA**
**(805) 564–5418**
**www.sbparksandrecreation.com**

Named for Francesco Franceschi, who made a name for himself in horticulture, the 18-acre park actually encompasses a portion of a nursery he owned until 1925.

In addition to an impressive botanical collection, the park offers a panoramic view of the city and ocean from its lookouts and winding walkways. Of special interest is Franceschi's home, built in 1905 and still within the park's boundaries. Plans are currently afoot to upgrade and improve the park, and there's a grassroots effort to restore Franceschi House. You'll also find a small picnic site and restrooms within the park, however, and it has its own parking lot. This is not necessarily a good "kid" park, however, as there is no play area and no lawn for romping.

**MacKenzie Park**
**State and De la Vina Streets**
**Santa Barbara, CA**
**(805) 564–5422**
**www.sbparksandrecreation.com**

MacKenzie Park, the site of El Mercado del Norte (the Northern Marketplace) during the annual Old Spanish Days celebration (see our Annual Events chapter), is pretty busy the rest of the year, too. In addition to one of the city's few lawn-bowling greens, plus an adjacent clubhouse, the 9-acre park has a playground, baseball diamonds, picnic areas with barbecues, and restrooms.

A recreational building in the park has a kitchen, fireplace, barbecue pit, and large patio and is available for meetings or other functions. Parking is available in an on-site lot.

**Mission Rose Garden**
**Los Olivos and Laguna Streets**
**Santa Barbara, CA**
**(805) 564–5418**
**www.sbparksandrecreation.com**

Tended carefully by local volunteers, the Mission Rose Garden and surrounding grassy area provide a popular place to toss the Frisbee around, stretch out for a nap, or literally stop and smell the roses. Inhale the fragrance of more than 1,500 rose plants in the garden, which is across the street from Mission Santa Barbara (see our Attractions chapter).You can also walk along the paths to several early historical sites nearby. This is a must for rose lovers. Park on the street.

**Oak Park**
**300 W. Alamar Avenue**
**Santa Barbara, CA**
**(805) 564–5418**
**www.sbparksandrecreation.com**

Oak- and sycamore-studded Oak Park, bisected by Mission Creek, plays host to all the city's ethnic festivals. It also provides a few extras, such as a raised dance floor where dancers from the festival of the moment can entertain the crowds.

When the park is not full of festival-goers, you'll find folks playing tennis on two public courts and kids splashing in the wading pool (open May through September) or romping on the playground. You can also play a serious game of horseshoes in the lighted horseshoe pit. The park has plenty of places to picnic and barbecue. Restrooms and a parking lot are also available.

**Orpet Park**
**Alameda Padre Serra and Moreno Road**
**Santa Barbara, CA**
**(805) 564–5418**
**www.sbparksandrecreation.com**

This charming park on the Riviera is filled with exotic plants and trees and is a good place for birding in the fall and spring. Park on Alameda Padre Serra,

**Insiders' Tip**

Tropical hibiscus is the official flower of the city of Santa Barbara, and the jacaranda and the coast live oak are the city's official trees.

then meander along the footpaths and enjoy the botanical wonders.

**Ortega Park**
**600 E. Ortega Street at Calle Cesar Chavez**
**Santa Barbara, CA**
**(805) 564–5418**
**www.sbparksandrecreation.com**

Ortega Park's 5 acres offer a softball field, a children's swimming pool and a wading pool (open daily May through September), a playground, picnic and barbecue facilities, and restrooms. The Ortega Welcome House is also here, accommodating up to 70 people for a meeting or other function. Parking is on the street.

**Pershing Park**
**100 Castillo Street at W. Cabrillo Boulevard**
**Santa Barbara, CA**
**(805) 564–5517**
**www.sbparksandrecreation.com**

Known primarily for its lighted ballfields and eight lighted tennis courts, Pershing Park is also home to the Old Spanish Days Carriage Museum (see our Attractions chapter). Other than that, you won't find a lot of recreational facilities, but you can spread a blanket out on the lawn and picnic. Restrooms are on-site, and there's a parking lot, but it fills up fast on weekends so you may have to park on the street.

**Rocky Nook Park**
**610 Mission Canyon Road**
**Santa Barbara, CA**
**(805) 568–2460**
**www.sbparks.org**

Donated to Santa Barbara County in 1928, 19-acre Rocky Nook Park is a charming spot for a stroll along the banks of Mission Creek or a quiet lunchtime picnic. Studded with oaks and sycamores and dotted with boulders, the park is almost completely shaded, which makes it a cool respite from the heat during the summer. It's also a great place for birding, especially in spring, when migrating birds gather in the dense foliage.

You'll find two large group picnic and barbecue areas here as well as several smaller picnic sites, and a small playground for the kids. Permanent restrooms are on-site, and parking is plentiful. After a relaxing picnic lunch, you can pop across the street to the Santa Barbara Museum of Natural History or stroll to Mission Santa Barbara, which is also within walking distance. You won't find any expansive lawns here, but that's part of the charm of this little "rocky nook."

**San Antonio Canyon Park**
**805 San Antonio Creek Road at Cathedral Oaks**
**Santa Barbara, CA**
**(805) 568–2460**
**www.sbparks.org**

Most of us call this county park "Tucker's Grove," which is actually the name of the lower section; the upper area is officially known as Kiwanis Meadow. Whatever you call it, the place is hugely popular with large groups, partly because of its easy access and partly because it has group picnic areas that can accommodate up to 400 people.

The lower portion of the park is almost completely level and covered with lawn, which means that it's easy to keep an eye on the kids, and they aren't likely to go climbing off someplace where you can't find them. On this level there's a large playground area, a volleyball court, horseshoe pits, and lots of picnic areas for large or small groups.

Kiwanis Meadow also has a very large group picnic area with a barbecue, play equipment, a ballfield, and a volleyball court. From Kiwanis Meadow you can hike up San Antonio Creek Canyon on foot or ride up on horseback (although you're responsible for getting the horse) all the way to San Marcos Pass Road. Both areas have permanent restrooms and parking lots, although the lots may fill up during large group events or on holidays.

**Skofield Park**
**1819 Las Canoas Road**
**Santa Barbara, CA**
**(805) 564–5418**
**www.sbparksandrecreation.com**

Nestled high in the Santa Barbara foothills, oak-studded Skofield Park is just below the trailhead for Rattlesnake Canyon Trail, the most popular hiking trail in Santa Barbara (and yes, you do need to watch out for rattlers in the spring and summer). You'll find lots of other trails here for mountain biking, walking, or hiking. Group picnic and barbecue facilities, restrooms, and on-site parking are available.

Skofield has a more rugged feel than some of our parks, but there is a wide expanse of lawn for those who don't want to rough it. One caution: Because of its foothill location, temperatures in the park during the day are often much warmer than those down below in the city, so dress accordingly.

**Shoreline Park**
**Shoreline Drive and La Marina**
**Santa Barbara, CA**
**(805) 564–5418**
**www.sbparksandrecreation.com**

One of the most popular parks in Santa Barbara, Shoreline Park encompasses 15 manicured acres that overlook the beach just west of the Santa Barbara City College campus. It's the perfect place to fly a kite (the annual Kite Festival happens here in March), or you can gaze out toward the Channel Islands and maybe see a whale going by (a bronze whale's tail marks the best vantage point for whale-watching).

The beach can be reached by going down stairs to the sand, or you can opt to stay in the park's grassy areas, which include facilities for picnics and barbecues. Kids will love the playground here, and you'll find restrooms on-site. The park has a fairly generous parking lot, so you usually don't have to go looking on the street.

**Stevens Park**
**258 Canon Drive**
**Santa Barbara, CA**
**(805) 564–5418**
**www.sbparksandrecreation.com**

Tucked into the foothills at the end of Canon Drive, Stevens Park is another great spot for hiking, birding (white-throated swifts can be found here almost all year long), and picnicking. A small playground sits along the banks of a creek, and the park has barbecues and restrooms. Parking is available in a small lot at the entrance. If you're going to hike, watch out for rattlesnakes, especially in spring and summer.

## Goleta

**Evergreen Open Space**
**Evergreen Street and Brandon Drive**
**Goleta, CA**
**(805) 568–2460**
**www.sbparks.org**

A greenbelt area in west Goleta, Evergreen has tennis courts and playground equipment and is a great spot for a picnic. It's the home of the only official 18-hole Frisbee (or "disc") golf course between here and Los Angeles. If that's your game, this is your place! Parking is on the street, and there are no restrooms.

**Goleta Beach Park**
**5986 Sandspit Road**
**Goleta, CA**
**(805) 568–2460**
**www.sbparks.org**

Located just east of the University of California at Santa Barbara campus, Goleta

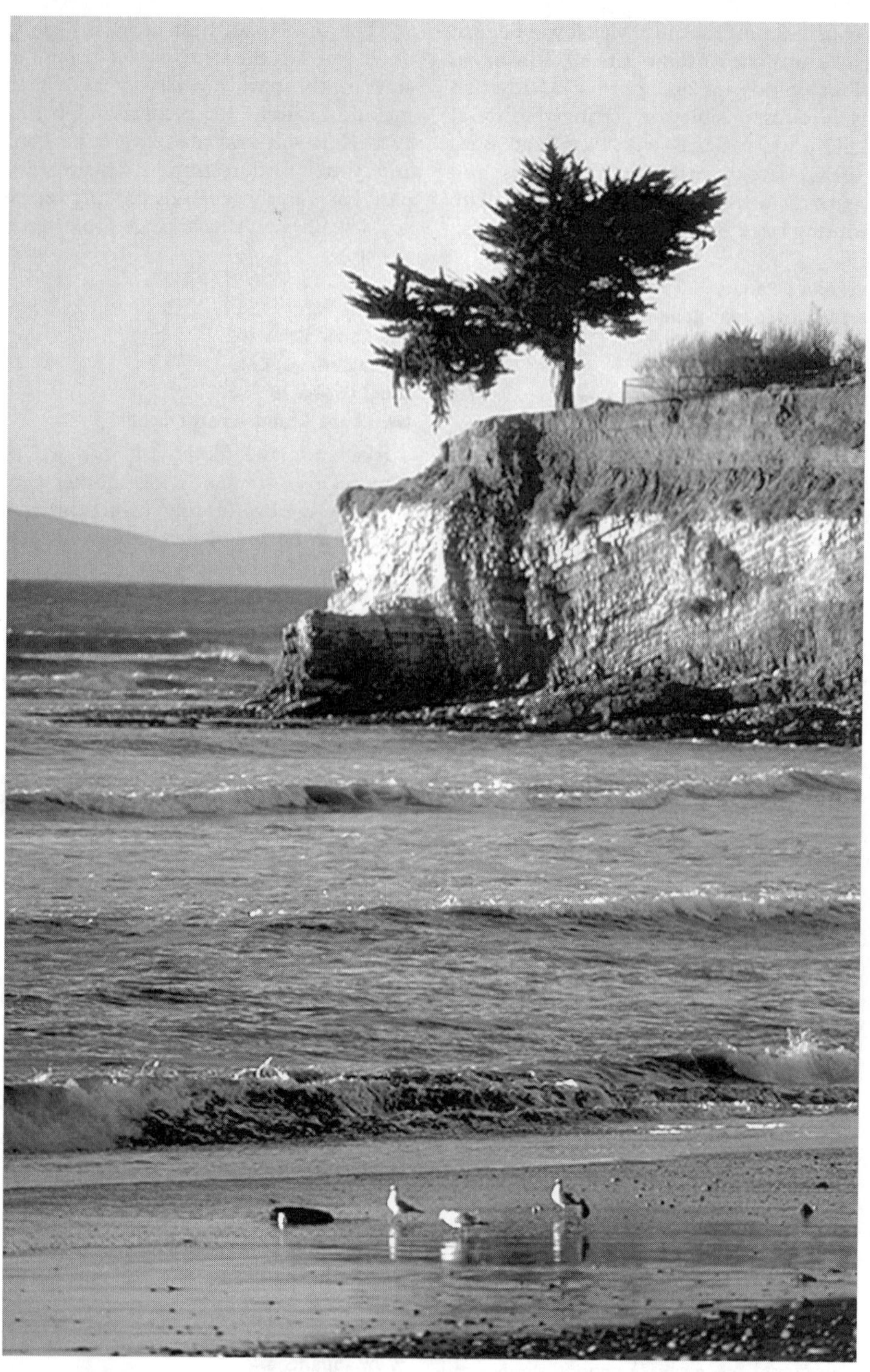

*The 15 manicured acres of Shoreline Park overlook the beach.* PHOTO: JOHN B. SNODGRASS

Beach sits at the entrance to the Goleta Slough, which makes it a great birding spot as well as a first-rate day-use facility for sunbathing, swimming, or fishing off the pier. Restrooms and ample parking are on-site, and the excellent Beachside Bar and Café (805-964-7881) sits right on the sand (see our Restaurants chapter). For more information about the park, see our Beaches and Watersports chapter.

**Lake Los Carneros Park**
**Los Carneros Road and Calle Real**
**Goleta, CA**
**(805) 568-2460**
**www.sbparks.org**

Lake Los Carneros, bounded by Los Carneros Road, Covington Way, Calle Real, and La Patera Lane, is a hidden jewel in the center of busy Goleta. The grounds include the lovely Stow House (see our Attractions chapter) and outbuildings, the restored Goleta Train Depot, which houses the South Coast Railroad Museum (also listed in our Attractions and Kidstuff chapters), and a 25-acre artificial lake that has been declared a natural preserve.

Pathways (either dirt, decomposed granite, or wood-chip-covered) go completely around the lake, making it easy to do the loop on foot or on a bike. At the north end of the lake, a wooden footbridge crosses the channel, offering the perfect vantage point for observing the birds, turtles, frogs, and other fauna that populate the area.

The garden around the Stow House, planted with a variety of exotic plants, is also a wonderful birding spot, especially in spring. There are fish in the lake, and some local fishermen swear that some of these are big fish, but we've never seen anything bigger than a large minnow. Still, you can take your chances by casting off the bank if you want. No swimming is allowed in the lake.

Near the railroad depot is a small picnic area, but people often eat lunch on the Stow House lawn, stretching out in the shade to enjoy the sights and sounds of nature. The park is a perfect place to exercise your dog, but please remember that he needs to be on a leash and should never be allowed to disturb the local wildlife by leaping into the lake.

You can park on any of the streets that border the park, but most people opt to use the parking lot on Los Carneros Road, between Cathedral Oaks and Calle Real. Restrooms are on-site.

**Stow Grove Park**
**580 La Patera Lane**
**Goleta, CA**
**(805) 568-2460**
**www.sbcountyparks.org**

Truly unique for the Santa Barbara area, Stow Grove is dominated by a large grove of 120-year-old California coastal redwood trees that tower over wood-chip-covered walkways lined with low wooden fences. Also scattered throughout the park are mature sycamores, oaks, and eucalyptus, and a small grove of giant sequoias has been planted north of the children's play area.

The south section of the park is newer, with a large redwood play area, lots of picnic tables, and a wide lawn sheltered by oaks and pines. The north section includes group picnic areas, a smaller playground, two volleyball courts, horseshoe pits, and a softball diamond. Stow Grove has a permanent restroom, and parking is available in the on-site lot. If the lot fills up, park on La Patera Lane or on the street north of Cathedral Oaks Road.

## Montecito

**Manning Park**
**449 San Ysidro Road**
**Montecito, CA**
**(805) 568-2460**
**www.sbcountyparks.org**

Divided into two distinct sections—upper and lower—Manning Park is a lovely shady spot in the middle of Montecito. It's a popular site for weddings and family celebrations. All of the vegetation in the park has been introduced, and California live oaks as well as native plant species such as toyon, coffeeberry, and maple trees have been planted.

In addition to the charm of its terrain, the park offers many recreational facilities, including three group picnic areas with barbecues (the largest accommodating up to 250 people), a softball field, a tennis court, a volleyball court, four horseshoe pits, and a playground. The upper park has a permanent restroom, while the lower park offers only a chemical toilet. Small parking areas are scattered throughout the park, or you can park on School House Road, which borders the southwest side of the upper park.

## Summerland

**Lookout Park**
**2297 Finney Road**
**Summerland, CA**
**(805) 568–2460**
**www.sbcountyparks.org**

Known for its spectacular view of the ocean and the Channel Islands, 4-acre Lookout Park is perched above the sea just north of Carpinteria. The beach below (you must descend a steep hill to reach the sand) has a secluded feel to it, and it's a great spot for swimming, surfing, or surf fishing. In the park area, you'll find two large picnic areas with a barbecue, a playground on a sand surface, volleyball courts, and restrooms.

**Toro Canyon Park**
**576 Toro Canyon Road**
**Summerland, CA**
**(805) 568–2460**
**www.sbcountyparks.org**

You are miles from the beach at this county park, but the rugged oak woodland provides for a pleasant change of scenery. The 74 acres have been left pretty much in their natural state, with only a small, 1-acre grassy area breaking up the chaparral, oak, manzanita, sage, and other indigenous plants.

Toro Canyon has two main parking areas, three large group picnic areas (one accommodating up to 200 people), and a network of paths and hiking trails throughout, one of which will reward you with an overlook gazebo at the end. Recreational facilities include horseshoe pits, two playgrounds, and a volleyball court.

A park ranger lives here year-round. Note: Fire danger can be extremely high here during the summer and fall.

## Carpinteria

**Carpinteria Bluffs**
**Bailard Avenue**
**Carpinteria, CA**
**(805) 684–5405**
**www.earthisland.com/bluffs/**

Perched high above the sparkling Pacific, this stunning expanse of wilderness is one of the largest tracts of open space left along the county's south coast. In October 2000, after a passionate fund-raising campaign by a local group known as Citizens for the Carpinteria Bluffs, this 52-acre property was officially deeded to the City of Carpinteria to be protected as a natural open-space preserve. Stretching west from Baillard Avenue, the bluffs encompass a spectacular area of quiet meadows, thick eucalyptus groves, and rugged sea cliffs. As you stroll along the hiking trails, you'll be treated to gorgeous views of the Carpinteria Valley, the Santa Ynez Mountains, and the Santa Barbara Channel. It's also a fantastic place to hike and look for wildlife. In a rocky cove below the bluffs lies one of only two publicly accessible harbor seal colonies in Southern California (see the Close-up in this chapter). Whales and dolphins regularly cruise the channel, and you can often catch a glimpse of red-tailed hawks hovering above the bluffs. The preserve is awaiting upgrades. Most of the area will remain undeveloped, but the city plans to improve the hiking-biking trails and may add playing fields in the future. To access the bluffs, take the Bailard

*The Carpinteria Bluffs offer panoramic views of Rincon Point and the Santa Barbara Channel.*
PHOTO: KAREN HASTINGS

Avenue exit, turn right, and park in the lot at the end of the street.

**Carpinteria State Beach**
**Linden Avenue and Sixth Street**
**Carpinteria, CA**
**(805) 684–2811**

In addition to camping spaces, this 48-acre park has a mile of beachfront perfect for swimming, fishing, tidepooling, surfing, beach volleyball, and soaking up the sun. If you'd rather not get sand in your shorts, there's a grassy play area that's relatively sand-free. Nearby, seals and sea lions are often visible, and occasionally you can even spot a whale going by. Stop by the visitor center to view natural history exhibits or take one of the scheduled nature walks.

**El Carro Park**
**El Carro Lane and Namouna Street**
**Carpinteria, CA**
**(805) 684–5405**
**www.ci.carpinteria.ca.us**

This small neighborhood park has a playground for the kids, a picnic area with a barbecue, a multi-use field, and restrooms. It's a great place to spread out a blanket, and there's plenty of room to run on the expansive lawn.

CLOSE-UP

## Sealing Their Future

As our human population swells, wildlife habitats shrink, so it's exhilarating to know wild places can still thrive in our midst. If you visit small-town Carpinteria, on the eastern reaches of Santa Barbara, and hike along the spectacular ocean-view bluffs, you can see one of these last fragile places. Tucked deep within a rocky cove is one of only two publicly accessible harbor seal colonies in Southern California. This is *National Geographic* stuff—right on our doorstep!

Harbor seals are perhaps the most easily seen of all Santa Barbara's six species of seals. On land, however, they are extremely skittish, so you need to approach the viewing area with care. If you visit the sanctuary in December through January you will see expectant mothers resting on the shore. In February to early May, the chubby doe-eyed pups are born and suckled amid the mossy rocks on the beach. By the end of May, the pups are independent. They are swimming and fishing on their own, ready to face a life of uncertainty in the sea.

Every year, more than ten thousand people come to the colony to see this cycle of life unfold. Why are we so fascinated by the seals? Perhaps when we watch them, we see a reflection of our own life's cycles and rituals: whether it's a birth, the nursing of a newborn, the bond between a mother and her offspring, or the daily struggle to survive.

Whatever your reason for visiting, as you watch the seals, inevitably you'll want to know more about them. Below, we've listed some of the questions most frequently asked of the volunteers who staff the colony. We hope the answers enhance your appreciation of these gentle creatures.

### How do I get to the colony?

Going south on Highway 101, take the Bailard exit. Turn right and park in the lot at the end of the street near the hot dog stand. Follow the path west along the bluffs for approximately a half-mile until you see a viewing area just before the pier. If you have a dog with you, tie it up before you enter the area. (Dogs scare the seals into the water.) Slowly and quietly approach the viewing area. You can usually spot the seals lying on the beach or resting on the large rock. Scan the water too. It's fun to watch them swimming and playing in the surf. Don't forget your binoculars, so you can see them up close and personal!

From the Carpinteria State Beach Campground, hike along the bluff-top trail parallel to the beach for about a quarter-mile. When you arrive at the private Venoco parking lot, follow the blue seal markers on the ground.

### What are harbor seals?

Harbor seals are mammals. They are called pinnapeds (Latin for "fin-footed ones") and belong to the group of seals known as phocids or true seals. On land, phocids crawl on their stomachs like giant caterpillars instead of using their flippers for mobility as sea lions and fur seals do. Look closely at their heads and you'll also notice that they lack external ear lobes.

## When is the best time to see the seals?

Your best chance to spot the seals is from December through May when the beach is closed to the public and the seals feel safe enough to rest on shore. From January to May, volunteers are there to protect the seals from any disturbances. Try to visit at low tide during these times. It's easier to spot the seals on the exposed beach.

## Why is the beach closed?

From December 1 through May 31, the beach is closed so that the pregnant seals can haul out on land to rest, give birth, and nurse their pups. Disturbances such as a loud noise, a sudden movement, or a dog barking can frighten the seals and send them crawling into the water. When this happens, spontaneous abortions can occur and any young pups left on shore are extremely vulnerable to predators. If separated for too long from their mothers, the pups are orphaned and can starve to death. Disturbances may also result in relocation of the colony.

## What work are the volunteers doing?

Volunteers are there to protect the seals, inform the public, answer questions, monitor the impact of disturbances, and collect data. Every 30 minutes the seals are counted. When you visit, estimate how many seals are on land and then ask the volunteer for the latest official count. We bet there's more than you think!

## Can I go onto the beach and touch the seals?

No. The seals are protected by both local and federal law. Under the Federal Marine Mammal Protection Act, you can be fined up to $10,000 for disturbing the seals. Dog owners are also liable for any injury inflicted by their pets.

## Are the seals here year-round?

Yes. Unlike some other species of seals, harbor seals are nonmigratory, so they use this cove as their home base throughout the year. However, they are difficult to see when the beach is open in summer and fall because people and animals frighten them into the water. Your best bet for spotting them at this time of the year is to visit the colony early in the morning.

## Where else are they found?

Harbor seals are found throughout the northern hemisphere in the Atlantic and Pacific Oceans. In the northeast Pacific they range from the Bering Sea to Baja. They also breed and give birth on some of the Channel Islands.

## How many seals live in this colony?

More than 300 seals have been counted here, but numbers fluctuate depending on the tides, the weather, and local disturbances.

## How big do they get?

Adult males can grow up to 6 feet in length and weigh up to 300 pounds. Females are slightly smaller.

*If you visit the Carpinteria seal colony between February and May, you may witness the birth of a harbor seal pup.* PHOTO: BRIAN HASTINGS

### How long do they live?

Harbor seals can live to be 30 to 40 years old.

### Why are they different colors?

It's a matter of genetics. Just as people are born with different hair color, seals are born with different-colored coats and variations in mottling. Some are a beautiful silvery gray or dark brown with many dark splotches. Others are cream, caramel, or white, with few markings. You can only see their colors on land when their coats are dry. In the water they all look shiny and black.

### What do they eat?

The diet of harbor seals consists mainly of fish, but they also eat shrimp, squid, crayfish, and crab. They can dive as deep as 600 feet underwater to find prey on the ocean floor, staying down for up to 20 to 30 minutes.

### What eats them?

In the water, killer whales and sharks—especially great white sharks—are common predators. On land, coyotes, domestic dogs, and eagles prey on juveniles or pups. For centuries, humans slaughtered harbor seals for meat and for their thick pelts, but the animals have been protected in the United States since 1972. Unfortunately though, we are still killing them indirectly. Ocean pollution has led to an increase in the incidence of disease, and in this colony, it's the most common cause of death.

### How big are the pups when they are born?

At birth, harbor seal pups weigh about 12 to 18 pounds.

### When can the pups swim?

Since they are born in intertidal zones, the pups can swim almost immediately after birth. They will spend roughly half their lives in water and half on land.

### How long do the pups stay with their mothers?

Harbor seal pups usually stay with their mother for about 4 to 6 weeks until they are weaned. After this they must find their own food and fend for themselves.

### Are there any males in this colony?

Yes, but since the difference in size between males and females is slight, they are difficult to identify.

### Where do they sleep?

Harbor seals prefer to sleep on land, however they are occasionally forced to sleep in the water during high tides or when hauling grounds are in short supply.

### Do the seals ever have twins?

Harbor seals rarely give birth to twins. When they do however, the chances of both pups surviving to adulthood are slim.

### How do seals communicate with each other?

Harbor seal pups sound a little bit like human babies. They make a bleating noise that sounds like "maaaaaaa, maaaaaaa," which helps their mothers identify them. The adults, while not as vocal as other species, communicate by grunting, yelping, growling, snarling, and making deep belching noises. They probably wouldn't make the best dinner-party guests!

### What should I do if I find a harbor seal on the beach?

The first thing you should do is leave it alone. If it's a pup, chances are its mother is in the water searching for food or waiting for you to leave so she can reunite with her baby. Staying too close to seal pups can result in them being orphaned. Also, you should *never* pour water on seals as they are prone to respiratory ailments. Note the exact location of the animal and call the Marine Mammal Center Hotline at (805) 687–3255.

### Are their numbers increasing?

Since the inception of the volunteer protection program, the number of pups born each year in this colony has increased. Only 6 pups were observed in 1991 and 46 were observed in 2001. It is difficult to tell if the adult population is increasing, but from the data collected, it seems safe to say it is not declining. As long as we treat the seals and their habitat with care and respect, they will continue to thrive here and the colony will remain for future generations to enjoy.

**Monte Vista Park**
**Bailard Avenue and Pandanus Street**
**Carpinteria, CA**
**(805) 684-5405**

If you're into playing horseshoes, this is the only park in Carpinteria with a pit. It also has a jogging trail, multi-use field, and playground. The park is set back behind some condominiums outside the city of Carpinteria, just above the Ventura County line.

## West of Goleta

We mention El Capitan, Gaviota, and Refugio beaches briefly here but for detailed information (including camping information) see our Recreation and Beaches and Watersports chapters.

**El Capitan State Beach**
**Off U.S. Highway 101, 17 miles west of Santa Barbara**
**(805) 968-1033**
**www.parks.ca.gov**

El Cap is open from dawn to dusk year-round and offers swimming (the beach is accessible via a stairway on the bluffs), fishing, picnicking, and camping as well as tidepooling and birding. The bike trail here connects with Refugio State Beach, 2.5 miles up the coast.

**Gaviota State Park**
**Off U.S. Highway 101, 33 miles west of Santa Barbara**
**(805) 968-1033**
**www.parks.ca.gov**

Made up of 2,700 acres that rise from sea level to the top of Gaviota Peak, Gaviota has recently renovated its campground facilities and parking lots. In addition to the normal beach activities, the park has great hiking trails, including one that takes you to Gaviota Hot Springs.

**Refugio State Beach**
**Off U.S. Highway 101, 23 miles west of Santa Barbara**
**(805) 968-1033**
**www.parks.ca.gov**

Just 2.5 miles west of El Capitan State Beach, Refugio is an excellent spot for surf fishing, picnicking, camping, and hiking. Refugio is also a good place for diving, with offshore reefs and kelp beds to explore.

## Santa Ynez Valley

**Cachuma Lake Recreation Area**
**Calif. Highway 154, 20 miles northwest of Santa Barbara**
**(805) 686-5054**
**www.sbparks.org**

Although the Santa Ynez Valley is technically out of Santa Barbara proper, we include this county park because it is a local favorite and less than an hour's drive from Santa Barbara. It is especially popular for fishing and camping (see our Fishing and Recreation chapters for details) as well as for boating and wildlife observation.

Boats (with or without motors) can be rented at the lake on a daily, weekly, or monthly basis, and private boat-launching facilities are also available. (Canoes, kayaks, and other boats less than 10 feet in length are not allowed on the lake.)

Because Cachuma is a domestic water reservoir, swimming, wading, waterskiing, sailboarding, and any other bodily contact with the water are not allowed, but there's a swimming pool in the campground that's open during the summer months. You can also rent a bike or arrange for horseback riding in the vicinity.

The Interpretive Nature Center features displays of local flora and fauna as well as Chumash Indian artifacts (the

Chumash Village of Ah-ke-tsoom once thrived in the area, but the site was covered with water after the construction of Bradbury Dam in 1953). For a fun family outing, join in the nature walks scheduled every Saturday afternoon during the summer. Some of the animals you might expect to see around the lake are deer, wild pigs, bears, and as many as 275 species of birds.

Cachuma is especially proud of its small but permanent American bald eagle population, and this is the only place in the county where you can reliably spot this majestic symbol of America. To get a close-up look at the eagles and other wildlife, we recommend taking a two-hour, naturalist-led Eagle Cruise aboard the *Osprey*.

Eagle Cruises (November through February) depart from the marina Wednesday through Sunday at 10:00 A.M., with additional trips Friday and Saturday at 2:00 P.M. The cost is $12 for adults; $5 for children 12 and younger. Wildlife Cruises (March through October), departing Friday at 3:00 P.M., Saturday at 10:00 A.M. and 3:00 P.M., and Sunday at 10:00 A.M., also originate at the marina and have the same admission prices as the Eagle Cruises. Be sure to make a reservation (805–686–5050), and bring your binoculars and a warm jacket, as it can be quite chilly on the lake. Because you are riding on a relatively flat surface, seasickness is generally not a problem.

Cachuma Lake is open for day use from 6:00 A.M. to 10:00 P.M.; admission is $5 a vehicle. Plenty of parking is scattered throughout, and restrooms (or chemical toilets) are available in each camping area, at the marina, and near the pool.

# Channel Islands National Park and National Marine Sanctuary



The Channel Islands are less than 30 miles from the mainland, but they're an entire world apart. When you step ashore, you feel as if you've traveled a century back in time to the pristine California land and seascapes that once dominated the coast. You won't see hotels, restaurants, and museums lining the shores. Instead, you'll find spectacular scenes of white-sand beaches, sea caves and hidden coves, vast grasslands, barren mountains, rocky reefs, and incredibly clear water.

Eight islands in the waters off the coast of Southern California make up the Channel Islands. Often referred to as the "American Galapagos," these remote islands and the waters surrounding them are filled with unusual species of marine creatures and wildlife, geological formations, archeological finds and other oddities that occur nowhere else on earth.

One reason the channel is so unique is because it is an unusual transition zone called the Southern California Bight. At Point Conception, the islands and the mainland run east-west rather than north-south. The waters lying between the islands and the mainland form the Santa Barbara Channel—a melting pot of currents from different directions. The California current brings cold waters from the Arctic into the channel from the north. Warm currents from Mexico come in from the south, carrying more subtropical marine life along with them.

The result of this complex blend of currents is an exceptional variety of cold-water and warm-water plants and animals, including giant kelp forests, sea birds, whales, seals, and sea lions. In addition, the remoteness of the islands has allowed plants and wildlife to evolve in isolation. This is the only part of the world where you'll find the Santa Cruz Island scrub-jay, the Channel Island fox (see the Close-up in this chapter), the Anacapa deer mouse, and many other unique species.

## From Isolated Islands to Protected Sanctuaries

For more than 11,000 years, the Chumash, or "island people," lived on these islands. They regularly traversed the channel in swift canoes called tomols to trade with mainland Indians. They lived in peaceful isolation on the islands until 1542, when explorer Juan Rodriguez Cabrillo cruised through the channel while leading an expedition for Spain. He supposedly fell on San Miguel and died as a result, but his body has never been found.

The 1700s and 1800s brought more explorers and eventually fur traders, hunters, settlers, and ranchers—all of whom threatened the Channel Islands' resources and habitats. It wasn't until the late 20th century that the incredible biodiversity, important cultural artifacts, and stunning natural beauty of the islands triggered a succession of moves to protect the region. In 1980, Congress officially recognized the significance of the region's natural and cultural resources and declared five of the islands—San Miguel, Santa Rosa, Santa Cruz, Anacapa, and Santa Barbara—and their surrounding 1 nautical mile of ocean as the Channel Islands National Park. Later that year, 1,252 nautical miles of ocean extending from mean high tide to 6 nautical miles offshore around each of the islands in the park were designated a National Marine Sanctuary.

The islands themselves fall under the jurisdiction of the National Park Service, while the National Oceanic and Atmospheric Administration (NOAA) administers the marine sanctuary program, and the National Park Service and the National Marine Sanctuary share jurisdiction of the nautical mile closest to the island shores. (In this chapter, Channel Islands National Park and Channel Islands National Marine Sanctuary are often referred to collectively for easier reading.)

## Continued Conservation

In 1988, The Nature Conservancy, a nonprofit international environmental organization, acquired the western 90 per cent of Santa Cruz Island from a private owner and formed the Santa Cruz Island Preserve. The National Park Service continued to own and manage the remaining eastern side of the island. Then in August 2000, The Nature Conservancy transferred 8,500 acres of its holdings on Santa Cruz Island to the National Park Service, a donation designed to reinforce the partnership between the two organizations. Since the transfer, the Conservancy owns and manages the western 76 per cent of the island, while the eastern 24 per cent is owned and managed by the National Park Service.

The 8,500 acres of Santa Cruz Island donated by The Nature Conservancy to the National Park Service adjoin the park's western boundary and includes the five-mile long narrow section of the island called the isthmus. The land transfer was great news for visitors to Santa Cruz Island, who now have much more land to explore. The public can come ashore on the isthmus at Prisoners' Harbor, hike the trails, explore the beach, and camp in the designated areas. The Nature Conservancy limits public access to the Santa Cruz Island Preserve due to recovering ecosystems in this part of the island. See the "Santa Cruz Island Project" section below for more information.

## Current Controversy

Currently the Channel Islands community is considering a controversial proposal to extend the boundaries of the existing marine reserve, a move that could create the largest marine sanctuary from commercial fishing grounds anywhere in the world. Driving the proposal is the disturbing decline of marine populations in areas outside existing reserves. Giant sea bass, black bass, rockfish, lingcod, and cowcod are vanishing from the kelp beds, and the succulent white abalone—which once graced menus across the country—now gets top billing on the endangered species list. Most people in the community agree steps to protect these populations should be taken. At issue here is the size of the proposed reserve. Citing recent studies, marine scientists and environmentalists say large no-take zones are critical for key species to recover. The fishing community, they argue, will ultimately benefit because a spillover effect will replenish fish stocks in neighboring waters. But many commercial fishermen and women want more research to be done before they turn over such a huge stretch of the waters on which their livelihood depends.

*Dolphins are a common sight in the Santa Barbara Channel.* PHOTO: CONDOR PHOTOS

## A Wealth of Natural Resources

In the areas of the Channel Islands that are currently protected, scientists have been following a remarkable comeback by Mother Nature. Native flowers and plants are beginning to bloom anew after years of grazing by cows and sheep. Sea lions and seals are multiplying, and fish are restocking their schools.

People come from all over the world to see and experience the wonders of the Channel Islands. The national park is home to more than 2,000 terrestrial plants and animals, and 145 of these are found nowhere else on earth. Thousands of sea birds nest on the islands because there are few other creatures to prey on them.

The marine life surrounding the Channel Islands is equally amazing. The giant kelp forest alone supports more than 800 species of marine life. Key species in the sanctuary include the California sea lion, elephant and harbor seals, blue and gray whales, dolphins, and the blue shark, brown pelican, western gull, abalone, garibaldi, and rockfish.

Pinnipeds (seals and sea lions) were once hunted nearly to extinction for their meat, fur, oil, and ivory. But the Marine Mammal Protection Act passed in 1972 made it illegal to kill, harm, or capture any kind of marine mammal without a permit. Six species of pinnipeds live and breed on the Channel Islands and in the surrounding waters.

More than 27 species of cetaceans (whales and porpoises) can be found in the sanctuary during the year. From December through April, thousands of gray whales swim through the channel on their annual migration from Alaska to Mexico and back. (See the "Whale-Watching" section of our Beaches and Watersports chapter if you'd like to go on a whale-watching trip). In the last decade, increased numbers of more unusual whales have shown up in the channel, including blue, minke, and humpback.

The common dolphin practically owns the channel. They travel in large groups and love to play and surf in the wake of passing boats. Sometimes you can spot a Dall's porpoise or Risso's dolphins. Other dolphins here include the Pacific white-sided and bottlenose dolphins.

More than 25 species of sharks have been sighted in the channel, but some only vacation here from time to time. Resident sharks include the giant basking, leopard, thresher, blue, horn, and Pacific angel.

We humans are invited to experience this natural wonderland in all its splendor—as long as we respect and care for its precious resources.

**Insiders' Tip**

Stay tuned to the weather! It changes quickly on the channel and around the islands. NOAA broadcasts weather reports at KIH-34 162.40 MHz.

## The National Park, Marine Sanctuary, and Nature Preserve

The National Park Service, the National Marine Sanctuary, and The Nature Conservancy all work to protect the fragile ecosystems of the islands and the sea, while educating the public about the plants, animals, marine life, and other natural phenomena. Following are descriptions of the special services each provides.

**Channel Islands National Park Headquarters and Visitor Center**
**1901 Spinnaker Drive**
**Ventura, CA**
**(805) 658–5730**
**www.nps.gov/chis**

The Channel Islands National Park Headquarters and Visitor Center is in Ventura, 35 miles southeast of Santa Barbara. Although it's not technically in the geographic area covered by this book, we do need to tell you about the visitor center, which is not only a one-stop resource for information about the islands, but also a fun and fascinating place to visit. Wander inside and you'll find a museum, a bookstore, a living tidepool and interactive touch-screen exhibit, telescopes, and other interesting displays. You can also see a 25-minute movie in the auditorium. The visitor center is open Memorial Day through November 1 daily 8:30 A.M. to 5:00 P.M. and weekdays 8:30 A.M. to 4:30 P.M. throughout the rest of the year.

On weekends and holidays, park rangers offer free public programs about park features such as tidepools and recreational opportunities within the park. You can even go on a visual journey to the undersea world of the kelp forest without getting wet! Here's how: On Tuesdays and Thursdays during the summer months, rangers dive into the Landing Cove on East Anacapa with a video camera. You can see exactly what the diver sees: sea stars, urchins, brilliant fish, etc., on video monitors placed on the dock at Anacapa and in the mainland visitor center auditorium. You can even ask questions; the diver is outfitted with a voice communication system, which is connected to both the dock and the visitor center.

**Channel Islands National Marine Sanctuary**
**113 Harbor Way**
**Santa Barbara, CA**
**(805) 966–7107**
**www.cinms.nos.noaa.gov**

The Channel Islands National Marine Sanctuary is one of only 13 National Marine Sanctuaries in the United States. Sanctuary programs are designed not only to protect the waters, but also to promote public awareness of marine issues and make the area available for recreational activities.

One such program is the Sea Center (805–962–0885), a marine museum on Stearns Wharf that the sanctuary sponsors

CLOSE-UP

## Islands Outfoxed

For years the sweet little Channel Island fox, a tiny cinnamon and gray version of its mainland cousin, flourished on the Channel Islands. Predators were nonexistent. Food was plentiful. Even the Chumash Indians lived in harmony with these diminutive mammals, probably adopting the kits as pets. Why then is the Channel Island fox, California's only endemic carnivore, now quivering on the brink of extinction?

Indirectly, you can blame it on the pigs. Feral swine have trampled the islands since the early 1800s when ranchers brought them over with cattle and sheep. The domesticated animals grazed the land of native brush, and the pigs ran wild and swelled in number. Then, in the late 1990s, the pigs attracted a new and dangerous kind of predator to these windswept shores, one that would feast on more than swine. Golden eagles, stalkers of the sky, swooped down upon the islands and are now playing a major role in the fox's decline. Without much native brush for cover, the once-fearless Channel Island fox makes an easy snack for this wily bird of prey, spicing up its pork-rich diet. In 1994, several hundred foxes roamed free on Santa Cruz Island and a similar number thrived on San Miguel. Five years later, those numbers dipped to less than 100 on Santa Cruz and a mere few dozen on each Santa Rosa and San Miguel Islands. Park officials realized that unless the pigs and eagles were removed, the island fox would vanish.

To tackle the problem, Channel Islands National Park Service is using a multi-pronged approach. By eradicating the non-native pig population, park officials are removing the food source that brought the golden eagle here in the first place and, in the process, helping to restore much of the islands' uprooted native fauna. But the golden eagles must also be removed. They are being relocated to the mainland, and to keep them out, the much bigger bald eagle, which once thrived on the islands before hunters and DDT depleted their population, are being reintroduced. Fish, not fox, is their main fare, and they will aggressively defend their territory from golden-feathered intruders. And what of the fox? Park officials are rebuilding their population through a captive breeding program. They are also seeking to have the Channel Island fox listed as an endangered species. Perhaps one day, when the pigs are long gone and the bald eagles patrol the skies again, the little fox will be top dog on the Channel Islands once more.

in partnership with the Santa Barbara Museum of Natural History (805-682-4711). See our Attractions chapter for a detailed description of the Sea Center, which is due to reopen in summer 2003 after an 18-month renovation.

The sanctuary, the Sea Center, and the Museum of Natural History all offer educational trips to the islands led by trained naturalists. Call each one directly for information about scheduled excursions.

**Santa Cruz Island Project of The Nature Conservancy**
**213 Stearns Wharf**
**Santa Barbara, CA**
**(805) 962–9111**
**www.nature.org**

The Nature Conservancy is a private, international nonprofit membership organization. Its mission is "to preserve the plants, animals, and natural communities that represent the diversity of life on Earth by protecting the lands and waters they need to survive."

Since 1951, The Nature Conservancy has protected more than 11 million acres in the United States, including some 900,000 in California. It currently owns and manages the Santa Cruz Island Preserve, which comprises 76 percent of the island. The Nature Conservancy Visitor Center on Stearns Wharf is open daily.

The Nature Conservancy also offers a variety of day-long and occasional overnight educational trips to the preserve through local museums. Call the above number for more information.

## What to See and Do

If you're looking for direct interaction with nature, you'll love the Channel Islands. They offer a fantastic array of recreational opportunities amid gorgeous scenery. You can hike, fish, camp, dive, snorkel, and even surf within the park. You can go diving, birding, whale-watching, and sailing, explore tidepools, and lounge on the beaches, which locals think are among the most beautiful in the world.

From certain overlooks on some islands, you can observe hundreds of seals and sea lions hauling onto the beaches. You can kayak in coves, sea caves, and lagoons or go on a ranger-led hike and discover the island's human history. Many Santa Barbara companies offer scuba diving, kayaking, and sailing trips—see our Beaches and Watersports chapter for details on the specific sport you're interested in. You'll also find complete information on angling in our Fishing chapter.

If you're interested in kayaking, contact the Channel Islands National Park Visitor Center at (805) 658-5730 and request its special sea kayaking information brochure. For guided camping adventures and customized tours contact Adventours Outdoor Excursions (805-899-2929, www.adventours-inc.com) or Santa Barbara Adventure Company (888-596-6687, www.sbadventureco.com).

## Camping

You can camp year-round in National Park Service-managed campgrounds on all five islands, but no camping is allowed in the Santa Cruz Island Preserve.

Camping reservations are required for all campgrounds and can be obtained by calling (800) 365-CAMP. Before you can reserve a campsite, however, you are required to arrange your transportation. That's because the boats tend to fill up before the campgrounds.

In 2001, the Channel Islands National Park raised the camping fee to $10 per campsite per night, with most of the money covering maintenance of the camping facilities as well as monthly water monitoring. Reservations can be made no more than three months in advance, and we recommend that you reserve well ahead of time, not only to ensure that you get a site, but also to allow time for the permit to travel in the mail. When you call, you will need to have some information at hand: camping dates, transportation information, and number of campers.

Facilities are very primitive. You will need to bring all your own water and food. You also have to carry your gear from landing areas to the campgrounds, so don't go overboard when packing. All campgrounds have picnic tables and pit toilets. Fires are not permitted except in designated areas on eastern Santa Cruz Island. Bring along an enclosed camp stove for cooking.

On Santa Rosa Island, you can enjoy the luxury of running water and even an open-air cold-water shower. But, to be safe, you should only use this water for cooking and washing—you should still bring your own drinking water.

The campgrounds on Santa Rosa and San Miguel islands are often visited by fierce winds. The National Park Service has built windbreaks to shield campers from their full force. You won't blow away, but your maps and lightweight items might, so stow them tightly away.

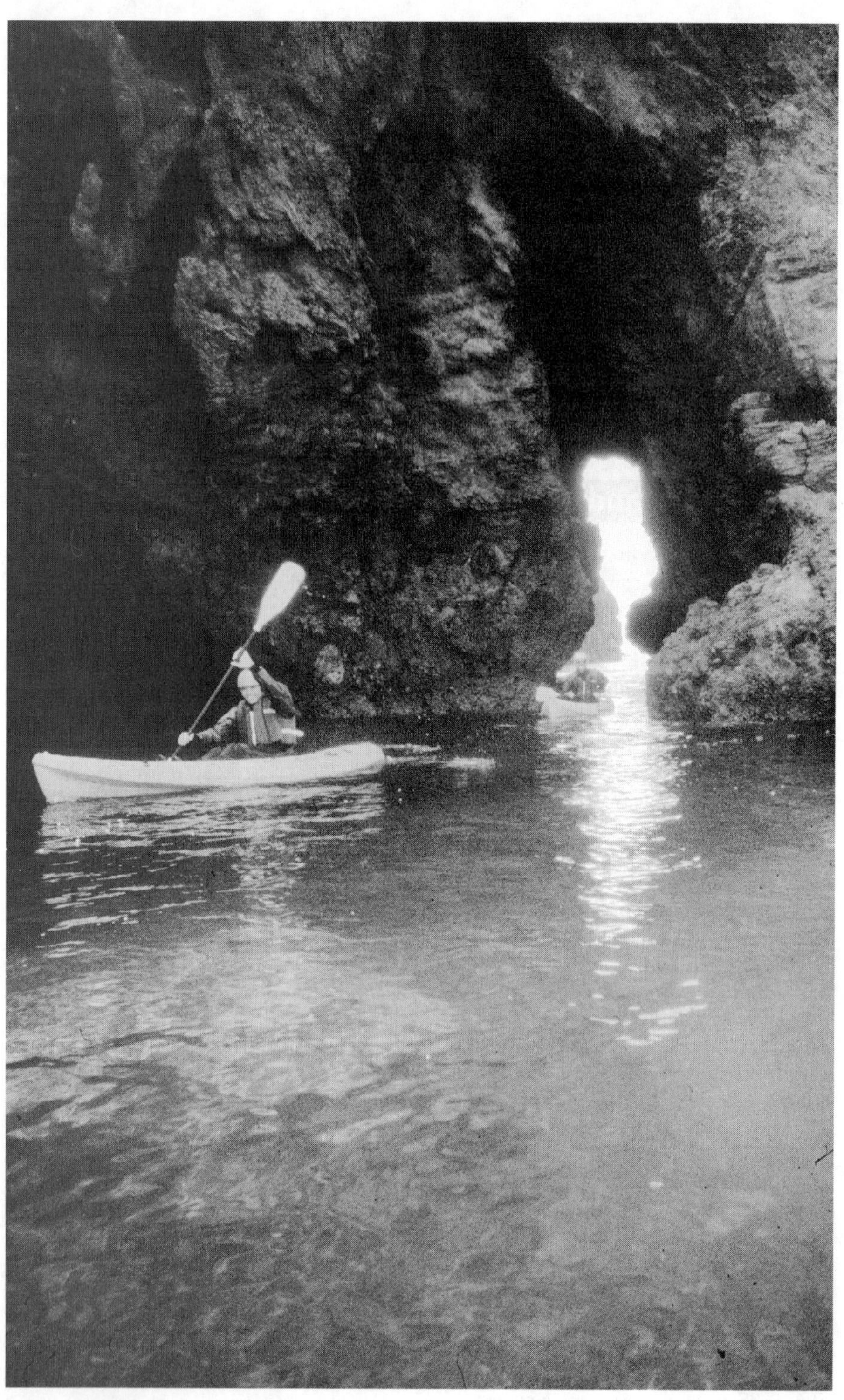

*Kayakers paddle through Channel Islands sea caves.* PHOTO: M. SCOTT MCGUIRE

The National Park Service can send you detailed camping information specific to each island as well as suggested packing lists. Call (805) 658–5730.

## Diving

The National Park and the Marine Sanctuary form a diver's paradise. Divers from all around the nation and the world come to explore the magnificent kelp forests and the incredibly diverse marine life. Visibility here is usually much better than off the mainland beaches.

Fall is usually the best time to explore the waters. At this time of year, seas are smoother, water temperature hovers in the higher ranges, and sunshine lights up the water. Visibility also tends to be better during the fall.

If you're a diver, contact the Channel Islands National Park or the Marine Sanctuary for special pamphlets on diving and on shipwrecks you can visit. Permits to dive are not required. For information on diving excursions, refer to the "Diving" section of our Beaches and Watersports chapter. In the meantime, here are a few guidelines to keep you safe in the sometimes-treacherous channel waters.

- Use standard safe diving procedures.
- Know the area.
- Be aware that changing weather affects currents and surge.
- Never dive alone.
- Always fly the diver's flag when underwater.

## Island by Island

While the Channel Islands have a lot in common with each other, each has distinct features that set it apart. Here are brief descriptions of each island. You also can request a detailed guide for each island from the Channel Islands National Park Visitor Center in Ventura (805-658-5730).

**Insiders' Tip**

Scenes from a number of famous films have been shot on the Channel Islands, including the Academy Award-winning *Mutiny on the Bounty* (San Miguel Island).

Note that there are no food and drink concessions on the islands. When you visit, you must bring all your own supplies, including drinking water. You will also need to pack out all your trash.

## Anacapa Island

Anacapa Island's name is derived from the Chumash Indian word "Eneepah," which means island of deception or mirage. That's because the island gives the illusion of changing shape when the weather is foggy or very warm. Anacapa is actually a chain of three small islets (East, Middle, and West Anacapa) connected by shallow sandbars. It's not very big—5 miles long and a half-mile wide—and the land area totals just 1 square mile. Since this island is closest to the mainland (Ventura), it's also the most visited. It's only about 90 minutes by boat from the mainland and is a good choice if you're visiting the islands for the first time.

Anacapa has 130 sea caves, 29 Chumash archeological sites, and towering cliffs. The island also boasts rich tidepool areas—the best is said to be near Frenchy's Cove on the southeastern tip of West Anacapa.

On East Anacapa Island you'll find ranger residences, a visitors center, a lighthouse, and a church-like building containing two 50,000-gallon redwood water tanks, all built before 1932. Until 1990, the lighthouse had a handmade Freshnel lens. It now uses a modern lighting system, but you can see the original lead crystal lens in the visitor center.

You can hike on about 1.5 miles of trails on East Anacapa. During the summer, the park rangers offer daily guided nature walks. A self-guided trail booklet is available at the visitor center trailhead. Picnic tables for day use are available in three areas on East Anacapa. You can snorkel and swim in the Landing Cove, but you might want to wear a wetsuit—the water's pretty cold, even in summer.

## Santa Cruz Island

Santa Cruz is the largest and most topographically diverse of all the Channel Islands. It's about 24 miles long, with a total of 62,000 acres of mountains, valleys, grasslands, woodlands, beaches, and dunes. Most visitors hike, camp, picnic, and explore on the eastern end of the island, which is managed by the Channel Islands National Park. Be prepared for a skiff landing on the beach—there are no piers at any of the landings.

A number of rugged hiking trails and roads lead you to bluffs and mountaintops for spectacular views, and along the 77 miles of coastline are sea caves, rocky ledges, reefs, and tidepools. On land, the island supports an exceptional array of flora and fauna. More than 600 plant types flourish here, and 8 types are found only on Santa Cruz Island. The most famous endemic plants include the Santa Cruz Island ironwood and the island oak.

More than 260 species of birds can be found on the island, including the endemic Santa Cruz Island scrub-jay—a bigger, bluer version of its mainland cousin. The Channel Island fox is the most famous mammal in these parts, next to the seals and sea lions that bask and play in the coves.

The island is a superb destination for swimming, snorkeling, diving, and kayaking. It lies right in the transition zone for warm currents from the south and colder currents from the north, so this is where you'll find a mingling of all worlds.

*Almost three times the size of Manhattan, Santa Cruz is the largest of the Channel Islands.*

PHOTO: BRIAN HASTINGS

**Insiders' Tip**

Santa Cruz Island is home to the largest and deepest known sea cave in the world—Painted Cave. Named for the colorful rocks and lichens covering its surface, the cave is 160 feet high at its entrance and extends a quarter of a mile into the side of the island. In the spring, a waterfall cascades down through its mouth. Depending on conditions, you might be able to enter the cave on a summer whale-watching cruise aboard the *Condor*. (See our Beaches and Watersports chapter.)

If you're in any type of kayak or a private boat and want to land or hike in the Nature Conservancy–owned preserve, you *must* apply for a day-use landing permit in advance. See the "Permits and Regulations" section later in this chapter.

## Santa Rosa Island

Santa Rosa is the second-largest island in the park (53,000 acres, or 84 square miles). It's also one of the most remote, which means you won't run into many people. Because of its size and seclusion, Santa Rosa is a great choice for multiday visits. Or you can take a daytrip over to fish for surf perch and halibut off the windswept beaches or wander the rugged trails. The island's many landscapes—mountains, canyons, sand dunes, grasslands, woodlands, and freshwater marsh—make hiking along the dirt roads and trails a real treat. Lobo Canyon Trail is especially rewarding. This 5-mile round-trip route passes through an old Chumash village site.

We've visited Santa Rosa in the summertime and especially enjoyed walking along the beautiful windswept beaches and up to the grove of Torrey pines—one of the rarest trees in the world. The only other Torrey pines on this half of the planet are found near San Diego, at the Torrey Pines State Reserve. The only native terrestrial mammals that make their home on the island are the Channel Island fox, spotted skunk, and deer mouse all of which are endemic to the Channel Islands.

Santa Rosa is also famous for its remains of the pygmy mammoth, a miniature mammoth that roamed the island during the Pleistocene era. A fossil skeleton of a pygmy mammoth discovered in 1994 on Santa Rosa is the most complete specimen ever found.

Santa Rosa Island was long home to a commercial cattle ranch, Vail & Vickers Company, which began ranching there in 1902. In 1986 the company sold the island to the National Park Service and negotiated a special-use permit allowing it to continue the business until 1998, when the last of the cattle were removed. Currently, the company holds a special-use permit allowing it to hunt introduced species such as deer and elk for a few months of the year.

Other characteristics unique to Santa Rosa include six endemic plant species that occur nowhere else on Earth, and extensive archaeological findings that tell us a great deal about the Chumash Indians who thrived on this island for thousands of years. Currently Santa Rosa is the only island that allows backcountry beach camping at certain times of the year.

*Wind-sculpted dunes fringe the beaches of Santa Rosa Island.* PHOTO: BRIAN HASTINGS

## San Miguel Island

San Miguel lies closest to Point Conception, the westernmost end of the channel. Since it is more exposed to prevailing northwest winds and blasting Pacific storms, this island is more barren and weather-beaten than the others. It's often foggy and windy, but if you can put up with the less-than-perfect weather, you'll be rewarded with scenes of wildlife you won't find anywhere else.

Animals like their privacy, and they know that San Miguel is about as private as you can get among the northern Channel Islands. San Miguel's major draw is the Point Bennett rookery and haul-out spot for pinnipeds (sea lions and seals), including Northern fur seals, California sea lions, elephant seals, Guadalupe fur seals, and stellar sea lions. At certain times of year, more than 30,000 of these pinnipeds crowd the beach. This is also the only place in the world where six species of pinnapeds congregate together.

Another unique thing about San Miguel is its caliche forest. Sort of a petrified forest in sand, it was formed by caliche (calcium carbonate) casts around plant roots and trunks. The plants are gone, but you can still see the very strange stone forms that enveloped them.

Between 1948 and 1970 the U.S. Navy used San Miguel as a bombing range, which didn't exactly do much for its natural environment. But Mother Nature has made a huge comeback on the island, and it is now a fertile and scenic preserve for all sorts of animals, birds, and plants. Whales (gray, killer, and blue), dolphins, and porpoises grace the surrounding waters, and zillions of birds, including western gulls, cormorants, pelicans, and auklets fill the skies during the spring and summer months.

Hiking is a fantastic way to experience San Miguel. However, if you leave the Cuyler Harbor and ranger station area, a park ranger must lead you.

## Santa Barbara Island

Santa Barbara Island lies much farther offshore than the other islands in the park, so be prepared for a longer boat ride (four or more hours). It's also the smallest of the group—only 1 square mile, or 640 acres. Most of the island is a giant mesa, surrounded by steep cliffs.

Although the island is small, it offers a surprisingly rich array of wildlife and scenery. We once asked a ranger which island she preferred in the park, and she named Santa Barbara as her perennial favorite.

Santa Barbara Island is most famous for its large sea lion rookery, and you can observe the seals and sea lions from a number of excellent overlook spots. The island is also an outstanding destination for birding, snorkeling, swimming, diving, and kayaking.

## Permits and Regulations

To protect the delicate resources of the National Park and Marine Sanctuary, all visitors are required to follow specific regulations and obtain appropriate landing, day-use, and camping permits. Here's an overview.

### Permits

#### Channel Islands National Park

Landing and hiking on the islands is limited, and in most cases (except day use on Anacapa and Santa Barbara Islands), you will need a permit to access an island beyond the beaches. All permits are issued free of charge and are available at the park's headquarters and visitor center in Ventura or by calling (805) 658-5730.

#### Santa Cruz Island Preserve

Access to the preserve is limited, and commercial vessels or commercial charter parties are not allowed to land or let passengers off here. However, if you go by private boat, you can apply for a permit that allows you to land and hike on this part of the island. Contact The Nature Conservancy at (805) 962-9111 to get an application and a list of the strict rules governing activity on the island. The Conservancy issues permits to owners or captains of private charter boats, but not to commercial vessels. Permits cost $60 for a calendar year or $20 for 30 consecutive days. You can also sign up for one of the naturalist-led daytrips to the island scheduled throughout the year or, if you represent an educational, research or nonprofit organization, you can organize a charter day trip. Contact Island Packers at (805) 642-1393 (see the listing under "By Boat" in this chapter).

### Rules and Regulations

Going out to the National Park and Marine Sanctuary is a fantastic way to view wildlife up close and personal. But you have to remember that all the island's natural resources are protected. The National Marine Sanctuary Program Synopsis of Regulations brochure summarizes the rules all visitors must follow. It's available at the National Park Service Visitor Center in Ventura or the Marine Sanctuary office in Santa Barbara.

Following are a few of the major regulations you should know about.

You may not feed, collect, harass, or otherwise harm the wildlife, plant life, or other natural and cultural resources of the Channel Islands National Park. That means you may not bring back any shells, plants, feathers, animals, Chumash artifacts, or other things you might be tempted to stash in your backpack. When you're tidepooling, don't collect anything. Take only pictures, and leave everything else where it is.

The water, too, is protected, so don't dump any type of refuse in the ocean.

Under federal law, it is illegal to disturb and/or harm marine mammals and seabirds in the National Park or the Marine Sanctuary at any time. They are very sensitive to any type of human disturbances, especially during nesting and pupping seasons. Kayakers, hikers, and other visitors should stay at least 100 yards away from marine mammals, both in the water and on the beaches.

CLOSE-UP

## Blue Whales—Repeat Visitors to the Santa Barbara Channel

At one time of year or another, 27 species of cetaceans (whales and porpoises) visit the Channel Islands National Marine Sanctuary. Among these are the rare and magnificent blue whales—the largest animals that have ever existed on Earth.

Blue whales (Balaenoptera musculus) have been on the endangered species list since 1966. Before the whaling industry severely depleted their numbers, about 400,000 blue whales cruised the world's oceans. Today, there are fewer than 10,000. About 2,000 are found off the coast of California—the greatest concentration of blue whales in the world.

In 1992, for reasons still not entirely understood by marine experts, blue whales began coming in increasing numbers to feed in the Channel Islands National Marine Sanctuary, usually from late May through October. Approximately 200 blue whales have been sighted at the peak of the feeding season, which is an incredibly large number considering that blue whales are usually very shy, very fast, and as a result, seldom seen. Also, they generally travel alone or in pairs, and their migratory patterns are not entirely predictable.

The whales that feed near the California coast typically go south in the winter (usually to Mexico) to breed and give birth. In the summer, they return to California to feed, traveling wherever they can find abundant krill, which are small, shrimplike crustaceans found mostly near continental shelf waters. It seems as though blue whales have discovered a sumptuous krill buffet in the Channel Islands National Marine Sanctuary, and they keep coming back for more.

The blue whale population in the Santa Barbara Channel has been steadily increasing since 1992. Now the captains of the *Condor,* a whale-watching and sport-fishing boat based at SEA Landing in Santa Barbara, usually see blues daily from May 15 to September 14. News of this trend has spread through the marine science world, and whale experts and whale lovers alike have begun to descend upon Santa Barbara for an almost guaranteed glimpse of these graceful behemoths in action.

Blue whales are truly amazing creatures. When a calf is born, it already weighs 2 to 3 tons and is 20 to 24 feet long. Adults weigh approximately 100 tons, which is equal to thirty elephants, 1,600 people, or four apatasauruses. They reach about 80 to 100 feet in length and eat 4 tons of krill every day (about 1.5 million calories).

An adult blue whale's heart is about the size of a VW Beetle, and its tongue is as large as an African elephant or hippopotamus. Despite their weight and girth, blues are incredibly fast swimmers, traveling at speeds of 8 to 20 knots. They can also dive up to 630 feet. When a blue whale blows, the spout rises up to 50 feet.

The jury's still out on why the blue whales have decided to become regular vacationers in the Santa Barbara Channel. One thing's for certain, though—they do like the gourmet krill the channel serves up. During the spring and summer months, there's something of a "krill machine" phenomenon in the channel, out near a deep canyon close to the Channel Islands. The winds cause an upwelling of dense, cold water that is rich in oxygen and nutrients. When the strong summer sunlight hits this

*The concentration of blue whales in the Channel Islands National Marine Sanctuary is one of the largest in the world.* PHOTO: CONDOR PHOTOS

nutrient-rich water, it triggers photosynthesis. The tiny plants that result in turn attract tiny, but slightly larger, animals such as krill, which feed on the plants. Two hundred krill weigh about one ounce; it takes about 3,200 to top a pound. They float around in swarms measuring about 330 by 660 feet. Blue whales simply flap their flukes, open their jaws wide, and swim fast through the swarm, and in a short time they pick up literally tons of krill and other marine life that happens to be in the way. One adult blue whale can eat up to 4 tons of krill a day.

Fred Benko, the owner of the *Condor,* has been following blue whales for years and has his own theory about why the blues have been frequenting the channel. According to Benko, blue whales have been here since historic times, but not in significant numbers since World War II, when the U.S. government conducted seismic testing in the Santa Barbara Channel. The tests initially used dynamite and later compressed air cannons. Both made a big boom.

Blue whales are particularly sensitive to low-frequency sound. They can hear certain frequencies, including the ones produced by the testing, for thousands of miles. The government ceased seismic testing in 1989, and, lo and behold, in 1992 the blue whales in the vicinity started increasing in numbers.

Furthermore, they started making friendly approaches (sidling up to a boat and checking it out for awhile) in Southern and Northern California—but not in Mexico or Costa Rica. Benko says that blue whales approach the *Condor* regularly, and he's convinced that they recognize the boat.

It seems that the blue whales will be around here for a time, since much of their feeding area lies within the protected waters of the Marine Sanctuary. Could it be the lack of disturbance or a larger volume of krill? No one knows for certain, but in the meantime, whale aficionados are trying to see them while they can.

You can see the 67-foot skeleton of an adolescent blue whale outside the Santa Barbara Museum of Natural History. But if you'd like to see the real thing, make a point of taking a cruise to the Channel Islands National Marine Sanctuary sometime during the blue whales' June through October feeding season. The sanctuary sponsors three to five cruises during the summer months; call (805) 966–7107 for information. You can also contact any of the companies listed in the "Whale-Watching" section in our Beaches and Watersports chapter.

Many thanks to the Channel Islands National Marine Sanctuary for providing most of the statistics and information for this Close-up.

Fishing in waters within the park and sanctuary requires a California fishing license. You can get one at any bait and tackle shop or when onboard a Truth Aquatics vessel (see subsequent listing under "By Boat"). (See our Fishing chapter for more specifics on licenses.)

The waters 1 nautical mile around Anacapa, San Miguel, and Santa Barbara islands are California State Ecological Reserves, where special fish and game regulations apply. In some areas of these reserves, marine life is totally protected—you can't fish or take game at all.

Abalone is now endangered and totally off limits to everyone for an indefinite period of time. Hands off!

Pets are not allowed onshore on any of the islands.

## Getting There

The easiest way to get to the Channel Islands is to hop aboard a commercial passenger boat operated by one of the two official park concessionaires. You can also fly to Santa Rosa Island or catch a ride on a private charter boat.

### By Boat

For years, Island Packers Company in Ventura was the sole concessionaire providing public boat transportation to the islands. In recent years the National Park Service added another, Truth Aquatics, located right in Santa Barbara, making it easier for locals and visitors to get out to the islands.

**Island Packers Company**
**1867 Spinnaker Drive, Ventura**
**(805) 642–1393 reservations**
**(805) 642–7688 recorded information**
**www.islandpackers.com**

Island Packers offers various trips to Anacapa and Santa Cruz Islands year-round, to Santa Barbara and Santa Rosa islands from April through November, and to San Miguel in April and June through October. Trips include half-day cruises, all-day excursions and camper transportation, kayaking expeditions, and nature discovery tours.

Weekend and holiday trips fill quickly during the spring and summer months, so you should make your reservations at least two weeks in advance. Fees range from $24 for a half-day trip to Anacapa Island to $180 for a two-day visit to San Miguel Island. Island Packers also operates a trip to Prisoners' Harbor, the new National Park–managed area of Santa Cruz, for $48. Discounts for children and seniors are available.

**Truth Aquatics**
**SEA Landing, 301 W. Cabrillo Boulevard**
**Santa Barbara, CA**
**(805) 962–1127, (805) 963–3564**
**www.truthaquatics.com**

Truth Aquatics has three fully equipped dive boats and has been taking divers on regular excursions to the Channel Islands for years. It started its official island transportation service in April 1998 and takes passengers from Santa Barbara Harbor to the islands year-round, usually several times a month from September through May and more often during the summer. Kayaks and snorkeling gear may be rented onboard.

For the time being, Truth Aquatics is focusing on trips to Santa Rosa, San Miguel, and Santa Cruz Islands.

A typical one-day excursion is a hiking trip on one of the islands. If you take a trip to Santa Rosa, for example, you depart at 4:00 A.M. (Truth Aquatics boats have sleeping berths) and arrive at Santa Rosa at 7:00 A.M. Then you can hike, kayak, snorkel, or explore until late afternoon, when the boat heads back to Santa Barbara.

You can also take a two-day weekend trip, for example to Santa Rosa and San Miguel. The boat departs from Santa Barbara at 4:00 A.M. and you arrive at one of the islands early in the morning. You reboard the boat for evening activities, slide shows, videos, or education workshops. After sleeping onboard, you wake up and spend the day exploring another island before returning to Santa Barbara. At times, campers can board the boat and hop off for two to six or more days of camping, depending on when the boat is scheduled to pick them up.

Daytrips to Santa Cruz Island cost $60 for adults and $45 for children 12 and younger and seniors 65 and older. Day trips to Santa Rosa or San Miguel are $75 for adults and $56 for children and seniors.

A two-day trip to Santa Rosa and San Miguel, including meals, costs $252 for adults and $190 for children and seniors.

## Other Commercial and Private Boats

A number of commercial and private boats offer island excursions—see our Beaches and Watersports chapter for an overview of your boating options. If you plan to take your own boat out to the islands, you can find navigational information in NOAA charts 18720, 18727, 18728, 18729, and 18756. If you need emergency assistance, call the Coast Guard on Channel 16 of your marine band radio. National Park Service patrol vessels regularly monitor the channel.

## By Air

**Channel Islands Aviation**
**Camarillo Airport, 305 Durley Avenue**
**Camarillo, CA**
**(805) 987–1301**
**www.flycia.com**

If you really can't face being on a boat or your time is limited, just cruise to the islands by air in only 25 minutes. Channel Islands Aviation offers year-round departures from Santa Barbara Airport (six-passenger minimum, daytrips only) and Camarillo Airport. It provides camper transportation, daytrips, and one-day and weekend camping and surf fishing safaris to Santa Rosa Island.

Camper transportation costs $163 per person. One-day trips to Santa Rosa cost $106 for adults and $84 for children ages 2 through 12. Infants and toddlers who sit on a parent's lap ride free. Charters are available.

*Anglers fly in for a day's fishing on the remote beaches of Santa Rosa Island.* PHOTO: BRIAN HASTINGS

# Recreation



For a city its size, Santa Barbara has an incredible number of recreational opportunities. Part of this is due to the number of tourists who come to town looking for fun, but it's also a result of the Santa Barbara lifestyle, which places a heavy emphasis on being health-conscious, active, and fit. We think you'll find just about everything you'd ever want to do listed below, but if you wake up one morning and get the urge to do something spur-of-the-moment, pick up the *Santa Barbara News-Press* and look in the "Public Square" section for a listing of the day's activities and events around town.

On Saturdays, check out the "Your Day in Santa Barbara" page in the "Life" section, with listings of recreational activities and attractions, and on Sundays look for the "What's Doing on the South Coast" calendar, which includes everything happening in the upcoming week. Also check "The Week" listings in *The Santa Barbara Independent* (distributed free each Thursday). Remember that such facilities as tennis, volleyball and basketball courts, gyms, pools and running tracks at local colleges may be available for limited public use. Call UCSB, (805) 893-3738 , the Santa Barbara City College Athletics Department, (805) 965-0581, ext. 2276, or the Westmont College Athletic Department, (805) 565-6010, for information.

This chapter begins with a list of local sports and recreation companies, facilities, and organizations, then covers area sports and activities alphabetically. The chapter ends with a list of local athletic clubs.

## Organizations and Facilities

The following companies, organizations, and facilities sponsor a variety of sports and recreational programs and events in Santa Barbara.

**Adventours Outdoor Excursions**
**(805) 899-2929**
**www.adventours-inc.com**

Adventours is an experienced outdoor recreation company specializing in customized group excursions. If you're looking for an alfresco adventure with a group of friends or colleagues, Adventours will gladly coordinate an itinerary to suit your interests and skills. Activities include mountain biking (for groups of eight or more), coastal and Channel Island kayaking (groups of four or more), hiking and backpacking tours, high-end rock-climbing, and sky diving. Adventours also offers customized multisport adventures; for example you can bike down a mountain in the morning then paddle the Pacific in the afternoon. Call in advance to schedule a tour and obtain a price quote. (See the subsequent listings for Adventours in the "Biking" and "Kayaking" sections of this chapter for more information on these activities.) If you're thinking of holding a conference in Santa Barbara, the company will coordinate corporate team-building and recreational programs such as beach Olympics, eco-challenges, and ropes courses. Adventours also runs the Santa Barbara County Triathlon (check the web site for more information).

**Louise Lowry Davis Recreation Center**
**1232 De la Vina Street**
**Santa Barbara, CA**
**(805) 897-2568**

**Carrillo Recreation Center**
**100 E. Carrillo Street**
**Santa Barbara, CA**
**(805) 897-2519**

Headquarters for the Senior Citizens Information Service, the Louise Lowry Davis Center offers weekday recreational activities for adults, with many programs specially designed for the older set. The center offers bridge, scrabble, bingo, "sit-and-be-fit" classes, porcelain painting, yoga, crochet, and knitting. The Carrillo Recreation Center also offers many classes for adults, including dance and fitness. Both centers are run by the Santa Barbara Parks and Recreation Department. You can pick up activity schedules for both centers at either location.

**Santa Barbara Adventure Company**
**(805) 452-1942, (888) 596-6687**
**www.sbadventureco.com**

Launched in 1998, Santa Barbara Adventure Company is a relatively new company offering a range of guided outdoor adventures. Trips are tailored to your interests, with activities ranging from kayaking, biking, hiking, surfing, and rock climbing to camping adventures, Channel Island trips, and wine country tours. The emphasis is on escaping crowds and getting back to nature. One of the most popular trips is the coastal kayaking excursion. Experienced guides lead kayakers along the spectacular Gaviota coast while sharing their knowledge of the area's natural history and marine ecology. Multisport adventures are also available (biking and kayaking, for example). Prices range from $60 per person for a three-hour kayaking tour to about $355 per person for a multisport three-day adventure. All trips include qualified guides, equipment, transportation, and any necessary permits. Day trips require reservations two days in advance. For overnight trips, book at least two weeks in advance. Call or visit the company's web site for more information.

**Santa Barbara City College Adult Education Program**
**310 W. Padre Avenue**
**Santa Barbara, CA**
**(805) 687-0812**
**300 N. Turnpike Road**
**Santa Barbara, CA**
**(805) 964-6853**
**www.sbcc.net/ce**

This comprehensive program of inexpensive classes is a huge hit with Santa Barbarans, who anxiously look forward to the quarterly Adult Ed schedule (it comes in the *Santa Barbara News-Press* or can be picked up at Adult Ed offices).

In addition to business classes, computer courses, lectures, foreign-language classes, and self-improvement courses, Adult Ed offers a plethora of recreational and arts classes, including dance, fitness, ceramics, drawing, painting, quilting, cooking, birding, nature walks, and music. We can only scratch the surface of the possibilities here, so call for a copy of the schedule of classes and tempt yourself to try something new.

**Santa Barbara Parks and Recreation Department**
**620 Laguna Street**
**Santa Barbara, CA**
**(805) 564-5418**
**www.sbparksandrecreation.com**

The Santa Barbara Parks and Recreation Department organizes a wide range of recreational activities for the whole family. Among these are the city's youth and adult sports leagues, dance classes, dog-obedience training, teen programs, fitness classes, aquatics, tours, and special programs for seniors (to name a few).

Information on all of the programs can be found in the free *Parks and Recreation Activity Guide,* which is issued twice a year (spring/summer and fall/winter); it's distributed inside *The Santa Barbara Independent* and the *Santa Barbara News-Press* and is also available at the Parks and Rec office. Fees vary according to the class or activity you choose but are generally very affordable. Disabled persons need not feel left out of the local recreation scene. In addition to hundreds of other events, Parks and Recreation sponsors adapted programs such as wheelchair tennis lessons, aquatic programs, and the popular Blister Bowl, a football game featuring wheelchair athletes, held in October. Call (805) 564-5421. Starting September 2001 you can register online for most recreational classes. Go to the web site listed above and click on "e-Recreation."

**Santa Barbara Sports Leagues**
**(805) 564-5422**
**www.sbparksandrecreation.com**

The Santa Barbara Parks and Recreation Department organizes city leagues in a variety of sports, including volleyball, basketball, soccer, softball, and tennis. Men's, women's and coed leagues are available, so get your friends together and join the fun. Registration fees vary depending on the type of league you join, but generally top out at about $200 for the season. Call for further information.

**Santa Barbara Semana Nautica Association**
**P.O. Box 5001**
**Santa Barbara, CA 93150**
**(805) 897-2680**
**www.semananautica.com**

Back in the mid-1930s, five Navy battleships were moored outside the Santa Barbara Harbor, filled with bored crew members. The locals hit upon an idea: Why not challenge the sailors to a series of contests on our beach, just for the fun of it?

Originally dubbed "Fleet Week," the celebration still happens every year around the Fourth of July weekend, but with a new name to honor Santa Barbara's Spanish heritage.

This festival spans several weeks and draws crowds of spectators, but we list it here for those of you interested in participating. With contests as diverse as swimming, tennis, yachting, cycling, softball, running, racquetball, paddleboarding, volleyball, cardboard-boat races, and sandcastle-building—to name a few—you are sure to find something you're good at. Designed for people of all ages and skill levels, the contests appeal to both serious athletes and weekend warriors, plus kids and older adults. Most events require entry fees, which vary widely depending on the event. For a brochure listing all events and contact phone numbers for entering, contact the Santa Barbara Semana Nautica Association at the address listed above or visit their web site.

The East Beach Bathhouse, 1118 E. Cabrillo Boulevard (805-897-2680), and the Santa Barbara Parks and Recreation Department, 620 Laguna Street, (805-564-5418), also have Semana Nautica brochures. This is Santa Barbara-style recreation par excellence, so start getting in shape now!

**University of California at Santa Barbara**
**Off Highway 217**
**Goleta, CA**
**(805) 893-3738**
**www.par.ucsb.edu**

UCSB's Department of Physical Activities and Recreation offers a packed schedule of recreational programs and classes held on the campus or nearby. Most are excellent, and all are open to the public, although you'll have to pay more if you're not a student (and you'll also have to pay for parking). Especially popular are the Leisure Arts classes (805-893-3738), which include everything from aquatics, dance, and group fitness to martial arts, sailing, and kayaking. Call for a current brochure or visit the department's web site for information.

## Insiders' Tip

Need a map? Look for the informative series of Santa Barbara Recreational Maps (there are seven in all) for the scoop on hiking, biking, and the San Rafael Wilderness and Dick Smith Wilderness areas. Maps are available at local bookstores and in bike and outfitting shops for $3.50 or less.

## Biking

As you might expect in a fitness-conscious city like Santa Barbara, there are miles of bike trails that will literally take you from the mountains to the sea (or from downtown Santa Barbara to Goleta). Nearly all county roads have bike paths marked by a solid white line on the right side of the road. These lanes must be kept clear of vehicular traffic, and by the same token, bikes are expected to stay out of the vehicle lanes.

A good investment is Map No. 7 of the Santa Barbara County Recreational Map Series, "Santa Barbara Road Bicycling Routes," available for about $3.50 from bookstores and bike shops (we suggest Bicycle Bob's, 15 Hitchcock Way; Open Air Bicycles, 224 Chapala Street; or Velo Pro Cyclery, 629 State Street). City maps are available at these locations for free. You can also receive a free map by calling Traffic Solutions at (805) 963–SAVE or by visiting its web site at www.sbcag/tf.htm and sending an e-mail request.

One of the favorite in-town spots to bike is the 3-mile, two-lane Cabrillo Bike Lane, which spans the entire waterfront from Leadbetter Beach to the east end of Cabrillo Boulevard. This path is open to bicycles, quadracycles, and in-line skaters, so it is often crowded, and you never know who you might (literally) run into.

Caution is the byword here, especially on weekends or holidays, when massive numbers of bikers and skaters (as well as many pedestrians who walk across bike paths) make for a harrowing ride. Of course, in addition to casual biking, many Santa Barbarans love cycling the county's rugged hills and canyons. To get the buzz on what's hot for training or racing, ask at any of the bike shops.

## Outfitters

The following companies organize biking trips.

**Adventours Outdoor Excursions**
**(805) 899–2929**
**www.adventours-inc.com**

Adventours organizes customized bike tours for groups of eight or more riders. Trips include exhilarating downhill rides from local peaks to the sea and single-track mountain-biking tours.

**Pedal and Paddle of Santa Barbara**
**(805) 687–2912**
**www.nvstar.com/pedpad**

Judy Keim, a local naturalist, leads bike and kayak excursions from Carpinteria to Gaviota. (See our Beaches and Watersports chapter for details on the paddle activities.) You can choose from several standard tours, or you can customize a tour if you wish.

In Santa Barbara, take the Wetlands Tour, a 25-mile round-trip exploration of local wetlands that includes a look at the monarch butterfly preserve in Goleta (December through February); the Hidden Art in Santa Barbara Tour, a 10-mile round trip; or the Art and Architecture Tour, a 20-mile round trip focusing on Montecito. Prices range from $25 for a two-hour Douglas Family Preserve Tour (7 miles round-trip) to $100 for a day-long excursion. Judy supplies all the equipment (plus water and snacks), and you get an $8 discount if you have your own bike and helmet.

**Santa Barbara Adventure Company**
**(805) 452-1942, (888) 596-6687**
**www.sbadventureco.com**

Bike through the back streets of town, cycle around the wine country across rolling hills and farmland, or bump your way along a rugged single-track forest trail. Santa Barbara Adventure Company offers a range of excursions for bikers of all levels, and they'll customize tours to suit your skills and interests. If you don't want to break a sweat climbing any hills, choose the Mountains to the Shore trip and zoom down hill with the wind in your hair.

### Rentals

**Beach Rentals**
**22 State Street**
**Santa Barbara, CA**
**(805) 966-6733**
**www.wheelfunrentals.com**

Quadracycles, cruisers, mountain bikes, and tandem bikes are offered at this lower State Street rental shop just a half-block from the beach and the waterfront bike paths. Rental prices range from $15 an hour for single quadracycles to $35 an hour for double (9-person) quadracycles.

**Cycles 4 Rent**
**101 State Street**
**Santa Barbara, CA**
**(805) 966-3804, (888) 405-BIKE**
**Fess Parker's Doubletree Resort**
**633 E. Cabrillo Boulevard**
**Santa Barbara, CA**
**(805) 564-4333**
**Radisson Hotel**
**1111 E. Cabrillo Boulevard**
**Santa Barbara, CA**
**(805) 963-0744**
**www.cycles4rent.com**

In addition to renting in-line skates (a popular way of getting around on the waterfront), Cycles 4 Rent offers the very popular quadracycles, which are four-wheeled canopied bikes that can hold up to three adults and two small children (single) or up to six adults and two children (double). Prices range from $10 for one hour on a single quadracycle to $60 for four hours on a double. Quadracycle drivers must be 18 or older. Also available are mountain bikes, tandem bikes, three-wheelers, scooters, kids' bikes, and all the accoutrements (helmets, locks, and bike seats for kids).

## Bowling

**Zodo's Bowling & Beyond**
**5925 Calle Real**
**Goleta, CA**
**(805) 967-0128**

Open around the clock, Zodo's Bowling & Beyond is the only bowling alley located in the South County. With 24 lanes, bumpers for kids, and the popular Glow Bowl (Sundays 8:00 P.M. to midnight, Tuesdays and Wednesdays 9:00 P.M. to midnight), and Galactic Bowl (9:30 P.M. to midnight each Friday), it's a popular place for birthday parties and recreational bowling. In addition, Zodo's organizes a variety of leagues, including men's, women's, mixed, and senior. The Galleon Room cocktail lounge and a coffee shop are also in the bowling complex.

## Camping

Camping is a fantastic way to experience Santa Barbara's famed natural environment. Few things are more exhilarating than waking up in the morning to the call of the birds and wildlife, then going for an early morning hike or walk along the beach, with views of the ocean, islands, and mountains everywhere you look.

Santa Barbara doesn't have many campgrounds, but they all offer excellent camping facilities as well as incredible scenery. Nearly all are situated on or near a beach, and several let you experience both the mountains and the beach at the same time.

One thing we can't emphasize enough: make reservations as early as possible. The state park campgrounds fill up very quickly, especially during the summer months and on holiday weekends. Many people make their summer reservations at least six months in advance.

Los Padres National Forest also has a number of campgrounds. Many of these sites are available on a first come, first served basis with varying fees depending on the facility. You will, however, need a permit to park or camp at most of these sites. For reservations, call (877) 444-6777 or visit www.reserveUSA.com. If you have any questions, you can call the Los Padres National Forest Service headquarters (805-968-6640) or the Santa Barbara Ranger District (805-967-3481). For a truly unique camping experience, try one of the Channel Islands. You'll find detailed information in our Channel Islands National Park and Marine Sanctuary chapter.

## State Parks

Four state parks with year-round campgrounds are in the area covered in this book. Three of them—El Capitan, Refugio and Gaviota—occupy prime beachfront along the scenic coastline that stretches northwest between Goleta and Gaviota. The fourth, Carpinteria State Beach, lies on the shores of Carpinteria, just 12 miles south of Santa Barbara. Each welcomes hundreds of thousands of day-use visitors and campers every year.

To reserve a site at El Capitan, Refugio, or Carpinteria, call Parknet (800-444-7275) or visit www.reserveamerica.com. We highly recommend reserving your campsite well ahead of time. You can make reservations up to seven months in advance (but do so at least two days before your planned arrival). Gaviota does not accept reservations; sites are available on a first come, first served basis.

You can camp in these parks for up to seven days from June 1 through September. At other times of year you can stay longer—up to 15 days. During the off-season and on weekdays you might be able to get a campsite without advance reservations, but don't count on it—these parks are amazingly popular, even during the winter months. Lifeguards are generally on duty at state beaches from mid-June through Labor Day weekend.

Keep in mind that all California state parks have strict regulations regarding noise, curfews, parking, trail access, and litter (you will be advised of these regulations when you arrive). Dogs are allowed on a 6-foot leash, but you may not take them on trails or beaches. Be prepared to pay a fine if you do. And don't forget to clean up after your pets!

**El Capitan State Beach**
**Off U.S. Highway 101, 17 miles northwest of Santa Barbara**
**(805) 968–1033**
**www.parks.ca.gov for information**
**(800) 444–7275**
**www.reservamerica.com for reservations**

"El Cap" ranks among the most beautiful state parks in Southern California. The 133-acre park was formerly the site of a large Chumash Indian village. Today it features 140 developed campsites and 4 group sites, restrooms, a snack bar, showers, barbecue grills, and open fire pits. Trailers up to 27 feet in length and campers to 30 feet in length are allowed to park here, but there aren't any hookups. Try to nab Site 75—if you're lucky and it's available, you're in for a real treat. *Sunset* magazine named the blufftop campsite the best beach campsite in Southern California, largely because of the awesome ocean and island views, shade trees, and easy beach access. Or try for Site 120, with stunning views to the west, toward Point Conception.

Rates from April through September are $12 per site per night year-round for a standard site. Firewood is available for $5 per bag. There's a lot to see and explore at El Cap. Walk down a path from the bluffs and you'll arrive at the sandy beach, where you can sunbathe, fish, sailboard, and explore tidepools. You can hike along nature trails or along the bluffs—and if you take the blufftop trail just 2.5 miles west you'll end up at Refugio State Beach. From June 19 through Labor Day, lifeguards patrol daily.

> **Insiders' Tip**
>
> No skating or skateboarding is allowed on any downtown city streets, sidewalks, or in any local shopping malls.

**Gaviota State Park**
**Off U.S. Highway 101, 33 miles west of Santa Barbara**
**(805) 968–1033**
**www.parks.ca.gov**

This sprawling, 2,700-acre park is smaller and a bit more primitive than El Capitan and Refugio, but it offers fantastic views from mountainside trails. It lies 33 miles west of Santa Barbara, close to where the coastline turns north at Point Conception. The 52 developed sites are available on a first come, first served basis. You will need to bring your own drinking water.

Park facilities include pay showers, food service, restrooms, and picnic areas. You can swim, fish off the pier, and hike on numerous trails, including one that leads to Gaviota Hot Springs. U.S. 101 cuts across the park. So does a railroad trestle (down by the day-use parking lot). Trailers up to 25 feet and campers as long as 27 feet may park here, but there are no hookups.

Camping fees are $12 per site per night year-round.

**Refugio State Beach**
**Off U.S. Highway 101, 20 miles northwest of Santa Barbara**
**(805) 968–1033**
**www.parks.ca.gov for information**
**(800) 444–7275, www.reserveamerica.com for reservations**

Palm trees line the beach and campgrounds at Refugio, so the place looks like a picture-postcard scene from Hawaii. The park offers 80 developed campsites and one group site on 155 acres, many picnic areas, excellent coastal fishing and nature trails, and a seasonal kiosk. Trailers up to 27 feet and campers up to 30 feet in length may park here, but there aren't any hookups.

Camping fees are $12 per site per night year-round.

Refugio is a great place for picnicking, diving, snorkeling, and exploring nature trails. A 2.5-mile bike trail connects Refugio with its neighboring state park, El Capitan.

**Carpinteria State Beach**
**5361 Sixth Street**
**Carpinteria, CA**
**(805) 684–2811**
**www.parks.ca.gov for information**
**(800) 444–7275**
**www.reserveusa.com for reservations**

Because of its excellent facilities and programs, Carpinteria State Beach is almost always booked to capacity throughout the summer and on every major holiday. The park has a visitor center with natural history exhibits and nature programs as well as a convenience store. Birding, swimming, fishing, hiking, surfing—you name it—are popular activities here.

The 48-acre park has more campsites and facilities than any other state park in the region. Each of the 261 narrow family campsites has a parking space, picnic table, and fire ring. Restrooms in each campground feature hot showers. Drinking water is available nearby. You'll find sites here for tents as well as campers, trailers, and motor homes up to 30 feet. Water, sewer, and electrical hookups are available in one of the campgrounds.

You can buy firewood at the park headquarters. Sites without hookups cost $12 per night year-round, those with hookups are an additional $6 per night. The rangers put on campfire programs several nights a week throughout the summer. They also organize a Junior Ranger program for kids ages 7 to 12. Adults and kids alike can sign up for naturalist-led nature walks to the shore and tidepools.

Check the schedule at the visitor center. The park is about 12 miles south of Santa Barbara off U.S. 101. Take the Casitas Pass exit to Palm Avenue and follow it three blocks into the park.

## Other Public Camping Areas

**Cachuma Lake Recreation Area**
**Calif. Highway 154, northwest of Santa Barbara**
**(805) 688–4658 recorded information**
**(805) 686–5054, (805) 686–5055**
**www.sbparks.com**

Cachuma Lake is a 3,200-acre county reservoir and recreation area that lies in the Santa Ynez Mountains about 20 miles northwest of Santa Barbara. It's the pride and joy of the Santa Barbara County park system, and you can count on friendly staff, gorgeous scenery, and diverse wildlife in the area at any time of year.

Tent and RV campsites are available year-round on a first-come, first-served basis. More than 550 regular campsites are available, each with a picnic table and barbecue pit. Ninety sites have full electrical, water, and sewer hookups. All campsites are close to showers, restrooms, and water. You can stay up to 14 days in the summer and up to two months in the winter. Group sites for 8 to 30 vehicles can be reserved up to a year in advance; call (805) 686-5050 for information.

For an unusual camping experience, you can reserve a yurt (pronounced YOORT), which is basically a tent covering the frame of a round cabin, for $35 to $50 per night. Fees vary, depending on the yurt size and season. Each yurt is insulated and has bunk beds, a skylight, and a wooden deck. The yurts are very popular with families and can be reserved up to a year in advance. Call (805) 686-5050 for reservations.

Cachuma Lake provides numerous facilities, including a fully stocked general store, a gas station, a laundromat, a snack bar and grill, a marina, a bait and tackle shop, bike rentals, boat rentals, and an RV dump station. You're allowed to bring a dog as long as it stays on a leash. You'll need to pay a $2 daily pet fee and show proof of rabies vaccination.

If you're looking for a place to pursue lots of different recreational activities while camping, you can't go wrong by choosing Cachuma. It's a recreational paradise, with boating, fishing, naturalist programs, wildlife and eagle cruises, and trails for horseback riding and hiking.

However, swimming, waterskiing, sailboarding, or any bodily contact with the lake is strictly forbidden because it's a reservoir, and much of the water ends up in someone's home down the mountain.

Rates range from $16 to $22 per night, depending on the type of site. A second vehicle at the same site costs an additional $8 (maximum two vehicles and eight people per site). If you're going to visit Cachuma more than once, you might consider buying a season pass at the entrance. Our Parks chapter contains a complete description of the Cachuma Lake Recreation Area.

**Los Padres National Forest**
**Various campsites off Calif. Highway 154, about 20 miles northeast of Santa Barbara**
**(805) 968–6640 headquarters**
**(805) 967–3481 Santa Barbara Ranger District Office**
**(877) 444–6777, www.reserveUSA.com for reservations**

Los Padres National Forest is a huge region (nearly 2 million acres) that stretches across the coastal mountain ranges for about 225 miles from Los Angeles County in the south to Monterey County in the north. You'll find 16 developed family campgrounds in the Santa Barbara Ranger District of this national forest; the closest to the city of Santa Barbara lie near Calif. Highway 154, near Paradise Road, the upper Santa Ynez River, and Cachuma Lake. Amenities at each site vary from rustic campgrounds with toilets (but no piped drinking water) to full-service sites with piped water, fire pits, toilets, paved roads, picnic tables, and stoves. You can also camp by permit in designated backcountry areas.

Reservation sites are Upper Oso, Paradise, and the group area at Sage Hill. All the other sites are available on a first come, first served basis, and the fees are about $12 per night. You will, however, need a permit to park and/or camp at most of these sites. For information, call the Forest Service office, 6755 Hollister Avenue, Suite 150, Goleta, at (805) 968-6640 or (805) 967-3481.

## Private Campgrounds

**Sunrise RV Park**
**516 S. Salinas Street**
**Santa Barbara, CA**
**(805) 966-9954, (800) 345-5018**

Sunrise is the only private RV park in Santa Barbara, and it's only 13 blocks from East Beach, 1.5 miles from State Street, and 3 blocks from a bus stop. It has been in operation for more than 40 years and has 33 RV sites. Each site offers full hookups (water, electricity, sewer, and even cable TV). The park has four restroom areas with free hot showers, laundry facilities, and two tent sites (the only tent sites within the city limits).

Rates start at $35 per night per person in an RV up to 30 feet in length. Each additional person costs $5 per night. If your rig is longer than 30 feet, you pay an extra $5 for each additional 5 feet. You can stay for as long as 28 days. After that, you can request an extension, which is sometimes available during the off-season. The ultimate maximum length of stay is six months.

Sunrise RV Park is booked year-round. Advance reservations are highly recommended. Pets are welcome as long as they remain leashed and owners clean up all pet messes.

## Dancing

The Santa Barbara Parks and Recreation Department offers an impressive lineup of dance lessons and dances, including modern, jazz, ballet, swing dance, and country-western. After you practice up, show off your steps at the Carrillo Recreation Center, at 100 E. Carrillo Street (805-965-3813). The center's ballroom is one of only two spring-loaded dance floors in the country. Ballroom dances are scheduled here every Saturday evening (except the last Saturday in a five-Saturday month). For $8 ($9 for nonmembers), you can dance to a live ballroom orchestra from 8:00 to 11:00 P.M.

Also at the Carrillo Recreation Center: free tea dances are held the first Sunday of each month from 2:00 to 5:00 P.M.; swing dances happen on the first and third Friday of the month from 8:00 P.M. to midnight, with lessons on Tuesday through Thursday evenings; and country, folk, line, and contra dancing is scheduled on Sundays from 6:30 to 10:00 P.M. Hip hop sessions take place Mondays from 5:30 to 6:30 P.M. and Wednesdays from 7:00 to 8:00 P.M. Ballet, tap, and tango classes are also available. Fees vary, but are generally less than $10 per session. For a schedule of dance programs, pick up an *Activity Guide* from Santa Barbara Parks and Recreation (see the listing at the beginning of this chapter) or download one at the department's web site, www.sbparksandrecreation.com. See our Nightlife chapter for more information on dancing.

## Hang Gliding

Hang gliding and paragliding are alive and well in Santa Barbara, and an active association in town promotes the sports. If you're new to gliding, you can take lessons (it costs about $190 for an introductory lesson) using the company's equipment. After that you'll have to decide whether or not to buy a glider, as they are usually not rented.

Local launch points include La Cumbre Peak, the Douglas Family Preserve, and the beloved 200-foot training hill—which is considered one of the best in the country—in an undeveloped area on the south side of Las Positas Friendship Park. Contact Fly Away Hang Gliding (805-957-9145) or Fly Above All AirSports

(805-965-3733, www.flyaboveall. com) to talk to real enthusiasts of the sport who are anxious to tell you all about it. (Also see the listing for the New Year's Day Hang Gliding and Paragliding Festival in our Annual Events chapter.)

## Hiking

Santa Barbara is a hiker's paradise. With miles of trails accessible year-round, you'd be hard-pressed to find a better place to take in the beauty of nature.

Maps and information (as well as permits needed for backcountry hiking) can be found at the Los Padres National Forest Headquarters, 6755 Hollister Avenue, Suite 150, Goleta (805-968-6640). Or you can pick up a copy of the *Santa Barbara Trail Guide* at a local bookshop or outdoor equipment store; it lists 25 hiking trails in the Santa Barbara area, including trail ratings, access information, descriptions, maps, and trail logs.

*Lizard Rock Point rewards hikers with spectacular sunset views.* PHOTO: NIK WHEELER, COURTESY OF SANTA BARBARA CONFERENCE & VISITORS BUREAU

**Insiders' Tip**

When hiking in the county, it's possible to run into a rattlesnake, especially in the spring and summer. So watch your step!

*Santa Barbara Day Hikes* by Raymond Ford, Jr., is also a good resource, as is Map No. 2 in the Santa Barbara County Recreational Map Series, titled "A Hiker's Guide to the Santa Barbara Front Country." Trail maps are also available at Pacific Travellers Supply, 12 W. Anapamu Street, Santa Barbara (805-963-4438), and Traffic Solutions, at (805) 963-7283. If you'd rather not go off by yourself, the Sierra Club (805-966-6622) sponsors a variety of day and evening hikes that range from easy to strenuous. These and other local club hikes are usually listed in the "Events Today" section of the *Santa Barbara News-Press.*

One of our favorite easy hikes is Rattle Snake Canyon, a serpentine 3-mile trail with waterfalls, pools, and plenty of shady picnic spots. The moderately easy Cold Springs Trail is also popular. Once a stagecoach route, this 9-mile trail begins in the shade by a cool running creek and ends with a steep and rocky climb up the mountain.

## Horseshoes

Horseshoe courts are available in the following parks: Monte Vista Park, Bailard Avenue and Pandanus Street, Carpinteria (one court); Manning Park, San Ysidro and East Valley Roads, Montecito (four courts); Oak Park, W. Alamar Avenue and Junipero Street, Santa Barbara (one lighted court); Goleta Beach Park, Sandspit Road, Goleta (four courts); Stow Grove Park, La Patera Lane and Cathedral Oaks Road, Goleta (two courts); Tucker's

Grove Park, San Antonio Creek Road and Cathedral Oaks, Santa Barbara (eight courts); Toro Canyon Park, Toro Canyon Park Road (two courts).

## Horseback Riding

**Circle Bar B Stables and Guest Ranch**
**1800 Refugio Road**
**Goleta, CA**
**(805) 968–3901**
**www.circlebarb.com**

Well known for its riotous dinner theater, the Circle Bar B, 20 miles north of Santa Barbara, offers 90-minute rides at 9:30 and 11:30 A.M. and 3:00 and 5:00 P.M. daily. The cost is $30 per person, and reservations are required. Children must be at least 7 years old to participate.

Half-day rides are also available and last from 9:00 A.M. to 1:00 P.M.; they cost $65 per person, including lunch. Enjoy views of the local canyons, ocean, and Channel Islands, or choose the special sunrise or sunset rides. Groups can also be accommodated.

From U.S. 101 take the Refugio State Beach exit and drive 3.5 miles toward the mountains. A large sign will be clearly visible on your right.

**Montecito Farms**
**455 Toro Canyon Road**
**Santa Barbara, CA**
**(805) 695–0480**
**www.horserentals.com/montecitofarms**

Always dreamed of galloping along a sun-drenched beach on horseback? Montecito Farms offers guided trail rides in Summerland, Montecito, Santa Barbara, and Carpinteria that include an exhilarating canter along the beach. They also offer lessons and pony rides. Call for more information.

**Rancho Oso Stables and Guest Ranch**
**3750 Paradise Road**
**Santa Barbara, CA**
**(805) 683–5110**
**www.rancho-oso.com**

You'll be riding into history at this old ranch, once a Spanish land grant in the local mountains. Rancho Oso offers trail riding starting at $28 for a one-hour ride. Little cowboys and cowgirls can practice their skills on hand-led pony rides for $10. On the weekends, the chuckwagon food service lets you refuel after your ride. Rancho Oso offers equestrian group camping as well as overnight accommodations in cabins and covered wagons. Reservations are required, so call ahead. Beginners and children are welcome. Event facilities are also available. Take Calif. 154 to Paradise Road and look for the sign approximately 5.5 miles from the turnoff.

## Jogging

The beach is the most popular jogging site in Santa Barbara, either on the sand, along the Cabrillo bike path, or along Shoreline Drive. If you're looking for something away from the coast, head for one of these parks, which have jogging trails: Monte Vista Park, Bailard Avenue and Pandanus Street, Carpinteria; and Las Positas Friendship Park, Las Positas Road and Jerry Harwin Parkway, Santa Barbara. If you're into serious running, see our listing for Adventours Outdoor Excursions in the "Organizations and Facilities" section at the beginning of this chapter.

## Lawn Bowling

Santa Barbara has two lawn bowls greens, and free instruction is offered at both. Since they are open on alternate days, it's possible to play every day if you're so inclined.

**MacKenzie Park Lawn Bowls Club**
**State Street at Las Positas Road**
**Santa Barbara, CA**
**(805) 563–2143**

This club has two greens, which are open to visitors as well as club members. Annual membership is $175, after which you can

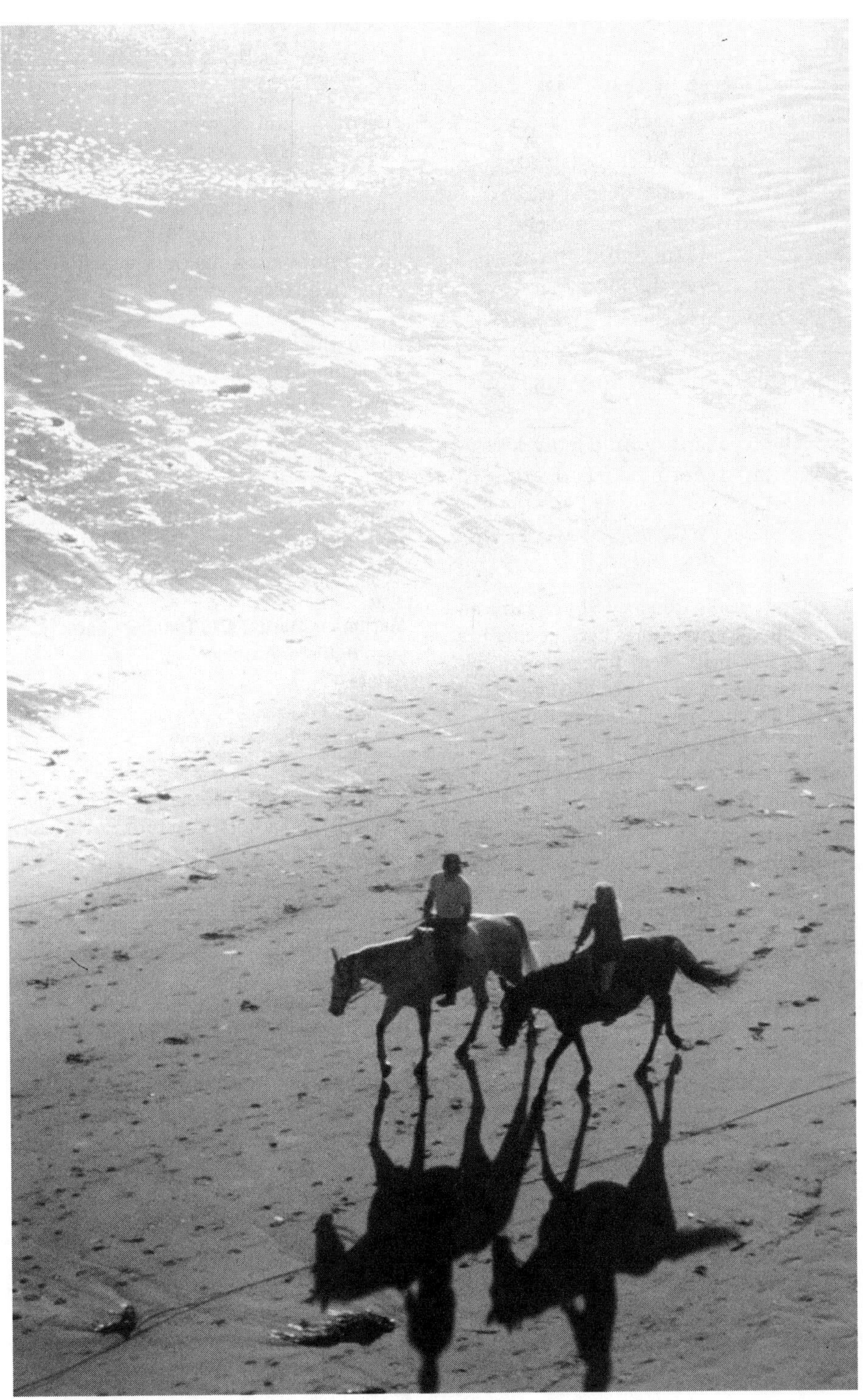

*Horseback riders enjoy a sunset trot on a deserted Santa Barbara beach.*
PHOTO: TOM TUTTLE, COURTESY OF THE SANTA BARBARA CONFERENCE & VISITORS BUREAU

**Insiders' Tip**

For information on Santa Barbara day hikes, beach strolls, town walks, bike trails, and wilderness areas, visit www.sb-outdoors.org. Have a question about recreation? "Ask the Outdoor Guy" by using the online e-mail form. He'll send you an answer in a couple of days.

bowl for free. Visitors pay $1 per game and are limited to five games per calendar year. Classes are held every few months, with free instruction and use of bowls, and individual instruction is also free. (After your lessons, you'll need to buy your own bowls.) Walk-ins are welcome. The club is open Monday, Wednesday, and Friday from 11:00 A.M. to 4:00 P.M., and Saturday from 10:00 A.M. to 4:00 P.M.

**Santa Barbara Lawn Bowls Green**
**1216 De la Vina Street**
**Santa Barbara, CA**
**(805) 965–1773**

The two greens here are open to club members and novices, who learn to bowl during a short training course. Out-of-town visitors need to be a member of a lawn bowls club to play and pay $1 per game. Walk-ins, either beginners or experienced lawn bowls club members, are welcome.

The annual membership for the local club is $150. The green is open Tuesday, Thursday, and weekends from 11:00 A.M. to 4:00 P.M.

## Martial Arts

Whether it's karate, tae kwon do, kung fu, t'ai chi, or sambo, you can find a variety of local schools willing to teach you the skills you seek. We've included a few and suggest you check the Yellow Pages of the local phone directory for others. Call for complete information on class schedules and prices, which vary widely.

**Aikido with Ki**
**255 Magnolia Avenue**
**Goleta, CA**
**(805) 967–3103**

Learn aikido and judo from a master at this small school, which has been in Goleta for more than 30 years. There's a free introductory lesson, and classes for men, women, and children are available.

**Macomber Martial Arts Training Center**
**5950 Hollister Avenue**
**Goleta, CA**
**(805) 687–2332**
**www.macomberkarate.com**

Macomber is a family martial arts center offering a range of classes for preschoolers, children, and adults. Call for information.

**Santa Barbara Martial Arts Academy**
**2610 De la Vina Street**
**Santa Barbara, CA**
**(805) 687–7488**

The Martial Arts Academy offers instruction in tae kwon do, kung fu, t'ai chi, kickboxing, and grappling. Free introductory classes are available.

**The Wu Shu Studio**
**23A W. Gutierrez Street**
**Santa Barbara, CA**
**(805) 965–5316**

This is the oldest martial arts studio in Santa Barbara, and is consistently voted the best martial arts studio in local newspaper polls. You'll find a good range of martial arts taught here, including kenpo, karate, kickboxing, kung fu, tai-chi, and jujitsu. There are classes for adults, children, seniors, and disabled persons.

## Skating

"Skating" is a rather passé term these days, as those clumsy old roller skates have given way to high-tech skateboards and in-line skates. Although Santa Barbara has no skating rinks, in-line skating is one of the most popular activities along the Cabrillo Boulevard waterfront. If you don't have your own, you can rent them from the places listed below. (Just remember to stay out of the way of bikes and quadracycles as you zip along the bike path.) All rentals include protective gear.

**Beach Rentals**
**22 State Street**
**Santa Barbara, CA**
**(805) 966-6733**

Rent your skates from this location, and you're a glide away from Cabrillo Boulevard. Rollerblades cost $7 for an hour, $3 for the second hour, $12 for 3 to 5 hours, and $20 for 24 hours.

**Cycles 4 Rent**
**101 State Street**
**Santa Barbara, CA**
**(805) 966-3804**
**Doubletree Resort**
**633 E. Cabrillo Boulevard**
**Santa Barbara, CA**
**(805) 564-4333**
**Radisson Hotel**
**1111 E. Cabrillo Boulevard**
**Santa Barbara, CA**
**(805) 963-0744**
**www.cycles4rent.com**

All three Santa Barbara locations of Cycles 4 Rent offer Rollerblades in addition to bikes and the popular quadracycles. Rental rates vary depending on the location, with the cheapest rates at 101 State Street. There, Rollerblade rental is $7 for one hour, and $12 for three to five hours.

## Rock Climbing

Set against the rugged backdrop of the Santa Ynez Mountains, Santa Barbara has some great crags for climbing. From huge boulders and steep sandstone cliff faces to dramatic overhangs and bluffs, avid climbers will find plenty to challenge them. If you're serious about the sport, we suggest you pick up a copy of *Rock Climbing: Santa Barbara and Ventura* by Steve Edwards. It lists more than 1,000 climbing routes in the area.

One of the most popular climbing spots in Santa Barbara is Gibraltar Rock. It's easily accessible and offers routes for climbers of all levels. To get there, wind up Mountain Drive past Sheffield Reservoir, veer left, and turn right on Gibraltar Road. Continue about 5 miles up Gibraltar Road and you'll see the rock on the left hand side. Painted Cave has some of the best bouldering in Santa Barbara. The boulders hang over Painted Cave Road off Highway 154. You'll find them about a mile before the Chumash Painted Cave Historical Park.

If you're just starting out in the sport or want to brush up on your skills, UCSB Adventure Progams (805-893-3737, www.par.ucsb.edu) offers instruction for climbers of all levels—from total beginners to more advanced climbers. For three-hour classes, prices range from about $75 to $109 ($45 to $75 for UCSB students with ID). UCSB also has an indoor climbing center. Test your skills on the bouldering wall with its contoured 40-foot traverse, clamber up the 22-foot vertical wall with three different routes, or train on the rock rings. The center provides all the hardware and ropes. All you need to bring is a harness and chalk. The climbing center is open Monday through Thursday. Call for

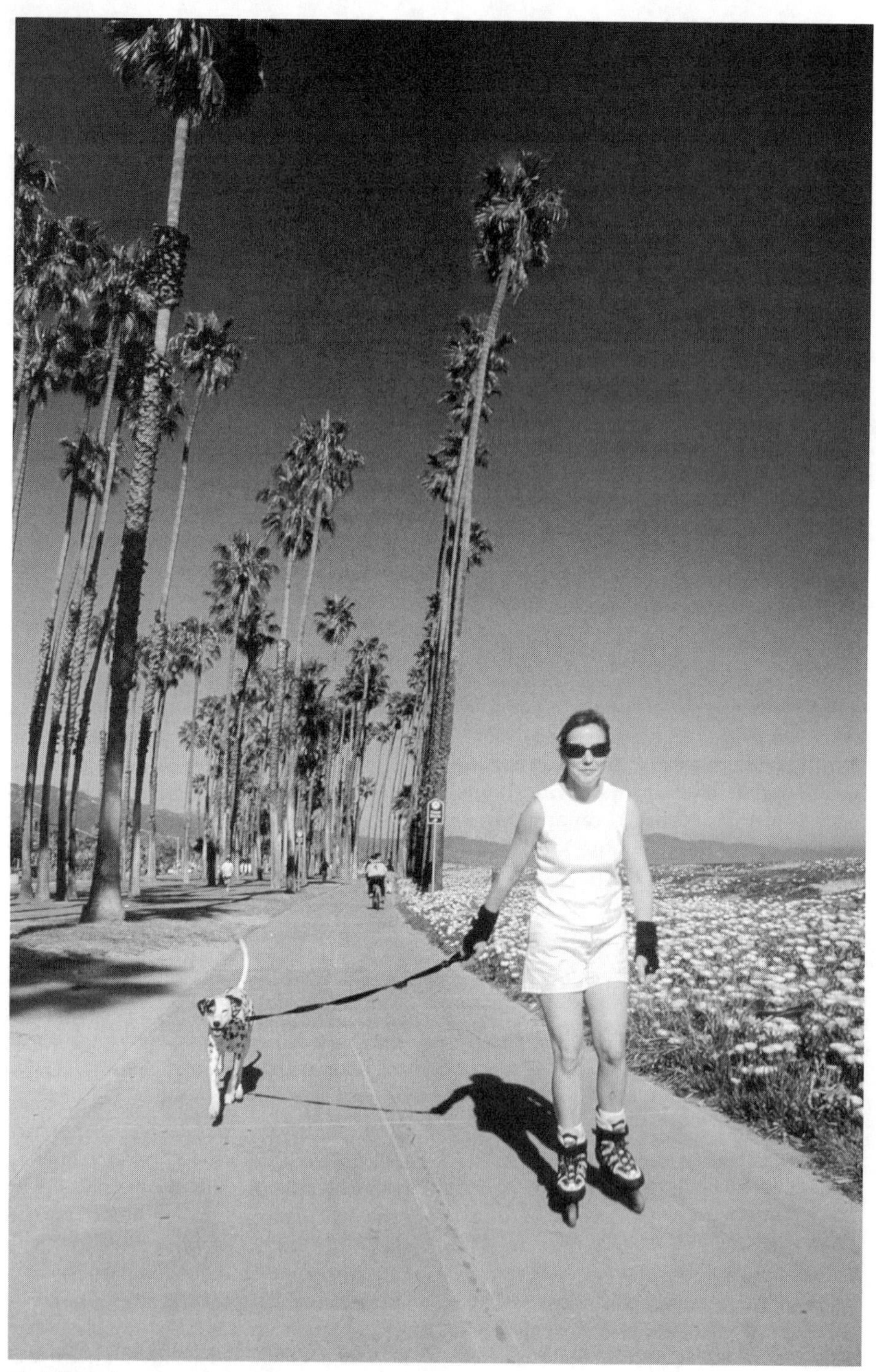

*The bike path at East Beach is a favorite spot for in-line skating.* PHOTO: BRIAN HASTINGS

more information. Adventours Outdoor Excursions (805-899-2929, www.adventours-inc.com) offers high-end rock-climbing trips for groups.

## Skiing

Although the nearest ski slopes are several hours away from Santa Barbara, you might want to contact the Santa Barbara Ski Club (P.O. Box 6751, Santa Barbara, CA 93160, www.sbski.org), a member of the Far West Ski Association. The club is open to people 21 and older, with annual dues of $40 for individuals, $70 for couples.

Meetings are held the first and third Wednesdays of the month during the ski season at the Chase Palm Park Center, and excursions to destinations such as Lake Tahoe, Vail, and Jackson Hole are regularly planned.

Also of interest is the Santa Barbara and Ventura County Ski and Snowboard Festival, which takes place at Ventura Fairgrounds each fall. It's a good place to see all the latest equipment and pick up brochures on your favorite skiing destinations. Call the fairgrounds at (805) 648-3376 or visit www.seasidepark.org for more information.

## Soccer

Soccer is one of the fastest-growing sports in Santa Barbara. There are countless leagues (both adult and children's—see the "Youth Sports" section in our Kidstuff chapter for information on children's leagues), and hard-fought matches take place all over town on just about any weekend. Soccer fields (called "multiuse" fields because they also accommodate a good old American football game as well as Ultimate Frisbee) are found in Santa Barbara at Chase Palm Park, E. Cabrillo and Santa Barbara Street; Dwight Murphy Field, Por la Mar Drive at Niños Drive; Las Positas Friendship Park, Las Positas Road and Jerry Harwin Parkway; MacKenzie Park, State Street and Las Positas Road; Pershing Park, Castillo Street and W. Yanonali Street; Shoreline Park, Shoreline Drive; Spencer Adams Park, Anapamu and De La Vina Streets; Girsh Park, Phelps Road, Goleta; Children's Park, Picasso Road, Isla Vista; Estero Park, Camino del Sur and Estero Road, Isla Vista. In Carpinteria, a field is located at Monte Vista Park, Bailard Avenue and Pandanus Street.

## Softball

Softball is actually more popular than baseball around here, and a number of city leagues (see the earlier Santa Barbara Parks and Recreation listing) take to the fields during the spring and summer season.

Even if you don't join a league, if the ballfields are not occupied by league play, you're welcome to round the bases at these locations in Santa Barbara (all fields are lighted): Cabrillo Ball Park, Cabrillo Boulevard; Dwight Murphy Field, Por la Mar Drive at Niños Drive (one field); Girsh Park, Phelps Road; Las Positas Friendship Park, Las Positas Road and Jerry Harwin Parkway (three fields); Ortega Park, E. Ortega Street and Calle Cesar Chavez (one field); and Pershing

### Insiders' Tip

Looking for a spot to kick a soccer ball, flick a Frisbee, or hit a few tennis balls? Visit www.totalsantabarbara.com. The site lists neighborhood parks, complete with colorful keys to all their facilities. Once you've found your destination, you can click on the link for maps and directions.

Park, Castillo Street and W. Cabrillo Boulevard (two fields).

Other area venues include El Carro Park, El Carro Lane and Namouna Street, Carpinteria (one field); Toro Canyon Park, Toro Canyon Park Road, Summerland (one field); Manning Park, San Ysidro and East Valley Roads, Montecito (one field); Stow Grove Park, La Patera Lane and Cathedral Oaks Road, Goleta (one field).

## Swimming

With all our sunshine and warm weather, swimming is a popular form of aerobic exercise in these parts, and there are a couple of public pools to choose from.

**Los Baños del Mar Pool**
**401 Shoreline Drive**
**Santa Barbara, CA**
**(805) 966–6110**

This 50-meter outdoor pool, opened in 1914 and formerly called "The Plunge," accommodates up to 300 swimmers every day. In 1997, the pool and deck were renovated, and a renovation of the showers, lockers, weight room, and plumbing was completed in the summer of 1998.

Especially popular with lap swimmers, the pool is used for Parks and Recreation programs such as year-round noon lap swims, adult swim lessons, aquamotion sessions, and coached morning and evening workouts. Fees vary, so call for complete information. Los Baños is open to the public only during limited summer afternoon hours.

**Carpinteria Valley Community Swimming Pool**
**5305 Carpinteria Avenue**
**Carpinteria, CA**
**(805) 566–2417**

Aqua aerobics, master classes, and children's swim lessons are just some of the activities and classes held at this community pool. Walk-ins are welcome for most classes and lap swimming usually goes on all day (6:00 A.M. to 7:00 P.M.). Recreational swimming is available from noon to 5:00 P.M. during the summer and every Saturday from noon to 4:00 P.M. At other times, call ahead and ask for availability.

## Tennis

In addition to its swanky private tennis clubs, the Santa Barbara area has a variety of public courts that are available on a first come, first served basis.

### Santa Barbara

In the city of Santa Barbara, permits are required for most public courts. They may be purchased on-site or from the Parks and Recreation Department at 620 Laguna Street. Daily permits are $3 per person; annual permits are $79 for adults and $69 for seniors 60 and older. Teens and children 17 and younger play free and do not need a permit. For information on any courts in the city of Santa Barbara, as well as on lessons, leagues, or local tournaments sponsored by the city, call (805) 564–5517.

The largest tennis facility in Santa Barbara is the Municipal Tennis Courts complex, at 1414 Park Place. You'll find 12 courts here, and the 1,000-seat center court stadium is the main venue for local tournaments. Open from dawn to dusk, the center has lockers, showers, restrooms, and equipment rentals. Three courts are lit until 9:00 P.M.

**Insiders' Tip**

Tennis anyone? The Santa Barbara Parks and Recreation Department (805-564-5418) offers classes and lessons and organizes singles, doubles, and team tennis leagues.

The Las Positas facility, at 1002 Las Positas Road, includes six lighted courts, backboards, showers, and restrooms, and is open until 9:00 P.M. nightly. The only other lighted courts in the city are at Pershing Park, 100 Castillo Street. The eight lighted courts here are used by the Santa Barbara City College tennis team and are open to the public only on weekends and on weekdays after 5:00 P.M. Play is available until 9:00 P.M. Monday through Friday. Oak Park, at 300 W. Alamar Avenue, has two unlighted courts open for public use daily from 6:00 A.M. to dusk.

### Montecito

Montecito has one public court in Manning Park, at San Ysidro and East Valley Roads. You can play for free here.

### Goleta

In Goleta, you'll find two courts at the Evergreen Open Space, in the 7500 block of Evergreen Drive; two at the Emerald Terrace Open Space, at Berkeley Road and Arundel Road; four at the Kellogg Tennis Courts, in the 600 block of Kellogg Avenue; and two in the Stow Open Space, located in the 6200 block of Stow Canyon Road.

## Ultimate Frisbee

Santa Barbara has been described as a hotbed of Ultimate Frisbee. In fact, UCSB's team, the Black Tides, have made it to the National Tournament 13 times and captured the National Championship 6 times. Every Saturday at 10:00 A.M. and Tuesday evenings at Chase Palm Park there's an informal pickup game, and intramural league play is big at UCSB—call (805) 893-3253 for information. There's a Frisbee Golf course in Goleta at the Evergreen Open Space, in the 7500 block of Evergreen Drive.

## Volleyball

Volleyball is big in Santa Barbara, especially on the beach, where you can show off your tan (and your body) while getting a good workout. The East Beach volleyball courts on E. Cabrillo Boulevard (there are 14 of them) are the most popular venues

*Beach volleyball is one of Santa Barbara's favorite pastimes.* PHOTO: BRIAN HASTINGS

for beach volleyball, and they are generally available on a first come, first served basis (although Courts 9 through 14 are reserved from noon to 1:30 P.M. weekdays for the Parks and Recreation Noontime Volleyball program).

Most major tournaments are held here, and tournament or league play sometimes takes up most of the courts, but you're welcome to snag one if it's free. Several other local beaches and parks have volleyball courts, including Manning Park in Montecito (one court); Leadbetter Beach in Santa Barbara (two courts); and Goleta Beach Park (one court), Stow Grove County Park (two courts), and Tucker's Grove Park (two courts) in Goleta. Other locations include Lookout Park in Summerland and Toro Canyon Park in Carpinteria.

Men's, women's, and coed indoor volleyball leagues are organized by Santa Barbara Parks and Recreation, with games at Santa Barbara City College and the Goleta Valley Youth Center. Call (805) 564-5422 for information.

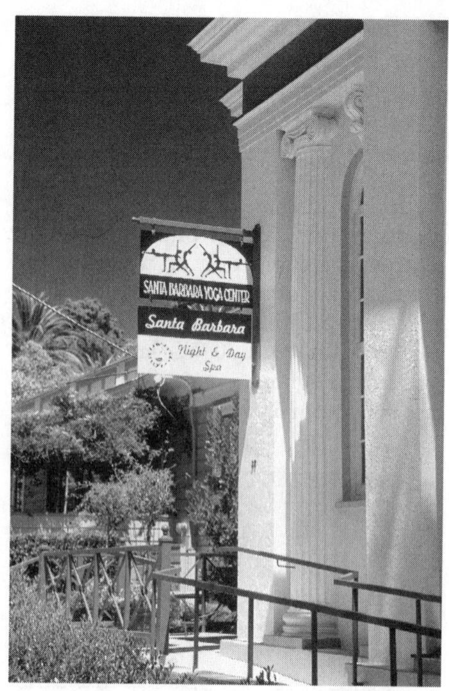

*Locals stay strong and supple at Santa Barbara's yoga centers.* PHOTO: BRIAN HASTINGS

## Yoga

**Santa Barbara Yoga Center**
**15 E. Micheltorena Street**
**Santa Barbara, CA**
**(805) 965-6045**
**www.santabarbarayogacenter.com**

You'll find more than 100 yoga classes a week at this busy center, including Gentle Hatha Yoga, Ashtanga, and Restorative Yoga just to name a few. Introduction to Yoga workshops are scheduled twice a month. Prices range from about $7 for a community class to $155 for a 30-day unlimited pass.

**The Yoga Studio**
**1911 De La Vina Street**
**Santa Barbara, CA**
**(805) 962-2234**
**www.theyogastudio.net**

Introductory classes are taught Tuesdays and Thursdays here, and you can surely find a class to match your strength and fitness level among the studio's 40 classes a week. Special packages are available for beginners, but class costs are normally $10 each, with a $69 pass entitling you to attend an unlimited number of classes each month.

## Athletic Clubs

The greater Santa Barbara area has a large number of health and fitness clubs with varied programs and facilities. Most will not quote membership prices over the phone, but require you to come in, take a tour, and then choose from several membership options.

Generally, individual and family memberships are offered at each club, and special packages and discounts are often available, so be sure to ask if you are considering joining. Many clubs also allow a complimentary session to familiarize you with the facilities. If you're in town for a few days, ask about day-use fees, which are also commonly available.

## Santa Barbara

**East Beach Bathhouse**
**1118 E. Cabrillo Boulevard**
**Santa Barbara, CA**
**(805) 897–2680**

Open 8:00 A.M. to 5:00 P.M. Monday through Friday and 10:00 A.M. to 5:00 P.M. on weekends, with extended hours during the summer, the bathhouse is situated right on the beach and offers weight rooms, beach volleyball courts, lockers, showers, and beach supplies and rentals. Best of all, there's no membership fee, and you can choose to pay a small fee by the day (about $2.50) or buy a $57 punch-card, which is good for 30 visits. Beach-friendly wheelchairs are also available here at no charge.

**Fitness Gallery**
**2285 Las Positas Road**
**Santa Barbara, CA**
**(805) 687–8222**

With its membership limited to women, the Fitness Gallery provides the kind of privacy that many women seek. More than 50 classes are scheduled each week, and equipment includes free weights, Stairmasters, treadmills, and everything else you'll need to get fit for swimsuit season. Childcare is also provided. Hours are 6:00 A.M. to 9:30 P.M. Monday through Thursday, 6:00 A.M. to 8:00 P.M. Friday, 8:00 A.M. to 6:00 P.M. Saturday, and 8:00 A.M. to 1:00 P.M. Sunday.

**Gold's Gym**
**21 W. Carrillo Street**
**Santa Barbara, CA**
**(805) 965–0999**
**3908 State Street**
**Santa Barbara, CA**
**(805) 563–8700**
**www.goldsgym.com**

Voted the "Best Gym in Santa Barbara" in a recent local newspaper poll, Gold's offers weight training, aerobics classes, personal trainers, a cardiovascular center, and a private women's gym. Childcare is available at the State Street location. Gold's is open 5:00 A.M. to 11:00 P.M.

*The historic East Beach Bathhouse offers fitness facilities right on the beach.* PHOTO: JOHN B. SNODGRASS

Monday through Thursday, 5:00 A.M. to 10:00 P.M. Friday, 7:00 A.M. to 9:00 P.M. Saturday, and 7:00 A.M. to 8:00 P.M. Sunday. The Carillo Street location is open an hour later on Friday and Saturday.

**Santa Barbara Athletic Club**
**520 Castillo Street**
**Santa Barbara, CA**
**(805) 966-6147**
**www.sbathleticclub.com**

Aerobics, yoga, and self-defense classes are available here as well as an outdoor lap pool, a weight room, and a spinning studio. You'll also find saunas, steam rooms, and spas, plus a childcare facility where you can leave the kids while you work out. A free towel and a locker are provided on each visit. The SBAC is open 5:30 A.M. to 10:30 P.M. Monday through Thursday, 5:30 A.M. to 10:00 P.M. Friday, 7:00 A.M. to 8:00 P.M. Saturday, and 8:00 A.M. to 8:00 P.M. Sunday.

**Santa Barbara Family YMCA**
**36 Hitchcock Way**
**Santa Barbara, CA**
**(805) 687-7727**
**www.Ciymca.org**

The usual family-oriented YMCA atmosphere prevails here, with classes and activities for the young and old. Serious fitness buffs will appreciate the circuit, free-weight, and cardio-training equipment and aerobics classes as well as the large pool, which is open for lap swimming, water aerobics classes, and recreational swimming.

The kids can take swim lessons or join in group recreational programs. Childcare is available. The Y is open weekdays 6:00 A.M. to 10:00 P.M., Saturday 7:00 A.M. to 7:00 P.M., and Sunday 11:00 A.M. to 6:00 P.M.

**Santa Barbara Gym and Fitness Center**
**615 Garden Street**
**Santa Barbara, CA**
**(805) 962-1544**

More of a "gym" in the traditional sense than a health club, the Santa Barbara Gym and Fitness Center offers free weights, Stairmasters, treadmills, rowing machines, stationary bikes, and much more, with doors that roll back to let in the fresh air and give you the illusion of being in the great outdoors. Hours are 5:00 A.M. to 10:00 P.M. Monday through Friday, and 7:00 A.M. to 7:00 P.M. weekends.

**World Kickboxing Gym**
**29 W. Anapamu Street**
**Santa Barbara, CA**
**(805) 963-7736**

Specializing in kickboxing, boxing, muay thai, sambo, and tae kwon do, the World Kickboxing Gym features a full weight room, boxing ring, and plenty of punching bags. It also has Stairmasters, treadmills, locker rooms, and showers. The gym is open 9:00 A.M. to 9:00 P.M. Monday through Friday and 11:00 A.M. to 5:00 P.M. Saturday and Sunday.

## Goleta

**Cathedral Oaks Athletic Club**
**5800 Cathedral Oaks Road**
**Goleta, CA**
**(805) 964-7762**
**www.calwestgroup.com/coac**

This popular family swim, tennis and athletic club features a full fitness area with Stairmasters, treadmills, stationary bikes, and free weights; two outdoor heated pools; a Jacuzzi; and 12 tennis courts, 8 of which are lighted. Also available are aerobics, step aerobics, aqua aerobics, and yoga classes, plus a variety of programs for children and teens.

There's a definite family feel here. It's open 5:30 A.M. to 9:30 P.M. Monday through Friday and 8:00 A.M. to 9:30 P.M. weekends.

**Gold's Gym**
**6144 Calle Real**
**Goleta, CA**
**(805) 964-0556**
**www.goldsgym.com**

This Gold's gym serves the Goleta and nearby UCSB student communities. Weight training, a cardio center, aerobics classes, and a private women's gym are all there for the serious fitness buff, and childcare is available.

Gold's is always voted one of the top gyms in Santa Barbara in local polls. It's open 5:00 A.M. to 11:00 P.M. Monday through Thursday, 5:00 A.M. to 9:00 P.M. Friday, and 7:00 A.M. to 8:00 P.M. Saturday and Sunday.

**Goleta Valley Athletic Club**
**170 Los Carneros Way**
**Goleta, CA**
**(805) 968–1023**
**www.gvac.net**

One of the largest fitness clubs in town, the Goleta Valley Athletic Club offers aerobics classes, fitness and cardiovascular equipment, free weights, handball, racquetball, yoga, kickbox aerobics, self-defense classes, and senior fitness classes. In addition, it has an outdoor lap pool, indoor and outdoor whirlpools, a sauna, and facilities for massage and yoga. Rock climbing and volleyball are also available. Hours are 5:00 A.M. to 11:00 P.M. Monday through Thursday, 5:00 A.M. to 9:00 P.M. Friday, and 8:00 A.M. to 8:00 P.M. weekends.

## Montecito

**Montecito Athletic Club**
**40 Los Patos Way**
**Montecito, CA**
**(805) 969–4379**

This 3,500-square-foot facility opened in February 1998 to rave reviews. Facilities include state-of-the-art Life Fitness equipment, free weights, a Pilates studio, custom-designed men's and women's locker rooms, a full-service cappuccino bar with an outdoor patio, and a second-floor mezzanine with the latest cardiovascular equipment. Hours are 5:00 A.M. to 9:00 P.M. Monday through Friday, 7:00 A.M. to 5:00 P.M. on weekends.

**Montecito Family YMCA**
**591 Santa Rosa Lane, Montecito**
**(805) 969–3288**
**www.ciymca.org**

The family-friendly atmosphere of the Y appeals to many, and you'll find a full lineup of youth lessons, classes and sports, as well as facilities for adults who are serious about keeping fit. Facilities include a large pool, free weights, and cardio training equipment, as well as tennis, handball, and racquetball courts. Aerobics and aqua aerobics are offered, and childcare is available. The Y is open 6:00 A.M. to 9:00 P.M. Monday through Friday, 7:00 A.M. to 6:00 P.M. Saturday, and noon to 6:00 P.M. on Sunday.

## Carpinteria

**The Firm Athletic Club**
**4945 Carpinteria Avenue**
**Carpinteria, CA**
**(805) 566–1003**

Carpinteria's only fitness club features Nautilus equipment, Jazzercise, a cardiovascular room, a massage studio, free weights, yoga, and tanning. There's also a juice and smoothie bar. The club is open 5:00 A.M. to 10:00 P.M. Monday through Friday, 7:00 A.M. to 7:00 P.M. Saturday, and 8:00 A.M. to 7:00 P.M. Sunday.

# Golf

Santa Barbara
Goleta
Carpinteria
Over the Pass

Santa Barbara is a great place to play golf. With the ocean to the south and the beautiful Santa Ynez Mountains to the north, you are practically guaranteed a gorgeous view no matter where you play, and our year-round sunshine makes for perfect playing conditions.

Although many local courses are private, a few hotels offer guest privileges at nearby private courses, so explore that option if you have your eye on a particular course. For example, Montecito Inn offers golf privileges at the Montecito Country Club.

There is also a good variety of public courses. Two relatively new ones are the Glen Annie Golf Club in Goleta and the Rancho San Marcos Golf Course, 12 miles north of Santa Barbara on Calif. Highway 154. Although the openings of these courses were widely heralded (they were the first regulation courses to open in Santa Barbara in 25 years), local golfers continue to complain that golf is too expensive in Santa Barbara. It's true that the greens fees for weekend play at one of the new courses are $140, and it costs more than $130 to play a round at the Sandpiper Golf Course, but you pay less if you play during the week, later in the afternoon, or at one of the less pricey public courses.

This chapter includes information on public courses in the greater Santa Barbara area as well as details about the Rancho San Marcos course, which is a bit farther out. If you're still looking for a bargain, drive up the coast to Lompoc's 18-hole La Purisima Golf Course (805–735–8395), which was rated one of the "Top 75 Affordable Courses" by *Golf Digest.*

Note that all fees listed here include the use of a cart, so you can expect to save money if you hoof it. Also, most courses offer discounts to Santa Barbara residents, seasonal specials, and lower twilight rates. Be sure to ask about specials when you call.

## Santa Barbara

**Hidden Oaks Golf Course**
**4760 Calle Camarada**
**Santa Barbara, CA**
**(805) 967–3493**

This picturesque little nine-hole, 1118-yard course is almost literally hidden in the oaks south of Hollister Avenue. Once a lemon orchard, Hidden Oaks is a rather hilly par 27, and you play the whole course with irons. This is a great little practice course, especially for chipping and putting. The longest hole is 173 yards. Fees are $10 on weekdays, $11 on weekends, with discounts available for junior golfers and seniors 62 and over. No electric carts are available, but you can rent a pull-cart if you wish. Hidden Oaks operates on a first come, first served basis.

**Santa Barbara Golf Club**
**Las Positas**
**3500 McCaw Avenue**
**Santa Barbara, CA**
**(805) 687–7087**

One of the most popular courses in town, the par-70, 18-hole Santa Barbara Golf Club is owned by the City of Santa Barbara. In addition to public golf, the 6009-yard course offers many activities including leagues for men, women, and couples. The club also sponsors a junior golf program in conjunction with the city's Parks and Recreation Department.

In 1998 the course began a series of improvements that will continue over the

*Santa Barbara has some of the most scenic golf courses in the country.* PHOTO: BRIAN HASTINGS

next several years, including upgrading greens 1 and 6 to PGA standards, installing new hitting stalls at the driving range, and building tee-to-green concrete cart paths for all holes. While these improvements are going on, however, you can still play this challenging course, which has several hilly sections and some strategically placed trees.

This course has been called the most affordable course of its quality in town, so it's definitely worth checking out. Also onsite are Mulligan's Cafe (with a banquet room), a putting green, and a 15-stall driving range. Fees are $28 on weekdays and $37 on weekends, with reduced twilight fees ($18 on weekdays and $23 on weekends) available after 2:00 P.M. in summer and 12:30 P.M. in winter. Soft spikes are required on the course. Reservations are recommended.

Santa Barbara County residents can purchase a resident card ($10 to $75, depending on the plan), which entitles them to a sizable discount on greens fees. Nine-hole rounds are also an option.

## Goleta

**Glen Annie Golf Club**
**405 Glen Annie Canyon Road**
**Goleta, CA**
**(805) 968–6400**
**www.glenanniegolf.com**

Making its debut in December 1997, the 6420-yard, par 72 Glen Annie Golf Club was expertly designed by Damian Pascuzzo and Robert Muir Graves. Snuggled into the foothills in west Goleta, it offers panoramic views and a large variety of unusual and personal services.

Your clubs are picked up when you arrive in the parking lot and are loaded into a cart, which will be ready to go when you reach the clubhouse. Each cart is equipped with a computer screen that shows the layout of each hole and the distance to the green, giving golfers an advantage in planning their shots.

Among the more challenging holes are the par-5 10th, which is the longest at 557 yards (uphill). A lake and 10-foot waterfall are visible on holes 4, 17, and 18.

In addition to a pro shop, a lighted 32-spot driving range, and other amenities, the club boasts an excellent restaurant, the Frog Bar & Grill (see our Restaurants chapter).

Fees for Santa Barbara County residents are $50 Monday through Friday, $60 on weekends. Proof of residency is required. Nonresidents pay $20 to $25 more. Twilight rates represent a significant savings over regular greens fees. Soft spikes are required on the course.

**Ocean Meadows Golf Club**
**6925 Whittier Drive**
**Goleta, CA**
**(805) 968–6814**

A nine-hole, par-36 course that has been operating in Goleta for more than 30 years, Ocean Meadows needs a bit of sprucing up, but it offers one of the most affordable games in town. There are two par-5 holes and two long par 3s, with water at the sides of most holes. Since the course borders Devereux Slough, you might even see some wildlife. Ocean Meadows has a driving range, putting and chipping greens, and sand bunkers for practicing, and you can arrange a lesson if you want to improve your game. Fees are $23 on weekdays and $25 on weekends for nine holes. Student, junior, and senior discounts are available, as are twilight rates.

**Sandpiper Golf Course**
**7925 Hollister Avenue**
**Goleta, CA**
**(805) 968–1541**
**www.sandpipergolf.com**

Sandpiper occupies a winning location next to the new Bacara Resort & Spa. But the course draws mixed reviews. Local golfers have called this par-72, 18-hole beauty everything from a giant rip-off to the best course in the world. While some complain about the high cost of a round of golf, the slow pace on the course, and fairways that are not always in tip-top shape, others say this seaside course provides the ultimate golfing experience.

Regardless of what the locals say, *Golf Digest* has rated Sandpiper among the top 25 public courses in the country (it was among the top 75 upscale courses in 1998), and the PGA scheduled a tour qualifying round here in 1996. Designed by William Bell and opened in 1972, the course is 6597 yards, and the back nine is literally on the edge of the Pacific.

Fees are $130 both during the week and on weekends. For a good deal, play between 3:00 P.M. and dark for the special twilight rate of $57 Monday through Thursday and $72 Friday through Sunday. Soft spikes are required.

**Twin Lakes Golf Course and Learning Center**
**6034 Hollister Avenue**
**Goleta, CA**
**(805) 964–1414**
**www.twinlakesgolf.com**

Twin Lakes, which sits near the bank of a Goleta creek, is a nine-hole, 1504-yard executive course. It has several challenging holes with water and tight dogleg turns, and a mere slip of the wrist may put you out of bounds.

Twin Lakes boasts one of the best driving ranges in the greater Santa Barbara area, with 30 high-tech driving stations that are lighted at night. In fact, it is estimated that almost 50 percent of the golfers who come to Twin Lakes do so for instruction and practice.

Greens fees are very affordable—$10 on weekdays and $11 on weekends. No carts are available.

## Carpinteria

Carpinteria doesn't have a golf course, but its Tee Time Driving Range, at 5555 Carpinteria Avenue (805–566–9948), is open for practice from 7:30 A.M. to 8:00 P.M. daily. The lighted range includes sand traps and putting greens, so you can practice all your skills. Golf lessons are also available. Fees are $4 for a small bucket of balls, $7 for a large bucket, and $12 for a jumbo bucket.

*Beautiful Sandpiper Golf Course skirts the Pacific.* PHOTO: NIK WHEELER, COURTESY OF SANTA BARBARA CONFERENCE & VISITORS BUREAU

## Over the Pass

**Rancho San Marcos Golf Course**
**4600 Calif. Highway 154**
**Santa Barbara, CA**
**(805) 683–6334**
**www.rsm1804.com**

You'll have to drive 12 miles north of Santa Barbara to reach Rancho San Marcos, but most golfers think playing a round here is worth it. The 18-hole, par-71 course, designed by Robert Trent Jones, Jr., opened in January 1998 to rave reviews.

It cost $16 million to build the course, and every penny is evident in the 7000-yard beauty, which offers views of Cachuma Lake, the Santa Ynez Valley, and the mountains. More than 1,700 oak trees dot the course, many of them two centuries old.

Every hole has a name, such as "The Vineyard" (the 524-yard, par-5 opening hole), "Long View" (No. 6, at 585 yards), and "Twin Oaks" (No. 8, which doglegs between two oak trees). Glen Griffith, Rancho San Marcos's PGA head pro, reports that the Pepsi and Buy.com tours have shown interest in the course. Casey Paulson, the club's Director of Operations is also a PGA pro. In addition to the 18 challenging and well-maintained holes, golfers will find a driving range, chipping and putting green, a clubhouse, and pro shop.

Although a cafe here serves food and beverages, no alcohol is available, to keep drivers who may be alcohol-impaired off dangerous Calif. 154 (see our Getting Here, Getting Around chapter for information on the dangers of traveling this road).

Fees are relatively steep: $119 Monday through Thursday, and $139 Friday through Sunday. Twilight rates are available after 2:30 P.M. at considerable discounts. In an effort to encourage local youngsters, Santa Barbara County kids 18 and younger can play the course for $19 Monday through Thursday and $39 Friday through Sunday. Soft spikes are required.

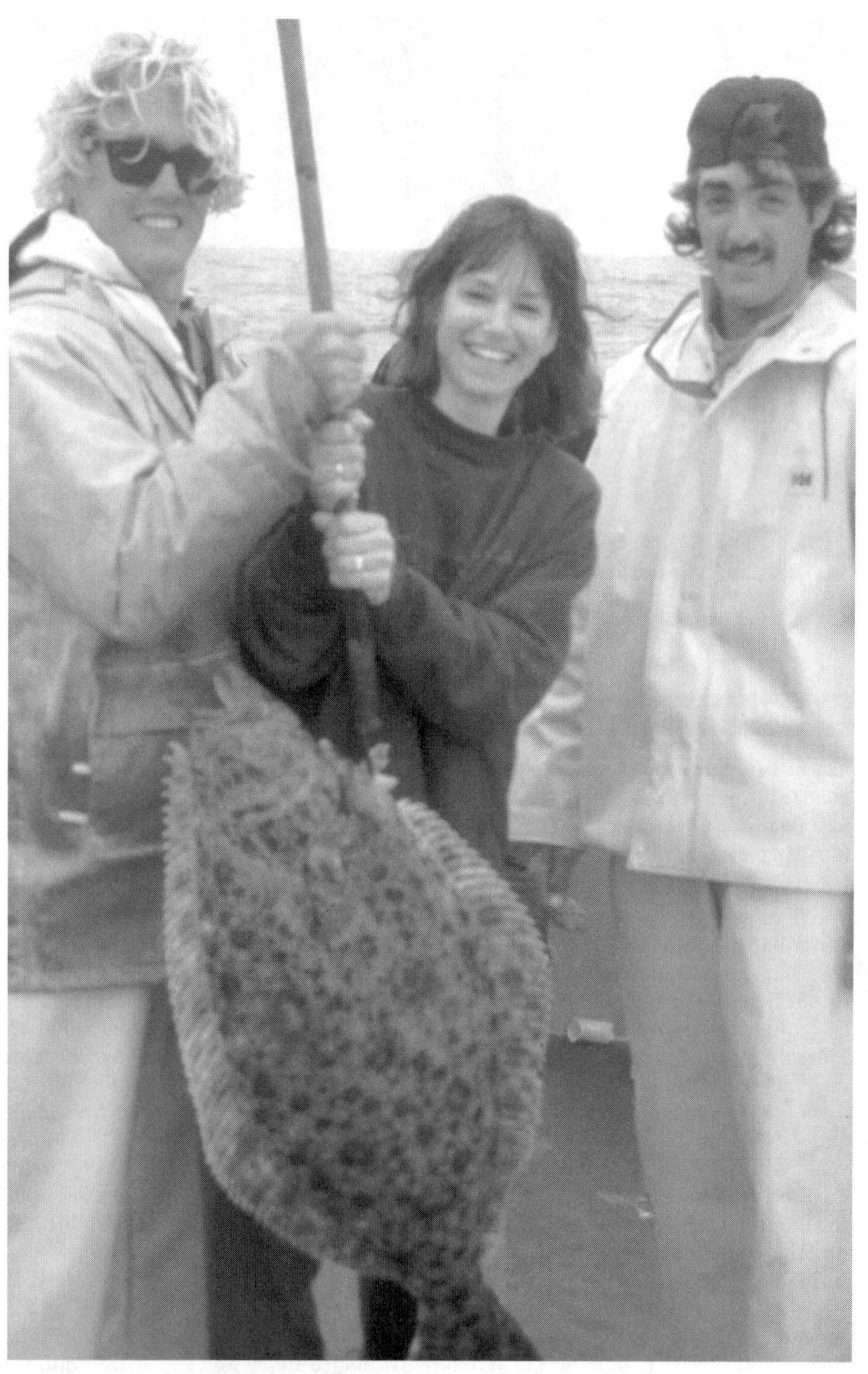

*A happy angler requires help displaying her prize.* PHOTO: CONDOR PHOTOS

# Fishing



Santa Barbara doesn't compare with some of the more famous sport-fishing areas of the world, for example Cabo San Lucas or the Florida Keys. We don't have many marlin, tuna, or dorado (although sometimes warm-water El Niño conditions send them this way). But the area does offer excellent opportunities to catch an array of fish in the ocean as well as in freshwater streams and artificial lakes.

Santa Barbara has always been blessed with an abundance of fish, mollusks, crustaceans, and other forms of marine life. The Chumash Indians found fish aplenty in the channel, rivers, and creeks. For more than a century, successful commercial fishing enterprises have supplied area homes and restaurants with a wide range of tasty bounty.

Given this bounty, angling is a local favorite pastime. You can cast your line from a party boat near the islands, off the Breakwater, into the surf, or beneath the calm waters of Cachuma Lake. And if Lady Luck passes you by, you can at least enjoy a few relaxing hours surrounded by incredibly beautiful scenery.

## A Channel Full of Surprises

Santa Barbara County is the northern part of what's called the Southern California Bight. From Point Conception about 50 miles to Ventura, the coastline stretches east-west rather than the north-south orientation that dominates the rest of the California coast.

About 25 miles off the coast lie the Santa Barbara Channel Islands, which also stretch from east to west. This unusual orientation has created the Santa Barbara Channel, an area often protected from the larger ocean swells of the open Pacific.

The channel is a crossroads where cold water masses from the north converge with warmer masses from the south. North of Point Conception, the water is cold most of the year because the prevailing northwest winds cause an upwelling of water. South of the point, ocean waters gradually warm, although Santa Barbara waters are cool most of the year.

As the channel waters warm and cool with the seasons, game fish from the north and south migrate in and out of the area, resulting in a fascinating potpourri of species. At certain times of year, for example, you might catch warm-water barracuda and cold-water king salmon on the same day. This is one of the only places in California where you'll find such a mix.

## Useful Guides

Pick up a free copy of the California Department of Fish and Game's *Guide to Ocean Sportfishing in Santa Barbara and Ventura Counties*. This clear, easy-to-read booklet is useful for any angler, but it especially targets novices and people who are unfamiliar with channel resources. It gives a general description of popular fishing sites, catch species, and fishing techniques. You can also pick up the *California Marine Fish Identification* guide. These guides are available at the Department of Fish and Game's office at 1933 Cliff Drive, Suite 9, Santa Barbara (805–568–1231).

To learn more about Pacific Ocean fish, you can purchase *Probably More than*

**Insiders' Tip**

The weather in the channel often turns nasty in the afternoon, when the winds pick up. Be sure to tune in to your weather radio or the Weather Channel (46) to get the latest forecast, especially if you're going out in a private boat.

*You Wanted to Know About the Fishes of the Pacific Coast: A Humorous Guide to Pacific Fishes* by Milton Love. It's available at most local bookstores.

## Fishing Licenses and Regulations

Anyone 16 or older needs a sport-fishing license to take any fish, including mollusks and crustaceans, from California waters. However, you do not need a license to take fish from a public pier. Everyone must adhere to catch and season restrictions and size limits. Ask for a current list of regulations when you buy your license.

### Fishing Licenses

**Annual: $30.45 for residents, $81.65 for nonresidents**

**Ten-day nonresident sport-fishing: $30.45 (valid for 10 consecutive days from purchase date)**

**Resident Pacific Ocean–only sport-fishing: $17.85**

**Two-day sport-fishing: $11.05 for residents and nonresidents (valid for fishing in both inland and ocean waters)**

**One-day Pacific Ocean–only: $6.55 for residents and nonresidents (allows you to take fin fish, but not mollusks or crustaceans)**

**One-day Pacific Ocean–only (fin fish only) with an Ocean Enhancement Stamp: $7.10 for residents and nonresidents (the stamp is required for ocean fishing south of Point Arguello)**

By state law, you must display your valid sport-fishing license by attaching it to your outer clothing at or above the waistline so that it is plainly visible. If you're diving from a boat or shore, you may leave your license on the boat or within 500 yards of shore. If you're caught fishing without a license, you risk a minimum $250 fine. So don't forget it!

Licenses can be obtained at authorized bait and tackle stores, most sporting goods stores, SEA Landing, and Harbor Tackle at the harbor, and most county and state campgrounds. You can also buy licenses on-line at www.dfg.ca.gov.

The *California Sport Fishing Regulations Book* provides details on the seasons, limits, and sizes allowed for each fish species. You should also ask about any supplements to this manual, as the state often issues periodic updates to be used in combination with the larger publication. Both books and supplements are available at bait and tackle shops and sport-fishing enterprises.

For more information regarding regulations and licenses, call or write the California Department of Fish and Game, 1933 Cliff Drive, Suite 9, Santa Barbara (805–568–1231). Better still, visit their Web site at www.dfg.ca.gov.

## Where to Fish

To help you become more familiar with the different places you can fish around Santa Barbara, we've divided this section into five areas: the Coast, the Islands, Pier Fishing, Surf Fishing, and Freshwater Fishing.

## The Coast

The three main habitats along the Santa Barbara coast are the kelp beds, sandy bays and beaches, and open waters up to several miles from shore.

The main characteristic of our coastal waters is the presence of giant kelp (actually an algae) that grows in waters from 20 to 80 feet deep. Although rooted mainly to rocky bottoms, kelp can take root in soft bottoms in the more protected regions of the coastline.

Giant kelp can create dense underwater forests that provide shelter for a variety of marine life. The tops of the kelp canopies look like glassy brown patches spread along the surface of the water. While a source of many catches for anglers, kelp beds can also be a huge source of frustration. Lines often get tangled and break in the rubbery strands.

Stretches of sandy beaches break up the kelp beds along the coastline, giving you a chance to troll freely for bottom species. Open waters generally encompass areas up to several miles offshore and provide an ideal home for more pelagic species.

In the kelp beds, the kelp (or calico) bass reigns as king of the coast. These delectable bass range from 2 to 10 pounds. They are generally found in dense kelp beds but also make their home in rocky reefs. Calicos can be caught in many ways; the most common is casting with scampi lures or live anchovies. Calicos are present just about any time of year but seem to be most active during summer and fall months.

The white sea bass is another prize catch in the kelp bed areas, but it's hard to find because its numbers are dwindling. White sea bass fishing usually occurs in short flurries, as schools of these croakers come and go quickly. White sea bass range from about 15 to 30 pounds, but can weigh as much as 75 pounds. Thanks to a restocking program in Southern California, the future of this fish looks bright. They are best caught with live bait such as anchovy or squid.

Other edible species that can be caught in the kelp bed areas include cabezon, sheepshead, a variety of rock fish, sculpin, and lingcod. The prime season to catch each species varies, but most are generally available year-round.

The California halibut is probably the most sought-after prize in Santa Barbara coastal waters. This flat fish tends to dwell on wide expanses of sandy bottoms, but you can also find it on sand patches in kelp forests. Although fish in excess of 40 pounds have been taken, large halibuts these days average about 25 pounds. The sweet, flaky flesh of this hard-fighting fish makes for excellent dining.

To maximize your chance of catching halibut, you should troll on the bottom with a salmon-type rig—a large flasher baited with an anchovy and weighted with a one- to two-pound sinker. Drifting and casting with a small flasher and anchovy or live anchovy can also produce a good catch. The best time of year to catch halibut is during the spring and summer, when the water warms and the fish begin to spawn.

Other fish that inhabit the sandy coastlines include barred sand bass, corbina, and barred surf perch.

In the open waters offshore, you can catch more pelagic species. One of the most popular is the Pacific bonito, but its numbers have seriously declined in recent years. This member of the tuna family ranges from about 3 to 12 pounds. You can catch it on live anchovy or by trolling a variety of lures, including green gobblers or "Cojo" flies.

Bonito make good table fare and are best when bled immediately upon catching and eaten fresh. Pacific mackerel, although generally less than two pounds, tastes great when you cut it into chunks and cook it using a shake-and-bake method.

Although smaller than its Atlantic cousin, the California barracuda still puts up a good fight and can weigh up to 15 pounds. You'll have the best luck catching

*Prized for their tasty white meat, halibut are a popular catch in Santa Barbara waters.* PHOTO: BRIAN HASTINGS

this fish with live anchovies, but you can also achieve success by trolling with a bright lure. The peak season for most pelagic species is during the summer and early fall.

Every few years during the spring, migrating salmon can be found in the waters off the Santa Barbara area. King and silver salmon are the two most common species. These elusive fish usually appear when the local water is coldest. Their preference for cold water keeps them at a depth of about 100 to 150 feet. When a salmon run arrives, Santa Barbarans hit the water en masse.

About the only way to catch these fish locally is to use a salmon rig with a flasher and a one- to two-pound weight with a quick release and baited with an anchovy. The slow troll required for salmon fishing can be extremely boring, but the rewards are more than worth the effort.

Occasionally during summers with very warm water temperatures, such as those produced by El Niño, more tropical species can visit the coast of Santa Barbara. The most consistent visitor of this group is the yellowtail, a member of the jack family. It's the sign of a landmark season when anglers can catch these prized fish within several miles of the coastline. Yellowtail range from 10 to 30 pounds, but the larger ones can reach a weight of 45 pounds.

The preferred areas for yellowtail fishing include the offshore oil rigs near Naples reef (west of Santa Barbara) and Carpinteria. Use live bait, such as squid, mackerel, or anchovy, for the best shot at catching these fish. However, you can also catch them by trolling white feathers and larger lures that look like mackerels.

## The Islands

Four islands in the Santa Barbara Channel Island group run in an east-west chain about 25 miles offshore from the Santa Barbara coast: Anacapa, Santa Cruz, Santa Rosa, and San Miguel. In general, these islands offer better fishing than along the mainland due largely to the diversity of habitats and lower fishing impact. This windswept region of rock and water is famous for bottom fishing, and anglers routinely come home with a gunnysack full of fish.

**Insiders' Tip**

The California Department of Fish and Game designates one day in June and one day in September as free fishing days when no fishing license is required. Dates are listed in the *California Sport Fishing Regulations Book*.

Species include several types of rock fish. The most popular species include the vermilion rockfish or red snapper (the meat-and-potatoes of island fishing), lingcod, ocean white fish, cabezon, sheepshead, and sculpin. It's not uncommon to see anglers reel up a rock cod rig of six hooks from the depths with a fish on each hook.

The peak season for bottom fishing is usually during the winter months, but any time of the year can be fruitful. Halibut fishing along some of the sandy stretches of the islands during the warmer months can produce trophy-size fish.

The easiest way to access the islands is to hop on a party boat from the Santa Barbara Harbor (see the "Charter/Party Boats" section later in this chapter). However, be prepared for cold temperatures and rough seas, as the exposed outer channel is typically much windier than the coastal waters.

## Pier Fishing

The traditional roots of most local anglers are in pier fishing. You can cast a line off

> **Insiders' Tip**
>
> For local saltwater fly fishing information and monthly fishing reports, check out www.garybulla.com. You can also purchase flies specially designed to lure local species on the site.

Stearns Wharf or the Breakwater at the Santa Barbara Harbor. Licenses are not required unless you step out onto the sand and/or use live bait. You can also pier fish at Goleta and Gaviota Beaches, about 10 and 30 miles west of Santa Barbara, respectively. Both piers lie on sandy bottoms.

Off the pier, you're most likely to reel in barred surf perch, with a sprinkling of halibut, mackerel, jack, smelt, white croaker, yellowfin, and spotfin croaker. During the summer months, pier anglers are occasionally rewarded with a run of bonito and barracuda.

## Surf Fishing

Casting from shore is a popular form of fishing, both at sandy beaches and rocky coastlines. Some of the best sandy beaches for surf fishing include Jalama and Gaviota Beaches, about 50 and 30 miles west of Santa Barbara, respectively, and Carpinteria, about 10 miles east of Santa Barbara.

The main catches at these beaches are barred surf perch and an occasional halibut. You can also catch cabezon in the rough waters of Jalama and the scrumptious corbina (whose northern range is Santa Barbara) in Carpinteria. The best bait for these fish varies, but sand crabs, which can be dug from these beaches, usually bring the most success. Flyfishers are an increasingly common site along the beaches in Santa Barbara and Carpinteria. If you want to try your luck with a fly line, you'll find that surf perch, halibut, yellowfin croaker, and corbina are especially partial to clouser minnow flies, sand crab imitations, and surf rat flies.

The rocky coastlines in the region can offer some profitable fishing for rock fish, calico bass, and cabezon. The reefy areas near Gaviota and Goleta, about 10 miles west of Santa Barbara, are prime spots. Many of the fishing techniques used for kelp beds apply here.

California grunion ranks as one of the wonders of the Southern California marine world. This 5- to 7-inch member of the silversides family has the unique habit of coming ashore through the surf onto sandy beaches to mate and bury its eggs. Between March and September, these fish spawn three or four nights following each full or new moon and then for a one- to three-hour period immediately after high tide.

Females swim onto the beach and dig themselves into the sand to lay their eggs, while males flop next to them and fertilize the eggs. They achieve all this in a matter of seconds, then ride back into the ocean in a passing wave.

Grunion fishing (or hunting, as many locals call it) has been equated to snipe hunting, as a person can search for a lifetime and never experience this amazing phenomenon. Many people claim that the whole thing is really a hoax. In reality, grunion running does occur, but mainly on the darkest nights and on the darkest beaches away from human development.

In the Santa Barbara region, the best places to see grunion runs are Goleta Beach and beaches in the Carpinteria area. It is legal to take grunion by hand. However, just seeing a grunion run is reward enough for most people, as very few can truthfully say that they've seen this remarkable quirk of nature.

## Freshwater Fishing

Drive 35 miles northwest of Santa Barbara and you'll come across Cachuma Lake—the best freshwater fishing area in the county and one of the best bass fishing lakes in Southern California. Cachuma was created when the Bradbury Dam was built in the 1950s on the Santa Ynez River.

Surrounded by the Santa Ynez Mountains, the lake offers spectacular scenery as well as great fishing. On the shores you can spot many types of wildlife, from mountain lions, mule deer, and endangered pond turtles to osprey, kingfishers, and golden eagles. At certain times of year, you can also view several pairs of nesting American bald eagles and their offspring.

The lake water provides plenty of action for serious and not-so-serious anglers. Here you can find trout, small- and largemouth bass, catfish, bluegill, crappie, and redear perch. The lake is stocked with trout from October through May. Approximately 150,000 rainbow trout are planted annually. Licenses, bait, and tackle are available at the marina along with fish-cleaning stations. You can also rent a boat by the hour or day (see the "Charter/Party Boats" section below).

If you're into stream trout fishing, you'll find a few opportunities at the Los Padres National Forest north of Santa Barbara. The main fishery is in the Santa Ynez River above Cachuma Lake, where trout are stocked occasionally during the cooler months of the year. Other smaller streams in the backcountry offer small trout, but expect to hike a long distance to reach many of the more productive areas.

All forms of fishing appear to result in some success, for example using flies, spinners, and natural baits. A small steelhead trout fishery once existed below Bradbury Dam on the Santa Ynez River, which created Cachuma Lake. Due to dwindling numbers, however, no fishing is permitted on any rivers from the coastal peaks to the ocean. That means no casting for any species, and steelhead are now protected—so hands off! Although Lake Casitas in Ventura County lies outside the geographic region covered in this book (it's about 20 miles east of Santa Barbara), it merits mention because it's one of the best spots in California for catching trophy-size largemouth bass. It's also a great place for trout, catfish, bluegill, crappie, and redear perch. Call the Casitas Bait Shop at the lake for more information, (805) 649-2043.

## Charter/Party Boats

If you want to fish the coastal waters and don't have access to a private boat—or you just want the luxury of having someone else do the driving—Santa Barbara offers several party boats of various sizes. All the boats operate from the Santa Barbara harbor.

Prices vary, depending on whether you take a half- or all-day trip and whether you hug the coast or go out to the islands. Coastal half-day trips run about $29 for adults and $23 for kids and seniors. All-day island trips cost approximately $62 to $70 on weekdays and $79 on weekends.

All the party boats listed below have full galleys and experienced crews to help beginners. They also offer limited charter engagements, and tackle is available on a rental basis from all operators. Ventura and Oxnard, about 30 miles south of

### Insiders' Tip

Tide books are available free at all local tackle shops and many other stores in Santa Barbara. If you have a PDA, you may also download local tide charts from www.toolworks.com/bilofsky/tidetool.htm.

*A fisherman displays his catch after a successful excursion on the* Condor. PHOTO: CONDOR PHOTOS

Santa Barbara, also offer party boat operations. Call Captain Hook's Sportfishing in Ventura Harbor, (805) 382-6233, and Cisco's Sportfishing in Channel Islands Harbor, (805) 985-8511, for details.

## Santa Barbara

**Condor**
**SEA Landing**
**301 W. Cabrillo Boulevard**
**Santa Barbara, CA**
**(805) 963-3564, (888) 77-WHALE**
**www.condorcruises.com**

From February through May, the 88-foot *Condor* is busy taking people out in the channel to look for gray whales (see Whale-Watching in our Recreation chapter). For a few months following this season, the 125-passenger boat takes folks out on full-day fishing trips to the Channel Islands. From about September through November (depending upon when the whale-watching season finishes), it leaves Sundays, Wednesdays, and Fridays at 6:00 A.M. and returns at about 4:00 or 5:00 P.M. The cost is $48 per person. The *Condor* sometimes offers additional full-day trips to San Miguel on Saturdays during these months for $79 per person. Call to confirm the current schedule.

The boat has 34 bunks, and it's filled on a first come, first served basis. You're welcome to board the boat any time after 10:00 P.M. the night before. If all the bunks are occupied, you can snooze on a bench in the dining area or wherever you can find a spot. On weekends the boat sticks to a 34-passenger maximum. Schedules may change during blue whale–watching season, June through August. Call to confirm the current schedule.

**Stardust**
**SEA Landing, 301 W. Cabrillo Boulevard**
**Santa Barbara, CA**
**(805) 963-3564**

The 65-foot *Stardust* offers half-day deep-sea fishing trips. In the summer (and on weekends and holidays the rest of the year) the boat goes out twice a day, from 7:00 A.M. to noon and from 12:30 to 5:30 P.M. A twilight trip is also offered during the summer from 6:00 to 9:30 P.M. Wednesday through Friday. On weekdays from October through May, the *Stardust* goes out once daily from 10:00 A.M. to 3:00 P.M.

**WaveWalker Charters**
**Marina 3 Gate at the harbor**
**Santa Barbara, CA**
**(805) 964–2046 home**
**(805) 895–3273 cellular phone**
**www.wavewalker.com**

Seasoned skipper and writer Captain David Bacon and his 31-foot custom sport fisher *Grady-White* are available for charter for small groups of four to six passengers. Fees are $475 for a half-day morning or twilight trip, $600 for a three-quarter day, and $700 for an all-day coastal or island trip.

## Cachuma Lake

**Cachuma Boat Rentals**
**Cachuma Lake Marina**
**(805) 688–4040**

If you're planning to fish at Cachuma Lake, you can rent boats right at the marina. Motorboat rates range from $32 an hour for a four-passenger, 5-horsepower boat to $66 for a full-day rental of a six-passenger, 9.9-horsepower boat. Boats without motors range from $12 an hour to $34 for a day. Patio deck boats start at $75 an hour for a 10-passenger, 25-horsepower boat to $200 for a full day on a 14-passenger boat.

## Bait and Tackle Shops

You can find bait and tackle shops near any of the piers, at the harbor, at charter boat landings, and at Cachuma Lake and Lake Casitas—here are two of the more popular ones in town.

**Hook, Line and Sinker**
**4010 Calle Real**
**Santa Barbara, CA**
**(805) 687–5689**

Hook, Line and Sinker is regularly named "Best Bait and Tackle Shop in Santa Barbara" in local media polls. It's conveniently situated near the intersection of State Street and Calif. Highway 154, which is right on the way to Cachuma Lake. The staff here know a lot about all types of fishing in the area as well as all over the United States and Mexico, and they dispense information readily to newcomers and visitors.

**Harbor Tackle**
**117A Harbor Way**
**Santa Barbara, CA**
**(805) 962–4720**

Harbor Tackle is probably the best source for local saltwater fishing information. Stop in here for fresh and saltwater tackle, frozen bait, rod and reel repairs, and custom rod building. It's open 7 days a week.

# Beaches and Watersports



Santa Barbara just wouldn't be Santa Barbara without the beach and the ocean. For most of us, the beaches, bluffs and the blue channel waters are a recreational and spiritual staff of life. Here we take long walks, sunbathe, frolic, relax, and pursue our favorite watersports, which run the gamut from boating to windsurfing.

Thanks to the temperate climate, Santa Barbarans can enjoy the outdoors most of the year. It's a glorious feeling to think about the rest of the country in the dead of winter, locked in the icy grip of subzero temperatures, while we play on the beach in shorts, T-shirts, and bathing suits.

But there is a slightly less-than-perfect side to our waters you should probably know about before you plunge into the ocean. The water temperatures are not like those off the shores of the Caribbean or Mexico, where they average in the upper 70s. During the summer months, water temperatures here tend to be in the mid-to-high 60s. During the winter months they drop about 10 degrees to the mid-50s.

Many people wear wetsuits so they can stay in the water for hours. Some hardy souls, however, dive and dip without any extra coverage every month of the year. If you find the water a bit cold for your taste, remember that these very temperatures allow for the incredible diversity of marine life in the channel.

In this chapter we give you an overview of where you can go and what you can do in, on, under, over, and next to the water. We start with descriptions of our most popular beaches and places where you can rent or buy beach equipment. Then we highlight the area's major watersports, listed alphabetically: boating (including sailing), boat excursions/sightseeing, diving and snorkeling, kayaking, jet-skiing, parasailing, waterskiing, whale-watching, surfing, and windsurfing.

If you're visiting between February and the end of April, you might want to check out the "Whale-Watching" section of this chapter right away. You won't want to miss the chance to view one of nature's most amazing events—the annual gray whale migration. You can view blue whales, humpback whales, and other types of marine mammals year-round. Whatever time of year you're here, our beaches and waters beckon you to enjoy and explore.

## Parking

Before you set out on your waterfront adventures, you have to actually get to the beaches and watersports within the Santa Barbara city limits. Which means you must find parking. Looking for a vacant, affordable spot can be a real frustration during the summer and on busy holiday weekends. Here are a few pointers to help your beach days get off to a smooth start.

The city operates a number of parking lots along the beach side of Cabrillo Boulevard: near East Beach, Chase Palm Park, Garden Street, at the harbor, and at Leadbetter Beach. Although these lots are extremely convenient (who wants to cross Cabrillo Boulevard with beach equipment and children in tow?), they can also be expensive if you park there for more than a few hours.

On off-season weekdays (November through April) you can park for free in the lots at Leadbetter, Garden Street, and Chase Palm Park. But from May through September, during holiday seasons, and on weekends you will have to pay $1 for each hour or any part of an hour, with a maximum of $7 per day. In the Cabrillo East, Cabrillo West, and Harbor West lots, the honor system applies year-round and the fees are slightly cheaper. For $2 you get three hours of parking, with a maximum of $7 per day. In these lots, look for the signs directing you to the collection boxes and drop your fee in the one that corresponds with your parking stall. The harbor lot is open 24 hours, so if you need to leave your car overnight while you're out on a boat, you don't have to worry. The Harbor Patrol cruises the lot regularly.

It's very difficult to find on-street parking, especially on busy weekends and throughout the summer months. In fact, you need a resident permit to park for more than 90 minutes on weekends on many of the streets in the waterfront area. Tickets are frequent, and fines are high, so you probably won't want to test your luck with the meter patrol.

If you're going to be here for a while, we recommend buying an annual parking permit, which allows you to park free at any of the beachfront city lots except on Stearns Wharf. The permit (a sticker that goes on your windshield) costs $60 a year and is valid from January through December. Buy your permit on December 1 when they go on sale, and it will be valid for 13 months of parking. Buy it mid-way through the year and the fee will be prorated. They're available from the kiosks at the parking lot entrances or at the Harbor Patrol Office above the Chandlery on the harborfront. For waterfront parking information, call (805) 564-5523.

**Insiders' Tip**

Don't forget to cover up or rub on the sunscreen when you're outdoors in Santa Barbara, especially when you're out on the water. The sun's rays have a habit of making their presence known, even in winter and on foggy summer days.

## Beaches

The Santa Barbara coastline stretches more than 50 miles between Gaviota and Carpinteria, and you'll find many excellent beaches all along the way. Some are ideal for a family day at the beach—they have full facilities, including restrooms, playgrounds, restaurants, snack bars, and showers. Others have no facilities but boast great tidepools, perfect surfing waves, and wide stretches of sand for sunbathing.

Even if the weather isn't conducive to sunbathing, our beaches can be fantastic places to enjoy the natural surroundings. Here we describe most of our favorite beaches. A few others are not listed because they have very limited parking in residential areas and/or difficult-to-explain access by trails or paths through private property. Besides, you can reach most of these "secret" beaches by walking from the beaches described here at low tide.

Lifeguards are on duty at most of the beaches listed here from 10:00 A.M. to 6:00 P.M. daily from Memorial Day weekend (or mid-June) through Labor Day weekend. They are also on duty other weekends in May and September and sometimes in

October if warm weather prevails. If lifeguards are not available at a beach, we've noted it in the description.

Please keep a few rules in mind during your day at the beach. Bottles are not allowed on Santa Barbara city beaches (cans are fine). The same goes for open fires and burying coals. Use the designated barbecue pits, if the beach has them. Dogs are not allowed at all on most city beaches, which include East Beach, West Beach, and Leadbetter Beach. Nor are they allowed on the beaches in the state parks including El Capitan, Gaviota, and Refugio Beaches. However, you can walk your dog on a county beach, as long as it's on a leash. Don't litter! That includes cigarette butts. Please collect all your trash and put it in one of the many trash cans lining the waterfront and beaches.

With that said, we wish you many happy hours in the sun, sand, and sea!

## Santa Barbara

**Arroyo Burro Beach Park**
**2981 Cliff Drive**
**Santa Barbara, CA**
**(805) 687–3714**
**www.sbparks.org**

Most Insiders call this "Hendry's Beach," and it's one of our favorites. It stretches beneath the bluffs of Hope Ranch and continues for nearly 2 miles west toward Goleta and a short way east toward the Mesa. It's a great place to surf, sailboard, fish from the shore, watch dolphins swim by, and look at tidepools. From February through May you might also spot some gray whales passing by (bring your binoculars).

At low tide you can walk or run as far as Goleta Beach Park to the west and Shoreline Park to the east. At high tide, especially during the winter, you might not be able to walk as far, but the views are still wonderful. You're allowed to walk dogs here as long as they're on a leash. Lifeguards are on duty every day from mid-June through Labor Day.

Arroyo Burro has restrooms, outdoor showers, public telephones, and a grassy area with picnic tables. The Brown Pelican Restaurant offers beachside seating, ocean views, good food, and a lively bar. It serves breakfast, lunch, and dinner and Sunday brunch inside or on the patio. There's also a snack bar window outside the restaurant.

The beach parking lot lies about a half-block west of the Cliff Drive/Las Positas Road intersection.

**East Beach**
**E. Cabrillo Boulevard**
**Santa Barbara, CA**
**(805) 897–2680**
**www.sbparksandrecreation.com**

East Beach, with a wide swath of glorious sand that stretches from Chase Palm Park toward the Bird Refuge and numerous facilities, is one of the most popular beaches in Santa Barbara. It's often acclaimed in various magazines as one of the best beaches in the nation.

*Palm trees line East Beach.* PHOTO: JOHN B. SNODGRASS

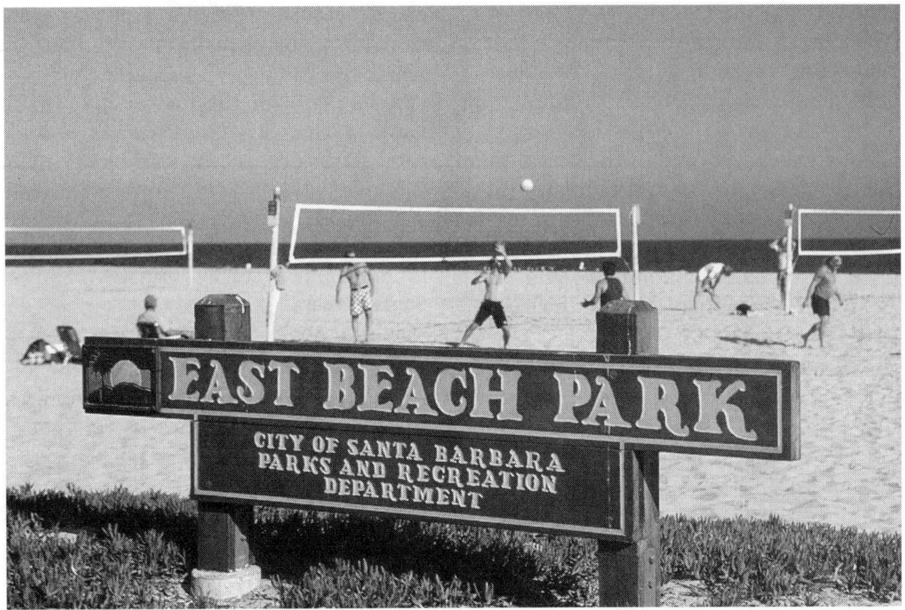


*East Beach is a popular volleyball spot.* PHOTO: BRIAN HASTINGS

Volleyball courts dominate the east end of the beach. This is where world-renowned beach volleyball champ Karch Kiraly (a native son) practiced and played for years. Big-time beach volleyball tournaments often take place here.

At the East Beach Bathhouse (beneath the Cabrillo Arts Pavilion) you'll find public restrooms, cold-water outdoor showers, equipment rentals (chairs, umbrellas, volleyballs, beach-friendly wheelchairs etc.), and a casual restaurant/snack bar. The beach also has a large picnic ground and playground. There's virtually no surfing here, but sometimes you can enjoy decent boogie-boarding.

Park in one of the city lots on either side of the Cabrillo Arts Pavilion.

**Leadbetter Beach**
**Shoreline Drive at Loma Alta Drive**
**Santa Barbara, CA**
**(805) 897-2680**
**www.sbparksandrecreation.com**

"Leds" is a fantastic family beach tucked between the harbor and Shoreline Park. The waves usually aren't very big except at the point near Shoreline Park, where beginner and intermediate surfers and boogie-boarders can usually count on catching some rides. When the breeze picks up, it's great fun watching the colorful sailboards, catamarans, and sailboats whiz by.

Volleyball courts, restrooms, outdoor showers, and a grassy expanse with family picnic areas and barbecues are all available here. You can buy breakfast, lunch, dinner, and drinks at the Shoreline Beach Cafe right on the beach. Park in the city lot right at the beach.

**West Beach**
**W. Cabrillo Boulevard**
**Santa Barbara, CA**
**(805) 897-2680**
**www.sbparksandrecreation.com**

If you walk directly west on the sand from Stearns Wharf toward the marina, you'll be treading across West Beach. This small, quiet expanse has hardly any waves (it's at the entrance to the harbor) and is ideal for swimming and watching the boats cruise in and out of the harbor. Several kayak rental outfits park themselves on West Beach during the summer (see the "Kayaking" section of this chapter for information). There are also a number of volleyball courts.

If the kids get tired of the beach, they can head over to the nearby playground and wading pool (open in the summer only) next to the Los Baños del Mar pool. Park in the harbor parking lot and walk toward Stearns Wharf to reach the beach.

## West of Goleta

The following three state beaches are just off U.S. 101 near Gaviota. They all have camping facilities and are therefore very popular. See the "Camping" section of our Recreation chapter for camping information.

**El Capitan State Beach**
**Off U.S. Highway 101, 17 miles west of Santa Barbara**
**(805) 968–1033**
**www.parks.ca.gov**

El Capitan was once the site of an extensive Chumash Indian village, and it's easy to see why the Chumash chose to live in this area for so long. At "El Cap" you can spend many hours exploring rocky tidepools, spotting sea lions and seals, and relaxing on the beach. The stands of sycamore and oak trees form a beautiful backdrop for swimming, fishing, surfing, and walking. From February through May you might even spot the gray whales that swim close to shore.

You can hike the nature trails in the adjacent park, and if you walk or ride a bike just 2.5 miles west, you'll arrive at Refugio State Beach.

**Gaviota State Park**
**Off U.S. Highway 101, 33 miles west of Santa Barbara**
**(805) 968–1033**
**www.parks.ca.gov**

This huge, 2,700-acre park lies 33 miles west of Santa Barbara, close to where the coastline turns north at Point Conception. It has a cove at the mouth of a creek where you can fish, swim, and picnic. You can also fish off the pier or hike up to Gaviota Hot Springs. Facilities include food service, restrooms, and picnic areas. (See our Parks chapter for more details.)

**Refugio State Beach**
**Off U.S. Highway 101, 23 miles west of Santa Barbara**
**(805) 968–1033**
**www.parks.ca.gov**

If you saw a picture of Refugio, you might think it was a tropical beach on a Hawaiian island because of the many palm trees planted along the beach and camping area. The beach stretches for 1.5 miles along the coast, next to a 39-acre park. It's a great place for picnicking, diving, snorkeling, and exploring nature trails.

Refugio lies just 2 miles west of El Capitan State Beach—a bike trail along the bluff connects the two. It's 23 miles northwest of Santa Barbara.

## Goleta

**Goleta Beach County Park**
**5990 Sandspit Road**
**Goleta, CA**
**(805) 568–2460**

This 29-acre county park has long been a favorite destination for families and UCSB students alike. A palm-lined grassy expanse fronts the wide, mile-long sandy beach. Waves tend to be small here, which makes the beach ideal for children and beginning surfers. You can fish off the pier (no license necessary), play volleyball on a court in the sand, and toss horseshoes in a designated area. Children can romp in the playground.

The park also has picnic facilities, barbecue areas, pay phones, dressing rooms, restrooms, and a snack bar. The Beachside Bar and Café serves lunch and dinner and drinks daily.

To reach the park, take the Ward Memorial Freeway from U.S. Highway 101

*Beachgoers soak up some rays on Goleta Beach.* PHOTO: BRIAN HASTINGS

toward UCSB. You'll see the Goleta Beach exit just before you get to campus. Park in the free parking lot at the beach.

## Montecito

**Butterfly Beach**
**End of Butterfly Lane**
**Montecito, CA**
**(805) 568–2460**

Butterfly Beach lies across the street from the posh Four Seasons Biltmore Hotel. If you're hoping to run into celebrities, you have a fairly good chance here. This is where many Montecito residents take beach walks because it's one of the only places along the shore where you're allowed to walk your dog.

Lots of celebrities also stay at the Biltmore and head to the beach for a few moments of R and R. It's a great beach for swimming and sunbathing, and when the tide is low you can walk to East Beach. You won't find any facilities here, but the Coast Village Road shopping area is just a few blocks away. If you do spot a celebrity, we recommend you do what Insiders do—leave him or her alone.

## Summerland

**Summerland Beach**
**2297 Finney Road**
**Summerland, CA**
**(805) 568–2460**
**www.sbparks.org**

Summerland Beach is quiet and clean and a great place for families to spend the day. Lookout Park sits on the bluffs above the beach. There you'll find picnic tables, barbecue areas, restrooms, telephones, and a playground. Walk down the path from the parking lot to reach the sand, where you can swim, sunbathe, and walk along the shore. (Be careful when you walk down the asphalt path to the beach—it's steep.)

Take the Evans Avenue exit from U.S. 101 and head toward the ocean. You'll dead-end into the Lookout Park parking lot. Parking is free.

> **Insiders' Tip**
>
> Remember, all "private" beaches are public below the mean tide line. You're free to be there, as long as you don't trespass on residents' property. Use the legal access trails to get there.

## Carpinteria

**Carpinteria City Beach**
**End of Linden Avenue**
**Carpinteria, CA**
**(805) 684-5405**

The City of Carpinteria's beach is very popular with families, since it's billed as the "world's safest beach." Protected by a natural reef breakwater, the beachfront waters are ideal for swimming, bodysurfing, and boogie-boarding. You can rent bikes, kayaks, and other equipment, buy snacks and lunch at the snack bar, and play volleyball on one of the beach courts.

**Carpinteria State Beach**
**Linden Avenue and Sixth Street**
**Carpinteria, CA**
**(805) 684-2811**
**www.parks.ca.gov**

Nearly 800,000 visitors trek to this 48-acre beach park every year to enjoy the glistening sands, tidepools, and campgrounds. It has day-use and camping facilities (restrooms, picnic areas, and telephones) and a visitor center with natural history exhibits and nature programs.

This is a fantastic place to watch birds—in fact, it's one of the best birding spots in the area. You can also swim and fish at the shore, hike on the beach and nature trails, and picnic in the grassy play area. There's an excellent swimming beach and a designated area for surfing. Day-use hours are from 7:00 A.M. to 7:00 P.M. during the winter and from 7:00 A.M. to 9:00 P.M. during the summer. For camping information, see the "Camping" section of our Recreation chapter.

**Rincon Beach Park**
**U.S. Highway 101 at Bates Road**
**Carpinteria, CA**
**(805) 568-2460**
**www.sbparks.org**

The point at the east end of this beach is world famous for its excellent surf waves (see the "Surfing" section of this chapter). But during the warmer months, when the waves are smaller, Rincon is a great beach for sunbathing and cooling off in the water, as long as you steer clear of the rocky point.

Rincon has public telephones, restrooms, and picnic tables. But bring your own picnic—there's no snack bar here.

To find Rincon, drive 3 miles east of Carpinteria and turn toward the ocean at the Bates Road exit, right at the Santa Barbara/Ventura County line. Park for free in the upper or lower Rincon Beach lots.

# Beach Supplies

We've included specialized stores (dive shops, kayak specialists) in their respective categories later in this chapter. Here, though, are a few shops that rent a variety of equipment you'll find useful at the beach. Smaller kiosk-type rental shops are located at some beaches.

**A-Frame Surf**
**3785 Santa Claus Lane**
**Carpinteria, CA**
**(805) 684-8803**

Run by two local brothers, this surf shop opened in 2000 right by Santa Claus Beach. You can wander in here and rent surfboards, body boards, wetsuits, fins, and skim boards, then stroll back out to the beach and hit the waves. Call for prices.

**The Beach House**
**10 State Street**
**Santa Barbara, CA**
**(805) 963–1281**

The Beach House is conveniently located near the intersection of Cabrillo Boulevard and State Street. It has soft surfboards, boogie boards, and springsuits for rent.

**Santa Barbara East Beach Bath House**
**1118 E. Cabrillo Boulevard**
**Santa Barbara, CA**
**(805) 897–2680**

The Bath House is situated right on East Beach. While it doesn't have beach equipment like surfboards and wetsuits for rent, it does rent out volleyballs for use on the beach and is the only place we know that provides beach-friendly wheelchairs. You can also use the showers for a small fee (about $2.50) and stash your belongings in the lockers. It's open 8:00 A.M. to 5:00 P.M. Monday through Friday and 10:00 A.M. to 5:00 P.M. on weekends, with extended hours during the summer.

**Surf Country**
**Calle Real Center**
**5668 Calle Real**
**Goleta, CA**
**(805) 683–4450**

Surf Country is a complete surf and beach shop with soft and hard surfboards, body boards, and wetsuits for rent. It also sells a variety of other beach gear such as clothes, sunglasses, hats, and accessories for men, women, and children.

## Boat Excursions/ Sightseeing Trips

Most of these boats also offer special whale-watching excursions. (See the "Whale-Watching" section later in this chapter.) Schedules and excursions vary, depending on the season, so it's always best to call ahead for current departure times. The schedules in this section reflect summer options and rates, unless otherwise indicated. We recommend you wear rubber-soled shoes and try to dress in layers so you're prepared for sudden changes in weather. Remember to bring a sweater, hat, sunglasses, sunscreen, and your camera. If you have binoculars bring those too, for a close-up glimpse of the wildlife.

**AKA *Sunset Kidd* Sailing**
**125 Harbor Way**
**Santa Barbara, CA**
**(805) 962–8222**
**www.sunsetkidd.com**

The *Sunset Kidd* is a 41-foot Morgan Out-Island ketch, Coast Guard–certified for 18 passengers who seek a truly tranquil sailing experience. Narration is kept to a minimum. *Sunset Kidd* takes people out on romantic sundowner cruises, two-hour coastal excursions, and overnight Channel Island trips. Two-hour trips along the coast cost $30 per person. The sunset-twilight sail also costs $30 per person. You can quench your thirst at the full-service bar on board, then relax and enjoy a quiet glide along the coast. *Sunset Kidd* is located at Cabrillo Landing in front of the Breakwater Restaurant at the harbor.

***Condor***
**SEA Landing**
**Cabrillo Boulevard at Bath Street**
**Santa Barbara, CA**
**(805) 882–0088, (888) 77–WHALE**
**www.condorcruises.com**

Watch the sunset and dine, dance, and drink cocktails on the 125-passenger, 88-foot *Condor*. It's the perfect party boat. You can charter the *Condor* for group sunset cocktail and dinner cruises. The boat has a large galley that will provide anything from light hors d'oeuvres to three-course meals, and the full bar will keep your guests well-imbibed. Bands and DJs can also be arranged. Rates for a three-hour cruise (7:00 to 10:00 P.M.) are $950 on weekdays and $1,150 on Friday and Saturday evenings.

**_Double Dolphin_/Santa Barbara Sailing Center**
**Next to the boat launch ramp at the harbor**
**Santa Barbara, CA**
**(805) 962–2826, (800) 350–9090**
**www.sbsailctr.com**

Sail in style on the 49-passenger *Double Dolphin,* a 50-foot catamaran. The *Double Dolphin* offers coastal trips, sunset Champagne cruises, jazz cruises, weekend dinner cruises, and Channel Island safaris. During the summer, coastal cruises are scheduled Monday through Thursday at 1:00 and 3:30 P.M., and the sunset Champagne cruises are at 6:00 P.M. The cost is $27 for adults and $17 for children 12 and under and you'll be treated to a free glass of champagne or the beverage of your choice. The two-hour trips include a narrated tour of the harbor, then a cruise past Stearns Wharf along the coastline towards Montecito. Jazz cruises are scheduled on Friday evenings at 6:00 P.M. and cost $38 for adults and $32 for children 12 and under. Dinner cruises are available on Saturday and Sunday from 6:00 to 8:00 P.M. during the summer months. Feast on tri-tip steak, chicken piccata, pasta dishes, fresh mixed vegetables, Caesar salad, and baguettes while you watch the sun sink into the sea.

Fares are $38 for adults, $27 for children 12 and younger. On Sundays, the *Double Dolphin* also takes passengers on full-day ocean safaris to the Channel Islands. The excursions include a trip to Painted Cave on Santa Cruz Island, one of the largest sea caves in the world. Tickets are $64 for adults and $38 for children 12 and under. Reservations are required. You can also charter the *Double Dolphin* for private cruises. Call for more information.

## Boating/Sailing

### Santa Barbara Harbor

If you're moving to Santa Barbara and want a permanent slip for your boat, we have bad news for you. There's a very long waiting list for permanent slips in the 1,000-slip harbor—some people have been waiting 20 years! Most people sell their boat and their permit together, so the list rarely shrinks. However, this situation may change in the near future, if City Council proposals that would speed up the wait time are approved. Call Waterfront Development (805–564–5531) to find out the latest developments.

If you're just visiting the area with your boat, you'll have better luck. Guest slips are available on a first come, first served basis. Call Visitor Slip Information at (805) 564–5530, regarding visitor slip assignments. Availability depends on the type of vessel.

If you arrive in Santa Barbara by boat and the marina is full, you can be put on a waiting list and then drop anchor in the open anchorage area to the east of Stearns Wharf. The list is updated daily.

Slip fees are payable in advance. The base rate for the first 14 days is 50 cents per linear foot per 24-hour day; the rate doubles after 14 days. The permit is valid until noon of the last day paid for. You can renew it by contacting the Harbormaster's Office (805–564–5530) before 11:00 A.M. of your checkout day.

You'll pay a $35 fine if your visiting vessel is tied up without permission and $5 per day for not paying for your visitor slip permit in advance. And if you leave the harbor owing visitor fees, you pay $10 plus double the amount you owe.

Alcoholic beverages are permitted in marinas but not on public sidewalks. Pets must be confined aboard your boat. Dogs must be leashed when walking to and from your boat. Parking (maximum vehicle length 20 feet) costs $1 an hour ($7 maximum per day). Boat trailers in the launch ramp cost $1 an hour ($5 maximum per day).

### Useful Numbers

These numbers might come in handy if you're boating or sailing in the Santa Barbara area:

*Sailboats skim past Stearns Wharf.* PHOTO: BRIAN HASTINGS

**Santa Barbara Marine Emergencies: 911**

**Coast Guard/Search and Rescue: (800) 221-8724, (310) 732-2044**

**Waterfront Department: (805) 564-5531**

**Harbor Patrol: (805) 564-5530**

**Marine Weather: (805) 897-1942**

## Public Boat Ramps

If you have a boat and want to put it in the water, you have only a few choices. The Santa Barbara Harbor maintains a boat launch ramp that can handle most types of boats. It's at the east end of the harbor parking lot, near the intersection of Cabrillo Boulevard and Bath Street.

There's a small-vessel (e.g., Jet Ski) launch in Carpinteria off Ash Avenue. You'll need to go to the Santa Barbara Harbor if you have a real boat.

The piers at Goleta and Gaviota have winches from which you can launch boats up to two tons.

## Power Boat Rentals

**Sailing Center of Santa Barbara**
**Next to the boat-launching ramp in the harbor**
**Santa Barbara, CA**
**(805) 962-2826, (800) 350-9090**
**www.sbsailctr.com**

The Sailing Center rents 13-foot Boston whalers as well as 36- to 50-foot yachts with skippers by the hour and day. Prices start at $35 an hour for the smaller boats and range up to $715 a day to charter a 42-foot sailing yacht with skipper.

## Sailing

Sailing the Santa Barbara Channel can be an incredible experience. As you cruise along the coastline, you'll see the Santa Ynez Mountains looming beyond the bluffs and the Channel Islands shimmering on the horizon. Although infrequently windy, the area has a wide range of challenging conditions.

Breezes along the coastline average 10 to 15 knots, and swells average 2 to 4 feet during most of the year. Out in the channel, especially close to the islands, it's very common to experience light winds in the morning and winds of 20 to 30 knots in the afternoon.

If you have any questions regarding sailing in the Santa Barbara region, you can call the Sailing Center of Santa Barbara or The Chandlery marine supply store (see subsequent listings). They both have expert sailors on staff who can help you navigate a safe course through our waters.

**Sailing Center of Santa Barbara**
**Next to the boat-launching ramp in the harbor**
**Santa Barbara, CA**
**(805) 962–2826, (800) 350–9090**
**www.sbsailctr.com**

The Sailing Center of Santa Barbara is one of the largest sailing schools on the West Coast. To get here, park in the harbor lot and walk to the Sailing Center docks by the boat-launch ramps.

The center offers one-stop shopping for sailboat rentals, group charters, cruises, and more. Its many other services include sailing lessons, from basic learn-to-sail classes to bareboat chartering certification; skippered and bareboat charters; and single- and multiple-day trips to the Channel Islands. Call for information and rates.

To rent a smaller boat, you'll need to pass a three-minute checkout to show that you won't hurt yourself or others and that you know how to get back to the dock. If you plan to rent a larger boat to sail to the islands, you'll need to complete a four-hour checkout. Rentals start at $28 per hour and $112 for a full day.

## Marine Supply Stores

**The Chandlery**
**132-B Harbor Way**
**Santa Barbara, CA**
**(805) 965–4538**
**www.chandlery.com**

Since 1946, The Chandlery has provided a full range of top-quality marine supplies. It's open daily and carries navigational maps and charts, marine hardware and electronics, rigging, installation, clothing, gifts, and just about everything related to the sailing and boating worlds, including new and used sailboats and power boats. You'll find The Chandlery on the breakwater at the harbor, near the Yacht Club.

## Diving

Scuba diving in the Santa Barbara Channel can be fantastic. There's an incredible diversity of marine life and many species are found nowhere else on earth. Along the coastline you can explore the kelp forests and shallow reefs. Many divers from all over the world head out to the Channel Islands Marine Sanctuary, which surrounds the Channel Islands (see our Channel Islands National Park and National Marine Sanctuary chapter). The experts at the following dive shops and companies are your best bet for getting the scoop on where to dive.

**Anacapa Dive Center**
**22 Anacapa Street**
**Santa Barbara, CA**
**(805) 963–8917**
**www.anacapadivecenter.com**

Lacy Lee Taylor and Michael Taylor own this full-service PADI dive center. Lacy is a NAUI instructor with training in both recreational and commercial diving and Michael is an experienced PADI instructor, so you'll be in good hands here. The center is one block from the beach in downtown Santa Barbara and offers instruction in the on-site heated pool as well as beach dives. Classes range from resort scuba courses and open-water SCUBA certification to more advanced courses. SCUBA courses for disabled divers are also available. In addition, Anacapa Dive Center rents and sells equipment, provides expert service, and arranges local and international dive trips. The center is open daily.

**Santa Barbara Aquatics**
**5822 Hollister Avenue**
**Goleta, CA**
**(805) 967–4456**
**www.sbaquatics.com**

Santa Barbara Aquatics has been around for more than 20 years and is one of the largest ocean sports centers in the area. It offers a full range of classes, plus equipment sales and rentals for scuba diving, kayaking, surfing, and swimming. You can take SSI, NAUI, or PADI courses in just about every type of diving: night, deep, drysuit, kayak and boat diving, navigation, search and recovery, rescue, assistant instructor, dive master, and instructor.

The shop also sells custom wetsuits as well as drysuits; rents skin-diving gear and assorted watersport accessories; and operates a repair station.

## Dive Boats

Nearly all the aforementioned dive shops and other groups arrange frequent trips along the coast and out to the Channel Islands. Just call any of them to find out what's on the schedule. The following company offers regular trips for all types of divers throughout the year.

**Truth Aquatics**
**301 W. Cabrillo Boulevard**
**Santa Barbara, CA**
**(805) 962–1127**
**www.truthaquatics.com**

Truth Aquatics operates three excellent dive boats from SEA Landing at the Santa Barbara Harbor: *Truth, Conception,* and *Vision.* All were designed and custom-built for divers. Truth Aquatics runs one- to five-day excursions to the Channel Islands year-round. A great thing about this company is that you can show up in just a bathing suit, and the staff will outfit you with everything you need.

One-day, open-party "experience dive" trips usually go out on Wednesdays. These trips are geared for divers who were recently certified and/or are unfamiliar with Santa Barbara Channel waters. Divers are taken to shallow, protected dive spots, usually off Santa Cruz Island. The boat departs from Santa Barbara at 6:00 A.M. and arrives at the dive site around 7:30 or 8:00 A.M. You dive until 3:00 P.M. and return to Santa Barbara around 5:30 P.M. You can buy inexpensive meals in the galley. These one-day trips cost $65 per person and include air fills.

On Thursday, Friday, Saturday, and Sunday, experienced divers can go on deeper dives, usually near Santa Rosa or San Miguel Islands (depending on the weather). The boat leaves at 4:00 A.M. and arrives at the dive site around 8:00 A.M. You can usually get in about four or five dives before the boat heads back for Santa Barbara, arriving about 5:30 P.M. Cost per person is $75, including air fills.

A popular three-day, limited-load trip is offered every few months, when the owner takes the boat out himself and shows the divers all his secret dive spots (the cost is $475 and includes air fills and gourmet meals). There are also regular Optaquatics trips geared toward underwater photography; underwater cameras and development equipment are on board.

Boats can also be chartered for groups for up to five days.

The Truth Aquatics monthly activities calendar lists all of its multiple-day trips six months in advance. You can pick up the calendar at any local dive shop, view it on the web site, or contact Truth Aquatics at the above number.

# Jet Skiing

**Jet Skiing**
**Santa Barbara Jet Boats**
**SEA Landing**
**301 W. Cabrillo Boulevard**
**Santa Barbara, CA**
**(805) 963–3564**

SEA Landing works in conjunction with Santa Barbara Jet Boats. It operates year-round out of the harbor, next to the boat-launch ramp near SEA Landing. You can rent a Sea-Doo jet boat (seats up to four, $120 per hour) or a WaveRunner III (seats one to three people, $85 to $95 per hour depending on the model). All prices include fuel, life vests, wetsuits, and safety orientation. You must be at least 18 years old to rent any watercraft, and a $500 security deposit with a credit card is required. Reservations are essential.

## Kayaking

The following firms offer kayak rentals and/or guided tours along the coast or out to the Channel Islands. Ocean kayaks are much more stable than the narrow, tippy river kayaks, so you don't need much experience to use one effectively. They're a fantastic way to explore the Santa Barbara coastline and marine world.

**Adventours Outdoor Excursions**
**(805) 899–2929**
**www.adventours-inc.com**

Adventours is a major outdoor recreation company specializing in custom group tours. It organizes and promotes numerous events and excursions and has teamed up with Aquasports (see next entry) to provide an extensive array of coastal and island kayak excursions. One-way or round-trip coastal kayaking tours typically originate at the harbor. Popular one-way routes include a scenic paddle from the harbor to the Four Seasons Biltmore Hotel, and one from Hendry's (Arroyo Burro) Beach back to the harbor. Adventours also offers excursions along the remote Gaviota coast. Group sizes range from four paddlers to more than 40, and the trips include a kayaking instruction clinic tailored to the group's experience. Beginners are welcome. All the guides are kayaking experts with extensive knowledge of the region's natural history. For an even wilder kayaking experience, ask about the single- and multi-day island tours for groups of five or more paddlers. The company works with various charter boats. Adventours also offers excursions that combine kayaking with mountain biking and other sports. You'll find a full description of Adventours in our Recreation chapter. Note that the company operates on an open calendar, so you usually have to book well in advance.

**Aquasports**
**111 Verona Avenue**
**Goleta, CA**
**(805) 968–7231, (800) 773–2309**
**www.islandkayaking.com**

Aquasports rents sea kayaks for groups and will deliver them to beaches from Goleta to Leadbetter Beach in Santa Barbara. Rental fees include an introductory lesson—no experience is required.

Aquasports also offers guided kayak trips along the Santa Barbara coast. Launch the kayak near Stearns Wharf and paddle out into the open ocean along the coastal bluffs for a two- to three-hour round-trip. Prices are about $79 per person for a group of four. Another trip takes you along the spectacular Gaviota coastline, a succession of small, secluded coves about 15 minutes west of Santa Barbara. This is a more remote experience—some of the beaches along here can only be accessed by kayak, so you'll really feel like you're getting back to nature. This trip costs about $89 per person for a group of four paddlers.

Guided kayak trips to the Channel Islands are also available (you cross the channel by power boat, then kayak off the islands). No special athletic ability or prior sea-kayaking experience are required.

Regularly scheduled trips take paddlers to Scorpion Ranch on Santa Cruz Island. The fee for a one-day trip is $179 per person, which includes the charter boat fee, all equipment, and guides. Two-day trips are $279, not including meals. The camping is very comfortable—in a huge eucalyptus grove in a valley. One-day trips to Santa Barbara Island, the most remote of the Channel Islands, are also available.

Custom trips may be scheduled with advance notice, and charter boats are available for groups of four or more.

*Kayakers set off for a sunset paddle.* PHOTO: NIK WHEELER, COURTESY OF SANTA BARBARA CONFERENCE & VISITORS BUREAU

**Paddle Sports**
**100 State Street**
**Santa Barbara, CA**
**(805) 899–4925**
**117-B Harbor Way**
**Santa Barbara, CA**
**(805) 962–6550**
**www.paddlesportsofsantabarbara.com**

Owned by a local kayak enthusiast, Paddle Sports is the oldest and largest kayak shop on the central coast of California. In 2001, the store added a convenient new location at the Santa Barbara Harbor. At this store you can rent all types of kayaks, both singles and tandems, as well as kayak-related gear (helmets, wetsuits, paddles, etc.). You can also launch your kayak on flat water a short stroll from the store. The original store, on lower State just a block north of Stearns Wharf, has an extensive selection of kayaks and kayaking equipment for sale. The staff are all experts in the sport and will outfit you with everything you need to get on the water. A single-person kayak rents for $20 for the first two hours and $5 for each additional hour. Rates for tandem kayaks are $30 for the first two hours and $5 per hour thereafter. Day, week, and group rates are available.

Paddle Sports has years of experience guiding kayakers in local waters. During the summer, the store offers guided trips to the Channel Islands National Park (call the State Street store). The trips focus on exploring the caves and rocky coves of the islands, some of which are only accessible by kayak. Paddlers travel at their own pace, taking time to enjoy their surroundings, so anyone can sign up regardless of skill level (minimum age is 18). Trips cost $179 per person and include powerboat transportation to the islands, instruction, wetsuits, helmets, and lights. Overnight stays are optional. If you prefer to explore the mainland coast, you have two options for guided tours: Paddle the 3.5 miles of remote coastline between Refugio and El Capitan, or glide from the harbor along the beautiful Santa Barbara coastline to the Four Seasons Hotel in Montecito. Both coastal trips cost $65 per person. Group and corporate rates are available.

**Pedal and Paddle of Santa Barbara**
**(805) 687–2912**
**www.nvstar.com/pedpad**

Instructor/leader Judy Keim has been exploring the coastline by kayak and bike since 1974. She loves to share her knowledge of nature with others and specializes in the coastline from Gaviota to Carpinteria. She also has great stories to tell—she's married to a fourth-generation Santa Barbaran and knows a lot about the area's history, famous people, and interesting local tidbits.

Participants set out in an open-cockpit, self-bailing kayak (no roll required). Anyone who knows how to swim and is in good health can sign up, but Judy generally recommends that beginners start out in the harbor, where there aren't any waves.

A two-hour trip (for example, from the harbor to Butterfly Beach with a shuttle back) costs $52 per person. Three-hour trips are $62, and half-day tours are $72. Full-day tours cost $100 per person. The price includes your kayak, paddle, life jacket, and guide escort. If you have your own kayak, you get an $8 discount.

Judy will customize tours to your interests and skill levels. She can arrange overnight tours; for example you can paddle from Gaviota to El Capitan, stay overnight at the campgrounds, and then paddle down to Goleta Beach. She also offers kayak/bike combination tours and bike-only tours (see our Recreation chapter for biking tour info).

**Sailing Center**
**Next to the boat-launching ramp in the harbor**
**Santa Barbara, CA**
**(805) 962–2826, (800) 350–9090**
**www.sbsailctr.com**

The Sailing Center rents kayaks and all the accessories starting at $10 per hour for a single kayak and $15 for a tandem. Full-day rentals are $40 and $50, respectively. The center also offers an Olympic-style rowing scull for $25 an hour or $100 per day.

**Santa Barbara Adventure Company**
**(805) 452–1942, (888) 596–6687**
**www.sbadventureco.com**

Launched in 1998, Santa Barbara Adventure Company offers a wide range of kayaking excursions led by experienced and knowledgeable guides. Choose from coastal paddling adventures along the spectacular Santa Barbara and Gaviota coasts, evening stargazing trips, and full- or multiday paddles around the sea caves and secluded coves of the Channel Islands. As you paddle, the guides share their knowledge of the area's natural history and marine ecology, so you'll enrich your mind as well as your spirit. The company will also customize trips to suit your skills and interests. Prices range from about $60 per person for a three-hour paddle to $350 per person for a three-day paddle around Santa Cruz Island. If you're not completely confident on a kayak, sign up for a lesson. Santa Barbara Adventure Company offers kayak instruction for beginners as well as kayak surfing and Eskimo roll classes for more advanced paddlers. If you're really adventurous, sign up for the Anacapa Island to Santa Cruz Island Self-Support trip, with an open-water crossing between the islands. All trips include qualified guides, equipment, transportation, and any necessary permits. The company operates on an open calendar, so daytrips require a two-day advance reservation. For overnight trips, book at least two weeks in advance. Call or visit the company's web site for more information.

**Santa Barbara Aquatics**
**5822 Hollister Avenue**
**Goleta, CA**
**(805) 967–4456**
**www.sbaquatics.com**

Santa Barbara Aquatics offers paddling and kayaking courses. It also sells and rents kayaks and accessories. Rentals average $35 a day for a single kayak and $50 a day for a tandem.

## Parasailing

**Blue Edge Parasail**
**Stearns Wharf**
**Santa Barbara, CA**
**(805) 966–5206**
**www.spydercide.com/blueedge**

Soar nearly 500 feet above the sea along the Santa Barbara coast on an approximately 10-minute, winch-directed parasail flight. A Coast Guard–licensed captain and crew will tow you 600 feet from the boat. Takeoffs and landings are soft, and you can stay completely dry. Two people can parasail together, and the boat holds up to six passengers at a time.

Flights start at $55 per person. Group discounts are available, and a $5 discount is applied before 10:00 A.M. and after 5:00 P.M. Young and old alike are invited to take flight—there's no minimum or maximum age. Blue Edge is open daily from May through September and weekends the rest of the year.

## Surfing

The Santa Barbara coast is one of California's premier surfing areas. The best waves hit the coast in the winter and fall, but good wave conditions for beginner to advanced surfers roll in regularly just about every month of the year.

The Channel Islands help protect the Santa Barbara coast from storm winds and create manicured conditions during strong winter swells. Unfortunately, these islands also block the coastline from almost all southerly swells, which tend to dominate during the warmer months. So from about May through September, the surf along the Santa Barbara coastline is typically quite small—perfect for beginners or intermediate surfers, but less than thrilling for experts.

Most local surfers are reluctant to share their favorite secret spots with anyone—crowds reduce their chances of catching the best waves. But we'll share a bit of Insider surf knowledge anyway, as

*A California surfer heads out to a long board break.* PHOTO: BRIAN HASTINGS

long as you promise to adhere to local surf etiquette. Usually the first person who catches the wave or is closest to the white water at the shoulder of the wave has the right of way. Most local surfers passionately enforce this unwritten rule. Be patient and wait your turn when it's crowded. And give a few waves away to be polite—you might be on the receiving end the next time.

Now for the surf scoop. Here's a brief overview of the main surf spots along the Santa Barbara coast, from east to west. We've tried to give you a good idea of their locations and basic information about access. For more details, call one of the surf shops listed after the surf spots—they can point you toward the best wave conditions for the day.

By the way, you will need a full-length wetsuit most of the year, although you can usually get away with a springsuit during the warmer months.

## Rincon Point

The Rincon is internationally renowned in the surfing world. It's located a few minutes' drive to the east of Carpinteria, right at the Santa Barbara/Ventura county line. Sometimes called the "Queen of the Coast," this wide, cobblestone point offers long, classic California point-break waves. It's mainly a winter break, and waves during the cooler months are often excellent, ranging from 2 to 20 feet (measured from the wave face).

Since Rincon has a rocky bottom along most of the break, and conditions are often very crowded, this break is most appropriate for intermediate to advanced surfers.

You can easily access the spot from the U.S. 101 Bates Road off-ramp. Park in the county or state parking lot.

## Leadbetter Point

You'll find this small point at the west end of Leadbetter Beach, just below Shoreline Park. It typically has small waves (2 to 8 feet) that break on a rocky bottom into a sandy beach. It's an excellent spot for beginner and intermediate surfers. You can access the break from the Leadbetter Beach parking lot on Shoreline Drive.

## Arroyo Burro Beach (Hendry's Beach)

This beach-and-reef break sometimes creates some decent surf waves during small to medium-size swells. It's also a good wind-swell spot (typically in the afternoons) and a fun spot for kids to catch some waves. Park in the Arroyo Burro Beach parking lot off Cliff Drive. The break is directly in front of the parking lot and the Brown Pelican restaurant and snack bar.

## Campus Point

Campus Point is a large point break named after the UCSB campus, which sits along its shore. It's one of the best breaks in Santa Barbara, with three or four sections that are good in nearly all conditions. Consequently, it offers great surfing for beginners to advanced surfers. However, it does have a rocky bottom, so it's not the safest place for beginners. It can also be packed with UCSB students.

To access Campus Point, take the Ward Memorial Freeway from U.S. Highway 101 to the UCSB campus gate, where you will need to pay a parking fee on weekdays. Once you're inside the gate, turn left. On weekends you can park in the first parking lot to the left. On weekdays, you're only allowed to use visitor parking spots, which are quite a distance from the beach.

Another approach is to take the Goleta Beach off-ramp, just before the entrance to UCSB. Park in the beach lot and walk west along the coast about a half-mile.

## Sands Beach

You'll find this sandy reef break just west of Isla Vista, the densely populated student community adjacent to UCSB. Sands offers very nice surfing experiences in a beautiful location. You can expect to find small to medium surf; the best conditions occur during wind swells. The only negative here is that you often have to put up with tar globs in the water and on the beach, thanks to offshore oil seeps.

To reach Sands Beach, take Del Playa Road to its west end, then walk about a half-mile to the trail, just past Devereaux Point (also a decent surf spot on occasion).

## El Capitan State Beach

The point at El Capitan ranks among the most beautiful surf spots along the Santa Barbara coastline. A small rocky point that ends in a sandy bay, this spot can have excellent and hollow surf up to 10 feet. Follow U.S. 101 north from Santa Barbara about 17 miles and take the El Capitan State Beach off-ramp. Go through the park gate (the day-use fee is $5), then take the beach trail east of the parking lot.

## Hollister Ranch

Known by name to most surfers on the planet, "The Ranch" has some of the best surf in California. It's located about 30 miles west of the city of Santa Barbara and stretches from Gaviota State Beach to Point Conception. Unfortunately (or fortunately for those lucky enough to get to surf there), access to this stretch of coastline is very limited. There are only two ways to get there: by boat or by driving through private, gated Hollister Ranch property.

Boaters usually launch their crafts from the winch at the end of the Gaviota Beach pier, just east of the ranch property. As you motor westward, you'll run into several breaks with varying surf conditions. Recent subdivision of ranch property has substantially increased the number of property owners (many of whom buy pieces of land just to have surf access) and the number of people who are allowed to drive to the pristine beaches by vehicle. Local surfers frequently try to cajole, entice, and bribe their fortunate friends who own ranch property to drive them into the ranch for a session.

## Jalama Beach

Although not in the geographic area covered in this book, Jalama State Beach is often frequented by Santa Barbara surfers. This coastal area is well exposed to the open Pacific waters, and unlike Santa Barbara, it catches swells from southerly to northerly directions. With often windier, colder, and rougher surf, Jalama challenges even the most experienced surfer. Beach and reef breaks occur all along this stretch of wild and scenic coastline.

To access the area, take U.S. 101 to just north of Gaviota, then take the Calif. Highway 1 turnoff. From there, go about 8 miles to the Jalama Road turnoff on the left, then follow this winding road 12 miles to the beach. The state campground offers day-use facilities as well as dozens of overnight camping spots.

## Surfing Equipment

**A-Frame Surf**
**3785 Santa Claus Lane**
**Carpinteria, CA**
**(805) 684–8803**

Run by two local brothers, this surf shop opened in 2000 right by Santa Claus Beach. The store sells short boards from local designers such as Progressive and Clyde Beatty as well as some hard-to-find smaller lines of surf- and beachwear for men, women, and children. You can also rent surfboards, body boards, wetsuits, fins, and skim boards here, and surf lessons are available year-round.

**Channel Islands Surfboards**
**29 State Street**
**Santa Barbara, CA**
**(805) 966–7213**

Tourists and surf experts alike shop at Channel Islands Surfboards. This is where you can find surfboards by Al Merrick, one of the best board designers and shapers in the surfing industry. You can also purchase a range of other surfing equipment and apparel.

**Surf Country**
**Calle Real Center**
**5668 Calle Real**
**Goleta, CA**
**(805) 683–4450**

This complete surf and beach shop is a good place to pick up Insider information on the best surf and beach spots. It rents soft or hard surfboards, body boards, and wetsuits. Rates are $25 a day and $10 for each additional day. Surfing lessons are also available.

## Windsurfing

Santa Barbara can be an excellent place to windsurf, but you have to be up on the changing conditions and be ready to travel. Most of the year, the southwest-to-west sea breeze of 8 to 12 knots prevails—fine conditions for beginners. But during the cooler months of the year, the passage of storm systems brings a wide variety of southeast to westerly winds, both moderate and strong.

West Beach is a decent spot to windsurf, as is Leadbetter Beach, which continues to serve as the most frequently used spot for local sailboarders (see the Beaches section earlier in this chapter for beach descriptions). Protected by Leadbetter Point, the waters off Leadbetter Beach are fairly flat during most of the year, making it the best spot to learn how to sail in Santa Barbara. Parking is available about 100 yards from the sandy beach, so you don't have to haul your equipment too far. An added bonus is the lawn next to the parking lot, good for rigging up.

Most of the other windsurfing spots in the area are more suited for advanced sailors, due to the increased wave conditions and/or inaccessibility. Some of these spots include Arroyo Burro Beach, Isla Vista, Jalama Beach in the North County, and C Street in Ventura. Be careful at these spots, as all of them can at times have treacherous surf.

If you want flat water (and warm water in the summer), you might consider Lake

Lopez, about two hours north of Santa Barbara and just east of Arroyo Grande in San Luis Obispo County. Lake Lopez offers a nice change of pace from the cooler and often fluky wind conditions in Santa Barbara.

Windsurfing was much more popular in Santa Barbara in the 1980s than it is today. There used to be several local windsurfing equipment stores, but, alas, not a single one exists today. The closest store is in Ventura.

## Whale-Watching

Every year in late September, about 28,000 Pacific gray whales begin migrating 5,000 miles south from Alaska to warm lagoons and bays in Baja California, where they mate and give birth. In early February, the adult males, pregnant females, and a few juveniles start heading back north to their summer Arctic feeding grounds. The new mothers and their calves hang around the lagoons a bit longer before following along.

This migration—among the longest of any mammal—is one of nature's most incredible spectacles, and you can get a ringside seat to watch it right here in the channel.

Going south, most of the gray whales pass between Santa Rosa and Santa Cruz Islands. On the way back north, usually from February through April, they tend to hug the Santa Barbara coastline, typically swimming from 1 to 5 miles offshore. Mothers and calves sometimes stay within a few hundred yards of the shoreline. It's truly amazing to watch these 80,000-pound giant mammals gracefully breach, spout, and cavort.

You also have an excellent chance of spotting whales at other times of year. If you take a cruise boat out to the islands from July through September you're almost guaranteed to spot humpback and blue whales, which often come through the channel, close to the islands, to feed on the krill. In fact, the largest concentration of blue whales in the world has regularly visited local waters in recent years. If you're lucky, you might also spot minke and pilot whales.

At any time of year you might see orcas, also known as killer whales. They come into the channel to feed on seals and

*A playful humpback whale waves its fluke.* PHOTO: CONDOR PHOTOS

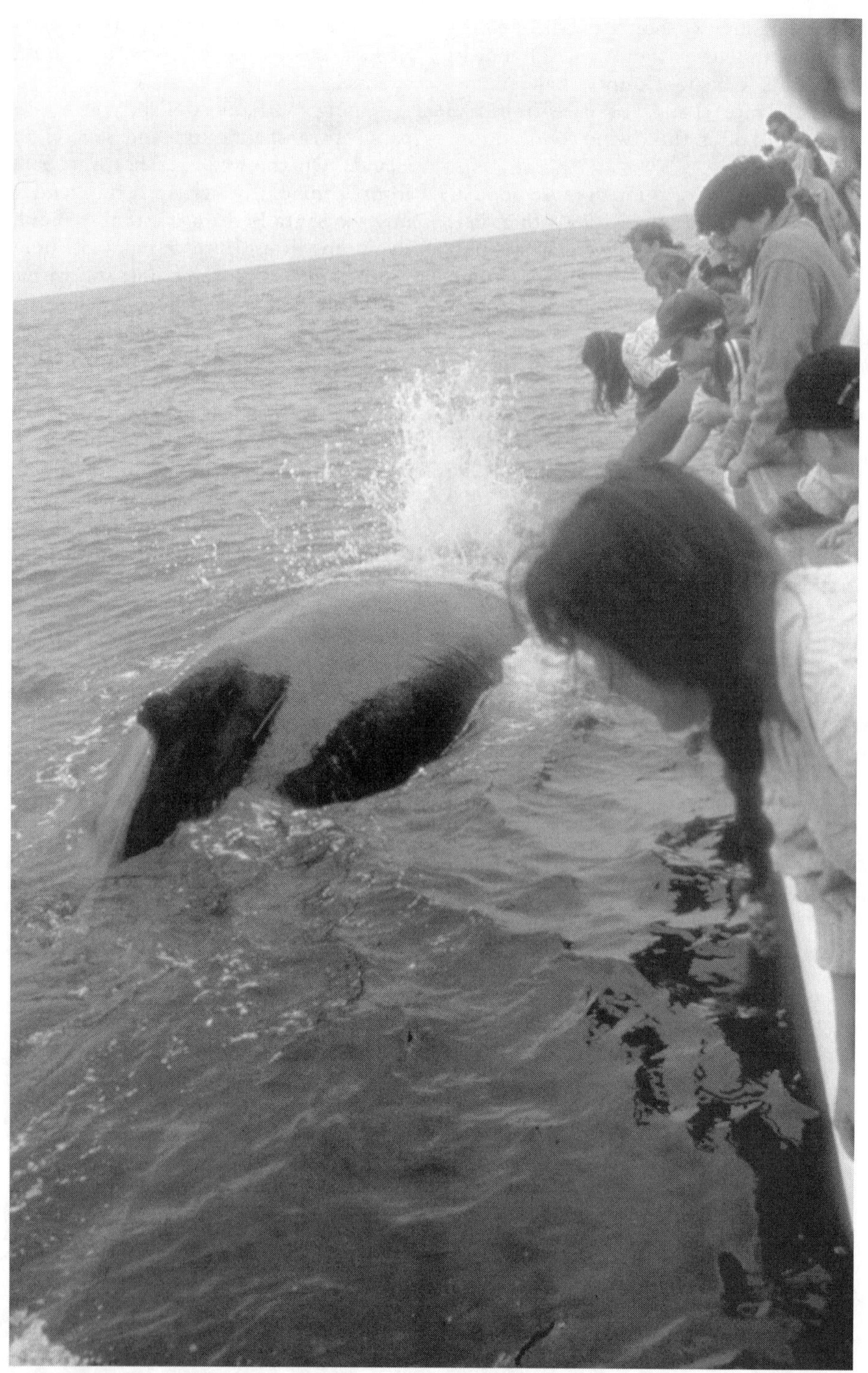

*A number of local boats offer whale-watching cruises.* PHOTO: CONDOR PHOTOS

**Insiders' Tip**

Heading out on a whale-watching trip? Take a windbreaker. It's cold on the water. Also bring binoculars if you have them so you can get a good look at the wildlife.

sea lions. In the spring, they sometimes attack migrating gray whales, especially cows and calves. That's when you might also encounter dolphins, porpoises, and basking sharks.

The following is a list of boats that will take you out to watch the whales and give you a bit of whale education in the process. It's a good idea to call to verify the current schedule, as departure days are often added or dropped, depending on how many whales are in the channel that week. All these boats work as a team. If one boat is enjoying a spectacular appearance by a whale or pod of whales, the captain will radio other whale-watching boats in the vicinity and share the sighting.

**AKA *Sunset Kidd* Sailing**
**125 Harbor Way**
**Santa Barbara, CA**
**(805) 962–8222**
**www.sunsetkidd.com**

*Sunset Kidd* is probably the least touristy of the whale-watching trips. This excursion is for those who love sailing and prefer the tranquility of gliding up to the whales on a wind-powered vessel (the motor is used as little as possible). Narration is kept to a minimum. The *Sunset Kidd,* a 41-foot Morgan OutIsland ketch, takes up to 18 passengers on two-hour whale-watching cruises daily from mid-February through May. The fare is $30 (no discounts for kids or seniors).

**Captain Don's Whale Watching**
**On the breakwater at the harbor**
**Santa Barbara, CA**
**(805) 969–5217**

Captain Don's power yacht, the 149-passenger *Rachel G,* has a full galley and bar, an upper deck with great views and seating, and a lower deck with indoor seating, air conditioning, and heating.

The boat goes out three times a day (9:00 A.M., noon, and 3:00 P.M.) from February through the end of the migration in May. Trips last about two-and-a-half hours. The adult fare is $27, children 12 and younger can board for $17, and seniors 65 and older pay $23 per trip.

From June through September, the *Rachel G* takes passengers out to the Channel Islands to visit with giant blue whales. You might also spot humpback whales, dolphins, porpoises, and sea lions. The cost is $65 for adults, $40 for children 12 and younger, and $55 for seniors 55 and over. The boat departs at 8:00 A.M. from Stearns Wharf pier and returns between 1:00 and 2:00 P.M. Reservations are requested.

***Condor***
**SEA Landing**
**301 W. Cabrillo Boulevard at Bath Street**
**Santa Barbara, CA**
**(805) 882–0088, (888) 77–WHALE**
**www.condorcruises.com**

The 88-foot, 125-passenger *Condor* is the only whale-watching vessel affiliated with and recommended by the Santa Barbara Museum of Natural History. It's also the only company offering a whale-watch guarantee. If you don't see whales or exceptional sightings of other marine animals on your trip, the captain will issue a "whale check," which is good for a free trip on another excursion during the same season. The boat offers three daily whale-watching cruises at 9:00 A.M., noon, and 3:00 P.M. throughout the gray whales' northerly migration season (February, March, and April). Each cruise lasts two-and-a-half-hours and includes an

CLOSE-UP

## A Whale of a Time with Captain Benko

If you're a passenger on the *Condor,* an 88-foot, 125-passenger boat that takes people on whale-watching trips throughout the year, you might be lucky enough to meet Fred Benko. Benko has owned the *Condor* since 1983 and was its main captain until he semi-retired in 1985. He still hops aboard several times a week to share stories, facts, and trivia about Santa Barbara Channel marine life with passengers.

Few Santa Barbarans know more about the Santa Barbara Channel—or about the whales who visit here—than Benko, a salty soul who has cruised the channel at least several times a week for more than 25 years. He is on the advisory board for the Channel Islands National Marine Sanctuary and has also spent more than 25 years actively helping to educate schoolchildren and adults about marine life.

One might think that after all these years on the water, Benko would be a bit bored or jaded. On the contrary—he still thrills at the sight of a breaching whale or a pod of dolphins, and his enthusiasm is downright infectious. After a trip with Benko, chances are you'll spend the rest of your life learning more about marine life and marveling at its wonders.

Benko has always been something of a free spirit, an adventurer in tune with the natural world. Born in 1939, he grew up in Ohio. At the ripe old age of 17 he joined the Marines and was trained as a meteorologist—a very handy vocation for a future sea captain. Benko was stationed at Iwakuni on Honshu in Japan and had his own sailboat. His job was typhoon forecasting, and he worked in shifts—24 hours on, 72 hours off—which gave him plenty of time to sail around the coast of Japan.

During his sailing trips he would often play the guitar for villagers he'd meet, and sing American and Japanese folk songs. Those years in Japan spurred a lifelong interest in all things Japanese. In fact his wife, Hiroko, is originally from Japan, although the couple met in Montecito.

After leaving the Marines, the prospect of full-time meteorology work did not appeal to Benko. Instead, he decided to travel the world. With his trusty guitar in hand, he traipsed through Europe, living out of the back of an MG and picking the guitar for beer money. After he returned to the United States, Benko earned an MBA degree at George Washington University in Washington, D.C. Then he spent 10 years working in Southern California with Pfizer Laboratories, an international pharmaceutical, agriculture, and chemical company.

A big life change for Benko came about when Pfizer wanted to transfer him to New York City. He said no way and decided to leave the company. He'd always been a fisherman and a diver and had owned a number of boats. So in 1973 he decided to devote himself to the life of the sea full time. He bought a couple of boats, including the *Hornet* and the *Condor,* and started S.E.A. Landing at the harbor. S.E.A. originally stood for Sport fishing, Excursion, and Adventure, but the periods after the initials were eventually dropped, and now some people capitalize it and others don't.

In 1986, Benko decided to retire and sold most of his boats and SEA Landing to Truth Aquatics. He held onto the *Condor,* though, so he could still keep in touch with his beloved channel firsthand. "I like being out there too much to stay away," he explains. "You never know what kind of surprise the channel will come up with on a

*Fred Benko, captain of the* Condor, *has spent nearly three decades educating Santa Barbara residents and visitors about marine life.* PHOTO: CHRIS CRABTREE

given day." Benko works on board two or three days a week. Ron Hart is now the regular captain of the *Condor,* and several other people fill in as well. "All the guys really know their stuff," says Benko, "and they're really good at educating the passengers about what they're seeing."

Somehow, whales in the Santa Barbara Channel seem to recognize the *Condor* and often approach the boat and play right next to it. Benko is convinced that the blue whales, especially, recognize the boat. "They see us as nonthreatening and interesting. We leave the engines idle because the sound comforts them. They also like the sound of the depth-finder."

Benko has always been committed to marine education and has been giving slide/video shows and talks at schools since 1974. He's currently on the advisory board for Los Marineros, a marine education program jointly administered by the Channel Islands National Marine Sanctuary and the Santa Barbara Museum of Natural History that reaches every 5th-grade student in the Santa Barbara School District.

The children learn about natural history and the marine environment through marine science classes, beach cleanups, trips to local tidepools, and whale-watching excursions. Los Marineros also provides education for elementary teachers through a series of marine education workshops.

Education, in fact, is a big reason why Fred still likes to hop aboard the *Condor* along with groups of schoolchildren. "We educate them about what's in their own backyard," he says. "We show them what's there, and we help them become more aware of their environment."

The diversity of marine life in the Channel is usually a real eye-opener for adults as well as kids. Benko says he meets lots of people who have lived in Santa Barbara for years but see the ocean as a big, dark mysterious place. Once they go out on the *Condor,* their perception changes forever. "They learn to see the channel not just as a big body of water, but as a living place," says Benko. "I love hearing people tell me 'Now I know the ocean is full of life.' It's a great feeling."

informative narration about the whales and other wildlife you might encounter on the trip. Fares are $27 for adults and $16 for children (4 through 12 years). Group rates are available. From June through to about the beginning of September (depending on when the whales arrive), the *Condor* also takes people out in the channel to see blue and humpback whales. This trip includes a stop at the spectacular Painted Cave on Santa Cruz Island, one of the largest sea caves in the world. Trips depart at 8:00 A.M. and return at 3:00 P.M. Tickets are $65 for adults and $35 for children. Call for the current schedule.

**Insiders' Tip**

For beach status reports, visit the Santa Barbara County Environmental Health Services website at www.sbcphd.org and click on the Beach Closures link. You can also call the Ocean Water Hotline at (805) 681-4949. To be safe, try to avoid contact with ocean and creek water for at least three days after a storm, when runoff pollutes the water.

***Double Dolphin*/Santa Barbara Sailing Center**
**Santa Barbara Harbor near the boat-launch ramp**
**Santa Barbara, CA**
**(805) 962–2826, (800) 350–9090**
**www.sbsailctr.com**

The *Double Dolphin,* a 50-foot catamaran, takes up to 49 passengers out for two-and-a-half-hour narrated whale-watching cruises at 9:00 A.M., noon, and 3:00 P.M. from mid-February through mid-May during the gray whale migration. Boarding passes are $27 for adults, $17 for children 12 and younger.

# Spectator Sports



Although Santa Barbara's cultural and arts scene displays big-city sophistication, when the subject turns to professional sports, you're still talking small town.

While this may be a disappointing fact for big-league sports fans, you can see all the pro sports in Los Angeles—just a few hours away—including Dodgers and Angels baseball, Lakers and Clippers basketball, Kings and Mighty Ducks ice hockey, and the renowned L.A. Marathon.

Not that Santa Barbara hasn't had big-league sports on its mind a time or two. Back in October of 1924, for example, Babe Ruth and Lou Gehrig were just a few of the players who came to Peabody Stadium (which now belongs to Santa Barbara High School) for a game that drew 2,000 fans. Tickets were a pricey $1.50, plus $1 for parking and a 10 percent war tax, but Santa Barbarans were more than ready to ante up for a big-time baseball game. Four years later, Laguna Park, a full-size major league ballpark, was built on East Cota Street in an effort to bring major league baseball to Santa Barbara on a permanent basis, and in 1941 a farm team of the Los Angeles Dodgers, the Santa Barbara Saints, began playing there. The park was closed down for a while at the beginning of World War II, and later the Dodgers moved their farm team to Bakersfield, which marked the beginning of the end for Laguna Park. After years of deterioration, it was torn down in 1970.

There's still some good baseball being played in Santa Barbara, though. The Santa Barbara Foresters, a semipro team in the California Coastal Collegiate League, play a June through August season at UCSB.

Football in Santa Barbara pretty much consists of local college and high school games, but don't underestimate the thrill of a good contest between crosstown rivals such as San Marcos and Dos Pueblos High, San Marcos and Santa Barbara High, or Carpinteria and Bishop Garcia Diego High. Santa Barbara City College also fields a good football team.

Horse racing was big in Santa Barbara in the mid-1850s, when Thomas Hope laid out California's first flat course for trotters and pacers at Hope Ranch. The first hurdle race in the state took place at Hope's track, which ran around the shores of Laguna Blanca. After his premature death in 1875, Hope's land was divided up, and Laguna Blanca later became the centerpiece of an 18-hole golf course at the La Cumbre Country Club, which opened in 1935.

Below are some of the local possibilities for spectating, along with some phone numbers for contacting L.A. teams about tickets and schedules. You can also check out the daily "Sports" section of the *Santa Barbara News-Press*.

## Semipro Sports

**Santa Barbara Foresters**
**Caesar Uyesaka Stadium**
**UCSB**
**Santa Barbara, CA**
**(805) 684–0657**
**www.sbforesters.org**

The Foresters are Santa Barbara's next best thing to professional baseball. Part of the Coastal Collegiate League, the Foresters play at UCSB's Caesar Uyesaka Stadium in a June-through-August season. Players come from college teams all over the country, including UCSB, USC, UCLA, Stanford, Florida State, and

> **Insiders' Tip**
>
> All UC Santa Barbara basketball games are broadcast live on KEYT radio, 1250 AM in Santa Barbara. You can also access them at www.broadcast.com or www.ucsbgauchos.com.

Wichita State. The Foresters are pretty good, too. The team is a seven-time California Coastal Collegiate League winner and three-time California State Champion. The team also finished in fifth place at the National Baseball Congress World Series in Wichita in 1997 and in seventh place in 1999 and 2000.

There's an old-time family atmosphere at Foresters games, with promotions, contests, and races between innings, so bring the kids and enjoy.

Tickets are available at the gate. Admission is $4 for adults, $3 for seniors, $1 for children under 12. Season and family passes are also available, making this a great deal for summertime family fun.

## College Athletics

Although nationally ranked teams and overflowing stadiums are not the rule in Santa Barbara, we're proud of our local schools and love to cheer them on. If there's a hot contest going, Santa Barbarans turn out in droves to support the home team, and everyone gets into the spirit. The cost for watching college athletic events varies—some events are free and others require an admission fee. Only UCSB offers tickets in advance, with Santa Barbara City College and Westmont selling tickets at the door or gate.

**Santa Barbara City College**
**721 Cliff Drive**
**Santa Barbara, CA**
**(805) 965–2262 (student activities and athletics)**

SBCC has fielded some fine football, volleyball, and basketball teams, and the public is always welcome to attend any sports event on campus. The Vaqueros' football team, which plays in La Playa Stadium, recently capped a winning season with a trip to the Holiday Inn Bowl.

SBCC also fields baseball and softball teams and has men's and women's golf, soccer, tennis, and volleyball teams. In recent years, the men's soccer team has won three conference championships and a state championship. Tickets to all SBCC athletic events can be bought at the door or gate and are not available in advance.

**University of California at Santa Barbara Athletics Ticket Office**
**(805) 893–8272**
**www.ucsbgauchos.com**

UCSB's Gauchos, who play in the Big West Conference, host a variety of sports events that are open to the public. The university's women's basketball team advanced to its seventh NCAA tournament in 2001 and entered the Mideast Regional as the 14th seed. The Lady Gauchos have won the Big West Conference regular season title for six straight seasons and received the conference's automatic bid for five straight years.

The men's basketball team hasn't been quite as sterling, but under coach Bob Williams, formerly of UC Davis, who coached his Davis team to an NCAA Division II championship, the future looks brighter. Join the Gauchos in the "Thunderdome," so-named because the thousands of stomping feet during a tight game rumble like thunder.

UCSB almost always has great men's and women's volleyball teams. In the past, the men's team has ranked among the top five teams in the nation and always ranks somewhere in the top 20. Other spectator sports on campus include baseball, softball, swimming, soccer, tennis, track and water polo. In 2001, UCSB won titles in men's and women's swimming and women's basketball and took second place in baseball, men's golf, and men's cross-country. This excellent track record earned UCSB its first Big West Commissioner's Cup as the Big West school with the best results in the 2000–01 season.

**Westmont College**
**955 La Paz Road**
**Santa Barbara, CA**
**(805) 565–6010 (athletics)**
**www.westmont.edu/sports**

Westmont's Warriors invite the public to basketball, soccer, volleyball, track, tennis, and other spectator sports events played by its men's and women's teams. Westmont has ranked ninth among more than 300 NAIA institutions in overall sports performance in the past six years that the Sears Directors' Cup has been awarded. (The Sears Cup awards points based on national results in each sport.) Part of the Golden State Athletic Conference, Westmont's men's basketball team almost always has a winning record, and has had 13 appearances at the NAIA national tournament. A women's team competed for the first time in the 1998–99 season.

Like UCSB, Westmont fields excellent volleyball teams, and its men's soccer team is a standout, with 16 NAIA tournament appearances and 28 district, conference, and regional titles. When athletic events have an admission fee, tickets are sold at the gate or the door.

## Polo

**Santa Barbara Polo and Racquet Club**
**3375 Foothill Road**
**Carpinteria, CA**
**(805) 684–8668**
**www.sbpolo.com**

The public is invited to watch Sunday afternoon matches during the polo season, which runs from April through October. Matches are played at 1:00 and 3:00 P.M., and admission is $10 at the gate for adults (children under 12 are free). Food and beverage service is available, or you can bring your own picnic.

## Satellite Wagering

**Earl Warren Showgrounds**
**U.S. Highway 101 and Las Positas Road**
**Santa Barbara, CA**
**(805) 682–2187**
**www.earlwarren.com**

Although you can't enjoy the thrill of the race in person unless you drive to Los Angeles, Earl Warren Showgrounds (affectionately called "Earl's Place" in this particular context) is open for satellite wagering daily except Monday and Tuesday. Races from several tracks, including Los Alamitos, Santa Anita, and Hollywood Park in the Los Angeles area, as well as some Eastern imports are beamed down via satellite—you can even wager on the Kentucky Derby. The box office opens at 10:00 A.M., with races scheduled throughout the day (call 805–682–1259 for schedules). Food and bar service are available, and you can check the day's race results any time by calling (805) 682–2187. General admission is $5, $4 for seniors and students with ID. Seniors over 55 are admitted free on Thursdays and women are admitted free every Saturday evening after 6:00 P.M.

## The Real Thing—L.A. Pro Sports

For big-city spectator sports, you'll have to drive to the Big City—Los Angeles in this case. Expect a two- to three-hour drive to L.A., and plan to arrive at least 30 minutes before the game begins, as you may have to negotiate parking, crowds, and long lines at ticket windows and/or food stands.

Many teams offer advance ticket sales through TicketMaster, and the number is listed where appropriate. Note that the TicketMaster number listed is a local call from Santa Barbara, but you can get tickets from any TicketMaster outlet. Tickets are also sold at the gate for most events. Toll-free numbers with the 800 or 888 prefix are listed when available, but you often need to make a toll call to reach the L.A. ticket office.

## Baseball

The Anaheim Angels play American League baseball at Edison International Field, Anaheim, April through September. Information: (714) 663-9000, TicketMaster (805) 583-8700, www.angelsbaseball.com.

The Los Angeles Dodgers are the city's National League baseball team. They play at Dodger Stadium April through September. Information: (323) 224-1448, www.dodgers.com.

## Basketball

The Los Angeles Clippers play NBA basketball at the Staples Center from October through May. Information: (213) 742-7555, TicketMaster (805) 583-8700, www.clippers.com.

The Los Angeles Lakers also play NBA basketball at the Staples Center in October through May. Information: (213) 480-3232, (714) 740-2000, TicketMaster (805) 583-8700, www.lakers.com.

## Horse Racing

L.A. racetracks: Hollywood Park, Inglewood (310-419-1500); Santa Anita Park, Arcadia (626-574-7223); Los Alamitos Race Course, Los Alamitos (714-995-1234).

## Ice Hockey

The Los Angeles Kings play NHL hockey at the Staples Center from October through April. Information: (888) KINGSLA, TicketMaster (805) 583-8700, www.lakings.com.

The Mighty Ducks, another NHL hockey team, take to the ice at the Arrowhead Pond, Anaheim, from October through April. Purchase tickets at the door, or call TicketMaster, (805) 583-8700, www.mightyducks.com.

## Running

The Los Angeles Marathon takes place in March. Information: (310) 444-5544, www.lamarathon.com.

# Neighborhoods and Real Estate

Neighborhoods
Real Estate
The Rental Scene

If you never leave your hotel near the beach, you probably won't be all that interested in the local real estate market or in the character of Santa Barbara's various neighborhoods (except to do a bit of sightseeing). Like a lot of visitors, though, you just might make a few trips to our fair city and begin to wonder about actually making Santa Barbara your permanent home.

Then you'll be interested in neighborhoods and real estate—in fact, you'll become obsessed with what each neighborhood has to offer, where the most affordable houses are, what locations are near parks and recreational facilities, and how far you'll have to commute to work. In this chapter, we provide a brief overview of each neighborhood within the greater Santa Barbara area and a broad idea of the home prices there. We touch on a few attractions or landmarks in each area, but to do a thorough job of fact-checking, you'll need a map and some time to explore on your own.

If you're in a home-buying mood, we also suggest you check out several other chapters in this book, including Kidstuff, Recreation, Shopping, Parks, and Education and Child Care, for information that may be of interest to prospective residents. Once you've decided on a neighborhood that sounds inviting, continue on to the Real Estate section of the chapter for the inside scoop on the local market, how to choose a real estate agent, and a list of local real estate companies that will help you find your dream house.

Before you begin your home-buying hunt, we should warn you that Santa Barbara is one of the most expensive locales in the state. In just the past couple years, prices in many markets here have more than doubled. But hey, you didn't expect paradise to come cheap did you? Remember, when you buy a place here, you're also paying for the sunshine, the palm trees, the beaches, and the great quality of life.

(If you absolutely can't afford a dream-house kind of commitment, take a look at our Vacation Rentals chapter and line up a condo for the summer. It's the next best thing to living here!)

## Neighborhoods

### Santa Barbara

If all you've ever seen of Santa Barbara is the touristy beachfront area, you've missed the flavor of the charming neighborhoods that make up our beautiful city. In fact, as you cruise the leafy streets of Santa Barbara, you'll discover many highly desirable residential areas—probably more than you'd expect for such a small town. Scenic enclaves such as the Mesa, downtown Santa Barbara, Mission Canyon, and the Riviera all evoke contrasting images for Insiders, and each is worth exploring. But let's start with an overview of the beachfront strip. Then we'll venture further afield.

#### The Beachfront

The Santa Barbara beachfront area along Cabrillo Boulevard is the most tourist-oriented section of the city. State Street and Stearns Wharf divide this strip into East Beach and West Beach, our classic palm-fringed stretches of sand. Not surprisingly, hotels and motels line the street

**Insiders' Tip**

Santa Barbara's strict building design guidelines arose from a stroke of Mother Nature's wrath. After a devastating earthquake in 1925, planners rebuilt the city in Spanish-Mediterranean style. Today the pale stucco facades, wrought-iron gates, and red tile rooftops of the city's historical district evoke the aura of its rich Spanish colonial past.

opposite the beach on the north side of Cabrillo. If you're not walking to the beach from one of these nearby accommodations, you will find parking a nightmare along here, especially on weekends when the Sunday Santa Barbara Arts and Crafts show is set up along East Cabrillo Boulevard. A few public parking lots are available if you're willing to pay; if not, get there early or park on a side street and walk.

East Beach has volleyball courts on the sand and is the site of many local tournaments. Across the street from these you'll notice some upscale condos. These are considered quite exclusive and rent for more than $2,200 per month.

West Beach includes the area west of Stearns Wharf to the Santa Barbara Harbor. This wide expanse of sand is home to beach-rental and kayaking concessions as well as a calm area for swimming. Across the street, motels and restaurants are jammed in from one end of West Beach to the other, drawing hordes of tourists during the summer. If you continue to the far west end, you'll hit SEA Landing, the boarding point for whale-watching trips.

This combined waterfront area is poised for big changes. After many revisions, Fess Parker's (aka Davey Crockett's) proposed new hotel near his DoubleTree Resort on East Beach has the thumbs up, and a few condominium projects are in the works. Perhaps the most controversial of these is Entrada de Santa Barbara (the "Levy project" as it's called in the papers), a proposed complex of time-share condos and retail outlets on lower State Street near Cabrillo. The project caused quite a stir. Among other issues, some locals argued the two- and three-story buildings would block precious mountain views. Despite all the protests, the project has been approved, and construction is slated to commence in the summer of 2002. Once complete, these developments will further cement this area's reputation as a tourist magnet.

### The Mesa

Heading west up the hill from the harbor lies the Mesa (Spanish for "table"), a large, family-oriented residential neighborhood bisected by Cliff Drive. Properties here range from Mediterranean and ranch-style homes to contemporary dwellings and shingled cottages with prices starting at about $500,000 for small single-family homes and reaching up to $2 million for larger homes on prime property with ocean views. You'll also find many apartments here rented by Santa Barbara City College students.

A thriving shopping district is located at the intersection of Meigs Road and Cliff Drive, and for recreation, Mesa residents head to Shoreline Park. This 15-acre stretch of rolling lawns, on a bluff overlooking the ocean, is a favorite venue for family outings and picnics. It's also one of the best places in Santa Barbara to watch the sunset. Perched on a Mesa bluff top to the east of Shoreline, you'll find Santa Barbara City College, which arguably has the best panoramic view of any educational institution in the country; its La

Playa Stadium is directly across the street from beautiful Leadbetter Beach and the Santa Barbara Harbor.

### Downtown

The retail center of downtown Santa Barbara lies on "lower" State Street, between Stearns Wharf and Carrillo Street. Its busy shops, restaurants, sidewalk cafes, theaters, and the palm-lined Paseo Nuevo outdoor mall are a natural draw for visitors.

On the outskirts of this downtown area is a mix of gorgeous historic homes, smaller single-family dwellings, apartment and condo complexes, and small California cottages. Especially lovely are the old Victorian homes and gardens interspersed throughout the city. Homes within the city boundaries can be reasonably priced (if you consider $500,000 reasonably priced) or soar into the millions, depending on the location.

Downtown Santa Barbara contains a large number of tourist attractions, including the historic Courthouse, the Presidio, and the Santa Barbara Museum of Art, so it's easy for a visitor to shop, dine, and see the sights within a fairly compact area. If you want to explore this historical district, we recommend the Red Tile Walking Tour (see our Attractions chapter for more details). Downtown always seems to be decked out with banners or decorations of some sort, adding to the neighborhood's festive feel. But the area can be frustrating to negotiate in a car. It won't take you long to notice that the streets are often narrow, in a state of disrepair (or of being repaired), and very busy. Parking is a huge problem almost everywhere downtown. Your best bet is to nab a spot in a public parking lot (if you can find one) and explore on foot. Better still, you can take the electric shuttle, which will whisk you around the downtown area for probably less than you'd spend to park in one of the pay lots. (See our Getting Here, Getting Around chapter for more information on local parking and transportation.)

### Upper State Street

If you continue your drive up State Street, you'll reach Mission Street, the beginning of the "upper" State Street district, a mix of commercial and residential properties extending to La Cumbre Road. Unlike the downtown area, upper State lacks the Spanish ambiance and has a much more modern feel. An exception is La Cumbre Plaza mall, which was revamped in an upscale Mediterranean style.

### San Roque

San Roque, between upper State Street and the foothills, is another charming residential neighborhood populated by a mix of families with young children and older retirees. Despite its close proximity to a busy shopping and commercial district, it manages to retain a quiet and secluded feel. Meticulously maintained homes with well-manicured lawns line the sunny streets, and you'll notice a variety of architectural styles, from imitation Tudor cottages and Spanish haciendas to classic ranch-style homes. Real estate (you're probably getting used to this by now) is expensive, and a three-bedroom house can sell for more than $600,000. Smaller two-bedrooms may go for $500,000 or more.

### Mission Canyon

Mission Canyon is the quiet, thickly wooded neighborhood around Mission Canyon Road and the adjacent foothills. It's a beautiful area of old oaks and sycamores, rocky streams, and hiking trails. Lured by the area's natural beauty, many artists, writers, and musicians make their home here. It's only a 10-minute drive to downtown, but the rugged wilderness makes it feel more remote. In lower Mission Canyon you'll find the Santa Barbara Museum of Natural History, Rocky Nook Park, and Mission Santa Barbara, while upper Mission Canyon is home to the Santa Barbara Botanic Garden. Architecture in the area tends to be more contemporary in style. Home prices range from $600,000 in the Mission Canyon Heights to well over a million for more

**Insiders' Tip**

Yammering loudly on your cell phone in public is considered big-city behavior in this laid-back town. So if you want to look like a local, you might want to tone it down a notch.

exclusive homes secluded in the woodlands.

### The Riviera

Driving up from Mission Canyon on meandering Alameda Padre Serra (Insiders call it "APS") puts you on the sunny Santa Barbara Riviera, with its magnificent views of the ocean, the Channel Islands (on a clear day), and the city of Santa Barbara. Not all the homes on the Riviera are large, but their location makes them expensive, with prices ranging from $700,000 to well over $3 million. The main campus of the Brooks Institute of Photography resides on prime property here, and just above Alameda Padre Serra you'll find El Encanto Hotel and Garden Villas, with its Mediterranean-style restaurant and spectacular views of the city and sea (find out more in our Hotels and Motels and Restaurants chapters).

## Goleta

Goleta (Go-LEE-ta, from the Spanish word for "schooner"—and yes, we know that is not the proper Spanish pronunciation) is a huge, family-oriented community that sprawls from a rather indistinct Santa Barbara city boundary somewhere between Patterson and Kellogg Avenues to another indistinct boundary "somewhere out there" past Winchester Canyon. Goleta has more industrial and high-tech firms than anyplace in the county, and many University of California Santa Barbara employees live here. It also includes the Santa Barbara Airport, which technically sits on a patch of the City of Santa Barbara carved out of the middle of Goleta (just to complicate things).

Goleta, or the Goleta Valley, as some prefer, has its own county beach, and you'll find several excellent golf courses here, including the celebrated Sandpiper Golf Course and the Glen Annie Golf Club. Camino Real Marketplace, a massive new retail center at Hollister and Storke Roads, draws throngs of shoppers, and the brand new Bacara Resort and Spa, a $200-million beachfront property, is Santa Barbara's most upscale resort, with rooms going for more than $400 per night.

As for tourist attractions, Insiders love Stow House, a two-story Victorian home built by Sherman P. Stow in 1872; the Goleta Lemon Festival, held each October on the Stow House grounds; and, of course, the cultural and educational hotbed that is UC Santa Barbara. (See our Arts and Education and Childcare chapters for more information.)

A water moratorium that started in the mid-1970s held down construction in Goleta for years, but in recent years the town has become the site of some major upscale developments. These include Cathedral Pointe, along Cathedral Oaks Road between Patterson and Kellogg Avenues, where homes originally sold for $460,000 to $590,000, and Winchester Commons, at Winchester Canyon Road and U.S. Highway 101, with properties originally priced upwards of $325,000. Like everywhere else in Santa Barbara, these homes have seen dramatic price increases since they were built.

These days, homes in Goleta can sometimes be had for as low as $400,000, depending on the neighborhood, while new homes in the area are now selling for $600,000 to $800,000.

Goleta is also the site of many apartment dwellings, especially in Isla Vista (pronounced EYE-la VIS-ta—and yes, we've tweaked the Spanish pronunciation again), where thousands of UC Santa Barbara students cram into several square blocks of rental complexes. New housing projects continue to sprout up all over Goleta but demand still far outpaces supply.

Goleta has been struggling for decades to find its own identity. In 2001, the County Board of Supervisors unanimously backed a proposal for Goleta cityhood and the issue went before voters in the November 2001 ballot. After rejecting different versions of the cityhood proposal three times since 1987, voters finally approved the measure, creating the second largest city in the south county behind Santa Barbara.

The most controversial part of the latest cityhood plan was where to draw the city boundaries. To increase the chances of passing the proposal, the new plan excluded many neighborhoods in the eastern Goleta Valley, which historically favored annexation to the city of Santa Barbara. The plan also excluded Isla Vista and UCSB due to concerns that the typically transient student population would sway election outcomes. The result is a city of about 29,000 people who share a strong desire to shape their own destiny and perhaps curb the troubling (to some) boom in development.

## Hope Ranch

Isolated between the area west of Modoc Road and the ocean, Hope Ranch, a ritzy Santa Barbara County neighborhood, is like a community unto itself. Sprawling ranch-style homes and secluded mansions line the main thoroughfare of Las Palmas Drive, and the scores of winding, maze-like roads make it easy to get lost if you don't know where you're going. This is probably just fine with Hope Ranch residents, who value their privacy and employ their own security police.

Homes here sell for very big bucks, with low-end properties in the $1-million range and the most extravagant estates zooming upwards of $10 million. In 2000, an estate here sold for a whopping $37 million, making it the biggest sale on the south coast for that year.

You won't find any commercial businesses or tourist attractions in Hope

*A colonnade of palms lines the entrance to the affluent neighborhood of Hope Ranch.* PHOTO: BRIAN HASTINGS

Ranch, but we recommend taking at least one sightseeing tour on Las Palmas Drive just to get a feel for the place. As you enter Las Palmas from Modoc Road (under the famous Hope Ranch gateway), to the left you'll see Laguna Blanca, a small lagoon that's part of the private La Cumbre Country Club. Originally the lagoon was surrounded by a horse-racing track designed by Thomas Hope, an Irishman who was granted the land in 1870.

You'll also notice a lot of bridle trails. Riding, as well as raising and showing horses, is a popular Hope Ranch pastime. Residents have access to bridle paths and a horse show ring as well as a private beach and tennis courts.

## Montecito

Lying between Carpinteria and the city of Santa Barbara, Montecito has a well-deserved reputation as an enclave of the rich and famous. Unfortunately for the curious, most of the wealth is hidden behind massive gates or at the end of long winding drives lined with trees or other lush vegetation. Movie stars do live here, but unless you are lucky enough to see them out shopping or browsing the local farmers' market, you won't get much of a look at them.

Montecito's sense of elegance and seclusion is carried over into its luxurious lodging places, including the exclusive San Ysidro Ranch, built in the 1930s and a vacation retreat for the likes of John and Jacqueline Kennedy, Jean Harlow, and Katharine Hepburn, and the posh Four Seasons Biltmore, a beautifully landscaped complex of elegant rooms and cottages constructed in 1927 and perched just above Butterfly Beach (for more details, see our Hotels and Motels chapter).

Shopping tends to be upscale and exclusive here, with two main shopping areas, the "lower village," along Coast Village Road, and the "upper village," at San Ysidro and East Valley Roads, which also contain galleries, high-end real estate offices, and restaurants. In our opinion, the most rewarding attraction in Montecito is Lotusland, a stunning collection of wildly imaginative gardens and exotic plants created by the eccentric Polish opera singer Mme. Ganna Walska. (See our Attractions chapter for more details.)

Two highly respected educational institutions, Westmont College and the Music Academy of the West, are located within the boundaries of Montecito, but unless you have big bucks, there's probably not much of a chance you'll be living here. Home prices range from about $1,000,000 (yes that's six zeros) way on up to the mega-millions. In fact, Montecito has always vied with Hope Ranch for the most stratospheric estate sales. Until recently, Hope Ranch held the record with that $37-million sale in 2000. Then Oprah came along. In 2001, she snapped up a 42-acre estate here for a reported $50 million, giving Montecitans cause to gloat over their lattes again. Not only is this a record real estate sale for the county, it's one of the biggest real estate transactions for a private home in U.S. history.

## Summerland

Rambling up the hillsides on the north side of Highway 101, between the exclusive enclave of Montecito and laidback Carpinteria, sits a community of funky Victorian-style houses, antique stores, restaurants, and brightly painted cottages. Blink and you might miss it. But in recent years, this cute little coastal enclave has become quite a hot spot. Homebuyers are scrambling for a prime piece of ocean-view property here, and its diminutive nature is a big part of its charm.

Tinged with a faintly bohemian air, Summerland (or "Spookville," as it was once called) used to be a stomping ground for spiritualists, who gathered here for séances in the late 1800s. Today it's a popular hangout for antique shoppers, surfers, and a steady gush of tourists who flock here on weekends to enjoy its quaint bed and breakfasts and friendly cafes. From the freeway, you can see the Big Yellow House, former home of the widow of Summerland's founder, which is now a popular family-style restaurant. (Some say a ghost haunts the dining room.) In 1992 Summerland basked in the media spotlight after President Clinton visited the rustic Nugget restaurant and bar here. Since then, real estate prices have soared. Take a look at the Cottages at Summerland, a new ocean-view housing project at the east end of the main drag, Via Real. Despite their location overlooking the freeway, prices for these units started at $925,000, with the most expensive going for $1.5 million. If you're lucky, you might be able to nab a small fixer-upper in Summerland for $600,000, but grander homes with the best sea views will certainly stretch your pocketbook.

## Carpinteria

An incorporated city located about 12 miles south of Santa Barbara, Carpinteria has a friendly, small-town feel. Named for the Chumash Indian carpenters that Gaspár de Portol encountered here on a 1769 expedition, "Carp" (as the locals call it) contains acres of flower fields, greenhouses, and avocado groves. The annual California Avocado Festival is held here each October (see our Annual Events chapter), and a weekly farmers' market also shows off the local bounty.

Several high-tech firms, such as QAD and Digital Sound, are headquartered here, diversifying employment opportunities while allowing the city to maintain the low-impact environmental profile that residents insist on.

Carp's main attraction is its natural beauty, but it does maintain a small historical museum and boasts the area's only polo fields, just north of the city at the Santa Barbara Polo & Racquet Club. The downtown area, situated around the intersection of Linden and Carpinteria Avenues, has small shops and restaurants, and a strip mall with more modern businesses occupies both sides of Casitas Pass Road. The area is especially good for antique hunting, and the city has an excellent beach, dubbed "The World's Safest Beach," with a wide sandy stretch and relatively riptide-free waters. Carpinteria State Beach Park is visited by about a million people annually. It boasts 4,000 feet of ocean frontage for swimming and tidepool exploring as well as facilities for picnicking, hiking, and surf fishing (see our Parks chapter).

Because everything is cheaper in Carpinteria, many families choose it over Santa Barbara for vacations, especially because it offers easy beach access, numerous motels, and better odds of finding a vacation rental. Historically, housing prices tend to be lower here than in Santa Barbara, but in 2000, according to the Santa Barbara Multiple Listing Service, the median price jumped by a record 31 percent, with an older three-bedroom home selling for about $500,000, and lavish homes on the beach or in the foothills running as high as $5 million.

A large condominium market thrives in Carp, with prices ranging from $250,000 and up for a one-bedroom to more than $1 million for a three-bedroom beachside condo.

# Real Estate

In 1974, a struggling young couple with a down payment provided by their parents bought a three-bedroom, 20-year-old Santa Barbara tract home for $36,500. Making the payments was a stretch, but they managed, even while the woman stayed home to raise the kids.

Almost 30 years later, the same home, now 47 years old and with only a new coat of paint and some new carpet to show for it, would sell for more than 12 times that amount. Mom and Dad, still living in the house, could not afford to buy it today, nor could they afford the mortgage payments, even though they're both working now. As for their grown-up children, they have to pack up and move out of town to be able to afford a home of their own.

And so it goes in Santa Barbara. Residents joke that they could sell their houses

## Insiders' Tip

The Community Housing Office at UCSB offers support for students renting off-campus apartments. Check out its bulletin board for rental listings and pick up a copy of its *Rental Housing Survival Guide* for rental tips and advice. You can stop by the office in The University Center, Room 3151, between 8:00 A.M. and 5:00 P.M. Monday through Friday, or call the office at (805) 893-4371. You can also call (805) 893-4376 for a recording of rental listings received during the previous day.

and buy mansions elsewhere, but the same scenario almost never happens the other way around. Facing a job transfer or other reason for relocation, many Santa Barbarans rent out their homes rather than sell and risk cutting off any chance of being local homeowners again if they ever come back. This tendency to hang on to local real estate is bad news for homebuyers. Demand far exceeds supply. Adding to the fierce competition for housing in recent years were cash-rich dot-commers, who liquidated stock options before the tech bubble burst and snapped up local real estate in the blink of an eye. (According to a recent article in the *News-Press,* in the year 2000 an incredible 400 sales exceeded the $1-million mark, a massive increase over the previous year.)

Another factor affecting housing demand is the tech effect. As advances in technology allow more businesses to operate away from big cities, high-tech companies and workers migrate to small towns like Santa Barbara, where crime rates are low and the quality of life is high. Welcomed by the county for their environmentally friendly business practices, more than 200 such companies have popped up here in recent years, earning Santa Barbara the nickname "Silicon Beach." And then there are all those ripe-aged baby boomers looking for a quiet place to retire. For them, Santa Barbara has it all: sun, sea, surf, and fabulous golfing.

With such high demand for property, 2001 began as a banner year for the Santa Barbara real estate industry. In the first quarter, the median home price zoomed to a record high of more than $626,000 according to the California Association of Realtors. That represents a 14.2 percent increase above the median price for the previous year. Of course, all those multimillion-dollar estates in Hope Ranch and Montecito skew the figures a bit (we hear you can't even find a decent estate around there for a measly $2 to $3 million anymore), but even at the lower end, homes in Santa Barbara County are out of reach for many buyers.

To give you an idea of the mortgage payments you might be looking at if you're house-hunting in the area, consider the following scenario, presented in a recent *News-Press* article. Let's say you've just arrived in town and you want to buy a house at the median price of around $626,000. After plunking down a 20 percent deposit of $125,200, you secure a $500,000 loan at 7.25 percent interest rate on a 30-year mortgage. So what will your monthly payments be? Including property taxes and fire insurance, you can expect to pay about $4,120 per month. That means you'll need to be earning at least $138,000 per year. Considering the average annual salary for a county resident in 2001 was estimated at $33,668, it's not surprising home buyers are frustrated. At these rates, most renters can only dream of owning a home in the area. Some government officials say the solution to high-cost housing is simple: build more houses! This scenario makes conservation-minded Santa Barbarans (and there are a lot of them) cringe. So when will the real estate rocket ride end? Historically, the market moves in cycles. But even during the dips here, demand remains relatively strong and prices are still high. Despite the recent economic decline, selling prices for the first nine months of 2001 were higher overall than the previous year and most Realtors expect the market to weather the recession quite well. After all, there's only one Santa Barbara in the world and a lot of people want to live here.

## Real Estate Firms

Whether you rent or buy, housing in Santa Barbara will take a tremendous toll on your budget. So it's important to find someone you trust to assist you in the process of home-finding. Santa Barbara is a relatively small town where everyone knows nearly everyone else in real estate, so word gets around fast if anything unscrupulous is going on—which is not often.

Many local real estate firms have been around for decades and have sterling reputations, while others are part of respected national chains. Several individually owned firms have also found their niche and are doing very well.

Given the good record of local companies, the real estate agents we spoke with think it's wisest to go shopping for an individual agent rather than a specific company. "Inventory moves quickly here so it's important to build a rapport with a Realtor who has the inside track," according to Timm Delaney, a local real estate expert and Director of Estate Sales, Relocation, and REO with Coldwell Banker. "Most of the Realtors in Santa Barbara are very experienced and dedicated and they'll work closely with you to find a property that suits your needs." Because it's important to have a good relationship with your real estate agent, you should spend time finding someone who makes you feel comfortable. Referrals are a great way to land an agent, whether it be from a Realtor in the town you are coming from or a personal or company referral.

If you don't have a reliable source for a referral, your best bet is to log on to the Internet, research various companies, and then call around and chat with some by phone. (Refer to the web sites on the listings below.) If you're a technophobe, try to stop in at a few open houses and chat with the agents you meet. You may find someone you click with. Or, call a few Realtors who advertise in *Casa,* a local real estate publication, or in the *Santa Barbara News-Press,* then stop by their offices, check out credentials, and pick one who makes you feel comfortable about your working relationship. Ask for references from his or her clients before making a final decision.

Avoid a real estate agent who wants to focus on only one part of Santa Barbara (unless it's your preferred location) and look for someone who knows the entire area and is willing to work around your needs. Agents who belong to the Santa Barbara Association of Realtors list homes in Goleta, Santa Barbara, Hope Ranch, Montecito, Summerland, and Carpinteria.

Be aware that the agent who is offering a house for sale is working for the seller, although that doesn't preclude him or her from securing the sale for you. In fact, no one knows the property better than the listing agent, so it's up to both of you to decide if that agent can also represent you in what should essentially be a "win-win" situation for both sides. However, since both buyers and sellers are trying to get the best possible deal, some listing agents believe they cannot fairly work in the best interest of both parties and prefer that buyers get their own agent to represent them in the negotiations. Remember that the seller almost always pays the sales commission, so you are not incurring any extra cost by getting your own Realtor.

CLOSE-UP

## Beautiful Homes, Bargain Prices

High on a grassy knoll in the coastal hamlet of Summerland sits a cluster of charming new houses and condominiums with sparkling Pacific vistas. This upscale housing project, known as The Cottages at Summerland, consists of 20 deluxe single-family homes, most of which will sell for more than $1 million. Adjacent, 10 similarly designed condos with the same million-dollar views start at $67,800. How can this be? It's all part of a creative approach to Santa Barbara's housing crisis. In exchange for permission to build more units than current zoning laws allow, the county requires developers of housing projects to add affordable units to the mix. These units sell for less than they cost to build, but the developers make up the loss by selling the extra luxury units at market prices. This isn't the first project of its kind in the area. Goleta is home to several others, and another exclusive Mediterranean-style development in mega-bucks Montecito with seven affordable housing units is sending would-be first-home buyers into a frenzy. Think you want to be in on this deal? Good luck! Prospective homebuyers must meet strict low-income criteria, live in the county, and enter a lottery for the privilege of purchase.

Nearly all real estate companies offer some type of relocation services. The large firms associated with national chains often have relocation departments or specialists, but independent Realtors work hard to meet relocation needs as well.

The Santa Barbara Chamber of Commerce (805–965–3023) offers two types of relocation packets that can be ordered when you call: a $25 personal packet that includes a map and real estate and demographic information, and a $40 business packet that contains an economic profile, contacts for commercial real estate, a calendar of local events, and information on the arts and cultural activities.

The companies below represent a partial list of real estate firms located in the greater Santa Barbara area. They are generally considered to have experienced agents who have good track records in assisting both buyers and sellers.

**Century 21**
**A Hart Realty Incorporated**
**3412 State Street**
**Santa Barbara, CA**
**(805) 687–7591, (800) 350–2733**
**www.century21ahart.com**

This well-respected office of 23 agents has won the coveted Centurion Award for outstanding customer service every year since 1983. The office specializes in residential real estate but it also handles commercial and investment properties in all areas of greater Santa Barbara. Among the experienced staff are two past presidents and the 2001 president of the Santa Barbara Association of Realtors as well as a real estate instructor. This office is independently owned, but offers the benefits of affiliation with a large chain, such as Century 21's national relocation program.

**Coastal Getaways Realty**
**1086 Coast Village Road**
**Montecito, CA**
**(805) 969–1258**
**768 Linden Avenue**
**Carpinteria, CA**
**(805) 684–8777**
**www.coastalrealty.com**

In business since 1993, Coastal Getaways has turned its extensive knowledge of the upscale vacation rental market into a successful "boutique" real estate venture. Specializing in Montecito, Hope Ranch,

Santa Barbara, and beach properties, the company's 16 agents deal in everything from $250,000 condos to $30-million estates. A licensed real estate attorney is also on the staff.

**Coldwell Banker**
**1515 Chapala Street**
**Santa Barbara, CA**
**(805) 963-7587**
**3902 State Street**
**Santa Barbara, CA**
**(805) 682-2477**
**1290 Coast Village Road**
**Montecito, CA**
**(805) 969-4755**
**www.coldwellbanker.com, www.cbsocal.com, www.previewsestates.com**

Recently voted Santa Barbara's best real estate company in two local newspaper polls, Coldwell Banker is a distinguished firm that sells multimillion-dollar estates as well as lower-priced family homes. The company has been in Santa Barbara for more than 30 years, and about 200 experienced agents work for the firm, which now includes Jon Douglas Company, Fred Sands, and Santana Properties. Coldwell Banker also has a national and international relocation department, a commercial division, an REO department, and a concierge service to help smooth your transition.

**Maizlish Realtors, Inc.**
**El Paseo**
**816C State Street**
**Santa Barbara, CA**
**(805) 963-9555, (888) 963-9556**

Co-owners Morton and Alicia Maizlish are both brokers and the sole employees of this independent firm established in 1980. They believe in the single-agency approach, which means the company will only represent one party in a transaction. Recently they have been specializing in downtown, upper east, and Riviera properties. The Maizlishs deal with a full range of real estate, from condos to estates, and limit transactions to between 20 and 25 a year in order to provide personalized service.

**T.H. Phelps Realtors**
**(805) 683-1222**

A top-producing agent with another local company before forming her own real estate firm in 1994, Helene Phelps has been in the real estate business in Santa Barbara since 1980. She and her husband, Tom, a broker since 1991, pride themselves on their personalized service and professionalism. Although T.H. Phelps Realtors specializes in Goleta, it serves all of the greater Santa Barbara area.

**Pitts & Bachmann Realtors**
**1436 State Street**
**Santa Barbara, CA**
**(805) 963-1391**
**1165 Coast Village Road**
**Montecito, CA**
**(805) 969-1133**
**1482 E. Valley Road**
**Montecito, CA**
**(805) 969-5005**
**www.pbrealtors.com**

Founded in 1962, Pitts & Bachmann is the largest and oldest independently owned real estate firm in the area. This full-service company handles all types of properties, from mobile homes to multimillion-dollar estates, all over the greater Santa Barbara area, including Santa Ynez. As a special bonus, its 180 full-time agents offer personal tours of the area for potential buyers contemplating a move to Santa Barbara.

**Prudential California Realty—Santa Barbara**
**3868 State Street**
**Santa Barbara, CA**
**(805) 687-2666, (800) 326-3483**
**1150 Coast Village Road**
**Montecito, CA**
**(805) 969-5026, (800) 201-4364**
**www.prucalresb.com**

Doing business in Santa Barbara since 1950 (and voted the best local real estate company five years in a row in past *Santa Barbara News-Press* polls), Prudential California Realty–Santa Barbara has 120 agents working out of two local offices. The company deals in all types of properties including residential, commercial,

> **Insiders' Tip**
>
> Housing prices in the North County (including Santa Maria and Lompoc) are lower than those in the South County (greater Santa Barbara), but consider the cost of gasoline and the extra driving time before you buy.

and investment properties and specializes in helping first-time homebuyers break into the market. Prudential's worldwide network of offices provides relocation assistance.

**RE/MAX Santa Barbara**
**1715 State Street**
**Santa Barbara, CA**
**(805) 687–2600**
**1205 Coast Village Road**
**Montecito, CA**
**(805) 969–2282**
**5652 Calle Real**
**Goleta, CA**
**(805) 964–2662**
**www.remax.com**

Part of a large national chain, this firm is a full-service agency handling a range of properties throughout the greater Santa Barbara area. Special divisions include relocation, estates, restaurants, residential, commercial, and investment properties. The company's broker has held many prestigious positions in the industry, including president of the California Association of Realtors in 2000. About 75 agents work out of three offices, and on average, they have a minimum of 12 years' experience in local real estate. Many are also multilingual. The company as a whole and its individual Realtors donate part of the commission from every sale to the local Children's Miracle Network.

**Village Properties**
**1250 Coast Village Road**
**Montecito, CA**
**(805) 969–8900**
**www.villagesite.com**

Established in 1996, Village Properties is a locally owned and operated independent agency. The company specializes in residential properties, including beachfront homes, estates, and new homes. Its 41 experienced agents serve Santa Barbara, Montecito, Goleta, Carpinteria, and the Santa Ynez Valley. Relocation experts are also on staff to assist newcomers to the area.

## Other Resources for Finding a Home

The real estate pullout section in the Sunday *Santa Barbara News-Press* is a great resource; it's published in cooperation with the Santa Barbara Association of Realtors. *Casa,* a free tabloid, features real estate ads and photographs of homes for sale as well as a schedule of open houses for the week and a few classified ads for rentals. It is available in real estate offices and at more than 250 street stands in Santa Barbara.

*Homes & Land* runs photos of listed properties along with ads for the real estate companies that are listing them, as does the glossy new *Real Estate* magazine. Ads for fancy estates on the market in Montecito and Hope Ranch can be found in the slick quarterly *Santa Barbara Magazine,* which often shows both interior and exterior shots. Price tags on these homes are seldom below $1 million (actually, you might get a small cottage or condo for $500,000) and are occasionally as high as $20 million.

## The Rental Scene

If you can't afford to buy, you may have to rent, but don't expect to get off without paying a lot of money. (Hey, this is Santa Barbara!) At the end of 2000, the average monthly rent for a three-bedroom apart-

## Insiders' Tip

Looking to rent? Good rentals are often gone by afternoon in Santa Barbara, so read the *Santa Barbara News-Press* classified ads early every morning (not just on weekends!) and call as quickly as you can.

ment in Santa Barbara county was more than $1,900. Home rentals start at about $1,500 a month, and there is literally no ceiling, with large mansions and beachfront properties renting for $20,000 a month or more. In addition, the rental market is as tight as the sales market, so you may have a difficult time finding what you want.

Use whatever network you have in place, as word of mouth is often the best way to find out what's available. Tell everyone you know that you're looking, and follow up on every lead. If you are a college student looking for an apartment or room to rent, your best bet is the student housing office at the college or university you will be attending.

Most Realtors, who have many local contacts, will gladly advise you on rentals, but bear in mind that in Santa Barbara a Realtor gets no commission on rental property. Whether you are looking for a house or an apartment, landlords are choosy about their tenants because the current market allows them to be. Several recent proposals aimed at making the market more equitable for renters are currently under review. Among them, a 60-day notice for changes in the rental contract, interest on security deposits, and monetary relocation assistance for tenants evicted due to landlord code violations.

But because of the tight demand, you need to show you're really serious to secure a place. Pick up a rental application from a local real estate office, fill it out accurately and completely, and when you visit a potential rental, leave a copy with the landlord if you are interested. Make copies so you don't have to fill out a new application each time you apply. Finally, you will need cash in the bank to cover required security and cleaning deposits, usually payable before you take occupancy.

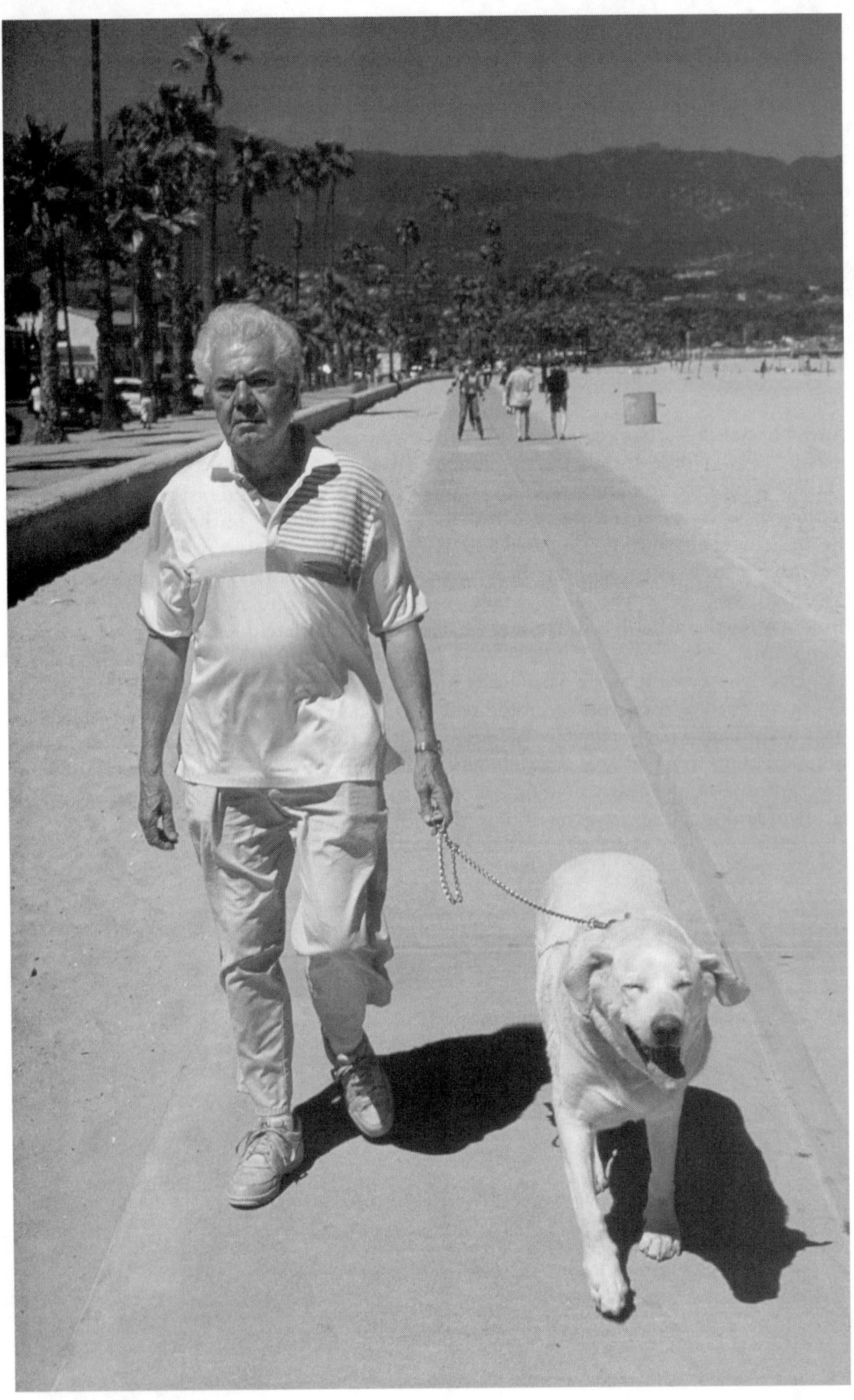

*With its sunny weather and beautiful beaches, Santa Barbara is a popular place to enjoy retirement.*
PHOTO: BRIAN HASTINGS

# Retirement



When people dream of retirement, they often envision a comfortable home in a warm, dry climate, a town or area with plenty of social, recreational, and cultural opportunities, excellent healthcare, friendly people, and beautiful scenery in which to spend the latter decades of life. Santa Barbara, by all accounts, matches this dream as an ideal retirement community. For more than a century, countless seniors and younger retirees from around the United States and, indeed, the world have packed their belongings lock, stock, and barrel and moved to Santa Barbara. In this chapter we focus on seniors, since they comprise the majority of retired folk in Santa Barbara.

Our over-60 crowd makes its presence known everywhere. They play a major role in politics, the arts and culture scene, and Adult Education classes. Senior volunteers serve as docents at the museums, the zoo, the Botanic Garden, and other attractions; as helpers at our numerous service agencies; as tutors, teachers, guides, and mentors to younger Santa Barbarans. Our seniors stay active as long as possible, in all senses of the word. Folks from age 60 to 100 regularly attend fitness classes—it's not unusual to see a grandmother "crunching abs" right next to a 20-year-old. They walk, jog, play tennis and golf, attend concerts, travel, study, and read.

And when seniors are no longer able to venture out as much as they'd like, Santa Barbara makes great efforts to bring services and activities to senior residences throughout the community.

Sound perfect? Well there's one catch. As we've mentioned elsewhere in this book, the cost of living here is exorbitant. In fact, its virtually impossible to live here on Social Security alone, and seniors on limited incomes find it extremely difficult to meet the costs of daily life. Housing and services for lower-income seniors have limited availability and long waiting lists.

Affordability aside, Santa Barbara offers many advantages to retired residents. In this chapter we give you a sampling of our services and programs for seniors—with a special focus on those that can help stretch limited dollars.

We start with general information resources; then move on to senior centers; ways to nourish body and mind; recreation; employment and volunteer opportunities; retirement communities; and housing. For information on Santa Barbara's extensive healthcare system, see our Healthcare and Wellness chapter.

## Tapping into the Senior Network

Your best resource for finding out about senior services and programs is the *Santa Barbara County Senior Resource Directory*. It includes listings of nearly all nonprofit and government agencies that provide services to senior citizens. Its contents are the foundation of this chapter, and you won't find a more comprehensive compendium of information of interest to seniors anywhere else in the county. To receive a copy, call (800) 510-2020 in California or (800) 350-6065 from elsewhere, or drop by one of the senior centers listed later in this chapter.

## Senior Resources

The following organizations provide information on a variety of topics of interest to seniors.

**American Association of Retired Persons (AARP)**
**Santa Barbara Chapter #72**
**333 Old Mill Road, Space 263**
**Santa Barbara, CA**
**(805) 964–3943,**
**(916) 446–AARP, regional headquarters**
**www.aarp.org**

AARP is the nation's leading organization for people age 50 and older. AARP's motto, "to serve and not be served," reflects its commitment to preserving the independence and autonomy of all older persons. It serves the needs of seniors through advocacy, research, and consumer information. An extensive network of local chapters and volunteers provides educational programs and community services for our nation's older population.

Local chapter meetings focus on senior issues and community concerns. Members of Chapter #72 take great pride in donating nearly 6,000 hours of service to the community every year.

**Area Agency on Aging/Central Coast Commission for Senior Citizens**
**208 W. Main Street, Suite B**
**Santa Maria, CA (headquarters)**
**(800) 510–2020, (805) 925–9554**
**www.centralcoastseniors.org**

The Older Americans Act (1965) and its subsequent amendments in 1973 gave birth to Area Agencies on Aging, a network of federal, state, and local agencies, all working together to help seniors maintain independence and dignity in the environments they choose. At the local level, the Area Agency on Aging works in tandem with other public and private agencies to provide senior citizens with a wide range of services.

The Area Agency on Aging for the Santa Barbara region is the Central Coast Commission for Senior Citizens. The organization, which is based in Santa Maria, provides information only over the phone and through its web site. Its programs include home-delivered meals, senior lunches, in-home support services, respite for caregivers, information and referral, transportation services, legal assistance, senior daycare services, senior citizen centers, home repair, and peer counseling.

Senior Connection is a special service of the Area Agency on Aging. The staff can give you information, refer you to appropriate programs and services, and help you with just about any question you have that relates to senior citizens.

**Family Service Agency Senior Outreach Program**
**123 W. Gutierrez Street**
**Santa Barbara, CA**
**(805) 965–1001**
**www.fsacares.org**

If you're older than 60 and live in Santa Barbara, Carpinteria, or Goleta, Family Services will send a professional counselor to your home to assess your needs. Then it will connect you with the appropriate community resources. It will also provide individual, group, and family counseling if you so desire.

The agency also sponsors SAIL—Seniors Aimed at Independent Living. Through SAIL, seniors and disabled persons receive help with home repairs and maintenance. The homeowner provides the material costs and pays a sliding-scale donation for labor based on monthly income. SAIL workers assist with general house upkeep, make safety modifications, and build wheelchair ramps.

**Santa Barbara County Geriatric Assessment Program (GAP)**
**300 N. San Antonio Road**
**Santa Barbara, CA**
**(805) 681–5266**

Are you over 60 and experiencing difficulty in your present living situation? GAP staffers will come to your home to assess your social, environmental, psycho-

## Insiders' Tip

Do you love to read? Santa Barbara's new web-based library reservation system makes hunting down that special book a breeze. Simply go to www.ci.santa-barbara.ca.us/departments/library; search by author, title, subject, or keywords; then request a pickup location at a library close by. You can also browse through more than 800 magazines and medical journals and track down CDs, videotapes, and large-type books. Happy reading!

logical, and health needs. They will also consult with family members, caregivers, and professionals about ways to preserve your independence.

## Frequently Called Numbers

Santa Barbara's senior citizens have access to a wealth of resources. Here's a list of telephone numbers that you'll probably want to have on hand for quick and easy reference.

**American Association of Retired Persons (AARP), (805) 964-3943**

**The Eldercare Locator, (800) 677-1116**

**Family Service Agency Senior Outreach Program, (805) 965-1001**

**Senior Citizens Law Center, (805) 966-4892**

**Senior Connection, (800) 510-2020**

**Senior Information and Referral Help Line, (805) 884-9820**

**Senior Services, (805) 967-7373**

## Senior Centers

All the area community senior centers provide a vast range of information and resources, and each center offers different types of services. Typical examples are lunch programs, community education, recreational activities, music, health screenings, arts and crafts classes, computer training, and health-insurance counseling. Senior centers are excellent places to meet with other seniors and stay active.

**Louise Lowry Davis Recreation Center**
**1232 De la Vina Street**
**Santa Barbara, CA**
**(805) 897-2568, (805) 965-3813 recreation information**

The Louise Lowry Davis Recreation Center is one of the most popular senior centers in the city. Located downtown on the corner of De la Vina and Sola Streets, the center serves as headquarters for the Senior Citizens Information Service. On fair-weather days, you can always see groups of smiling, laughing seniors bowling on the adjacent lawns. You can walk in and join various activities (e.g. chess and bridge) or sign up for weekday recreation programs. The center has a kitchen area, serving area, meeting rooms, restrooms, and on-site parking.

**Insiders' Tip**

Put your name on the waiting list at a senior apartment complex or retirement community as early as possible. And don't be discouraged if the list is long—sometimes the wait is relatively short.

## Other Senior Centers

Other area senior centers also provide social, educational and recreational services and facilities.

### Santa Barbara

**Community Recreation Center**
**100 E. Carrillo Street**
**Santa Barbara, CA**
**(805) 965-3813 (main venue for senior fitness classes)**

**Franklin Neighborhood Community Center**
**1136 E. Montecito Street**
**Santa Barbara, CA**
**(805) 963-7605**

**Westside Community Center/Senior Center**
**423 W. Victoria Street**
**Santa Barbara, CA**
**(805) 963-7567**

### Goleta

**Goleta Senior Center**
**5679 Hollister Avenue**
**Goleta, CA**
**(805) 683-1124**

### Carpinteria

**Carpinteria Senior Center**
**941 Walnut Avenue**
**Carpinteria, CA**
**(805) 684-6090**

# Nutrition

## Grocery Resources

Call the Senior Connection at (800) 510-2020 for a list of stores in your area that deliver or for the names and phone numbers of services that will do your shopping for you.

## Meals Delivered to Your Home

**Community Action Commission Mobile Meals**
**5681 Hollister Avenue**
**Santa Barbara, CA**
**(805) 692-4979**
**www.cacsb.com**

For a suggested donation of $2.25, Mobile Meals delivers a hot noontime meal Monday through Friday to homebound seniors ages 60 and older. Frozen meals for weekends are also available. The delivery area includes Santa Barbara, Goleta, and Carpinteria.

**Meals-on-Wheels**
**(805) 683-1565**

Meals-on-Wheels delivers hot midday meals to homebound seniors every day year-round, including holidays. They charge a modest fee for each meal—call for more information between 9:00 A.M. and noon.

**Senior Brown Bag Program**
**4554 Hollister Avenue**
**Santa Barbara, CA**
**(805) 967-7863**

A project of the Santa Barbara County Food Bank, Brown Bag distributes market-size bags of groceries twice a month to area seniors. The bags are meant to supplement seniors' grocery shopping and include a variety of food items, including produce and bread. To be eligible, you must be 60 or older, have a limited income, and be in an independent-living situation. Singles or couples may apply.

## Dining with Friends

**Cliff Drive Senior Luncheon**
**1435 Cliff Drive**
**Santa Barbara, CA**
**(805) 965-4286**

Join other seniors for lunch every Thursday at noon during the fall, winter, and spring months. A donation is requested.

## Community Action Commission Senior Nutrition Sites

If you're 60 or older, you're eligible for hot lunches at a nutrition site. You need to make reservations 24 hours in advance. Meals are free, but donations are suggested. If you need a ride to the site, transportation may be available. Call the commission headquarters for information and to make reservations at any of the following sites. It's located at 5681 Hollister Avenue in Goleta (805-692-4979, www.cacsb.com).

### Santa Barbara

**Franklin Senior Center**
**1136 E. Montecito Street**
**Santa Barbara, CA**

**Pilgrim Terrace**
**649 Pilgrim Terrace Drive**
**Santa Barbara, CA**

**Presidio Springs**
**721 Laguna Street**
**Santa Barbara, CA**

**Westside Senior Center**
**423 W. Victoria Street**
**Santa Barbara, CA**

### Goleta

**Goleta Senior Center**
**5679 Hollister Avenue**
**Goleta, CA**

### Carpinteria

**Carpinteria Senior Center**
**941 Walnut Street**
**Carpinteria, CA**

## Recreation

Santa Barbara's recreational opportunities are available to active people of every age. See our Recreation chapter for a detailed overview of your many options. Many facilities offer senior discounts—be sure to ask whenever you inquire for information or pay fees.

**Senior Recreation Services Club**
**Santa Barbara Parks and Recreation**
**100 E. Carrillo Street**
**Santa Barbara, CA**
**(805) 897-2519, (805) 965-3813**
**www.sbparksandrecreation.com**

If you're 60 years of age or older, you can join the Senior Recreation Services Club for only $23 a year ($33 per couple). You'll receive a monthly newsletter with details on classes, special events, and an extensive tour and travel program. Members are eligible for discounts on tours and free admission to a range of fitness and personal-enrichment classes.

Most fitness activities take place at the Carrillo Recreation Center, 100 E. Carrillo Street. Others take place at the Louise Lowry Davis Center, 1232 De la Vina Street, and the MacKenzie Park Adult Building in MacKenzie Park, where Las Positas Road and State Street intersect.

Fitness activities include yoga, badminton, table tennis, various exercise classes, t'ai chi, dancercise, slow-pitch softball, lawn bowling, and horseshoes. The stretch and tone class is particularly popular. Personal enrichment classes and social events include dances, bingo, movie days, social luncheons, language classes, ceramics and painting classes, support groups, chess and bridge games.

*Santa Barbara offers recreational activities for people of all ages and interests.* PHOTO: JOHN B. SNODGRASS

## Education

There's no age limit for expanding the mind, and Santa Barbara offers virtually unlimited educational possibilities (see our Education and Childcare chapter for more information). You'll find a variety of lectures, classes, forums, and poetry readings. Here we would like to highlight one of Santa Barbara's shining educational stars—the Adult Education Program—which actually targets seniors and provides special educational programs just for the over-50 set.

**Santa Barbara City College Continuing Education Division**
**Alice E. Schott Center**
**310 W. Padre Street**
**Santa Barbara, CA**
**(805) 687–0812**
**www.sbcc.net/ce**

The Continuing Education Division of Santa Barbara City College, a.k.a. Adult Ed, offers an incredible range of noncredit and community services classes. During fall, winter, spring, and summer sessions, Adult Ed classes meet weekday mornings, afternoons, and evenings as well as Saturdays. More than 36,000 people enroll in Adult Ed classes every year.

Most classes take place at the Alice Schott Center. Others meet at the Selmer O. Wake Center, 300 N. Turnpike (805–964–6853), and at more than 100 locations in the greater Santa Barbara area. Most Adult Ed classes are free, with occasional minimal fees for materials.

Many of the classes are specially designed for seniors. Subjects include the arts, business, finance, real estate, job training, computers, cooking and wine, crafts, current events and world affairs, literature, writing, home and garden, humanities, languages, music, and photography. The Omega Program, developed especially for seniors and frail elderly community residents, offers classes and workshops related to the subject of aging. The Omega Program fosters self-esteem and dignity and helps seniors develop an appreciation of their past roles. Examples of classes include Body/Mind Awareness; Beautiful World, Beautiful People; Our Lives and Times; Music for All Seasons and Reasons; and Words for Thought.

If you enjoy traveling, sign up for some of Adult Ed's popular trips and tours. Local trips enabled groups to explore the new Getty Center museum in Los Angeles and to visit Casa del Herrera, Santa Barbara's premier Spanish Colonial Revival residence. Trips abroad have been offered as well.

## Employment

**AARP Foundation/Senior Community Service Employment Program**
**411 E. Canon Perdido Street #1**
**Santa Barbara, CA**
**(805) 963–1949**
**www.aarp.org**

AARP Foundation is a special, separate branch of the AARP, the American Association of Retired Persons. It arranges hiring, training and placement of seniors in part-time paid positions in public and private nonprofit agencies. You must be at least 55 years old and meet limited-income requirements.

## Volunteer Opportunities

Give the gift of your talent, skills, and time to the community. Many human service agencies such as hospitals, museums, homeless shelters, children's programs, wildlife agencies, and libraries rely on volunteers to keep things running. Here are two clearinghouses for volunteer opportunities. You can also try calling specific programs directly—*The Santa Barbara News-Press* publishes a feature called "Lighting the Way" in the Sunday "Life" section that highlights volunteer opportunities and includes a partial list of nonprofit organizations in Santa Barbara County.

**Non-Profits, Inc.**
**Harmony House**
**1235-B Veronica Springs Road**
**Santa Barbara, CA**
**(805) 563–9111**

This group maintains a list of available volunteers and offers it to community organizations for review. It also maintains a list of community organizations that are seeking volunteers. If you wish, the agency can match you with an organization in which you have special interest and/or that needs someone with your particular skills.

**Retired Senior Volunteer Program (RSVP)**
**Santa Barbara**
**35 W. Victoria Street**
**Santa Barbara, CA**
**(805) 963–0474**

RSVP places seniors in volunteer positions at schools, hospitals, service agencies, senior centers, and other senior programs.

## A Roof Over Your Head

It's very difficult for anyone to find affordable, available housing in Santa Barbara County. Low-cost rentals for seniors are available, but they are in extremely high demand and have long waiting lists. If you have a bit of a nest egg put aside, you may be able to buy or rent a home in your choice of neighborhoods (see our Neighborhoods and Real Estate chapter).

But if you're like many seniors, you may be seeking the security and comfort of a retirement community where you can socialize with peers and take advantage of services that make daily life a bit easier. All the retirement communities below offer, at the minimum, 24-hour security and housekeeping services. We've focused on communities with independent-living residences, although many of these also offer facilities for assisted living as well as skilled nursing.

People who opt for "assisted living" don't need full-time nursing care, but do need some help with dressing, bathing, eating, taking medications, and mobility. Assisted-living facilities provide these services while allowing residents to retain privacy and independence.

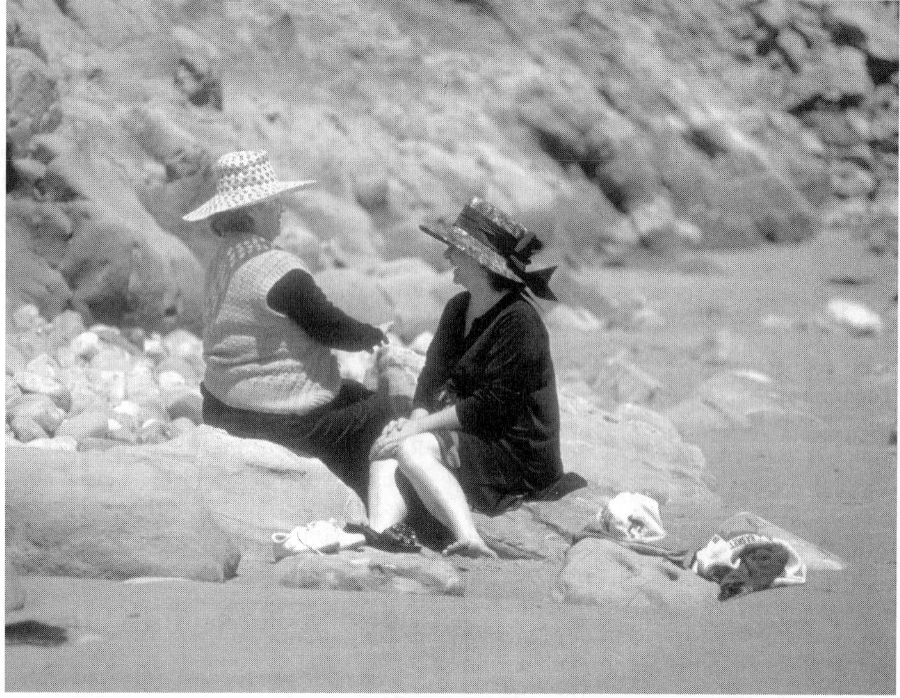

*Retirees enjoy a sunny afternoon on the beach.* PHOTO: JOHN B. SNODGRASS

We do not cover skilled-nursing homes here. We recommend that you call the Senior Connection at (800) 350-6065 if you need information about this level of care in the community. If you're not sure what type of residence is best for you, just ask for guidance. The experienced staff will be more than happy to help.

## Continuing Care Retirement Communities

These facilities offer a continuum of care: independent residential apartments or homes and separate facilities for assisted-living and skilled-nursing care. Costs vary significantly. Some require hefty entry fees plus monthly payments for services. At others, you pay month to month without a significant entry fee or endowment. Be sure to inquire about all the financial requirements when you request information.

### Santa Barbara

**The Samarkand**
**2550 Treasure Drive**
**Santa Barbara, CA**
**(805) 687–0701, (800) 370–5357**
**www.covenantretirement.com**

This Christian retirement community is situated on a 16-acre, centrally located campus in a residential neighborhood bordered by Oak Park, Las Positas Road, and State Street. The Samarkand property originally was a boys' school, which closed in 1920. The land then was subdivided, and the complex became a resort hotel, which was named after the capital city of the Mongol conqueror Tamerlane. A group of local businessmen converted the property to a retirement community in 1955 and sold it to the Evangelical Covenant Church in 1966.

Today the Samarkand is one of 12 Covenant Retirement Communities run by a not-for-profit corporation whose stated mission is to "provide excellent, loving, and personalized care for each resident." The Samarkand campus has about 400 residents in independent-living apartments, a 52-bed assisted-living residence, and a skilled-nursing facility and special care unit. Amenities include a 24-hour emergency call system, housekeeping, linen service, three meals a day, health services, and much more.

Residents of Samarkand can keep busy in the swimming pool and Jacuzzi, exercise room, library, billiard room, woodworking workshop, and hobby room or they can participate in organized activities and adult education programs. Community areas include a 220-seat fellowship hall, a private lounge for small groups, a dining room, and a chapel.

The Samarkand also has scheduled transportation for church, shopping, and appointments, as well as a gift shop, chaplain services, and a barber/beauty shop. Apartments and cottages range from studios to two-bedroom units. Custom apartments are available.

**Valle Verde**
**900 Calle de Los Amigos**
**Santa Barbara, CA**
**(805) 687–1571**

Valle Verde's 65-acre campus rests in the hills of the serene Hidden Valley neighborhood near Hope Ranch and Arroyo Burro Beach. It's owned and operated by American Baptist Homes of the West, a nonprofit corporation that has provided retirement housing and health care services since 1949. Valle Verde opened in 1966 and today offers several levels of care. About 275 of the 420 residents live independently in cottages. The remainder live in an assisted-living complex and the nursing facility.

Many residents ride bikes, golf carts, or motorcycles to get around the sprawling campus, which seems like a country club on a golf course. Amenities include a solar-heated pool and Jacuzzi, library, theater, beauty/barber shop, and a sundries store. It also has a craft room and hobby shop, putting green, hiking trails to the beach and foothills, coach service and city bus service. Activities include adult education and exercise classes.

All apartments feature an emergency call system that connects directly with Valle Verde's Health Center, where registered gerontology professionals are always available. The wellness department arranges weekly clinics with the medical director and provides basic nursing services. The dietary department can design a special diet if you need one.

If your needs change, you can move to assisted living quarters in Quail Lodge or to the Health Care Center, a skilled-nursing facility. Each spacious suite in Quail Lodge has a living area and private bath, along with a call bell system that connects you with staff 24 hours a day. The lodge serves three meals a day in a common dining room, and meals are tailored to the individual dietary requirements of each resident. It also provides housekeeping and maintenance services as well as activities. At the Health Center, licensed nurses and certified nursing assistants are on duty around the clock. They provide postoperative and rehabilitative care and other support services.

**Villa Santa Barbara**
**227 E. Anapamu Street**
**Santa Barbara, CA**
**(805) 963–4428**

Villa Santa Barbara is located just a few blocks from the heart of downtown Santa Barbara's arts and culture district. Residents can walk to the Arlington Theatre, cafes, restaurants, the central library, bookstores, movie theaters, shopping, churches, and the Museum of Art.

Villa Santa Barbara's spacious apartments are available for rent on a monthly basis, with no initial investment other than a security deposit. The monthly fee covers 24-hour staffing, tableside dining service (three meals a day, plus a 24-hour snack and beverage bar), housekeeping and linen services, transportation, and a full recreation program. Activities such as

## Insiders' Tip

Direct Relief International, one of the world's most admired humanitarian-aid organizations, is headquartered right here in Santa Barbara. Founded in 1948 by two Eastern European immigrants escaping WWII, this nonprofit organization ships medical resources to victims of natural disasters, health epidemics, and war. For more information or to volunteer, call (805) 964-4767 or visit www.directrelief.org.

t'ai chi and craft classes, international dinners, and beach walks are available on-site or within walking distance.

Choose from studio or one-bedroom apartments, each with a kitchenette and a terrace overlooking the garden. On-site facilities include a hair salon for both men and women, a library, a TV room, billiards, a theater/music room, and a roof-garden terrace. Villa Santa Barbara is located near doctors' offices, St. Francis Hospital, Cottage Hospital, and Sansum Medical Clinic; the staff provides transportation to appointments. Villa Santa Barbara also offers assisted-living accommodations in its Garden Court.

**Vista del Monte**
**3775 Modoc Road**
**Santa Barbara, CA**
**(805) 687–0793**

Vista del Monte is owned and operated by FACT Retirement Services, a not-for-profit organization that grew from a California teacher's service program established in 1928. Opened in 1964, this serene complex features beautiful landscaping, expansive lawns, and stately pines. It's open to anyone 62 and older. The complex is located next to Hope Ranch, near the Santa Barbara community golf course, hiking trails, and Arroyo Burro Beach.

Vista del Monte offers spacious independent-living apartments, assisted-living accommodations, and a skilled-nursing facility. It boasts a fitness and aquatic center, an adult education program, and an active residents' association. If you need limited assistance with daily activities, you can arrange for a home attendant to come to your residence. In assisted-living apartments, staff is available to help around the clock.

### Montecito

**Casa Dorinda**
**300 Hot Springs Road**
**Montecito, CA**
**(805) 969–8011**
**www.casadorinda.com**

This lush retirement community on 48 beautifully landscaped acres is the ultimate place to spend your golden years. Casa Dorinda was selected as one of the "USA's Top 10" retirement communities in 1995 by *New Choices Magazine.* It originally operated as a for-profit institution, but since 1988 it's been owned and operated by the Montecito Retirement Association, a community-sponsored, not-for-profit corporation serving seniors through estate retirement living.

Casa Dorinda was originally designed by Carleton Winslow for Anna Dorinda Bliss and her husband, William, wealthy New Yorkers who relocated to Montecito in the early 1900s. The grand mansion had more than 80 rooms surrounding a central patio and was once a focal point of Montecito social life. It opened as a retirement community in 1975. Today, more than 300 residents enjoy one of four levels of retirement care, from independent living to hospital care.

Casa Dorinda offers an on-site swimming pool and Jacuzzi, croquet, lawn bowling, a fitness center, transportation services, food service, maintenance, housing care, healthcare, and walking trails through 24 acres of sycamore and oak groves. A full-time activity director plans trips to the theater, symphony, and other cultural events, including excursions to the Los Angeles area. Beaches, bikeways, and mountain trails are all nearby.

The wide selection of apartments ranges from studios to two-bedrooms, all professionally updated and prepared for each resident. You can use the reception rooms for your own parties and to entertain guests. Other facilities include a nursing center, a separate clinic for everyday matters, a 40-room Personal Care Unit, and a state-of-the-art medical center with 52 private rooms, completed in 1997. You must be at least 62 years old at time of entry and meet the entry requirements.

## Senior Apartments

These comfortable apartments appeal to active seniors who want to maintain total independence in a community with their peers.

**Rancho Franciscan Apartments**
**221 Hitchcock Way, #107**
**Santa Barbara, CA**
**(805) 563–0343**

Rancho Franciscan apartments are open to seniors only (minimum age 55). Built in 1988, the Spanish-Mediterranean-style complex is located in the upper State Street area. It's right next door to the Santa Barbara YMCA, which offers Rancho Franciscan residents discounted senior memberships, and it's a few short blocks to grocery stores, La Cumbre Plaza Mall, movie theaters, and restaurants. The MTD bus stops in front.

Rancho Franciscan's 111 units are divided among four stucco buildings with red-tile roofs. You can choose from one- and two-bedroom apartments in two- and three-story buildings (three of the buildings have elevators). Each apartment has a private verandah and modern kitchen facilities.

Fees are by the month and range from approximately $1,059 for a one-bedroom to $1,271 for a two-bedroom apartment, including utilities. Shared amenities include a Jacuzzi, a recreation center, and outdoor barbecue grills. A full-time social director organizes activities such as movie screenings, visits to local art galleries, and picnics.

**Shepard Place Apartments**
**1069 Casitas Pass Road**
**Carpinteria, CA**
**(805) 684–5589**

This senior apartment complex is owned by the same people who own Rancho Franciscan. It features 169 garden-style apartments (one- and two-bedroom), a swimming pool, a spa, and activities. Shephard Place is within walking distance of downtown Carpinteria and the beach. Residents sign a 12-month lease, then rent on a month-to-month basis after the lease expires. Monthly fees range from $985 to $1,020 for one-bedroom apartments and $1,260 to $1,295 for two-bedroom units.

## Door-to-Door Transportation

**Easy Lift Transportation**
**423 W. Victoria Street**
**Santa Barbara, CA**
**(805) 568–5114**
**www.rain.org/~easylift**

Easy Lift is a nonprofit organization providing curb-to-curb, wheelchair-accessible van transportation service for frail elderly and handicapped people who cannot ride the bus. Service is available weekdays from 6:00 A.M. to midnight. Weekend service can also be arranged. The cost is $2 per one-way trip (exact change is required); discount ticket books are available.

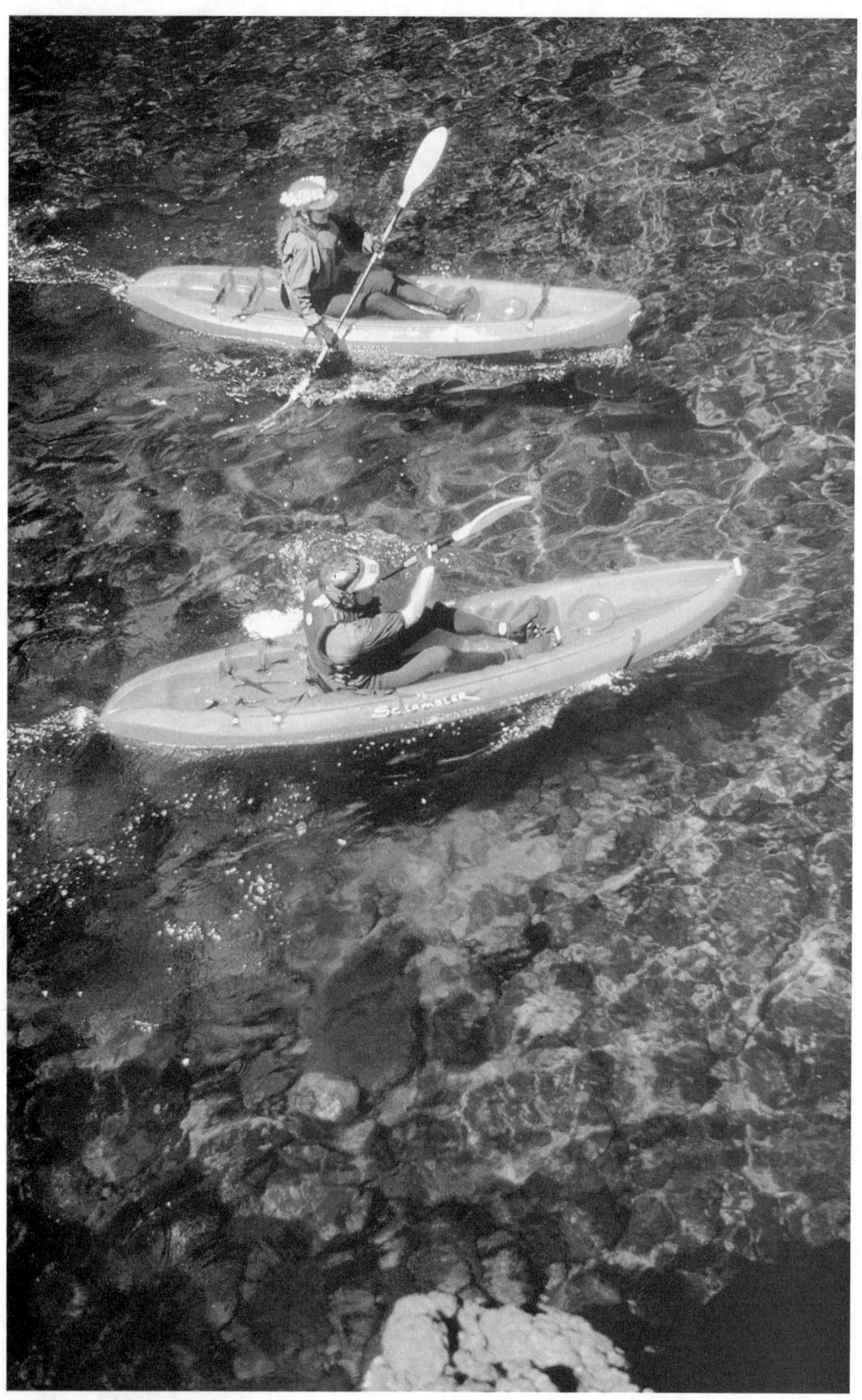

*Thanks to Santa Barbara's fine weather and many parks and beaches, many residents pursue a healthful, active lifestyle.* PHOTO: M. SCOTT MCGUIRE

# Healthcare and Wellness



Illness and injury are rarely on anyone's agenda. But if the unexpected happens while you're in Santa Barbara, it's reassuring to know that you have quick access to first-rate healthcare. The city offers the best concentration of healthcare facilities on the California coast between Los Angeles and the San Francisco Bay area. Every day, people from all parts of the state—and other areas of the country and the world, for that matter—come to Santa Barbara seeking quality healthcare services.

Many of our hospitals and clinics date back a century or more, and our physicians and other healthcare practitioners rank among the best in the nation. It has always been easy to attract top physicians to the area—given the choice, wouldn't anyone rather raise a family in Santa Barbara than in one of the crowded urban centers that many of the major teaching hospitals are located in?

About the only medical services you won't have access to here are treatment for serious burns and organ transplants, and even those types of care can be found at highly rated institutions just an hour or two south of the county line.

Our community emphasizes preventive healthcare and offers many classes and services designed to promote good health. A "Health Calendar" with an extensive listing of nearly all wellness programs, support groups, and services appears every Tuesday in the *Santa Barbara News-Press*.

Most hospitals and clinics accept major insurance plans. However, HMOs are growing rapidly in the area, and along with the growth have come many changes, especially regarding physician choice. It's best to call and check beforehand with the individual hospital, clinic or physician and your insurer to discuss coverage.

We begin this chapter with an overview of our main hospitals and affiliates, followed by descriptions of major clinics and alternative healthcare resources. We've also included handy lists of walk-in clinics, emergency numbers and support services.

## Hospitals

### Cottage Health System

The nonprofit Cottage Health System (www.cottagehealthsystem.org) consists of Santa Barbara Cottage Hospital, Goleta Valley Cottage Hospital (both described below), and Santa Ynez Valley Cottage Hospital. Together they are the largest healthcare provider on the California coast between Los Angeles and the San Francisco Bay area.

Until the mid-1990s, the system's hospitals were all separate institutions. Santa Barbara Cottage Hospital merged with the smaller, community-based facilities so they could share services, save money, and expand their lists of health-insurance providers. So far the merger has proved very successful, and you can count on excellent care at all affiliated centers.

The Cottage System presents a year-round wellness program (as do many of the facilities described below). The program's many offerings include Stop Smoking courses, depression screenings,

**Insiders' Tip**

UCSB Student Health Service (805-893-3371) offers a wide range of affordable health services to registered students, including dental care, x-rays, eye care, physical therapy, gynecology, psychiatry, and health education. Not sure whether you need a doctor? Chat with a nurse advisor first. He or she will assist you with healthcare decisions.

flu shots, community CPR classes, mobile mammography, and tot safety classes.

**Santa Barbara Cottage Hospital**
**Pueblo at Bath Street**
**Santa Barbara, CA**
**(805) 682–7111, (805) 569–7210 emergency department**
**www.cottagehealthsystem.org**

Cottage Hospital is Santa Barbara's oldest and largest hospital. In the 1880s, a group of civic-minded women came up with a radical concept for the times: a group of small cottages, each housing a separate medical department. Together they would provide medical care in a cozy, homelike atmosphere that would help patients recover faster. They decided to call it Santa Barbara Cottage Hospital. Although the cottage-style construction never happened (a single building was constructed instead), the name stuck.

Since 1888, Cottage has grown from a 25-bed facility to a 436-bed, nonprofit acute-care medical center and teaching hospital that admits about 18,000 patients a year. Cottage has been nationally recognized for superior service. Press, Ganey Associates (a national rating company comparing peer hospitals) ranked the Cottage Emergency Department, Cardiac Care Unit, and Outpatient Surgery Center in the top 2 percent of the nation's hospitals in 2000. Cottage Hospital has one of the only graduate medical education programs between the San Francisco Bay area and Los Angeles, with sought-after residencies in internal medicine, general surgery, and radiology.

Cottage Hospital's services run the gamut. It provides immediate trauma response and 24-hour in-hospital coverage for illness and accidents as well as complete psychiatric and chemical-dependency services. About 500 specialists in all major clinical areas make up the hospital's medical staff. Cottage is particularly renowned for its cardiac care (including open-heart surgery), as well as its pediatric and maternal/child services. The hospital boasts a new radiology wing and surgical suites.

Cottage Children's Hospital includes a Childbirth Center (where some 2,500 babies are delivered each year) with a comprehensive maternal/child health program, neonatal and pediatric intensive-care units, a perinatal center for high-risk pregnancies, a perinatal/pediatric ambulance, pediatric surgery, a pediatrics unit, and pediatric GI and pediatric hematology/oncology departments. Outpatient services include cardiac care (a chest pain center, cardiac electrophysiology, heart catheterization labs, and cardiac rehabilitation), an eye center, an outpatient surgery center, a diabetes center, a wound clinic, a biofeedback program, diagnostic ultrasound, CT body scanning, and magnetic resonance imaging. The laboratory, radiology, and physical therapy services offer convenient extended hours.

**Goleta Valley Cottage Hospital**
**351 S. Patterson Avenue**
**Goleta, CA**
**(805) 967–3411**
**www.cottagehealthsystem.org**

Many residents love this small, neighborhood hospital for the friendly, personalized care it has offered since 1966. Formerly called Goleta Valley Community Hospital, the 122-bed institution joined forces with Santa Barbara Cottage Hospital in 1996, but maintains its intimate, community-based character and services. About 2,000 patients check into the hospital every year.

Goleta Valley Cottage Hospital offers a full range of services, including a 24-hour emergency department and heliport, a comprehensive critical care unit, specialized medical/surgical services for both inpatients and outpatients, a breast care center with specialized diagnostic and treatment programs, and an occupational health center. The comfortable, homey Birth Center at Goleta Valley attracts many women with low-risk pregnancies (about 300 babies are born here every year). In fact, Goleta Valley is one of only a handful of hospitals in the United States to receive a Baby-Friendly designation from the U.S. Committee for UNICEF. That's largely because the maternity nurses offer an optimal level of lactation care. They help new moms breastfeed their babies right from the start, and they even visit moms and babies at home to ensure continued breastfeeding success.

## Other Area Hospitals

**The Rehabilitation Institute at Santa Barbara**
**2415 De La Vina Street**
**Santa Barbara, CA**
**(805) 687-7444 ext. 2317**
**www.risb.org**

This beloved, nonprofit community institution has cared for thousands of patients with major disabilities as well as their families. The institute's goal is to return patients to maximum independence. Established in 1967, it provides specialized inpatient, outpatient, and community-based programs for people with brain injury, spinal cord injury, stroke, neurological and orthopedic problems, and other disabling conditions resulting from injury or illness.

The institute's brain injury, spinal cord injury, and comprehensive rehabilitation programs are accredited by the Commission on Accreditation of Rehabilitation Facilities (CARF), the Joint Commission on Accreditation of Healthcare Organizations (JCAHO), and California Children's Services.

The institute is the only freestanding rehabilitation facility between Los Angeles and San Francisco. Therapy schedules are individually tailored to the particular medical condition. Each patient has a treatment team composed of physicians, a rehabilitation nurse, an occupational therapist, a psychologist/neuropsychologist, a case manager, a physical therapist, a recreation therapist, and a speech/language pathologist as appropriate. Families are also involved in education and treatment.

As a "hospital without walls," the institute provides a continuum of treatment, delivering various levels of care in many settings. The continuum begins with acute rehabilitation at the institute's 38-bed main hospital, coordinated by board-certified physicians who specialize in physical medicine and rehabilitation and internal medicine.

Outpatient services are also provided at the Keck Center (805-569-8900) at the main institute site. An affiliate of the institute, The Coast Caregiver Resource Center, at 5350 Hollister Avenue, Goleta (805-967-0220), assists caregivers of adults with brain impairment.

Institute programs also extend to rehabilitation services in retirement communities and skilled-nursing facilities.

**Saint Francis Medical Center of Santa Barbara**
**601 E. Micheltorena Street**
**Santa Barbara, CA**
**(805) 962-7661, (805) 568-5712 emergency department**
**www.saintfrancis.org**

Perched on a Riviera hillside, St. Francis hospital offers state-of-the-art medical care in a friendly, intimate atmosphere. Because of extra-attentive personal care,

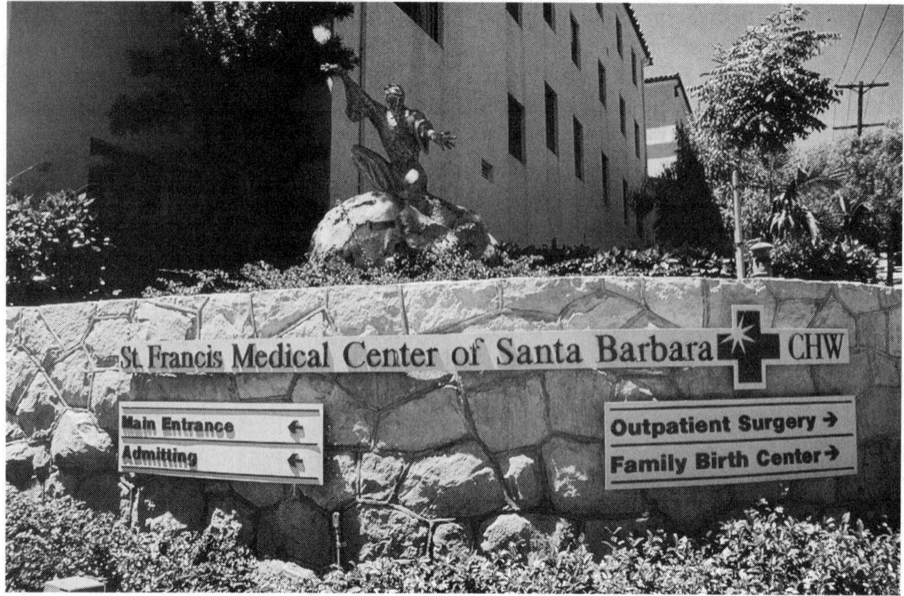


*With its sweeping city views, Saint Francis Medical Center is a favorite local hospital.* PHOTO: BRIAN HASTINGS

supermodern facilities, and fantastic city, ocean, and island views that cheer up recovering patients, Saint Francis is a favorite choice among residents.

Founded in 1908, the 85-bed, nonprofit hospital is now part of the Catholic Health Care West System. About 450 physicians are on the Saint Francis medical staff. The Emergency Department provides 24-hour emergency care for adults and children.

Other Saint Francis features include an intensive-care and cardiac-care unit, magnetic resonance imaging, a catheterization laboratory, a short-stay surgery department with its own waiting and recovery rooms, and an outpatient diagnostic and treatment center.

The surgical department is equipped to handle various types of orthopedic surgery, eye surgery, and cystoscopy. General surgery rooms have laser equipment and closed-circuit television. Saint Francis has a sight-hearing clinic and departments in occupational therapy, physical therapy, outpatient surgery, and radiology. Saint Francis also operates Villa Riviera, a residential care home that provides assisted living for seniors.

Saint Francis presents a regular schedule of wellness programs—call Community Relations at (805) 568–5730. Its Healthscreen program offers free and low-cost screenings several times a year for cholesterol, glaucoma, nutrition, and other needs. The hospital also offers classes for the general public and healthcare providers, for example, adult and pediatric CPR. The Speaker's Bureau and Tour Program arranges for physicians and other healthcare providers to speak at meetings, seminars, or other events.

## Clinics

**The Cancer Foundation of Santa Barbara**
**300 W. Pueblo Street**
**Santa Barbara, CA**
**(805) 682–7300**
**www.ccsb.org**

This nonprofit cancer treatment center, founded in 1949, offers radiation therapy, chemotherapy, and nuclear medicine for cancer patients. It also provides extensive support services for cancer patients and their families and friends. All support services are free and include counseling, home visits, a patient library, relaxation and stress management, support groups, and visitors programs.

**Sansum–Santa Barbara Medical Foundation Clinic**
**Corporate Office: 470 S. Patterson Avenue**
**Santa Barbara, CA**
**(805) 681–7700**
**www.sansum.com**

In October 1998, Santa Barbara witnessed the merger of two of the oldest medical groups in the region: Sansum Medical Clinic and Santa Barbara Medical Clinic. The parent organization is now called Sansum-Santa Barbara Medical Foundation Clinic and serves in an administrative capacity for the newly formed medical group of more than 130 physicians.

Sansum Medical Clinic was established in 1924 by William David Sansum, M.D., who is widely credited as the first American to successfully isolate, produce, and administer insulin to treat diabetes. For decades, Sansum Medical Clinic has enjoyed a local, regional, national, and international reputation as a leading healthcare provider for medical evaluation, diagnosis, and treatment.

Santa Barbara Medical Clinic was founded in 1921 by three physicians. They succeeded in forming a carefully designed group practice to make comprehensive specialty care available to all segments of Santa Barbara at a time when solo practitioners provided most of the care. In 1973, the physician-owners entrusted the clinic's assets, buildings, administrative operations, and contractual agreements to the nonprofit Santa Barbara Medical Foundation Clinic. The physician group kept the name Santa Barbara Clinic, Inc., and was retained by the foundation as a multispecialty physician group to administer health services.

In a nutshell, the merger of these two groups means that you are likely to find excellent healthcare that matches your needs, no matter what ails you or what type of health plan you have.

Sansum-Santa Barbara Medical Foundation Clinic operates the following facilities in Santa Barbara's South Coast region:

**Sansum Clinic**
**317 W. Pueblo Street**
**Santa Barbara, CA**
**(805) 682–2621, (800) 472–6786**

**Foundation Clinic**
**215 Pesetas Lane**
**Santa Barbara, CA**
**(805) 681–7500**

**Ophthalmology Branch/Optical Shop**
**29 W. Anapamu Street**
**Santa Barbara, CA**
**(805) 681–8950;**
**(805) 681–8969, Laser Eye Care Center;**
**(805) 681–8980, Optical Shop**

**Obstetrics/Gynecology Branch**
**515 W. Pueblo Street**
**Santa Barbara, CA**
**(805) 681–8911**

**Sansum Gynecology Branch**
**317 W. Pueblo Street**
**Santa Barbara, CA**
**(805) 898–3282**

**Pueblo Primary Care Branch**
**301 W. Pueblo Street**
**Santa Barbara, CA**
**(805) 898–3291**

**Hitchcock Branch**
**51 Hitchcock Way**
**Santa Barbara, CA**
**(805) 563–6100;**
**(805) 563–1995, pediatrics, community medicine;**
**(805) 563–6100, urgent care;**
**(805) 563–6190, Center for Wellness**

**Santa Barbara Pulmonary and Critical Care Branch**
**601 E. Arrellaga Street #101**
**Santa Barbara, CA**
**(805) 963–2029**

**Goleta Family Practice**
**122 S. Patterson Avenue**
**Goleta, CA**
**(805) 681–1733**

**Immedicenter**
**101 S. Patterson Avenue**
**Goleta, CA**
**(805) 898–3311**

**Montecito Branch**
**1270 Coast Village Circle**
**Montecito, CA**
**(805) 566–5051**

**Carpinteria Branch**
**4806 Carpinteria Avenue**
**Carpinteria, CA**
**(805) 566–5080; (805) 566–5000, urgent care**

Preferential hotel and transportation rates in Santa Barbara are available to Sansum-Santa Barbara Medical Clinic patients and guests. Visit www.sansum.com for a list of participating providers.

**Planned Parenthood of Santa Barbara**
**518 Garden Street**
**Santa Barbara, CA**
**(805) 963–5801**
**www.ppsbvslo.org**

The local Planned Parenthood center offers complete and confidential family-planning services at affordable rates. Services include pregnancy testing, counseling, birth control, infertility treatment, gynecological services, and education programs.

## Walk-In Clinics

Urgent care centers are located throughout Santa Barbara County. These smaller medical facilities provide services for a range of health and wellness needs. They are usually open every day and often have extended hours, typically 8:00 A.M. to 8:00 P.M. weekdays and shorter hours on weekends.

In most cases, you can just walk in—no appointment necessary. If you need quick treatment for minor accidents and emergencies or general family medical care, these are convenient places to go.

Sansum-Santa Barbara Medical Foundation Clinic Urgent Care Centers:

**Immedicenter**
**101 S. Patterson Avenue**
**Goleta, CA**
**(805) 898–3311**
**51 Hitchcock Way**
**Santa Barbara, CA**
**(805) 563–6100**
**4806 Carpinteria Avenue**
**Carpinteria, CA**
**(805) 566–5000**

**MedCenter**
**2954 State Street**
**Santa Barbara, CA**
**(805) 682–7411**

### Insiders' Tip

Lifeline, a wireless device worn around the neck and connected to the telephone, can help elderly or physically-challenged people live independently at home. It's available through Cottage Hospital to anyone who lives from Carpinteria to Santa Ynez for only $30 a month. Call (805) 569-7572.

**MedCenter**
**319 N. Milpas Street**
**Santa Barbara, CA**
**(805) 965–3011**

## Alternative Medicine

Many Santa Barbarans regularly turn to alternative medical treatments, and they don't have to go far to find them. You can find skilled practitioners in nearly every area of alternative healthcare, including naturopathy, homeopathy, clinical nutrition, acupuncture, and herbology. There are also numerous therapists with years of experience in massage, rolfing, shiatsu, and all types of bodywork therapy.

The weekly *Santa Barbara Independent* is a great resource for alternative medical services. You can also consult the Yellow Pages for listings.

## Physician Referral Services

Call any of these numbers to find out which physicians or dentists meet your particular medical and insurance needs.

**Cottage Health System Physician Referrals, (805) 683–5333**

**Dental Society of Santa Barbara-Ventura County, (805) 684–1220**

**Santa Barbara County Medical Society Physician Referral, (805) 683–5333**

**St. Francis Medical Center Physician Referral, (805) 568–5783**

## Numbers to Call

Refer to this list if you are experiencing an emergency situation or need information and assistance regarding community resources. Crisis lines are answered 24 hours a day.

**Emergencies, 911**

**Fire Stations**
**Santa Barbara, (805) 965–5254**
**Gaviota, Goleta, and Isla Vista, (805) 681–5500**
**Carpinteria, (805) 684–4591**
**Montecito, (805) 969–7762**
**Summerland, (805) 684–4591**

**Police or Sheriff Departments**
**Santa Barbara, (805) 897–2300**
**Gaviota and Goleta, (805) 681–4100**
**Isla Vista, (805) 681–4179**
**Montecito and Summerland, (805) 684–4561**
**Carpinteria, (805) 684–4561**

**American Cancer Society, (800) 227–2345**

**California Poison Control, (800) 876–4766, (800) 972–3323 TTY**

**Cottage Hospital 24-Hour Psychiatric/ Substance Abuse Hotline, (800) 895–7800**

### Insiders' Tip

Traveling overseas? If you need help with immunizations, malaria prevention, altitude sickness, or motion sickness, contact the Travel Center of Sansum—Santa Barbara Medical Foundation Clinic, 215 Pesetas Lane, Santa Barbara (805-681-7639). The center provides medical assistance to travelers and up-to-date travel-related health information.

## Insiders' Tip

The *Santa Barbara Independent* lists a wide range of free health services and self-help providers. It's available free at shops and businesses around town.

**Crisis/Suicide Intervention 24-Hour Helpline, (805) 692–4011**

**Coalition to End Domestic and Sexual Violence 24-Hour Hotline, (805) 656–1111**

**Hospice of Santa Barbara, (805) 563–8820**

**National HIV and AIDS Hot Line, (800) 342–2437**

**Pollen and Mold Spore Hotline, (805) 961–3951**

**Santa Barbara Rape Crisis Center 24-Hour Hotline, (805) 564–3696**

**Santa Barbara Council on Alcoholism and Drug Abuse, (805) 963–1433**

**Santa Barbara County Adult and Child Protective Services, (805) 737–7078**

**24-Hour Anger Management Hotline, (805) 656–4861**

# Education and Childcare



Given the intellectual atmosphere of the town, it should come as no surprise that Santa Barbarans have always placed great emphasis on high-quality education. For a relatively small community, Santa Barbara offers incredible educational breadth and diversity. If you're moving here, you'll have access to excellent schools, educational facilities, and programs for all ages, from preschool through retirement years.

At the preschool, elementary, and high school levels, parents have many choices for their children within the public and private sectors. At the higher-education level, Santa Barbara is home to a University of California campus, one of the world's top photographic schools, a highly rated Christian college, and the prestigious Music Academy of the West. Santa Barbara also has one of the nation's leading community colleges as well as a number of continuing education and professional schools.

This chapter provides an overview of the many educational options available in Santa Barbara. We begin with elementary and high school education (public and private), then describe our higher education institutions, including schools that specialize in photography, music, law, and other fields. Finally, we give you a brief overview of resources for finding appropriate childcare and preschools for infants, toddlers, and pre-kindergartners.

## Public Elementary and High Schools

About 25,000 students are currently enrolled in public schools in South Santa Barbara County, the area of focus in this book. Despite the funding cuts that have affected virtually every public school in California over the last 20 years, Santa Barbara's public schools have managed not only to stay afloat but, in many cases, to thrive. At schools where "extra" programs have been eliminated, parents and local school districts have rallied to find innovative ways to raise funds to support them. Hardly a week goes by without a car wash, a jog-a-thon, an auction, or some other form of fund-raising event for local schools.

Many of our schools have earned California Distinguished School status over the years—a designation awarded to only 4 percent of all public schools in the state of California. It's a sure sign of excellent and innovative programs. A high proportion of our schools have also earned the prestigious National Blue Ribbon Award in the last five years (see the individual school districts below). Only about 200 schools in the United States achieve this prestigious designation following a rigorous application and screening process.

Most schools and/or districts in the area also offer GATE (Gifted and Talented Education), and all schools have special education programs. Santa Barbara also has three charter schools—public schools that operate free of many state statutes and regulations—and an Open Alternative School with an alternative curriculum and structure.

Legislation passed in July 1996 provides California public schools with incentive funding to reduce class size in the primary grades to improve instruction and student performance. The law made funds available to elementary schools so that they can reduce class size to 20 students or fewer in first and second grades and then in either kindergarten or third grade, at the school's discretion. Most elementary schools in the county, seizing the opportunity to create smaller classes, quickly arranged for extra classrooms and teachers. At nearly all schools, you can count on classes of 20 or fewer in kindergarten through third grade. Class sizes for grades 4 to 6 are typically 26 to 28 students.

If you're researching public schools in the area, be sure to call individual schools and request their School Accountability Report Card. School boards issue the Report Card annually across the state. It provides information about each school's resources, operations, successes, and areas of growth and improvement. Contents include a school profile, student achievement statistics, class sizes, budgets, expenditures, and other useful information. Most of the school districts in Santa Barbara County also post their report cards on the web. Go to www.sbceo.org/schools and click on the "School Accountability Report Card" link.

## Current Issues in the Public School System

The biggest issues Santa Barbara public schools face today are budget challenges due to rising costs and declining enrollment in our elementary schools. Like everywhere else in the state, California's power squeeze sapped funds from Santa Barbara school districts during the 2000–2001 school year. In addition, school boards predict a substantial increase in medical benefits, property insurance, and liability insurance premiums over the next few years—expenses which represent a significant chunk of the districts' budget. To combat these rising costs, districts are finding ways to conserve resources—especially power. Santa Barbara School Districts, for example, have introduced energy-management systems, completed electrical retrofitting, and installed more efficient heating and cooling systems. Strategies like these will help ease funding pressures, but districts must still find ways to slice dollars from the budget.

As if all this wasn't enough, the Santa Barbara Elementary School District is suffering from declining enrollment. In the 1999–2000 school year, enrollment dropped by at least 100 students and the district expects this trend to continue for the next 10 years. Despite per-student funding allocations, certain expenses such as utilities and some staff salaries remain fixed regardless of student numbers. When enrollment declines, school districts have less money to meet these costs. Why are students leaving? One reason may be that the high cost of living in South Santa Barbara County has forced many families to settle in more affordable satellite suburbs. At the same time, those who can afford to live here often choose to enroll their children in private schools. It's a problem that contributed to a $1-million deficit in the Elementary School District for the 1999–2000 school year and put even more pressure on school boards to cut costs. So now for the burning question—where will the money come from? It's a problem that's been haunting Santa Barbara's school boards for months.

Faced with the reality of more budgetary pressures, parents and school officials have rummaged to find creative ways to meet these new demands without sacrificing the quality of education. In 2001, after toying with the idea of cutting music programs and eliminating librarians to shave money from the budget, the school district finally found another way out. They voted to dispense with several administrative positions and reduce funds for certain supplies. Most welcomed the decision, recognizing that it ultimately had the students' best interests at heart. But no matter which path the school boards take, it usually ends up being a painful one. Everybody seems to agree, though, that the students are the priority and as long as this drives future budgetary decisions, Santa Barbara's schools will continue to enjoy the excellent academic track record they have in the past.

Another very sensitive issue now simmering on the back burner is bilingual education. In June 1998, California voters approved a California state initiative that basically dismantled bilingual education in all California public schools. Since then, most district schools have implemented a number of successful reform initiatives to improve the reading levels of Limited English Proficiency (LEP) students. For example, the Santa Barbara School District implemented an English Acquisition Plan in 1998. Prior to this, only one-third of the districts' third-grade students ended the school reading at or above grade level. With the current focus on literacy, the district's scores have been steadily rising each year and the school districts hope they will continue to do so.

## Public School District Overview

In this section we focus on the major school districts on the South Coast: Santa Barbara and Hope in Santa Barbara; Carpinteria; Cold Spring and Montecito Union in Montecito; and Goleta Union.

### Santa Barbara

The Santa Barbara Elementary School/High School districts are separate districts governed by a single Board of Education. Under the California Education Code, the board operates independently from city or county governments. It has adopted an open-enrollment policy, meaning parents may enroll students at the school of their choice as long as space permits.

**Santa Barbara Elementary School District**
**720 Santa Barbara Street**
**Santa Barbara, CA**
**(805) 963–4331**
**www.sbsdk12.org**

The Santa Barbara Elementary School District covers about 22 square miles in the City of Santa Barbara—and provides instruction for children in kindergarten through sixth grade. It serves more than 6,000 students in 14 schools, including three charter schools (public schools that operate free of many state statutes and regulations) and an Open Alternative School (kindergarten through eighth grade), which has an open structure and curriculum. Some of the schools in this district have earned a string of prestigious awards. In the last five years, Washington and Monroe Elementary received California Distinguished School status, and both were also recipients of the National Blue Ribbon award, along with Peabody Charter School, a two-time recipient. These awards honor only the most exemplary of schools.

In 1999 the district opened Santa Barbara Community Academy, a year-round elementary school requiring uniforms, which now enrolls about 180 students in kindergarten through fourth grade. Additional grade levels up to sixth grade will be added each year until 2003–2004. The academy emphasizes a challenging academic curriculum, including foreign-language instruction starting in the early grades. Student applicants are selected via a lottery system.

In the fall of 2000, the Cesar Estrada Chavez Dual Language Immersion Charter School opened its doors with an enrollment of 39 students. The school uses a 50-50 balance of both English and Spanish to teach a curriculum that meets state standards in all subjects. Most schools in the district offer a number of special programs, including GATE (Gifted and Talented Education) and Mentor Teacher programs. On average, the district's student to teacher ratio is 20 to 1 in kindergarten through grade 3, and 27 to 1 in grades 4 through 6. Since about 40 percent of students do not speak, read, or write English proficiently, the district provides specialized programs such as the English Acquisition Plan to help these students improve their English language skills.

**Santa Barbara High School District**
**720 Santa Barbara Street**
**Santa Barbara, CA**
**(805) 963-4331**
**www.sbsdk12.org**

The Santa Barbara High School District serves approximately 10,800 students in grades 7 through 12. This district covers a much wider region than the elementary district—about 136 square miles—and draws students from all neighborhoods stretching from Goleta to Montecito. The district schools include four junior or middle schools (La Cumbre, La Colina, Santa Barbara, and Goleta Valley), three high schools (Dos Pueblos, San Marcos, and Santa Barbara) and one continuation high school.

Each school offers a comprehensive curriculum that meets all state and district standards. GATE, Advanced Placement, and ESL classes are available and many of the schools have earned distinguished awards. In the past five years, La Colina Junior High, Goleta Valley Junior High, and Dos Pueblos High attained California Distinguished School status; Santa Barbara Junior High was a first-time recipient of this impressive award in 2001. Dos Pueblos High and Goleta Valley Junior High also received the illustrious National Blue Ribbon Award. In addition, the district produced 14 National Merit Scholarship finalists in 2001.

Consistently a standout in this impressive lineup of schools is Dos Pueblos High. For the past eight years, students from the school earned the highest average SAT scores in the county: 119 points higher than the state average and 113 points higher than the national average. The Academic Performance Index places Dos Pueblos in the top 10 percent of all high schools in the state. Average scores at the other local high schools are slightly lower, but also well above the national average.

Over the last few years, the district has launched some innovative on-campus academies or "school-within-a-school" programs. These academies are designed to prepare students for various careers. Santa Barbara High School has on-campus academies for the visual arts, multimedia arts, and horticulture. In the fall of 2001, San Marcos High School introduced a Health Careers Academy, and in 2002, Dos Pueblos High School will launch an Engineering Academy. Students wishing to enroll in these programs must submit an application for review.

All schools in this district offer a full range of athletic and extracurricular activities and are fully wired for the computer and Internet age. Classes typically have about 18 students to each teacher.

**Hope School District**
**3970 La Colina Road**
**Santa Barbara, CA**
**(805) 682-2564**
**www.sbceo.k12.ca.us/hopesd/**

With more than 1,300 students enrolled in kindergarten through grade six, this small district consists of three excellent elementary schools in the Hope Ranch/San Roque/La Cumbre area: Monte Vista, Hope, and Vieja Valley. Hope Elementary School reopened in September 1997 after being closed for more than 20 years. Monte Vista and Vieja Valley have both been named California Distinguished Schools in the last decade, and Monte Vista was recognized as a National Blue Ribbon School in 1997. To receive this award , a school must demonstrate a strong commitment to educational excellence for all students. At these schools, median test scores in reading, math, and language in grades 2 through 6 regularly rank in the high-70th to 80th percentiles nationally.

The Hope District provides a number of special programs, including GATE, Esperanza, and assistance for students with learning differences. Each school has computer labs with networked computers, and every classroom has a Macintosh computer with CD-ROM capabilities. The average number of students per teacher is 20 for kindergarten through grade 3 and 27 for grades 4 through 6. The Hope District spent $4,100 per student in 2000.

## Insiders' Tip

Researching Santa Barbara schools? Check out the Santa Barbara County Education website at www.sbceo.org. You'll find links to public and private schools, as well as API reports, School Accountability Report Cards, STAR test results, and other resources for parents, teachers, and students.

### Goleta

**Goleta Union School District**
**401 N. Fairview Avenue**
**Goleta, CA**
**(805) 681–1200**
**www.goleta.k12.ca.us**

The Goleta Union School District has 10 schools with more than 4,500 students enrolled in kindergarten through grade 6. It has nationally recognized programs in bilingual education, composition, computer literacy, and mathematics. All the district's schools offer technology programs as well as music, art, and physical education. GATE is offered in grades 4, 5, and 6 and special education programs are available throughout the district.

Goleta Union parents and community members are very supportive and active participants in the schools, and the students' academic performance reflects this involvement. In school year 1999–2000, of the 11 schools in the county that attained the statewide API (Academic Performance Index) of 800 or above, four were in the Goleta Union School District. The district also ranks consistently above the national average and state average in academic tests. In 2001, Mountain View was designated a Blue Ribbon School, the highest national honor bestowed upon a public or private school. Average number of students per teacher is typically 20 from kindergarten through grade 3, and 28 in grades 4 four through 6. In 2000–2001, the district spent $6,302 per child. All the schools in this district have undergone extensive refurbishments in recent years. The Goleta community passed a $26-million school construction bond measure in November 1996, and the money was used to repair and upgrade school infrastructures, build new classrooms and libraries, and replace the oldest school (Isla Vista) with a new facility for 700 students.

### Montecito

**Cold Spring School District**
**2243 Sycamore Canyon Road**
**Montecito, CA**
**(805) 969–2678**
**www.sbceo.k12.ca.us/~coldspring/**

Tucked in the leafy foothills of Montecito, Cold Spring School is a one-school district serving approximately 240 students in kindergarten through 6th grade. Student academic performance at this excellent school consistently ranks in the top 10 percent to 15 percent of all elementary schools in California. In addition to its core teaching staff, the school employs a technology specialist; three resource specialists for reading, special education, and language; and professional musicians and artists who provide instruction in visual arts, ceramic sculpture, drama, and music. New to the school is a tech lab with 28 computers, and if they wish, students can hone their computer typing and chess skills in an after-school enrichment program. In 2000–2001, the nonprofit Cold Spring School Foundation raised approximately $105,000 to support these programs. The school has also established a working relationship with nearby Westmont College, whose students serve as teacher's aides for extracurricular activities. Average number of students per teacher is 20 or fewer for kindergarten through grade 3 and 25 in grades 4 through 6. In 2000–2001, total expenditure per pupil was approximately $6,700.

**Montecito Union School District**
**385 San Ysidro Road**
**Montecito, CA**
**(805) 969–3249**
**www.sbceo.k12.ca.us/~montecit/**

Set on a beautiful eight-acre site in an exclusive neighborhood, Montecito Union is a highly regarded one-school district with grades kindergarten through 6. Enrollment is approximately 510 students. The district has an outstanding academic record. In 2000–2001, students achieved the highest Academic Performance Index (API) of any school district in Santa Barbara County. Students in all grade levels also regularly rank in the 80th and 90th percentiles nationally in reading, language, and math tests. In 1998, the school was awarded California Distinguished School status. It was one of only two schools in California to receive a perfect score on all 11 areas of evaluation. Montecito Union offers a GATE program and hires specialists to teach computer sciences, music, art, Spanish, physical education, and ESL. Budding musicians can join one of two school bands and students can use the resources of a new media center with a well-stocked library and a state-of-the-art computer lab. In 2000, the district upgraded the campus, adding seven new classrooms and replacing six portable ones. Parents can expect an average of 20 students per teacher in kindergarten through grade 3, and 22 students per teacher in grades 4 through 6.

### Carpinteria

**Carpinteria Unified School District**
**1400 Linden Avenue**
**Carpinteria, CA**
**(805) 684–4511**
**www.cusd.net/home**

Carpinteria Unified serves the communities of Carpinteria, Santa Claus Lane, Serena, and Summerland from the Rincon to Ortega Ridge Road and the Pacific Ocean to the Los Padres National Forest. The district's eight schools include the Early Childhood Learning Center (kindergarten only) and Foothill High School, an alternative school. About 3,100 students are enrolled in grades kindergarten through 12. In 2001, Carpinteria Middle School received the prestigious California Distinguished School award for the 2000–2001 school year. The Early Childhood Learning Center is said to be one of the best in the nation, and Carpinteria students in the primary and elementary grades consistently score above the state average on standardized tests. Approximately 90 percent of high school graduates continue on to college, enroll in an apprenticeship program, or join the armed forces.

The district places a strong emphasis on integrating the tools of technology into its academic programs. Special education programs include GATE and assistance for those challenged in areas of learning, communication, and physical abilities. In addition, all English language learners receive primary language support through their core academic classes. Average number of students per teacher for the district is 20 for kindergarten through grade 3, 30 for grades 4 through 5, and 28 for grades 6 through 12. In 2000–2001, the district spent approximately $6,235 per student.

## Private Schools

Santa Barbara's private schools range from small, affordable nonsecular schools to very expensive high schools that prepare students for entry into the best universities in the country. If you're looking into private schools, you'll have no trouble finding one that suits your children's academic interests and personalities. It might be difficult, however, to find one that pleases your pocketbook.

Typical annual tuition at private elementary schools ranges from $8,000 to more than $13,000. Parochial schools are sponsored by parishes and usually cost considerably less. Many private schools offer some form of financial aid for qualified students—be sure to ask for information if your funds are limited.

Before you begin your search, be forewarned that application to one of Santa Barbara's private schools does not guarantee admission. The most sought-after schools typically have only one or two classes per grade and are flooded with applicants. Some schools can have as many as 100 applications for a single, 25-student kindergarten class, which is often already filled with siblings of older students.

We recommend you apply to several schools to widen your options. At most independent schools, a child must be at least 5 and sometimes 5.5 years by September 1 in the year he or she enters kindergarten.

Santa Barbara also has a number of parish-supported elementary schools (Catholic, Episcopalian, and other denominations). Tuition at these schools is generally more affordable than at other independent schools. Keep in mind, however, that admission preference is given to registered active members of the parish. If you're interested in enrolling your children in a particular parochial school, we suggest you contact the parish directly.

Following is a roundup of many of the finest private schools in the area. All are co-educational. You can also check the Yellow Pages under "Schools" for a comprehensive list of local educational institutions.

## Santa Barbara

**The Anacapa School**
**814 Santa Barbara Street**
**Santa Barbara, CA**
**(805) 965–0228**
**www.anacapaschool.org**

The Anacapa School is a college-preparatory day school for grades 7 through 12. Founded in 1981, the school is very small (only 72 students), so students receive a great deal of personal attention. The student-to-teacher ratio is 6-to-1 and class sizes average 12 students.

The curriculum emphasizes critical thinking and writing skills and offers a wide range of classes from core academics to electives such as animation and organic gardening. Students go on regular field trips, day excursions, and two camping trips a year. Almost 100 percent of Anacapa graduates continue on to college and many have gained admission to some of the nation's top tertiary institutions.

The school is located right in downtown Santa Barbara, so visits to the main library, the Museum of Art, the Courthouse, and other downtown facilities are incorporated into the school's activities schedule.

**Bishop Garcia Diego High School**
**4000 La Colina Road**
**Santa Barbara, CA**
**(805) 967–1266**
**www.bishopdiego.org**

Bishop Garcia Diego is a Catholic high school (grades 9 through 12) with an enrollment of approximately 340 students. It was founded in 1940 as Santa Barbara Catholic High and was later renamed to honor California's first bishop, Francisco Garcia Diego y Moreno. It operates in the Catholic tradition, teaching moral virtues and stressing a philosophy of scholarship and Christian service. The academic program offers a traditional, challenging, and comprehensive curriculum in three tiers: college preparatory with honors, college preparatory, and high school. Advanced Placement classes are available to qualified students in English, American History, Calculus, and Spanish. More than 98 percent of Bishop graduates are accepted at colleges and universities throughout the country. The school also offers a state-of-the-art technology program as well as courses in the creative arts. Average class size is 18 students, and the student-to-teacher ratio is 12 to 1.

Bishop Garcia Diego is Santa Barbara's only Christian high school and admits students of all races, religions, and ethnic origins.

**Laguna Blanca School**
**4125 Paloma Drive**
**Santa Barbara, CA**
**(805) 687–2461**
**www.lagunablanca.org**

Founded in 1933, Laguna Blanca School is a top-notch college-preparatory day school for students in kindergarten through grade 12. In September 2000, the kindergarten through grade 4 classes moved to the former Howard School campus at 260 San Ysidro Road in Montecito. Grades 5 through 12 remain on the school's 29-acre campus in the heart of the affluent Hope Ranch neighborhood. Since the move, most of the extra space on the Hope Ranch grounds has been converted to a Middle School Campus and additional facilities such as a state-of-the-art computer lab, an additional classroom, a student store, offices, and a new art room. The school offers 21 Advanced Placement courses, an outstanding visual and performing arts program, a community-service component, interscholastic athletic competitions, student exchange opportunities, and a host of extracurricular activities. Not surprisingly, admission to Laguna is highly competitive. The school has a total capacity of about 430 students (330 in Hope Ranch and 100 in Montecito) with a maximum class size of just 15 students. Each year 100 percent of Laguna graduates are accepted to college. Out of 29 students in Laguna Blanca's class of 2001, an unprecedented 44 percent received National Merit Scholarship recognition. The class produced one winner, four finalists, seven commended scholars, and one National Hispanic Recognition Scholar Finalist.

**Marymount of Santa Barbara**
**2130 Mission Ridge Road**
**Santa Barbara, CA**
**(805) 569–1811**
**www.marymountsb.org/**

Marymount is set on 10 acres of wooded grounds that once belonged to an old Riviera estate. The school enrolls about 250 students and welcomes qualified applicants of good character from all religious traditions, races, and ethnic origins for grades kindergarten through 8.

Marymount was founded in 1938 by the Religious of the Sacred Heart of Mary. Today it's a nonprofit corporation governed by a board of trustees and is one of the oldest and most respected private schools in Santa Barbara. Its two-track religion program (Catholic Studies and Religious Studies) grows from the Judeo-Christian tradition and emphasizes moral development and community service. Students may choose an appropriate track, depending on their religious backgrounds.

The strong academic curriculum (which includes Latin instruction as of 2001) and small classes (averaging about 20 students) are designed to promote self-esteem and the love of learning in each student. The school has an iMac computer lab and employs a learning specialist for students with special needs. Academic performance consistently ranks in the 50th percentile and above among the nation's independent schools. Marymount encourages creative expression and emphasizes physical fitness and good sportsmanship.

**Santa Barbara Middle School**
**2300-A Garden Street**
**Santa Barbara, CA**
**(805) 682–2989**
**www.sbms.org/**

Founded in 1976, Santa Barbara Middle School spans grade 6 through 9 and seeks to develop well-rounded and well-grounded teenagers through an innovative curriculum incorporating outdoor team trips. On a typical day, students attend challenging academic classes in the morning and engage in creative arts and sports activities in the afternoon. In addition, they participate in three "rite of passage" field trips a year linked to their academic course of study. The fall and mid-year trips are usually a week in length. The end-of-year trip lasts from 10 days to two weeks.

In the Rite of the Wheel portion of the program, for example, students bicycle more than 1,500 miles in seven states during the course of their enrollment. They hike and backpack, travel, eat and camp with their headmaster and teachers. The annual trips teach students about the history, culture, and geography of a particular region and help them learn teamwork, self-confidence, and self-reliance (for example, they learn to repair their own bikes).

Advanced Placement classes are offered in all core subjects. The school also boasts an excellent drama department and supplements its challenging academic curriculum with technology courses in computers, digital animation, and digital filming. It also provides a Learning Difference program for special needs students. The 150 students enrolled at the school are organized into age-appropriate academic villages with an average class size of about 15. Students also participate in a one-week work internship in the community.

**The Waldorf School of Santa Barbara**
**2300-B Garden Street**
**Santa Barbara, CA**
**(805) 569–2558**
**www.waldorfsantabarbara.org/**

The Waldorf School of Santa Barbara is one of at least 750 Waldorf Schools in 35 countries. It opened in 1984 and is now a complete elementary school with about 170 students in pre-kindergarten through grade 8. The 6-acre campus lies on a beautiful historical site between Mission Santa Barbara and the Natural History Museum.

Waldorf teaching methods are based on the approach of Rudolf Steiner, an Austrian philosopher/teacher. They emphasize disciplined creativity, as well as reverence and respect for the beauty of all living things. Specialty classes supplement traditional core subjects. They include Spanish and German (from grade 1); handiwork such as knitting and crochet to develop logical thinking and concentration; Eurythmy, in which words are expressed through dance; Bio-Dynamic gardening; and music instruction such as flute, recorder, violin, cello, and chorus. The curriculum is presented in a supportive, structured, and noncompetitive environment, and support programs are offered to children with special needs. In addition, Waldorf teachers move with the classes (which average about 19 students) from grade 1 all the way through to grade 8. Financial adjustments for lower-income families are available.

## Goleta

**Montessori Center School**
**401 N. Fairview Avenue #1**
**Goleta, CA**
**(805) 683–9383**
**www.sbceo.k12.ca.us/~mcssb/**

Founded in 1965, The Montessori Center School is a nonprofit organization offering pre-primary, primary, and elementary education for approximately 250 students from 18 months of age through grade 6.

Set amid beautiful gardens, the school follows a traditional Montessori curriculum, which emphasizes independent, self-paced learning. Montessori students learn to manipulate specially designed learning tools at an early age to experience concrete principles and then move to higher degrees of complexity and abstraction. These methods aim to foster self-awareness, leadership, teamwork, and creativity in thinking. Each class incorporates three different grade levels. Montessori advocates believe this allows children to learn from one another. In this mixed-age environment, older children can act as role models and reinforce their own skills by sharing their knowledge with younger children. The school also aims to foster an appreciation for the environment and offers children the chance to participate in frequent camping trips. Spanish and French are taught to children at a very young age, all classes learn sign language, and programs are offered for students with special needs. Adult to child ratios are typically 1 to 6 in pre-primary classes and 1 to 12 in primary, lower-, and upper-elementary. In annual standardized tests, upper-elementary students at the Montessori Center School consistently average results between two and three years above their grade level.

**Santa Barbara Christian School**
**4200 Calle Real**
**Goleta, CA**
**(805) 967–1269**
**www.sbceo.k12.ca.us/%7Esbcs/contact.htm**

Established in 1960, the Santa Barbara Christian School in Goleta provides a program of high-quality, nondenominational Christian education. The curriculum focuses on helping students (grades kindergarten through 8) attain a balance of rigorous intellectual competence, healthy character development, and a personal commitment to Jesus Christ. Children from both Christian homes and those with no church affiliation are welcome.

The school emphasizes biblical doctrine, spiritual lifestyle, and excellent academics. It also provides instruction in art, music, foreign language, and athletics, and students have access to a computer lab. Although the school offers no special education programs or GATE, students are tested for learning differences and the school works with private tutors. Currently the school is located on two campuses: kindergarten through grade 5 are in interim housing at 4200 Calle Real in Goleta, and grades 6 through 8 (middle school) are at a new location at Shoreline Community Church, 935 San Andres, Santa Barbara. The proposed new location for K to grade 5 is the Emanual Lutheran Church, 3721 Modoc Road, Santa Barbara. The total enrollment is about 265 students with an average of about 18 students per teacher.

## Montecito

**Crane School**
**1795 San Leandro Lane**
**Montecito, CA**
**(805) 969–7732**
**www.sbceo.k12.ca.us/~crane/**

Set on 11 beautiful acres in affluent Montecito, Crane School offers a challenging academic curriculum for grades kindergarten through 8. The school was established in 1928 and has an excellent reputation. Crane's teachers encourage independence and creativity while helping students use their education to become kind and responsible human beings. The school teaches a traditional curriculum using a stimulating and innovative approach. Art, drama, music, and athletics are critical facets of the syllabus, and the school offers a bevy of special programs in areas such as technology, library media, visual arts, and physical education.

Total enrolment is 229 students. Grades kindergarten through 5 have a maximum 20 students per class and grades 6 through 8 are divided into sections of 12 to 16 students. Because Crane insists on small class sizes and has only one class per grade level, admission is extremely competitive.

## Carpinteria

**Cate School**
**1960 Cate Mesa Road**
**Carpinteria, CA**
**(805) 684–4127**
**www.cate.org**

Cate School is regularly ranked among the top college-preparatory boarding schools in the nation. The four-year high school (grades 9 through 12) was established in 1910 and boasts a gorgeous, 150-acre campus set on a mesa overlooking the ocean and the Carpinteria Valley.

About 260 students from all over the world are enrolled at Cate, and approximately 220 of them live on campus. Average class size is 12 students, and the school offers Advanced Placement courses in more than 18 subjects.

Admission is competitive: for the 2000–2001 school year, about 450 students applied and only 145 were accepted for enrollment. Nearly 25 percent of the student body receives financial aid. In recent years Cate students have won National Merit Scholarships, National Science Scholarships, and numerous other awards. One hundred percent of Cate graduates go on to four-year colleges and universities such as Stanford, Harvard, UC Berkeley, and Brown.

## Higher Education

**University of California at Santa Barbara**
**Santa Barbara, CA**
**(805) 893–8000**
**www.ucsb.edu/**

UCSB is one of the nine campuses that form the University of California system—widely regarded as the nation's leading public system of higher education. UCSB is unquestionably the educational jewel of the Santa Barbara area. Its presence extends well beyond the campus, influencing community arts, athletics, the intellectual scene, politics, and more.

UCSB offers an array of undergraduate majors, more than 50 master's degree programs, and nearly 35 doctoral programs. The campus includes three colleges: Letters and Science, Engineering, and Creative Studies. It's also home to two professional schools: the Graduate School of Education and the School of Environmental Science and Management.

The university "family" includes about 16,700 undergraduates, 2,200 graduate students, and more than 900 faculty members. About 2,500 students live on campus and most of the others live in adjacent Isla Vista, a high-density student community with shops, restaurants, and a zillion bicycles.

Since the campus consists of nearly 1,000 acres of prime coastal property on the edge of the Pacific, replete with beaches, palm trees, lagoons, and meadows, one might wrongly assume that academics are a low priority compared with surf, sun, and fun. On the contrary—since UCSB was founded in 1944, it has firmly established itself as a world-class research center and teaching institution.

A recent national study of America's top research universities ranks UC Santa Barbara as one of the top two public universities nationwide based on criteria such as research dollars, prestigious fellowships, and number of publications.

UCSB is also an elected member of the Association of American Universities, which includes 61 leading institutions of higher learning in the United States and Canada, including Stanford, Harvard, and UC Berkeley. The Carnegie Foundation for the Advancement of Teaching also ranks UCSB as one of America's top research institutions.

### Insiders' Tip

Counseling and Career Services at UCSB are not just for campus-related problems. If you're a student of the university and are having trouble with relationships, stress, homesickness, or depression, they can help. Call (805) 893-4411 or visit the office in Building 599.

The university is best known for interdisciplinary research. It's small enough for different colleges and departments to collaborate, which leads to more discoveries. This makes it easier to get funding, which in turn makes it easier to attract experts and more money. In recent years, UCSB's faculty members dazzled the academic community by winning three Nobel prizes in chemistry and physics. The faculty also includes fellows of the National Endowment for the Humanities, recipients of the National Medal of Science, and members of the National Academy of Arts and Sciences, the National Academy of Sciences, and the National Academy of Engineering.

UCSB has eight national research centers and institutes, including the Institute of Theoretical Physics, the Center of the Study of Quantized Electronic Structures, the Marine Science Institute, and the Institute for Crustal Studies (earthquake research). Seven of the centers are sponsored by the National Science Foundation. UCSB also has an excellent reputation for teaching.

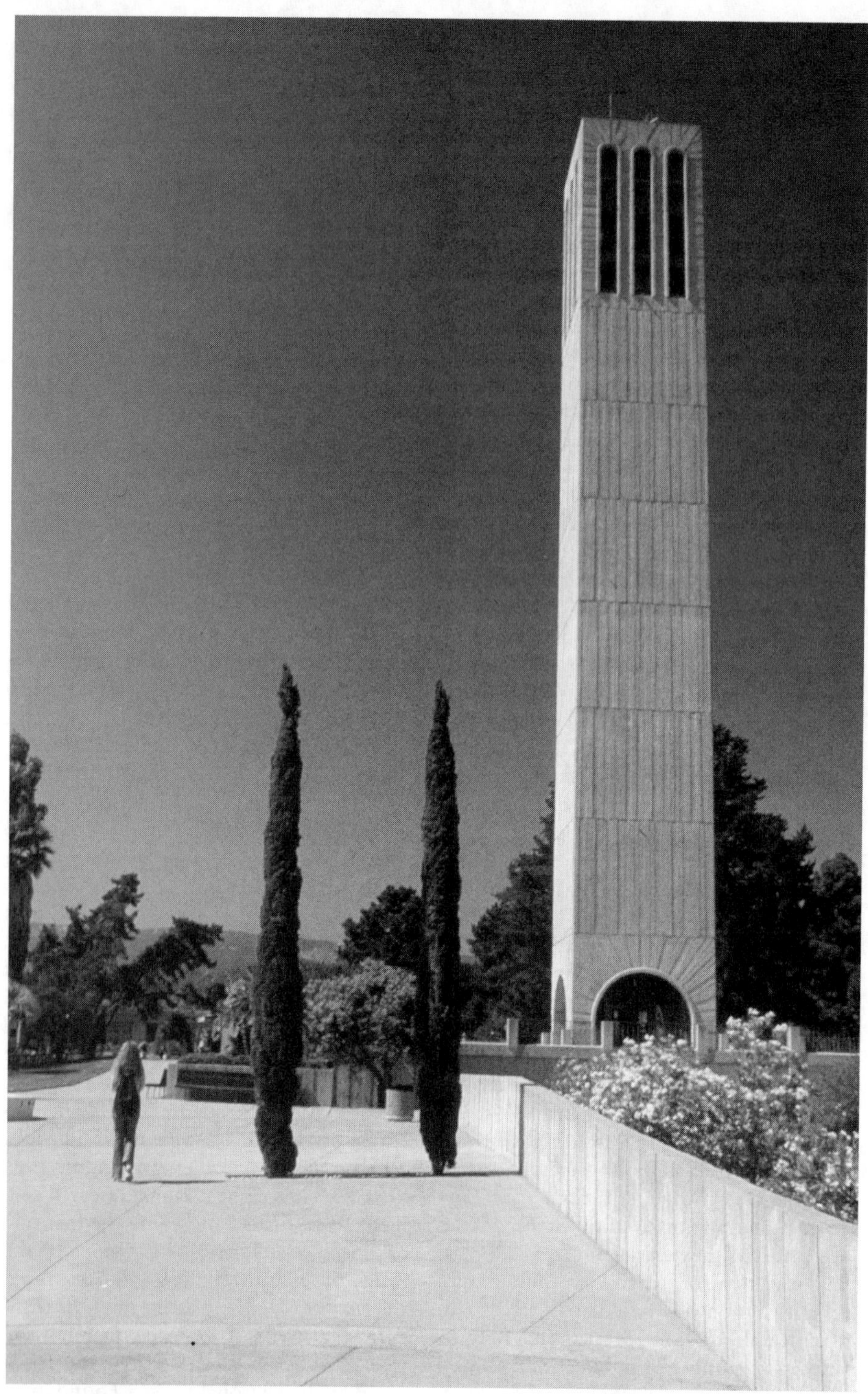

*UCSB's Storke Tower Carillon has 61 bells and an observation deck offering panoramic views.*
PHOTO: BRIAN HASTINGS

The university is particularly renowned for its accomplishments in the realm of science and technology. According to Science Watch ranking by the Institute for Scientific Information, UCSB rates among the top 10 federally funded universities in the nation. In addition, Governor Gray Davis selected UCSB as the first of three California Institutes for Science and Innovation in December 2000. This university research partnership with UCLA will receive $100,000 annually to produce scientific advances in areas upon which California's economic health depends.

In the 2001 edition of *U.S. News and World Report*'s "America's Best Colleges" guide, UCSB was also named the 13th-best public university in the nation. That's quite a feat for an educational institution basking in one of the country's most beautiful but potentially distracting locales.

Not surprisingly, undergraduate admission to UCSB is highly competitive. In the fall of 2000, UCSB received a record 31,000 applications for freshman admission. Of these applicants, the university admitted 47 percent and enrolled only 23 percent. That freshman class was one of the most academically gifted entering classes in the university's history, with average total SAT scores of 1189 and average high school GPAs of 3.72. Considering the university's excellent academic reputation (not to mention its palm-studded setting) it's no wonder students are scrambling to sign up.

**Insiders' Tip**

Be safe. If you're traveling alone between the UCSB campus and Isla Vista at night, call (805) 893-2000 for a free escort. Community Service Officers will accompany you anywhere on campus or in IV between dusk and 4:45 A.M.

## Community Colleges and Continuing Education

**Santa Barbara City College**
**721 Cliff Drive**
**Santa Barbara, CA**
**(805) 965–0581 ext. 7222**
**www.sbcc.net**

Widely regarded as one of the leading two-year community colleges in the state and the nation, seaside SBCC offers more than 90 degree and certificate programs to more than 12,000 students from Santa Barbara, virtually every state in the country, and more than 60 countries worldwide. The college also boasts one of the most breathtaking settings of any educational institution in the country. It's set high on bluffs overlooking the Santa Barbara Harbor.

Credit programs are open to any student who is at least 18 years of age or has earned a high school diploma or the equivalent. Students can receive an associate's degree; develop vocational, technical, and career skills; or prepare for transfer to a four-year university.

Nonresidents of California may attend City College, but they have to pay higher fees. To establish residency in California, you must be physically present in California for one year plus one day prior to the start of the semester and prove that you intend to make California your permanent place of residence.

To prove intent, you need to provide documentation, e.g., California State Income Tax returns, voter registration dates, California driver's license and registration, and W-2 forms with a California address. You will have to complete and file a residency questionnaire, a statement of financial independence, and evidence of permanent California residency no later than two weeks prior to your registration date.

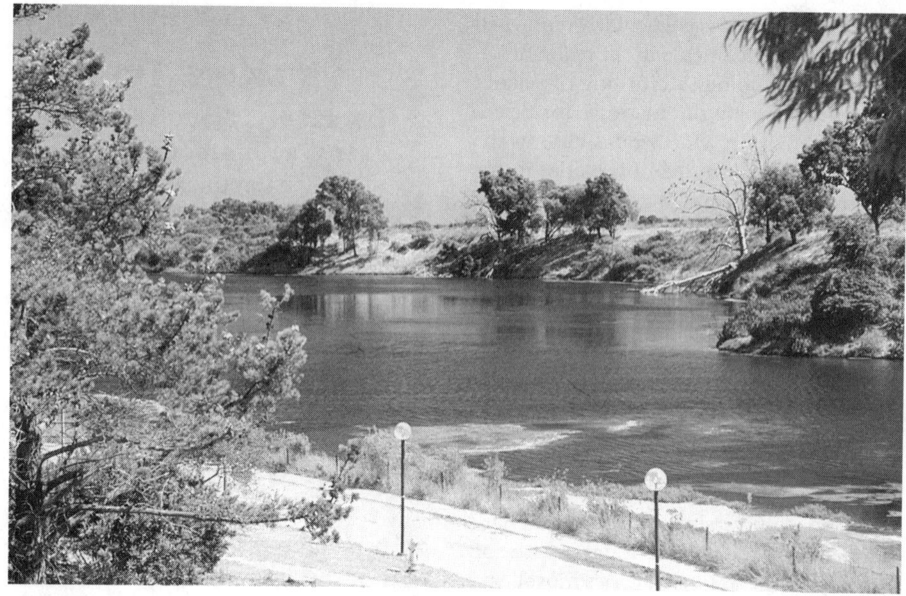

*The UCSB campus boasts nearly 1,000 acres of coastal property, including lagoons alive with plants and wildlife.* PHOTO: BRIAN HASTINGS

**Santa Barbara City College Continuing Education Division**
**Alice E. Schott Center**
**310 W. Padre Street**
**Santa Barbara, CA**
**(805) 687–0812**
**www.sbcc.net/ce**

Adult Ed (as the Continuing Education Division of Santa Barbara City College is more commonly known) is one of the best educational resources in Santa Barbara. It offers an incredibly wide range of noncredit and community services classes, and they're usually free, with occasional minimal fees for materials.

Subjects include the arts, business, finance, real estate, job training, computers, cooking and wine, crafts, current events and world affairs, literature, writing, home and garden, humanities, languages, music, and photography.

More than 42,000 people enroll in Adult Ed classes every year—an amazing number, since that's about one out of every three residents in the greater Santa Barbara region. During fall, winter, spring, and summer sessions, Adult Ed classes meet weekday mornings, afternoons, and evenings as well as Saturdays.

Most classes take place at the Alice Schott Center. Others meet at the Selmer O. Wake Center, 300 North Turnpike (805-964-6853), and at more than 100 other locations around the greater Santa Barbara area.

Adult Ed also organizes popular trips and tours. In the past it has sponsored trips to France, the Ashland Shakespeare Festival, Ireland, and Hawaii. Local excursions enable groups to explore the new Getty Center museum in Los Angeles and Casa del Herrera, Santa Barbara's premier Spanish Colonial Revival residence.

**University of California at Santa Barbara Extension**
**6550 Hollister Avenue**
**Goleta, CA**
**(805) 893–4200**
**www.unex.ucsb.edu**

UCSB Extension offers university-level certificate programs, courses, and seminars designed for professional training and career advancement. The wide range of courses includes art and design, business and management, computers and technology, education, environmental management, behavioral and health sciences, and legal studies.

Through the UCSB Extension, you can earn university credits and certificates and fulfill professional continuing-education and relicensure requirements. Courses are offered every quarter, year-round.

## Private Colleges, Universities, and Specialty Schools

### Santa Barbara

**Antioch University Santa Barbara**
**801 Garden Street**
**Santa Barbara, CA**
**(805) 962–8179**
**www.antiochsb.edu**

Antioch University Santa Barbara is an extension of Antioch University, which was founded in Yellow Springs, Ohio, in 1852. The Santa Barbara campus opened in 1977. Most of the 270 students enrolled at Antioch are working adults who wish to earn an undergraduate or graduate degree. The average student is 35 years old, and more than 70 percent of the students receive financial aid. Antioch offers a B.A. program in Liberal Studies and M.A. programs in organizational management, psychology, and clinical psychology.

**The Fielding Institute**
**2112 Santa Barbara Street**
**Santa Barbara, CA**
**(805) 687–1099, (800) 340–1099**
**www.fielding.edu**

The Fielding Institute is a regionally accredited graduate school offering degree programs in clinical psychology (Ph.D.), human and organization development (Ph.D., Ed.D.), educational leadership and change (Ed.D.), and organizational management (M.A.). It also offers certificates in neuropsychology, psychopharmacology, and respecialization in clinical psychology as well as continuing professional education programs in graduate teacher training and mental health.

The Fielding Institute was founded in 1974 on the principles of adult learning. Its scholar-practitioner model is designed to serve mid-career professionals who must maintain multiple commitments to family, work, and community while earning an advanced degree. Its educational model builds on students' existing learning and professional experience. It features collaborative, competency-based learning and assessment, as well as flexible scheduling.

A networked learning community is formed by means of electronic communications combined with periodic face-to-face meetings at various locations. Approximately 1,200 students are enrolled at Fielding.

**Santa Barbara College of Law**
**20 E. Victoria Street**
**Santa Barbara, CA**
**(805) 966–0010**
**www.santabarbaralaw.edu**

Conveniently located in the heart of downtown, the Santa Barbara College of Law opened in 1975. The school provides high-quality legal education through an affordable part-time evening program, leading to a Juris Doctor degree and eligibility to sit for the California State Bar Examination. The faculty are all experienced attorneys or judges, and the campus includes an extensive library and computer facilities. Students usually complete the program in three-and-a-half to four years.

### Montecito

**Brooks Institute of Photography**
**801 Alston Road**
**Montecito, CA**
**(805) 966–3888**
**www.brooks.edu**

Brooks is a world leader in professional photographic and motion picture education, with state-of-the-art resources, an outstanding faculty, and five beautiful campuses: three in Santa Barbara, one in Montecito, and one in Ventura.

Ernest H. Brooks, Sr., a professional photographer, founded the school in 1945 after his return from military service. Today the school has a faculty of more than 40 experts who pass on their knowledge to more than 700 men and women from around the world. In the photography world, the institute is reputed to have the finest professors and facility in the nation.

Brooks prepares students for careers in the diverse disciplines of professional, commercial, and still photography and filmmaking. It also has programs geared toward the working photographer who seeks new skills to advance within the industry.

Great emphasis is placed on a well-rounded general education; courses in communications, marketing, and business teach skills essential for success in the competitive marketplace. Students have access to the latest technology and practices in the field.

The institute offers B.A. and M.S. degrees and a diploma in a variety of photographic disciplines and recently added a new Visual Journalism major. Brooks has a rolling admissions policy with six entering dates each year (except motion picture/video majors, who may enter in January, April, and September only). Once every two years, Brooks students travel abroad on an international documentary project (for example, to China, Africa, India, Mexico, or Cuba) and put on an exhibit when they return.

**Music Academy of the West**
**1070 Fairway Road**
**Santa Barbara, CA**
**(805) 969–8773**
**www.musicacademy.org**

The Music Academy of the West is one of the finest summer music schools in the country. It was established in 1947 by a group of dedicated art patrons and celebrated musicians, including legendary German opera singer Lotte Lehmann.

The academy's eight-week Summer School and Festival provides gifted young musicians with the opportunity for advanced study and performance under the guidance of internationally known faculty artists.

During the past 50 years, the school has attracted a stellar lineup of performing and teaching talent (for example Metropolitan Opera star Marilyn Horne, director of the academy's voice program, and piano pedagogue Jerome Lowenthal) and thousands of gifted students, many of whom later established critically acclaimed careers. More than 5,000 graduates have passed through the academy's gates, and they fill the ranks of major symphony orchestras and opera houses throughout the world. All those accepted to the academy through its rigorous audition process are awarded full scholarships, covering tuition, lodging, and meals for the entire eight weeks.

The academy's permanent campus is located at Miraflores, a Mediterranean-style estate on a bluff overlooking the Pacific Ocean. It occupies 10 acres of wooded, beautifully landscaped grounds and gardens.

**Westmont College**
**955 La Paz Road**
**Santa Barbara, CA**
**(805) 565–6000**
**www.westmont.edu**

Founded in 1937, Westmont College is a residential four-year college committed to the Christian faith. It provides a high-quality undergraduate liberal arts program in a residential campus community. About 1,300 students from 24 states, 16 countries, and 33 denominations are currently enrolled at the school. The student/faculty ratio is 13 to 1.

Westmont offers bachelor of arts and bachelor of science degrees in 26 liberal arts majors; 10 pre-professional programs; a fifth-year credential program; and numerous internships and practica. The extensive list of majors includes art, psychology, theater art, religious studies, kinesiology, biology, chemistry, and neuroscience, just to name a few. The gorgeous campus occupies 133 wooded acres—a collection of grounds from two former estates and a school for boys—in the Montecito foothills off Cold Spring Road. Westmont organizes numerous creative and performing arts programs, lectures, and sports events.

### Carpinteria

**Pacifica Graduate Institute**
**249 Lambert Road**
**Carpinteria, CA**
**(805) 969–3626**
**www.pacifica.edu**

Pacifica Graduate Institute provides graduate degree programs in depth psychology (Ph.D.), clinical psychology (Ph.D.), counseling psychology (M.A.), and mythological studies (M.A., Ph.D.). The school occupies a tree-studded, 13-acre campus in the Carpinteria foothills replete with wildlife-friendly plants, organic orchards, and vegetable gardens.

Reflecting the belief that human experience is diverse and multifaceted, Pacifica offers degree programs that are interdisciplinary in nature. Literature, religion, art, and mythology supplement the science of psychology, while students of mythology also develop an awareness of ecological issues and depth psychology. During the fall, winter, and spring quarters, students attend classes on campus during a three-day learning retreat once a month. Most programs also include a one-week summer session. Between sessions, students continue their coursework through reading, research, and practicum experiences in their homes. This unique educational format is particularly suited to people who wish to pursue graduate education while continuing their current professional and personal commitments.

**Insiders' Tip**

Want to meet other moms whose babies are the same age as yours? Call PEP—Postpartum Education for Parents—at (805) 564-3888. It'll put you in contact with a local group.

## Childcare

If you're working or just need time to get some "adult" things done, you'll be happy to know that Santa Barbara has many excellent facilities where your children can learn, play, and socialize with their pals under the careful supervision of qualified childcare providers. Your options range from licensed homes to large, church-affiliated centers, to on-site childcare programs at businesses or institutions.

We must advise you, however, that most childcare facilities have long waiting lists, especially those with affordable fees and/or excellent reputations. It's not uncommon for parents to sign up their kids as soon as they're born—or even earlier. Many parents find it necessary to arrange for alternative care in their own homes (nannies, babysitters) until a child reaches preschool age.

Santa Barbara has many outstanding preschools, which typically accept children from 2 years through age 5. If you have a baby or toddler, we recommend that you visit the schools and get on the waiting lists as early as possible—ideally at least a year ahead of the actual enrollment.

When choosing a preschool, don't immediately write off a school that isn't accredited. Preschool accreditation is a fairly new program. The National Academy of Early Childhood Programs (part of the National Association for the Education of Young Children) administers this voluntary accreditation system, which evaluates whether a program meets nationally recognized criteria for high quality. Accreditation is available to all types of preschools, kindergartens, childcare centers, and school-age childcare programs. But only a few local centers are currently accredited–it costs money to apply and the process is lengthy.

The best resources for finding out about childcare are described below. You can also pick up *Santa Barbara Family Life,* a free monthly magazine that includes listings and ads on childcare, preschools, and after-school day care; call (805) 965-4545. The *Santa Barbara News-Press* publishes a daily section called "Household and Personal Services" (in the Classified pages). Look under Child Care (Licensed) and watch for openings.

**Children's Resource and Referral Program**
**1124 Castillo Street**
**Santa Barbara, CA**
**(805) 962-8988**

The Children's Resource and Referral Program is administered through the Santa Barbara Family Care Center. It's one of more than 60 Resource and Referral Programs founded by the California Department of Education. The program provides information about all types of licensed childcare centers and private providers and distributes informational materials on choosing quality childcare. It also has a lending library with videos, toys, and resources for caregivers, parents, and community members. Telephone and walk-in referrals are available Monday through Friday from 8:00 A.M. to noon and 1:00 to 3:00 P.M.

**ChildTime Professional Nanny Placement Service**
**536 Brinkerhoff Avenue**
**Santa Barbara, CA**
**(805) 962-4433**
**www.childtimenanny.com**

ChildTime is a licensed and bonded nanny placement agency that specializes in matching nannies with families. Established in 1985, ChildTime sets high standards for its nannies. Selection is based on a careful screening and interview process. References, DMV records, and backgrounds are checked. Nannies are required to have CPR certification and to take a Nannies Skills Class.

Nannies are available for full-time or part-time positions on a live-in or live-out basis. ChildTime also has on-call temporary nannies who will come to your hotel or residence.

## After-School Care

All public and most private schools in the area offer after-school care, either on-site or at convenient locations in the vicinity of schools. When you enroll your child at a school, be sure to ask about your options. Some after-school care programs fill quickly, so be sure to do your research well in advance.

# Media



Let's face it: Santa Barbara doesn't have enough people to represent a huge media market on its own, but its well-educated and well-to-do citizens are hungry for big-city news and entertainment.

Luckily, Los Angeles is a mere 100 miles to the south and has enough electrical juice to send plenty of the above right up the coast and into local radios and TVs. And you can even find a big-city newspaper, the *Los Angeles Times,* on your doorstep in the morning. So see, you haven't missed out on a thing by choosing quiet little Santa Barbara.

This chapter includes a bit of local history and some insight into the city's "media beginnings," as well as the scoop on what's out there for you today. So, grab a cup of java or one of those fabulous Santa Barbara blended juice drinks, and read all about it.

## Newspapers

The *Santa Barbara Gazette* began a long tradition of excellence in hometown newspapers when it hit the streets on May 24, 1855. After struggling to survive with a small reader base, it eventually sold out to new owners, who moved to San Francisco and thereafter delivered the paper by steamship.

This wasn't acceptable to subscribers, who sometimes got the "news" when it was weeks old, and the *Gazette* soon went out of business.

In 1868, the weekly *Santa Barbara Post* began publishing locally, but just over a year later, it was bought out and the name was changed to the *Santa Barbara Press.* In 1871, it became Santa Barbara's first daily newspaper. Other newspapers that packed some clout in their day included the *Morning Press,* the *Daily News,* and the *Daily Independent.* Thomas M. Storke, a local boy and Stanford graduate with deep Santa Barbara roots, owned all of these publications at one time or another, and in 1938 the *Santa Barbara News-Press,* which folded all of these newspapers into one publication, was born. In 2000, local billionaire environmentalist Wendy McCaw sent ripples through the community by purchasing the paper from *The New York Times,* which had acquired it in 1985. For the first time in 36 years, the newspaper is locally owned, bucking a recent trend for conglomerate takeovers in the industry. The details on this and the greater Santa Barbara area's other fine publications appear below.

### Santa Barbara

#### Dailies

***Los Angeles Times***
**1421 State Street**
**Santa Barbara, CA**
**(800) 634–7776**
**www.latimes.com**

For big-city news and investigative reports as well as world and some local coverage (Santa Barbarans receive the paper's Ventura County regional edition), opt for the *Los Angeles Times.* This well-respected metropolitan newspaper covering all of Southern California is the largest city paper in the country, with a daily circulation of more than one million. It also boasts one of the most comprehensive news sites on the World Wide Web. In 2000, when the Tribune Company merged with Times Mirror, the paper became a Tribune Publishing Company. If you're looking for employment anywhere in the region, this is the paper to buy; the Sunday classifieds are exhaustive. The *Times* also has an excellent travel section. Subscriptions start at about $2.50 per week depending upon the area. Newsstand price is 50 cents Monday through Saturday and $1.50 on Sunday.

***Santa Barbara News-Press***
**De la Guerra Plaza**
**Santa Barbara, CA**
**(805) 564–5200**
**www.newspress.com**

The *Santa Barbara News-Press* is the city's main daily paper, with a circulation of nearly 44,600 during the week and 48,300 on weekends. It's a morning paper covering international, national, state, and local news. In 2000, big changes occurred at the *News-Press.* Local billionaire environmentalist Wendy McCaw purchased the paper from *The New York Times* through her privately held investment company, Ampersand Holdings. McCaw, a libertarian, hasn't really changed the format of the paper significantly, but some may argue that its political bent has swerved. Traditionally the paper was known for taking a conservative stance, although it seemed to be more middle of the road in recent years. For the moment, it remains in a period of transition.

In 2001, a new managing editor, Jesse Chavarria, was appointed. He plans to give even greater weight to local stories—especially investigative pieces. In general, the paper is well-respected and is an excellent source of news and information on Santa Barbara happenings. The Friday pull-out "Scene" section covers the local music, nightlife, theater, and arts scenes and runs reviews of movies and local restaurants. The "TV Week" television guide (in the Saturday edition) gives a complete lineup of local stations and programming.

Look for Public Square in the "Local" section, which lists the upcoming day's events, the agendas of local government meetings, a rundown of any roadwork that might affect your commute, and even a list of Santa Barbara citizens celebrating a birthday.

The excellent Fiesta edition (see Old Spanish Days in our Annual Events chapter) will fill you in on all the events and parties happening in conjunction with the annual August celebration. It's published the Sunday prior to Fiesta and is also

*The* Santa Barbara News-Press *office is the headquarters for the city's main daily newspaper.*
PHOTO: BRIAN HASTINGS

## Insiders' Tip

The *Santa Barbara News-Press* web site at www.newspress.com is one of the best online resources for local information. You can search the online classifieds, browse local real estate listings, or click on the links for information on local shops, businesses, community services, schools, and attractions. You can also access online versions of special features such as the Readers' Choice Awards and the Wedding Guide.

available at information booths throughout the city. For the online edition, log on to the *News-Press* web site. Weekly subscriptions to the paper start at about $2.87 for the daily delivery and $2.05 for weekend delivery. Newsstand costs are 50 cents weekdays and $1 on Sunday.

### Weekly

***The Santa Barbara Independent***
**1221 State Street**
**Santa Barbara, CA**
**(805) 965-5205**
**www.independent.com**

*The Independent,* published every Thursday, calls itself "The County's News and Entertainment Paper," and you'd be hard-pressed to find more information anywhere on Santa Barbara happenings.

This tabloid-style paper is packed with mostly local news; and oodles of information on the theater, arts, nightlife, sports, and dining scenes; and liberal social commentary (we like the Angry Poodle Barbecue column—which has nothing whatsoever to do with angry poodles or barbecue—written thoughtfully and sometimes venomously by the news editor, Nick Welsh).

The liberal slant of *The Independent* is carried over into its classified ads, where you'll find everything from Men Seeking Men and Women Seeking Women in the "Romance Lines" to a small section of more traditional classified ads. *The Independent* is crammed with local advertisements, which is how the publishers make money—the paper is distributed free to readers.

Circulation is almost 40,000, and it's a common sight in Santa Barbara to see folks sitting at a juice bar or deli reading *The Independent,* which is found on racks and in book and music stores all over the county. Even confirmed *News-Press* readers often nab *The Independent* on Thursday, because it's a great read.

## Carpinteria

***Coastal View***
**4856 Carpinteria Avenue**
**Carpinteria, CA**
**(805) 684-4428**
**www.coastalview.com**

*Coastal View* is a small tabloid-type weekly that serves the Carpinteria Valley with news of local business, education, and community events. Its circulation is about 6,000, with free copies available at newsstands and other locations in Carpinteria, Summerland, Montecito, and Santa Barbara.

Carp events (except for major happenings like the annual California Avocado Festival, listed in our Annual Events chapter) don't always get good coverage in the Santa Barbara press, so this is a great place to get the scoop on what's going on in Santa Barbara's neighbor to the south.

## Goleta

***Valley Voice***
**5786 Hollister Avenue**
**Goleta, CA**
**(805) 683–7657**
**www.goletavalleyvoice.com**

The *Valley Voice* is a free weekly covering all the local news in Goleta. Over the years, several newspapers have failed to succeed in Goleta, but as Goleta residents considered cityhood in 2001 (see our Neighborhoods and Real Estate Chapter), the *Valley Voice* emerged as an important community forum.

In its first-anniversary issue, published in February of 1998, the paper promised to expand its effort to "celebrate what is best about Goleta and tell our readers the news of their hometown," and so far it's lived up to this pledge.

The *Voice* is a small publication with a circulation of about 14,500, but it gives a nod to the local arts scene, events around town, and Goleta sports teams. Most residents like reading the "Sheriff's Blotter," which reports on Goleta's (mostly petty) crimes. You can pick up a copy at local businesses throughout Goleta or downtown in county buildings, post offices, and the public library.

## Magazines

***Montecito Magazine***
**1144 Edgemound Drive**
**Santa Barbara, CA**
**(805) 682–8335**
**www.montecitomag.com**

Montecito history, real estate, shops, galleries, restaurants, and entertainment are covered in this quarterly publication, available by subscription or at newsstands.

***Santa Barbara Magazine***
**2064 Alameda Padre Serra**
**Santa Barbara, CA**
**(805) 965–5999**

*Santa Barbara Magazine* is a slick quarterly geared to the well-to-do. In addition to several feature stories and columns about local people, celebrities, and events, you'll find a large section of ads for expensive Santa Barbara homes, and ads for private schools, art galleries, expensive automobiles, fine jewelry, and upscale shops.

In every edition you'll find a pullout "Insider's Guide" advertising supplement with a map showing the scenic drives, major parks, and other attractions. The magazine also often includes special inserts, such as a "Performing Arts Guide" or a pullout about the Santa Barbara Wine Auction. The photography is generally outstanding.

## Special Interest Publications

All of the publications listed below are free and are generally distributed at local bookstores (Chaucer's is always a good bet) or newsstands. Visitor information publications are usually available at hotels and tourist stops such as Santa Barbara Hot Spots, 36 State Street (805–564–1637).

***The Bulletin***
**126 East Haley Street**
**Santa Barbara, CA**
**(805) 963–3636**
**www.pacificpridefoundation.org**

A monthly publication of the Pacific Pride Foundation, the *Bulletin* provides coverage of events and issues of interest to the gay and lesbian community. In addition to news, feature stories, and columns, it includes a listing of community resources for Santa Barbara, Ventura, and San Luis Obispo Counties.

***Food & Home***
**3887 State Street #27**
**Santa Barbara, CA**
**(805) 563-6780**
**www.food-home.com**

Limiting the scope of its coverage to the Santa Barbara dining and bar scene (with a few recipes and details on attractions thrown in), this quarterly publication will help you keep up with local restaurant happenings. The "Appetizers" column gives the buzz on the restaurant scene, and the "Wine Country" column includes a winery tasting guide and a section called "Top Cellars" where local wine shops tout their best picks. Restaurants often include their menus in the advertisements, so you can really get an idea of what to expect.

***Montecito Journal***
**1122 Coast Village Circle**
**Montecito, CA**
**(805) 565-1860**

Calling itself "the voice of the village," the *Montecito Journal* is a biweekly tabloid that covers major social events, political issues, restaurants, and real estate, in addition to featuring several interesting columns by local writers. Pick up a copy for the scoop on all the "village" goings-on. You can find it at local businesses in Montecito including hotels and restaurants, and at select locations in other areas.

***Passport Gateway Magazine***
**331 N. Milpas Street, Suite F**
**Santa Barbara, CA**
**(805) 899-2200**
**www.passportmag.com**

Shopping, art galleries, performing arts, dining, points of interest, nightlife, a waterfront guide, a calendar of events, a listing of local phone numbers, and a cable TV guide are all included in this quarterly publication.

***This Month in Santa Barbara County***
**1900 State Street, Suite J**
**Santa Barbara, CA**
**(805) 687-1997**

Published quarterly and sold by subscription to local hotels, restaurants, and newsstands, *This Month* is distributed free to readers. It covers special events, cultural performances, the local art scene, shopping (including antiques stores), nightlife, the wine country, golf, and tours, and it lists more than 60 restaurants.

***The Whole Person Calendar of Events in Southern California***
**(805) 682-6948, (800) 962-0338**
**www.wholepersoncalendar.com**

Everything you'd ever want to know about upcoming events on astrology through Zen are listed in this rather ambitious monthly publication, which you can pick up at health food stores, bookstores, and libraries. Flip through the pages for information on holistic lectures, classes, support groups, or anything related to spiritual disciplines and alternative healing. Most of the events are New Age–oriented, although there are many traditional events listed, so pick up a copy and nourish your whole person!

## Radio

The oldest continuously broadcasting station in Santa Barbara is KDB (93.7 FM), which began operations in the Daily News building in 1926 under the call letters KFCR. (When the station was bought in 1929 by George Barnes, he changed the call letters to KDB, his wife Dorothy's initials.)

After several changes in physical locations and formats, KDB began broadcasting classical music exclusively in 1980, and has been doing it 24 hours a day ever since.

More than 10 years after KDB hit the air, KTMS, another of publishing magnate T. M. Storke's projects (the call letters are his initials), was broadcasting throughout the Santa Barbara area, with the inaugural program hitting the air waves on October 31, 1937. Beginning in August 1998, KTMS, which had been on the air for more than 60 years, became KEYT News Radio 1250 AM, broadcasting all news and local talk. Subsequently, the former KQSB 990 AM picked up the KTMS call letters, deeming them of too much historical significance to be allowed to fade into oblivion.

While you can find just about any kind of music on Santa Barbara radio stations, news and talk prevail. Nationally known shows with hosts such as Rush Limbaugh and Dr. Laura Schlessinger are available to local listeners, although the programs occasionally bounce from one network to the other. In general, the Santa Barbara radio market is made up of local people who are deeply committed to the Santa Barbara area and who are always getting involved in some event or celebration.

The local market is enhanced by many Los Angeles stations that have enough power to be heard in Santa Barbara, although several may fade in and out depending on the weather or your reception. Nonetheless, for your listening pleasure, we've included some of those in the list below.

## Adult Contemporary

**KSBL, 101.7 FM, "K-Lite"**
**KRUZ, 103.3 FM**

## Children

**KDIS, 710 AM, Radio Disney**

## Christian

**KDAR, 98.3 FM**

## Classical

**KFAC, 88.7 FM**
**KDB, 93.7 FM**

## College Radio

**KCSB, 91.9 FM**
**University of California at Santa Barbara**

## Country

**KHAY, 100.7 FM**

## Jazz

**KMGQ, 97.5 FM, "Smooth Jazz"**

## News/Talk

**KFI, 640 AM**
**KABC, 790 AM**
**KTMS, 990 AM**
**KNX, 1070 AM**
**KEYT News Radio, 1250 AM**
**KTRO, 1520 AM**

## Oldies

**KRTH, 101.1 FM, "K-Earth 101"**
**KKSB, 106.3 FM**
**KIST, 107.7 FM**
**KZBN, 1290 AM**
**KVEN, 1450 AM**

## R&B

**KCAQ, 104.7 FM, "Q-1047"**

## Rock/Alternative Rock

**KJEE, 92.9 FM**
**KOCP, 95.9 FM, "The Octopus"**
**KTYD, 99.9 FM**

## Spanish

**KOXR, 910 AM**
**KSPE, 94.5 FM**
**KTNQ, 1020 AM**
**KBKO, 1490 AM**
**KXSP, 1590 AM**

## Sports

**KXXT, 1340 AM, "Xtra Sports"**

**Insiders' Tip**

Local radio station KTYD (99.9 FM) marks Christmas with a 30-hour Beatles music marathon that starts on Christmas Eve at 6:00 P.M. (A 12-hour Rolling Stones marathon starts at 6:00 P.M. on New Year's Eve.)

## Television

Thomas M. Storke, who was on hand during the infancy of both the newspaper and radio businesses in Santa Barbara, seemed destined to be involved in the development of local television as well. It was not to be, however, and Harry Butcher, owner of a local radio station, along with several members of a new media corporation, beat Storke to the punch by going on the air first in the early 1950s.

The new station, which reportedly cost "many thousands of dollars," was KEYT, Channel 3, which is still Santa Barbara's only homegrown commercial television station.

Today an ABC affiliate, KEYT covers Ventura, Santa Barbara, and San Luis Obispo Counties. It is the only TV station that you can tune in to without at least basic cable, and even with cable, you don't always get good reception.

### Cable TV

Cox Communications (805-683-6651) provides cable service to all of Santa Barbara County. If you like to watch TV, you'll need to do business with Cox, which will charge you from about $20 a month for limited basic cable (38 channels) to around $40 for expanded cable (69 channels), depending on the package you select.

Each premium movie channel (HBO, Showtime, Cinemax, etc.) adds about $13 to your monthly bill unless you opt for the expanded cable package, which includes them for an extra $6 apiece.

### Satellite Companies

If you want to beam programs from hundreds of stations down to your TV set via your own private satellite dish, you'll find two full-service satellite equipment stores in Santa Barbara: SIA (805-965-4888) and Super Cellular (805-898-0987). You can also call the 800 number for any national company listed in the Yellow Pages under "Television-Cable & Satellite-Systems & Services."

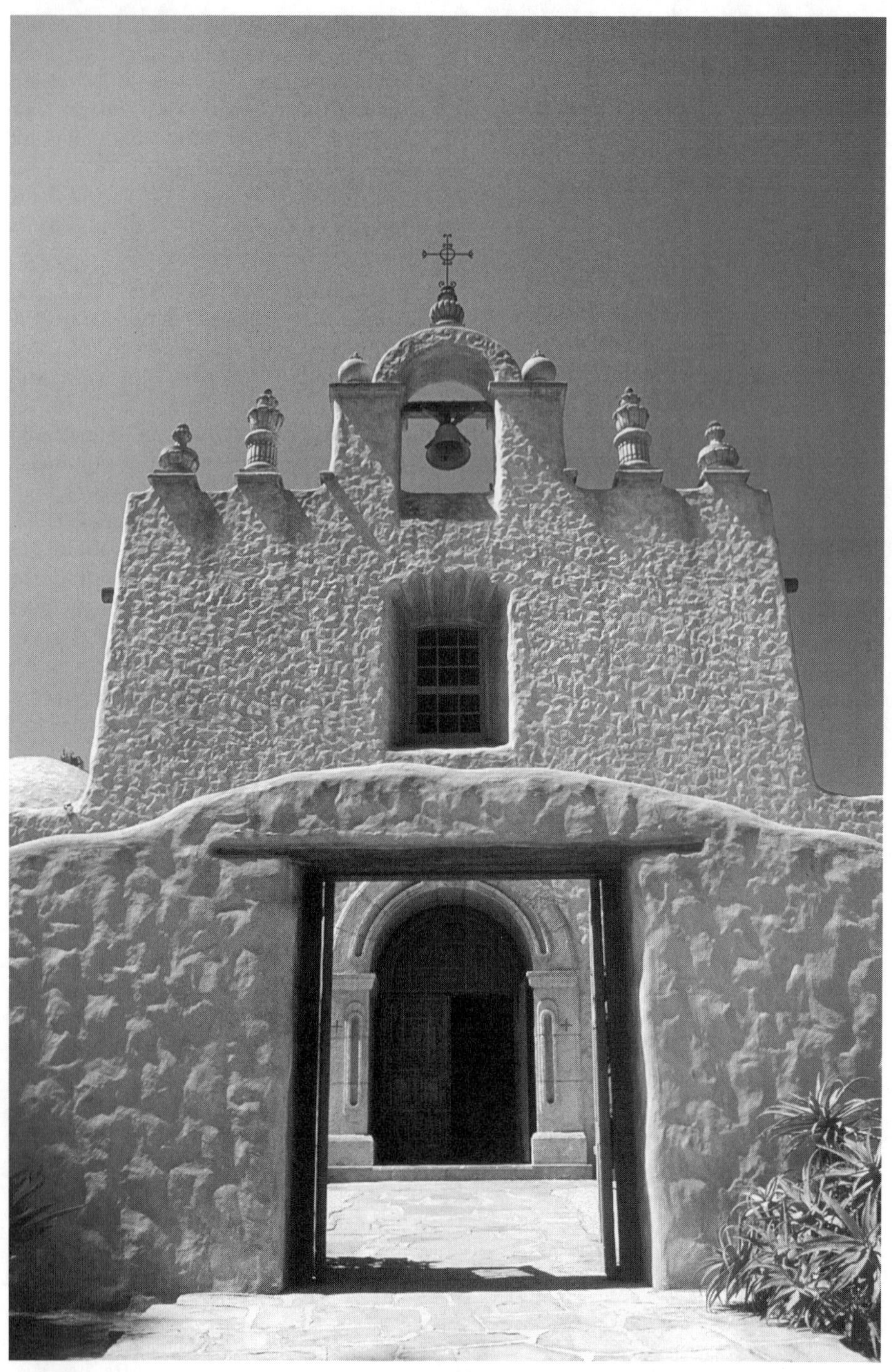

*Founded in 1936, the beautiful adobe-style Our Lady of Mount Carmel Catholic Church in Montecito is an evocative venue for Sunday mass.* PHOTO: BRIAN HASTINGS

# Worship

Santa Barbara is a diverse and tolerant community and its rich mix of religious and spiritual organizations reflects this fact. From Assemblies of God to Unitarian Universalist and everything in between, you're likely to find a congregation of people here who share your beliefs. Most of the organizations mentioned in this chapter welcome newcomers and offer fellowships, spiritual retreats, and social groups designed to help you bond with other members.

The city's spiritual evolution happened over time, of course. Santa Barbara's early residents, the Chumash Indians, consulted the local shaman for spiritual advice and flourished in harmony with the earth until the arrival of the Spaniards, who made it a top priority to convert them to Christianity. The raising of the cross and the blessing of the Mission Santa Barbara site in December 1786 signaled the beginning of the end of the Chumash's religion, not to mention their culture.

As the city evolved through its Spanish, Mexican, and American periods (see our History chapter for a more detailed account), religions other than Roman Catholicism were introduced to Santa Barbara and other churches were built, creating the cosmopolitan mix of religious and spiritual orientations that exists today.

A large Catholic population still congregates here and Mission Santa Barbara remains the best-known religious edifice in the city for its historical value as well as its beauty. St. Barbara's Parish still holds masses there on weekday mornings, Saturday afternoons, and Sundays under the direction of the Franciscan fathers, and it's a popular site for weddings and community events. In addition to the Mission, other local Catholic churches include Holy Cross Church, Our Lady of Mount Carmel, St. Mark's in Isla Vista, St. Raphael's in Goleta, and St. Joseph's in Carpinteria.

The first Protestant sermon to be preached in Santa Barbara was reportedly given by the Rev. Adam Bland, a Methodist minister who addressed a small group in the old adobe courthouse in 1854. The Methodists did not formally organize here until 14 years later, however, lagging behind the Congregationalists, Episcopalians, and Presbyterians, who organized in 1866. After these first churches were formed, others followed in rapid succession: the Baptists organized in 1874 with 19 charter members; a Unitarian Society church was founded here in 1885; Seventh-Day Adventists opened a church in 1887; the First Christian Church was organized in 1888; the First Church of Christ, Scientist boasted 16 members when it organized in 1900; Norwegian immigrants founded the Scandinavian Evangelical Lutheran Church in 1902, followed by the Grace Lutheran Church in 1903; and the African Methodist Episcopal Church was founded at Haley and Olive Streets in 1905. The rest, as they say, is history.

If you've just arrived here and are looking to connect with people who share your faith or ideology, you'll find Baptist, Christian Science, Congregationalist, Eastern and Greek Orthodox, Episcopal, Methodist, Jehovah's Witness, Lutheran, Pentecostal, Presbyterian, Religious Science, Seventh-Day Adventist, and Unitarian congregations within the Santa Barbara area. B'nai B'rith Temple on San Antonio Road serves the largest Jewish congregation in town, and in December 1998, a Jewish Community Center opened downtown at 524 Chapala Street. You'll also find Baha'i, New Age, Buddhist, Scientologist, and Vedanta temples, groups, and centers, and several nondenominational churches with local memberships.

## Information, Please

One of the best places to look for a particular religious organization is the Yellow Pages of the local phone book—check the listings under "Churches" or "Religious Organizations." Most churches are also listed by name in the white pages.

The *Santa Barbara News-Press* features a comprehensive "Religion" section in its Saturday edition that includes a detailed Religion Calendar in which local religious organizations list special events and ongoing classes or workshops. Individual places of worship also advertise the schedule of services and sometimes include the subject of the next day's sermon.

The *News-Press*'s Cinema in Focus column, also in the "Religion" section, features a local pastor's evaluation of a current commercial film.

The paper is especially helpful at religious holiday seasons, when special events such as sunrise services or midnight masses are advertised in the Holiday Services pages.

The *Santa Barbara Independent* is a great source for information about less traditional spiritual and religious organizations and events, with small blurbs and ads for New Age workshops, meditation seminars, and the like. It also has a Spirituality listing that covers everything from the Adi Da Samraj Way of the Heart Area Study Group to the Women's Full Moon Ceremony, with a few more conventional organizations represented as well.

### Insiders' Tip

Craving some solitude? Perched high on a mountain ridge above Santa Barbara, Mount Calvary Monastery and Retreat House welcomes people of all religious traditions who want to rest, reflect, and regroup. The guesthouse is run by the Benedictine monks and is available for prayer, study, working, or individual retreats as well as spiritually oriented conferences. For information, visit the monastery web site at www.mount-calvary.org or call between 8:30 A.M. and 6:00 P.M. Tuesday through Friday at (805) 962-9855 ext. 10.

# Index

# About the Author

One scorching summer's day in 1990, Karen left her home in Sydney, Australia, with an overstuffed backpack and a one-way ticket to London. Wanderlust struck at an early age. But now, with a degree in communications and psychology under her belt, Karen felt it was finally time for a "walkabout." "She'll probably be back in a couple of months," sobbed her family as her plane left the tarmac at Sydney Airport. Little did they know.

More than 10 years later, Karen is still living and working overseas, thanks to someone she bumped into along the way. About three months after leaving Sydney, Karen met her future husband, Brian, over après-ski drinks in Whistler, Canada. From that moment on, her fate was sealed. A photographer and proud second-generation Santa Barbaran, Brian shared her passion for travel and adventure. Together they spent the next eight years roaming the globe.

From Canada to Europe to Africa they wandered, supporting their travel addiction with odd jobs along the way. Over the years, they lived and worked in a ski chalet in the French Alps, co-managed a game lodge in Namibia, camped their way around Australia, dived the Cayman Islands, fly-fished in Belize, and crisscrossed southern Africa in a temperamental old Land Rover. In 1995, Karen scored an assignment working as a foreign correspondent for Cahners Travel Group. During this post, she reviewed more than 280 upscale hotels and resorts throughout Africa, Central America, and the Caribbean.

In between hotel-hopping, Karen and Brian frequently returned to Brian's hometown of Santa Barbara. For Karen, the beautiful beaches, eucalyptus groves, sports-loving lifestyle, and laid-back attitude evoked fond memories of her native Australia. She felt instantly at home. Eventually Karen and Brian decided to abandon their nomadic ways and settle down in sunny Santa Barbara.

Today Karen continues to work as a freelance travel writer from her adopted home. In 1999, she wrote the corporate meeting planner for the Santa Barbara Conference & Visitor's Bureau and penned updates through 2001. Her work has also appeared in the *San Diego Union Tribune, Star Service,* and various corporate travel publications. She lives with her husband Brian in a little cottage on the beach and tries to visit her family and friends in Australia every year.